AF868527

Lecture Notes in Computer Science 13117

Founding Editors

Gerhard Goos
Karlsruhe Institute of Technology, Karlsruhe, Germany

Juris Hartmanis
Cornell University, Ithaca, NY, USA

Editorial Board Members

Elisa Bertino
Purdue University, West Lafayette, IN, USA

Wen Gao
Peking University, Beijing, China

Bernhard Steffen
TU Dortmund University, Dortmund, Germany

Gerhard Woeginger
RWTH Aachen, Aachen, Germany

Moti Yung
Columbia University, New York, NY, USA

More information about this subseries at http://www.springer.com/series/7409

Yueh-Min Huang · Chin-Feng Lai ·
Tânia Rocha (Eds.)

Innovative Technologies and Learning

4th International Conference, ICITL 2021
Virtual Event, November 29 – December 1, 2021
Proceedings

Springer

Editors
Yueh-Min Huang
National Cheng Kung University
Tainan, Taiwan

Chin-Feng Lai
National Cheng Kung University
Tainan, Taiwan

Tânia Rocha
University of Trás-os-Montes
and Alto Douro
Villa Real, Portugal

ISSN 0302-9743 ISSN 1611-3349 (electronic)
Lecture Notes in Computer Science
ISBN 978-3-030-91539-1 ISBN 978-3-030-91540-7 (eBook)
https://doi.org/10.1007/978-3-030-91540-7

LNCS Sublibrary: SL3 – Information Systems and Applications, incl. Internet/Web, and HCI

© Springer Nature Switzerland AG 2021
This work is subject to copyright. All rights are reserved by the Publisher, whether the whole or part of the material is concerned, specifically the rights of translation, reprinting, reuse of illustrations, recitation, broadcasting, reproduction on microfilms or in any other physical way, and transmission or information storage and retrieval, electronic adaptation, computer software, or by similar or dissimilar methodology now known or hereafter developed.
The use of general descriptive names, registered names, trademarks, service marks, etc. in this publication does not imply, even in the absence of a specific statement, that such names are exempt from the relevant protective laws and regulations and therefore free for general use.
The publisher, the authors and the editors are safe to assume that the advice and information in this book are believed to be true and accurate at the date of publication. Neither the publisher nor the authors or the editors give a warranty, expressed or implied, with respect to the material contained herein or for any errors or omissions that may have been made. The publisher remains neutral with regard to jurisdictional claims in published maps and institutional affiliations.

This Springer imprint is published by the registered company Springer Nature Switzerland AG
The registered company address is: Gewerbestrasse 11, 6330 Cham, Switzerland

Preface

The International Conference of Innovative Technologies and Learning (ICITL), provides a platform for those who are working on educational technology to get together and exchange experiences. Benefiting from a variety of emerging innovative technologies, the e-learning environment has become highly diversified in recent years. Diversified innovative technologies have fueled the creation of advanced learning environments by adopting appropriate pedagogies. Moreover, these technologies not only facilitate learning but also actively help students reach maximized learning performances. However, due to the rapid evolution of new technologies, how to make best use of these technologies whilst still complying with effective pedagogies to create adaptive or smart learning environments remains an area of interest. Therefore, this conference series intends to provide a platform for those researchers in education, computer science, and educational technology to share experiences of effectively applying cutting-edge technologies to learning and to further spark brightening prospects. It is hoped that the findings of each work presented at the conference will enlighten relevant researchers or education practitioners to create more effective learning environments. ICITL is always ready to share the proceedings with the public.

Due to the unfolding coronavirus (COVID-19) outbreak and travel restrictions, this year's conference (ICITL 2021) was held virtually and interactively. Therefore, all accepted papers were presented in a fully virtual format, with each session held interactively in a virtual meeting room. This year we received 110 submissions from authors in 21 countries worldwide. After a rigorous double-blind review process, 59 papers were selected as full papers and two papers were selected as short papers, yielding an acceptance rate of 55%. These contributions covered the latest findings in the following areas: 1) Artificial Intelligence in Education; 2) Augmented, Virtual, and Mixed Reality in Education; 3) Computational Thinking in Education; 4) Design Frameworks and Models for Innovative Learning; 5) Education Practice Issues and Trends; 6) Educational Gamification and Game-based Learning; 7) Innovative Technologies and Pedagogies Enhanced Learning; 8) Multimedia Technology Enhanced Learning; 9) Online Course and Web-based Environments; and 10) Science, Technology, Engineering, Arts and Design, and Mathematics. Moreover, ICITL 2021 features two keynote presentations by renowned experts and scholars: Lin Lin and Matthieu J. Guitton. We are grateful for their insights on the topics of "Bridging Human Intelligence and Artificial Intelligence for Education and Future Workforce" and "Learning in a Post-COVID Era: The Challenges of Digital Inequalities".

We would like to thank the Organizing Committee for their efforts and time spent to ensure the success of the conference. We would also like to express our gratitude to the Program Committee members for their timely and helpful reviews. Last but not least, we would like to thank all the authors for their contribution in maintaining a high-quality conference – we count on your continued support in playing a significant role in the Innovative Technologies and Learning community in the future.

November 2021

Yueh-Min Huang
Joao Barroso
Frode Eika Sandnes
Chi-Cheng Chang
Tânia Rocha
Chin-Feng Lai
Mu-Yen Chen

Organization

Honorary Chair

Yueh-Min Huang	National Cheng Kung University, Taiwan

Conference Co-chairs

Joao Barroso	University of Trás-os-Montes e Alto Douro, Portugal
Frode Eika Sandnes	Oslo Metropolitan University, Norway
Chi-Cheng Chang	National Taiwan Normal University, Taiwan

Technical Program Co-chairs

Tânia Rocha	University of Trás-os-Montes e Alto Douro, Portugal
Chin-Feng Lai	National Cheng Kung University, Taiwan
Mu-Yen Chen	National Cheng Kung University, Taiwan

Finance Chair

Ting-Ting Wu	National Yunlin University of Science and Technology, Taiwan

Website Chair

Shih-Yeh Chen	National Taitung University, Taiwan

Executive Chair

Chia-Chen Chen	National Chung Hsing University, Taiwan

Publication Chair

Yu-Sheng Su	National Taiwan Ocean University, Taiwan

Program Committee

Ana Balula	University of Aveiro, Portugal
Andreja Istenic Starcic	University of Ljubljana, Slovenia
António Coelho	University of Porto, Portugal

Arsênio Reis	University of Trás-os-Montes e Alto Douro, Portugal
Chantana Viriyavejakul	King Mongkut's Institute of Technology Ladkrabang, Thailand
Claudia Motta	Federal University of Rio de Janeiro, Brazil
Constantino Martins	Polytechnic Institute of Porto, Portugal
Danial Hooshyar	University of Tartu, Estonia
Daniela Pedrosa	University of Aveiro, Portugal
Grace Qi	Massey University, New Zealand
Gwo-Dong Chen	National Central University, Taiwan
Hana Mohelska	University of Hradec Kralove, Czech Republic
Hanlie Smuts	University of Pretoria, South Africa
Hugo Paredes	University of Trás-os-Montes e Alto Douro, Portugal
João Pedro Gomes Moreira Pêgo	University of Porto, Portugal
José Cravino	University of Trás-os-Montes e Alto Douro, Portugal
José Alberto Lencastre	University of Minho, Portugal
Jui-Long Hung	Boise State University, USA
Jun-Ming Su	National University of Tainan, Taiwan
Leonel Morgado	Universidade Aberta, Portugal
Lisbet Ronningsbakk	UiT The Arctic University of Norway, Norway
Manuel Cabral	University of Trás-os-Montes e Alto Douro, Portugal
Margus Pedaste	University of Tartu, Estonia
Paula Catarino	University of Trás-os-Montes e Alto Douro, Portugal
Paulo Martins	University of Trás-os-Montes e Alto Douro, Portugal
Qing Tan	Athabasca University, Canada
Rustam Shadiev	Nanjing Normal University, China
Satu-Maarit Frangou	University of Lapland, Finland
Shelley Shwu-Ching Young	National Tsing Hua University, Taiwan
Synnøve Thomassen Andersen	UiT The Arctic University of Norway, Norway
Ting-Sheng Weng	National Chiayi University, Taiwan
Wu-Yuin Hwang	National Central University, Taiwan
Yi-Shun Wang	National Changhua University of Education, Taiwan
Yu-Cheng Chien	National Cheng Kung University, Taiwan
Yuping Wang	Griffith University, Australia

Main Organizers

Co-organizers

Contents

Artificial Intelligence in Education

Oral Practice Language Learning Companion Implementation on Voice Assistant Platform 3
Hsiang-Jen Chung

Amending Dynamic Capability Theory for Information Systems Research on the Reskilling of Coal Miners in an AI-Driven Era 10
Lloyd Letlhogonolo Koikoi Modimogale, Jan Hendrik Kroeze, and Cornè Johandia van Staden

Exploring the Impact of Artificial Intelligence Learning Platforms on Interest in and Attitudes Toward Learning 22
Hua-Xu Zhong, Chin-Feng Lai, Yu-Che Huang, Pei-Hsuan Wu, and Jui-Hung Chang

Lightening Up a New AI Cognitions and Performances for Engineering Students' Problem-Based Learning in Nature General Education Programs . . . 30
King-Dow Su

Use Object-Detection to Identify Materials and Tools for STEAM Hands-on Activity 39
Hsin-Yu Lee, Yu-Cheng Chien, Pei-Yu Chang, Danial Hooshyar, and Yueh-Min Huang

Perusall's Machine Learning Towards Self-regulated Learning 49
Manuela Francisco and Cristina Amado

Augmented, Virtual and Mixed Reality in Education

Developing an AR Tutoring System to Support Maker Education 61
Wei-Tsung Lin, Yong-Ming Huang, and Chao-Chun Chen

Facilitating 3D Geometry Learning with Augmented Reality in Authentic Contexts 67
Wu-Yuin Hwang, Rio Nurtantyana, and Muhammad Trio Maulana Putra

A Simulation Learning in Communication Technique Skill by Virtual Reality - Certification of Telecommunication Line Plant 74
ChinLun Lai

Integration of Mixed Reality in Teaching and Learning Effectiveness: A Systematic Literature Review of the Analyses 85
Ching-Yun Tseng, Yu Shu, Tien-Chi Huang, Wen-Chiao Hsu, and Pei-Ling Chien

A Study of Learner's Scientific Thinking Using Constructivist Virtual Learning Environment for Grade 11 Students 95
Kodchakorn Lamsombat and Issara Kanjug

Regarding the Virtual Reality Environment Design and Evaluation Based on STEAM Learning 102
Chih-Chao Chung, Yuh-Ming Cheng, and Shi-Jer Lou

Using STEAM-6E Model in AR/VR Maker Education Teaching Activities to Improve High School Students' Learning Motivation and Learning Activity Satisfaction 111
Yu-Hsuan Lin, Hao-Chiang Koong Lin, and Hsin-Lan Liu

Computational Thinking in Education

The Use of E-learning Tools in a Basic Logic Course During the COVID-19 Lockdown 121
Peter Øhrstrøm, Steinar Thorvaldsen, Ulrik Sandborg-Petersen, Thomas Ploug, and David Jakobsen

Improve University Humanities Students' Problem-Solving Ability Through Computational Thinking Training. 131
Jim-Min Lin, Zeng-Wei Hong, Zong-Kun Song, Wei-Wei Shen, and Wai-Khuen Cheng

The Development of a Computational Thinking Learning Package that Integrates a Learning Experience Design for Grade K 144
Chinnaphat Junruang, Issara Kanjug, and Charuni Samat

Development of Online Learning to Enhancing Computational Thinking for High School Students 152
Non Jarungsiraway, Nutthakarn Moeikao, Issara Kanjug, and Charuni Samat

Exploring the Usability of Web-Based Java Compiler as a Learning Tool . . . 161
Yu-Lin Jeng, Sheng-Bo Huang, Chin-Feng Lai, and Andreja Istenič Starčič

Young Kids' Basic Computational Thinking: An Analysis on Educational Robotics Without Computer 170
Pao-Nan Chou and Ru-Chu Shih

Design Framework and Model for Innovative Learning

The Validation of Constructivist Web-Based Learning Environment Model to Enhance Creativity Thinking for Undergraduate Student with Integration of Pedagogy and Neuroscience 183
Jetbordin Jitsopitanon, Sumalee Chaijaroen, and Pornsawan Vongtathum

Resource Designing Framework of Constructivist Web-Based Learning Environment to Enhance the Problem-Solving for Robot Programming in Secondary Grade 3 189
Kriangsak Pongsuphan and Sumalee Chaijaroen

AHP4Edu: An AHP-Based Assessment Model for Learning Effectiveness of Education 196
Yu-Lun Huang and Yu-Hsin Wu

A Designing Framework for Flipped Classroom Learning Environment Model Combined with Augmented Reality to Enhance Creative Thinking in Product Design for High School Students 206
Sathaporn Wongchiranuwat, Charuni Samat, Issara Kanjug, and Suchat Wattanachai

Development of Constructivist Web-Based Learning Environment Model to Enhance Critical Thinking: Integration Between Pedagogy and Neuroscience Topic on Substance for Primary Students 219
Pimwarun Nunthaitaweekul, Sumalee Chaijaroen, and Romwarin Gamlunglert

Using Design Patterns to Teach Conceptual Entity Relationship (ER) Data Modelling 228
Lizette Weilbach, Mariė Hattingh, and Komla Pillay

Education Practice Issues and Trends

Conceptualising a Model for Meaningful Digital Pedagogy 241
Janne Väätäjä and Satu-Maarit Frangou

Research on the Data Literacy Index System of Pre-service Teachers Under the Background of Big Data 252
Peiyao Su, Huimin Chen, Xiaoying Deng, Han Lin, and Zhe Li

An Integrated Conceptual Framework to Assess Small and Rural Municipalities' Readiness for Smart City Implementation: A Systematic Literature Review 262
Nkhangweni Lawrence Mashau, Jan H. Kroeze, and Grant R. Howard

Digital Application Literacy 274
LeAnne J. Schmidt

Big Data in the Innovation Process - A Bibliometric Analysis 283
Zornitsa Yordanova

The Student Role in Technology Supported Learning 293
Lisbet Rønningsbakk

Effects of E-recruitment Interface Attributes on the Attractiveness of Taiwanese Job Seekers 303
Judy F. Chen, Clyde A. Warden, and Jia-Wen Liou

Evolution of Lean Startup over the Years – A Bibliometric Analysis. 310
Zornitsa Yordanova

Educational Gamification and Game-Based Learning

Effect of Game Elements on Game-Based Learning for Computer Programming Using Task-Technology Fit 323
Wei-Tsong Wang and Mega Kartika Sari

A Development of Smart Coding Creative Kit to Enhance Creative Problem Solving Thinking for Children 333
Pornsawan Vongtathum, Charuni Samat, and Suchat Wattanachai

Board Game and Family Involvement Motivate Target Language Learning 343
Yingling Chen

Gamifying Digital Learning Platform for Information Security Awareness . . . 352
Thanawat Rintanalert and Arthorn Luangsodsai

A Study on the Application of Collaborative Learning by Using Moment Cam to Improve Mathematics Acceptability 365
Ting-Sheng Weng, Mu-Fen Chao, and Chien-Kuo Li

Developing an Application for Teaching Mathematics to Children with Dyscalculia: A Pilot Case Study 377
Diana Carvalho, Tânia Rocha, Paulo Martins, and João Barroso

Innovative Technologies and Pedagogies Enhanced Learning

Analytical Skills in Statistical Applications Based on End-of-Term Students' Self-evaluations 389
Jane Lu Hsu and Melchior Antoine

Exploring Affordances and Student Perceptions of MALL in Familiar Environments 397
Rustam Shadiev, Taoying Liu, Narzikul Shadiev, Mirzaali Fayziev, Elena Gaevskaya, Roza Zhussupova, and Olimboy Otajonov

The Study of Smart Coding Creative Kit to Enhance Creative Problem Solving Thinking for Children 413
Pornsawan Vongtathum, Charuni Samat, and Pinyarat Singha

Learner's Ill- Structures Problem Solving with a Constructivist Web-Based Learning Environment Model 422
Chan Singkaew and Sumalee Chaijaroen

The Development of Internet of Things Learning Kit to Enhancing Programming Skills for High School Students 430
Nutthakarn Moeikao, Non Jarungsirawat, Issara Kanjug, and Charuni Samat

Computer Integrated Education Evaluation: A Case Study 439
Corlia Smuts and Hanlie Smuts

Impact of the IRS Idiom Teaching on Elementary Students' Learning Achievement and Motivation 450
Mei-Jie Lai, Hong-Ren Chen, and Sen-Chi Yu

Multimedia Technology Enhanced Learning

On the Convenience of Speeding Up Lecture Recordings: Increased Playback Speed Reduces Learning 461
Ida Ness, Kathinka Opdal, and Frode Eika Sandnes

My Morning Routine: An Interactive UDL Compliant E-Book on Health and Hygiene for Learners with Visual Difficulties 470
Azka Rizwan, Mohsina Abid, Noor Us Subah Quidwai, and Midhat Noor Kiyani

Applying E-Book System to Facilitate Student' Flipped Learning Performance in Software Engineering Courses 483
I-Chun Lin, Tz-Chi Wang, and Yen-Ting Lin

Effectiveness of Online Multimedia Courses for Improving Children's Self-regulation Through Social-Emotional Learning 491
Fu-Rung Yang, Mei-Hsin Wu, Jih-Hsin Tang, and Chih-Fen Wei

Combining Flipped Learning and Formative Assessment to Enhance the Learning Performance of Students in Programming 498
Shu-Chen Cheng, Yu-Ping Cheng, Yueh-Min Huang, and Yeongwook Yang

Online Course and Web-Based Environment

The Framework for Development of the Constructivist Learning Environment Model to Enhance Ill-Structured Problem Solving in Industrial Automation System Supporting by Metacognition 511
Samrit Thima and Sumalee Chaijaroen

Using the Diffusion of Innovation Theory to Explain Foundation Phase Teachers' Perceptions of Online Zoom Classes During a Pandemic – A Case of a South African Private School 521
Komla Pillay and Tania Prinsloo

Enhancing Learners' Creative Thinking in the Massive Open Online Course (Moocs) Learning Environment Model for Higher Education 533
Benjaporn Sathanarugsawait, Charuni Samat, and Suchat Wattanachai

Designing of Learning Environment Model to Enhance Student' Self Regulation by Using Massive Open Online Course 542
Benjaporn Sathanarugsawait and Charuni Samat

Higher Education Students' Perceptions Towards Using Facebook as a Learning Platform. 548
Rdouan Faizi and Maria Rudneva

STEAM Education

Gender Differences in Engineering Design Thinking in a Project-Based STEAM Course 557
Wan-Hsuan Yen, Chi-Cheng Chang, and John Willliams

STEM Learning in Digital Higher Education: Have It Your Way!. 567
Margarida M. Pinheiro and Vanda Santos

Bilingual Instruction Model for a STEAM Course: A Preliminary Study 579
Fu-Rung Yang

Employing STEAM 6E Teaching Methods to Analyze the Academic Emotions of the Digital Video Practice Course 584
Yu-Chen Liang, Koong Hao-Chiang Lin, and Cheng-Tsung Li

Satisfaction of Engineering Design Thinking Course for High School Students. 593
Charuni Samat, Sathaporn Wongchiranuwat, Issara Kanjug, Pornsawan Vongtathum, Sumalee Chaijaroen, and Suchat Wattanachai

Author Index 601

Artificial Intelligence in Education

Oral Practice Language Learning Companion Implementation on Voice Assistant Platform

Hsiang-Jen Chung(✉)

Graduate Institute of Network Learning Technology, National Central University, Taoyuan, Taiwan
ryanchung@ncu.edu.tw

Abstract. Oral practice for language learning usually needs to find partners or teachers to accompany, no matter how patient they are, it's not easy to stay for a long-time conversation practice. This study tries to implement an energetic oral practice language learning companion on voice assistant platform, it can always be with you to practice English conversation. It uses natural language processing and voice recognition technology to tell if you are repeating the same sentence, help students can practice conversation by themselves.

Keywords: Language learning · Learning companion · Virtual companion · Voice assistant · Artificial intelligence · Education technology

1 Introduction

1.1 Motivation

The best way to learn language is practicing with real people and makes you get into the whole foreign environment. But sometimes we do not have chances or budgets to do so. No matter gets a foreign friend or foreign place, it costs. So, if there comes a learning companion can be with learner to practice English every day, let learner know if he is doing right or not, that would be great helpful to every demand learner to practice by himself.

1.2 Literature Review

Learning companion is a type of Intelligent Tutor System [1]. It can simulate the teaching way like classmates, partners. It can help students to get more ideas, better than the experience of studying alone. Using machine learning to build the learning companion, there are still some details need to figure out [2]. When design the learning companion, we should take these in mind: Cognitive, Motivation, Sociability, Attitudes and Ethics [3].

Taking the voice assistant for education is just about the beginning stage. Students can use it as Q&A station, timer…We also believe it is also good for special education, because the feature of voice interface [4]. For knowledge query, mental support and recreation, the voice assistant platform can play a good role for learning companion [5].

© Springer Nature Switzerland AG 2021
Y.-M. Huang et al. (Eds.): ICITL 2021, LNCS 13117, pp. 3–9, 2021.
https://doi.org/10.1007/978-3-030-91540-7_1

2 Design & Implementation

2.1 Voice Assistant

The voice assistant has several features just match the human beings; the following Table 1 gives the comparison.

Table 1. Voice assistant vs. Human beings

Function	Voice assistant	Human beings
Talk	Speaker	Mouth
Listen	Microphone	Ears
See	Camera (only specific types)	Eyes
Show	Monitor (only specific types)	–

Since the voice assistant can listen and talk basically, we are trying to make it as the conversation practice partner who never feels tired. At first, let us check how the voice assistant works (Fig. 1).

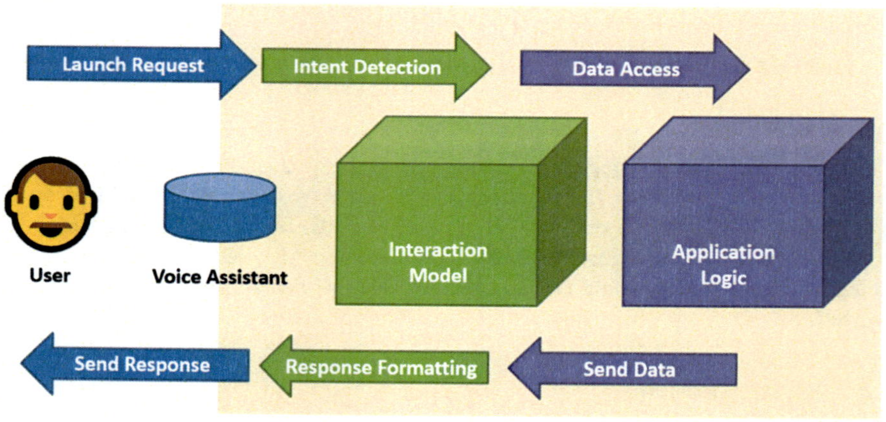

Fig. 1. How the voice assistant works

When the user reaches to voice assistant, he can wake up the voice assistant device with the invocation name like Alexa, OK Google, …. Then shoot the skill invocation name to enter specific skill. After the device get what user says, interaction model will recognize the sentence to matched intent, and get the keywords (also called slots or entities). The application logic usually designed by developer, to determine what kind of data to get and executes corresponding condition-based operation. After the operation, sends back the data to interaction model to transfer to the suitable data format (voice, text, image, video…) to user.

Based on this infrastructure, the researcher wants to design an oral practice language learning companion, when user needs to practice, he can wake up the machine and do the conversation practice, it never tired. The system design diagram below (Fig. 2).

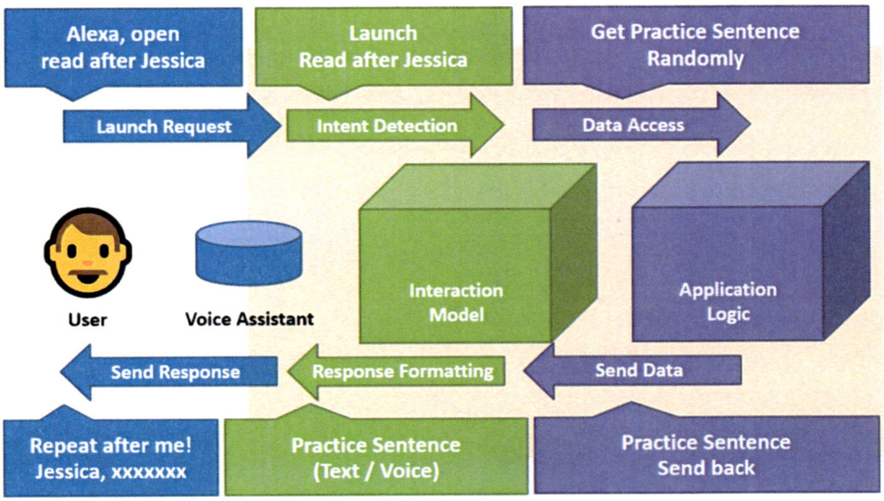

Fig. 2. How the oral practice language learning companion works

Let us go to the details for the interaction model and application logic. About the interaction model, we need to clarify what user says, and match to the right intent to get the next step. In this skill, we design 5 custom intents in the interaction model (Table 2).

Table 2. Intents in the read after Jessica

Intent name	Trigger	Purpose
HelloWorldIntent	When user says something like hi, hello,...	Launch the practice
RepeatIntent	When user request to say it again	Repeat the sentence
AnswerIntent	When user says "Jessica, xxxxx"	Check user's answer
AMAZON.YESIntent	When user gives positive response	Go to next sentence
AMAZON.NextIntent	When user ask for next question	Go to next sentence

The core operation logic is in the handler for AnswerIntent, we will talk about it later. Let us review the user – voice assistant interaction flow first (Fig. 3).

Fig. 3. The interaction flow between user & voice assistant

In our design, the user needs to repeat exactly what the voice assistant says. So, it makes user to say the sentence very carefully. But sometimes the problem may incur from the voice recognition system or the microphone hardware. There are still lot of spaces to improve in this design scheme. Now let us go to see the details in the AnswerIntent (Fig. 4).

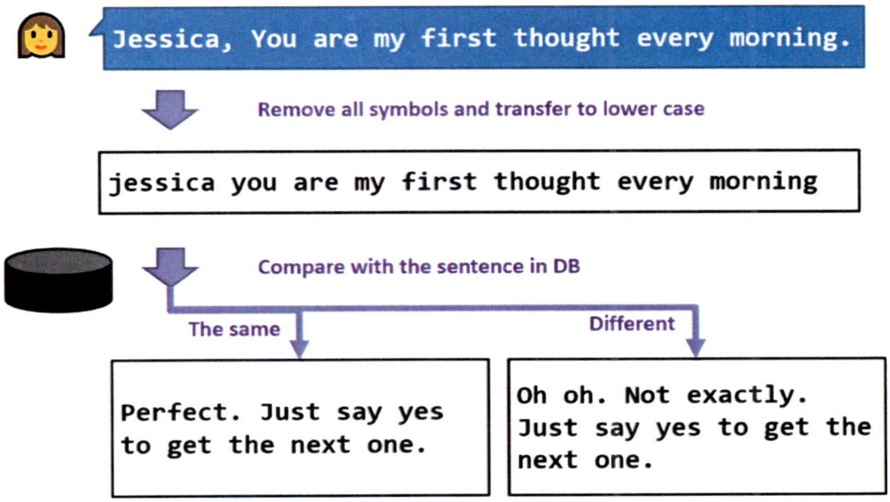

Fig. 4. The logic operation in AnswerIntent

When the voice assistant gets the practice sentence from user, the voice recognition system transfers it to text. Then the system determines which intent it belongs to. When it goes to AnswerIntent, it will firstly remove all symbols and change it all to lower case. The purpose for this step is for comparison later. Then the system will compare the sentence user spoken and the sentence in database, to see if it is the same or different. When it is the same, user will get the positive response, to know he is speaking right completely. Or user will get negative response, in those devices which have monitor, we also show what the system got from user, let user sees how far it is between with the right answer. This adding visual feature part is useful for language learner.

3 Results and Discussion

In this very early version of "Read after Jessica", the researcher made it public to Amazon Alexa skill store.

Here is the result for the first month (Table 3):

Table 3. Users testing result

Test number	Test record (5 times/unit)	Correct rate
1	XXXXX	0%
2	XOOOO	35%
3	XXOXX	20%
4	XXOXX	20%
5	OXXXO	40%
6	XXOOO	60%
7	XXOXO	40%
8	XXXXX	0%
9	XXXXX	0%
10	XXXXO	20%
11	XOOOO	80%
12	XXOXX	20%
13	XXOXX	20%
14	XXXXX	0%
	Average correct rate	28.6%

We let them to interact with the voice assistant, and take 5 sentences as unit, no matter what the English level of user, for 5 sentences, user get the exactly right sentence are only around 1 ~ 3. According to the user response shows in the monitor, The common difference factors we list below (Table 4):

Table 4. The common difference from users

Factors	System
Spell error	Can vs. can't, mine vs. mind...
System error	Amazon will transfer one to 1 from user
Recognition error	Due to the volume or the quality of microphone
Speak too slow	The system will stop listening to your input

4 Conclusion

It is the very beginning version of "Read after Jessica", but we found the voice platform is a good way to simulate the oral practice learning companion. You can use it in any time you want, to get practice by your own. Although it just like a very strict teacher, you can only get encourage when you get 100% right. But it can show you what you just said on the screen to check and do the oral practice repeatedly and continuously.

There are still some types of errors are nothing to do with users, so we can still improve the voice assistant platform, and add guidance to users who almost speak the same sentence.

References

1. Chan, T.W., Baskin, A.B.: Studying with the prince: the computer as a learning companion. In: The Proceedings of International Conference of Intelligent Tutoring System, ITS 1988, pp. 194–200. Montreal, Canada (1988)
2. Chan, T.W., Baskin, A.B.: Learning companion systems. In: Frasson, C., Gauthier, G. (eds.) Intelligent Tutoring Systems: At the Crossroads of Artificial Intelligence and Education, Chapter 1. Ablex Publishing Corporation, New Jersey (1990)
3. Chan, T.W.: Learning companion systems, social learning systems, and the global social learning club. J. Artif. Intell. Educ. **7**(2), 125–159 (1996)
4. George, T., Maya, S.: Voice assistants and smart speakers in everyday life and in education. Inf. Educ. **19**(3), 473–490 (2020). https://doi.org/10.15388/infedu.2020.21
5. Chung, H.J., Chan, T.W.: Virtual Learning Companion Feature Practicability on AI Voice Assistant Platform. Taiwan E-Learning Forum (2021)

Amending Dynamic Capability Theory for Information Systems Research on the Reskilling of Coal Miners in an AI-Driven Era

Lloyd Letlhogonolo Koikoi Modimogale(✉), Jan Hendrik Kroeze, and Cornè Johandia van Staden

School of Computing, University of South Africa, PO Box 392, Pretoria UNISA 0003, South Africa
modimoll@endiansys.co.za, {kroezjh,vstadcj1}@unisa.ac.za

Abstract. Due to digitalization and disruptive technologies, the business landscape has changed. The change will influence the nature of work across all industries. The South African mining sector is going through a modernization process to stay relevant. The paper explores Dynamic Capability Theory (DCT) as a suitable theory for the reskilling of coal miners. The paper will define the theory and related concepts to get a better understanding and explore the link with information systems. It amends existing dynamic capability frameworks and proposes a modified model that can be used to guide the reskilling of mineworkers for the new era. The amended framework can be used to mitigate the foreseen consequences of the use of robotics and automation in the mining industry in South Africa. The inclusion of human aspects in DCT is especially important to facilitate the Africanization of information systems within the mining sector on the continent. As a result, this will increase the understanding and learning of transitioning skills within the context of using a variety of emerging innovative technologies fueled by the new era.

Keywords: Dynamic capability · Dynamic Capability Theory (DCT) · Digitalization · Human resource development (HRD) · Coal mining · Information Systems (IS) · Information technology (IT)

1 Introduction

Disruptive technologies and digitalization are driving change and innovation in the business landscape [1, 2]. Digitalization is changing the nature of work, the skills needed and the way the work is done [3]. A major impact of this change is a reduction in the workforces of companies due to robotics, automation, artificial intelligence (AI) and autonomous vehicles which have replaced numerous manual jobs such as mine workers', truck drivers' and receptionists' jobs. The most affected industries will be those with routine and repetitive jobs [4]. To address this problem, Stubbings and Williams [1] suggest taking deliberate action in driving technological development whilst exploring

© Springer Nature Switzerland AG 2021
Y.-M. Huang et al. (Eds.): ICITL 2021, LNCS 13117, pp. 10–21, 2021.
https://doi.org/10.1007/978-3-030-91540-7_2

innovative solutions to unemployment. According to Valsamis et al. [5], the net impact of the changes on the nature of work is still unknown and more studies need to be done to determine it. As much as technology threatens the current workforce, it has also created new jobs that require the adaptation of manual skills into new digital skills. This means that the reduction in the workforce is not as drastic as might have been expected, because technological advancement has proven to be viable due to job relocation [5]. This creates a fertile learning environment for identifying new skills and reskilling opportunities.

To determine the impact of digitalization, the paper focuses on coal miners in South Africa. This is largely because the South African mining sector is a key contributor to the South African economy and it is also responsible for the employment of many low-skilled South African workers [6]. Hence, the impact of digitalization in this sector will be massive for the South African labor market. Manual laborers, including mineworkers, should be taught new skills that are directly or indirectly related to the digital work environment, e.g., how to operate or program mining robots. The use of Africanized information systems, that are intuitive to use in local environments, could facilitate and ease such a reskilling process. Such a deserving endeavor should be founded on a suitable and rigorous Information Systems (IS) theory. Vartiainen and Hansen [7] point out that most change drivers today are IS-enabled. Therefore, the research question of this paper is: *What is a suitable theory to guide the reskilling of coal miners in the digital era?*

The authors explore Dynamic Capability Theory (DCT) as a foundation for research on how to keep coal mines competitive in the ever-changing mining business. DCT has been gaining popularity over the years across multiple disciplines, including the information systems and information technology space [8]. DCT was initially published by Teece, Pisano and Shuen [9] in the strategic management space where it was built to enhance the Resource-based View theory (RBV). Unlike its predecessor, DCT takes into consideration market dynamics, such as technology developments, changes in laws, innovation, and so on.

To begin with, the paper discusses the background of DCT, with specific reference to its origins and its relation to information systems, followed by the definition of the different concepts related to dynamic capabilities. The paper then explores the drivers of dynamic capabilities as well as the key constructs of dynamic capabilities and how they relate to human resource development (HRD). Finally, an amended dynamic capability model is proposed to be used to guide the reskilling of coal miners for the new digital era.

2 Background

According to Gumede [10], there is a need for basic mechanization or modernization geared towards the mining process to leverage it through digitalization in South Africa. Mechanization refers to the process of replacing physical tasks done by people or animals with machinery [10]. "Automation is the next phase of mechanisation, where the interaction between humans and tasks are further reduced through modern information and control systems" [10]. With this as a backdrop, the firm has two main groups of business capabilities. Firstly, operational capabilities address the day-to-day running of the business; secondly, dynamic capabilities drives the development of new operational capabilities and thereby effectively change the way the business functions [11]. However, the classification differs from one firm to another, depending on the firm's strategic outlook and the use of the capability or capabilities concerned. If the capability is strategic, it is classified as a dynamic capability, and if it has an operational nature, it is identified as an operational capability [11, 12]. Dynamic capabilities are made up of the following: dynamic managerial capabilities, dynamic integration, dynamic organization capabilities, dynamic reconfiguration, and dynamic learning. It's important for these dynamic capabilities to be cognizant of the information system landscape. IS capabilities are the abilities to acquire, deploy and leverage information system or information technology resources to strengthen business strategy and they form part of other capabilities (operational or dynamic) depending on usage [7].

Teece, Pisano and Shuen [9] introduced the DCT in their seminal 1997 paper which defined dynamic capabilities as "the firm's ability to integrate, build, and reconfigure internal and external competences to address rapidly changing environments" [9]. Since then, the theory has evolved and gained popularity [13, 14], with some authors dismissing it as "fuzzy" and "tautological" and others recommending it as a good base [15]. DCT expands on the resource-based view of the firm which states that the firm's ability to be competitive depends on the bundling of resources and capabilities that it has [8]. The resources of the firm are typically tangible or intangible assets that are used to develop or control input to the production of value in a specific market [16]. The challenge with RBV is that it is static and ignores the influence of the market dynamism. Besides, it fails to explain how resources are converted to be competitive instruments [11, 16].

Furthermore, DCT provides an ideal lens for studying how a firm can adjust its resource-base to take advantage of opportunities in the long-term [17]. Dynamic capabilities facilitate valuable, rare, inimitable and non-substitutable (VRIN) resources to ensure competitiveness and performance [11].

Since the introduction of dynamic capabilities in 1997, literature has shown a continuous increase in usage of this theory [11, 15]. This has been particularly evident in the information systems and information technology space due to the increased impact of digitalization and the fourth industrial revolution in the business landscape. The main influence of dynamic capabilities is on the resource-base, and generally resources are viewed from a technical aspect and overlook human resource (HR) as one of the critical resources in an organization. Information systems is defined as the use of information technologies by humans in conducting the affairs of the organization [18]. Human resources are a key component of this definition and it has a direct positive impact on the performance of the firm [19, 20]. A correlation exists between firm performance and human resources [12, 19], as confirmed by Breznik [13] who insists that the deployment of human resources as a dynamic capability will result in sustained competitiveness. Thus, organizational performance can be achieved by setting up human resource development (HRD) practices that enable HR as a dynamic capability. The relationship between human-resource development practice and dynamic capabilities is, however, not discussed sufficiently in existing literature [7, 21]. Neither does it break down the concept of the resource base into lower levels or show the multi-level construct nature of DC on job responsibilities as highlighted by Vartiainen and Hansen [22]. These knowledge gaps are addressed in the paper (see Sects. 5 and 6 below).

3 Definition of Dynamic Capabilities

There are several definitions of dynamic capabilities. These definitions have evolved, but the essence remains. The original definition provided by Teece, Pisano and Shuen [9] refers to "the firm's ability to integrate, build, and reconfigure internal and external competences to address rapidly changing environments" [9]. Eisenhardt and Martin [23] further expand this definition as follows: "The firm's processes that use resources — specifically the processes to integrate, reconfigure, gain and release resources — to match, and even create market change. Dynamic capabilities thus are the organizational and strategic routines by which firms achieve new resource configurations as markets emerge, collide, split, evolve, and die." Therefore, the key highlight of this definition is that dynamic capabilities influence a firm's strategic routines and processes.

Similarly, in an attempt to simplify dynamic capability definitions, Helfat et al. [15] redefined dynamic capabilities as follows: "A dynamic capability is the capacity of an organization to purposefully create, extend, or modify its resource base". Furthermore, recent papers have simplified the definition of dynamic capabilities to three main constructs: sense; seize (orchestrate the design of the business); and transform (implement a business model) [16, 24–26].

Additionally, DCT states that capabilities represent resources within the organization. To this end, the dynamic capability conceptualization of company resources and the evolving business environment is generative for grasping how resources are utilised to remain competitive. As a result, this supports the reason why any company adopts information systems, which is the use of information technology, people and organizational processes to be competitive.

According to Teece [25], dynamic capabilities are divided into 'microfoundation' and 'macro-level capabilities'. The former deals with new product development, expansion into new regions, and obtaining new resources through acquisitions and alliances [27]. Microfoundation refers to the analysis of dynamic capabilities in its lowest form. Carnahan et al. [28] provide a more comprehensive definition of the microfoundation as follows: "The microfoundations of dynamic capabilities — distinct skills, processes, procedures, organizational structures, decision rules, and disciplines — which undergird enterprise-level sensing, seizing, and reconfiguring capacities are difficult to develop and deploy" [28]. Contrary to this, the macro-level capabilities are higher-level processes that help the organization achieve its daily operational abilities to attain its goals [15, 21, 28]. These higher-order capabilities deal with changing and rebuilding the ordinary capabilities of the organization.

Fallon-Byrne and Harney [21] oppose the popular view by highlighting the need to further expand on the concept of microfoundation of dynamic capabilities at a lower level. They believe that sensing, seizing and reconfiguration are at a macro level and not a micro level, as demonstrated in their model [25, p. 26]. This is in direct contradiction with Teece's [28] perspective which is based on the dynamic capability framework which will be discussed later on. Fallon-Byrne and Harney's [21] model uses an innovation perspective and it argues that an innovation strategy represents human resources [21].

There are four main themes within the dynamic capabilities for innovation model as discussed by Fallon-Byrne and Harney [21]: organizational innovation strategies, climate (i.e., innovation and affective behaviors), dynamic capabilities and outcomes. The first two themes represent microfoundations of the organization while the last two themes are represented by dynamic capabilities and innovation outcomes respectively, and it can be deduced that they are macrofoundations. The bottom part of the dynamic capabilities for innovation model [25, p. 26] illustrates the link between the following human resource views: intended managerial strategy, employee perspective, employee behavior, dynamic capability, and organizational outcomes. This view is instrumental in the contextualization of the relationships between macro and micro-processes. This demonstrates that microfoundations are multi-layered [21] and Teece [25] supports this argument. According to Teece [25], sensing, seizing and transforming can be seen as the top layer of the microfoundation.

3.1 Definition of Capability

Capability is defined as the ability to perform a particular task or activity [15]. Firms use capabilities to achieve their goals, as highlighted by Helfat et al. [15] and Teece [28]. Also, there are different types of capabilities as listed below:

Substantive capabilities [8] are the abilities to solve business problems.

Higher-order capabilities [25, 26] are "the abilities to change the way the firm solves its problems" [29].

Innovative capability is "the ability to develop new products or markets" [30]. In the context of this paper, this refers to using new technologies to create new products, processes and markets.

Absorptive capabilities refer to "the ability of a firm to recognize the value of new, external information, assimilate it, and apply it to commercial ends" [11]. In the context of this paper, this means the ability to identify emerging disruptive technologies and how they will affect the business landscape.

Adaptive capability [11, 30] is the firm's ability to identify and take advantage of emerging market opportunities such as technology.

Dynamic managerial capabilities are the abilities of the firm's management to motivate their skills and experience for the management of a changing landscape.

Dynamic organizational capabilities [8, 25, 31] refer to the ability of the organization to deal with changing business landscapes.

It is, therefore, apparent that the above-mentioned capabilities are especially relevant in this digital age as they can be categorized into one of either operational type of capabilities or dynamic type of capabilities (see Table 1). The former enables the organization to earn a living by running the day-to-day routines. In contrast, the latter is concerned with the future adaptability of the organization [15]. Therefore, it supports the original argument by Teece, Pisano and Shuen (1997) that operational capabilities ensure that the company delivers on its value proposition on a daily basis.

Table 1. Operational vs. dynamic capabilities.

Operational capabilities	Dynamic capabilities
Substantive capabilities	Innovative capability
Higher-order capabilities	Absorptive capability
Human resource capabilities	Adaptive capability
First-order capabilities	Dynamic managerial capabilities
Human resource development (HRD)	Dynamic organizational capabilities
IS capabilities	IS capabilities
	Strategic human resource development (SHRD)

4 Constructs of Dynamic Capabilities

The key constructs and elements of dynamic capabilities shown in Teece's [21] dynamic capability framework illustrate the ability to sense changes in the business environment and to seize the change advantageously by designing a refined business model and committing the necessary resources to finally transform the organization by realigning and influencing its culture. These abilities are crucial, particularly in the digital era where information technologies are affecting the business model. Taking into consideration the current strategy of the Minerals Council South Africa to modernize mining operations [10], mines' management needs to go through a process of sensing new technologies relevant for the mining industry, such as robotics, artificial intelligence (AI), autonomous driving and the like [32]. They should then seize any opportunities for modifying their business models to ensure adoption of the digital technologies. Once that is done, they need to realign the mining culture with the new technologies.

According to DCT, the three main processes for dynamic capabilities are:

Sense, which is defined as the continuous scanning of the environment internally and externally for opportunities brought by market dynamism [13, 15, 24].

Seize, which refers to the firm's ability to take advantage of the opportunities by designing and refining the business model and ensuring that resources are committed to take advantage. (Breznik [13] highlights that seizing is about making a good decision in uncertain times.)

Transform, which refers to the firm's ability to realign and re-configure its routines, processes, structures and culture [13, 15, 24].

According to Teece's [21] framework, the above three processes are also referred to as "microfoundations" as they enable internal knowledge and skills development to gain a competitive advantage. Furthermore, it has become apparent that the success of dynamic capabilities is dependent on the role, skills and competences of the manager [13, 25]. Management has developed into a sub-field of dynamic managerial capabilities [25] which, in turn, has led to the dynamic managerial capabilities (DMC). DMC refers to senior management's abilities to effectively alter company routines, processes and resources configuration [29]. Therefore, a manager's perspective concerning dynamic capabilities is crucial for orchestrating and enabling change to take advantage of opportunities [29]. To be effective in the transformation journey, the manager needs to be adaptive, absorptive and to possess innovative capabilities [11].

A firm-specific process, such as integration, reconfiguration, renewal and recreation, together with the above capabilities, will regulate the firmness of the dynamic capabilities within the firm. It can therefore be concluded that higher performance and appropriate change in the organization is reliant on the viability of the dynamic capabilities.

Wang and Ahmed's [13, p. 39] research model of dynamic capabilities shows that market dynamism triggers dynamic capabilities. Dynamic capabilities are made up of two main parts: the common features depicting component factors, and firm-specific processes depicting underlying processes. The higher the dynamic capabilities the firm shows, the more likely it will be to build new capabilities over time. As a result, the development of these new capabilities will be directed by the firms. It is also important to note that capability development differs from business to business as it is simultaneously directed by the strategy and the dynamic capabilities of the firm concerned.

Capability development has a direct influence on the performance of the firm, as per the research model [13, p. 39].

Notably, the influence of dynamic capabilities on performance generally takes place over the long-term rather than the short-term [11].

As a result, capability development deals with the development of strategic dynamic capabilities – such as strategic human resource development (SHRD), dynamic management, dynamic learning and others – that will move the firm into the future.

5 Discussion

It is therefore apparent that similarities exist between Teece's [25] dynamic capabilities framework and Wang and Ahmed's [11] research model of dynamic capabilities. Wang and Ahmed's [11] model takes a wider view on their modelling to include market dynamism and capability development. In contrast, Teece's [25] model focuses on the dynamic capabilities, business model and strategy. It can also be seen that the firm-specific process that forms part of Wang and Ahmed's research model reflects the dynamic capability process, which itself resembles Teece's dynamic capability framework. Both models show the influence of strategy on the dynamic capabilities, but Teece [25] expands on the strategy discussion by explaining the relationship between the strategy and the business model.

Teece [25] and Wang and Ahmed [11] discuss the importance of human resource development and dynamic managerial capabilities, however, their models do not reflect this. Consequently, this creates a misconception of human resources and dynamic managerial capabilities as equivalent to other dynamic capabilities. Furthermore, as mentioned earlier, the manager's perspective is crucial, and it needs to be technology conscious. Hence, Wang and Ahmed's [11] model discusses common features which are constituent factors for management, adaptive capability, absorptive capability and innovative capability. These constituent factors are therefore crucial in establishing SHRD practice which will develop the human resources in the firm or establish if additional ones are needed. This means that features common to both can be expanded to effectively reflect the dynamic managerial capabilities and SHRD. Therefore, this paper expands the dynamic capability framework to incorporate the proposed additions, as indicated in the proposed model in Fig. 1. Also, the literature review exposes a gap between the relationship of human resource development practice and dynamic capability [19, 33]. This indicates a need for further studies to be conducted in this area. Furthermore, dynamic capability literature describes the resource base as a significant element of DCT, but it does not break down the concept of the resource base into lower levels [15]. It does, however, describe resource-base elements, such as assets, equipment, relationships and human resources.

This paper aims to break down the aspect of the resource base and focuses, in particular, on the human-resource aspect. According to the findings of Kareem and Mijbas [33], the relationship between HRD and organizational effectiveness is not direct in changing the business environment but indirect through the facilitation of dynamic capabilities.

HRD has been defined as "a process of developing and unleashing expertise to improve individual and teamwork processes, and organizational systems" [12]. Kareem and Mijbas [33] expand on the definition to includ deliberate plan for developing an employee's knowledge, skills and abilities to increase organizational effectiveness concerning the adoption of information systems. This is, however, rejected by Garavan and Carbery [12] who distinguish between HRD and SHRD. Garavan and Carbery [12] insist that the former looks at HRD from an operational perspective while the latter has a strategic perspective of the HRD.

6 Proposed Model

Figure 1 proposes a model that takes into account dynamic management capabilities and strategic human resource development. The proposed model shows dynamic management capabilities as an extension of dynamic capabilities because the manager's perspective is essential for sensing changes and for developing relevant SHRD. This is important so as to ensure that managers can recognize emerging technologies and react appropriately to empower employees with the right knowledge and skills through the SHRD. The relationship between dynamic management capabilities and SHRD practice is a continuous loop to influence human resource development. Senior management must understand the components of information systems and their impact on the business. SHRD will influence seizing and transformation to ensure competitiveness.

The output of the transformation process is the alignment of existing processes and/or investment in additional capabilities. The arrows in the model show the flow of information and influence exercised by the items described in the various boxes.

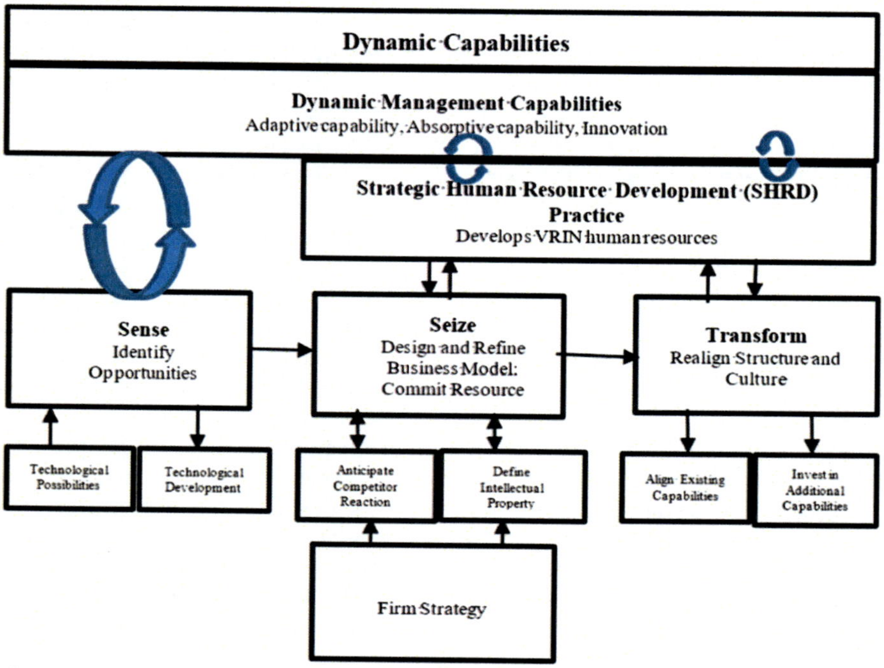

Fig. 1. Proposed dynamic capability model.

7 Conclusion

The paper developed the proposed framework that can be used to help reskill coal miners for the digital era to mitigate the societal impact of emerging mining technologies. Applying the proposed dynamic capability model (see Fig. 1) to the coal mining industry could lead to a position that enables the leadership of a mine to develop high strength dynamic capabilities to ensure that the reskilling of the coal miners will take place.

The assumption is that mining companies will adopt disruptive technologies as part of the mechanization of mines. The Minerals Council South Africa is promoting the modernization strategy of the mines by embracing automated and autonomous technologies among others, which will have a huge impact on skills and labor markets [34].

In line with the literature, coal mines need to develop dynamic capabilities within the firm to sense market changes and thereby see opportunities and threats. For example, the mechanization of the mining industry and the resulting decrease in profit margins make it difficult for businesses to realize value [34]. Coal mines will, therefore, need to seize the opportunity to mechanize their business to stay relevant and profitable. This will require dynamic managerial capability from the mines' management teams. Lastly, the mines will need to transform or reconfigure some of their capabilities and develop new capabilities. This will be done through reconfiguring human resources. One of the biggest resources in a coal mine is the human resource – the miners who go through the process of extracting coal from the ground. In future, miners will be expected to use new digital technologies to perform their duties. This paper has attempted to highlight the need for a transformation process and to develop a conceptual framework that could guide the reconfiguration of coal miners for the future. "Substantial changes to the organizational structures and business processes will work in concert with technology improvements to enable a substantial shift in the way mining enterprises work" [35]. The organization and its people need to work together to identify changes that digitalization (prompted by the fourth industrial revolution) is bringing to the company.

A limitation of this paper is that no empirical evidence yet exists to support the design of the proposed conceptual framework. In future work, qualitative research should be conducted to provide this evidence and to refine the framework even further, based on the results of such empirical work. The specific needs of the African continent and its divergent cultures should be taken into consideration when the proposed framework is refined and implemented. It is anticipated that this paper will spark interest in learning about the impact of innovative technologies on current skills sets in the coal mining sector, and the adjustment thereof by using e-learning technologies.

Acknowledgements. This work is based on research supported in part by the National Research Foundation of South Africa (Grant Number 132180) and the University of South Africa's Research Professor Support Programme. The grant holder acknowledges that opinions, findings and conclusions or recommendations expressed in the article are that of the authors, and that the NRF/Unisa accepts no liability whatsoever in this regard. We would like to thank the editors, programme chairs and reviewers for their feedback that guided us to improve the article.

References

1. Stubbings, C., Williams, J., Sethi, B., Brown, J.: Workforce of the future: the competing forces shaping 2030. www.pwc.com (2017)
2. Brundrett, S.: Industry analysis of autonomous mine haul truck commercialization (2014). https://doi.org/10.1007/s13398-014-0173-7.2
3. OECD: Going digital: making the transformation work for growth and well-being. https://ec.europa.eu/futurium/en/system/files/ged/going_digital_longflyer_jan_2017.pdf (2017)
4. OECD: Future of work and skills (2017)
5. Valsamis, D., de Coen, A., Vanoeteren, V., Van der Beken, W.: Employment and skills aspects of the digital single market strategy. Eur. Parliament (0), 1–67 (2015)
6. Statistics South Africa: National accounts: mineral accounts for South Africa: 1990–2010. https://www.destatis.de/EN/FactsFigures/NationalEconomyEnvironment/NationalAccounts/DomesticProduct/Tables/GrossValueAddedIndustries_BWS.html (2013)
7. Vartiainen, K., Hansen, L.K.: Dynamic capabilities in information systems research – a literature review. Selected Papers of the IRIS, Issue Nr 9 (2018), vol. 2 no. 9 (2019)
8. Barreto, I.: Dynamic capabilities: a review of past research and an agenda for the future. J. Manage. **36**(1), 256–280 (2010). https://doi.org/10.1177/0149206309350776
9. Teece, D.J., Pisano, G., Shuen, A.: Dynamic capabilities and strategic management. Strateg. Manage. J. **18**(7), 509–533 (1997). https://doi.org/10.1142/9789812796929_0004
10. Gumede, H.: The socio-economic effects of mechanising and/or modernising hard rock mines in South Africa. South Afr. J. Econ. Manage. Sci. **21**(1), 1–11 (2018)

11. Wang, C.L., Ahmed, P.K.: Dynamic capabilities: a review and research agenda. Int. J. Manage. Rev. **9**(1), 31–51 (2007). https://doi.org/10.1111/j.1468-2370.2007.00201.x
12. Garavan, T.N., Carbery, R.: Strategic human resource development. J. Eur. Ind. Train. **15**(1), 23–44 (2012). https://doi.org/10.1108/EUM0000000000219
13. Breznik, L.: Deploying human resource capability for sustainable performance : a dynamic capabilities framework. In: Human Capital without Borders: Knowledge and Learning for Quality of Life, pp. 561–570. Portoroz, Slovenia (2014)
14. Helfat, C.E., Peteraf, M.A.: Understanding dynamic capabilities: progress along a developmental path. Strateg. Organ. **7**(1), 91–102 (2009). https://doi.org/10.1177/1476127008100133
15. Helfat, C., et al.: Dynamic Capabilities: Understanding Strategic Change in Organizations. Blackwell, Malden, MA, USA (2007)
16. Ahmad, M., Papert, M., Pflaum, A.: Dynamic capabilities related implementation skills for internet of things solutions in the digital economy. In: Proceedings of the 51st Hawaii International Conference on System Sciences, pp. 3996–4005. Hawaii (2018). https://doi.org/10.24251/HICSS.2018.502
17. Doherty, N., Morgan, T., Jobs, S., Doherty, N.F.: Incremental innovation by design: a dynamic capabilities perspective. In: UK Academy for Information Systems Conference Proceedings, p. 14. Spring, UK (2016)
18. Paul, R.J.: What an information system is, and why is it important to know this. J. Comput. Inf. Technol. **18**(2), 95 (2010). https://doi.org/10.2498/cit.1001800
19. Garavan, T., Shanahan, V., Carbery, R., Watson, S.: Strategic human resource development: towards a conceptual framework to understand its contribution to dynamic capabilities. Hum. Resour. Dev. Int. **19**(4), 289–306 (2016). https://doi.org/10.1080/13678868.2016.1169765
20. Kamoche, K.: Strategic human resource management within a resource – capability view of the firm. J. Manage. Stud. **33**(2), 213–233 (1996). https://doi.org/10.1111/j.1467-6486.1996.tb00158.x
21. Fallon-Byrne, L., Harney, B.: Microfoundations of dynamic capabilities for innovation: a review and research agenda. Ir. J. Manage. **36**(1), 21–31 (2017). https://doi.org/10.1515/ijm-2017-0004
22. Vartiainen, K.: In search of the? How? Of dynamic capabilities in digital transformation: contradictions as a source of understanding. In: 26th Americas Conference on Information Systems, AMCIS 2020, pp. 0–5 (2020)
23. Eisenhardt, K.M., Martin, J.A.: Dynamic capabilities: what are they? Strateg. Manage. J. **1121**(21), 1105–1121 (2000)
24. Arora, S.K., Li, Y., Youtie, J., Shapira, P.: Measuring dynamic capabilities in new ventures: exploring strategic change in US green goods manufacturing using website data. J. Technol. Transfer **45**(5), 1451–1480 (2019). https://doi.org/10.1007/s10961-019-09751-y
25. Teece, D.J.: Business models and dynamic capabilities. Long Range Plann. **51**(1), 40–49 (2018). https://doi.org/10.1016/j.lrp.2017.06.007
26. Mikalef, P.: IT-enabled dynamic capabilities, environmental uncertainty, and competitive performance: a configurational approach. In: Americas Conference on Information Systems AMCIS, pp. 1–10 (2018)
27. Garavan, T.N.: A strategic perspective on human resource development. Adv. Dev. Hum. Resour. **9**(1), 11–30 (2007). https://doi.org/10.1177/1523422306294492
28. Teece, D.J.: Explicating dynamic capabilities: the nature and microfoundations of (sustainable) enterprise performance. Strateg. Manage. J. **28**(13), 1319–1350 (2007). https://doi.org/10.1002/smj.640
29. Zahra, S.A., Sapienza, H.J., Davidsson, P.: Entrepreneurship and dynamic capabilities: a review, model and research agenda. J. Manage. Stud. **43**(4), 917–955 (2006). https://doi.org/10.1111/j.1467-6486.2006.00616.x

30. El Gizawi, N.: The dynamic capabilities theory: assessment and evaluation as a contributing theory for supply chain management. In: 3rd IBA Bachelor Thesis Conference, pp. 1–15 (2014)
31. Konlechner, S., Müller, B., Güttel, W.H.: A dynamic capabilities perspective on managing technological change: a review, framework and research agenda. Int. J. Technol. Manage. **76**(3/4), 188 (2018). https://doi.org/10.1504/IJTM.2018.091285
32. O'Callaghan, J., et al.: We need to talk about the future of mining (2017)
33. Kareem, M.A., Mijbas, H.A.: Mediating role of dynamic capabilities on the relationship between human resource development and organizational effectiveness. Organizacija **52**(3), 187–203 (2019). https://doi.org/10.2478/orga-2019-0012
34. Leeuw, P., Mtegha, H.: The significance of mining backward and forward linkages in reskilling redundant mine workers in South Africa. Resour. Policy **56**, 31–37 (2018). https://doi.org/10.1016/j.resourpol.2018.02.004
35. Bassan, J., Srinivasan, V., Knights, P., Farrelly, C.T.: A day in the life of a mine worker in 2025. In: 1st International Future Mining Conference and Exhibition, no. 10, pp. 71–78 (2008)

Exploring the Impact of Artificial Intelligence Learning Platforms on Interest in and Attitudes Toward Learning

Hua-Xu Zhong[1], Chin-Feng Lai[1], Yu-Che Huang[1], Pei-Hsuan Wu[3], and Jui-Hung Chang[2](✉)

[1] Department of Engineering Science, National Cheng Kung University 1, University Road, Tainan 701, Taiwan, R.O.C.

[2] Department of Computer Science and Information Engineering, Department of Electrical, Engineering, National Cheng Kung University 1, University Road, Tainan 701, Taiwan, R.O.C.
changrh@mail.ncku.edu.tw

[3] Department of Computer Science and Information Engineering, National Cheng Kung University 1, University Road, Tainan 701, Taiwan, R.O.C.

Abstract. Artificial Intelligence (AI) learning technologies and research in deep learning are rapidly expanding, and there is a lack of AI learning platforms to support students in related courses. At present, an understanding of the impact of learning on AI learning platforms on student interest in and attitudes towards learning is still unclear. This has thus become an important research topic in the field of AI. This study implemented an AI learning platform (Ladder) to deliver AI courses to students using two questionnaires (interest in learning and attitude towards learning). The study was implemented to survey 65 university students (males = 55, females = 10) at a national university in southern Taiwan, where 65 students were surveyed to obtain their opinions on their interest in learning and attitudes towards learning after learning on the AI learning platform. The results of the survey showed that about 40% of the students were interested in learning and had a positive attitude towards the AI learning platform. In addition, undergraduate university students may not always attach importance to AI. The findings of this study provide researchers and teachers with a better understanding of students' perceptions of their interest learning and attitudes toward learning.

Keywords: Artificial intelligence · Machine learning · Learning interest · Attitude toward attitude · Learning platform

1 Introduction

As one of the most successful machine learning methods in supervised learning, neural networks (NNs) have changed modern everyday life radically and have had a huge impact on even the most basic of our actions [1]. Because of its relative opaqueness, a neural network is known as a 'black box,' which makes it impossible to know the entire mode of operation, which has been the focus of discussion in recent years [2, 3]. An artificial

© Springer Nature Switzerland AG 2021
Y.-M. Huang et al. (Eds.): ICITL 2021, LNCS 13117, pp. 22–29, 2021.
https://doi.org/10.1007/978-3-030-91540-7_3

intelligence learning tool based on deep learning and a plat-form that enables developers and learners to quickly reuse resources are the trends of the future [4]. If the students combine their learning with practical application exercises, they can enhance their basic knowledge of deep learning techniques, and their level of enthusiasm in this field will increase.

Deep learning has a minimum learning threshold related to basic programming skills, and students also encounter programming problems and challenges during the learning process. The process of learning a program can cause a variety of learning issues related to a lack of programming experience or a misunderstanding of the pro-gram, which can lead to negative attitudes toward learning [5]. The relevant literature on programming indicates that different teaching methods [6, 7] and teaching tools [8, 9] can be used to influence students' attitudes towards learning. Students interested in the process of learning a program are encouraged to have a positive learning attitude and to participate in the course [10] because attitude toward learning is one of the important factors that affects learning outcomes [7]. Furthermore, if new pro-gramming concepts attract the interest of students, they will learn them with a positive attitude [5]. However, the current understanding of students' interest in learning and their attitudes towards artificial intelligence is still unclear.

Therefore, in the current study, an AI learning platform (Ladder) was implemented to provide students with AI courses intended to enhance students' interest in learning and improve their attitude toward learning. According to this research purpose, we attempted to answer the following research question: After learning on an AI learning platform, what are university students' perceptions of their interest in and attitudes toward learning?

2 Literature Review

2.1 Artificial Intelligence (AI)

Traditional machine learning techniques are limited to processing data in its raw form. In contrast, deep learning allows models consisting of multiple processing layers to learn the features of data. This method has improved the state of speech recognition, graphic recognition, object detection, and many other such techniques [11]. A broad deep neural network-work (DNN) architecture consists of an input layer, sever-al hidden layers, and an output layer. In each layer, there are several units called neurons, which receive multiple inputs, weight their inputs, and generate output values by means of an activation function. Each neuron has a vector of weights associated with its input size and a bias optimized during training [12, 13].

2.2 AI Learning Platforms

Relevant AI learning platforms and research on this topic are rapidly developing. One such effort is a systematic review of studies by [14] that analyzed the last seven years (from 2014 to 2020) of AI adaptive learning systems, and identified key topics in the visualization of AI research objectives, AI learning interventions, and AI learning analyses. The fundamentals of deep learning techniques are important to college students in related professions. Students need to acquire not only basic deep learning knowledge, but also must experience practical application of the acquired knowledge to complete learning tasks and develop a complete concept of deep learning.

Artificial intelligence learning systems provide different functions to help students learn and solve problems [14]. For example: [15] proposed the DL-OIET system to provide students with personalized learning and used neural networks to plan learning for students in order to enhance their English learning outcomes. [16] Used a deep neural network to propose an assessment of an e-learning platform and examined students' flow experience in order to facilitate personalized learning. [17] Investigated the implementation of a virtual learning environment and proposed an artificial neural network model intended to improve examination pass rates.

3 Research Method

3.1 Sample

In this study, an AI learning platform was implemented in a top national university in southern Taiwan for 65 students (male = 55, female = 10) with consent from all students. The students all had programming experience but no relevant AI experience.

3.2 Research Platform

Description of the Functions of the Artificial Intelligence Learning Platform (Ladder). In this study, an artificial intelligence curriculum was implemented for university students on an artificial intelligence learning platform (Ladder). This learning plat-form (Ladder) is a model-building platform using graphical machine learning structures with the following functions:

Layer Operations. The convolution layer is mainly composed of many different kernels that perform the convolutional operations on the input image, as shown in part (a) of Fig. 1. In this section, the user can adjust the number of neurons (Hidden Size) in the convolutional layer.

A convolutional layer is a set of parallel feature maps, which are formed by sliding different kernel sizes over the input image and performing certain operations. Thus, the user can adjust the number of neurons (Hidden Size), the Filter Width (also called the kernel size), stride, the Keep dimension (the same as padding), and other values to determine the output of the layer.

Learning Parameters. As shown in part (b) of Fig. 1, the neuron takes multiple inputs and adds them together by weighting each input, and optimizing the bias values during the training process. Then, the resulting values are passed through an activation function to pro-duce the output values. Therefore, the user can choose between the weight and bias modes, and the two learning parameters can be fine-tuned with more detailed variable settings.

Layer Proceedings. As shown in part (c) of Fig. 1, batch normalization can be standardized for each batch of data, and Dropout mode can be entered to randomly turn off some neurons to significantly reduce overfitting. Users can also choose a preferred activation function to non-linearly transform the neuron output values, which can all be used to mitigate the gradient disappearance problem in the depth model.

Output Manipulations. As shown in part (d) of Fig. 1, the user can select whether to flatten the output matrix or to output it in a specified shape to ensure that the next layer receives the out-put matrix shape.

Use of the Artificial Intelligence Learning Platform (Ladder). The actual operation process of this platform (Ladder) is shown in Fig. 1: (1) Step 1: The user enters the local data source. (2) Step 2: When the user adds a layer, a dialog box with default values will pop up, and the user can decide whether to adjust the values related to the layer operations related. (3) Step 3: The user can click on the new layer to display the attributes (a ~ d) on the right side and make changes. (4) Step 4: The user selects the type of task to be performed, e.g., indicates the number of categories if it is a category task. (5) Step 5: After editing the model, the user can download the model code and run the file locally for training.

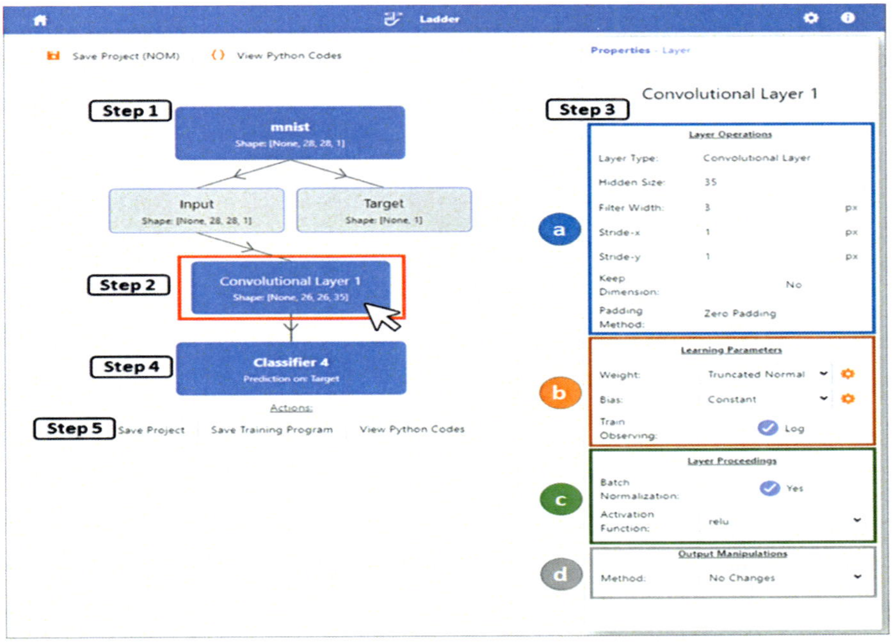

Fig. 1. Artificial intelligence learning platform (Ladder) functional interface and operation process.

The user can upload the training results to the platform and directly see if the loss function has been successfully converged and if the accuracy of the results has been stabilized in the visualization of the model training curve and in the presentation of the actual test results. The learning platform helps users build their models and produce a clear picture of the results for observation and analysis, further enhancing their impression of the effectiveness of deep learning.

3.3 Research Instrument

The instrument was modified from a study by [18], which had two variables including seven questionnaire items on learning attitudes and six questionnaire items on learning interests (Table 1).

Table 1. Descriptive statistics for learning interest, and learning attitude.

Dimension ($N = 65$)	Items	Percentages (%)					Mean	S.D.
		1	2	3	4	5		
Learning interest	Lint 1 AI courses are interesting to learn	0.0	3.1	33.8	44.6	18.5	3.78	0.78
	Lint 2 Learning about relevant AI knowledge is interesting	0.0	1.5	26.2	47.7	24.6	3.95	0.759
	Lint 3 Learning about AI-related concepts and knowledge is interesting	0.0	0.0	23.1	53.8	23.1	4	0.685
	Lint 4 It is interesting to practice the practical AI tasks in the AI course	0.0	0.0	40.0	41.5	18.5	3.78	0.739
	Lint 5 The teacher's guidance and teaching instructions attracted my attention in the AI course	0.0	1.5	40.0	41.5	16.9	3.74	0.756
	Lint 6 For me, AI courses are more interesting than other programming courses	3.1	0.0	46.2	33.8	16.9	3.62	0.878
Learning attitude	Latt 1 AI courses are valuable and worth taking	0.0	0.0	20.0	43.1	36.9	4.17	.741

(*continued*)

Table 1. (*continued*)

Dimension ($N = 65$)	Items	Percentages (%)					Mean	S.D.
		1	2	3	4	5		
	Latt 2 It is worth learning about AI	0.0	0.0	15.4	38.5	46.2	4.31	.727
	Latt 3 It is worth taking this AI course	0.0	0.0	21.5	43.1	35.4	4.14	.747
	Latt 4 It is important to understand the relevant AI information, including modelling, design models, and AI concepts	0.0	0.0	15.4	46.2	38.5	4.23	.702
	Latt 5 It is important to understand the concepts and applications of AI	0.0	1.5	16.9	41.5	40.0	4.20	.775
	Latt 6 I would actively seek out more relevant AI concepts and applications	0.0	0.0	36.9	43.1	20.0	3.83	.741
	Latt 7 It is important for everyone to take an AI course	4.6	15.4	29.2	29.2	21.5	3.48	1.13

4 Results

The findings of this study show that the students' learning interest in the AI course was positive. Almost 40% of students chose option 4, and others chose options 3 and 5. Only a few students chose options 1 and 2. The mean value of the questionnaire items ranged from 3.74 to 4, indicating a positive evaluation of students' interest in the AI learning platform. The results of the study showed that the AI learning plat-form can engage students' interest in AI.

In addition, the results show that students' learning of the AI course aroused positive learning attitudes among students. About 40% of the students chose option 4, and the other students chose option 3 and option 5. The mean value of the questionnaire item ranged from 3.48 to 4.31, which indicates that the students had a positive attitude towards learning when using the AI platform. In particular, for the Latt 7 item, the results showed that the percentage of students choosing the option varied across students. This means that undergraduates may not always value AI as a career path, depending on their own personal interests and career goals.

5 Conclusions

The purpose of this study was to implement an artificial intelligence learning platform (Ladder) and to identify students' perceptions of their learning interests and attitudes. The artificial intelligence learning platform provided students with systematic learning about AI and helped them to understand the concept of AI. The results showed that about 40% of the students positively evaluated their learning interest and learning attitude. They also showed an interest in and a positive attitude towards learning on the AI learning platform. In addition, the results indicated that undergraduate university students may not always value and move towards artificial intelligence as a career path. This study provides researchers and teachers with an AI learning platform for students and a better understanding of students' perceptions of their learning interests and attitudes. There are, however, some limitations to this study. The students were recruited from top national universities in the Department of Computer Science and Information Engineering, and some of the students may thus have already had positive learning interests and attitudes towards AI. This might have biased the results of the study. More importantly, future research could consider the implementation of AI learning platforms for university students from other disciplines and explore the impact of other variables.

Acknowledgment. We thank the anonymous reviewers for their constructive comments. This research work was supported in part by the Ministry of Science and Technology of Taiwan, ROC. (MOST 108-2221-E-006-173-MY2).

References

1. Shiloh-Perl, L., Giryes, R.: Introduction to Deep Learning. arXiv:2003.03253 (2020)
2. Samek, W., Wiegand, T., Müller, K.-R.: Explainable Artificial Intelligence: Understanding, Visualizing and Interpreting Deep Learning Models. arXiv:1708.08296 (2017)
3. Marcus, G.: Deep Learning: A Critical Appraisal. arXiv:1801.00631 (2018)
4. Muniasamy, A., Alasiry, A.: Deep learning: the impact on future eLearning. Int. J. Emerg. Technol. Learn. **15**(01), 188 (2020)
5. Yang, J., Wong, G.K.W., Dawes, C.: An exploratory study on learning attitude in computer programming for the twenty-first century. In: Deng, L., Ma, W.W.K., Fong, C.W.R. (eds.) New media for educational change. ECTY, pp. 59–70. Springer, Singapore (2018). https://doi.org/10.1007/978-981-10-8896-4_5
6. Hooshyar, D., Malva, L., Yang, Y., Pedaste, M., Wang, M., Lim, H.: An adaptive educational computer game: effects on students' knowledge and learn-ing attitude in computational thinking. Comput. Hum. Behav. **114**, 106575 (2021)
7. Tisza, G., Markopoulos, P.: Understanding the role of fun in learning to code. Int. J. Child-Comput. Interact. **28**, 100270 (2021)
8. Yukselturk, E., Altiok, S.: An investigation of the effects of programming with Scratch on the preservice IT teachers' self-efficacy perceptions and attitudes towards computer programming. Br. J. Edu. Technol. **48**(3), 789–801 (2017)
9. Papavlasopoulou, S., Sharma, K., Giannakos, M.N.: How do you feel about learning to code? Investigating the effect of children's attitudes towards coding using eye-tracking. Int. J. Child-Comput. Interact. **17**, 50–60 (2018)

10. Sun, J.C.-Y., Rueda, R.: Situational interest, computer self-efficacy and self-regulation: their impact on student engagement in distance education. Br. J. Edu. Technol. **43**(2), 191–204 (2012)
11. LeCun, Y., Bengio, Y., Hinton, G.: Deep learning. Nature **521**(7553), 436–444 (2015)
12. Chollet, F.: Deep Learning with Python. Simon and Schuster (2017)
13. Al-Garadi, M.A., et al.: A survey of machine and deep learning methods for internet of things (IoT) security. IEEE Commun. Surv. Tutorials **22**(3), 1646–1685 (2020)
14. Kabudi, T., Pappas, I., Olsen, D.H.: AI-enabled adaptive learning systems: a systematic mapping of the literature. Comput. Educ. Artif. Intell. **2**, 100017 (2021)
15. Sun, Z., Anbarasan, M., Praveen Kumar, D.: Design of online intelligent english teaching platform based on artificial intelligence techniques. Comput. Intell. **37**(3), 1166–1180 (2020)
16. Semerci, Y.C., Goularas, D.: Evaluation of students' flow state in an e-learning environment through activity and performance using deep learning techniques. J. Educ. Comput. Res. **59**(5), 960–987 (2020)
17. Rivas, A., et al.: Artificial neural network analysis of the academic performance of students in virtual learning environments. Neurocomputing **423**, 713–720 (2021)
18. Hwang, G.-J., Chang, H.-F.: A formative assessment-based mobile learning approach to improving the learning attitudes and achievements of students. Comput. Educ. **56**(4), 1023–1031 (2011)

Lightening Up a New AI Cognitions and Performances for Engineering Students' Problem-Based Learning in Nature General Education Programs

King-Dow Su[1,2](✉)

[1] Hungkuo Delin University of Technology, New Taipei, Taiwan
su-87168@mail.hdut.edu.tw
[2] Chung Yuan Christian University, Taoyuan, Taiwan

Abstract. The purpose of this research focused on designing artificial intelligence (AI) life learning texts for problem-based learning (PBL). Starting students in life AI scientific knowledge experience of practical value. This research used the effective evaluation tool to evaluate the learning results and feedback of 83 university students, and obtained the following four results: (1) to design three AI teaching units on the social application situational issues in life science; (2) to develop authentic tools with a good validity and reliability (Cronbach's α, 0.946) for students' open-ended questions of the AI course PBL learning results and PBL attitude questionnaire with AI situational issues; (3) to present students' logical reasoning and activation ability, and improve the cognitive levels of problem-solving by quantitative analysis of learning achievements; (4) to show that the factor of students disposition AI courses is the most important for their impact on learning attitudes by one-way ANOVA.

Keywords: Artificial intelligence · Problem-based learning · Cognitive levels · Learning performances

1 Introduction

The 21st century is the innovation era of knowledge economy, the rapid rise of new technology industry, in order to meet the fourth era of scientific and technological revolution, Artificial Intelligence (AI), Internet of Things (IOT) and 5G are quietly entering our life circle. With the rise of AI around the world, AI will bring unprecedented changes to human society, AI has become the current learning. In recent years, students' interest in the meaning of AI in social applications has continued to grow, making AI not only appear in their own fields, but also play an interdisciplinary role in the application of tools (Rihtaršič et al. 2016). However, most students' cognition and application of AI is still limited, how to face the talent demand in the new century when AI becomes the core of the fourth scientific and technological revolution, so that students can grasp the

© Springer Nature Switzerland AG 2021
Y.-M. Huang et al. (Eds.): ICITL 2021, LNCS 13117, pp. 30–38, 2021.
https://doi.org/10.1007/978-3-030-91540-7_4

development trend and context of AI, learn and experience new technology, has become the focus of attention in many countries around the world.

According to this, advanced countries have been actively involved in AI research and development and education site integration (Alimisis 2013). Then, the AI in the information teaching education research is not so much and teaching integration at the university level is more limited. The current AI curriculum and teaching still have some problems that students on AI's social and historical literacy still only stay in the knowledge concept of the machine itself (Benitti 2012). Further general teaching strategy activation, construction and learning effectiveness analysis still need to invest in more research and development (Altin and Pedaste 2013; Sullivan and Heffernan 2016). Educators believe that activated learning strategies are an important way to improve the learning effectiveness of students in the higher education system (Prince 2004; Nasr et al. 2017). The importance of these strategies according to the interest of students will have a real need to be selected. However, PBL is a student-centered teaching strategy to improve their learning effectiveness (Mundilarto 2018; Savery 2006). The strategy has been applied to various subjects teaching and learning by educators.

To sum up, this study designs PBL in the social application of AI (AI-PBL) life situation teaching texts to provide the experience of authenticity problems. Students will through active learning group discusses to propose their learning issues, to determine the scope of knowledge required, and to conduct the necessary research in order to present their problem-solving skills. The narrative skills of engineering students will be enhanced by the PBL strategy in the course "Science and Technology Society and Life". Therefore, students' learning achievement, attitude and interviews will be conducted to improve students' experience of scientific knowledge, cognitive understanding, and their learning performances of AI society's practical value in life in this research.

2 Research Purposes and Question

In summary, the main purpose of this study is to design the life situational teaching texts of AI society application in PBL. Students take the initiative and cooperate in learning to start their experience of scientific knowledge for the AI practical value in life, to enhance cognitive understanding, and to successfully complete the problem-solving in teaching. In order to make teaching more diverse and interesting, and learning to become more meaningful, thereby improving the effectiveness of students in science learning. Therefore, the focus questions of this research is as follows:

1. How to design and develop AI social application life situation experience teaching texts of PBL?
2. How to develop an evaluation tool with validity and reliability for students' pretest and posttest test items, learning attitude questionnaire and interview test items to assess their learning performances?
3. How to explore students' independence variables of different argument gender, enrollment, frequency of using 3C products, disposition of AI issues, 3C equipment and AI-related knowledge background for their cross-disciplinary experience learning attitude statistical analysis after PBL strategic teaching?
4. What is students' feedback reflection in interview of PBL strategic learning?

3 Literature Review of PBL

PBL teaching strategy is a problem-based and student-centered collaborative teaching method (Prince and Felder 2006; Jansson et al. 2015). This method is a case learning which is often varied according to teaching objectives and design (Prince and Felder 2006). In PBL, students acquire problem-solving skills; and in group learning, increase their self-confidence. PBL teaching method also enhances students' self-learning and lifelong learning skills (Hung et al. 2008). The biggest difference between PBL teaching and other methods lies in PBL use ill-structured problem as a learning situation, to start students' learning process, to link learning experience through learning problems in life, and to stimulate their motivation. Therefore, a meaningful learning process is obtained by PBL learning strategies, such as actively identify learning issues, apply self-learning, problem reasoning and solution (Savery 2006).

In the process of PBL teaching, students play an active role in learning, identifying problems, constructing problems and solving problems, while teachers play the role of promoters, supporters and monitors of learning, constructing a safe learning environment and assisting students in their learning functions (Dolmans and Schmidt 2006). Researchers (Belt et al. 2002; Yoon et al. 2014; Jansson et al. 2015) point out that PBL strategy can help improve students' problem solving, self-learning and self-assessment skills, increase students' learning and in-depth understanding of the subject in science. (Gunter and Alpat 2017) also found that PBL has significant results for students' scientific achievements. (Selco et al. 2003) designed the study of PBL learning strategy for seawater analysis and found that students were able to produce high-quality study reports. (Sendag and Odabasi 2009) using online PBL courses, found that this strategy does improve student critical thinking.

Based on these studies, this research takes PBL as the teaching strategy to design AI's life teaching texts applied in society as the learning connotation, and tries to explore students' learning processes, problem-solving abilities, learning attitude and feedback analysis.

4 Methodology

4.1 Participants of Research and Ethical Approval

Participants include engineering students and experts in the relevant fields, divided into the following:

In students, this research takes the students of author's school as research samples, mainly from the sophomore students who take the general course of "Technology Society and Life". Students from different departments of the three colleges of the whole school, a total of 83 students participated (distributed gender from 48 boys and 35 girls; age about 20–22 year-old), the curriculum discussion in a group of 6 to 8 people, homogeneity divided into six experimental groups by group cooperative learning.

In the relevant fields of experts, including scientific education experts, sociology experts and psychology experts, such as a total of seven in three fields, and seniority in more than 10 years, mainly in assisting the questionnaire question logic, focus and fluency of the examination, in order to construct the appropriate expert content validity.

4.2 Instrument Design

The instrument of this research contains open-ended questions and PBL learning attitude questionnaire. All the design instructions for the research evaluation instrument are as follows:

Development of Open-Ended Questions. This study designs the draft of the open-ended questions which invites 1 scientific education scholar, 3 information education communication scholars, 1 humanities education scholar and 2 artificial intelligence education scholars, and a total of seven people to conduct the question content and logical examination. The first draft has been revised to form an expert content validity. The open-ended questions are designed to assess students' cognitive understanding of AI in life social application situational issues.

Development of Learning Attitude Questionnaire. The learning attitude questionnaire consists of two parts, the first part is the basic background information of the students, and the second part is Likert structured learning attitude questionnaire. The Likert five scale consists of five options: "very agree", "agree", "ordinary", "disagree" and "very disagree".

Basic background information of students aims at providing the independent variable of the research framework. Then, six aspects of the learning attitude questionnaire provide the dependent variable of the research. The first draft of the "AI Situational PBL Attitude Questionnaire" was adapted from author's questionnaire (Su 2016) and the seven experts were invited to conduct substantial review, revision and deletion. The revised questionnaire is examined in 109 academic-year. A total of 44 students participated in the pilot test. Attitude questionnaire with the main component analysis, Bartlett spherical test reached significant, indicating suitable for factor analysis. There are six aspects considered in main component analyses of the questionnaire. The Eigenvalue obtained is above 1.0 with an accumulative explanation variation of 71.85%. The total scale score of the Cronbach's α 0.946 reached the satisfactory degree of internal consistency in accordance to students' learning attitude. According to the research of (Salta and Tzougraki 2004) reliability, the result of coefficient reliability over 0.900 gave better indication of learning scale which confirmed the high internal consistency of this questionnaire (Su 2008, 2018).

All findings of factor analyses were classified into six dominating dependent variables of learning attitude: A1 (attitude towards situation-based PBL courses), A2 (attitude towards science instructors), A3 (attitude towards multimedia learning environment), A4 (attitude towards AI-PBL students), Qa5 (attitude towards self-evaluation), and A6 (attitude towards statistical results) and these six variables are designed for further SPSS analytical developments. A total 31 test items in this questionnaire is used to explore affected factors of learning attitudes. A total result of pilot test indicated that mean score is 4.000, the standard deviation is (SD) 0.688, Cronbach's α value is greater than 0.9, according to the literature shows that the internal consistency of the scale is excellent (Salta and Tzougraki 2004; Su 2008, 2018).

4.3 Data Analysis

The data collected before and after the AI-PBL experimental teaching were computer coded (Arabic numerals in English) and viewed. The statistical method includes the internal consistency of the Cronbach's α, descriptive statistical analysis and one-way ANOVA. All statistical information is carried on the file of SPSS for MS Windows 22.0 software.

5 Results and Discussion

5.1 Designing AI-PBL Innovative Texts

PBL-guided multi-learning texts of AI life issues, such as face recognition system, self-driving cars and robots, were designed with Ausubel (1968) construction learning theory in this research. Instructor is the role of promoter and guide, design authentic AI in life social application situation teaching texts, the application of PBL to guide students to interactive learning, so that students ponder over and over again, strengthen the concept of cognition and application.

5.2 Analysis of Pretest and Posttest for Open-Ended Questions

Students' learning effectiveness are assessed and compared with pretest and posttest of open-ended questions. The scores are based on the design of Gunter and Alpat (2017). The percentage of students' response results shown in Table 1 and improved the overall conceptual cognitive level for pretest ones.

Table 1. Analysis of students' average responses rate (%) for open-ended questions between pre-tests and post-tests.

Cognitive level	Score	Mean	
		Pretest	Posttest
I	0	3.7	0
SM	1	29.2	15.7
PUSM	2	58.2	67.8
PU	3	8.1	14.8
CU	4	0.8	1.7

In summary, after the application of PBL conducted AI situation-based teaching posttest, the results showed that the blank volume students who did present incomprehension (I) decreased from 3.7% to 0%, the specific misconception (SM) students decreased by 13.5%, partial understanding with specific misconception (PUSM) increased by 9.6%, partial understanding (PU) students who increased by 6.7%, and clearly understood (CU) increased by 0.9%. Su' study (2017) suggested that aids help students to cultivate their problem-solving skills and demonstration of reasoning ability. Cracolice et al. (2008) also pointed out that students' reasoning ability is related to the improvement of problem-solving skills. However, PBL teaching on AI situational issues is indeed very important for students' logical reasoning and active learning (Eichler and Peeples 2016; Sadler et al. 2016).

5.3 Analysis and Discussion for Learning Attitude Questionnaire

Descriptive Statistical Analysis. Effective recovery rate of the students' learning attitude questionnaire is 81.9%. The descriptive statistical analysis showed that overall mean (*M*) value is 3.713, the standard deviation(*SD*) is 0.596, and the total scale score of the Cronbach's α is 0.960. There were totally 31 items in the questionnaire which could be classified into six dominant aspects: A1, A2, A3, A4, A5 and A6.

- A1: students' learning attitude towards AI situation-based PBL courses.
- A2: attitudes towards teachers
- A3: attitudes to the multimedia learning environment
- A4: attitudes towards AI-PBL students
- A5: attitudes towards self-learning AI-PBL courses
- A6: views on AI-PBL course results

The mean (M) value above 3.50 revealed that students' learning attitudes were positive attributes (Su 2008), and the overall Cronbach's α value of 0.960 for the internal consistency in total scales which reached a good satisfactory degree of statistic results (Salta and Tzougraki 2004). This finding was an important echo for scholars' research (Adesope and Nesbit 2012; Lin and Atkinson 2011). Thus, PBL-guided learning could help students enhance their positive learning attitude (Adesope and Nesbit 2012).

One-Way ANOVA. Owing to AI-PBL group's blocking variable, a series of ANOVAs were guided for the multi-variants of the Wilks' Lambda parameter upon attitude survey samples of the six subscales in this research. Accordingly, a brief summary of individual learning attitude with the F-ratios, p-values, effect sizes (f), and Scheffé's post hoc comparisons was provided from independent variable of gender of students and disposition of AI courses.

Independent variable of gender of students (male, 24; female, 44) in six dependent variables, only aspect A4 has significant (F, 4.563; p, 0.036; f, 0.264), and girls are better than boys, Cohen's (1988) effect size f above medium (>.25), other dependent variables do not differ significantly.

The blocking variable for students' AI-PBL course disposition (very positive, 17; positive, 39; neutral, 12; negative, 0; very negative, 0) toward AI-PBL learning attitude stemmed from a series of ANOVA and combined participants. All six significant aspects, A1(7.644, 0.001, 0.491), A2(8.088, 0.001, 0.498), A3(4.699, 0.012, 0.380), A4(6.800, 0.002, 0.457), A5(3.253, 0.045, 0.316) and A6(5.712, 0.005, 0.418), were fit together in determining students' learning disposition toward AI-PBL nature general course. The dependent variables from A1 to A6 in Scheffe's post hoc comparisons showed that students had expressed more learning attitudes in "very positive" orientations than those in "neutral" ones.

Students show a positive learning attitude from descriptive statistical analysis. Furthermore, in terms of students' learning attitude shows that the independent variable of AI-PBL course disposition is significant to all six dependent variables, representing students who like AI courses, and the influence on learning attitude is positive. Scholars (Alan et al. 2019; Mohtar et al. 2019) emphasize that integrating cross-disciplinary learning can help students improve their self-efficacy, ensure sustained interest in learning, and create better products.

6 Conclusions

After this research, developed a reliability assessment tool to evaluate engineering students' learning performances. According to the results of research and analysis, put forward the following some findings:

1 Texts designing will help the majority of students, so that they can learn and guide through
2 interaction, enrich their own learning connotation, and improve their learning visions.
3 Instrument developing will assess students' logical reasoning and activation ability, improve the cognitive level of problem solving, and make learning results better.
4 The descriptive statistical analysis of students' learning attitude shows positive thinking attributes.
5 One-way ANOVA indicates that the factors of students' natural science course disposition have an important influence on learning attitude.

This research introduces new thinking for problem-solving to promote engineering students' cognitive levels and become a decision maker. The future research will focus on integration of academic resources and cross-discipline leaning (such as STEM) in engineering classroom.

Acknowledgements. The author's sincere thanks must also be given to the patronage of the Ministry of Education (under Grant No. PGE 1090526) and the Ministry of Science and Technology in Taiwan (under Grant No. MOST 110-2511-H-237-001). Without their help and financial support, this research could not have been completed in the present form.

References

Adesope, O.O., Nesbit, J.C.: Verbal redundancy in multimedia learning environments: a meta-analysis. J. Educ. Psychol. **104**, 250–263 (2012)

Alan, B., Zengin, F.K., Keçeci, G.K.: Using STEM applications for supporting integrated teaching knowledge of pre-service science teachers. J. Balt. Sci. Educ. **18**(2), 157–170 (2019)

Alimisis, D.: Educational robotics: Open questions and new challenges. Themes Sci. Technol. Educ. **6**(1), 63–71 (2013)

Ausubel, D.P.: Educational Psychology: A Cognitive View. Holt, Rinehart & Winston, New York (1968)
Belt, S.T., Evans, E.H., McCreedy, T., Overton, T.L., Summerfield, S.: A problem based learning approach to analytical and applied chemistry. Univ. Chem. Educ. **6**(2), 29–36 (2002)
Benitti, F.B.V.: Exploring the educational potential of robotics in schools: a systematic review. Comput. Educ. **58**(3), 978–988 (2012)
Cohen, J.: Statistical Power Analysis for the Behavioral Sciences, 2nd edn. Erlbaum, Hillsdale, NJ (1988)
Cracolice, M.C., Deming, J.C., Ehlert, B.: Concept learning versus problem solving: a cognitive difference. J. Chem. Educ. **85**, 873–878 (2008)
Dolmans, D.H.J.M., Schmidt, H.G.: What do we know about cognitive and motivational effects of small group tutorials in problem-based learning? Adv. Health Sci. Educ. **11**(4), 321–336 (2006)
Eichler, J.F., Peeples, J.: Flipped classroom modules for large enrollment general chemistry courses: a low barrier approach to increase active learning and improve student grades. Chem. Educ. Res. Pract. **17**(1), 197–208 (2016)
Gunter, T., Alpat, S.K.: The effects of problem-based learning (PBL) on the academic achievement of students studying 'Electrochemistry.' Chem. Educ. Res. Pract. **18**(1), 78–98 (2017)
Hung, W., Jonassen, D.H., Liu, R.: Problem based learning. In: Spector M., Merrill D., Van Merrienboer J., Driscoll M. (eds.), Handbook of Research on Educational Communications and Technology, pp. 485–506, 3rd edn. New York, NY: Erlbaum (2008)
Jansson, S., Söderström, H., Andersson, P.L., Nording, M.L.: Implementation of problem-based learning in environmental chemistry. J. Chem. Educ. **92**, 2080–2086 (2015)
Lin, L., Atkinson, R.K.: Using animations and visual cueing to support learning of scientific concepts and processes. Comput. Educ. **56**, 650–658 (2011)
Mundilarto, H.I.: Effect of problem-based learning on improvement physics achievement and critical thinking of senior high school student. J. Balt. Sci. Educ. **16**(5), 761–780 (2018)
Nasr, Z., Paravattil, B., Wilby, K.J.: The impact of antimicrobial stewardship strategies on antibiotic appropriateness and prescribing behaviours in selected countries in the middle east: a systematic review. East. Mediterr. Health J. **23**(6), 430–440 (2017)
Prince, M.: Does active learning work? A review of the research. J. Engl. Educ. **93**(3), 223–231 (2004)
Prince, M.J., Felder, R.M.: Inductive teaching and learning methods: definitions, comparisons, and research bases. J. Engl. Educ. **95**, 123–138 (2006)
Rihtaršič, D., Avsec, S., Kocijancic, S.: Experiential learning of electronics subject matter in middle school robotics courses. Int. J. Technol. Des. Educ. **26**(2), 205–224 (2016). https://doi.org/10.1007/s10798-015-9310-7
Sadler, T.D., Romine, W.L., Topçu, M.T.: Learning science content through socio-scientific issues-based instruction: a multi-level assessment study. Int. J. Sci. Educ. **38**(10), 1622–1635 (2016)
Salta, K., Tzougraki, C.: Attitudes toward chemistry among 11th grade students' in high schools in Greece. Sci. Educ. **88**, 535–547 (2004)
Savery, J.R.: Overview of problem-based learning: definitions and distinctions. Interdiscip. J. Probl. Based Learn. **1**(1), 9–20 (2006)
Sendag, S., Odabasi, H.F.: Effects of an online problem based learning course on content knowledge acquisition and critical thinking skills. Comput. Educ. **53**, 132–141 (2009)
Selco, J.I., Roberts, J.L., Jr., Wacks, D.: The analysis of seawater: a laboratory-centered learning project in general chemistry. J. Chem. Educ. **80**(1), 54–57 (2003)
Su, K.D.: The effects of a chemistry course with integrated information communication technologies on university students' learning and attitudes. Int. J. Sci. Math. Educ. **6**, 225–249 (2008)

Su, K.D.: Strengthening strategic applications of problem-solving skills for Taiwan students' chemistry understanding. J. Balt. Sci. Educ. **15**(6), 662–679 (2016)
Su, K.D.: Enhancing students' corresponding reasoning of cognitive performances by animated concept mapping in electrochemistry. J. Balt. Sci. Educ. **17**(4), 662–673 (2018)
Sullivan, F.R., Heffernan, J.: Robotic construction kits as computational manipulatives for learning in the STEM disciplines. J. Res. Technol. Educ. **48**(2), 105–128 (2016)
Yoon, H., Woo, A.J., Treagust, D., Chandrasegaran, A.L.: The efficacy of problem-based learning in an analytical laboratory course for pre-service chemistry teachers. Int. J. Sci. Educ. **36**(1), 79–102 (2014)

Use Object-Detection to Identify Materials and Tools for STEAM Hands-on Activity

Hsin-Yu Lee[1], Yu-Cheng Chien[1], Pei-Yu Chang[2], Danial Hooshyar[3], and Yueh-Min Huang[1](✉)

[1] Department of Engineering Science, National Cheng Kung University, Tainan, Taiwan
huang@mail.ncku.edu.tw
[2] Department of Information Management, Tamkang University, New Taipei, Taiwan
[3] School of Digital Technologies, Tallinn University, Tallinn, Estonia

Abstract. The STEAM is an educational concept of interdisciplinary curriculum integration, which involves the knowledge and skills of science, technology, engineering, arts, and math courses. Countries worldwide are actively promoting STEAM education plans, as well as related education policies and teaching strategies. Influenced by the idea of learning by doing, STEAM education centered on hands-on learning has gradually been disseminated and promoted. However, previous research was generally used scales or questionnaires for quantitative analysis to evaluate the learning performances. That may be prone to be biased by people's self-awareness. In order to obtain Intuitive data, this study first uses object detection to identify various materials and tools through recording the videos of learners in STEAM hands-on activities. This report can be used as the basic prototype of the application of computer vision in STEAM education. The ultimate goal is to identify and judge learners' participation in STEAM activities.

Keywords: STEAM education · Hands-on · Object-detection · Image recognition

1 Introduction

With the many countries in the world pay more attention to STEAM education, it reflects the importance of all countries in the world to interdisciplinary courses. Several researchers, educators, governments, and industrial and commercial organizations emphasize the beneficial effects of STEAM disciplines and related skills in cultivating creativity and innovation positively impact the future society and economy [1–3]. STEAM education aims to cultivate the ability to integrate knowledge in science, technology, engineering, arts, and mathematics. Learners use what they have learned in these fields to identify and solve problems that cannot be solved by a single-disciplinary approach [4].

STEAM education is not only limited to integrating multiple disciplines but also needs to incorporate cross-field knowledge into problem-solving capabilities to solve various problems in life [5]. The general teaching strategy is project-based learning,

© Springer Nature Switzerland AG 2021
Y.-M. Huang et al. (Eds.): ICITL 2021, LNCS 13117, pp. 39–48, 2021.
https://doi.org/10.1007/978-3-030-91540-7_5

which mainly involves a specific course or activity with the concepts of constructivism, contextual learning theory, cognitive psychology [6]. Influenced by the idea of learning by doing, STEAM education centered on hands-on learning has gradually been disseminated and promoted [7]. The hands-on in STEAM can cultivate learners' core competence in engineering through the practice of the production process of the product and even serve as a bridge between learners' theory and reality [8, 9]. Moreover, compared to traditional teacher-centered teaching methods, hands-on learning can stimulate learners' creativity and independent learning ability [10].

On the other hand, in order to evaluate the learning performances of learners, scales or questionnaires are commonly used for quantitative analysis [11–15], but this method is prone to be biased by people's self-awareness [16]. Therefore, this study is a pilot study that uses object-detection to identify various materials and tools by recording the videos of learners in STEAM hands-on activities. In this way, this study can be used as the basic prototype of computer vision application in STEAM education. Its ultimate goal is to identify and judge learners' participation in STEAM activities.

2 Related Work

2.1 STEAM Education

With the launch of the first artificial satellite by the Soviet Union, countries began to realize the importance of integrating science, mathematics, and technology; they thus sought to keep up with the development of technology and engineering to avoid military threats from other countries [17]. Furthermore, to maintain the country's leading position in the rapidly changing and expanding global economy. The leaders of various countries have begun to regard the innovation and production of industrial, and consider it a necessary condition for economic progress and national competition. A series of educational reform projects for science, mathematics, and technology have been proposed [18, 19].

The most representative is STEM education proposed by National Science Foundation (NSF) in the 1990s. The term "STEM" education represents the abbreviations for Science, Technology, Engineering, and Math, which present that education is no longer an independent subject teaching model, meaning further towards integrating multiple subjects through the combination of science and engineering [5]. STEM integrates basic science and mathematics knowledge into engineering and technology and extends it to other fields [20, 21].

On the other hand, Yakman [22] indicated that most STEM education only regards various disciplines as independent fields without achieving proper integration; and the previous STEM emphasizes the knowledge and skills represented by multiple disciplines, while culture and humanities were often overlooked in the process from concept to implementation [23]. Therefore, Yakman [22] proposed integrating the arts into STEM to create a STEAM framework for teaching across disciplines (see Fig. 1). The STEAM framework establishes more effective interdisciplinary associations and improves learning mode within and between disciplines [24–26].

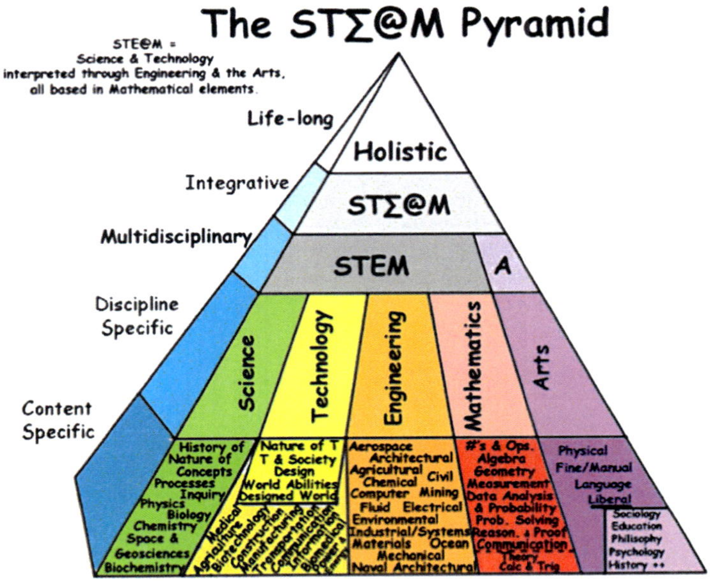

Fig. 1. A framework for STEAM education [22].

2.2 STEAM Hands-on Learning

Hands-on learning originated from the early garage culture in the United States. In the hands-on process, learners must be able to use their senses and make by themself to practice products, and then test their learning [27]. Learners will form an abstract concept or theory from the experience of trial, knowledge, and thinking to achieve reflective thinking through analysis and induction [28]. Holstermann, Grube, and Bögeholz [29] reported that learners with hands-on experience could show higher interest and learning motivation than others. It also has a significant positive impact on learning difficulties [30, 31].

The core of STEAM education is to cultivate learners using cross-domain knowledge to solve different challenges from the real world. Meanwhile, ghallenge and interesting learning situations tgnite curiosity and desire to explore and find specific solutions [32]. However, the traditional teacher-centered approach is ineffective on particular topics for STEM or even STEAM education [33–35]. Many studies thus have integrated hands-on learning into STEAM education, trying to find the most suitable teaching method in STEAM education [7, 36].

3 Methodology

3.1 Participants

InTheMicro:bit Obstacles Avoidance Car training workshop was held as an experimental activity. In this study, a total of 28 students were recruited to participate in this experiment from elementary schools in southern Taiwan, including 17 boys and 11 girls. All participants were asked to engage in a series of STEAM activities related to hands-on learning, which are the obstacles avoidance car tasks. Due to three students could not complete the experimental procedure, the total number of students after excluding their experimental data is 25 students. Then, 25 students were assigned to a homogeneous grouping of three persons according to the scores of the past achievement, which means a group of people with similar scores to ensure that they will have better interaction to complete every tasks. The detailed grouping information is shown in Table 1.

Table 1. The details of grouping in this study.

	Boys	Girls	Total
High-achievement	4	2	6
Middle-achievement	8	1	9
Low-achievement	4	6	10

3.2 STEAM Activity

In this experiment, the micro:bit obstacles avoidance car activity was designed by shallower to the deeper, which guides the learners to gradually understand the operation and concept of the obstacles avoidance car and obtain micro:bit and makecode programming-related information. The details of the task design and arrangement are shown in Table 2.

Table 2. The task of Micro:bit obstacle avoidance car in STEAM activity.

Tasks	Content
Basic programming	Micro:bit and makecode
Assembly and drive	Use programs to control the movement of obstacles avoidance car
Follow the line	Programming the makecode to control gray value sensor to complete the track and move
Avoid obstacles	Programming the makecode to control ultrasonic sensors to avoid obstacles on the track

3.3 System Design

Based on the excellent detection speed and accuracy of the YOLOv4 model [37] in the field of object detection, this study thus uses the YOLOv4 model to identify objects commonly used in STEAM hands-on activity. This study used the generated STEAM hands-on activities and its collected videos as training data, which targeted the human keyboard, mouse, tablet PC, obstacles avoidance car, mobile phone, and pen, a total of 7 objects for marking. The marking tool named LabelImg used is a set of open-source marking software developed based on Python [38]. LabelImg can be accessed through Mark the target object by frame selection, which the operation process is shown in Fig. 2. The final output is the bounding box of each object in the images denoted $BBox_i$, which contains the category number $Class_i$, the center point of images X coordinate and Y coordinate, the image size X_i and Y_i, the width of the bounding box W_i and the height H_i. A total of five data in YOLO format (see Fig. 2).

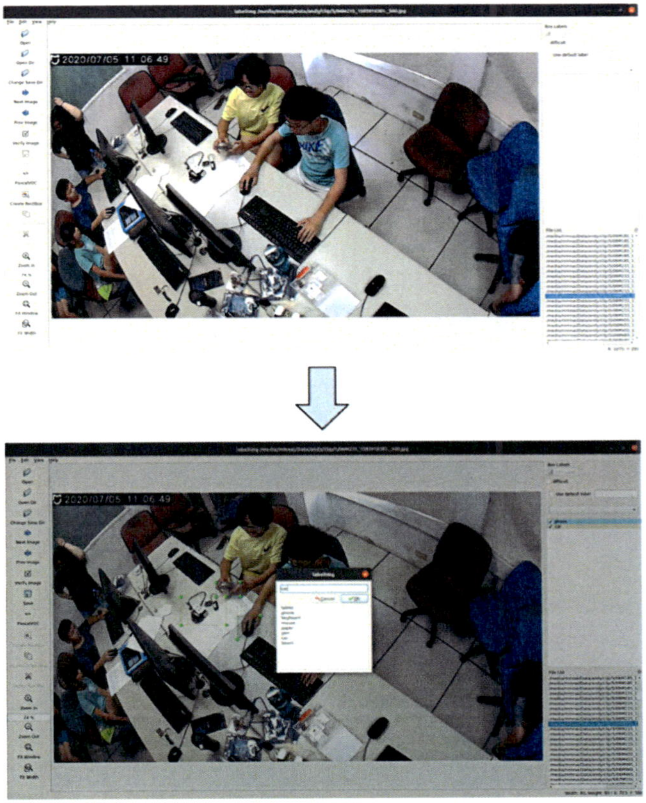

Fig. 2. The marking process of LabelImg.

The proposed approach is the original labeled training dataset, and the testing dataset was simply trained through the model of YOLOv4-Large [39], the YOLOv4-Large then trained the original YOLOv4. In this way, the object features learned by the YOLOv4-Large were granted to the original YOLOv4 and finally achieved the same detection speed and improve the recognition accuracy of small objects without increasing the cost of marking time. Restated, the YOLOv4-Large uses a deeper network architecture to overlay and adjust the input image size to 1280 × 1280, which can record the characteristics of more objects. As the input image size increases, the parts of small objects can be recognized.

4 Results

4.1 The Description of Datasets

This research uses YOLOv4 to identify the operated objects in Micro:bit Obstacles Avoidance Car activities, the learning materials, and tools include: 1) human; 2) keyboard; 3) mouse; 4) tablet; 5) car; 6) mobile phone; and 7) pen.

In the datasets, 872 labeled images captured by the field were cut, and all images were divided into 785 training dataset and 87 testing dataset at a ratio of 9:1. As Fig. 3, Fig. 3(a) is the number of various objects in the training dataset, which shows the distribution of objects is relatively uneven, especially the least number of mobile phones (class #1) and pen (class #5). Figure 3(b) is the distribution of the center points of the training set, and it can be found that the objects in the training dataset are evenly scattered throughout the screen. Figure 3(c) is the aspect ratio distribution of the objects in the training dataset. The result denoted that the objects in the training dataset are mostly small objects.

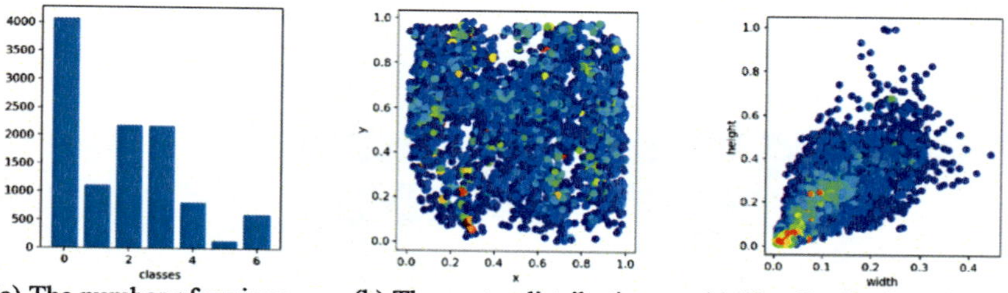

(a) The number of various objects (b) The center distribution of the object (c) The distribution of object size ratio

Fig. 3. The description of the training dataset.

4.2 The Results of YOLOv4 Object Detection

Due to images are taken from the same video for training and testing, the images in the training dataset and the testing dataset may cause similarity, and then, the results of accuracy calculated from the testing dataset may be too good to evaluate the accuracy of the model accurately. Therefore, to ensure that the testing dataset is completely independent of the training dataset, and its validity of the accuracy of the evaluation. The random segmentation is not used when splitting the training dataset and the testing dataset. In other words, the images in the training dataset and the testing dataset are from different groups; for example, some part of the training data may come from the 1st group, and some part of the testing data comes from the 3rd group. This way of datasets classification can avoid the problem of excessive similarity, and the validity of the accuracy evaluation can be further ensured.

After training 20,000 epochs, the final average loss is 2.8, and the mAP(Mean Average Precision) in the testing dataset is 88.7%. The accuracy of each type of object are: 1) human = 98.9%; 2) keyboard = 98.3%; 3) mouse = 98.1%; 4) tablet = 93.6%; 5) car = 93.5%; 6) phone = 62.7%; and 7) pen = 76.0%. The recognition result is shown in Fig. 4, which can find that the recognition effect of larger objects is better, but for small objects, such as pens and phone, the recognition results are relatively poor and often unrecognizable.

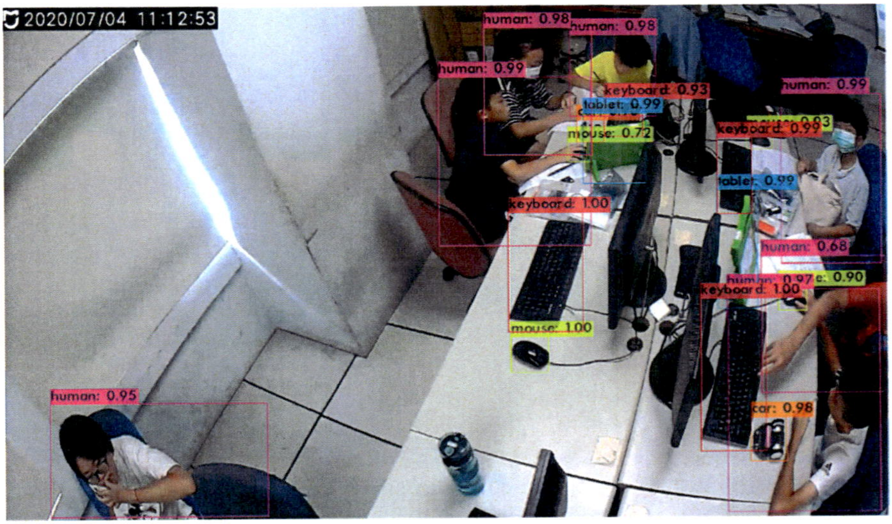

Fig. 4. A sample of the result in YOLOv4 object detection.

4.3 The Results of YOLOv4-Large Object Detection

In this study, the proposed approach is an original labeled training dataset, and testing dataset were simply trained through the model of YOLOv4-Large.Notably, if the YOLOv4-Large is directly used as the object detection model, the detection time will be lengthened because the model becomes relatively complex. That is, the original 30-FPS (Frames Per Second) is reduced to 10-FPS, which means that 20 images reduce the number of images detected per second. This phenomenon of speed loss will affect the operation speed of the subsequent overall motion recognition system and cause a bottleneck; therefore, this study only uses the YOLOv4-Large as an automatic labeling model. In other words, YOLOv4-Large will automatically label the remaining images and uses the results of automatically labeled images as a new training dataset to retrain the original YOLOv4 model.

Finally, after 20,000 epoch training, the average loss is 2.2 and mAP in the testing dataset is 96.1%. The accuracy of various objects are: 1) human = 99.1%; 2) keyboard

= 98.6%; 3) mouse = 99.3%; 4) tablet = 95.5%; 5) car = 98.3%; 6) phone = 87.4%; and 7) pen = 94.7% . The comparison results of different models in STEAM hands-on activity for object-detection are shown in Table 3.

Table 3. Comparison of different models on STEAM hands-on activity

	Human	Keyboard	Mouse	Tablet	Car	Phone	Pen
YOLOv4	98.9%	98.3%	98.1%	93.6%	93.5%	62.7%	76.0%
YOLOv4-Large	99.1%	98.6%	99.3%	95.5%	98.3%	87.4%	94.7%

5 Discussion and Conclusion

Overall, although the original YOLOv4 is used as a model to recognize objects in STEAM hands-on activity, the recognition effect is better for larger objects; however, due to the complexity of the STEAM, there are often smaller objects that are not easy to identify. Therefore, this study proposed a solution to train small models (i.e., YOLOv4) in the form of large models (i.e., YOLOv4-Large) to improve the recognition accuracy of small objects while maintaining the same detection speed and not increasing the cost of marking time.

Compared to YOLOv4, the findings of this study show that the mAP of YOLOv4-Large increased by 7.4%. Moreover, the accuracy of smaller objects in STEAM obtained improving, that is, the mobile phone increased by 24.7%, and the pen increased by 18.7%. Based on this solution, objects of large and small sizes can be accurately identified in STEAM implementation activities to facilitate the implementation of advanced systems, such as human pose and behavior recognition.

References

1. Bybee, R.W.: What is STEM education? Science **329**(5995), 996–996 (2010)
2. English, L.D.: STEM education K-12: perspectives on integration. Int. J. STEM Educ. **3**(1), 1–8 (2016)
3. Kelley, T.R., Knowles, J.G.: A conceptual framework for integrated STEM education. Int. J. STEM Educ. **3**(1), 1–11 (2016)
4. Martín-Páez, T., Aguilera, D., Perales-Palacios, F.J., Vílchez-González, J.M.: What are we talking about when we talk about STEM education? A review of literature. Sci. Educ. **103**, 799–822 (2019)
5. Sanders, M.: Integrative STEM education: a primer. Technol. Teach. **68**, 20–26 (2009)
6. Tseng, K.-H., Chang, C.-C., Lou, S.-J., Chen, W.-P.: Attitudes towards science, technology, engineering and mathematics (STEM) in a project-based learning (PjBL) environment. Int. J. Technol. Des. Educ. **23**, 87–102 (2013)
7. Ziaeefard, S., Miller, M.H., Rastgaar, M., Mahmoudian, N.: Co-robotics hands-on activities: a gateway to engineering design and STEM learning. Rob. Auton. Syst. **97**, 40–50 (2017)

8. Chien, Y.-H.: Developing a pre-engineering curriculum for 3D printing skills for high school technology education. Eurasia J. Math. Sci. Technol. Educ. **13**, 2941–2958 (2017)
9. Fan, S.-C., Yu, K.-C.: How an integrative STEM curriculum can benefit students in engineering design practices. Int. J. Technol. Des. Educ. **27**(1), 107–129 (2015)
10. Thunberg, H.M., Salmi, H.S., Bogner, F.X.: How creativity, autonomy, and visual reasoning contribute to cognitive learning in a STEAM hands-on inquiry-based math module. Think. Skills Creat. **29**, 153–160 (2018)
11. Chien, Y.-C., Liu, M.-C., Wu, T.-T., Lai, C.-H., Huang, Y.-M.: Enriching search queries to construct comprehensive concept maps for online inquiries: a case study of a food web. J. Internet Technol. **17**, 19–27 (2016)
12. Chien, Y.-C., Su, Y.-N., Wu, T.-T., Huang, Y-Min.: Enhancing students' botanical learning by using augmented reality. Universal Access Inf. Soc. **18**(2), 231–241 (2019)
13. Liu, C.-J., Huang, C.-F., Liu, M.-C., Chien, Y.-C., Lai, C.-H., Huang, Y.-M.: Does gender influence emotions resulting from positive applause feedback in self-assessment testing? Evidence from neuroscience. J. Educ. Technol. Soc. **18**, 337–350 (2015)
14. Liu, M.-C., Huang, Y.-M., Chien, Y.-C.: Facilitating vocabulary note taking on computers through the deep processing strategy. J. Educ. Comput. Res. **56**, 1296–1323 (2019)
15. Shadiev, R., Chien, Y.-C., Huang, Y.-M.: Enhancing comprehension of lecture content in a foreign language as the medium of instruction: comparing speech-to-text recognition with speech-enabled language translation. SAGE Open **10**, 2158244020953177 (2020)
16. Paulhus, D.L., Vazire, S.: The self-report method. In: Handbook of Research Methods in Personality Psychology 1, pp. 224-239 (2007)
17. Haugsbakk, G.: From Sputnik to PISA shock–new technology and educational reform in Norway and Sweden. Educ. Inq. **4**, 23222 (2013)
18. National Commission on Excellence in Education: A Nation at Risk: The Imperative for Educational Reform. The National Commission on Excellence in Education, Washington, DC (1983)
19. Ritz, J.M., Fan, S.-C.: STEM and technology education: international state-of-the-art. Int. J. Technol. Des. Educ. **25**(4), 429–451 (2014)
20. White, D.W.: What is STEM education and why is it important. Florida Assoc. Teach. Educators J. **1**, 1–9 (2014)
21. Li, Y.: Journal for STEM education research – promoting the development of interdisciplinary research in STEM education. J. STEM Educ. Res. **1**(1–2), 1–6 (2018)
22. Yakman, G.: What is the point of STE@ M? – A brief overview. Steam: A Framework for Teaching Across the Disciplines. STEAM Education 7 (2010)
23. Robelen, E.W.: STEAM: experts make case for adding arts to STEM. Educ. Week **31**, 8 (2011)
24. Clapp, E.P., Jimenez, R.L.: Implementing STEAM in maker-centered learning. Psychol. Aesthet. Creat. Arts **10**, 481 (2016)
25. Patton, R.M., Knochel, A.D.: Meaningful makers: stuff, sharing, and connection in STEAM curriculum. Art Educ. **70**, 36–43 (2017)
26. Perignat, E., Katz-Buonincontro, J.: STEAM in practice and research: an integrative literature review. Think. Skills Creat. **31**, 31–43 (2019)
27. Piaget, J., Grize, J.-B., Szeminska, A., Bang, V.: Epistemology and Psychology of Functions. Springer Netherlands, Dordrecht (1977). https://doi.org/10.1007/978-94-010-9321-7
28. Dewey, J.: Experience and education. In: The Educational Forum, pp. 241–252. Taylor & Francis (1986)
29. Holstermann, N., Grube, D., Bögeholz, S.: Hands-on activities and their influence on students' interest. Res. Sci. Educ. **40**, 743–757 (2010)
30. Brigham, F.J., Scruggs, T.E., Mastropieri, M.A.: Science education and students with learning disabilities. Learn. Disabil. Res. Pract. **26**, 223–232 (2011)

31. Salmi, H., Thuneberg, H., Vainikainen, M.-P.: Learning with dinosaurs: a study on motivation, cognitive reasoning, and making observations. Int. J. Sci. Educ. Part B **7**, 203–218 (2017)
32. Thuneberg, H., Salmi, H., Fenyvesi, K.: Hands-on math and art exhibition promoting science attitudes and educational plans. Educ. Res. Int. **2017**, 1–13 (2017)
33. Chen, W., Shah, U.V., Brechtelsbauer, C.: A framework for hands-on learning in chemical engineering education—training students with the end goal in mind. Educ. Chem. Eng. **28**, 25–29 (2019)
34. Freeman, S., et al.: Active learning increases student performance in science, engineering, and mathematics. Proc. Natl. Acad. Sci. **111**, 8410–8415 (2014)
35. Waldrop, M.M.: Why we are teaching science wrong, and how to make it right. Nat. News **523**, 272 (2015)
36. Christensen, R., Knezek, G., Tyler-Wood, T.: Alignment of hands-on STEM engagement activities with positive STEM dispositions in secondary school students. J. Sci. Educ. Technol. **24**(6), 898–909 (2015)
37. Redmon, J., Divvala, S., Girshick, R., Farhadi, A.: You only look once: unified, real-time object detection. In: Proceedings of the IEEE Conference on Computer Vision and Pattern Recognition, pp. 779–788 (2016)
38. Lin, T.: labelImg [v1.8.4]. https://github.com/tzutalin/labelImg (2020)
39. Wang, C.-Y., Bochkovskiy, A., Liao, H.-Y.M.: Scaled-yolov4: scaling cross stage partial network. In: Proceedings of the IEEE/CVF Conference on Computer Vision and Pattern Recognition, pp. 13029–13038 (2021)

Perusall's Machine Learning Towards Self-regulated Learning

Manuela Francisco[1,2](✉) and Cristina Amado[3]

[1] Laboratory of Distance Education and eLearning, Universidade Aberta, Lisbon, Portugal
maria.francisco@uab.pt
[2] Center for Studies in Education and Innovation, Politécnico de Leira, Leiria, Portugal
[3] Universidade Aberta, Lisbon, Portugal

Abstract. This current work presents exploratory research related to Perusall activity. One of the objectives of this study was to analyze the Perusalll's features, with emphasis on peer work, which can increase individual motivation facilitating self-regulation learning. Perusall is a social web tool that uses a machine learning algorithm, which assesses the quality of annotations and students' engagement. This tool was integrated with the LMS of Universidade Aberta (Portugal) and it was used as a pilot project in a Curricular Unit, from the 2nd year of the Education undergraduate program. We designed a collaborative activity inspired by Inquiry-based Learning and peer-instruction, to be performed on Perusall. 115 students, from 2 classes, were involved. To assess students' work, their engagement and motivation (basis for self-regulation) we analyzed Perusall´s reports and scoring based on 6 different components. We also asked students to report positive and negative aspects related to their experience with Perusall. Our findings confirm that collaborative reading tools can help students to get more involved in self-learning, as well machine learning can help instructors work, namely monitoring and assessment tasks.

Keywords: Machine learning · Perusall · Collaborative learning · Self-regulated learning · Distance education

1 Introduction

Technology is today, more than ever, an intrinsic component of education, namely in distance education and eLearning [1–3], not only because of the pandemic situation that has been going on since 2020 [4], but also because of the variety of educational resources and tools available for education. In addition to these factors, we have a new students' profile, who uses technology, namely mobile devices in all contexts of daily life. As such, it is inevitable that the education system will adopt technology more massively and equitably. However, the use of technology must be appropriate to the context, the pedagogical approach, and the learning objectives [5, 6]. Furthermore, the integration of

Financed national funds through FCT – Fundação para a Ciência e a Tecnologia, I.P., under the projects UIDB/04372/2020 e UIDP/04372/2020.

© Springer Nature Switzerland AG 2021
Y.-M. Huang et al. (Eds.): ICITL 2021, LNCS 13117, pp. 49–58, 2021.
https://doi.org/10.1007/978-3-030-91540-7_6

technology that uses Artificial Intelligence (AI) can play a fundamental role in virtual learning contexts, particularly in monitoring and assessment tasks, providing planning and managing time, and adequacy for more meaningful learning strategies.

These emerging and easily accessible educational opportunities should be structured and appropriate for the student profiles. In addition to achieving the objectives to which they are proposed and to be applied with effective quality for learning, it is necessary to carry out studies and evaluate the contexts of their application. This aspect can be supported by the potential of artificial intelligence (AI) and more specifically machine learning (ML). ML is a sub area of AI [7] which enables computers to learn autonomously. This capability is ensured by algorithms aimed at ML, and allows the identification of patterns in existing information, construction of models for prediction without having to be effectively programmed for this purpose. As argued [8], ML is supported by algorithms and its most valuable aspect is the capability for predictive modeling. The implementation of predictive models is developed based on information and historical data to obtain future and new data. In fact, ML is an emerging technical field in AI based on the computational, statistical and data sciences, considered essential for more accurate and learning-optimizing education [9]. ML algorithms can help to identify patterns and student profiles, enable the construction of new perspective models, and make predictions [10]. The application of AI and ML techniques are conducive to learning analysis to improve the quality of teaching and student learning, being crucial for Precision Education (PE) [11, 12]. As reinforced by these authors, PE includes steps of diagnosis, prediction, data processing and prevention that are associated with the process of identifying learning patterns and student behavior, predicting learning outcomes based on the collected data. These steps allow the timely intervention in the teaching-learning process, by the instructor, instructional design if planned according to different progresses and profiles, as well as enabling the student to have greater involvement and regulation of their learning process.

Self-Regulated Learning (SRL) consists of the intentional, dynamic, and persevering supervision of the students' own actions [13]. As mentioned, student involvement in their learning process includes intentional adaptations and regulation at the level of cognition, behavior, emotions, and motivation itself, adapting strategies.

Another aspect related to distance education is the way in which the student assumes the orientation of their individual learning processes. As advocated [14], SRL is a self-directed process of transforming and adapting a student's mental abilities into task-related skills in distinct areas of learning. Throughout the learning process, the student understands how to act in order to achieve learning goals and adjusts processes and strategies accordingly. This autonomy, which allows the achievement of learning goals, conveys and stimulates the student's motivation in guiding their knowledge [15–17]. This type of regulation is associated with metacognition by self-assessment of antecedent cognitive activities. Thus, when regulation is initiated and managed by the student, it becomes self-regulation. In learning contexts, the self-regulation of processes to acquire and build knowledge itself is considered SRL. SRL is highlighted in online learning, and as verified in previous studies, the students' motivation and goals are important in the way they "conceptualize the purpose of a course, which in turn influences their perception of the learning process" [11]. However, the pedagogical approach used can be decisive for the student's motivation and involvement in their learning process. Of the various learning theories associated with distance learning, we consider that collaborative approaches can be more effective in the individual and social construction of knowledge, as expressed in literature [18–20]. Some authors [21–23] point out that collaborative learning places students in an active role through the development of activities that promote work among peers in the search for solutions and understanding of a given subject, making these practices more effective than the traditional method of knowledge transmission and explanation. It is also reported that collaborative activities, in addition to benefiting the individual cognitive learning process, contribute to the development of social skills, as well as to group metacognition [24] and for self-regulation [25].

One of the collaborative learning strategies adopted for a more meaningful learning and, also, promoting the SRL, is the realization of questions elaborated by students and answered by the group mates [26, 27]. Previous studies [28, 29] report that inquiry-based learning allows students to become aware of what they already know and what they want to deepen or need to solve a given problem. If the answer is presented by those who explain according to how they learned (peer-instruction), the process of understanding is facilitated and becomes more significant [30].

Based on these concepts, a collaborative activity was designed, inspired by inquiry-based learning and peer-instruction, which took place on the Perusall platform. This free online social platform, developed by Harvard University, allows collaborative reading and annotation, asynchronous communication between students and provides various interaction features with learning resources (document or video) and with the classmates' annotations and comments. It uses ML to assess the quality of students' annotations and their interactions with the document or other learning material and with peers, as well as providing activity reports and statistics for teachers. The pedagogical potential of this platform has been documented in several studies [31–36], not only due to the diversity of strategies that can be adopted, but also due to the level of involvement of students with the topic under study. Students' activity reports and "confusion report" can be very useful to adapt strategies according to the subjects that generated more interactions or provide support mechanisms for students who showed greater difficulties.

2 Methodology

Considering that data analysis from learning environments has advantages in the study of SRL student behavior in an online environment, the present study focuses on holistic assessment based on machine learning and on reports generated by Perusall, having been complemented with students' testimony about using this platform.

Perusall was integrated in the LMS (Moodle) of Universidade Aberta, having been used as a pilot project in the Curricular Unit (CU) Accessibility in Education and Training, 2nd year of the Education undergraduate program. The course is entirely online, and interaction is fundamentally asynchronous. CU foresees 2 assessment moments throughout the semester with a weight of 20% each, and a final assessment moment with a weight of 60%. A collaborative reading activity was designed in Perusall, which took place between April and May 2021. A 43-page document (PDF) on Web Accessibility Guidelines and strategies for creating accessible digital content was made available. The instructions for carrying out this activity asked each student to elaborate 3 questions throughout the document, answer 2 questions from other participants and vote on the 3 questions they considered most interesting and that related theory to practice or that would motivate further research on the topic. The activity was evaluated according to Perusall's holistic assessment parameters and had a weight of 20% in the student's final grade. The group consisted of students from 2 classes with a total size of 115 students. To facilitate the annotation process and interaction between students, 2 groups were randomly defined per class with approximately 30 participants in each group. After the activity, students answered open-ended questions about their experience using Perusall. The aim of this study was, on one hand, to assess the advantages of using the Perusall platform, both for student and for teacher, and on the other hand, to understand whether platforms that use ML can contribute to greater involvement and motivation of students, thus contributing to SRL.

3 Data Analysis

In this study we used information from 2 different sources: 1) reports and grades obtained by Perusall, 2) questionnaire on the difficulties experienced and advantages in using the platform. The questionnaire had 2 open-ended questions, not restricted to word limit. To analyze the answers, a qualitative content analysis methodology was adopted, which allows more freedom to students and to obtain less distorted information [37]. In this syntactic content analysis, words and expressions highlighted by the students were identified, which were grouped into main categories [38] (Perusall, learning methodology, and overall activity). The expressions and words that best characterized the student's opinion were highlighted, and synonyms and expressions were grouped. In general, the most used expression was established as a parameter to be analyzed. This strategy allowed us to use qualitative values and apply a quantitative analysis that translates the parameters into the students' responses. For parameter evidence, the "non-observance" of the comment assumes the value "0", the "observance" the value "1" and the non-conclusive opinion we named as "neutral" assumes the value "2". The obtained data were organized in a spreadsheet and treated using functions for counting the absolute frequency of occurrences.

The data obtained in Perusall was based on holistic assessment, with 50% being assigned to each of the 6 parameters (Annotation content component, Opening assignment component, Reading component, Active reading time component, Getting responses component, Upvoting component). The reports generated by Perusall were also analyzed: Confusion report, Student activity report, Annotation submission time, Overall assignment progress).

4 Results

There were 115 students enrolled in Perusall, but only 84 participated partially or fully in the activity and answered the questionnaire, being the majority female (80%).

Based on data obtained from Perusall, the students' activity related to their involvement and performance, including final grade (score) was analyzed, as shown in Table 1 and Table 2.

Table 1. Students' report.

Evidence	Class 1	Class 2
Students who have accessed Perusall	57	58
Students who have exceeded the requested tasks	34	35
Students that completed all requested tasks	2	10
Students who performed some of the requested tasks	1	2
Students who did not perform any of the requested tasks	20	11
Total active reading time in course	4 h 52 min	5 h 04 min
Average score	13.72	14.38

Table 2. Overall assignment progress.

Evidence	Class 1	Class 2
Completed with maximum score	58.9%	58.9%
Completed but not maximum score	3.6%	17.9%
Some work submitted	1.8%	3.6%
No work submitted	35.7%	19.6%
Comments	275	366
Questions	105	140
Unanswered questions	32	47
Average reading time	2 h 23 min	2 h 44 min

When checking students' habits, it is interesting to analyze the time intervals of participation, not only because of how this participation is distributed throughout the month in which the activity took place, but also in the most active hours of the day, as shown in the Perusall report (Fig. 1).

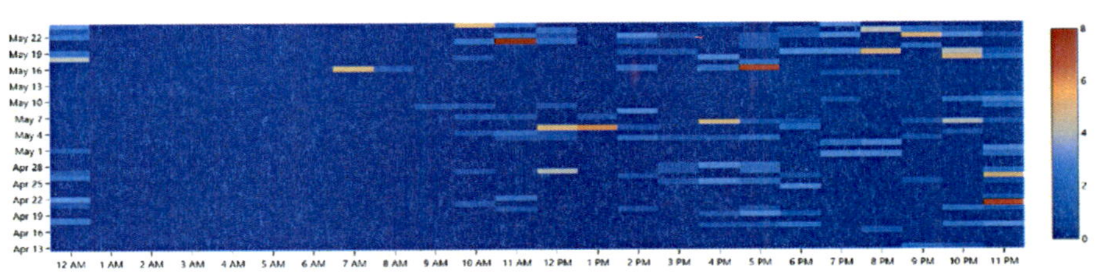

Fig. 1. Annotation submission time heat map (Class 1)

As shown in Fig. 1, participation over time was balanced, although weaker at the beginning and more participatory in the last days of the activity. In terms of daily schedule, 3 periods (Lisbon time) are highlighted: in the morning, between 11:00 and 13:00, in the afternoon between 16:00 and 17:00, concentrating at night between 20:00 and 23:00. This performance is very similar to class 2.

Other interesting data are related to the most voted comments and the level of student involvement. In the information presented by Perusall, the most voted comments and the most active students are also available. The observation of data from the top 10 comments and the top 10 most active students in the class does not show evidence that there is a relationship between them, since the most voted comments were not placed by the most active students.

The data obtained in the automatically generated "Confusion Report", show that the first chapter of the document proposed for reading, related to the Web Content Accessibility Guidelines (WCAG), was the one that summarized more interactions in both classes, namely new questions, and voting. Chapters 2 and 3, related to interfaces and visual content, were also very participated and gained more comments. Chapter 3 was also the one that triggered the most external information sharing (hyperlinks and images) with proposals for alternative texts and long descriptions of shared images.

Regarding the qualitative analysis of the answers to open-ended questions, Tables 3 and 4 present the percentage results obtained for each evidence identified by the students. Most students considered the use of Perusall to be advantageous, as they considered it to facilitate learning and enhance peer interaction, as shown in Table 3.

Table 3. Positive evidence about Perusall.

Evidence	Observed	Not observed	Neutral
Advantageous	86%	12%	2%
Learning enhancer/facilitator	39%	61%	0%
Increased interactivity/interaction with peers	54%	46%	0%
Easier access to content	15%	85%	0%
Collaborative and cooperative learning/participation	62%	38%	0%
Increased proactivity	11%	89%	0%

The less favorable aspects about Perusall are related to the difficulties experienced, namely at the beginning of the activity, as shown in Table 4.

Although 48% mentioned difficulties at the beginning, relating to the fact that they were using the platform for the first time, the majority said that they had been overcome. 4% of students referred to the existence of several features without specifying whether they were an advantage or a disadvantage. Some students mentioned that, despite the tool being interesting, they prefer to have the document printed on paper to read and annotate.

Table 4. Negative evidence about Perusall.

Evidence	Observed	Not observed	Neutral
Just at the beginning	48%	48%	4%
Unintuitive	13%	87%	0%
Interface language	10%	90%	0%
Browser incompatibilities	4%	0%	0%

5 Final Considerations

In general, we can state that most students feel motivated to learn with collaborative and cooperative activities in an eLearning context. The fact that this activity took place on a new platform, which, despite being intuitive, proved to be a little complex at first for some students, seems to have contributed to a balanced involvement throughout the activity. Still considering the difficulties, more studies should be carried out to understand the writing problems in the conversation text editor (the cursor does not move) reported by some students who used Google Chrome as they were overcome when they switched to Mozilla Firefox. We were unable to identify the problem that was probably related to a specific browser extension. However, despite the difficulties, students enjoyed the experience they considered to be a learning facilitator due to interactive annotation, further study to support their comments and keeping updated with their own performance automatically generated by Perusall. When comparing their opinion with data obtained from Perusall, namely the student activity reports, we found a high level of adherence to the proposed activity and most students had higher involvement than expected. Regarding collaborative reading, some students expressed the need for prior individual reading and printed documents, as they are used to highlighting information and taking notes in this more traditional way.

As instructors, we have identified several advantages in using the platform, namely in the ease of monitoring the learning process, identification of chapters (subjects) that need further development and excellent help in the difficult task of evaluating student contributions and engagement. We were pleased by the quality algorithm that, although the tool is only available in 4 languages, not including Portuguese, student comments were able to be assessed by this algorithm. This type of processes or algorithms based on information created by students and on interactions generated during their participation, that is, during the collaborative reading activity, is referred to as a machine learning technique, which in fact brings numerous advantages for the education. It should also be mentioned that the data generated by Perusall can bring several contributions to distance education, allowing the creation of individual learning paths according to the rhythms, schedules, interests, and difficulties of each student.

In this pilot project, we used the reports generated by Perusall to analyze the students' performance (interactions, quality of comments and grades), which showed us a high level of involvement. The grades (scores) attributed by Perusall allowed us to verify the potential of machine learning used in Perusall (based on the quality algorithm). Once the activity was completed, these reports were made available to students so that they could be aware of their performance. In the future, it is intended to make these reports available to students throughout the activity, so that students can have greater control of their learning.

We recognize that the data obtained in this pilot study enable multiple analyses, however we highlight in this work the role of student motivation. It is also intended to continue this activity by combining pedagogy and technology so that more specific conclusions can be drawn for self-regulated learning. Although we did not highlight the pedagogical approach in the present paper, we believe that the strategy inspired by Inquiry-Based Learning may have helped and motivate students in their first interactions in Perusall. Also, the fact that the activity is assessed may have influenced the level of participation. Data suggest that more active and collaborative pedagogical strategies, combined with technology, in particular with the Perusall platform, can increase motivational levels and student engagement, contributing positively to self-regulated learning.

References

1. McGreal, R., Elliott, M.: Technologies of online learning (E-learning). In: T. Anderson, F. Elloumi (eds.), Theory and Practice of Online Learning (chapter 5). Athabasca University. Retrieved from http://cde.athabascau.ca/online_book/ch1.html (2004)
2. Bates, A.W.: Technology, e-learning and Distance Education, 2nd edn. Routledge, New York (2005)
3. Garrison, D.R., Anderson, T.: E-learning in the 21st Century: A Framework for Research and Practice. Routledge, London (2003)
4. OECD: Education responses to covid-19: embracing digital learning and online collaboration. OECD (2020). https://doi.org/10.1787/d75eb0e8-en
5. Laurillard, D.: Digital technologies and their role in achieving our ambitions for education. Institute of Education, University of London, London. Retrieved from http://eprints.ioe.ac.uk/628/1/Laurillard2008Digital_technologies.pdf (2008)
6. Mentis, M.: Navigating the e-learning terrain: aligning technology, pedagogy and context. Electron. J. e-Learn. **6**(3), 217–226. Retrieved from http://www.ejel.org/issue/download.html?idArticle=76 (2008)
7. Maini, V., Sabri, S.: Machine Learning for Humans. Ebook (2017)
8. Brownlee, J.: Machine Learning Performance Improvement Cheat Sheet. [Blog]. Retrieved from https://machinelearningmastery.com/ (May 22, 2019)
9. Jordan, M., Mitchell, T.M.: Machine learning: trends, perspectives, and prospects. Science **349**(6245), 255–326 (2015)
10. Luan, H., Tsai, C.-C.: A review of using machine learning approaches for precision education. Educ. Technol. Soc. **24**(1), 250–266 (2021)
11. Yang, A.C.M., Chen, I.Y.L., Flanagan, B., Ogata, H.: From human grading to machine grading: automatic diagnosis of e-book text marking skills in precision education. Educ. Technol. Soc. **24**(1), 164–175 (2021)
12. Yang, S.J.H.: Precision education: New challenges for AI in education [conference keynote]. In: 27th International Conference on Computers in Education, XXVII–XXVIII. Asia-Pacific Society for Computers in Education (APSCE), Kenting, Taiwan (2019)
13. Pedrosa, D., Cravino, J., Morgado, L., Barreira, C.: Self-regulated Learning in Computer Programming: Strategies Students Adopted During an Assignment. In: Allison, C., Morgado, L., Pirker, J., Beck, D., Richter, J., Gütl, C. (eds.) iLRN 2016. CCIS, vol. 621, pp. 87–101. Springer, Cham (2016). https://doi.org/10.1007/978-3-319-41769-1_7

14. Zimmerman, B.J.: Self-regulated learning: theories, measures, and outcomes. In: Wright, J.D. (Ed.), International Encyclopedia of the Social & Behavioral Sciences, pp. 541–546. Elsevier, Oxford (2015). https://doi.org/10.1016/B978-0-08-097086-8.26060-1
15. Winne, P.H., Hadwin, A.F.: Self-regulated learning and socio-cognitive theory. In: Peterson, P., Baker, E., McGaw, B. (Eds.). International Encyclopedia of Education, 3rd ed., pp. 503–508. ISBN 97.80080448947 (2010)
16. Ahmed, W.: Motivation and self-regulated learning: a multivariate multilevel analysis. Int. J. Psychol. Educ. Stud. **4**(3), 1–11 (2017)
17. Panadero, E.: A review of self-regulated learning: six models and four directions for research. Front. Psychol. **8**(422) (2017). https://doi.org/10.3389/fpsyg.2017.00422
18. Bandura, A.: Social cognitive theory. Handbook of Social Psychological Theories, pp. 349–373 (2011)
19. Vygotsky, L.S.: Mind in Society: The Development of Higher Psychological Processes. Harvard University Press, Cambridge, MA (1978)
20. Siemens, G.: Connectivism: a learning theory for the digital age. Int. J. Instruct. Technol. Distance Learn. **2**(1), 3–10 (2005)
21. Smith, B.L., MacGregor, J.T.: What is collaborative learning? In: Goodsell, A., Maher, M., Tinto, V., Smith, B.L., MacGregor, J.T. (Eds.), Collaborative Learning: A Sourcebook for Higher Education. Pennsylvania State University, USA: National Center on Postsecondary Teaching, Learning, and Assessment Publishing (1992)
22. Laal, M., Ghodsi, S.M.: Benefits of collaborative learning. Procedia Soc. Behav. Sci. **31**, 486–490 (2012). https://doi.org/10.1016/j.sbspro.2011.12.091
23. Law, Q.P.S., So, H.C.F., Chung, J.W.Y.: Effect of collaborative learning on enhancement of students' self-efficacy, social skills and knowledge towards mobile apps development. Am. J. Educ. Res. **5**(1), 25–29. Retrieved from http://pubs.sciepub.com/education/5/1/4 (2017)
24. Biasutti, M., Frate, S.: Group metacognition in online collaborative learning: validity and reliability of the group metacognition scale (GMS). Educ. Tech. Res. Dev. **66**(6), 1321–1338 (2018). https://doi.org/10.1007/s11423-018-9583-0
25. Zimmerman, B.J.: From cognitive modeling to self-regulation: a social cognitive career path. Educ. Psychol. **48**, 135–147 (2013). https://doi.org/10.1080/00461520.2013.794676
26. Hu, S., Kuh, G.D., Li, S.: The effects of engagement in inquiry-oriented activities on student learning and personal development. Innov. High. Educ. **33**, 71–81 (2008)
27. Butler, D.L., Schnellert, L.: Collaborative inquiry in teacher professional development. Teach. Teach. Educ. **28**, 1206–1220 (2012)
28. Zafra-Gómez, J., Román-Martínez, I., Gómez-Miranda, M.: Measuring the impact of inquiry-based learning on outcomes and student satisfaction. Assess. Eval. High. Educ. **40**(8), 1050–1069 (2015)
29. Spronken-Smith, R., Angelo, T., Matthews, H., O'Steen, B., Robertson, J.: How Effective is Inquiry-Based Learning in Linking Teaching and Learning. International Policies and Practices for Academic Enquiry. Marwell, Winchester, UK (2007)
30. Mazur, E.: Peer Instruction: A User's Manual. Prentice Hall, Upper Saddle River, NJ (1997)
31. Cecchinato, G., Foschi, L.C.: Perusall: university learning-teaching innovation employing social annotation and machine learning. Qwerty: Open Interdiscipl. J. Technol. Cult. Educ. **15**(2) (2020). https://doi.org/10.30557/QW000030
32. Biro, S.: Reading in a time of crisis: using Perusall to facilitate close reading and active discussion in the remote philosophy classroom. Teach. Philos. (2021)
33. Adams, B., Wilson, N.S.: Building community in asynchronous online higher education courses through collaborative annotation. J. Educ. Technol. Syst. **49**(2) (2020)
34. Walker, A.S.: Perusall: harnessing AI robo-tools and writing analytics to improve student learning and increase instructor efficiency. J. Writing Analytics **3** (2019)

35. Suhre, C.J.M., Winnips, J.C., de Boer, V., Valdivia, P., Beldhuis, H.J.A.: Students' experiences with the use of a social annotation tool to improve learning in flipped classrooms. In: 5th International Conference on Higher Education Advances (HEAd 2019) (2019)
36. Lee, S.C., Yeong, F.M.: Fostering student engagement using online, collaborative reading assignments mediated by Perusall. Asia-Pacific Scholar **3**(3) (2018)
37. Krippendorff, K.: Content Analysis: An Introduction to its Methodology, 2nd edn. Sage, Thousand Oaks, CA (2004)
38. Berg, B.L., Lune, H.: Qualitative research methods for the social sciences, 9th ed. Pearson Education Limited (2017). ISBN 10: 129-2-16439-5

Augmented, Virtual and Mixed Reality in Education

Developing an AR Tutoring System to Support Maker Education

Wei-Tsung Lin[1], Yong-Ming Huang[2](✉), and Chao-Chun Chen[1]

[1] Department of Institute of Manufacturing Information and System, National Cheng Kung University, Tainan, Taiwan, R.O.C.

[2] Department of Multimedia and Entertainment Science, Southern Taiwan University of Science and Technology, Tainan, Taiwan, R.O.C.

Abstract. Maker education has been regarded by scholars as one of the most important topics, which is committed to turning ideas into reality. With the development of maker education, many makerspaces have been established to promote maker education. However, the number of teachers in makerspace is limited, so students can't learn how to use maker tools effectively. Thus, we found that the current challenge in maker education is the "lack of teachers" in makerspace. For this reason, we developed an AR system which can be used in maker education. This system can help teacher to guide students in maker education. In addition, we conducted a series of analyses. Based on the results of the analysis, we boldly assume that the system is helpful to students' learning in maker education. Finally, we have listed the problems and solutions encountered during the development process for future developers' reference.

Keywords: Augmented reality · Maker education · Unity

1 Introduction

Maker has been regarded by scholars as one of the most important topics [7], and itis committed to bringing ideas to life [8]. Maker, also known as "self-maker," is derived from the American garage culture in the 19th century [3]. The garage is a place where self-builders can give full play to their creativity. This visceral, non-profit-orientedculture is regarded as the origin of the third industrial revolution [17]. However, the word maker, it was proposed in 2005 by Dale Dougherty, the founder of Make Magazine in the United States [4]. Dougherty believes that as long as you do it yourself, the person who realizes the idea can be called a maker. In addition, former U.S. President Obama held the Maker Fair at the White House for the first time [15], and set June 18th each year as the National Maker Day [16]. Besides, the United States had more than 400 maker spaces in 2016, including maker spaces in schools, libraries, and universities [6]. Therefore, maker is one of the core concepts in the United States to cultivate talents for future generations, and it also redefines the public's view of learning. More importantly, students can learn creativity in the process of creation, thereby enhancing their 21st century abilities [9].

Due to the importance of maker, many scholars have applied it in education, and makerspace has been established one after another to promote maker education [11].

© Springer Nature Switzerland AG 2021
Y.-M. Huang et al. (Eds.): ICITL 2021, LNCS 13117, pp. 61–66, 2021.
https://doi.org/10.1007/978-3-030-91540-7_7

Maker education is a teaching strategy based on creation, which emphasizes that studentsshould be immersed in the process of creation [19]. In other words, students should learn through hands-on experience, and connect the knowledge with life, in short, is unite knowledge and action. For example, some elementary school students use Scratch tocontrol Lego devices and use actuators to animate their puppets, and it also allows students to dvelop collaboration and communication skills, thereby enhancing their expressive skills [1]. Then we see another case, some elementary school students conducte an after-school learning activity called "robot building", and the results show that this activity can improve students' knowledge of programming, thereby improving their problem-solving ability [2]. However, these teaching strategies of case are different from the traditional strategies, so they require a special teaching environment. Therefore makerspace was born, it can provide student with an environment based on creative learning [5].

However, the teacher in makerspace is quite limited, so students can't learn how to use the maker tools effectively [13]. Professor Zhu Zhiting said that the lack of teachers is an important problem in maker education [21]. He also said that in some schools,teachers must use their time after school to work on maker education, which means that they may not be experts in this field [21].In addition, the scholar said that the "lack of teachers" is a problem in maker education [14]. And he also said that schools should hire experts in the field of maker education to design the courses, this is the way to effectively train creative students [14]. Moreover, the scholar's study mentions that there are some problems in maker education, such as: lack of teachers and courses, incomplete teaching system, etc. [10]. Furthermore, USC Rossier and some teachers created the guide for maker education, and in the guide there is mention of an elementary school teacher who said that managing over 30 students at a same time for maker activitie is a difficult task [18].

Based on the above, we find that the current challenge in maker education is the lack of teacher in maker space. For this reason, we designed an AR animator teaching program that can be used for maker education, including AR system and animation machine. Specifically, students must use the system to complete the assembly of the animation machine. In other words, when students encounter problems in maker activities, they can use the system to solve them. Therefore, the problem of "lack of teachers" in maker education has been solved. In addition, we conducted a series of analyses. Based on the results of the analysis, we have made some suggestions for our system. Finally, we have listed the problems and solutions encountered during the development of the system for future developers' reference.

2 Application Development

2.1 Development Enviroment

Figure 1 shows the development environment of AR system, which contains four software. The first one is Unity 2020.3.0f1, which is a game engine developed by Unity Technologies, and it can be used to develop AR system, so we will use it as the development platform of the system. The second is Vuforia 9.8.8, which is an AR software toolkit developed by Qualcomm, it can support Unity, so we will use it as an AR development tool. The third is Illustrator, which is a vector-based drawing software developed by Adobe. It is not only easy to operate but also powerful, so we will use it to designthe

2D interface of the system. The fourth is Blender, which is a free 3D graphics software that can run on different platforms and has rich features, so we will use it to design 3D models and animations in the system.

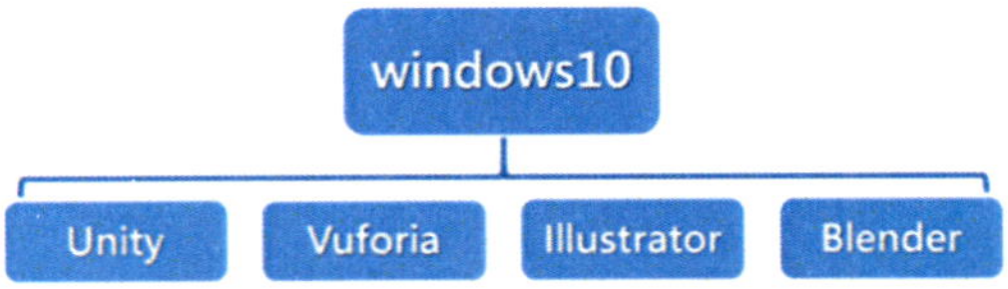

Fig. 1. Development environment

2.2 System Diagram

Figure 2 shows the schematic diagram of the system, which lists the most important five pages. Figure 2 (a) is the animation book page, which explains to the students how to draw the story. Figure 2 (a) shows the text description in the bottom left corner, the required tools in the bottom right corner, and the progress bar of the current work in the top. Figure 2 (b) shows the animator page, which shows students how to assemble the animator. below the AR movie are virtual buttons that students can touch to control theprogress of the movie. Figure 2 (c) is the motor page, which shows the students how

(a) Story

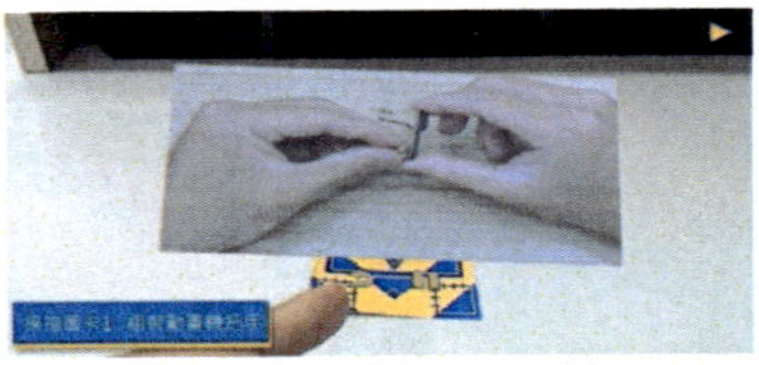

(b) Animachine machine

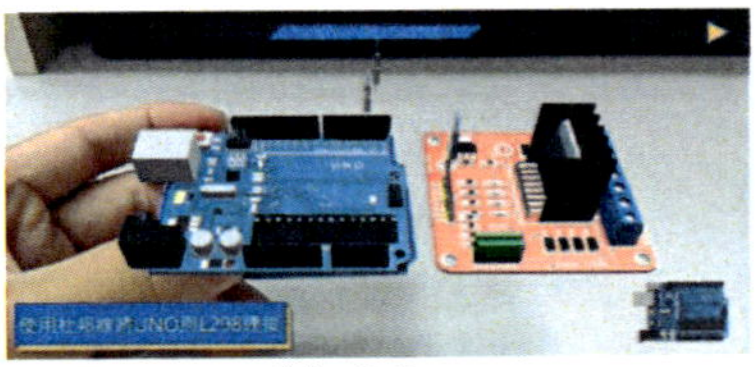

(c) Motor

(d) Integration

(e) Demonstration

Fig. 2. System diagram.

to assemble the motor. The bottom right corner of Fig. 2 (c) shows the required parts. Students can place the parts in front of the camera of the phone and the system will show the assembly animation. Figure 2 (d) is the integration page, which shows students how to integrate the motor and the animator. Finally, Fig. 2 (e) is the display page where students can interact the animation machine with the system.

3 Discussion and Suggestion

3.1 System Analysis

Figure 3 shows the AR systems of other scholars, and we find two systems to discuss.Fig. 3 (a) is used to learn the geometric concepts of chemical molecules. Specifically,the student has to use the phone to scan the identification card of the molecule, and then the screen will show the model of the molecule, and the student has to view the model to learn the geometry of the chemical molecule. The results showed that the studentfound his system easy to use and would recommend it to other students [12]. In other words, it is very helpful for learning. Figure 3 (b) is used to learn the use of the sewing machine. Specifically, the student has to use the phone to scan the identification card and then an AR video is displayed on the screen and the student has to watch the AR video to learn how to use the sewing machine. The results showed that the AR video improved students' learning efficiency and understanding of complex tasks [20]. In otherwords, it is also useful for learning. In summary, their studies show that the AR system is useful for students' learning, so we boldly assume that our system is useful for students' learning.

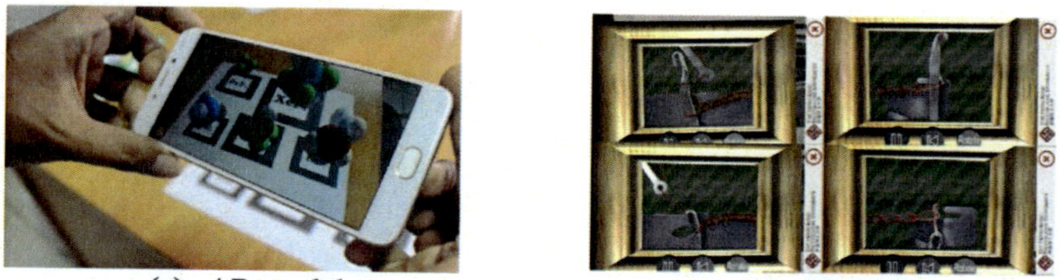

(a) AR model (b) AR Video

Fig. 3. AR learning system

3.2 Development Suggestion

Table 1 shows the problems we encountered in our development. First, the Windows user name and folders are named in English to avoid problems in Unity. Second, at present, the personal version of Unity can only be used if you get a license from Unity Hub, if you don't get a license to start Unity, it will not be able to run. Third, when compiling the apk, the API level should match the Android SDK version, otherwise it will not be compiled. Fourth, in the AR video, the virtual button should be placed in the center of the recognition card, if it is too far from the center, it will not work. Fifth, if you want to display the expanded objects step by step, you can use SetActive to control the objects under the Target Image, but don't control the objects of Target Image or Vuforia, otherwise there will be problems. Sixth, if you want to develop a new teaching system, you can get familiar with all the functions of AR before you start designing the system.

Table 1. Suggestion list

Problem	Solution
Unity compiler	File naming in English
Unity license	Go to Unity Hub to get the license
Compiling the apk	Versions must match
Virtual button	Virtual button design in the center of the card
AR step-by-step guide	Program control to expand objects
How to design in the future	Familiar with all the functions of AR

4 Conclusion

We developed an AR system, which can solve the problem of "lack of teachers" in maker education. In addition, based on the analysis results, we boldly assume that our system will be helpful for students' learning in maker education. Moreover, we expect that the development proposal will help future developers. Finally, we propose to improve the recognition capability of the system, such as the speed or accuracy of recognition.

Acknowledgments. The authors would like to thank the Ministry of Science and Technology of the Republic of China, Taiwan, for financially supporting this research under Contract No. MOST 109-2511-H-218-004-MY3.

References

1. Bull, G., Schmidt-Crawford, D.A., McKenna, M.C., Cohoon, J.: Storymaking: combining making and storytelling in a school makerspace. Theory Practice **56**(4), 271–281 (2017)
2. Chou, P.N.: Skill development and knowledge acquisition cultivated by maker education: evidence from Arduino-based educational robotics. EURASIA J. Math. Sci. Technol. Educ. **14**(10), em1600 (2018)
3. Daqin, D.: On makers and historical genes of the maker culture. Soc. Sci. Beijing **8**, 22–28 (2015)
4. Dougherty, D.: The maker movement. Innov. Technol. Gover. Global. **7**(3), 11–14 (2012)
5. Hsu, Y.C., Baldwin, S., Ching, Y.H.: Learning through making and maker education. TechTrends **61**(6), 589–594 (2017)
6. Irie, N.R., Hsu, Y.C., Ching, Y.H.: Makerspaces in diverse places: a comparative analysis of distinctive national discourses surrounding the Maker Movement and education in four countries. TechTrends **63**(4), 397–407 (2019)

7. Konopasky, A., Sheridan, K.: The maker movement in education. Oxford Research Encyclopedia of Education (2020)
8. Lakind, A., Willett, R., Halverson, E.R.: Democratizing the maker movement: a case study of one public library system's makerspace program. Ref. User Serv. Q. **58**(4), 234–245 (2019)
9. Lille, B., Romero, M.: Creativity assessment in the context of maker-based projects. Des. Technol. Educ. Int. J. **22**(3), 32–47 (2017)
10. Liu, W., Jin, S., Li, Y.: Cultivation of maker teachers under coordinated development. Int. J. Emerg. Multidiscipl. Res. **3**(4), 25–31 (2019)
11. Mersand, S.: The state of makerspace research: a review of the literature. TechTrends **65**(2), 174–186 (2020). https://doi.org/10.1007/s11528-020-00566-5
12. Nazar, M., et al.: Development of augmented reality application for learning the concept of molecular geometry. J. Phys. Conf. Ser. **1460**(1), 012083 (2020)
13. Paganelli, A., et al.: The makerspace experience and teacher professional development. Prof. Dev. Educ. **43**(2), 232–235 (2017)
14. Tao, L.: Research on the Significance and Path Optimization of the Cultivation of Maker Education Based on Multiple Interactions (2019)
15. The White House: Fact sheet: President Obama to host first-ever white house maker faire. Office of the Press Secretary. Retrieved from https://www.whitehouse.gov/the-press-office/2014/06/18/fact-sheet-president-obama-host-first-ever-white-house-maker-faire (2014)
16. The White House: Nation of makers. Retrieved from https://www.whitehouse.gov/nation-of-makers (2016)
17. Troxler, P.: Making the 3rd industrial revolution. FabLabs: Of Machines, Makers and Inventors. Transcript Publishers, Bielefeld (2013)
18. USC Rossier: 5 Challenges in Maker Education (and How to Overcome Them). Retrieved from https://rossieronline.usc.edu/maker-education/5-maker-ed-challenges/
19. Xianmin, Y., Jihong, L.: The potential value of maker education and its disputes. Modern Distance Educ. Res. **2**, 23–34 (2017)
20. Yip, J., Wong, S.H., Yick, K.L., Chan, K., Wong, K.H.: Improving quality of teaching and learning in classes by using augmented reality video. Comput. Educ. **128**, 88–101 (2019)
21. Zhang, Y.: SHENZHEN DAILY: experts share views on maker education. Retrieved from https://www.chmakered.com/newsinfo/721247.html (2018)

Facilitating 3D Geometry Learning with Augmented Reality in Authentic Contexts

Wu-Yuin Hwang, Rio Nurtantyana(✉), and Muhammad Trio Maulana Putra

Graduate Institute of Network Learning Technology, National Central University, Zhongli, Taiwan

Abstract. In this study, we developed 3D-UG with augmented reality (AR) to facilitate students while learning 3D geometry in authentic contexts. 3D-UG provided exploring activity with real-time measuring the authentic 3D objects in surrounding with AR. Students learn 3D geometry, measure 3D objects and calculate the volume or surface of the authentic 3D objects in their home during pandemic Covid-19 for one month. Participants were forty fifth-grade elementary schools' students that divide into two groups, twenty students in the experimental group (EG) used our purpose 3D-UG and twenty students in the control group (CG) used ruler. The results found that students in EG have improved geometry ability and outperformed compared with CG. Students in EG has a better understanding of geometry concept than CG. In addition, students in EG made fewer mistakes in their formula input and calculation process. It is because students carefully complete the solution and 3D-UG has clear steps to accomplish the solution. Therefore, our 3D-UG with AR could facilitate students to learn geometry learning in their home during Covid-19, exploring 3D objects their surroundings, and experienced 3D object measurement with augmented reality to enhance their geometry ability.

Keywords: Geometry learning · Authentic contexts · Augmented reality

1 Introduction

Recognizing and making a shape or measuring shape in geometry learning could increase student motivation because they feel playful with lots of fun [1]. However, students need to have a good understanding of 3D geometry thinking skills to visualize, to interpret, and to form representations of 3D figures [2]. Students will have the capability to recognize 3D objects as well by understanding the concepts of geometry and the measurement of geometry objects such as measuring volume and surface areas.

On the other hand, the students should have the capability to engage their understanding of 3D geometry with real 3D objects in their surroundings [3]. Several studies showed that learning geometry in authentic contexts could improve students learning achievement and students' abilities, including geometry ability, estimation ability, and spatial ability [4].

A problem in the learning process, especially in 3D geometry learning, is the lack of students' understanding of geometry [5] and interaction between students and real 3D objects in the surrounding [6]. In authentic contexts, students will be easy to understand

© Springer Nature Switzerland AG 2021
Y.-M. Huang et al. (Eds.): ICITL 2021, LNCS 13117, pp. 67–73, 2021.
https://doi.org/10.1007/978-3-030-91540-7_8

the types of 3D objects which surround them and to classify the objects according to their shape. However, very few studies addressed the issue of learning 3D geometry in authentic contexts and investigated learning behaviors of measuring 3D objects to know their influence on learning achievement. This is because there are difficulties when the students measure objects which are large if they only use a ruler. This issue could solve to use augmented reality technology which has the capability to measure the real world through cameras [7].

Based on the problems above, researchers developed an innovative system named 3D-UG to facilitate geometry learning in authentic contexts. The following are research questions to answer in this study:

1. Are there any significant differences in learning achievement between experimental group using 3D-UG and control group using a conventional method with a ruler?
2. What are the relationships between learning behavior and learning achievement in experimental group?

2 Literature Review

2.1 Geometry Learning in Authentic Context

There are several kinds of 3D objects like a cube, cuboid, cylinder, pyramid, etc. In addition, recognizing 3D shapes, measuring volume and surface area of 3D objects in daily life with and without standard units is also important to students because this real experience of applying geometry in daily life can consolidate understanding of geometry concepts [8].

Learning geometry can improve students' understanding when interacting with objects around them. Nowadays, understanding how to measure the volume and surface area of an object is very important and can be used in certain conditions. For example, when traveling that requires carrying a suitcase, but with limited baggage, we can estimate the volume of our suitcase so that it is not overloaded. But commonly, geometry is taught using textbooks, blackboard, and 2D images can be effective, but measuring volume and surface area are not highly effective [9, 10].

2.2 Geometry Ability in Geometry Learning

To visualize, to interpret, and to form representations of 3D figures, students should have good 3D geometry ability [2]. There are several dimensions of 3D geometry ability, including the ability to recognize and create 3D shapes, the ability to manipulate and translate representations of different views of 3D solids, the ability to structure 3D arrays of cubes, the ability to determine the properties of 3D geometric shapes, the ability to calculate the volume and area of 3D solids, the ability to compare features of 3D shapes. In this study, we conducted 3D geometry ability, including the ability to manipulate, to recognize, to structure, to determine properties, and to calculate volume and surface area of 3D objects.

2.3 Augmented Reality for Geometry Learning in Authentic Context

Augmented Reality (AR) is a technology that displays virtual objects produced by computers in the real world using camera sensors [11]. For example, ARCore that developed by Google to build AR app for Android devices [7]. As a platform to build AR, ARCore has been widely used to build authentic learning media based on AR. It is because can understand the surrounding environment and easier to integrate. Based on the feature of ARCore above, in this study, we provide AR with ARCore technology in our app. It will be more powerful for measuring 3D objects in the real world.

3 System Design

We developed 3D-UG to facilitate geometry learning with AR. Our 3D-UG app has features such as learning, measuring 3D objects with AR, and calculation. Figure 1 shows the learning material including theory, 3D representation, and calculation. The theory will give students learning material to learn the formula either for volume or surface area. The virtual 3D representation will show a virtual 3D object that students can make interaction with. The calculation will show students the step how to calculate, this function like a calculator that will show the step.

After students learn, students continue to measure real time 3D objects with AR that shown in Fig. 2. For example, students measure the volume and surface area of a suitcase in the real world, then students adjust the properties of virtual 3D objects such as the length, width and height to know the real properties. Finally, students calculate the volume or surface of 3D object to complete the geometry learning.

Fig. 1. Learning material on 3D-UG app

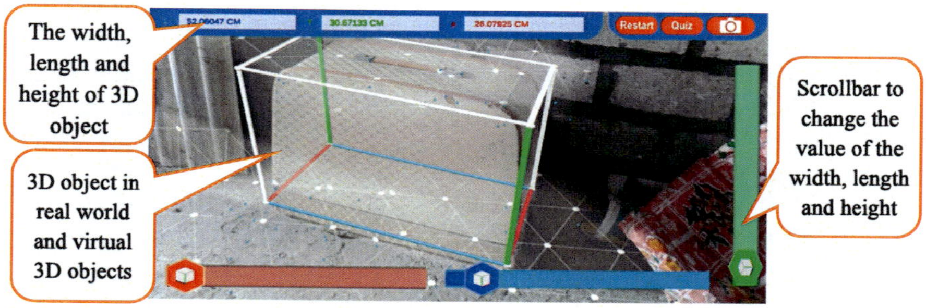

Fig. 2. Measuring 3D objects with 3D-UG app

4 Methodology

The participant of this research is forty people of fifth-grade elementary students which separated into two groups. The experiment group (EG) consisted of 20 students using 3D-UG app and the control group (CG) consisted of 20 students with a ruler. Students learn concepts of 3D Geometry and measuring volume and surface area in authentic contexts. The experiment conducted 1 month with pretest, learning with exploring activity and posttest. All activities were conducted in students' home because of pandemic Covid-19 situations and assisted with a teacher with an online meeting. In details, the teacher gave the pretest and the tutorial of use the 3D-UG via online meeting in the 1st week. In the 2nd until 3rd week, the students used 3D-UG app to explore and measuring 3D object in their surroundings. In the 4th week, teacher gave posttest content and submit it via online meeting. The topics for this study were measuring volume and surface area of cube and cuboid. As seen in Table 1, the research variables about learning behavior and learning assessment to measure 3D geometry ability. The analysis uses ANOVA to analyze the significant differences between EG and CG in both pretest and posttest. In addition, Pearson correlation analyze will conduct to know the relationship learning behaviors from 20 students in EG with post-test. The learning behaviors data collected from two weeks activities. At least, students measure and calculate both one volume and surface of cube and cuboid.

Table 1. Research variables

Variable	Description
Learning achievement	
1. Geometry ability	Ability to visualize, interpret, and form representations of 3D [2]
Learning behavior	
2. Error calculation	The number of errors in the calculation process
3. Error formula	The number of errors in the formula while trying to calculate volume & surface area
4. Number attempts	The number of trying to calculate the volume & surface area

5 Results and Discussions

5.1 Learning Achievement of Geometry Learning Between EG and CG

The ANOVA analysis was conducted to test in between the EG and CG, as shown in Table 2. It shows that students' prior knowledge not significantly different ($p > 0.05$) between EG and CG on the pretest. In other hand, the results found that there is a significant difference in geometry ability ($F = 12.434, p < .05$) also students' geometry ability in EG outperformed CG. This indicates that students significantly improved their geometry ability after using 3D-UG app.

A possible reason is that 3D-UG app with AR facilitated students which can identify the 3D object in their surroundings and define the properties such as length, width, and height and do the calculation. Therefore, students in the EG can understand the concept of geometry better than students in the CG.

Table 2. Learning achievement between EG and CG.

Group	*N*	Pretest				Posttest			
		M	*SD*	*F*	*Sig*	*M*	*SD*	*F*	*Sig*
EG	20	27.200	7.179	.525	.410	34.850	2.231	12.434	.001
CG	20	25.400	6.468			30.150	3.528		

5.2 Learning Behavior of Geometry Learning in EG

The correlation analysis in Table 3 shows that error calculation has a negatively significant correlation with geometry ability ($r = -.521, p = .018$). The results show that students who got higher scores were made fewer mistakes in the calculation process. It indicates that students need to be aware of their calculation process when they tried to solve the geometry problem in authentic contexts.

Table 3. Learning behavior on EG

	1	2	3	4
Learning achievement				
1. Geometry ability	1			
Learning behavior				
2. Error calculation	−.521*	1		
3. Error formula	−.446*	.318	1	
4. Number attempts	.178	−.391	−.239	1

The number of error formulas also has a negatively significant correlation with geometry ability ($r = -.446, p = .049$). The results shows that most students who got higher scores were made fewer mistakes in the formula. It indicates that students should make sure that the formula is correct before they do the calculation.

6 Conclusions

Regarding research question one, the results show that there is a significant different between EG with our 3D-UG app augmented reality and CG with a ruler. Our 3D-UG app with augmented reality can help students to learn geometry concepts and improved their geometry ability on learning achievement. Furthermore, the EG outperform in their learning achievement' score compared with CG. It is because EG can understand the concept of geometry learning when learning with 3D-UG.

Regarding research question two, the results found there is relationship between learning achievement and learning behavior. The results found that students in EG checked the calculation carefully before submitting the solution and checked the formula before the calculation.

In addition, the limitation in this study, students learning with 3D-UG on their home because of pandemic Covid-19 situations that imply the difference of 3D object that measured by students. The geometry learning in this study was limited to measure volume and surface on cube and cuboid. We analyze the learning behavior only in the EG group. We suggested that the future study can use collaborative measurement because students in their home and 3D-UG extend with other 3D objects.

References

1. Jones, K.: Issues in the teaching and learning of geometry. In: Haggarty, L. (ed.) Aspects of Teaching Secondary Mathematics: Perspectives on Practice, pp. 121–139. Routledge, London (2002)
2. Pittalis, M., Christou, C.: Coding and decoding representations of 3D shapes. J. Math. Behav. **32**(3), 673–689 (2013)
3. Chen, G.-D., Nurkhamid, Wang, C.-Y., Yang, S.-H., Lu, W.-Y., Chang, C.-K.: Digital learning playground: supporting authentic learning experiences in the classroom. Interact. Learn. Environ. **21**(2), 172–183 (2013)
4. Hwang, W.-Y., Purba, S.W.D., Liu, Y.-F., Zhang, Y.-Y., Chen, N.-S.: An investigation of the effects of measuring authentic contexts on geometry learning achievement. IEEE Trans. Learn. Technol. **12**(3), 291–302 (2019)
5. Özerem, A.: Misconceptions in geometry and suggested solutions for seventh grade students. Procedia Soc. Behav. Sci. **55**, 720–729 (2012)
6. Le, H.-Q., Kim, J.-I.: An augmented reality application with hand gestures for learning 3D geometry. In: 2017 IEEE International Conference on Big Data and Smart Computing, BigComp 2017, pp. 34–41 (2017)
7. Glover, J.: Unity 2018 Augmented Reality Project. Packt, United Kingdom (2018)
8. Mooney, C., Ferrie, L., Fox, S., Hansen, A., Wrathmell, R.: Primary Mathematics: Knowledge and Understanding, 8th edn. SAGE Publications, New York (2018)
9. Hwang, W.-Y., Su, J.-H., Huang, Y.-M., Dong J.-J.: A study of multi-representation of geometry problem solving with virtual manipulatives and whiteboard system. J. Educ. Technol. Soc. **12**(3), 229–247 (2009)

10. Noreen, R., Rana, A.M.K.: Activity-based teaching versus traditional method of teaching in mathematics at elementary level. Bull. Educ. Res. **41**(2), 145–159 (2019)
11. Azuma, R., Baillot, Y., Behringer, R., Feiner, S., Julier, S., MacIntyre, B.: Recent advances in augmented reality. IEEE Comput. Graph. Appl. **21**(6), 34–47 (2001)

A Simulation Learning in Communication Technique Skill by Virtual Reality - Certification of Telecommunication Line Plant

ChinLun Lai(✉)

Communication Engineering Department, Asia Eastern University of Science and Technology, Taipei, Taiwan
fo001@mail.aeust.edu.tw

Abstract. In this paper, a simulated learning strategy in communication skill is implemented by virtual reality technology and is applied to the course of telecommunication line plant certification which is the important skill training course in communication engineering. The proposed system is implemented as a full automatic evaluation system to demonstrate the effect of the brand new learning strategy for field test in telecommunication skills to validate the learning performance and efficiency. It is observed, from the experimental results, that the learning strategy can not only improves the student's learning performance and interest in skill training but also provide a stress-free and unlimited learning environment than the traditional teaching methods. That is, due to the strong extension to variety applications, it is very suitable for complementing physical training courses to achieve the best learning effect.

Keywords: Simulation learning · Self-skill training · Telecommunication line plant certification · Virtual reality technology

1 Introduction

Telecommunications technology refers to the use of electronic technology to transfer information between different locations which includes different long-distance communication methods such as radio, telegraph, television, telephone, data communication, and computer network, etc. Communication technologies mainly include transmission access, network switching, mobile communication, wireless communication, optical communication, satellite communication, support management, private network communication and other technologies. The above communication technologies are composed of the most basic carrier telecommunications lines. Different countries and regions around the world use dense telecommunication lines to achieve connectivity. At present, the main communication lines are still mainly copper cables, but more and more high-speed lines are replaced by optical fibers.

In Taiwan, the connection of communication lines requires professionals who have been passed the certifications which are called regulatory licenses. For example, the

© Springer Nature Switzerland AG 2021
Y.-M. Huang et al. (Eds.): ICITL 2021, LNCS 13117, pp. 74–84, 2021.
https://doi.org/10.1007/978-3-030-91540-7_9

"Communication Technique Skill", (also named as "Telecommunication Line Verification") level B and C skill certification of the Ministry of Labor of the country are included. The state actively promotes the cultivation of such professionals through the establishment of professional certification sites, and then integrates certification with international standards, promotes international labor mobility, and trains students with practice ability and technique in telecommunications, Internet, and optical fiber communications through the implementation of verification tests. The scope of work of a certified communication technology (telecommunication line) technician includes the erection, installation, and simple maintenance of various telecommunication lines and their terminal equipment.

As mentioned above, in order to obtain a professional license for telecommunication lines plant, students must learn a lot of basic knowledge. In addition to a lot of parts and materials that need to be known, the complicated steps of practical exercises are very cumbersome. Moreover, different designated topics require a variety of different skills and knowledge which should be familiar in advanced, and it is necessary to increase proficiency through repeated practice before it can be completed within the time limit. Therefore, in addition to being a big challenge for candidates, the time, materials, and related equipment and other resources required for the practice process are all extremely heavy burdens. For example, in order to obtain a license, students usually need to participate in special training courses. In addition to spend a considerable amount of practice time in a specific laboratory, the expenses for related consumables and training often cost more than hundreds of US dollars, which is a heavy burden to students.

On the other hand, the simulated learning and training method is a fast growing and powerful strategy in modern education, which replicates the context of real case in a safe environment and provides interactive and feedback activities for students to achieve better learning effect, especially for clinic and nursing education fields [1–6]. The students who participated in such activity gained "great interest" and "encouragement" from the VR supportive teaching materials, thus demonstrating enhanced skills and confidence in performing real practice. Most research shows that most students also agree that the VR-supported skill learning system provides clear and standardized steps. Since the system provides students with unlimited access time and practice time, it reduce the space and time limitation in the conventional skill learning model. In addition, students who are beginners can use the system to fast understand the whole process and reduce the pressure of learning. Moreover, the learning feedback can also be obtained from the system by notifying the wrong operations automatically. Since the risk-free VR environment is suitable for adaptive teaching strategies, it improves the ability of trainers to solve complex teaching problems. This innovative educational tool can shorten the distance between student theory and practice by reducing student anxiety and patient safety issues [7, 8] In addition, VR provides unlimited access to risk-free simulated presence scenarios, thereby reducing students' anxiety and improving students' self-confidence. Students participating in VR scenarios said that they are not under the pressure usually caused by the presence of teachers and can follow their own learning progress. In addition, students are no longer afraid of being embarrassed or scolded by their tutors for their mistakes, thus greatly reducing learning anxiety. These results include our previous work [9–11] disclose that the VR system can be a good learning assistance for skill training. On the other hand, using VR as the other professional skills training such as first responder training, military training, and workforce training, etc., as well as the common assessment tests and evaluation methods for validating the VR training effectiveness are also reviewed and well discussed [12–15].

In view of this, this paper proposes a telecommunication line skills verification practice system based on virtual reality to train the complicated and professional skills of telecommunication line plant. The training system combines functional modules including image recognition, voice recognition, gesture control, interactive immersive situations, automated assessment, and practice data analysis to build an immersive VR environment for self-training and auto-assessment purpose in telecommunication line plant certification field. In addition, for students who use this system to practice, preliminary exploration of changes in learning interest, motivation, and effect are carried out to verify the performance of the VR learning system.

2 Research Methodology

Descriptions of the research methodology include two aspects: namely the system construction and the study of learning effectiveness, which are described as follows:

2.1 Building up the VR Training System

In order to realize an automated VR skill training and verification system, the research team needs to complete 3D modeling of scenes and objects to realize the training space, equipment, and training materials required in the real world. The required 3D scenes and objects are first produced by Maya software package, and then imported into the Unity3D platform to complete the relevant scenes, equipment, and materials.

The VR training system uses Unity3D as a platform for script design and execution. Once the 3D scenes and objects are completed, the next step is to program and implement training scripts. The training operation script is realized one by one according to the content of the necessary completion work items and the evaluation standard description file in the skill verification specification. Once the operation script is completed, it is implemented in a programming language (C#) to verify its operation function in the Unity environment. For example, the basic and necessary work such as "instrument and tool use" item. Under this item, the evaluation standard description includes the usage of "three-purpose meter", "oscilloscope", "light source power meter"... etc. In another example, the necessary completion work 'line engineering" item includes "cable testing", "cable connection", and "basic wiring". Once all the operating scripts had been programmed and undergone the functional verification, the user can use the VR helmet with the control handle to perform skill training in the virtual scene.

2.2 Discussion on Learning Effect

A small number of trained students are invited to conduct a preliminary discussion on the difference of learning interest, motivation, and effect caused by using VR training system for self-skill training. This paper uses interviews to understand students' learning motivation, interest, effectiveness, and feedback from the experience of using this self-study system. The guiding questions are modified from part of [11, 16] which includes the subjective differences compared with traditional training methods, the subjective learning results caused by the training system, the experience of learning activity using VR systems, as well as the difficulties encountered during the self-learning process. A lecturer from the Department of Communication Engineering served as the moderator for interview questionnaire design and data collection, and the lecturer was trained to conduct focus group quantitative research. The questionnaire process ensures the anonymity of the data to ensure that students' responses do not affect their assessment of course performance. In addition, due to the impact of the COVID-19 epidemic, all interviews are conducted using online questionnaires. The guiding questions are described as follows:

Learning Effectiveness and Satisfaction:

1. This training system has achieved my individual learning goals.
2. I have acquired a deeper understanding by the participation of the training system.
3. My academic performance level will rise as a result of my attendance to this training system.
4. I am satisfied with the educational content in the training system.

Training System in This Course:

1. The system creates an appropriate educational and training environment.
2. The system organizes the training sessions properly to make the most use of the training sessions.
3. The training system was equipped with the highest standards of quality.
4. I will recommend others using this system for VR development.

The above questions are evaluated by adopting the 5-point Likert Scale, ranging from 5 (Strongly Agree) to 1 (Strongly Disagree). On the other hand, in order to collect subjective feelings of the users for comparison of the difference between the practical training and the virtual training, the following two questions are asked:

1. In your opinion, what are the advantages of using a VR system for automated skill training (examination) compared with actual on-site practice (examination)?
2. In your opinion, what are the disadvantages of using a VR system for automated skill training (examination) compared with actual on-site practice (examination)?

3 Experimental Results and Discussions

The proposed VR training system is implemented under the Unity3D 2019 platform. The hardware architecture includes high-end laptops (with Intel Core i9 CPU, 16G DDR RAM, and NVIDIA GeForce graphics accelerator GTX1080) and a VR helmets set (HTC VIVE Pro). In the teaching content part, the designated assessment items in the communication technology verification test are implemented as the content of skill exercises. Users need to wear helmets and handles to enter the simulated training classroom and complete all the designated assessment items. During the operation, students can terminate, suspend, or re-practice at any time. In the simulated classroom, in addition to the optional prompt board for displaying the operation steps, the correctness of each operation step will be judged and can be feedback to the user. All step prompts and operation feedback functions is optional for user. After completing all the operations, the system will automatically record the students' practice results, including the number of exercises, wrong step points, total score, number of wrong steps, and the statistical value of the error rate for each steps. Students can also use the video playback function to watch the wrong steps and the corresponding standard operation, so as to practice their skills repeatedly until they become proficient. The related system architecture, operation process, and content to be provided are displayed in Figs. 1, 2, 3, 4, 5, 6 and 7.

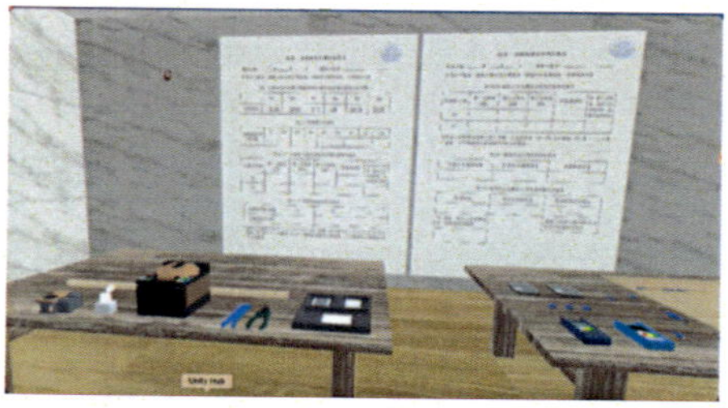

Fig. 1. The implemented VR scene of telecommunication line examination, including all the tools, consumables, and test questions.

Fig. 2. Snapshots of the scene, note that the hint display board can be activated or not by the user.

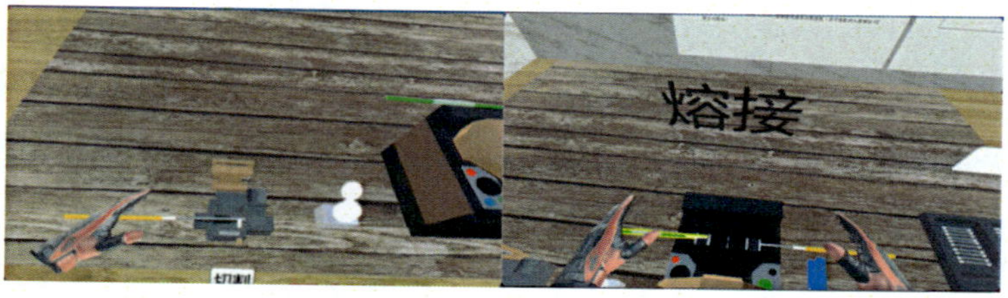

Fig. 3. Demonstration of operation steps of the optical fiber cutting (left) and fusion (right).

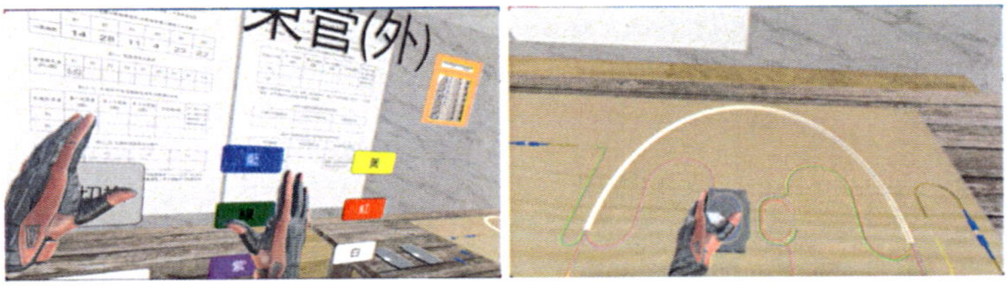

Fig. 4. Demonstration of operation steps of the optical fiber plant (left) and assembled (right).

Fig. 5. Learning feedback from the VR system during the training process, operation is correct (left) and operation is incorrect (right).

Fig. 6. The user can follow the directions list in the displayed board step by step to complete the whole process. The system will automatically check every step (left) until the examination is finished (right).

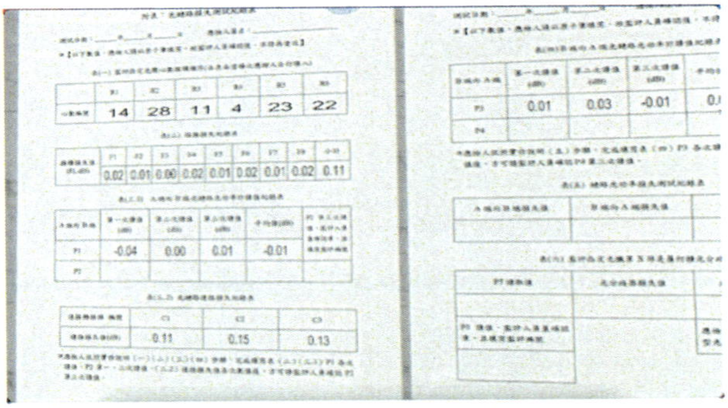

Fig. 7. All the evaluation work of the examination/training process is automatically done according to the given response of the user, no instructor is needed.

In the part of system effectiveness verification, this research adopts questionnaire analysis method for evaluation. A total of 25 students from the four-year university department are collected from questionnaires (limited by the number of students had taken the entity verification course). The average age of the participants is 21 years old, who are selected from those have taken the telecom line verification course. These students have actually participated in the physical practice operation of the telecom line verification, therefore, after inviting these students to carry out the line plant operations in the VR training system, their opinions are collected to compare the subjective feelings after physical training and VR virtual training. After analyzing the results of the questionnaire, the students' opinions on using the VR system for skill verification and training, the quantitative results are presented in Table 1.

Table 1. Summary of response to 8 survey questions using 5-point Likert Scale.

Survey questions	Strongly agree (5)	Agree (4)	Neutral (3)	Disagree (2)	Strongly disagree (1)	Mean value
This training system has achieved my individual learning goals	13(52%)	5(20%)	6(24%)	1(4%)	0	4.2
I have acquired a deeper understanding by the participation of the training system	14(56%)	7(28%)	4(16%)	0	0	4.4
My academic performance level will rise as a result of my attendance to this training system	12(48%)	8(32%)	5(20%)	0	0	4.3
I am satisfied with the educational content in the training system	14(56%)	7(28%)	4(16%)	0	0	4.4
The system creates an appropriate educational and training environment	13(52%)	6(24%)	5(20%)	0	1(4%)	4.2

(*continued*)

Table 1. *(continued)*

Survey questions	Strongly agree (5)	Agree (4)	Neutral (3)	Disagree (2)	Strongly disagree (1)	Mean value
The system organizes the training sessions properly to make the most use of the training sessions	12(48%)	8(32%)	4(16%)	1(4%)	0	4.2
The training system was equipped with the highest standards of quality	12(48%)	8(32%)	2(8%)	3(12%)	0	4.2
I will recommend others using this system for VR development	14(56%)	6(24%)	2(8%)	3(12%)	0	4.2

Observing from the results presented in Table 1, it is noted that the effectiveness of the students' skills training using the VR system reached 4.2, 4.4, and 4.3 points respectively (Rows 2–4), while their satisfaction with the use of the system (Row 5) reached 4.4 points. In addition, the evaluation of system context design (Row 6), content provision (Row 7), and operating functions (Row 8) reached 4.2 points equally. If we view the first two columns (Strongly Agree and Agree) of each question as positive response, then 80% of the users give positive response to verify the "learning effectiveness and satisfaction item" while 79% of the users give positive response to verify the "training system item".

On the other hand, in the qualitative subjective description part, it can be divided into the following five categories: convenient practice, fast skill learning process, reduced learning pressure, friendly to the environment, and lack of realism, etc.

Opinion 1: Practice is Very Convenient, but It Takes Time to Adapt. Most of the students stat that since no physical space and materials are needed in the VR simulation environment, it is more convenient to prepare for practice. However, despite simplifying the learning process, students still have to spend time learning and adapting to the operation of the VR system.

Opinion 2: The Process of Skill Learning Can Be Completed Quickly. The students expressed that they can acquired the operation process hint on the prompt list displayed in the VR skills learning system. by stepping through each step of the procedure, students can learn and know where they made a mistake. when a student makes an operation error, the system will give the alarm to remind them of mistakes immediately, thus made the students who are not familiar with the practice procedure can understand the complete operation steps through repeated practice. This make students can achieve the goal of operation step learning quickly. In addition, some students suggested that the VR skills practice should be carried out before the physical skills operation course, which will enable students to understand all the procedures before the actual operation, thus to help students to make more precise actions during the physical training process.

Opinion 3: Offering the Stress-Free Learning Environment. Through skill teaching and feedback demonstration, teachers are very important in physical training courses. However, teachers on the spot also make students feel nervous, fearful or lack of confidence, which affects their performance. However, in the automated VR training system, since no real instructor appear to perform incorrect instructions and correct demonstrations, students can arrange their own schedule, practice times and self-correction. Therefore, students generally F that the VR system can provide a much stress-free and independent learning environment and makes learning activity easier.

Opinion 4: More Friendly to the Environment. Most students pointed out that since the physical teaching process requires the construction of laboratories, supervisors, a large amount of consumable materials, and expensive equipment, the cost of learning is extremely high and inconvenient. In addition, due to the expensive materials, students must be cautious in the practice process, and it is not easy to pay for the expenses required for repeated practice, which prevent students from completing skill exercise. However, in the VR training system, not only the VR system requires no consumables, but also students can repeat the exercise process indefinitely without limitation of time and space. Since the VR system can greatly saves time (students' waiting time for practice), human resources (teacher's supervision) and material resources (the cost of equipment and consumables), it is extremely friendly to the environment.

Opinion 5: Lack of Real Body Sense. Almost all students stat that there is a greater sense of reality and in traditional training methods. the students pointed out that the hand operation/touch mode of the VR environment cannot provide the actual touch feeling and force feedback as students experienced in the actual practice, and the operation process cannot achieve the feeling of real wiring, stripping, knocking, etc., While the detailed operation movements cannot be achieved thus it is not easy to extend the virtual experience of the practice to the practical situation of the physical exercise. In addition, the VR system cannot provide actual circuit state measurement, so it cannot predict and respond to unexpected situations in future implementations.

It is observed from the above experimental results that the learning effectiveness, user satisfaction, completeness of content provision, and good operating functions as well as environment of this VR training system can be effectively verified. Moreover, in addition to the lack of real sense of body, students generally believe that the VR training system can provide a more concise and effective skill practice environment with properties of stress-free, free from time and space constraints, and friendly to the environment. It is very suitable for combining with physical practice courses as a supplementary usage for fast, intensive, and independent learning. In summary, the VR skills training assistance system can replace students with traditional skills teaching methods and serve as an auxiliary tool for future students to learn independently. Since students do not often have the opportunity to physically train their skills, they can use the VR skills training system to accumulate operations experience, hence to help to strengthen the effectiveness during the physical training.

4 Conclusions

This paper proposes a telecom line plant skill verification practice system based on virtual reality technology to assist the professional skill training. The virtual training system combines functional modules including image recognition, voice recognition, gesture control, interactive immersive situations, automated assessment, and practice data analysis to build an immersive VR skills training and verification environment, thus achieves the goal of automated professional skills training and assessment. Regarding the verification part of the system, a questionnaire evaluation method is adopted to collect opinions for analysis from students who had undergone both the physical training and virtual training process. The experimental results show that over 80% of the users verify that the VR training system has good performance for students' learning effectiveness, learning integrity, and user satisfaction. In addition, due to the characteristics of the VR system itself, it can provide a more stress-free, environment friendly, and less time-space limitation strategy while attending the autonomous and self-learning goal. Finally, due to the strong extension to variety applications, it is very suitable for complementing physical training courses to achieve the best learning effect.

References

1. Jeffries, P.R.: Simulation in Nursing Education: From Conceptualization to Evaluation. National League for Nursing, New York (2007)
2. Waxman, K.: The development of evidence-based clinical simulation scenarios: guidelines for nurse educators. J. Nurs. Educ. **49**(1), 29–35 (2010). https://doi.org/10.3928/01484834-20090916-07
3. Landeen, L., Nielson, A.: Focus on simulation-integrating simulation into teaching practice. J. Nurs. Educ. **47**(11), 487–488 (2008)
4. Khalaila, R.: Simulation in nursing education: an evaluation of students' outcomes at their first clinical practice combined with simulations. Nurse Educ. Today **34**, 252–258 (2014). https://doi.org/10.1016/j.nedt.2013.08.015
5. Ahn, H., Kim, H.: Implementation and outcome evaluation of high-fidelity simulation scenarios to integrate cognitive and psychomotor skills for Korean nursing students. Nurse Educ. Today **35**(5), 706–711 (2015)
6. Handwerker, S.M.: Transforming nursing education: a review of current curricular practices in relation to Benner's latest work. Int. J. Nurs. Educ. Scholars. **9**(1), 21 (2012). https://doi.org/10.1515/1548-923X.2510
7. Freina, L., Ott, M.: A literature review on immersive virtual reality in education: state of the art and perspectives. In: Proceedings of eLearning and Software for Education (eLSE), Bucharest, April 23–24 (2015)
8. Hussein, M., Nätterdal, C.: The Benefits of Virtual Reality in Education-A Comparison Study, Bachelor Dissertation. Chalmers University of Technology. University of Gothenburg, Sweden (2015)

9. Lai, C., Chang, Y.-M.: Improving the skills training by mixed reality simulation learning. In: Wu, T.-T., Huang, Y.-M., Shadieva, R., Lin, L., Starčič, A.I. (eds.) ICITL 2018. LNCS, vol. 11003, pp. 18–27. Springer, Cham (2018). https://doi.org/10.1007/978-3-319-99737-7_2
10. Lai, C., Chang, Y.-M.: A testing case of simulation learning in nursing by virtual reality - subcutaneous injection training. In: Huang, T.-C., Wu, T.-T., Barroso, J., Sandnes, F.E., Martins, P., Huang, Y.-M. (eds.) ICITL 2020. LNCS, vol. 12555, pp. 109–118. Springer, Cham (2020). https://doi.org/10.1007/978-3-030-63885-6_13
11. Chang, Y., Lai, C.L.: Exploring the experiences of nursing students in using immersive virtual reality to learn nursing skills. Nurse. Educ. Today. **97**, 1–7 (2020)
12. Xie, B., et al.: A review on virtual reality skill training applications. Front. Virtual Real. **2**, 645153 (2021). https://doi.org/10.3389/frvir.2021.645153
13. Abidi, M.H., Al-Ahmari, A., Ahmad, A., Ameen, W., Alkhalefah, H.: Assessment of virtual reality-based manufacturing assembly training system. Int. J. Adv. Manuf. Technol. **105**(9), 3743–3759 (2019). https://doi.org/10.1007/s00170-019-03801-3
14. Akdere, M., Jiang, Y., Lobo, F.: Evaluation and assessment of virtual reality-based simulated training: exploring the human-technology frontier. Eur. J. Train. Dev. (2021). https://doi.org/10.15405/epsbs.2021.02.17
15. Harrison, A., Derwent, G., Enticknap, A., Rose, F.D., Attree, E.A.: The role of virtual reality technology in the assessment and training of inexperienced powered wheelchair users. Disabil. Rehabil. **24**, 599–606 (2002). https://doi.org/10.1080/09638280110111360
16. Chiang, M.-T., Kung, Y.: The study of 2012 curriculum and teaching satisfaction in national Pingtung university of education. Forum. Educ. Admin. **5**(2), 1–24 (2013)

Integration of Mixed Reality in Teaching and Learning Effectiveness: A Systematic Literature Review of the Analyses

Ching-Yun Tseng[1], Yu Shu[2], Tien-Chi Huang[1](✉), Wen-Chiao Hsu[1], and Pei-Ling Chien[3]

[1] Department of Information Management, National Taichung University of Science and Technology, Taichung 404, Taiwan
tchuang@gm.nutc.edu.tw
[2] College of Languages, National Taichung University of Science and Technology, Taichung 404, Taiwan
[3] Global Communication Faculty, Kobe Gakuin University, Kobe, Japan

Abstract. In this study, a literature review was conducted on the trends in applying mixed reality (MR) technologies to education over the past decade (2011–2021) and to examine the learning outcomes achieved. This in-depth research project and examination included 64 articles in total, and an integrated analysis was performed based on six dimensions: year of publication, research discipline, educational stage of subjects, location of experimental subjects, learning orientation, and experimental design. The research results indicated that MR was mostly applied to teaching, practical training, and auxiliary experiences in the fields of health and wellbeing and science took the form of using simulation experiences during teaching and practical training and assisting students in visualizing abstract concepts. To improve students' learning cognition and enhance their practical abilities. In addition, relevant suggestions for mixed reality in education future research are proposed. The experimental data compiled in this study can be used for follow-up analysis, which will clarify the key moderating variables affecting the effectiveness of the application of MR technologies to teaching.

Keywords: Reality technologies · Mixed reality · Learning effectiveness · Literature review

1 Introduction

The robust development of science and technology in recent years has facilitated the integration of new technological equipment into the field of teaching, leading to qualitative and quantitative improvements in research on educational technologies. At the same time, the application of reality-altering technologies—virtual reality (VR), augmented reality (AR), and mixed reality (MR)—to education has become more frequent and extensive due to falling equipment costs. These technologies can be used to assist teachers and supplement, but not completely replace, classroom teaching. They can also

© Springer Nature Switzerland AG 2021
Y.-M. Huang et al. (Eds.): ICITL 2021, LNCS 13117, pp. 85–94, 2021.
https://doi.org/10.1007/978-3-030-91540-7_10

be used to promote interest in various industries and professions and can be used to enhance education, medical technology simulations, design, military training, tourism, architecture, and entertainment.

VR is a completely immersive experience: the equipment isolates users from the real world while a computer system simulates a virtual environment that is realistic, thereby providing them with an all-encompassing experience that mimics personal involvement in a scenario. However, VR is limited by its inability to create connections with real spaces. This shortcoming was eventually addressed by the emergence of AR, which is a partially immersive experience. Its technical principle involves superimposing virtual objects (such as digital audio and video or text) onto the real world using cameras along with recognition and positioning technologies. This creates the illusion of virtual objects existing in the real world. However, AR lacks the ability to mimic immersion in an alternate environment, as with VR.

Through the environment that they create, MR technologies compensate for the shortcomings of VR and AR. They provide a partially immersive experience, with users seeing virtual objects in real environments through head-mounted display units. The immersiveness of VR and the real-life environment of AR are equally emphasized: through the integration of the real and virtual worlds, users can interact naturally with virtual objects in the real environment with their hands. Past studies have concluded that MR better stimulates students' multi-sensory memory, and it is being introduced to traditional education [1–3], This has encouraged many researchers to focus on finding ways to use MR technologies to teach more effectively and improve learning efficiency. An overview of the research conducted in recent years revealed that some studies found MR to be helpful at enhancing learning motivation, which in turn improved learning effectiveness. Other researchers, however, did not identify any major difference (did not reach significance) between the learning effectiveness of reality-altering technologies and traditional teaching methods [4]. Consequently, the opinions on the topic can be divided into two groups.

In this study, the literature review method was adopted to collate and analyze the related articles published over the past decade. It is hoped that, through the findings of this research, researchers in related fields can clearly understand the trends in the application of this type of technology to today's educational context as well as its advantages, flaws, and limitations.

2 Method

2.1 Literature Collation Process

The Web of Science (WOS) database was used for the literature search. The keywords, defined to target the learning effectiveness of MR in education, were TS = (Mixed Reality in Education), OR TI = (Mixed Reality in Education), OR KP = (Mixed Reality), AND language (English) AND document type (Article). The time range for the search was 2011–2021. Eventually, a total of 389 articles were retrieved from the WOS database for follow-up analysis and examination. A flowchart of the literature search is shown in Fig. 1.

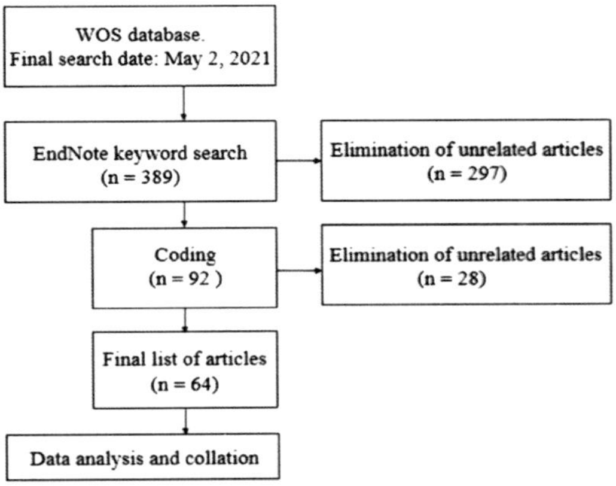

Fig. 1. Flowchart of the literature search process

2.2 Establishing the Selection and Exclusion Criteria

The following criteria were set for the screening of articles:

1. All articles whose subject and content were related to research on the application of MR technologies to education were included, with no restrictions on the field.
2. The articles could not be mere descriptions of VR or AR technologies being applied to education.
3. The articles needed to be complete papers with content that included the impact and results of integrating MR technologies into education. Literary analyses and literature reviews were excluded from the types of article that could be selected.

2.3 Screening for Usable Articles

The first stage of this research involved searching the WOS database using keywords; 389 articles were retrieved. Next, a preliminary screening was performed based on the articles' titles and abstracts before the articles found using the WOS database were imported into EndNote. The latter's search panel function permits searching of articles based on titles, abstracts, and keywords so that matching documents can be identified easily. Only MR-related documents were retained; those that did not mention MR or only mentioned VR or AR were excluded. The final number of articles was 92.

The second round of screening was carried out according to the previously mentioned selection and exclusion criteria. For collation, the 92 articles were coded in order. During the process, the articles were screened, and the following types were excluded: those that were not related to MR in educational research, those that did not constitute complete papers, and those that were focused only on VR and/or AR. The final number of articles was 64, all of which were included in the follow-up collation and analysis.

3 Results

3.1 Trends of Articles on MR in Education

Many articles not relevant to this study had already been excluded during the self-designed screening process. It is obvious from Fig. 2. that, in recent years, research on MR in the educational environment has exhibited a consistent upward trend. The decline in the results for 2021 was due to the lack of data for the year, since the final search period of this study was April-May 2021.

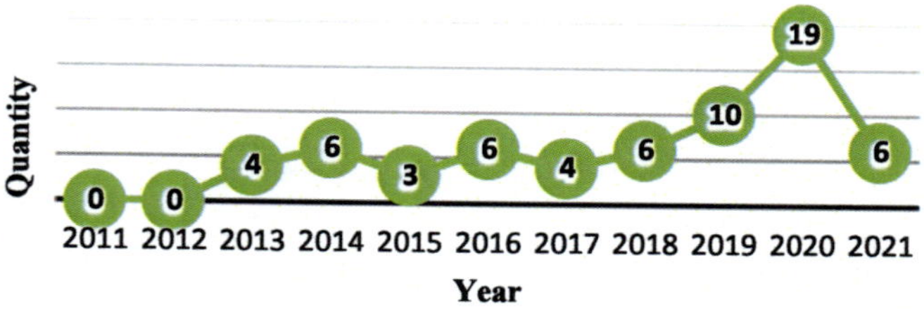

Fig. 2. Number of articles on MR in education by year

3.2 Trends in the Educational Field

In this study, the categorization of articles' disciplines was based on the fields in education defined in the International Standard Classification of Education (ISCED), which was proposed by the United Nations Educational, Scientific, and Cultural Organization's (UNESCO) Institute of Statistics in 2012 [5]. The statistical data of the categorized articles are shown in the Table 1. The educational subjects classified as part of the "services" discipline included leisure tourism, transportation services, and environmental protection. Two articles were classified as "others" because one only described the experience and process of game development during the application of MR in educational games; the other listed examples of MR in education but mentioned many subjects without focusing on any specific topic.

The results showing the discipline-related trends indicated that the health and well-being and science fields accounted for most of the articles, followed by the education and engineering and construction fields. There was no relevant article on the agricultural field. Research on the introduction of MR technologies to medical education was increasingly common: besides helping medical students visualize medical theories to facilitate their understanding, MR also allows learners to practice performing medical operations and other related simulations more easily.

Table 1. Statistical breakdown by discipline

Discipline	Article	Quantity
Education	Loup et al. (2017); Dawson et al. (2017); Vince et al. (2016); Dieker et al. (2014); Walker et al. (2016); Mateu et al. (2014)	6
Humanities and arts	Tang et al. (2020); Shin et al. (2020)	2
Social sciences, business, and law	Gonzalez et al. (2021); Wang et al. (2018); Seaborn et al. (2020)	3
Science	Duan et al. (2020); Barrett et al. (2018); Allcoat et al. (2021); Lindgren and Johnson (2013); Danish et al. (2020); Burleson et al. (2017); Lindgren et al. (2016); Johnson et al. (2016); Mateu, Lasala and Alamán (2015); Freschi et al. (2015); Alzahrani et al. (2014); Beyoglu et al. (2020); Weng et al. (2019); Langbeheim and Levy (2018); Mavilidi et al. (2017); Johnson et al. (2014); Arango et al. (2019)	17
Engineering, manufacturing, and construction	Tumkor (2018); Dai et al. (2021); Wu et al. (2020); Wu et al. (2019); Bosché et al. (2016); Wong et al. (2013)	6
Agriculture		0
Health and wellbeing	Kim et al. (2020); Rositi et al. (2021); Proniewska et al. (2021); Hauze et al. (2019); Coelho et al. (2019); Schoeb et al. (2020); Schneider et al. (2020); Ruthberg et al. (2020); Martin et al. (2020); House et al. (2020); Hammady et al. (2020); Galati et al. (2020); Antoniou et al. (2020); Zorzal et al. (2019); Zhang et al. (2019); Qin et al. (2019); Coelho et al. (2018); Birt et al. (2017); Dunnington et al. (2015); Hooten et al. (2014); Hochman et al. (2014); Chuah et al. (2013); Sampson et al. (2021); Hauze et al. (2019); Wang et al. (2020); Wainman et al. (2020); Aruanno et al. (2019)	27
Services	Gralak (2020)	1
Others	Lee et al. (2016); Mateu and Alamán (2013)	2

The science field focuses on inference, thinking abilities, and the need to understand many abstract concepts. The incorporation of MR technologies facilitates students' understanding of abstract concepts, which allows them to easily integrate theory and virtual elements and enjoy a high level of interactivity with objects in their environment.

This form of supplementary teaching improves learning effectiveness.

Simulation and teaching training are common teaching methods used in the education and engineering and construction fields. MR technologies are used to enhance students' learning experiences and strengthen their practical abilities. Students can explore learning strategies that cannot be easily conveyed through traditional learning methods. Through operating virtual equipment in a virtual environment, they can also easily simulate the performance of skills that are more complex and reflect and improve upon every action that they execute. The use of real-world equipment further enables learners to become familiar with tools' operation, thereby reducing risks during actual operation in the future.

3.3 Educational Stage

The statistical data of articles categorized according to educational stage are shown in Table 2. In terms of educational attainment, the research subjects had generally completed college, and some had attained more education. "Pre-employment" refers to those who had received training after graduation but prior to entering the workplace, while "on-the-job" refers to employees or professionals who had undergone educational training while working. The educational stages of the subjects in specific articles were varied, and they ranged from students to members of general society. Therefore, the category of "mixed age" was introduced. For several articles, the age of the subjects was not provided or the topic did not concern teaching experiments. Since these data could not be categorized, they were labelled as "Unknown."

Table 2. Educational stage of the experimental subjects

Educational stage	High school and below	College	Pre-employment	On-the-job	Mixed age	Unknown
Quantity	14	11	7	10	17	5

3.4 Location

This item refers to the region of, or location within, the country of origin of the experimental subjects. The data were categorized according to both geographical location and the demographic characteristics of the various regions. The results of are shown in Table 3. Most of the articles were focused on North America and Europe, with the number of studies on the integration of MR technologies into education conducted there far outnumbering the number in other regions. At the other end of the spectrum, there were no articles from Africa. This disparity may stem from the fact that well-known firms in North America and Europe have traditionally held the patents for VR, AR, and MR equipment and remain engaged in continuous research, innovation, and investment in related technologies. Another related factor was the presence of inter-country variations in education systems and levels of economic development.

Table 3. Locational distribution

Location	North America	South America	Europe	Asia	Oceania	Africa	Not stated
Quantity	25	2	19	11	5	0	2

3.5 Learning Orientation of the Courses

The data were coded to identify the learning orientation of educational contexts involving MR. The cognitive, affective, and skills orientations are explained as follows. "Cognitive orientation" includes the learning, understanding, application, analysis, integration, and evaluation of knowledge [6]. "Affective orientation" refers to the positive and negative psychological responses to external stimuli and includes learning attitudes and motivations. For example, one's likes or dislikes tend to influence one's behaviors. "Skills orientation" refers to the clearly visible performance of behavioral actions that are focused on the learning of skills. In addition, some of the articles involved dual orientations, so the total number for this item did not match the total number of articles analyzed in this study.

The statistical data of the articles categorized according to learning orientation in teaching are shown in Table 4. Cognitive and skills learning orientations accounted for the majority. MR technologies have the advantage of concretizing abstract theoretical concepts, which supplements students' learning during the teaching process. Such technologies can also enhance learners' practical abilities by simulating the environment in which they will practice a skill.

Table 4. Learning orientation of the courses

Orientation	Cognitive	Affective	Skills
Quantity	30	11	29

3.6 Experimental Design of the Courses

The data showing whether the articles involved an experimental design are shown in Table 5. "Experimental design" refers to a study showing the sample numbers, means, and standard deviations of the experimental and control groups. In the future, articles with an experimental design could be included in the follow-up analysis to obtain more effective results when calculating the overall effects of MR on education.

Table 5. Breakdown by experimental design

Experimental design	Article	Quantity
Yes	Tang et al. (2020); Gonzalez et al. (2021); Duan et al. (2020); Allcoat et al. (2021); Lindgren et al. (2016); Beyoglu et al. (2020); Weng et al. (2019); Langbeheim et al. (2018); Mavilidi et al. (2017); Johnson et al. (2014); Dai et al. (2021); Wu et al. (2020); Wu et al. (2019); Kim et al. (2020); Schoeb et al. (2020); Schneider et al. (2020); Ruthberg et al. (2020); House et al. (2020); Antoniou et al. (2020); Birt et al. (2017); Wang et al. (2020); Wainman et al. (2020); Walker et al. (2016); Tumkor (2018)	24
No		40

4 Discussion

The main purpose of this study was to analyze the advantages and disadvantages of applying MR technologies to education to examine the status of such applications. Most of the results related to the use of MR technologies in education were positive, and such technologies helped to improve learning effectiveness. The conclusions drawn by researchers in the fields of medicine, teaching and training, and the natural sciences showed that the integration of virtuality and reality through information technologies created effective simulated learning environments. Learners could undergo training and practice in simulated environments and could easily try various new methods without incurring any risks during experiments. They could perform simulation activities an unlimited number of times in an MR environment without any risk of being harmed. In addition to greatly reducing the safety risk of experiments, such an environment also elevated their sense of immersion in the course, helping them improve their practical experiences and abilities [7–12].

For courses based on theories or abstract concepts, such as research in the fields of social sciences or management, integrating MR into the teaching of theories represented a break with the past, when learners had to rely on diagrams and supplementary information or videos on the Internet to understand abstract concepts by themselves. Besides creating a visual environment, MR technologies can also produce a high level of interactivity with objects in students' environment, allowing them to use visually simulated effects that are realistic to understand abstract concepts. Doing so not only increases students' interest in learning but also improves their learning cognition [13–15].

Currently, applications of MR technologies face several limitations. One issue is the user's comfort while wearing the simulation device: when worn for long durations, the pressures exerted on the body tend to affect the subsequent learning process and its effectiveness [16, 17]. Another issue is the stability of network connections during the learning process. MR devices must be connected through the Internet, so poor connectivity affects students' learning experiences [18]. Other issues include the cost of MR equipment and the complexity of course preparation. If such technologies cannot generate significant differences from traditional teaching, there will be negative impacts on the overall effectiveness of learning [4]. These issues are key factors determining whether MR can be widely applied to teaching.

5 Conclusion

A review of the trend of integrating MR technologies into education from 2010 to 2021 was conducted in this study, and the data were analyzed and described using six types of codes that were self-designed. The research results showed that the application of MR technologies to the educational field exhibited an increasing trend every year, with the main research regions being North America and Europe. Within the education discipline, the health and wellbeing and science fields accounted for most of the data. The trend of applying MR to education predominantly took the form of using simulation experiences during teaching and practical training and assisting students in visualizing abstract concepts. The purpose was to improve the knowledge gained in the classroom and enhance learners' practical experiences and abilities. Although most of the results of our analysis were positive, there were some shortcomings revealed, which were related to considerations regarding equipment costs, the comfort level of wearable devices, and the stability of Internet connections. These are key factors that will determine whether MR technologies can truly be integrated into teaching in the future and be adopted in regions outside North America and Europe. The findings of this study can be used for follow-up analysis and research: the sample numbers, means, and standard deviations in the experimental data can be collated to calculate the strength of effects and conduct related research to verify the moderating variables using the Q test. Doing so would clarify the key moderating variables affecting the effectiveness of integrating MR into teaching environments.

References

1. Chang, C.W., Lee, J.H., Wang, C.Y., Chen, G.D.: Improving the authentic learning experience by integrating robots into the mixed-reality environment. Comput. Educ. **55**(4), 1572–1578 (2010)
2. Helle, S., Lehtonen, T., Woodward, C., Turunen, M., Salmi, H.: Miracle handbook: Guidelines for mixed reality applications for culture and learning experiences (2017)
3. Sugimoto, M.: A mobile mixed-reality environment for children's storytelling using a handheld projector and a robot. IEEE Trans. Learn. Technol. **4**(3), 249–260 (2011)
4. Langbeheim, E., Levy, S.T.: Feeling the forces within materials: bringing inter-molecular bonding to the fore using embodied modelling. Int. J. Sci. Educ. **40**(13), 1567–1586 (2018)
5. UNESCO Institute for Statistics: International standard classification of education: ISCED 2011. Comparative Social Research, 30 (2012)
6. Bloom, B.S., Krathwohl, D.R., Masia, B.B.: Bloom taxonomy of educational objectives. In: Allyn and Bacon. Pearson Education (1984)
7. Antoniou, P.E., et al.: Biosensor real-time affective analytics in virtual and mixed reality medical education serious games cohort study. JMIR Serious Games **8**(3), e17823 (2020)
8. Dawson, M.R., Lignugaris, K.B.: Meaningful practice: generalizing foundation teaching skills from TLE TeachLivE^{TM} to the classroom. Teach. Educ. Spec. Educ. **40**(1), 26–50 (2017)

9. Dieker, L.A., Rodriguez, J.A., Lignugaris, K.B., Hynes, M.C., Hughes, C.: The potential of simulated environments in teacher education: current and future possibilities. Teach. Educ. Spec. Educ. **37**(1), 21–33 (2014)
10. Hammady, R., Ma, M., Strathearn, C.: Ambient information visualisation and visitors' technology acceptance of mixed reality in museums. J. Comput. Cult. Herit. (JOCCH) **13**(2), 1–22 (2020)
11. Vince Garland, K.M., Holden, K., Garland, D.P.: Individualized clinical coaching in the TLE TeachLivE lab: enhancing fidelity of implementation of system of least prompts among novice teachers of students with autism. Teach. Educ. Spec. Educ. **39**(1), 47–59 (2016)
12. Weng, C., Rathinasabapathi, A., Weng, A., Zagita, C.: Mixed reality in science education as a learning support: a revitalized science book. J. Educ. Comput. Res. **57**(3), 777–807 (2019)
13. Gonzalez, D.A.Z., Richards, D., Bilgin, A.A.: Making it real: a study of augmented virtuality on presence and enhanced benefits of study stress reduction sessions. Int. J. Human. Comput. Stud. **147**, 102579 (2021)
14. Seaborn, K., Pennefather, P., Fels, D.I.: Eudaimonia and Hedonia in the design and evaluation of a cooperative game for psychosocial well-being. Human-Comput. Interact. **35**(4), 289–337 (2020)
15. Wang, W., Wu, X., Chen, G., Chen, Z.: Holo3DGIS: leveraging microsoft Hololens in 3D geographic information. ISPRS Int. J. Geo Inf. **7**(2), 60 (2018)
16. Rositi, H., et al.: Presentation of a mixed reality software with a HoloLens headset for a nutrition workshop. Multimed. Tools App. **80**(2), 1945–1967 (2020). https://doi.org/10.1007/s11042-020-09687-8
17. Mateu, J., Lasala, M.J., Alamán, X.: Developing mixed reality educational applications: the virtual touch toolkit. Sensors **15**(9), 21760–21784 (2015)
18. Martin, G., et al.: Use of the HoloLens2 mixed reality headset for protecting health care workers during the COVID-19 pandemic: prospective, observational evaluation. J. Med. Internet. Res. **22**(8), e21486 (2020)

A Study of Learner's Scientific Thinking Using Constructivist Virtual Learning Environment for Grade 11 Students

Kodchakorn Lamsombat and Issara Kanjug(✉)

Department of Educational Technology, Faculty of Education,
Khon Kaen University, Khon Kaen, Thailand
issaraka@kku.ac.th

Abstract. Scientific thinking could be explained as the important skill which emphasizes logically thinking through validation with reliable references. The process of scientific thinking occurred during the observation from the real situation (Scientific investigation) and allows them to adapt with the change in the way of life in society surrounded by science. The purpose of this research is to compare the scientific thinking of students before and after the class by using constructivist virtual learning environment following component; (1) Problem base (2) Resource (3) Science Laboratory (4) Collaboration tools (5) Scaffolding (6) Coaching. The research participants were 30 grade 11 students year 2020 of Kanlayanawat school, Thailand. The instrument used in the experiment was the Constructivist Virtual Learning Environment in the topic of solar energy. Data collection used the Scientific Thinking test for grade 11 students. The results showed that: students had the improved scientific test score after learning by constructivist virtual learning environment than before which has a statistical level of 0.01.

Keywords: Constructivist learning environment · Virtual learning · Scientific thinking · Digital learning · Mobile learning

1 Introduction

Scientific thinking is a thinking that emphasizes logically thinking through validation with reliable references. Scientific thinking can help individuals to verify the accuracy and reliability of information they received and assists them to adapt with the change in the way of life in society surrounded by science (Perjan and Sanduleac 2018). In the present, the science learning focuses on developing students to learn about real-world issues, emphasis on thinking skills, problem solving, self-seeking and use of technology (McFarlane 2013).

Learning environment is the model of learning management that focuses on learners to explore. It also stimulates learners to think and create understanding about things they have learnt by themselves which learners build from interactions based on experience and knowledge from various sources (Thitima and Sumalee 2012). The learning management is consistent with constructivist theory which has the idea that learners must practice

© Springer Nature Switzerland AG 2021
Y.-M. Huang et al. (Eds.): ICITL 2021, LNCS 13117, pp. 95–101, 2021.
https://doi.org/10.1007/978-3-030-91540-7_11

with enthusiasm and create their own knowledge. Each person will create knowledge through interaction with the environment. This is rooted in the theory of philosophers which have Piaget J and Vygotsky L.S. The constructivist virtual learning environment is a model of learning management that adopted the theory of group constructivist learning, which consists of Cognitive Constructivist and Social Constructivist as a basis for design by connecting with virtual reality technology (Virtual reality), which simulates the real environment into a virtual reality through the perception of sight, sound and touch (Baxter and Hainey 2019).

From the reason and importance that mentioned above, the learning management for Physic subject will help learners learn about the change of intelligence, a way of thinking development especially scientific thinking (Lu and Lin 2017). It also assists students to have an important skill to explore the knowledge, solve the problems systemically, able to make decisions based on diverse information and verifiable testimony (Kuhn 2010) Moreover, students can also keep up with advances in science and technology and are the ones who create new knowledge all the time (Jensen 2017). Therefore, the researcher is interested in studying and developing constructivist virtual learning environment that promotes scientific thinking.

2 Literature Review

2.1 Scientific Thinking

Scientific thinking is cognitive processes in which learners create substitutes for knowledge that lead to the understanding of electrical energy. It was assessed from a scientific thinking test based on the concept of Khun (2010) which has four steps: Step 1; Inquiry, which is to identify problems related to electric power. Step 2; Analysis, the ability to explain the solution and make the data which related with problems such as the concept of using solar energy to produce electric power. Step 3; Inference, the ability to rationalize and reject irrational evidence such as the principle of using solar energy to generate electricity. Step 4: Argument, refers to the ability to discuss the consequences after applying a solution to what the outcome is. By applying the results obtained to interpret and conclude in accordance with the hypothesis, for example, scientific reasoning in accordance with the principles of electric power generation.

2.2 Constructivist Virtual Learning Environment

Form of a learning environment which is created based on constructivist theory, cognitive theory and principles of scientific thinking form the basis for design (Thitima and Sumalee 2012). It is a print media which is compatible with media attribution and media symbol system combined with Virtual Reality technology that uses media attribution for the design.

3 Method and Result

3.1 Research Participants

The target group in this research were obtained from a purposive sampling as 30 Grade 11 students in the second semester of the academic year 2020 at Kanlayanawat School, Muang District, Khon Kaen.

3.2 Assessment Tool – Scientific Thinking Test

Scientific Thinking test of learners who learn with a constructivist virtual learning environment that promotes scientific thinking include of four steps which are Step 1: Inquiry, Step 2: Analysis, Step 3: Inference, and Step 4: Argument. The Scientific Thinking test sheets were developed by teachers. There is a way to find quality by experts checking. For the evaluation, there are 4 steps which are 1) Study theoretical frameworks and research related to scientific thinking from Kuhn (2010) 2) Construct a scientific thinking test which is a subjective test. It also related to the content and learning objectives 3) Create scores for the evaluation of each test item, consisting of 3 ranges from 0–2 points. 4) Present a scientific thinking test. to advisors and experts to verify the accuracy and correctness of the content, consistency of questions and the appropriateness of language use and interpretation. After that, improvements were made according to the recommendations.

3.3 Experimental Process

Implementing a constructivist virtual learning environment that promotes scientific thinking used in the learning management process. The learning management process is as follows: The teacher encourages students to be ready to learn and pay attention to the class by link the old knowledge and new knowledge. Then, ask about experiences that occur in the students' daily life including explaining about how to learn with a constructivist virtual learning environment which promotes scientific thinking on solar energy and takes a scientific thinking test before the class. Then, let students learn by using constructivist virtual learning environment that promotes scientific thinking on electric power. The learners will study problem situations and find solutions or answers from scientific thinking in the experiment. During learning, learners will work together to find and discuss together to conclude a solution of the problem. The researcher will be as a coach to keep motivating students about problem solving and guide students who need educational assistance. After studying in a constructivist virtual learning environment that promotes scientific thinking completely. Students take a scientific thinking test after class. Data collection process can be summarized as shown in Fig. 1.

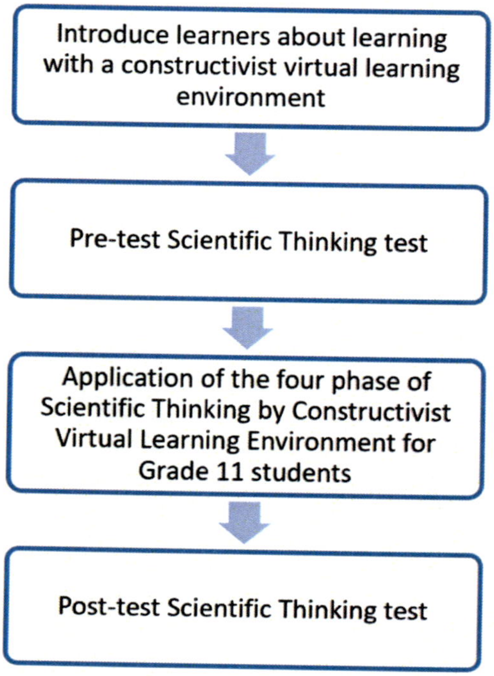

Fig. 1. Experimental process.

3.4 Learning Assistive

The constructivist virtual learning environment consists of the following components: (1) Problem base, which focuses on students to have an intellectual structure stimulation with problem cases for learners to try solving problems and guidelines for the solution of each problem in Virtual Reality (VR) using mobile phones. (2) Resources, which are sources of content information that students need to use in problem situations, and it is also the resource that include things which students need to acquire knowledge and find some answers that could be in the form of a learning resource which student study through video in the form of Virtual Reality (VR). (3) Science Laboratory, which aims to encourage learners to use science methods and scientific process skills in experiments to solve missions and problem situations (4) Learning Exchange Center (Collaboration) is to encourage students to exchange and learn with others to expand your perspective. Collaborating in the search for knowledge and solving problems will support learners, tutors, and experts to share their learning experiences with each other. (5) Scaffolding, is to support learners in problem solving. The assistance will consist of a conceptual help base, thinking help base, process assistance base and strategic assistance base. (6) Coaching. as guidance assistance. For learners, it is a practice for learners by educating learners in terms of providing problems (Fig. 2).

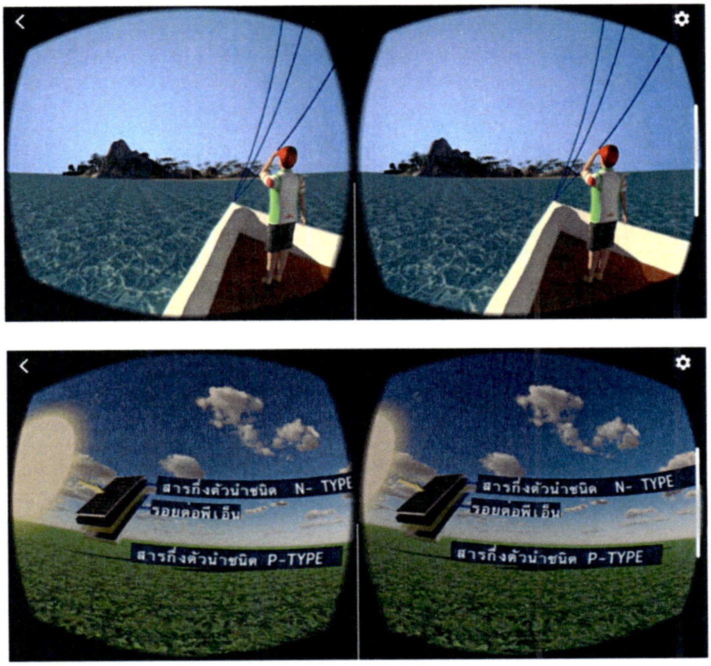

Fig. 2. Example of constructivist virtual learning environment.

4 Results and Discussion

4.1 Scientific Thinking

After using a constructivist virtual learning environment to manage learning. It was found that the pre-test scores of Scientific Thinking for thinking aspects to identify problems with the highest average score of 6.27 and scores on the Scientific Thinking test after learning to thinking aspects to identify problems has the average score as 1.96 and Table 1 found that scientific thinking in the area of thinking to identify problems, thinking to create hypotheses, thinking to test hypotheses, and thinking to interpret data and conclude before and after learning has statistically significant difference at 0.01 and the total of the scientific thinking test average score before learning was 19.67 and after was 29.07. The students had higher scores on the Scientific Thinking test after learning by constructivist virtual learning environment than before learning which is statistically significant at 0.01 level as shown in Table 1 (Fig. 3).

Table 1. The results of scientific thinking test.

List assessment	Average score before learning	Average score after learning	*t*-test
Inquiry	6.27	7.93	6.11**
Analysis	5.57	7.50	5.04**
Inference	3.83	7.33	9.87**
Argument	4.00	6.30	6.77**
Total	19.67	29.07	14.16*

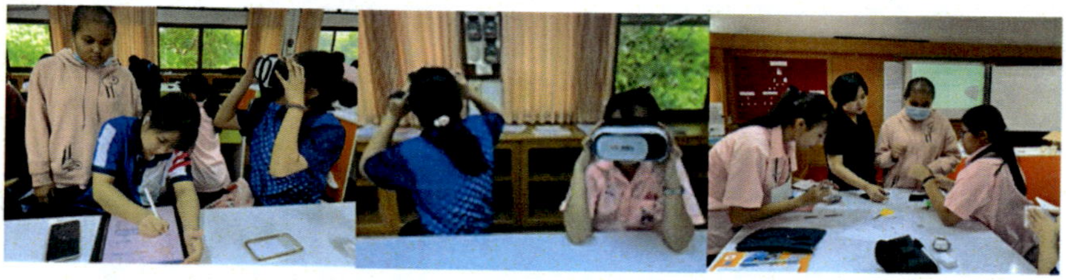

Fig. 3. Learning management using constructivist virtual learning environment.

4.2 Discussion and Future Work

From the research results, it was found that the constructivist virtual learning environment is able to develop students' scientific thinking with 4 steps: Step 1: Inquiry, Step 2: Analysis, Step 3: Inference, and Step 4: Argument. It is related with research by Ammar AL-Nawaiseh (2020), which investigated the effect of a Learning Management System (LMS) model on scientific thinking in chemistry subject. The learning management model Learning Management System (LMS) is learning through applications that contain content, course description, assignments and exercises which teachers can create and develop in learning management. The results of this research has shown that students who study with the Learning Management System (LMS) and regular format exams were statistically different levels of scientific thinking, and Cholarutai Thaweesang (2016) studied the results of using a learning management model based on the concept of meta-level to promote scientific thinking in the first graders. The results of the research revealed that the scientific thinking of learners who learned with a meta-level based learning management model to promote scientific thinking were significantly higher than before learning at the .01 level.

Future work includes in-depth discussion and analysis the constructivist learning environment that promotes other thinking skills such as problem solving and analytical thinking.

Acknowledgements. This work was supported by the Innovation and Cognitive Technology Research Center, Faculty of Education, and the Research and Technology Transfers Affairs Division, Khon Kaen University.

References

AL-Nawaiseh, A.: Impact of Using Developed Learning Management System on Student's Scientific Thinking Skills: Applied Study on 10th Grade Chemistry Class (2020)

Baxter, G., Hainey, T.: Student perceptions of virtual reality use in higher education. J. Appl. Res. Higher Educ. **12**, 413–424 (2019)

Perjan, C., Sanduleac, S.: Increasing the quality of Unversity studie through the development of students' scientific thinking. Appl. Res. Techn. Technol. Educ. **16**(2), 195–201 (2018). https://doi.org/10.15547/artte.2018.02.017

Dunbar, K.: How scientists think: online creativity and conceptual change in science. In: Ward, T.B., Smith, S.M., Vaid, S. (eds.) Conceptual structures and processes: Emergence, discovery and Change. pp. 24–38. Washington DC (1997)

Hanafin, M., Land, S., Oliver, K.: pen learning environments : foundations, methods , and models. In: Reigeluth, C.M. (Eds.). Instructional-Design Theories and Models Volume II A New Paradigm of Instructional Theory, pp.115–140. Lawrence Erlbaum Associates, Mahwah, New Jersey (1999)

Jensen, C.G.: Collaboration and dialogue in virtual reality. J. Probl. Based. Learn. Higher. Educ. **5**(1), 85–110 (2017)

Jonassen, D.H.: Designing constructivist learning environments. In: Reigeluth, C.M. (Ed.) Instructional-Design Theories and Models: A New Paradigm of Instructional Theory, Volume II, pp. 215–239. Lawrence Erlbaum Associates, New Jersey (1999)

Kuhn, D: What is scientific thinking and how does it develop? In: The Wiley-Blackwell Handbook of Childhood Cognitive Development, pp. 497–523. Wiley-Blackwell, Oxford, UK (2010)

Kuhn, D., Dean, D.: Is developing scientific thinking all about learning to control variables? Psychol. Sci. **16**(11), 866–870 (2005)

Lu, H.-K., Lin, P.-C.: A study of the impact of collaborative problem-solving strategies on students' performance of simulation-based learning — a case of network basic concepts course. Int. J. Inf. Educ. Technol. **7**(5), 361–366 (2017)

McFarlane, D.A.: Understanding the challenges of science education in the 21st century: new opportunities for scientific literacy. Int. Lett. Soc. Human. Sci. **4**, 35–44 (2013)

Mayer, R.E.: Systematic thinking fostered by illustrations of scientific text. J. Educ. Psychol. **81**, 240–246 (1989)

Power, S.M., Mitechell, J.: Student Perceptions and Performance in a Virtual Classroom Environment (1997). http//ericir.syr.edu. Accessed 5 May 2005

Relan, A.G., Bijan, B.: Web-Based Instruction and the Traditional Classrom; Simila and Differences (2004). Accessed 17 Sep 2005

Thitima, G., Sumalee, C.: Scientific thinking of the learners learning with the knowledge construction model enhancing scientific thinking. Proc. Soc. Behav. Sci. **46**, 3771–3775 (2012)

Regarding the Virtual Reality Environment Design and Evaluation Based on STEAM Learning

Chih-Chao Chung[1], Yuh-Ming Cheng[2], and Shi-Jer Lou[3](✉)

[1] General Research Service Center, National Pingtung University of Science and Technology, Neipu, Taiwan, ROC
[2] Department of Computer Science and Information Engineering, Shu-Te University, Kaohsiung City, Taiwan, ROC
[3] Graduate Institute of Technological and Vocational Education, National Pingtung University of Science and Technology, Neipu, Taiwan, ROC
lou@mail.npust.edu.tw

Abstract. This study aims to design a STEAM virtual reality (VR) learning environment for engineering students, as well as evaluate the practicability of the learning environment. This study adopted Fuzzy Delphi Method by inviting six experts in the fields of VR application, STEAM education, and engineering education to execute the expert questionnaire survey, in a bid to build up a capability indicator of STEAM education and carry out the STEAM VR environment practicability evaluation serving as a foundation of the further development of curriculum. According to our study findings, the most important capability indicator in STEAM is "Hands-on Skills", followed by "Problem Solving", "Daily Life Application", "Sensory Learning" and "Interdisciplinarity". In terms of the practicability evaluation of STEAM VR learning environment establishment, the highest scoring element is "Interactivity", followed by "Engagement", with "Imagination" being the lowest. This study serves as a reference for future educators and researchers in establishing a STEAM VR learning environment.

Keywords: Virtual reality · Environment design · STEAM · Education reform · STEAM learning

1 Introduction

The public's reliance on the convenience brought by technology exacerbates as our information and communication systems develop and improve. Upon the impact of the COVID-19 epidemic, breakthroughs and improvement in knowledge and skills require urgent support by technology, which highlights the importance of education and development in the engineering field. Nonetheless, in this century with ever-changing technology, more and more innovative and creative talents are desired. It urges the cultivation of STEAM students to become a critical education practice among governments [1].

© Springer Nature Switzerland AG 2021
Y.-M. Huang et al. (Eds.): ICITL 2021, LNCS 13117, pp. 102–110, 2021.
https://doi.org/10.1007/978-3-030-91540-7_12

To this end, an increasing number of countries are proposing divergent education strategies to train students in their interdisciplinary STEAM skills, including using intelligent studying products [2] such as Skilled-based Learning, Robot-based Education, Artificial Intelligence, Augmented Reality and Virtual Reality. It is hoped that students can be equipped with interdisciplinary integrating minds when nurturing their problem-solving skills in daily life and arousing their creativity and imagination through the assistance of technical tools to prepare for transformations in the social environment.

Despite STEAM education integrates subjects in different areas, it can be challenging for sole educators to implement the approach and develop STEAM ability in students [3]. It was pointed out by many that designing student-centered situated teaching can effectively cultivate their abilities in STEAM such as Interdisciplinarity, Hands-on Skills, Daily Life Application and Problem Solving [4]. Therefore, it is predicted that the application of sensory stimulation and highly interactive and immersive VR technology in education will be the major development trend in assisted instruction in the future [5, 6].

In conclusion, this study will design the STEAM VR learning environment and carry out its evaluation while adopting the emerging technology of VR and holding the prime aim of educating engineering students. Two objectives included are as below:

(1) Constructing a STEAM capability indicator
(2) Evaluate the practicability of a STEAM VR learning environment

2 Literature Review

STEAM- and VR-related literature revolving around our objectives are reviewed. Demonstrations are as below:

2.1 Definition of STEAM

STEAM is the integrated education combining scientific investigation, technology, engineering design, artistic creations and mathematics analysis [7]. It aims to improve problem-solving and critical thinking skills and creativity among students using mathematic and scientific based engineering and designing practices in order to remedy problems in the real world. It also encourages the reconstruction of current art education into inquiry-oriented teaching, as well as creative problem solving [1]. It is to equip the students with the five abilities in STEAM specified in Table 1.

To conclude, this study held the notion that to promote STEAM learning of students, a VR environment can be established to guide the students through entertaining simulation independently. During the exploring process, students can improve their five primary abilities of Interdisciplinarity, Hands-on Skills, Daily Life Application, Problem Solving and Sensory Learning.

Table 1. Definition of STEAM Capability Indicator.

No	Capability Indicator	Definition
1	Interdisciplinarity	Nurture practical ability in interdisciplinary learning through task-based learning
2	Hands-on Skills	Nurture hands-on skills and active inquiring ability
3	Daily Life Application	Able to integrate information and resources and apply knowledge in daily life
4	Problem Solving	Willing to resolve issues with positivism and problem-solving skills
5	Sensory Learning	Able to make use of the five senses, namely touch, sight, hearing, smell and taste, to learn

2.2 Definition of VR

VR is the technology to stimulate the reality world, with visualized expression being the most compatible with the instinctive visual exploration. It could promote experience and connection between learners and their practical reality environment [8]. VR possesses three features, according to Table 2, to provide users with a first-person perspective in a virtual situation, therefore allowing users to enjoy its merriment as experienced personally [5, 6, 9].

To sum up, this study brought the Immersion, Interaction, Imagination features of VR technology into play to establish a study-friendly STEAM environment for students in order to boost learning effectiveness in STEAM.

Table 2. Definition of VR.

No	Features	Definition
1	Immersion	Allow users to immerse in virtual scenes as if experiencing personally
2	Interaction	A prerequisite for virtual environment
3	Imagination	Simulation of the reality, filled with extra imagining possibilities

3 Research Design

Citing the result of literature review, the framework of "STEAM capability indicator" and "STEAM VR learning environment" practicability evaluation respectively are as below:

3.1 Research Structure and Subjects

This study framework (as shown in Fig. 1) adopted the Fuzzy Delphi Method by inviting six experts (more than six years of experience) in the fields of VR application, STEAM education and engineering to collaborate jointly and provide consultations in order to execute the Delphi expert questionnaire survey. Thus the STEAM capability indicator construction and the STEAM VR learning environment establishment practicability analysis are completed and serve as a foundation of future development of the curriculum.

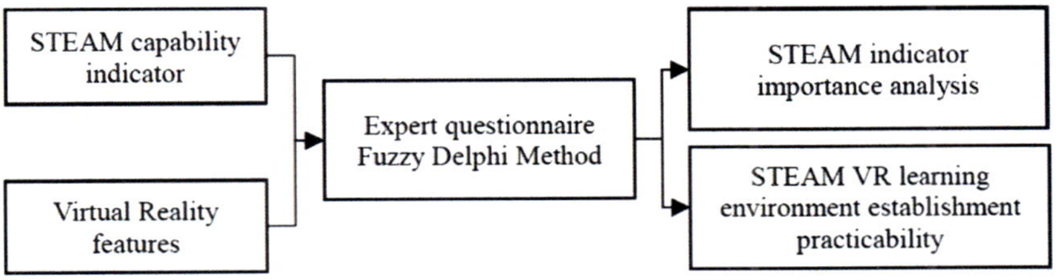

Fig. 1. Research structure.

3.2 Research Method

Fuzzy Delphi Method (FDM) is the combination of Delphi Method and Fuzzy Logic to use Triangular Fuzzy Number for ameliorating the shortcoming of traditional Delphi Method. It eliminates the limitations of humanity fuzzification and is an effective way to establish an indicator [10]. Hence, this study adopted the Fuzzy Delphi Method in the construction of STEAM capability indicator and STEAM VR learning environment practicability analysis.

4 Results and Discussion

The result analysis of executing the Fuzzy Delphi expert questionnaire survey based on the objective in establishing a STEAM VR learning environment is below:

4.1 Analysis of the Importance of STEAM Capability Indicator

For the "Establishment of STEAM capability indicator", after obtaining subjective value judgments and assessing scores from six experts of the Fuzzy Delphi expert questionnaire survey, the analysis results are as in Table 3. The scores in the importance of STEAM capability indicator ranged between 0.718 and 0.757. The highest scoring item is "Hands-on skills" with a score of 0.757, followed by "Problem-Solving" scoring 0.757, "Daily Life Application" scoring 0.753, "Sensory Learning" scoring 0.744, and ends by "Interdisciplinarity" scoring 0.718.

4.2 STEAM VR Learning Environment Practicability Analysis

This study delved into the practicability of establishing a STEAM VR learning environment. The analyzed result by Fuzzy Delphi Method experts is shown in Table 4.

Table 3. Scores in the importance of STEAM capability indicator.

Number	Item	*L*-value	*R*-value	Total	Rank
1	Interdisciplinarity	0.379	0.816	0.718	5
2	Hands-on skills	0.339	0.853	0.757	1
3	Daily life application	0.343	0.849	0.753	3
4	Problem solving	0.339	0.853	0.757	2
5	Sensory learning	0.352	0.840	0.744	4

In respect to the practicability of Interdisciplinarity VR learning, the scores ranged from 0.718 to 0.730. The item with the highest practicability is Interactivity, which scored 0.730.In respect to the practicability of Hands-on Skills VR learning, the scores ranged from 0.733 to 0.773. The item with the highest practicability is Interactivity, which scored 0.773.In respect to the practicability of Daily Life Application VR learning, the scores ranged from 0.724 to 0.759. The item with the highest practicability is Interactivity, which scored 0.759.In respect to the practicability of Problem Solving VR learning, the scores ranged from 0.718 to 0.766. The item with the highest practicability is Interactivity, which scored 0.766.In respect to the practicability of Sensory Learning VR learning, the scores ranged from 0.703 to 0.750. The item with the highest practicability is Interactivity, which scored 0.750.

Table 4. Scores in STEAM VR learning environment practicability analysis

NO	Item	VR Feature	*L*-value	*R*-value	Total	Rank
1	Interdisciplinarity	Immersion	0.379	0.816	0.718	3
		Interaction	0.367	0.827	0.730	1
		Imagination	0.377	0.818	0.720	2
2	Hands-on skills	Immersion	0.339	0.853	0.757	2
		Interaction	0.322	0.868	0.773	1
		Imagination	0.363	0.830	0.733	3
3	Daily life application	Immersion	0.343	0.849	0.753	2
		Interaction	0.336	0.855	0.759	1
		Imagination	0.373	0.821	0.724	3
4	Problem solving	Immersion	0.339	0.853	0.757	2
		Interaction	0.329	0.862	0.766	1
		Imagination	0.379	0.816	0.718	3
5	Sensory learning	Immersion	0.352	0.840	0.744	2
		Interaction	0.346	0.846	0.750	1
		Imagination	0.395	0.801	0.703	3

4.3 STEAM Competency Assessment Criteria and VR-Assisted Learning Planning

According to the above-mentioned expert consultation and fuzzy Delphi analysis results, the "Learning Effectiveness of STEAM Skills Questionnaire" is developed, and "STEAM VR Assisted Learning Activities" are planned, which are described as follows:

1. Learning Effectiveness of STEAM Ability Questionnaire

   In order to understand students' learning status of STEAM skills, the "Learning Effectiveness of STEAM Skills Questionnaire" is developed, which includes 5 dimensions: cross-domain, hands-on, life application, problem solving, and five sense learning. This research invites two experts and scholars to test the expert validity of the questionnaire, evaluate the validity of the initial draft of the questionnaire, and revise it according to the suggestions. In terms of reliability analysis, after the inconsistent items are deleted, as shown in Table 5, which has 21 questions in total. The overall Cronbach's alpha value of "Learning Effectiveness of STEAM Skills Questionnaire" is .861; among them, there are 3 questions (.860) in the "cross-domain" dimension, 4 questions in the "hands-on" dimension (.882), and 4 questions in the "life application" dimension (.821), 5 questions (.875) in the "problem solving" dimension and 5 questions (.840) in the "Five Senses Learning" dimension, which indicates that this questionnaire has good reliability and high consistency.

Table 5. Reliability analysis of STEAM ability learning effectiveness questionnaire.

Dimension	Item
Interdisciplinarity	1 I learn interdisciplinary knowledge and application in the curriculum
	2 I will integrate more than two kinds of interdisciplinary knowledge and thinking operations
	3 I think it is important to learn the interdisciplinary integration capability
Hands-on skills daily	4 I can practice and explore the principles of curriculum knowledge
	5 I construct knowledge from hands-on practice
	6 I like hands-on practice
	7 I am good at using hands-on practice to learn knowledge
Life application	8 This curriculum can cultivate my curiosity about daily life problems
	9 I can disassemble and analyze daily life problems
	10 I can apply the curriculum knowledge to my daily life
	11 I can judge the effect of problem-solving methods under certain conditions
Problem solving	12 I can identify problems and make systematic statements
	13 I can collect data and take appropriate information to collate the problem

(continued)

Table 5. (*continued*)

Dimension	Item
	14 I can put forward assumptions and multiple feasible solutions according to problems
	15 I can carry out the division of labor, process planning, and planned operation
	16 I can test and correct according to the proposed assumptions
Sensory learning	17 This curriculum can provide me with diversified learning stimulations
	18 This curriculum can cultivate my comprehensive learning through my 5 senses
	19 This curriculum can stimulate my potential and learning capabilities
	20 This curriculum can cultivate my imagination
	21 This curriculum can cultivate my creativity

2. STEAM VR assisted learning activity planning
   Taking the auxiliary teaching material "STEAM VR Smart Greenhouse" as an example, this research carries out STEAM curriculum design and VR-assisted teaching in accordance with the course objectives, course content, and expert advice of the "Smart Greenhouse" unit, and plans three-stage auxiliary learning activities, "Teacher Show", "Student Exercises" and "Student test". As shown in Table 6, it can help students develop practical ability in smart greenhouse practice. The instructions are as follows:

- Teacher presentation stage: The teacher will show the teaching of "STEAM VR Smart Greenhouse" to let students understand the relevant functional design of the smart greenhouse and to develop their interest and curiosity in the field learning of the smart greenhouse in the future, and cultivate the students' ability to apply what they have learned to the real field.
- Student practice stage: "STEAM VR Smart Greenhouse" assists students in their course of learning and provides students with hands-on practices and repeated exercises. Students can explore the knowledge of smart greenhouses, construct knowledge and understand the principles. "STEAM VR Smart Greenhouse" also strengthens students' hands-on practical ability.
- Student test phase: This research plans the "STEAM VR Smart Greenhouse" student test to assist them in the ability verification, including smart greenhouse category selection, artificial lighting system, ventilation system (the right photographs in Table 6), inner shading system (the left photographs in Table 6), and sprinkler system, as a reference basis to examine whether students are qualified for the practical examination of the smart greenhouse.

Table 6. STEAM VR assisted learning activity planning.

Name	Description
Teacher presentation stage	The teacher introduces their functions and displays according to the types of smart greenhouses 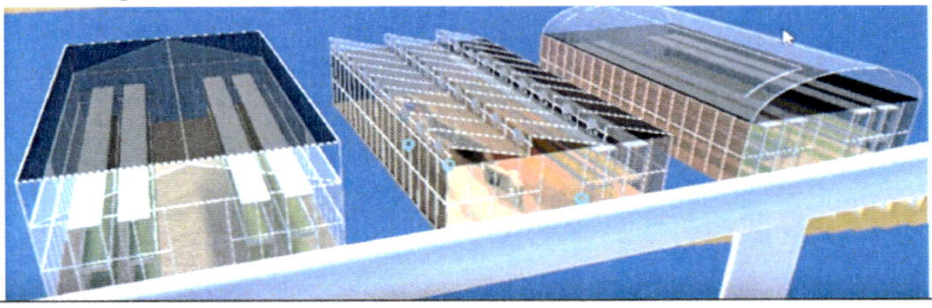
Student practice stage	Students explore the functions of the smart greenhouse and construct related knowledge on their own  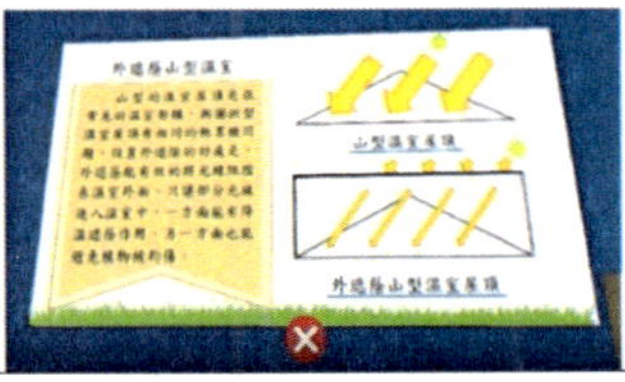
Student test phase	Students participate in the simulation test for smart greenhouses to verify their familiarity with the operation steps 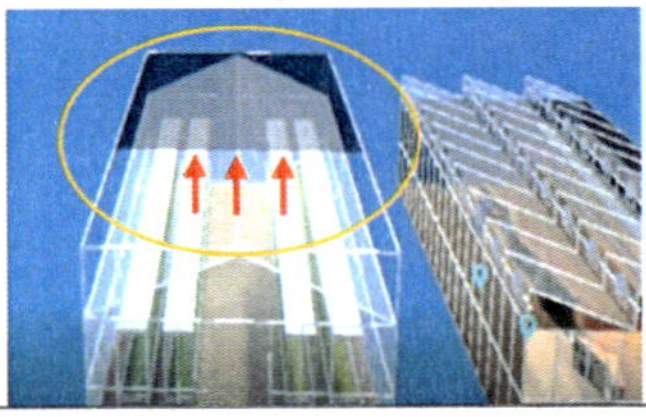 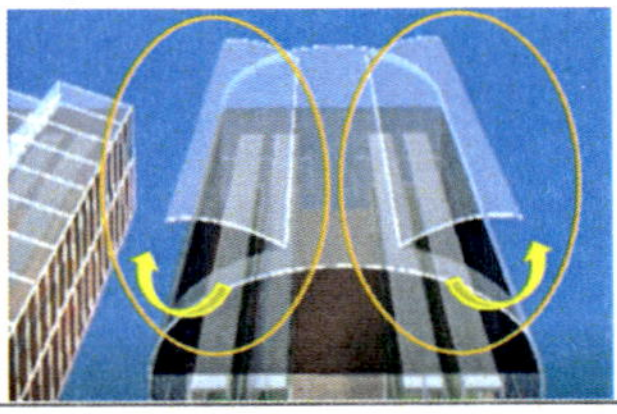

5 Conclusion and Suggestions

This study adopted VR technology in assisting STEAM ability cultivation and learning environment scheduling. After investigations and analysis of the Fuzzy Delphi expert questionnaires, in regard of building emphasis in the five STEAM abilities with the aid of VR technology, the highest scoring item is "Hands-on Skills", followed by "Problem Solving", "Daily Life Application", "Sensory Learning" and "Interdisciplinarity". Among the items, for the practicability of the featured VR-aided "Hands-on Skills" education, the highest scoring element is "Interactivity", followed by "Engagement" and "Imagination". By this means, this study serves as a reference for future educators and researchers in scheduling students' STEAM ability cultivation, as well as interdisciplinary studying and developments.

References

1. Chung, C.-C., Huang, S.-L., Cheng, Y.-M., Lou, S.-J.: Using an iSTEAM project-based learning model for technology senior high school students: Design, development, and evaluation. Int. J. Technol. Des. Educ. **10**, 1–37 (2020). https://doi.org/10.1007/s10798-020-09643-5
2. Adkins, S.S.: The 2016–2021 Worldwide Self-Paced eLearning Market: Global eLearning Market in Steep Decline. Ambient Insight, Monroe, WA (2016)
3. Lou, S.J., Liang, C.P., Chung, C.C.: Effectiveness of combining STEM activities and PBL: a case study of the design of fuel-efficient vehicles. Int. J. Eng. Educ. **33**(6), 1763–1775 (2017)
4. Chung, C.C., Lin, C.L., Lou, S.J.: Analysis of the learning effectiveness of the STEAM-6E special course-a case study about the creative design of IOT assistant devices for the elderly. Sustainability **10**(9), 1–16 (2018)
5. Huang, C.Y., Lou, S.J., Cheng, Y.M., Chung, C.C.: Research on teaching a welding implementation course assisted by sustainable virtual reality technology. Sustainability **12**(23), 10044 (2020). https://doi.org/10.3390/su122310044
6. Chung, C.C., Tung, C.C., Lou, S.J.: Research on Optimization of VR welding course development with ANP and satisfaction evaluation. Electronics **9**(10), 1673 (2020)
7. Pease, S.: ARCADE: STEM + A = STEAM. ARCADE, 31(2) (2013). http://cargocollective.com/speasedesign/ARCADE-STEM-A-STEAM
8. Olshannikova, E., Ometov, A., Koucheryavy, Y., Olsson, T.: Visualizing big data with augmented and virtual reality: challenges and research agenda. J. Big Data **2**(1), 1–27 (2015). https://doi.org/10.1186/s40537-015-0031-2
9. Burdea Grigore, C., Coiffet, P.: Virtual Reality Technology. Wiley-Interscience, London (1994)
10. Ishikawa, A., Amagasa, M., Shiga, T., Tomizawa, G., Tatsuta, R., Mieno, H.: The max-min Delphi method and fuzzy Delphi method via fuzzy integration. Fuzzy Sets Syst. **55**(3), 241–253 (1993)

Using STEAM-6E Model in AR/VR Maker Education Teaching Activities to Improve High School Students' Learning Motivation and Learning Activity Satisfaction

Yu-Hsuan Lin[1(✉)], Hao-Chiang Koong Lin[2], and Hsin-Lan Liu[3]

[1] General Research Service Center of National Pingtung University Science and Technology, Neipu, Taiwan
yu.hsuan@mail.npust.edu.tw

[2] Department of Information and Learning Technology, National University of Tainan, Tainan, Taiwan

[3] Department of Engineering Science, National Cheng Kung University, Tainan, Taiwan

Abstract. The Ministry of Education has also actively promoted STEM maker education in recent years. As a result, the maker teaching resources in secondary schools have flourished. STEM is composed of Science, Technology, Engineering and Mathematics. This research mainly introduces STEAM & Maker Education into the class and plans a "STEAM-6E Model" set to incorporate AR/VR Maker Education courses. Learn about theory, application, and implementation through courses. Integrate resources near the school and apply the knowledge learned to solve problems for the community practically. The subjects of the study are 60 high school third-year students in two classes. One class is the experimental group using STEAM-6E teaching and the control group uses traditional briefing teaching, conducting experiments. The MSLQ (Motivated Strategies for Learning Questionnaire) and the ASQ (Activity Satisfaction Questionnaire) are applied to acquire quantitative data for examination. The results showed that the experimental group had differences in learning motivation and satisfaction with learning activities.

Keywords: STEAM-6E · Augmented reality · Virtual reality · Maker education

1 Introduction

STEM education originated in the United States in the twentieth century. The Ministry of Education has also actively promoted STEM maker education in recent years. As a result, the maker teaching resources in secondary schools have flourished. STEM is composed of Science, Technology, Engineering and Mathematics. In recent years, the education industry has added Art to become the current STEAM. Barry [1] adds a dimension based on the 5E teaching model, puts students as the center, and proposes the 6E teaching model further to strengthen the design and inquiry capabilities in STEM education. This

© Springer Nature Switzerland AG 2021
Y.-M. Huang et al. (Eds.): ICITL 2021, LNCS 13117, pp. 111–118, 2021.
https://doi.org/10.1007/978-3-030-91540-7_13

research uses STEAM as the main shaft and joins the 6E instruction model. Plan a set of STEAM-6E Model. Gradually deepen students' integration of interdisciplinary content. Develop the concept of applying what they have learned.

With the advancement of science and technology, the maker's threshold has been lowered, making maker education combine the practice and cultivation of skills, humanities, arts, knowledge. However, STEAM education and maker education are increasingly popular educational innovation models worldwide in recent years. And gradually an educational boom on and off-campus.

The application fields of VR and AR include medical care, nursing, education, tourism, culture, military, architecture, design, engineering, scenic spot guide, game industry, entertainment [2, 3].

Based on the above content, build a learning model and plan a "STEAM-6E Model" to carry out AR and VR innovative teaching. Make STEAM education content more diversified. Through the Maker Education 3D printing teaching, from understand the application of the principles and implementation. In addition, to plan a set of STEAM-6E Model, it also evaluates students' learning motivation and satisfaction with learning activities.

Based on the background and motives of this study as well as the abovementioned discussion, the objectives of this study were as follows:

1. To discuss the effect of integrating STEAM-6E into AR/VR Maker education on learning motivation.
2. To discuss the effect of integrating STEAM-6E into AR/VR Maker education on learning activity satisfaction.

2 Literature Review

The researchers of this study effect of integrating STEAM-6E into AR/VR Maker education to facilitate learning. The literature review thus aims to introduce the following concepts STEAM-6E, STEAM & Maker, Virtual Reality and Augmented Reality.

2.1 Steam-6E

STEAM is composed of Science, Technology, Engineering, Art, and Mathematics. STEAM is widely advocated and implemented in education. Students are influential in STEAM interdisciplinary learning [4]. It's also regarded as one of the important factors to improve education and promote national progress. STEAM can attract and inspire different audiences. It helps students understand and learn more concepts [5]. Kaniawati and Suryadi [6] research found that integrating STEM education in the 6E pedagogy contributes to problem-solving skills. Chung et al. [7] pointed out that STEAM-6E special courses can enhance students' ability to integrate STEAM knowledge and improve their learning efficiency in each subject. Each cycle of the 6E teaching model represents a complete teaching unit. In the process, students must constantly think, so the teaching procedure is suitable for STEAM teaching. This research adopts the 6E teaching model to conduct STEAM courses, guiding students to gradually complete the creative design and production of AR/VR and maker education and obtain more specific knowledge about AR/VR and maker education.

2.2 STEAM and Maker

STEAM adds Art to STEM [8]. In the spirit of maker education, students will practice the creativity generated by combining these fields in actual practice. The energy and results stimulated by such a cross-field approach are surprising. Therefore, in recent years, a wave of global education has been set off. This research is also integrating the spirit and philosophy of STEAM education and maker education. It is hoped that more cross-disciplinary talents can be cultivated to meet the latest social and international trends.

2.3 Virtual Reality (VR)

The environment is simulated by a computer, which can be viewed and interacted with through a VR device, and the displayed images are all virtual. Guttentag [9] study mentioned that VR provides many useful applications for the tourism industry, which tourism researchers and professionals deserve more attention. Guerra et al. [10] pointed out that virtual reality is often used in tourism and heritage. Virtual reality may be a good way to travel and understand world tourism.

2.4 Augmented Reality (AR)

Incorporating virtual objects into the real scene. Many studies have explored the impact of AR integration on the tour guide experience [11–14]. AR can supplement the information that is not enough in the real environment in navigation and teaching. Kim et al. [15] studied augmented reality tourism systems to display 3D virtual characters. Tourists provide a more authentic guided tour experience.

3 Research Methods

3.1 Research Process

As shown in Fig. 1, the two groups of students were randomly allocated into the control and experimental groups in the research process flowchart. Before the teaching, a 10 min pre-test was used MSLQ Scale was implemented. The teaching course time was 900 min, A total of 18 classes. The experimental group uses STEAM-6E to integrate AR/VR maker education, and the control group uses traditional teacher-guided AR/VR maker education. 20 min post-test was implemented after the completion of the teaching activities. The questionnaire included: MSLQ and ASQ, measuring learning motivation and student satisfaction to evaluate the feasibility of this teaching activity.

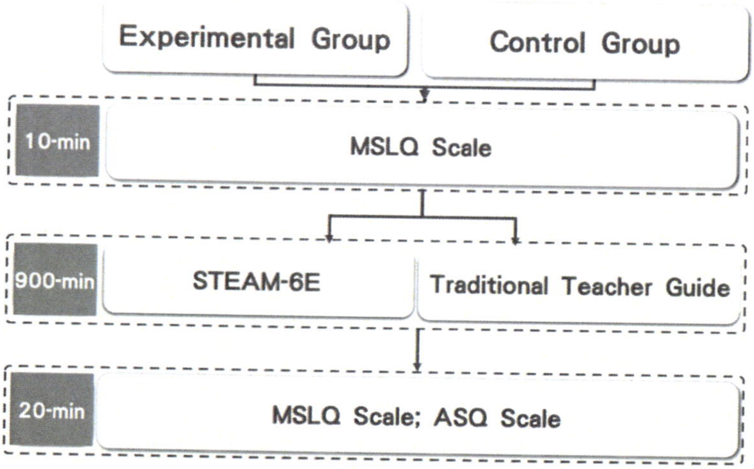

Fig. 1. The research process flowchart

3.2 Subjects

The participants of the study were undergraduates at a high school located in south-ern Taiwan. The sample size was 60, and the ages ranged from 17 to 18. The students were divided into the control group and the experimental group, with 30 students in the control group, and 30 students in the experimental group.

3.3 Research Tool

This research uses pre-/post-tests as instruments, as described below:

Motivated Strategies for Learning Questionnaire (MSLQ). To explore the students during the experience of the AR/VR maker education their learning motivation regarding the teaching from this study, we adopted the instructional materials motivation survey, which was designed by Pintrich et al. [16]. The Questionnaire includes Intrinsic Goal Orientation, Extrinsic Goal Orientation, Task Value, Control of Learning Beliefs, Self-efficacy for Learning and Performance and Test Anxiety. This is a Likert-scale questionnaire.

Activity Satisfaction Questionnaire (ASQ). In order to explore the learners' activity satisfaction during the experience of the AR/VR maker education, we adopted the flow questionnaire designed by Lewis [17]. The questionnaire has three questions which are treated as constituent items for summative or Likert scales. The items are 7-point graphic scales.

4 Results

4.1 Evaluation of Learning Motivation

As shown in Table 1, The interaction terms for the independent variables and the covariances were $F = 0.008$, $p = 0.931 > 0.05$, and a significance of $0.873 > 0.05$, which did not render a significant level, indicating that the linear relationship between the independent variables and the dependent variables from each group was consistent. Thus, an analysis of covariance could be implemented.

Table 1. Differences in learning motivation of the two groups

Source of variation	*SS*	*df*	*MS*	*F*	*p*
Group	.037	1	.037	.162	.689
Pre-test	.374	1	.374	1.656	.203
Group*Pre-test	.002	1	.002	.008	.931
Error (between groups)	12.650	56	.226		

As shown in Table 2, the results of the covariate analysis were $F = 12.855, p = .001 < .05$, and a significance of $0.001 < 0.05$, which implied that the differences between groups reached a significant level, thereby indicating that there were significant differences in the learning motivation between the two groups undergoing different learning methods.

Table 2. Analysis of covariance: learning Motivation of two groups.

Source of variation	*SS*	*df*	*MS*	*F*	*p*
Group	.381	1	.381	1.718	.195
Pre-test	2.853	1	2.853	12.855	.001
Error (between groups)	12.652	57	.222		

4.2 Evaluation of Learning Activity Satisfaction

From the average results of the learning activity satisfaction of the control and experimental groups, it is found that the learning activity satisfaction in the AR/VR maker education of the two groups is satisfied. Additionally, the obvious performance in the experimental group shows that learners get an average of more than 5 in each criterion, and the overall score is 5.46 (Table 3).

Table 3. Average and standard deviation of each dimension of learning activity satisfaction ($n = 60$).

Group	Dimension	*Mean*	*SD*
Experimental group	Effectiveness	5.23	.898
	Efficiency	5.37	.928
	Overall satisfaction	5.77	1.006
	Learning activity satisfaction	5.46	.899
Control group	Effectiveness	4.23	1.223
	Efficiency	4.47	1.196
	Overall satisfaction	4.60	1.133
	Learning activity satisfaction	4.43	1.132

Table 4 shows the results of the learning activity satisfaction analysis of the two groups in the AR/VR maker education using a paired sample t-test; there were significant differences in the post-test learning activity satisfaction between the experimental group and the control group, t (50) = − 3.874, p = 0.000. There were significant differences between the post-test acceptance score (M = 4.43, SD = 0.1.132) of the control group and the post-test acceptance score (M = 5.46, SD = 0.899) of the experimental group, with a significance of 0.000 < 0.05 between the two, which implied that there were significant differences between the two groups.

Table 4. Independent sample t-test for the ASQ.

	Mean *(SD)*		*df*	*t*	*p*
	Control group ($N = 30$)	Experimental group ($N = 30$)			
ASQ	4.43(1.132)	5.46(0.899)	58	58	3.874

5 Conclusion

This research mainly introduces STEAM & Maker Education into the class and plans a "STEAM-6E Model" set to incorporate AR/VR Maker Education courses. Learn about theory, application, and implementation through courses. Integrate resources near the school and apply the knowledge learned to solve problems for the community practically. The subjects of the study are 60 high school third-year students in two classes. One class is the experimental group using STEAM-6E teaching and the control group uses traditional briefing teaching, conducting experiments. The results of the study found that whether AR/VR maker education is combined with STEAM-6E, there are the following differences:

There is a significant difference in the learning motivation of combining STEAM-6E into AR/VR maker education. Incorporating STEAM-6E into AR/VR education can help learners increase their learning motivation more effectively. The results confirm those of previous studies, in which AR has been shown to enhance learning motivation [18]. Therefore, it can be speculated that using STEAM-6E as a learning instruction model can attract learners.

There is a significant difference in the learning activity satisfaction of combining STEAM-6E into AR/VR maker education. The results of this study show that introducing the STEAM-6E teaching method in the experimental group has a higher degree of satisfaction in learning than the traditional briefing teaching. Incorporating STEAM-6E into AR/VR education can help learners increase their learning activity satisfaction more effectively. The results confirm those of previous studies, in which STEAM-6E has been shown to enhance learning activity satisfaction [19, 20].

In the future, we should explore the effects of board games on learning effectiveness, flow, creativity, or analyze learning behaviors during activity to understand participants' learning processes better.

References

1. Barry, N., Burke, D.: 6E Learning by Design Model. Technology and engineering Teacher, 14–19 (2014)
2. Azuma, R.T.: A survey of augmented reality. Presence: Teleoper. Virtual. Environ. **6**(4), 355–385 (1997)
3. Azuma, R., Baillot, Y., Behringer, R., Feiner, S., Julier, S., MacIntyre, B.: Recent advances in augmented reality. IEEE Comput. Graphics Appl. **21**(6), 34–47 (2001)
4. Eger, J.: The Congressional STEAM Caucus may turn STEM to STEAM in the reauthorization of ESEA. Huffington Post (2015). Recuperado de www.huffingtonpost.com/john-m-eger/stem-may-become-steamoffi_b_8634126.html
5. Casasanto, V.A., Campbell, B., Manrique, A., Ramsayer, K., Markus, T., Neumann, T.: Lasers, penguins, and polar bears: novel outreach and education approaches for NASA's ICESat-2 mission. Acta Astronaut. **148**, 396–402 (2018)
6. Kaniawati, D.S., Suryadi, S.: Integration of STEM Education in Learning Cycle 6E To Improve Problem Solving Skills on Direct Current Electricity. Proc. ICMSE **3**(1), M-106-M–109 (2016)
7. Chung, C.C., Lin, C.L., Lou, S.J.: Analysis of the learning effectiveness of the STEAM-6E special course—a case study about the creative design of IoT assistant devices for the elderly. Sustainability **10**(9), 3040 (2018)
8. Perignat, E., Katz-Buonincontro, J.: STEAM in practice and research: an integrative literature review. Thinking Skills Creativ. **31**, 31–43 (2019)
9. Guttentag, D.A.: Virtual reality: Applications and implications for tourism. Tour. Manage. **31**(5), 637–651 (2010)
10. Guerra, J.P., Pinto, M.M., Beato, C.: Virtual reality-shows a new vision for tourism and heritage. Eur. Sci. J. ESJ **11**(9), 1–10 (2015)
11. Fenu, C., Pittarello, F.: Svevo tour: The design and the experimentation of an augmented reality application for engaging visitors of a literary museum. Int. J. Hum Comput Stud. **114**, 20–35 (2018)
12. Keil, J., Zollner, M., Becker, M., Wientapper, F., Engelke, T., Wuest, H.: The House of Olbrich—an augmented reality tour through architectural history. In: 2011 IEEE International Symposium on Mixed and Augmented Reality-Arts, Media, and Humanities (2011)

13. Lo, J.H., Gong, G.Z.: Touring system using augmented reality-a case study of Yilan cultural industries. In: 2020 3rd IEEE International Conference on Knowledge Innovation and Invention (ICKII), pp. 204–207. IEEE, August 2020
14. Martínez-Graña, A.M., et al.: Augmented reality in a hiking tour of the Miocene Geoheritage of the central Algarve cliffs (Portugal). Geoheritage **9**(1), 121–131 (2017)
15. Kim, K., Seo, B.K., Han, J.H., Park, J.I.: Augmented reality tour system for immersive experience of cultural heritage. In: Proceedings of the 8th International Conference on Virtual Reality Continuum and its Applications in Industry, pp. 323–324 (2009)
16. Pintrich, P.R., Smith, D.A., Garcia, T., McKeachie, W.J.: Reliability and predictive validity of the Motivated Strategies for Learning Questionnaire (MSLQ). Educ. Psychol. Measur. **53**(3), 801–813 (1993)
17. Lewis, J.R.: Psychometric evaluation of an after-scenario questionnaire for computer usability studies: the ASQ. ACM Sigchi Bulletin **23**(1), 78–81 (1991)
18. Chang, C. P. A.: Study on the Impact of Using Gamification 6E Model for IoT Hands-on Activity to High School Students' Learning Attitude, Learning Effectiveness and Behavior Pattern. Master's thesis, National Taiwan Normal University (2020)
19. Chung, C.C., Lin, C.L.: Research on development of STEAM-6E project course. In: 2018 1st International Cognitive Cities Conference (IC3), pp. 118–122. IEEE (2018)
20. Lin, C.L., Chiang, J.K.: Using 6E model in STEAM teaching activities to improve university students' learning satisfaction: a case of development seniors IoT smart cane creative design. J. Internet Technol. **20**(7), 2109–2116 (2019)

Computational Thinking in Education

The Use of E-learning Tools in a Basic Logic Course During the COVID-19 Lockdown

Peter Øhrstrøm[1(✉)], Steinar Thorvaldsen[2], Ulrik Sandborg-Petersen[1], Thomas Ploug[1], and David Jakobsen[1]

[1] Department of Communication and Psychology, Aalborg University, 9000 Aalborg, Denmark
{poe,ulrikp,ploug,davker}@hum.aau.dk
[2] Department of Education, Uit The Arctic University of Norway, 9037 Tromsø, Norway
steinar.thorvaldsen@uit.no

Abstract. This paper describes a study of the development and use of e-learning tools in the context of a basic logic course that was taught during the COVID-19 lockdown in 2021. The tools were used to compensate for learning and teaching limitations brought about by the lockdown. We compare a course that was taught in February and March 2020 (before the lockdown in Denmark) with a similar course that was taught in 2021 during the lockdown. In terms of exam results, the students from the 2021 course did significantly better than those in the 2020 course. This paper considers possible explanations for this difference. Among other things, we analyse the data collected from the students via a questionnaire.

Keywords: A basic logic course · E-Learning tools · Syllogistics · Propositional logic · Validity of arguments · Teaching during the COVID-19 lockdown

1 Introduction

Since the 1980s, various versions of a basic logic and argumentation course have been offered to students studying communication and digital media at Aalborg University, Denmark. This course emphasises the study of the logical validity of arguments from basic propositional logic and Aristotelian syllogistics. One important learning goal in this context is that students should obtain the needed skills to analyse an arbitrary propositional or syllogistic argument that is formulated in natural language in terms of symbolic logic to evaluate its logical validity. For this purpose, students should use truth tables and semantic trees to analyse propositional arguments and Venn diagrams and basic inference rules to analyse syllogistic arguments.

One of the authors of this paper (Peter Øhrstrøm) has taught versions of the course throughout this entire period from the 1980s to 2021, whereas two of the other authors (Thomas Ploug and David Jakobsen) have only been involved as teachers for a few years. A joint textbook [3] was used for the course, along with two learning tools, Syllog and Proplog, which were developed by Ulrik Sandborg-Petersen specifically for this course. These tools were employed during logic exercises to make the learning experience game-like and enjoyable (see [4]). The interface of the present version of the Syllog tool is shown in Fig. 1.

© Springer Nature Switzerland AG 2021
Y.-M. Huang et al. (Eds.): ICITL 2021, LNCS 13117, pp. 121–130, 2021.
https://doi.org/10.1007/978-3-030-91540-7_14

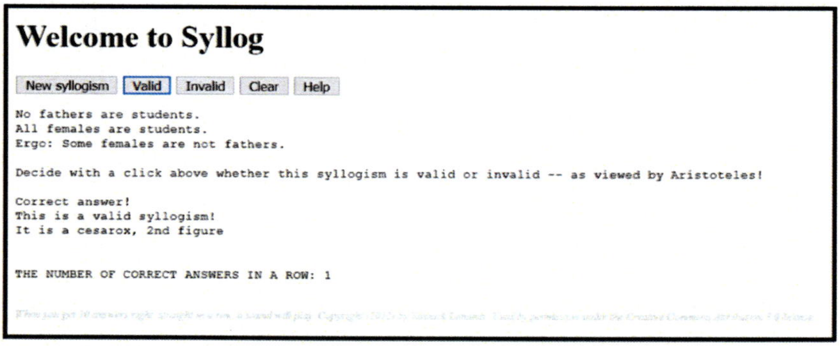

Fig. 1. Interface of the *Syllog* tool. Note that in the case of a valid syllogism, the system will give the classical medieval name of the argument (see [2] and [3]). The student may compare these names with the Aristotelian theory presented during the course lectures. The interface of the *Proplog* tool is similar. In both *Syllog* and *Proplog*, valid and invalid arguments occur with the same frequency.

The *Syllog* user can click on 'New syllogism' to get a new syllogism presented on the screen. The user must then decide whether the syllogism presented is valid or invalid (i.e. whether the conclusion follows the premise in any possible/thinkable scenario). *Proplog* works in a similar manner with a similar interface. See [3] for more information on the course.

In both 2020 and 2021, *Syllog* and *Proplog* were not only used along with the teaching during the courses, but it was also used to establish the individual exams after the courses. The students were asked to produce 15–20 random propositional and syllogistic arguments using *Syllog* and *Proplog* and then follow with analysing and discussing the arguments to document their validity or invalidity carefully. Ultimately, students of a basic logic course should not only be able to identify a valid/invalid argument but should also be able to understand and explain why a particular argument is valid/invalid.

The 2020 exam results revealed that several students needed a clearer understanding of what it takes to demonstrate that a syllogistic argument is valid, and they appeared to have an even weaker understanding of how to show that a syllogistic argument is invalid.

In 2020, the course's teachers had to invest significant energy into presenting and training students on the use of Venn diagrams as well as basic inference rules in syllogistic reasoning because many students seem to find these topics rather difficult. This was done in lectures and traditional exercises to be carried out and discussed in groups of 2–3 students under the teacher's supervision. For the 2021 version of the course, the COVID-19 lockdown made it unrealistic to apply a strategy involving exercises in small groups under the supervision of a teacher. Instead, two learning tools, *Proof* and *Venn*, were developed and used. The tools should make it possible to obtain the same knowledge and skills alone while only using a personal computer. The *Proof* tool should support the user in the construction of a proof documenting the validity of a syllogism, and the *Venn* tool should support the documentation of the syllogisms' invalidity.

In Sects. 2 and 3, we discuss the design of the two tools and their theoretical background as well as the practical use of the tools in the course. In Sect. 4, the results of the exams in 2020 and 2021 are considered and compared. Section 5 focuses on the results from a questionnaire designed to study the students' learning experiences during the course. Finally, in the conclusion, we offer some perspectives on possible compensation from the digital tools and teaching problems that can arise if teachers are limited to online communication with their students. The conclusion also answers some open questions and suggests interesting topics for further research.

2 The *Proof* Learning Tool

The Proof tool makes it possible for the user to construct indirect syllogistic proofs using a formal language involving four types of syllogistic propositions:

a(X, Y): 'All X are Y'
i(X, Y): 'Some X are Y'
e(X, Y): 'No X are Y'
o(X, Y): 'Some X are not Y'

The negation of a(X, Y) is o(X, Y), whereas the negation of e(X, Y) is i(X, Y). Additionally, we may reduce the number of proposition types if we allow for the negation of terms because the following may be argued:

$e(X, Y) \equiv a(X, \text{non-}Y)$
$o(X, Y) \equiv i(X, \text{non-}Y)$

Using the *Proof* tool, the user may be able to reason within the framework of a modern version of classical Aristotelian syllogistics (see [1, 2]). The three straightforward inference rules mentioned in Fig. 2 (i.e. TRANS, MUT and EX) are available. TRANS can be presented as:

$$(a(X, Y)\ \&\ a(Y, Z)) \rightarrow a(X, Z)$$

Clearly, if non-Z is substituted for Z we obtain:

$$(a(X, Y)\ \&\ e(Y, Z)) \rightarrow e(X, Z)$$

MUT can be presented as:

$$i(X, Y) \rightarrow i(Y, X)$$

By contraposition and renaming we obtain:

$$e(X, Y) \rightarrow e(Y, X).$$

EX can be presented as:

a(X, Y) → i(X, Y)

Clearly, if non-Y is substituted for Y we obtain:

e(X, Y) → o(X, Y)

As shown in Fig. 2, the user may prove the validity of a syllogism with two syllogistic premises and one syllogistic conclusion indirectly, demonstrating that the assumption of the premises along with the negated conclusion will lead to a contradiction. The present example shows that the combination of the propositions o(M, P), a(M, S) and a(S, P) leads to a contradiction. This follows the inference rule TRANS. Thus, we have demonstrated the validity of the syllogism from the premises o(M, P) and a(M, S) to the conclusion o(S, P), which is the negation of a(S, P). It is well known that any valid syllogism formulated in this classical way may be proved in this manner.

Notably, the user may play with the various possible applications of the inference rules to obtain practical experiences with what it means to prove something in syllogistic reasoning. The student may carry out this kind of playful and game-like activity alone, using their computer as a kind of dialogue partner. This possibility became quite relevant for learning during the COVID-19 lockdown. However, it seems that such tools may also be useful when the learning situation is more 'normal' because at least some students would like to study alone, even if traditional group work under supervision is offered.

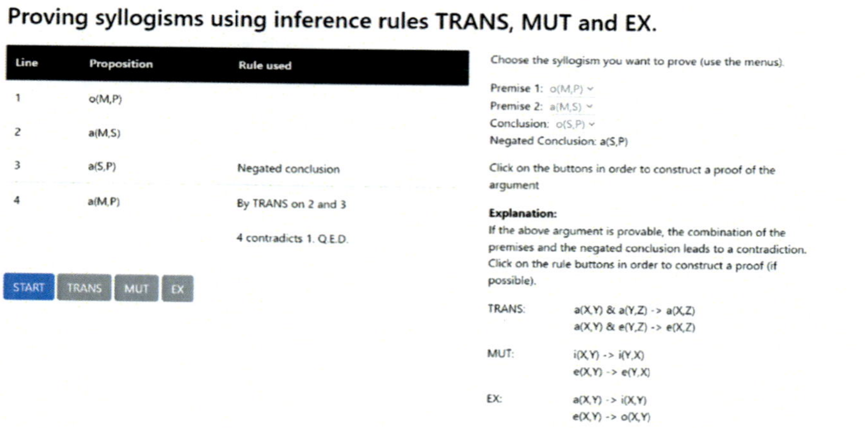

Fig. 2. Interface of the Proof tool. Note that the user can apply three different inference rules, TRANS, MUT and EX, to obtain a contradiction in order to produce an indirect proof. It is well known that all classical syllogisms can be proved in this way.

3 The Venn Learning Tool

The Venn learning tool allows the user to construct a Venn diagram designed to show that a certain syllogism is invalid. The diagram corresponds to a set of elements belonging to some universe of discourse. Seven subsets of this basic set are parts of the basic set. The user makes the diagram online using ' +' to indicate that a particular subset is non-empty and '−' to indicate that the subset is empty.

It should be mentioned that while John Venn (1834–1923) suggested another way of marking the subsets in the diagram (see [6]), we find his original approach inadequate as a basis for building a practical and interactive digital tool. For this reason, we chose a more useful but still equivalent method for constructing the Venn tool:

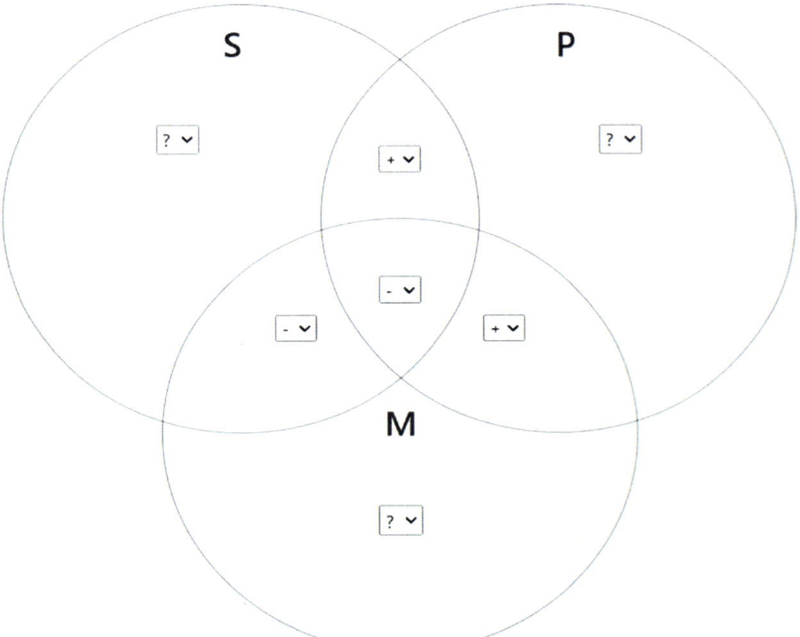

Fig. 3. Interface of the Venn tool. Note that the user can change the indications regarding the seven subsets in the diagram from '?' to ' +' or '−'. Then, the user can evaluate the propositions involved in the syllogism in question. If the premises are true and the conclusion is false, then we have documented the invalidity of the syllogism. – It should be noted that this kind of diagrammatical reasoning makes it possible to reason on the basis of incomplete knowledge – something which was in fact very important to John Venn himself (see [6]).

In the beginning all the subsets in the diagram are marked with '?', because it is as a start unknown whether or not they contain elements. Then the user can add the information that some of the subsets are empty (marked as '−'), whereas others are non-empty (marked as ' +'). When at least some of the subsets (or some of them) have been marked with ' +' or '−', we may evaluate any syllogistic proposition (a, i, e or o) based on M, P and S as 'true', 'false' or 'unknown' relative to the diagram. This makes it possible to look for a diagram that documents that a certain syllogism is invalid (i.e. it has true premises and a false conclusion relative to the diagram).

In the example shown in Fig. 3, the propositions i(M, P) and e(S, M) both turn out to be true, whereas e(S,P) is clearly false given the signs indicated in the diagram. This means that this Venn diagram documents the invalidity of the syllogism from the premises i(M, P) and e(S, M) to the conclusion e(S, P). It is well known that if a classical syllogism is invalid, then there is a Venn diagram according to which the premises are true and the conclusion is false; the student just has to find it.

As with the learning tool *Proof,* this approach to Venn diagrams can easily lead to a playful and game-like activity that the students can carry out alone, with their computers as their only counterpart.

4 Exam Comparisons

The exams in 2020 and 2021 were organised in almost the same way, making it interesting to compare the results. The course lectures in propositional logic and syllogistics were offered to second-year students studying communication and digital media at Aalborg University in Aalborg and Copenhagen during February and the first week of March 2020 (i.e., before the COVID-19 lockdown). In 2020, 121 students participated in the exam. In 2021, all the lectures were given during the COVID-19 lockdown, and 132 students participated in the exam. After the evaluation of the exam, each student received a written statement explaining how well they had done. These statements were rather formal and brief; thus, they were easily categorised as 'Good', 'Acceptable' and 'Weak'. The results of the exams in 2020 and 2021 are shown in Table 1.

Table 1. A chi-square test of independence showed that there was a significant association between year and result. The chi-square statistic (2, N = 253) is 6.292, p-value = 0.0430. The result is significant at $p < 0.05$ in favour of the year 2021.

	Good	Acceptable	Weak
2020	86	29	6
2021	108	23	1
p-value	0.0430		

Importantly, all assignments were evaluated by the same person, making the comparison of the results from the exams in 2020 and 2021 extremely reliable.

It is interesting that the learning results were significantly better in 2021 during the lockdown than those obtained in 2020, when teaching occurred before the COVID-19 lockdown. Multiple factors may have contributed to this difference in performance. We conducted a brief focus group interview with 8 students from the Copenhagen group.

A consensus was reached on three interrelated explanatory factors, namely the *uninterrupted time* spent on doing logic exercises in direct *continuation* of classes. The students stressed the importance for their learning process of being able to do exercises in direct continuation of classes without being interrupted by fellow classmates. They estimated that they ended up having spent more time doing logic exercises than they would otherwise have done, due to the unimpeded time right after the logic classes and the readily available exercises. The tools *Venn* and *Proof* played a key part in this change in the students' study behaviour, as they provided the students with platforms for conducting logic exercises. The changes in study behaviour partly enabled by E-learning tools indicates that the serious challenges to traditional university teaching caused by the COVID-19 lockdown can be overcome.

5 The Questionnaire

A group of 84 students (the Aalborg group) was asked to complete a questionnaire. Unfortunately, only 40 responded. For this reason, we should use these results with some caution. On the other hand, they may give some indication of the situation, and we may still use the results as some sort of descriptive statistics. In particular, the students' answers to two of the questions should be noted, because they relate directly to the two tools we have introduced during the COVID-19 lockdown. Table 2 refers to the Proof tool:

Table 2. The students were asked to consider the following statement: 'Proof has given me a better understanding of what it means to document the validity of a syllogistic argument with a direct proof'.

Strongly agree	5%
Agree	22.5%
Somewhat agree	12.5%
Neither agree nor disagree	10%
Somewhat disagree	7.5%
Disagree	30%
Strongly disagree	12.5%

Although around half of the students who have responded don't think that the use of the tool has given them a better understanding of syllogistic validity, there is still around 40% of the students who find that the tool has helped them in this regard. Furthermore, the Proof tool is very new, and its user interface may not be fully satisfactory. It should also be noted that its use of indirect proof may be a complication. As a consequence, some of the students may not fully have understood what precisely the tool does. In fact, this may be the reason why the majority of the students were unable to benefit from the use of the Proof tool.

Table 3 refers to the *Venn* tool, and it appears that the use of this tool has been helpful to an even bigger group of the students working with the course material. It appears from Table 3 that 52.5% of the students stated that they could benefit to some extent from the use of *Venn*.

Table 3. The students were asked to consider the following statement: '*Venn* has given me a better understanding of what it means to document the invalidity of a syllogistic argument with a Venn diagram'.

Strongly agree	12.5%
Agree	30%
Somewhat agree	10%
Neither agree nor disagree	10%
Somewhat disagree	10%
Disagree	12,5%
Strongly disagree	15%

Graphically, this may be illustrated in the following manner (Fig. 4):

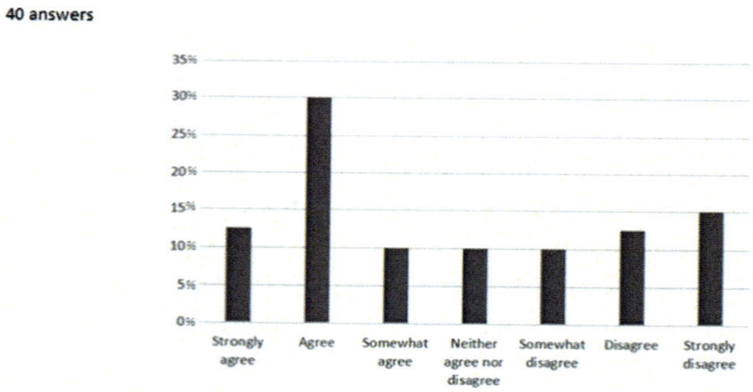

Fig. 4. Graphical illustration of the results included in Table 3. The students were asked to consider the following statement: '*Venn* has given me a better understanding of what it means to document the invalidity of a syllogistic argument with a Venn diagram'

The difference between the numbers in Tables 2 and 3 is in fact rather close to what we expected. At least it is fully consistent with our impression during the 2020 course and in particular during the 2020 exam, according to which many of the students found it relatively easy to prove the validity of a syllogism, whereas they felt more uncertainty about making a Venn diagram, by which we may document that a syllogism is invalid.

6 Conclusion

The finding that the 2021 students did significantly better on the logic exam than the 2020 students is a bit surprising considering that the 2021 students had more challenges due to the COVID-19 lockdown. One possible explanation may be that the students who were locked down were rather isolated and had few social distractions, which may have motivated them to study more. While likely part of the explanation, it is probably not significant enough to explain the notable difference between the exam results in 2020 and 2021. However, it is quite likely that the better exam results in 2021 were due to the introduction of the new learning tools *Proof* and *Venn*, the latter in particular. It is difficult to draw definite conclusions due to the low number of responses, but the answers seem to lend some support to the impact of the tools, with around half the students answering that the use of the tools led to a deeper and better understanding of the validity and invalidity of syllogisms.

In conclusion, this study clearly documents that, at least in some cases, when traditional teaching procedures and methods are or must be abandoned, being creative and innovative may allow us to design new teaching tools that can give rise to significantly better learning results than those occurring before the teaching situation changed. The outcome of an innovation sparked by change may even be useful and relevant when the normal teaching situation has been re-established. Thus, it will be meaningful to take advantage of all innovative ideas that emerge during a special and changed teaching situation, such as the one generated by the COVID-19 lockdown. As indicated by the present case, it will be relevant to create tools that can support students' work with propositional arguments, even if such tools have to be designed and developed after the COVID-19 lockdown. The analysis of the propositional arguments shows that many students lack a clear understanding of how propositional validity and invalidity can be demonstrated. This indicates that there is a need for an even stronger emphasis on the analysis of arguments in terms of truth tables and semantic trees. We may even consider building a tool based on the so-called existential graphs suggested by C.S. Peirce (see [7, pp. 165–181]).

The material for our basic logic course has been very much inspired by the works of A.N. Prior (1914–69). In particular, we have found his *Formal Logic* [8] from 1955 very useful. (More on the tools and topics chosen for the course can be found on our site on Prior's basic ideas on logic, www.logic.aau.dk). However, it is still an open question how many of Prior's ideas should go into our basic logic course.

No matter what, we should consider the development of tools for the part of the course material dealing with propositional logic as well. Such new tools should be carefully tested and evaluated. It is very likely that the use of such tools may improve the learning results even more, whether or not there is a lockdown.

References

1. Aristotle: Prior analytics, Translated by A.J. Jenkinson. The Internet Classics Archive (1994–2000). http://classics.mit.edu/Aristotle/prior.html
2. Parry, W., Hacker, E.: Aristotelian Logic. State University of New York Press (1991)
3. Øhrstrøm, P., Ploug, T., Jakobsen, D.: Logisk Set, 2nd edn. Metaphysica, Aalborg (2019)

4. Øhrstrøm, P., Sandborg-Petersen, U., Thorvaldsen, S., Ploug, T.: Teaching logic through web-based and gamified quizzing of formal arguments. In: Hernández-Leo, D., Ley, T., Klamma, R., Harrer, A. (eds.) EC-TEL 2013. LNCS, vol. 8095, pp. 410–423. Springer, Heidelberg (2013). https://doi.org/10.1007/978-3-642-40814-4_32
5. Øhrstrøm, P., Thorvaldsen, S., Sandborg-Petersen, U., Ploug, T.: Teaching propositional and syllogistic logic using e-learning tools. In: Rønningsbakk, L., Wu, T.T., Sandnes, F., Huang, Y.M. (eds.) ICITL 2019. LNCS, vol. 11937. Springer, Cham (2019). https://doi.org/10.1007/978-3-030-35343-8_89
6. Venn, J.: Symbolic Logic. Macmillan and Company, London (1881)
7. Malpass, A., Mafori, M.A. (eds.): The History of Philosophical and Formal Logic. From Aristotle to Tarski. Bloomsbury, London (2017)
8. Prior, A.N.: Formal Logic, Oxford University Press, Oxford (1955)

Improve University Humanities Students' Problem-Solving Ability Through Computational Thinking Training

Jim-Min Lin[1(✉)], Zeng-Wei Hong[1], Zong-Kun Song[1], Wei-Wei Shen[2], and Wai-Khuen Cheng[3]

[1] Department of Information Engineering and Computer Science, Feng Chia University, Taichung City, Taiwan
jimmy@fcu.edu.tw

[2] Department of Foreign Language and Literature, Feng Chia University, Taichung City, Taiwan

[3] Faculty of Information and Communication Technology, Universiti Tunku Abdul Rahman (UTAR), Kampar, Malaysia

Abstract. Humanities students are often considered to have lower problem solving ability and information application skills. This may be due to the fact that many humanities students receive basic computer education that only teaches word processing or other information software. In this paper, we want to investigate whether university humanities students' problem-solving ability could be improved through the computational thinking (CT) training. The experiment was divided into 2 phases. The first phase was to investigate whether the students' problem solving abilities could be affected by the CT education comparing with the training of MS-Office operating skills adopted in the traditional "Introduction to Computers" course. The result of this investigation showed that the experimental group received the CT training had significantly better achievement than the control group in both problem-solving ability and IT application ability.

Keywords: Computational Thinking (CT) · Problem-solving ability · Information application ability · Bebras challenge · Scratch programming

1 Introduction

In the information age, everyone should have a certain degree of information ability, including the ability to use computational tools to solve practical problems. In Taiwan, university humanities students are generally considered to be inadequate in Information Technology (IT) skills. The reasons may be: lack of interest, lack of IT skill or confidence; lack of logical thinking training for a long time in their school education; current computer-related courses do not attract students' interest; and few contact with the latest IT; and so on. It has always been a trouble for teachers who conduct computer-related courses, such as the "Introduction to Computers", in the liberal arts departments. Moreover, many humanities students have already given up the study of computer programming, or even the study of information-related knowledge. But these large groups

© Springer Nature Switzerland AG 2021
Y.-M. Huang et al. (Eds.): ICITL 2021, LNCS 13117, pp. 131–143, 2021.
https://doi.org/10.1007/978-3-030-91540-7_15

of humanities and social science students actually have good cultural literacy in language, literature, society, history and so on. If these students can be guided to integrate into the modern information society and give full play to their cultural abilities, they can enhance not only their own employability, but also their information skills. It can be helpful to the quality and connotation of the information industry. Therefore, how to improve these humanities students' IT concepts/mindset to solve their real problems in life, and then give full play to their ability to apply IT, will be a very meaningful task. In order to achieve the above-mentioned goals, "Computational Thinking (CT)" [1], which has become a trend in recent years, may be a feasible method and strategy.

Professor Jeannette M. Wing, a former Chair of the Department of Computer Science at Carnegie Mellon University (CMU), first proposed the term Computational Thinking (CT) in 2006. She proposed "CT is the use of basic computer science concepts to solve problems, design systems, and understand the thinking mode of human behavior." She stated that CT is also the basic qualities that everyone in modern society should have, as well as the computer science skills and knowledge necessary for future life [1]. She emphasized that the ability of computational thinking is as important as 3R (Reading, wRiting, and aRithmetics). It is not only a necessary ability for computer scientists, computer workers, or programmers, it is also the basic skill of every modern person. Computational thinking means a computerized problem-solving ability. This ability has four aspects [2]:

1. Decomposition: Disassemble data, workflow, or actual problems into small, operationally manageable parts.
2. Pattern Recognition: Observe phenomena such as the characteristic pattern, trend and overall pattern presented by the data.
3. Abstraction: Identify and establish the general principles of these patterns.
4. Algorithm Design: Design the implementation methods and steps to solve a problem or similar problems.

The computer introduction courses of the humanities department in Taiwan have always been teaching the operation and use of software tools, such as MS-Office, Web page creation, or simple APP programming design. The content is mostly boring input and operation following the teacher's examples. For students, there is only practice on skills, and no training on their problem-solving ability. Such a course does not motivate students on the one hand, and on the other hand, the effect of improving students' problem-solving ability is limited, and the expected results are not obtained. In general, students' course satisfaction is therefore not high. Therefore, the teachers are all trying their best to find a more suitable computer introduction course content for the humanities students. Therefore, if this study can confirm that the training of CT can achieve some help and effects for university humanities students, then one can consider, in the future, incorporating the content of the computer introduction course of the humanities department into the CT training and applications. On the other hand, the same CT training model can be transplanted to students of other disciplines, as well as the college students with low information learning achievements, so as to enhance the IT ability of college students; therefore, the results of this research can be of reference value for future IT education.

Therefore, for humanities students who are relatively inadequately trained in sciences such as mathematics, physics, and logic, the purpose of this paper is to study whether they can, by cultivating CT concepts, not only improve their ability to think, analyze, and find solutions to problems in life, but also improve their ability to think, analyze, and find solutions by using IT. This research hopes to take the social robot application system, a TA robot, as an example, to produce their own information tools designed and implemented by ourselves. In this research, we will take students of foreign language department as an example.

This paper is organized as the following: some related works are listed in Sect. 2; An experiment is reported in Sect. 3; The experimental results and discussion are addressed in Sect. 4. Finally, a brief conclusion is made in Sect. 5.

2 Related Works

The Computer Science Teachers Association (CSTA) and the International Institute of Educational Technology (ISTE) have defined a series of concepts encompassed by computational thinking and practice. These concepts are subdivided into data collection, data analysis, data representation and analysis, abstraction, analysis and model verification, automation, testing and verification, algorithm & process, problem decomposition, control structure, parallelization and analogy. Other scholars and organizations have also put forward their own definitions and opinions [3–5]. In addition, computational thinking is also a thinking process involved in formulating problems, so it is necessary to find computational steps and algorithms from its design and analysis to solve useful and more complex problems [3]. Korkmaz et al. further clarified that computational thinking can be defined as the necessary knowledge and skills, as well as the effective use of computers to illustrate the attitude of solving life problems [6].

Table 1 is based on the connotation of computational thinking proposed in the literature of many scholars [3–5, 7, 8], and the connotation of computational thinking that is currently generally accepted in private information technology education, such as: Google for Education Exploring Computational Thinking website [9] and Bitesize which is a website under the British Broadcasting Corporation BBC that provides free online learning resources for students [10].

It can be seen from Table 1 that the computational thinking proposed by scholars and the computational thinking proposed by private IT education resources have a high degree of overlap in Abstraction, Algorithm, and Decomposition, which means that These connotations are the consensus on the connotation of computational thinking in current research and education. Also, because the Ministry of Education (MOE) in Taiwan is also promoting learning computational thinking in education, the connotation of computational thinking that was used in this study should be as close as possible to the educational policy of Taiwan MOE.

Table 1. Connotation of computational thinking

	Wing [3]	Barr and Stephenson [4]	Selby and Woollard [7]	Google [9]	Bitesize [10]
Abstraction	✓	✓	✓	✓	✓
Algorithm		✓	✓	✓	✓
Automation	✓	✓			
Data		✓			
Decomposition		✓	✓	✓	✓
Evaluation			✓		
Generalization			✓		
Pattern recognition				✓	✓
Parallelization		✓			
Simulation		✓	✓		

3 Experiment

3.1 Research Questions

We have two research questions raised in this research:

1. Can CT education improve university humanities students' problem solving abilities by comparing with the MS-Office operating skills training in the traditional "Introduction to Computers" course?
2. Can CT education improve university humanities students' information application ability by comparing with the MS-Office operating skills training in the traditional "Introduction to Computers" course?

3.2 Participants

The experimental targets of this research were 20 students from the third and fourth grades (13 juniors and 7 seniors) foreign language department of a university in Taiwan. Before starting the experimental teaching, all participants took a pretest to assess their initial level of computing thinking ability, and then we used random grouping to divide them into the experimental group (EG) and the control group (CG). Levene's test was used to test the homogeneity of the variance. The test results showed no significant difference between the two groups' pretest, where $p = .596$. The equal variance was used, which means that the two groups were similar before the start of teaching, and the experiment can continue. Table 2 shows the Levene's test results of the two groups.

Table 2. Analysis confirms that there is no difference between the two groups before teaching

EG (*N* = 10)		CG (N = 10)		*P*
Mean	*SD*	*Mean*	*SD*	
139.50	42.911	100.56	25.427	.596

3.3 Procedure

Figure 1 shows the experimental procedure. The experiment was divided into two phases. The first phase is for the first research question, and while the second phase is for the second research question. The whole experiment lasted for 14 weeks, and one hour a week. The first week is the explanation of the experimental precautions, informing the students of their rights and obligations, and the CT pretest (and also a placement test). The CT pretest used the "2016 The Bebras International Computational Thinking Contest" (Bebras 2020) questions in the Senior Group (11th and 12th grade). In the training stage (Weeks 2–3), we had a CT training for experimental group compiled by

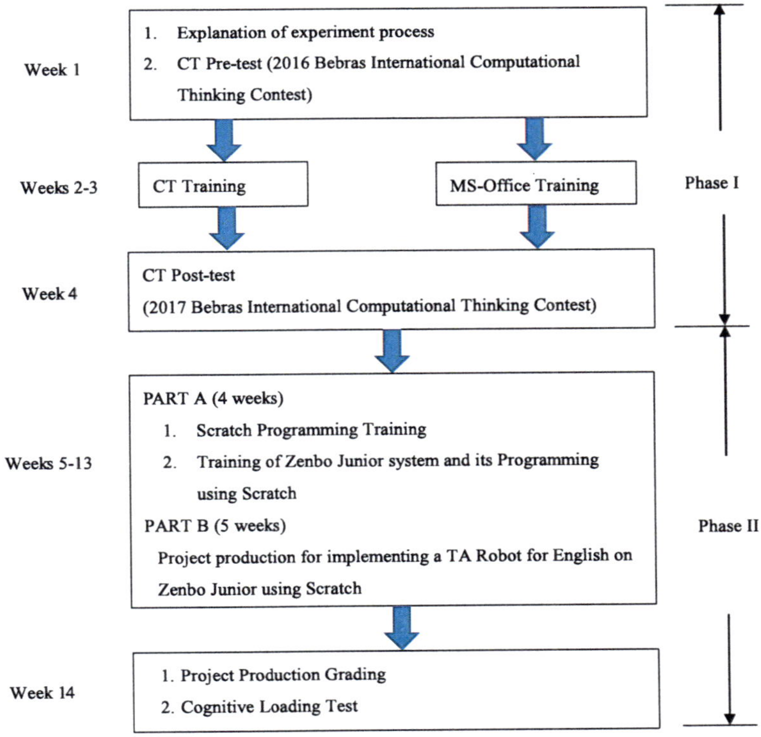

Fig. 1. Experimental process

this research and implemented the MS-Office training for the control group. The MS-Office training is a common training in the course - "Introduction to Computer Science" for university humanity students in Taiwan. Week 4 was the CT posttest using the "2017 The Bebras International Computational Thinking Contest" (Bebras 2020) questions in the Senior Group (11th and 12th grade). Weeks 5–13 was for the test of CT concept application. We would like to know whether the CT concept is helpful for university humanity students in increasing their ICT application ability. It included four weeks of Scratch programming training and then 5 weeks of project production of implementing a Robot Teaching Assistant (TA) for English. In the last week, students were required to submit their project production demonstration, the reports, and presentations for scoring.

3.4 Materials

Computational Thinking Training. Since there is no existing material for university humanity students' CT training, we decided to refer to documents in MOE, Taiwan, and then produce self-compiled CT materials, in forms of PowerPoint Slides [11, 12]. The contents of CT training materials included:

- CT basic concepts:
  - What is CT;
  - Why CT;
  - Introduction to CT components: Decomposition, Pattern Recognition, Abstraction, Algorithm Design;
- CT examples and applications that are related to humanity students' life and knowledge;
- Basic programming concepts that are introduced in the Computational Thinking test (CTT): Sequence, Loops, Events, Parallelism, Conditionals, Data, and Operators [13].

Some material examples are shown in Figs. 2, 3 and 4.

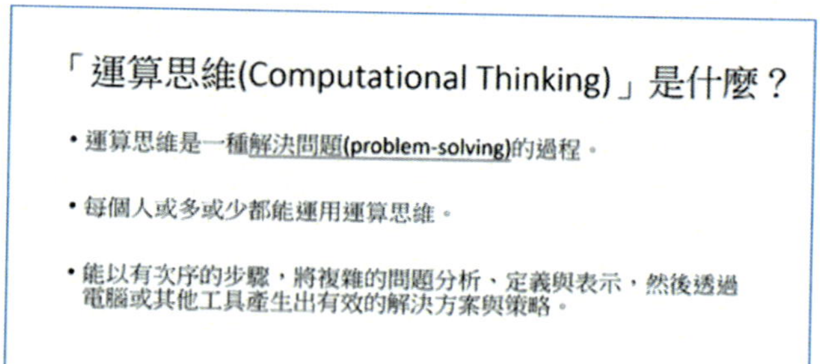

Fig. 2. Example PPT slide of the teaching materials - Introduction to computational thinking

After introduction to CT, we explained the composition of CT to the students. The conceptual elements explained here were the decomposition, pattern recognition, abstraction, and algorithm design. Then we explained the details of each part one by one. In order to prevent students from having difficulty in understanding because they only listened to the explanation of the textual meaning of the lesson, we used examples close to daily life to help students to understand CT more easily.

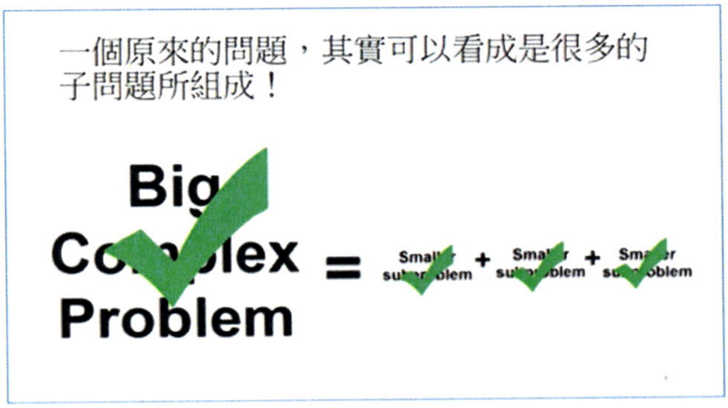

Fig. 3. Decomposition

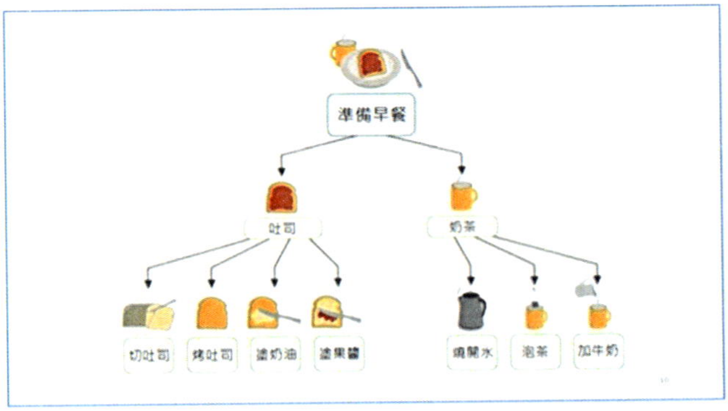

Fig. 4. Example of teaching slides of CT components

Figure 3 was used to introduce the concept of "decomposition" in CT. It explains that an original complicated problem could be divided into several smaller and easy-to-solve sub-problems such that a big and complicated problem could be conquered easily. To prevent students from just listening to the explanation and feeling that the concept is too abstract and difficult to understand, Fig. 4 was an example of decomposition presenting the preparation of breakfast in daily life. More supplementary examples close to daily life were given in the materials to help students understanding CT concepts.

Scratch Training. Scratch is regarded as a popular tool for cultivating elementary school students' computational thinking. It uses visualization tools to realize program construction through the simple building operation of building block instruction modules, and thus can effectively improve students' independent thinking ability. Since there have been lots of ready textbook for Scratch in Chinese, we choose one textbook that is appropriate for university humanity students.

3.5 Instruments

To know students' problem-solving ability in two groups before and after the CT training course, an assessment tool, the International Contest on Informatics and Computational Thinking (Bebras Contest), for measuring CT concepts was adopted. The Bebras competition originated in Lithuania. "Bebras" means "beaver" in Lithuanian, so the whole question type is based on beaver. What does Computational Thinking involve? From Bebras Web site: "The Bebras challenge promotes problem solving skills and Informatics concepts including the ability to break down complex tasks into simpler components, algorithm design, pattern recognition, pattern generalisation and abstraction. More about computational thinking" (Bebras 2020). The first Beblas Challenge was officially held in Lithuania in October 2004. There were 3470 students of different ages from 146 schools participated in the competition. From then to 2018, according to official statistics, 54 countries around the world have implemented this event. The competition accumulates nearly 3 million participants, and it is held only once a year, held by the locals of various countries, and more online competitions are used.

The difficulty age groups currently held in Taiwan are:

- Benjamin (fifth and sixth grade) (added since 2016)
- Cadet (seventh and eighth grade) (added since 2016)
- Junior (ninth and tenth grade)
- Senior (eleventh and twelfth grade)

For all age groups, there are 5 questions for each of the 3 difficulty levels: easy, medium and difficult, for a total of 15 questions. It is considered that the experimental students are college students and the highest level of the questions is only up to the high school stage, so a total of 10 questions with medium and difficult levels are selected to form test questions. The scoring method applied in this research was also based on the original contest scoring rules, but the part, difficult, was not included, and the full score was adjusted from 300 points to 225 points. This study used the 2016 and 2017 Taiwan Bebras Contest Senior Group questions as the Pretest and Posttest respectively to evaluate the computational thinking ability.

4 Results

4.1 Analysis of Computational Thinking Scores

In experiment phase 1, the experimental group implemented the computational thinking materials compiled by this research, while the control group implemented the general tradition of MS-Office training. After the experiment, checked by using Box plot [14], there are 3 invalid samples outlier caused by the large difference with the values of other students in the experiment process. Therefore, there are only 17 valid samples: 8 students in experimental group and 9 students in control group. Due to the small number of students in the experiment, it is necessary to use the non-maternal test analysis. Two independent sample groups are statistically analyzed by the Mann-Whitney U test. The null hypothesis of this test is "the two groups have the same degree of CT performance". The analysis results are shown in Table 3.

Table 3. Analysis of computational thinking scores

EG (N = 8)			CG (N = 9)			Mann-Whitney U test	
Mean	*SD*	Mean Rank	*Mean*	*SD*	Mean Rank	*U*	*P* [2*(single tail)]
141.25	36.228	11.75	100.56	25.427	6.56	14.000	.036*

Note: * $p < .05$

The results showed that the average rank (Mean Rank = 11.75) of the experimental group (N = 8) was greater than the average rank of the control group ($N = 9$) (Mean Rank = 6.56), with statistical significance ($U = 14.000, p = .036 < .05$), that rejects the null hypothesis. This result shows that in the Bebras test performance, the experimental group was significantly better than the control group. It means that the problem-solving ability of experimental group with CT training was better than that of the control group with traditional MS-Office training.

4.2 Analysis of Student Project Productions

The second phase of the experiment was to assess students' information application ability by observing how the students to apply their problem-solving skills with their majors in the Department of Foreign Languages to produce an IT-related project in which an English Teaching Assistant (TA) Robot should be designed and implemented by themselves. In the end, all students in both groups completed their robotics project. System demonstration and viewing of Scratch source programs will be performed to determine students' level of problem-solving and information application ability.

Scratch programming training has been commonly used to cultivating children's CT ability. In the research, we want to observe the performance difference in problem-solving between experimental group and the control group in which the former received CT training and Scratch programming training while the latter just received Scratch programming training only.

The grading standard is as shown in Table 4. The grading method is to directly observe the program codes submitted by the students, and award a score for each item corresponding to one of the four CT components. Each scoring item has a maximum of 5 points, and there are 20 points in total for four scoring items. Scoring was done by 3 IT experts separately, and then a final average score was obtained.

Table 4. Metrics for Scoring the Programming Part in Students' Projects

Evaluation item	Performance in corresponding programming	Example
Decomposition	Check the amount of functional blocks implemented in the program codes	Students can separate the small functions from the entire program instruction sequence, and then make these small functions into reusable functions
Pattern recognition	Check the amount of looping structures in the program codes	Students can streamline the sequential program/instructions into one or more looping blocks without redundant sequential process instructions
Abstraction	Check the amount of variables are defined and how complex the data structures are in the program codes	Check if the students can convert 5W: people (Who), events (What), times (When), places (Where), and things (Which) in real world into the corresponding program variables and data structures in the cyber world?
Algorithm design	Combination of the above three parts. Instructor can examine the core problem solving process in student's programs and check if the program codes matching with concepts shown above	In designing a 9 * 9 multiplication table, an instructor could check: • If the data types of the multiplicand and the multiplier is properly defined? • If the operation of multiplying the multiplicand by the multiplier are put into the structure of a double-loop program codes

The program codes were measured by mainly observing whether the students had used the program instructions learned in the Scratch training and practice. Using the instruction blocks that were not taught in training and practice didn't affect the score of this part, so as to prevent these additional performances from deviating from the scoring standard.

After all the students' programming works were scored, the scores of the two groups were then analyzed by Mann-Whitney U test. Table 5 shows the results of the analysis. The results showed that the average rank of the experimental group ($N = 8$) (Mean Rank

= 13.50) and the average rank of the control group ($N = 9$) (Mean Rank = 5.00) showed a statistically significant difference, where $U = .000$ and $p < .001$). This means that the project production programs coded by the experimental group students who were trained with CT is very significantly better than the control group students who were trained MS-Office in Phase I.

Table 5. Analysis of the CT performance on students' projects production

EG ($N = 8$)			CG (N = 9)			Mann-Whitney U test	
Mean	*SD*	Mean Rank	*Mean*	*SD*	Mean Rank	*U*	*p* [2*(single tail)]
17.875	0.856	13.50	13.780	3.113	5.00	.000	.000*

Note: * $p < .001$

Figure 5 is an example of the execution screen output of students' works: Robot Zenbo teaches English in elementary schools - thematic teaching.

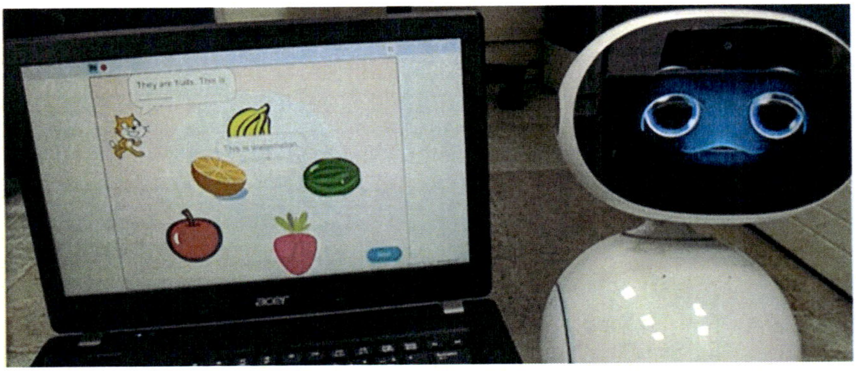

Fig. 5. Robot Zenbo teaches English in elementary schools - thematic teaching

5 Discussion and Conclusion

This paper aimed to improve university humanity students' abilities of problem-solving and information application through CT training. Brief conclusions that reflect two research questions are made as the following:

1. Compared with the traditional computer introduction course MS-Office training, the humanities students can indeed improve their problem-solving ability after receiving CT training. The difference is significant ($p < .05$).

2. Compared with the traditional computer introduction course MS-Office training, the humanities students can indeed improve their information application ability after receiving CT training. The difference is very significant ($p < .001$).

Although university humanities students are often considered to have lower problem solving ability and information application skills, this research shows their problem-solving ability and information application ability could be significantly improved through the CT training. Therefore, we would like to suggest that CT education should be considered to be added into the "Introduction to Computers" course in humanity departments, such as Department of Foreign Language and Literal, Department of Chinese Studies, Department of History, and other similar departments, in order to promote humanities students' problem solving ability in modern life.

In addition to the experimental results, we also collected feedback from students participating in the experimental courses. Students' feedback combined with the experimental results are useful for our future related research, experimental methods, and improvement of teaching materials.

Since the number of students in the experiment is small, it is easy to be suspicious to extend the results obtained to a larger scope. Therefore, it is recommended that the number of samples in the experiment should be expanded as much as possible to obtain more representative data when conducting related research in the future.

Most of the participants found that the CT training and topic production were moderately difficult and interesting, and they had done exercises, and felt a sense of accomplishment. A few students felt that the content of the textbook was a bit complicated and the teaching process was a bit stressful. We will make appropriate adjustments to the teaching materials based on the opinions of students, and hope that in the future, it can be provided to interested teachers of computer courses in the humanities department to meet the needs of most humanities students.

References

1. Wing, J.M.: Computational thinking. Commun. ACM **49**(3), 33–35 (2006)
2. Wing, J.M.: Computational thinking and thinking about computing. Philos. Trans. R. Soc. A Math. Phys. Eng. Sci. **366**(1881), 3717–3725 (2008)
3. Aho, A.V.: Computation and computational thinking. Comput. J. **55**(7), 832–835 (2012)
4. Barr, V., Stephenson, C.: Bringing computational thinking to K-12: what is Involved and what is the role of the computer science education community? ACM Inroads **2**(1), 48–54 (2011)
5. Sengupta, P., Kinnebrew, J.S., Basu, S., Biswas, G., Clark, D.: Integrating computational thinking with K-12 science education using agent-based computation: a theoretical framework. Educ. Inf. Technol. **18**(2), 351–380 (2013)
6. Korkmaz, O., Çakir, R., Ozden, M.Y.: A validity and reliability study of the computational thinking scales (CTS). Comput. Hum. Behav. **72**, 558–569 (2017)
7. Selby, C., Woollard, J.: Computational thinking: the developing definitions. In: 45th ACM Technical Symposium Proceedings on Computer Science Education. ACM, Canterbury (2013)
8. Zhang, L., Nouri, J.: A systematic review of learning computational thinking through Scratch in K-9. Comput. Educ. **141**, 103607 (2019)

9. Google Computational Thinking for Educators. https://computationalthinkingcourse.withgoogle.com. Accessed 10 Sept 2021
10. Bitesize Introduction to computational thinking. https://www.bbc.co.uk/bitesize/guides/zp92mp3/revision/1. Accessed 10 Sept 2021
11. Taiwan MOE Computational thinking in Taiwan. http://compthinking.csie.ntnu.edu.tw/. Accessed 10 Sept 2021
12. Computational thinking for K12. https://ctfork12.ice.ntnu.edu.tw/conception.html. Accessed 10 Sept 2021
13. Román-González, M., Pérez-González, J.C., Jiménez-Fernández, C.: Which cognitive abilities underlie computational thinking? Criterion validity of the computational thinking test. Comput. Hum. Behav. **72**, 678–691 (2017)
14. Tukey, J.W.: Exploratory Data Analysis. Addison Wesley, MA (1977)

The Development of a Computational Thinking Learning Package that Integrates a Learning Experience Design for Grade K

Chinnaphat Junruang[1], Issara Kanjug[2](✉), and Charuni Samat[2]

[1] Khon Kaen University Demonstration School, Faculty of Education, Khon Kaen University, Khon Kaen, Thailand

[2] Department of Educational Technology, Faculty of Education, Khon Kaen University, Khon Kaen, Thailand

issaraka@kku.ac.th

Abstract. Computational thinking is the one important skill of 21 century it means a structured and proven method designed to identify problems regardless of age or computer literacy level. The purpose of this research was to study the learner's preference learning experience about the characteristics of the elements of the learning Package material and to develop the Computational Thinking Learning Package Integrated Learning Experiences Design for Kindergarten Education. The research participants were 40 kindergarten academic year 2020 students of Demonstration school of Khon Kaen University and 3 experts to evaluate the learning package. Experimental research was employed in this study. The instruments used in the experiment were Computational Thinking Learning Package. Data collection used the learner's preference about the characteristics of the elements of the learning Package materials and the quality of Computational Thinking Learning Package. The results revealed that: the utilization of learning Experience about the learner's preference and designing Computational Thinking Learning Package Integrated Learning Experiences Design for Kindergarten Education and there were 6 elements as follows 1) Problem base 2) Resources 3) Collaboration tools 4) Scaffolding 5) Coaching 6) Computational thinking game. The result of the learning package revealed that elements and function were appropriate in 3 aspects follows as contents, media, and design.

Keywords: Learning experiences design · Learning environment · Computational thinking · Learning innovation · Kindergarten education

1 Introduction

The advancement of various technologies that have evolved by leaps and bounds in today's world has resulted in Work systems and technologies have been developed to facilitate and support many aspects of human work. If the work system or technology is able to think rationally, make decisions and learn by itself. Will lead to the application of various solutions which will be very useful to humans these are Challenging human

© Springer Nature Switzerland AG 2021
Y.-M. Huang et al. (Eds.): ICITL 2021, LNCS 13117, pp. 144–151, 2021.
https://doi.org/10.1007/978-3-030-91540-7_16

thinking in creating "smartness" for technology. The idea of creating a brain or artificial intelligence as intelligent as humans causing a branch of science computer science called "Artificial Intelligence (AI)", so to be able to exist in a dynamic world and is constantly changing is computational thinking Computational Thinking [1], which is a thinking ability that should be cultivated in the citizens of the country. This is because it is a fundamental ability that every citizen should have in order to effectively solve complex problems [2]. Therefore, it is necessary to cultivate computational thinking from the kindergarten level in order to prepare according to the theory of age-related development. To the next complex step. to create new researchers and innovators of the country in the future and current system Education around the world attaches great importance to the teaching and learning of Computing Science, which consists of Computer Science, Information and Communication Technology (ICT) and Digital Literacy for learning about Computer Science in the kindergarten level have to focus on 2 parts: Part 1 Using Thinking computational (Computational thinking) [1, 3] to solve problems like It is procedural and systematic. which consists of Breaking down a big problem into problems/sub-tasks (Decomposition), considering patterns of problems or methods of solving problems (Pattern recognition), considering the essence of the problem (Abstraction), and designing algorithms (Algorithms), and part 2, programming (Programing) with an emphasis on Write code without a computer. The child is going to encounter problems in their everyday life, and they're eventually going to have to learn how to solve them on their own. These problems can be simple – like learning how to brush their teeth – or slightly more complex, such as what to do when they're injured or scared. Being able to navigate complex information by recognizing it and breaking it down into more manageable data is an essential skill that complements further technological and practical processes. It's not an exaggeration when we say that computational thinking can serve as the foundation for most skills, abilities, and subject matter. The name alone links CT to Computer Science courses like coding, information theory, software development and testing, and IT infrastructure. But computational thinking is more than just technology and the internet. Computational thinking is a mindset that encourages children to scrutinize a problem and intentionally build a solution for it. This is a general problem solving that can be integrated with other fields like Mathematics, Science, and Communication [18]. Learning environment Package Is a new context in teaching design in which designers have to create situations or important events for learners with evaluation By allowing students to interact with various sources of knowledge In a variety of ways In which the learners are actively involved in the learning process And the new trend of learning theories that give more importance to learning than teaching is constructivist, Therefore, the principles of environmental design in learning are based on constructivist concepts [4, 5]. As basic principles in design to promote computational thinking in conjunction with Learner experience design is an emerging approach to learning design that uses methods borrowed from related design disciplines such as user experience design and service design thinking. User experience design can be described as the design of a user's perceptions and responses to their interaction with an object, product, service, or system through an interface [6]. Service design is aimed at providing a holistic experience to a user as they interact with the organization and combines design, management, and process engineering [7]. From this one could conclude that service design is a subset of user experience design. However, in practice, user experience design is often associated with product design while service design is associated with the design of organizational services. In learning design particularly for learning package solutions, learning designers often need to orchestrate the design for products (such as learning resources), systems (such as a course shell in a learning management system), and services (such as timely feedback or discussion facilitation). "Experience is not about good industrial design, multi-touch, or fancy interfaces. It is about transcending the material. It is about creating an experience through a device" [8]. Learner experience design aims to create the opportunity for a good learning experience proposed learning design solutions and setting up feedback mechanisms. Therefore, the principles of the constructivist learning environment in accordance with the Learning Experiences Design are used as the basis for the Learning Pack-age design to promote computational thinking. For students in kindergarten.

2 Purpose

To study the learner's preference learning experience about the characteristics of the elements of the learning Package material and to develop the Computational Thinking Learning Package Integrated Learning Experiences Design for Kindergarten Education.

3 Methodology

3.1 Research Participants

There were 3 experts for evaluation the quality of the Computational Thinking Learning Package in 3 domains, contents, media, and instructional design. There were 40 students in kindergarten level 2, Demonstration School, Khon Kaen University. Kindergarten Department That are currently studying in the first semester, academic year 2020. For explore the elements of learning materials using learning experience design. The sample was chosen by Purposive Sampling.

3.2 Research Instruments

For designing integrated learning experiences design for Kindergarten Education were used the learner's preference about the characteristics of the elements of the learning Package material a questionnaire form. For evaluation of Computational Thinking Learning Package Integrated Learning Experiences Design for Kindergarten Education was used the model evaluation form to evaluate the quality in 3 domains as follows: content, instructional design, and media.

3.3 Data Collection and Analysis

The elements of designing integrated learning experiences design for Kindergarten Education were collected by 40 students and were analyzed by using summarization, interpretation description. And evaluation of Computational Thinking Learning Package Integrated Learning Experiences Design for Kindergarten Education were collected by 3 experts and were analyzed by using summarization, interpretation description.

4 Results

4.1 Learning Experience About the learner's Preference

After applying questionnaire form learner's preference about the characteristics of the elements of the learning Package material. the results of the learner's preference about the characteristics of the elements of the learning Package material were analysis using Average and S.D. is listed in Table 1. As shown in Table 1, The learner's preference about the characteristics of the elements of the learning Package materials.

Table 1. Learner's preference about the characteristics of the elements of the learning Package materials.

No.	List assessment	Average	S.D.
1.	Active learning activities	4.78	0.42
2.	Game-based learning model	4.85	0.61
3.	Working in group work	4.50	0.37
4.	Video learning media	4.88	0.34
5.	Challenging learning missions	4.69	0.47
6.	Using digital technology devices	4.78	0.31
7.	The learning mission is competitive	4.70	0.41
8.	Meaningful activities available in daily life	4.76	0.48
9.	Clear scoring point	4.49	0.29
10.	Activities are beautiful and fun	4.84	0.31

According to Table 1, Learners' preferences regarding the nature of the elements of the learning package. From the analysis and summary of the data We have used the evaluation items to create the composition of the Computational Thinking Learning Package.

4.2 Development of the Computational Thinking Learning Package Integrated Learning Experiences Design

Computational Thinking Learning Package Integrated Learning Experiences Design was produced based on the designing framework comprised of 6 components [9] as follows: (1) Problem base, (2) Resources, (3) Collaboration, (4) Computational thinking game, (5) Scaffolding, and (6) Coaching obtaining as description of each key element is shown in Table 2.

Table 2. The key elements and descriptions learning environment

Key elements	Description
1. Problem base & learning task	It was shown Problem base for enhancing the learners to construct knowledge and computational thinking learning tasks [10, 11]
2. Resources	It was shown Resources to provide just-in-time information to help learners comprehend and solve the problem [12, 13]
3. Collaboration	It was shown Collaboration for supporting the learners to share their experience with experts by using Facebook and Google Classroom for expanding their multiple perspectives [14]
4. Computational thinking game	It was shown Computational thinking game centre for enhancing Computational thinking [1]
5. Scaffolding	It was shown Scaffolding for enhancing students to solve problems, to learn and construct the knowledge by themselves [15]
6. Coaching	It was shown Coaching by teachers and experts in learning content with computer principles with best practice [16]

The constructivist learning environment based on universal design for learning to develop computational thinking was produced based on the designing framework, as shown in Fig. 1, 2, 3, 4 and 5.

(A) (B)

Fig. 1. (A) (B) The box of computational thinking learning package integrated learning experiences design for kindergarten education.

4.3 The Quality of the Computational Thinking Learning Package Integrated Learning Experiences Design

The quality of the Computational Thinking Learning Package Integrated Learning Experiences Design for Kindergarten Education were evaluated by 3 experts in 3 domain as follow: learning content, media, and instructional design. The results revealed that in Table 3.

(A) (B)

Fig. 2. (A) (B) Problem base center.

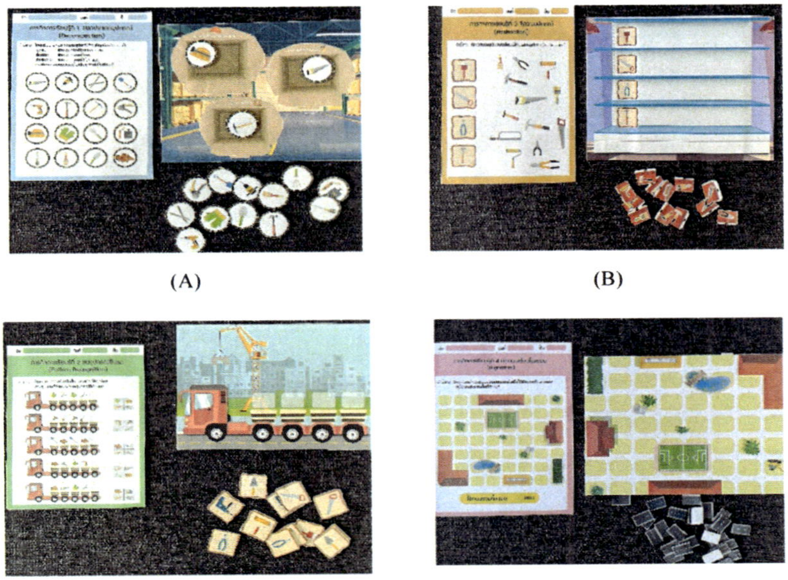

(A) (B)

(C) (D)

Fig. 3. (A) (B) (C) (D) Learning task center.

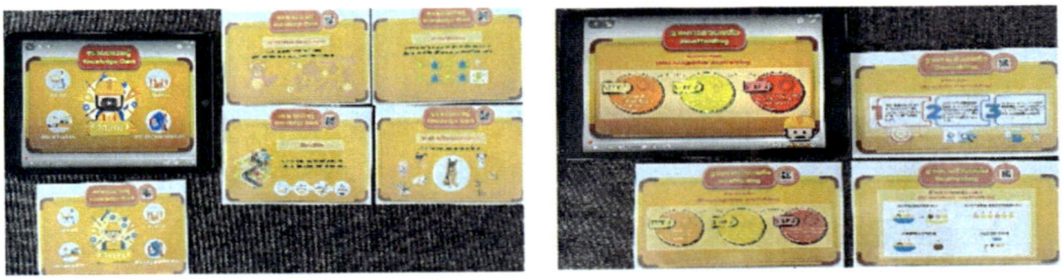

(A) (B)

Fig. 4. (A) Resources, knowledge bank center. (B) Scaffoloding center.

Table 3. The quality of computational thinking learning package

No.	List assessment	Expert no. 1	Expert no. 2	Expert no. 3
1	Learning content			
	1.1 Appropriate learning content	+1	+1	+1
2	Media			
	2.1 Appropriate navigation icon	+1	+1	+1
	2.2 Appropriate composition art	+1	+1	+1
	2.3 Appropriate images and animation	+1	+1	+1
	2.4 Stability	+1	+1	+1
3	Instructional design			
	3.1 Simulation problem base	+1	+1	+1
	3.2 Resource center/Knowledge bank	+1	+1	+1
	3.3 Collaboration center	+1	+1	+1
	3.4 Computational thinking game	+1	+1	+1
	3.5 Scaffolding center	+1	+1	+1
	3.6 Coaching center	+1	+1	+1

According to Table 3, learning content aspect, experts agreed that the content is appropriate for learners. For media aspect, experts agreed that the navigator icon, composition art, images and animations are appropriate and stability. The last aspect, instructional design, experts agreed that all components are appropriate and functional.

5 Discussion

According to the above findings, the results of this study as shown above, may cause from instructional design: ID Theory. This is the instructional designs which are based on the principles and theory. It can be showed by the quality of the Computational Thinking Learning Package Integrated Learning Experiences Design for Kindergarten Education that assessed by expert review. The quality was shown in several aspects: the content is accurate and appropriate; Media were designed to support the knowledge construction and Instructional design appropriate was based on learning theory. In addition, In designing the learning package, the principles of constructivist learning environment design were applied. together with the user (student) experience design to be appropriate and consistent with learning needs Based on the researcher's assessment questions based on observations and experiences in learning design and management [17], the results of the data analysis were used to create elements of the Learning package to promote Computational thinking for further research data collection.

References

1. Computational thinking. Commun. ACM **49**(3), 33–35. http://www.cs.cmu.edu/afs/cs/usr/wing/www/publications/Wing06.pdfMarkB. Accessed 22 Mar 2020
2. McKenna, V.B., Sixsmith, J., Barry, M.M.: The relevance of context in understanding health literacy skills: findings from a qualitative study. Health Expect. **20**, 1049–1060 (2017)
3. Phuworawan, Y.: What is computational science? The latest basic compulsory subjects for children with chapters 86 interview from the founder (2018). https://school.dek-d.com/blog/?p=656
4. Jonassen, D.H.: Designing constructivist learning environments. In: Reigeluth, C.M. (ed.) Instructional Design Theories and Models: A New Paradigm of Instructional Theory, Volume II, pp. 215–239. Lawrence Erlbaum Associates, Mahwah (1999)
5. Samat, C., Chaijaroen, S., Kanjug, I., Vongtathum, P.: Design and development of constructivist multimedia learning environment enhancing skills in computer programming. In: Proceedings - 2017 6th IIAI International Congress on Advanced Applied Informatics, IIAI-AAI 2017, Japan (2017)
6. Law, E., Roto, V., Hassenzahl, M., Vermeeren, A., Kort, J.: Understanding, scoping and defining user experience: a survey approach. In: Communication présentée à l'International Conference on Human Factors in Computing Systems, Boston, Etats-Unis, pp. 719–728 (2009)
7. Stickdorn, M., Schneider, J., Andrews, K., Lawrence, A.: This is Service Design Thinking: Basics, Tools, Cases. Wiley, Hoboken (2011)
8. Hassenzahl, M.: Experience design: technology for all the right reasons. Synth. Lect. Hum. Cent. Inform. **3**, 1–95 (2010)
9. Junruang, C., Kanjug, I.: A study of learner's computational thinking using constructivist universal design learning package for kindergarten education. In: Huang, T.-C., Wu, T.-T., Barroso, J., Sandnes, F.E., Martins, P., Huang, Y.-M. (eds.) ICITL 2020. LNCS, vol. 12555, pp. 219–226. Springer, Cham (2020). https://doi.org/10.1007/978-3-030-63885-6_25
10. Piaget, J.: The Construction of Reality in the Child. Ballantine Books (1975)
11. Brown, J., Collins, A., Duguid, P.: Situated cognition and the culture of learning. Educ. Res. **18**(1), 32–42 (1989)
12. Winn, W.: Cognitive perspectives in psychology. In: Jonassen, D.H., (eds.) Handbook of Research for Educational Communications and Technology: A Project of the Association for Educational Communications and Technology, pp. 79–112 (2004)
13. Sweller, J.: Cognitive load theory. In: Mestre, J.P., Ross, B.H. (eds.) The Psychology of Learning and Motivation: Vol. 55. The Psychology of Learning and Motivation: Cognition in Education, pp. 37–76. Elsevier Academic Press (2011)
14. Hannafin, M., Land, S.M., Oliver, K.: Open learning environments: foundations, methods, and models, instruction. In: Reigeluth, C.M. (ed.) Instructional-Design Theories and Models: A New Paradigm of Instructional Theory, vol. II. Lawrence Erlbaum Associates, NJ (1999)
15. Vygotsky, L.S.: Mind in Society: Development of Higher Psychological Processes. Harvard University Press (1978)
16. Collins, A., Brown, J.S., Holum, A.: Cognitive apprenticeship: making thinking visible. Am. Educ. **15**(3), 1–18 (1991)
17. John Martin, A., Maria Dominic, M., Sagayaraj Francis, F.: Learners classification for personalized learning experience in e-learning systems. Int. J. Adv. Comput. Sci. Appl. (IJACSA) **12**(4) (2021). https://doi.org/10.14569/IJACSA.2021.0120485
18. Computational Thinking For Kids | Why is it Important? https://codakid.com/computational-thinking/. Accessed 05 Sept 2021

Development of Online Learning to Enhancing Computational Thinking for High School Students

Non Jarungsiraway[1], Nutthakarn Moeikao[1], Issara Kanjug[2](✉), and Charuni Samat[2]

[1] Demonstration School, Faculty of Education, Khon Kaen University, Khon Kaen, Thailand
[2] Educational Technology, Faculty of Education, Khon Kaen University, Khon Kaen, Thailand
issaraka@kku.ac.th

Abstract. This research proposes to Develop the Online Learning to Enhancing Computational Thinking. The research design is model research about Model validation composed. The results collected both in quantitative and qualitative data. The data are analyzed and summarized by synthesizing the protocol, interpretating summaries and descriptive statistics. The outcomes of the study proved that 1) the model has validity in the learning contents, the media, and the design of the model. The model holds all six components whose quality is consistent with the synthesis of a theoretical framework and conceptual framework for designing and developing the online learning environments model. 2) the validity of this model is confirmed by the impact of the learning paradigm on students. The computational thinking shows that the students were able to create knowledge representation and understanding the programming. The students' opinion towards Online Learning showed that the learning contents, the media, and the design are suitable and supported to enhance the Computational Thinking.

Keywords: Online learning · Computational thinking · Learning environments · Computer · Programming

1 Introduction

Nowadays, the world is changing and changing fast. One of the most considerable changes that have affected everyday life is technology. The other change which is resulted from technology is in the fields of education. Technology has created fantastic innovation and resources in education, improving the pattern of teaching and learning. There have many factors affecting learning and teaching management, such as school activities, transportation, safety, environment, or academic competitions, especially on the internet, which is growing by leaps and bounds. This benefit of technology is useful to apply in education. Therefore, online learning is developed to improve the quality of education. The development of digital technology influenced to learning behavior of people in the present has many changed. Many academic institutions have modified teaching methods that focus on learning, which students can apply. This teaching method has the integration of different disciplines. Learners are searching for flexible learning

© Springer Nature Switzerland AG 2021
Y.-M. Huang et al. (Eds.): ICITL 2021, LNCS 13117, pp. 152–160, 2021.
https://doi.org/10.1007/978-3-030-91540-7_17

styles and innovations to respond to the needs of learners quickly and appropriately. In the 21st-century, the knowledge of the world developed and became a dynamic evolution of knowledge. Digital technology is a tool of the era that allows people to access knowledge, other experiences, and practices on the network instantly. The needed learning outcomes of learners in this century consist of thinking skills, cognitive skills, digital literacy, technology skills, and modern life-career skills.

Education in the digital era is not only preparing and educating, but also improving the learner's moral values. This concept can describe as, besides giving knowledge, the learners should have morality and be able to live with others as well. The skills comprise analytical thinking and learning dispositions that have been placed as being required for success in 21st-century society and workplaces. Therefore, education reform is needed in Thai learners, especially in curriculum and Instruction. Currently, the Ministry of Education is updating the curriculum to be used in the academic year 2018, from previously studying eight subject groups to learn in some subjected as same as the past. The curriculum's content will depend on the knowledge in the modern world, focusing and deep on the essential topics. This situation may affect to create new subjects such as Computing which will be learning about programs which are controlling the operation of machinery. These subjects will enhance the learners' ability to innovate, keep up with technology, and increase the knowledge of engineering and new science. Finally, the learners can apply this knowledge to establish innovation in the age of Creative and Innovation technology, focusing on creating Thai students can think by themselves.

From the literature reviews, the principle of online learning environments designing is focusing on learners. The learners create the knowledge by themselves from the environment which set up from the instructor. The principle of constructivist learning environments presents the learning content that is comprehensive and sufficient to solve problems. This content presentation has the order in a sequence and summarizing it into the essences. This principle helps to design the structure of learning environments on the network, which is easily accessed to resources. Accordingly, the attribution of constructivist learning environments enhances learners to create knowledge representatives as a mental model. The mental model defines the simple representation of knowledge created by learners during studying in the content. The model can be presented in an image or sign that supports the learners in understanding. The learners create the mental model from the interaction between their experience and new knowledge from various resources [2]. The characteristics of constructivist learning environments help create knowledge and enhance the mental model of learners. The mental model and programming from various problem bases in Subject 237216 Constructivism is used to integrate with technology and innovation or media to enhance the efficacy of learning and give students the skills to create knowledge [2].

The problems of learning and teaching Computer science in many schools are that the computer teacher has not enough knowledge in the field or did not complete all computer science pure major requirements. Secondly, the topics in the subject are not standard because the content is set depending on the competition program trend. Thirdly, students did not learn programming throughout the curriculum in some schools. Fourthly, due to the Ministry of Education's announcement, Computing science, which focuses on programming, is included in Basis Education Core Curriculum 2008 [5] in every school. Thus, the researcher is interested in using online learning environments to develop the instructional model. The online learning environments focus on developing students' ideas and collaboration, which design by using three theories i.e., Philosophy of Education (epistemology and social constructivism), Educational Psychology (behavioral, cognitive, social-psychological, and non-cognitive) and Educational Technology. In the expectation that the use of online learning environments for programming will affect the cognitive process of learners related to learning in the digital age and 21st-century skill.

For these reasons, the researcher is aware of the importance and need to develop the Online Learning for Enhancing Computational Thinking using the Theoretical framework. The information about many theories and previous studies of computational thinking is applied to design and develop the online learning. This media focuses on the learners to study the content with programming, mainly in the cognitive process. The outcomes from this study lead to the development of the learners' quality of programming and continuous self-development at every stage in life [3].

Therefore, the principles of constructivist learning environment in accordance with the Learning Experiences Design are used as the basis for the Online Learning to Enhance computational thinking [1]. For students in High School Students.

2 Purpose

Study the learners perceive about the characteristics of the elements of the Online Learning and to develop the Online Learning to Enhancing Computational Thinking for High School Students.

3 Methodology

3.1 Research Participants

1. The target group for evaluation the quality of the Online Learning in 3 domains, contents, media, and instructional design was 3 experts.
2. The target group was 35 students who were studying in the Demonstration School of Khon Kaen University, Thailand. The students were specifically selected from High School Students in the first semester of the academic year 2020. The selection of students was purposive sampling which had no significant differences between students' proficiency.

3.2 Research Instruments

The instruments which were used in the study was Online Learning. The process of design and development included 1) studying the principles Computational Thinking, and knowledge construction. 2) studying learning management system of learner, teacher, and curriculum. 3) synthesizing of theoretical framework which comprised of included psychology of learning, context, technology, computational thinking, and pedagogy by using the principles and theoretical and context. 4) synthesizing the designing framework by using theoretical framework 5) synthesizing the component of the Online Learning which were problem base, resource, scaffolding, cognitive tool, collaboration, and coaching from designing framework 6) designing and developing the Online Learning extracted from the previous data and 7) evaluating the efficacy of the Online Learning from contexts, media and model designing.

3.3 Data Collection and Analysis

1. The data was collected inspecting the quality of the model. The Online Learning was evaluated by using the survey from the experts in 3 fields which were content, media, and model designing. The results of the study showed that the quality of six components were qualified according to the quality of the synthesis of the theoretical framework and the framework of the basis for the design and development of the learning environment model on the network.
2. The data was collected using the Online Learning as a tool in this study. The model which was modified were utilized in lesson which learners studied by using the Online Learning as a tool to study the learners perceive. The learning opinions from the Online Learning were also examined in this part. The process of the study could be described as shown in Table 1:

Table 1. The process of using the online learning.

Online Learning	Learning Process	Activities
Online Pre-class (Self-Learning)	- Learning process though Online Learning by themselves. - Students perform tasks in accordance with the learning situation on the Online Learning. - Teachers, coaches via zoom meeting and answers questions via inbox Facebook.	 
Online During-Class	- Live teachers teach online via Zoom Meeting. - Presenting a critical example of the mission submitted in the Online Learning. - Reflection + Summary.	 
Online Post Class	- Teachers follow the online summary. - Students review knowledge. - Students reflect knowledge by sharing their mission in the Online Learning.	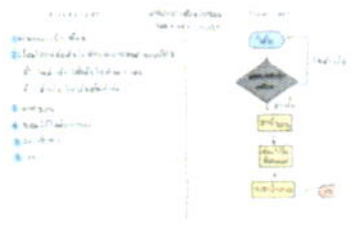

The process of using Online Learning was shown in Table 1. The student priorly studied by themselves through the Online Learning before going to the online class. Then the students and teacher perform the activity in the class together in the activity who practice problem, join discussion, and summarize the activity which they learned together. After the activity, the teacher and student summarized and shared the knowledge which the students have learned independently with the Online Learning using the Zoom Meeting.

3. The elements of designing were collected by 35 students and were analyzed by using summarization, interpretation description. And evaluation of Online Learning was collected by 3 experts and were analyzed by using summarization, interpretation description. And processed shown in Fig. 1

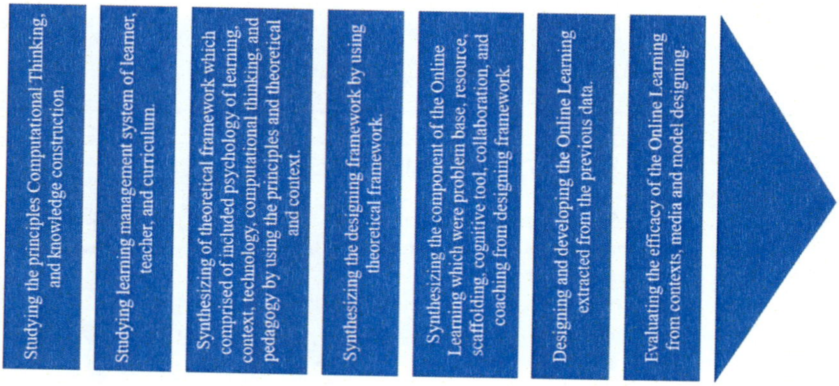

Fig. 1. Data collection process

4 Results

4.1 Development of the Online Learning to Enhancing Computational Thinking

Online Learning to Enhancing Computational Thinking Design was produced based on the designing framework comprised of 6 components as follows: (1) Problem Base, (2) Resource, (3) Scaffolding, (4) Cognitive tool, (5) Collaboration, and (6) Coaching obtaining as description of each key element is shown in Table 2.

Table 2. The key elements and descriptions learning environment.

Elements	Description
1. Problem base	Problem base could boost the learners' involvement in a situation resulting in initiative solution. The involvement occurred during learning process could be applied to real-world problems. Moreover, it was predictable that the students would be able to develop a broader knowledge and more learning framework. (Fig. 2)
2. Resources	The resource and the illustration which were systematically organized and were divided into distinctive categories promoted ease of access and search. Furthermore, they had different contents which contributed to a variety of ideas to solve problems. (Fig. 5 A)
3. Cognitive tools	Cognitive tools supported the learners in selecting the tool during learning and/or doing the mission to acquire additional knowledge. (Fig. 5 B)
4. Collaboration	Collaboration was considered as supporting the exchange of knowledge and co-working which students could discuss via chat room (Fig. 6 A)
5. Scaffolding	Scaffolding can stimulate the learners to solve the problem. (Fig. 7 A, B)
6. Coaching	Coaching was used to support, help, and advise the learners besides it could assist the communication between teachers and learners in seeking and finding various answers. These findings confirmed that the environment learning which was designed by using constructivist theory significantly encourage, support, enhance, and help build the student's knowledge of computational thinking [1]. (Fig. 6 B)

The constructivist Online Learning based on universal design for learning to develop computational thinking was produced based on the designing framework, as shown in Figs. 2, 3, 4, 5, 6, and 7.

(A) (B)

Fig. 2. (A) (B) The online learning to enhancing computational.

(A) (B)

Fig. 3. (A) (B) Problem base.

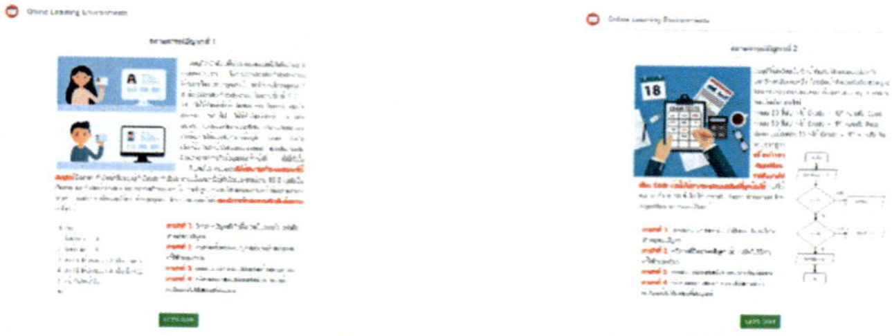

(A) (B)

Fig. 4. (A) (B) Learning task.

(A) (B)

Fig. 5. (A) Resources. (B) Cognitive tools.

(A) (B)

Fig. 6. (A) Collaboration. (B) Coaching.

(A) (B)

Fig. 7. (A) (B) Scaffloding.

4.2 The Quality of the Online Learning to Enhancing Computational Thinking

The quality of the Online Learning to Enhancing Computational Thinking was evaluated by 3 experts in 3 domains as follow: learning content, media, and Model design. The results revealed that in Table 3.

Table 3. The quality of online learning

No.	List assessment	Expert no. 1	Expert no. 2	Expert no. 3
1	Learning content			
	1.1 Appropriate learning content	+1	+1	+1
	1.2 Appropriate realistic context	+1	+1	+1
2	Media			
	2.1 Appropriate navigation icon	+1	+1	+1
	2.2 Appropriate composition art	+1	+1	+1
	2.3 Appropriate images and animation	+1	+1	+1
	2.4 Flexibility	+1	+1	+1
3	Model design			
	3.1 Problem base	+1	+1	+1
	3.2 Resource	+1	+1	+1
	3.3 Collaboration	+1	+1	+1
	3.4 Cognitive Tools	+1	+1	+1
	3.5 Scaffolding	+1	+1	+1
	3.6 Coaching	+1	+1	+1

According to Table 3, learning content aspect, experts agreed that the content is appropriate for learners. For media aspect, experts agreed that the navigator icon, composition art, images and animations are appropriate and stability. The last aspect, instructional design, experts agreed that all components are appropriate and functional.

5 Discussion and Future Work

The result of validation showed that the six components of Online Learning have the consistency according to the synthesis of a theoretical framework and conceptual framework for designing and developing the Online Learning on the network. Due to the result of the evaluation, the online learning had validity. From these internal results showed that internal validity of theoretical framework, designing framework and learning environment was consistent with the previous research [7].

The results of the validation from the evaluation of the experts in media and model design found that the Online Learning had the quality in every component of the model and were consistent with the theoretical framework and conceptual framework for designing and developing the online learning environments model.

References

1. D.: Development of computational thinking skills through unplugged activities in primary school. In: Proceedings of the 12th Workshop on Primary and Secondary Computing Education, pp. 65–72 (2017)
2. Chaijaroen, S.: Instructional Design: Principles and Theories to Practices. Anna Offset, Khon Kean (2014)
3. Jonassen, D.: Learning with Technology: A Constructivist Perspective. Prentice-Hall, Toronto (1999)
4. Moeikao, N., Samat, C.: Synthesis of designing framework for constructivist learning environments model to enhancing programming problem solving for connecting internet of thing devices. In: Wu, T.-T., Huang, Y.-M., Shadieva, R., Lin, L., Starčič, A.I. (eds.) ICITL 2018. LNCS, vol. 11003, pp. 253–260. Springer, Cham (2018). https://doi.org/10.1007/978-3-319-99737-7_26
5. Richey, R.C., Klein, J.: Design and Developmental Research. Lawrence, New Jersey (2007)
6. Maneeratana, A.S., Chaijaroen, S.: Designing framework of constructivist web-based learning environments model to enhance scientific thinking for secondary students. In: Huang, T.C., Wu, T.T., Barroso, J., Sandnes, F.E., Martins, P., Huang, Y.M. (eds.) ICITL 2020. LNCS, vol. 12555, pp. 391–398. Springer, Cham (2020). https://doi.org/10.1007/978-3-030-63885-6_44
7. Singkaew, C., Chaijaroen, S.: Development of constructivist web-based learning environment model to enhance problem-solving and transfer of learning on student in industrial: integration between pedagogy and neuroscience. In: Huang, T.C., Wu, T.T., Barroso, J., Sandnes, F.E., Martins, P., Huang, Y.M. (eds.) ICITL 2020. LNCS, vol. 12555, pp. 399–408. Springer, Cham (2019). https://doi.org/10.1007/978-3-030-63885-6_45

Exploring the Usability of Web-Based Java Compiler as a Learning Tool

Yu-Lin Jeng[1,4](✉), Sheng-Bo Huang[2,4], Chin-Feng Lai[2,4], and Andreja Istenič Starčič[3,4]

[1] Department of Information Management, Southern Taiwan University of Science and Technology, Tainan, Taiwan
jackjeng@stust.edu.tw
[2] Department of Engineering Science, National Cheng Kung University, Tainan, Taiwan
N98074037@ncku.edu.tw, cinfon@ieee.org
[3] Faculty of Education, University of Primorska, Koper, Slovenia
[4] Faculty of Electrical Engineering, University of Ljubljana, Ljubljana, Slovenia

Abstract. Computer programming learning is an important course for students to foster critical thinking and logical thinking ability. However, most students don't have enough learning ability to learn programming automatically. In this study, we developed a program assistant teaching system for students to learn program easily. We built a Web-based Java Compiler Module for students to code online. We use this learning module to collect the information during students' coding. After students test on the learning module, we invited 15 domain experts to evaluate the proposed learning system with the view of teacher/administer. The results of questionnaire survey show positive outcomes and indicate the benefit of the system for students.

Keywords: Programming learning · Java compiler · Learning feedback

1 Research Background and Purpose

With the progress and development of information technology, smart mobile devices are ubiquitous. Almost everyone has handheld devices such as smartphones and tablet computers. That is to say, the application of mobile APP has spread to people's lives, and smart mobile devices or wearable technology have become an indispensable part of people. On the other hand, the popularity of smart mobile devices has also brought a lot of convenience to people's life. Under this trend, the development and application of mobile APP have gradually become a hot topic. As a result, all walks of life are promoted to develop relevant applications, and even in teaching, some schools have integrated smart mobile devices to develop e-book systems to help students learn, so as to improve teaching effectiveness (Huang et al. 2012). This also shows the importance of program-related capabilities. Therefore, all countries in the world are investing heavily in programming education courses. The purpose is to cultivate relevant information talents to cope with the development of technology and application.

© Springer Nature Switzerland AG 2021
Y.-M. Huang et al. (Eds.): ICITL 2021, LNCS 13117, pp. 161–169, 2021.
https://doi.org/10.1007/978-3-030-91540-7_18

However, in terms of the teaching of programming, most colleges and universities nowadays focus on the teaching of the program grammar structure and the program algorithm theory, which also means that students have fewer opportunities to practice. Therefore, students lack practice-related studies in the traditional teaching environment, which also causes students to have insufficient experience in program implementation. However, programming is a professional course, with relatively high difficulty in learning (Mayer et al. 1986; Winslow 1996). Therefore, in view of the teaching of programming, the researcher noted that in the process of teaching students programming, teachers should use a step-by-step teaching method. Rahmat et al. (2012) mentioned that programming is a class capability. Therefore, Rahmat et al. (2012) suggested that students should have certain background knowledge before taking advanced courses. Students cannot obtain learning effectiveness if learning programming without certain background knowledge. On the other hand, many scholars also discussed how to effectively assist students in the development of programming capabilities in terms of the teaching of programming courses (Ahmadzadeh et al. 2005; Bancroft and Roe 2006; Tseng and Weng 2010; Michaelson 2015; Koorsse et al. 2015; Van and Webb, 2016; Kunkle and Allen 2016; Papadakis et al. 2016; Erol and Kurt 2017). However, most of the studies focused on the establishment of program concepts and algorithm theory (Kordaki et al. 2008). In other words, the teaching strategy focusing on theory was still very limited in the cultivation of programming capabilities. Therefore, how to take into account the knowledge concepts of different programming dimensions at the same time, how to effectively cultivate students' problem-solving capabilities, accumulate students' practical experience, and cultivate professional knowledge, have become important topics in the teaching of practical programming capabilities at present.

In terms of previous traditional curriculum teaching, the assessment of learning effectiveness was mostly based on test scores. However, in programming-related courses, due to its wide range of skills cultivated, other different methods were more suitable to be used to assess students' capabilities in other aspects. For example, in programming courses, the logical capabilities, thinking capabilities, and problem-solving capabilities of students should be cultivated (Schollmeyer 1996). In addition, in the process of learning programming, students would have different mistakes in learning programming due to their different knowledge backgrounds. For example, the most common situation when students write programs is that the programs cannot be executed. Thereby, students are often at a loss and feel frustrated in learning. In addition, in the process of practicing programming, students cannot recognize the debugging message displayed by the editor due to their lack of background knowledge, which not only leads to students' failure of independent completion of learning tasks but also bring frustration about learning to students. Eventually, students' learning willingness will be affected. The researcher also mentioned a similar view in this study that for beginners, programming learning is difficult because learners do not have enough background knowledge to independently identify error messages (Koorsse et al. 2015). Ahmadzadeh et al. (2005) carried out a study on the problems often encountered in programming, which collected and analyzed the program history records of 10,865 students. According to the results of this study, in terms of the most common errors made in programming by most students, 63% of students make Syntax Errors, while 46% of students make Semantic Errors, among which the most common situation is that learners fail to define variables, and only 1% of students make Lexical Errors. Therefore, in the teaching of programming, teachers can add constructive debugging methods or corrective feedback to help students learn (Bancroft and Roe 2006). The purpose is to enable students to solve problems through the feedback content in the programming environment and complete learning activities independently, so as to achieve the objective of cultivating computational thinking capabilities.

For this reason, in this study, a Web-based Java Compiler (WJC) was established. This WJC system integrated a Java programming language compiler, which was provided to students through a web interface. Compared with traditional Java teaching, the trouble of installing Java environment was reduced to lower the learning threshold. Meanwhile, by virtue of the advantages of web-based programming, the system will analyze the collected keywords of errors by collecting the program error message Log file, and then provide timely learning advice and assistance, so as to achieve adaptive teaching. Finally, in this study, the students' feedback on the Web-based Java Compiler (WJC) was assessed as the basis for the integration of the system into teaching activities in the future.

2 Literature Review

The learning process is used to explore various situations that occur during learners' learning process, which mainly refers to what happens during students' learning process, or refers to the learning process that affects the learning capabilities (Doz 1996). At present, the concept of the learning process is widely used in North America and European countries. The purpose is to enable students to record their previous learning materials anytime and anywhere, and to achieve the growth and development of learning capabilities by reflecting on the precious learning process records. Therefore, colleges and universities are actively promoting the e-learning process file at present. On the other hand, the e-learning process (or e-portfolio) is a very important tool for students, which can not only show students' learning capabilities and academic achievements, but also train students' basic information literacy capabilities, data integration capabilities, integration capabilities, logic capabilities, and the most basic writing and communication capabilities in the process of building their own learning processes. In addition, in terms of the process classification, most classifications are personal learning record data and course learning process data. Therefore, the learning process file becomes a clear context of the learning experience. Moreover, with the progress and development of information technology, the traditional learning process in the past has been gradually transferred to the online learning process platform. Nowadays, as for the common learning process platforms in colleges and universities, most of them can record students' learning process, which roughly includes the process of course taken, personnel licenses, activity participation, association participation, and learning planning. However, the contents recorded on the platform are the learning results, without special records of the behaviors in the learning process (Freire and Macedo 2013). Compared with the learning results, the behaviors of learners in the learning process are more meaningful to the teacher, mainly because the teachers can revise the teaching strategies with reference to the learners' reactions and behaviors in the course, Moreover, learners can also reflect and revise their learning strategies through the behaviors in the learning process.

Generally speaking, the learning process is mainly used to record the learning process of the actual situation, and teachers can observe the actual learning process of learners through the learning process file, including their learning achievements and methods to solve problems (Wilcox and Tomei 1999). Therefore, the learning process plays a very important role in teachers' teaching. Based on the records of the learning process, teachers can help students in learning, assist students in learning, and assess learning effectiveness. On the other hand, teachers can also make the learning process a reference for improving teaching strategies. However, with the emergence of more and more e-learning platforms, Hewitt (1995) suggested that the learning process file should include the following seven functions: (1) use for further studies, (2) use for teachers' inspection on students, (3) display of students' performance or work achievements, (4) provision of tangible evidence about students' efforts, (5)encouragement of students' target setting, (6) display of students' growth or progress, and (7) use for teachers' self-inspiration and understanding of students. On this basis, the WJC system put forward in this study would collect the relevant learning history data of learners on the platform, including the learners' use information and the historical records of program code writing. The purpose is to collect the behaviors of learners. On the one hand, teachers can refer to the data as a reference for textbook revision; on the other hand, through the presentation model for the learning process, the WJC system can provide teachers and learners with suggestions and warnings on learning, so that learners can adjust their learning methods to reduce the situation that students cannot keep up with the progress of curses or have unsatisfactory grades.

3 Research Method

Figure 1 is a system function module put forward by this study, which will continue to be developed based on the above-mentioned platform structure. In order to support students to practice Java programs on the platform, the platform will implement the function of a Web-based Java Compiler through an Open Source package. In this way, students can write Java program code through the WJC platform. Meanwhile, the history time, program code content, error messages after compilation for students' program code writing can be collected to be used for follow-up study and analysis. The diagram of the Web-based Java Compiler (WJC) is shown in Fig. 2. While this functional module is implemented, relevant modules will also be implemented to record the history of students' program code writing, including program code writing time, error message record, program history record, debugging behavior record, and program recommendation module. The records collected through these five functional models can be used as data for predicting future learning results, and can also provide teachers with visual methods for improving teaching strategies. Details are described as follows:

- Program code writing time: Generally speaking, if students use Java Integrated Development Environment (IDE) such as Android Studio or Eclipse, due to the independence of these tools, teachers are difficult to track the students' actual operation processes such as when to start writing programs, and when to press the compile button.

If the time of students' writing programs can be understood and be displayed through charts, teachers will be helped to understand the behavior analysis of students' writing programs and improve the teaching on this basis.

- Error message record: In case of an error detected during execution under a general program development environment, a Stack Trace will be printed for the developer to debug the program. Stack Trace means that a series of program Methods called by the application in the process of error will be printed, but such a message is still too complicated for students or beginners. The Web-based Java Compiler implemented in this study can provide real-time monitoring Log recorded by the backend server, and make further collection and analysis to identify compilation error types and runtime error types through simple string filtering and comparison methods. In addition to knowing their current error types, students can also link program errors with error types, and also return the error information to the back-end server, so that the back-end server can recommend useful debugging information to students through error messages.
- Program history record: For a program project or operation, the problem-solving processes of students in view of their known problems, are helpful to the cultivation of students' computational thinking capabilities, which are also important for teachers. The Web-based Java Compiler (WJC) developed in this study can record the program code, sequence, correct times, and error times of students' program code writing. This information is very useful for this study to recommend materials, analyze students' capabilities and predict learning results.
- Debugging behavior record: In case of a program error, for beginners, the most difficult thing is to identify the correct debugging direction, which usually comes from the aforementioned Stack Trace. The Web-based Java Compiler (WJC) developed in this study is expected to be able to parse the Stack Trace and analyze the suitable keywords. On the one hand, the system provides the keywords of error types to students to search for answers on the Internet by themselves and enables students to understand the program error and which keywords can be used to search for relevant network resources. The process of students from making mistakes to writing the correct program code can be recorded by the module so that the system or teachers can know the students' debugging behavior record, and help students solve the program problems encountered by cooperating with the program recommendation module.
- Program recommendation module: Through the aforementioned modules, the system can filter out the messages of students when program errors occur. These messages can help students further solve problems by searching or asking their peers. However, students may not know how to debug when they see too many error messages. This module can provide assistance. For example, Fig. 3 is a common run-time error. A content that exceeds the array index is to be printed by the program, so an error will occur during program code execution. Therefore, in the Stack Trace, an error message for the array index exceeding prompted by Java is listed, namely ArrayIndexOutOfBoundsException. Therefore, the Web-based Java Compiler (WJC) implemented in this study can identify suitable keywords of errors through string comparison and filtering, so that students will not be overwhelmed by such a long series of error messages.

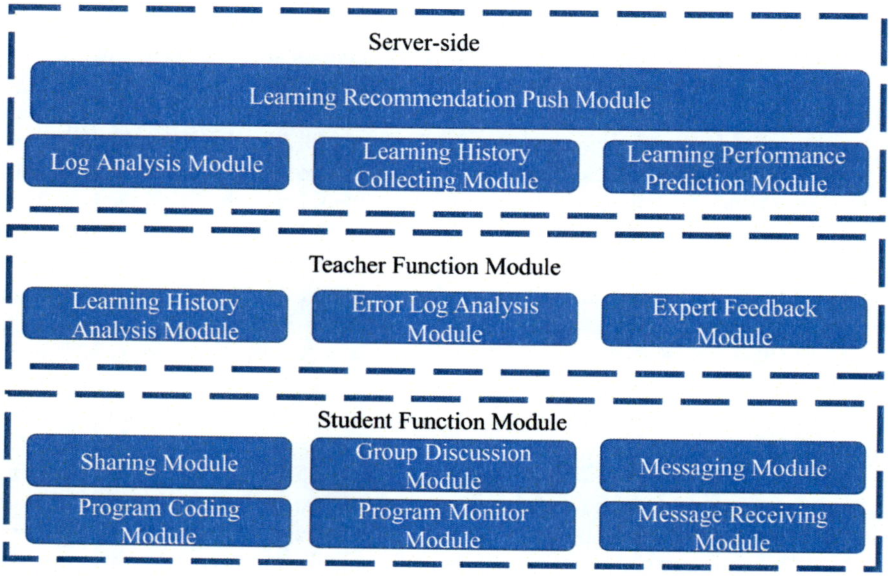

Fig. 1. System function modules

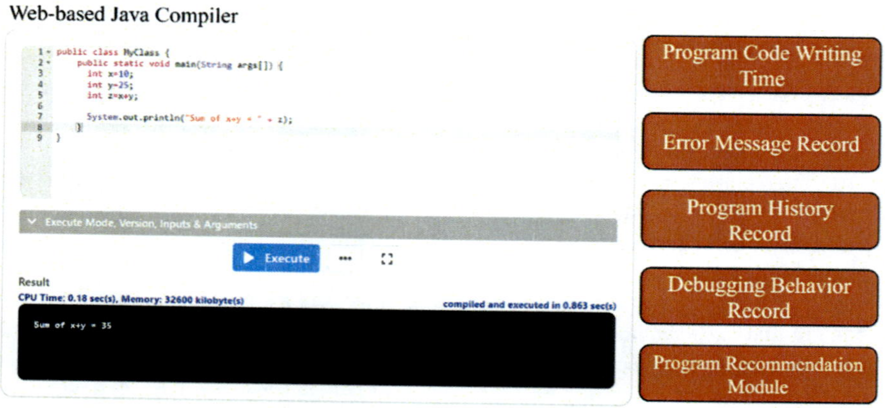

Fig. 2. Web-based Java compiler layout

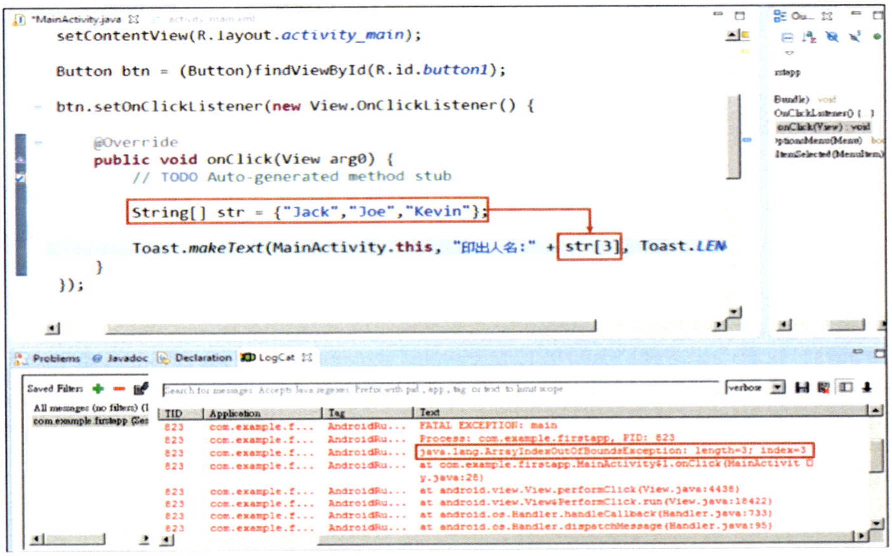

Fig. 3. Common run-time error sample

4 Evaluation and Discussion

In order to explore the usability and the effectiveness of the proposed five modules in WJC, we invite several experts to evaluate the system by replying questionnaires. A total of 15 experts who have strong programming teaching experience and professional in the area of e-learning research were invited to participate in the experimental assessment. The response portion of each question in the questionnaire was designed using a 5-point Likert scale. Typically, an item in a Likert scale is given as a statement and the invited experts need to respond the statement using a scale from 1 to 5, in which 5 stands for "strongly agree" and 1 stands for "strongly disagree". The 5 level responses also stand for the score of each question thus we can calculate the mean value of each item. The questionnaire item and statement includes:

1. Program code writing time module is important to students.
2. Error message record module is important to students.
3. Program history record module is important to students.
4. Debugging behavior record module is important to students.
5. Program recommendation module module is important to students.

The responses data from experts were collected from online questionnaire system and it can be further analyzed and discussed. The statistical results were presented in Table 1. The 5th column describes the percentage of each item score that are greater or equal to 4.

The statistics results show that the mean value of Item (2), (4), and (5) are higher than 4. The mean value of Item (1) and (3) are 3.667 and 3.8 separately. Therefore, the

Table 1. Questionnaire results

Item	*Mean*	Stand deviation	*Variance*	Score >= 4
1	3.667	0.471	0.222	67.00%
2	4.133	0.340	0.116	100.00%
3	3.800	0.400	0.160	80.00%
4	4.067	0.249	0.062	100.00%
5	4.467	0.499	0.249	100.00%

responses to Item (2), (4), and (5) indicates that the experts agree the proposed system modules are benefit to students' program learning. However, responses to Item (1) and (3) are relative lower than other responses. The results show that the experts don't agree program code writing time and program history record are the key factors in students' program learning.

5 Conclusions

This research proposed and implemented a programming learning system which supports web-based Java compile module. The authors developed a programming learning system for students to learn programming and to write code in web-based application. In the way, system can collect students' coding history and provide real-time support according to the history analysis results. The questionnaire survey from experts show that most proposed system modules can help the process of programming learning. However, experts don't agree program code writing time and program history record are the key factors in students' program learning. Therefore, in future work, we will evaluate the effectiveness of the proposed system modules with the view of students and to provide sufficient learning assistance information during the learning process.

Acknowledgement. The authors would like to thank the Ministry of Science and Technology of the Republic of China, Taiwan, for financially supporting this research under Contract No. MOST 110-2511-H-218-004-MY3.

References

Ahmadzadeh, M., Elliman, D., Higgins, C.: An analysis of patterns of debugging among novice computer science students. In: Proceedings of the 10th Annual SIGCSE Conference on Innovation and Technology in Computer Science Education, pp. 84–88 (2005)

Bancroft, P., Roe, P.: Program annotations: feedback for students learning to program. In: Proceedings of the 8th Australasian Conference on Computing Education, vol. 52, pp. 19–23. Citeseer (2006)

Doz, Y.L.: The evolution of cooperation in strategic alliances: initial conditions or learning processes? Strateg. Manag. J. **17**, 55–83 (1996)

Erol, O., Kurt, A.A.: The effects of teaching programming with scratch on pre-service information technology teachers' motivation and achievement. Comput. Hum. Behav. **77**, 11–18 (2017)
Hewitt, G.: A Portfolio Primer: Teaching, Collecting, and Assessing Student Writing. ERIC (1995)
Huang, Y.-M., Liang, T.-H., Su, Y.-N., Chen, N.-S.: Empowering personalized learning with an interactive e-book learning system for elementary school students. Educ. Tech. Res. Dev. **60**, 703–722 (2012)
Koorsse, M., Cilliers, C., Calitz, A.: Programming assistance tools to support the learning of IT programming in South African secondary schools. Comput. Educ. **82**, 162–178 (2015)
Kordaki, M., Miatidis, M., Kapsampelis, G.: A computer environment for beginners' learning of sorting algorithms: design and pilot evaluation. Comput. Educ. **51**, 708–723 (2008)
Kunkle, W.M., Allen, R.B.: The impact of different teaching approaches and languages on student learning of introductory programming concepts. ACM Trans. Comput. Educ. (TOCE) **16**, 1–26 (2016)
Mayer, R.E., Dyck, J.L., Vilberg, W.: Learning to program and learning to think: what's the connection? Commun. ACM **29**, 605–610 (1986)
Michaelson, G.: Teaching programming with computational and informational thinking (2015)
Papadakis, S., Kalogiannakis, M., Zaranis, N., Orfanakis, V.: Using Scratch and App Inventor for teaching introductory programming in secondary education. A case study. Int. J. Technol. Enhanc. Learn. **8**, 217–233 (2016)
Rahmat, M., et al.: Major problems in basic programming that influence student performance. Procedia Soc. Behav. Sci. **59**, 287–296 (2012)
Schollmeyer, M.: Computer programming in high school vs. college. ACM SIGCSE Bull. **28**, 378–382 (1996)
Tseng, S.-S., Weng, J.-F.: Finding trustworthy experts to help problem solving on the programming learning forum. Interact. Learn. Environ. **18**, 81–99 (2010)
Van Niekerk, J., Webb, P.: The effectiveness of brain-compatible blended learning material in the teaching of programming logic. Comput. Educ. **103**, 16–27 (2016)
Wilcox, B.L., Tomei, L.A.: Professional Portfolios for Teachers: A Guide for Learners, Experts, and Scholars [with CD-ROM]. ERIC (1999)
Winslow, L.E.: Programming pedagogy—a psychological overview. ACM Sigcse Bull. **28**, 17–22 (1996)

Young Kids' Basic Computational Thinking: An Analysis on Educational Robotics Without Computer

Pao-Nan Chou(✉) and Ru-Chu Shih

Graduate Institute of Technological and Vocational Education,
National Pingtung University of Science and Technology, Pingtung, Taiwan
pnchou@g4e.npust.edu.tw

Abstract. Educational robotics without computer was widely adopted for young kids 'computational thinking training. This study aimed to investigate how different instructional strategies influenced young children's basic computational thinking skills through two research case scenarios. A true-experimental posttest with control group was used to fulfill the research purpose. Two experiments involved 3-h educational training. 36 first graders (6-year-old) from two public elementary schools in Taiwan voluntarily participated in the study. A mouse-shape robot kit (Code & Go Robot Mouse) and a car-shape robot kit (Botley Robot) were two instructional tools in the study. Two types of instructional strategies were developed: with or without visual aid. Three levels of computational thinking challenges (Easy, medium and hard) were designed. The findings from two case scenarios yielded that different types of instructional strategies only produce different learning outcomes for a hard learning task. It was suggested that students needed visual aids to support their learning process when solving more complex computational thinking problems.

Keywords: Educational robotics · Instructional design · Computational thinking · Elementary education

1 Introduction

In recent years, our research team (Maker Education Lab in NPUST) had put an effort on using educational robotics with computer (ERC) to support elementary school students in engaging engineering design activities. For example, one previous study showed that 30 fifth graders significantly improved their electrical engineering knowledge and computational thinking skills after receiving 16-week ERC training [1]. In another prior research [2], 11 third graders demonstrated accurate engineering knowledge and obtained basic programming skills during immersing in a 5-week ERC lesson. However, even though positive learning outcomes identified in those studies, inappropriate learning behaviors, such as playing non-learning related applications (App), often appeared in learning contexts [3]. Whether or not educational robotics "without" computer (ERWC) may yield a better learning effect is worthy of further investigation.

© Springer Nature Switzerland AG 2021
Y.-M. Huang et al. (Eds.): ICITL 2021, LNCS 13117, pp. 170–180, 2021.
https://doi.org/10.1007/978-3-030-91540-7_19

ERWC was widely adopted in early childhood curriculum because some parents or instructors extremely concerned young children's eyesight. Commercial simple robots with animal or car forms, played a major role in ERWC learning activities. Although ERWC have less technology functions, the educational values were still powerful. In Lieto et al.'s study [4], 12 kindergarten kids participated in a 6-week ERWC program. The results showed that a bee-shape robot (Bee-Bot) significantly enhanced kids' visuo-spatial working memory and inhibition skills. In Sullivan and Bers' [5] study, 98 preschool children participated in a 7-week ERWC curriculum. The findings also revealed that children mastered programming concepts by using a car-shape robot (KIBO). However, pedagogy issues such as the development and application of instructional strategies were uncommon in the ERWC literature.

Based on the background information abovementioned, the purpose of the study was to investigate how different instructional strategies influenced young children's computational thinking performances through two research scenarios. In the first case scenario, a mouse-shape robot was adopted as an instructional tool. The second case scenario repeated the research procedure of the first scenario with similar robot kit. All participants were first graders at elementary schools. Specifically, the research question was:

- Did students immersing in different types of ERWC instructional strategies produce different learning outcomes?

2 Basic Computational Thinking Skills

Brennan and Resnick [6] proposed that students receiving Scratch programming training might obtain seven computational thinking skills, including sequence, loop, event, parallelism, conditional, operator, and data (see. Table 1).

Table 1. Computational thinking skills proposed by Brennan and Resnick.

Computational thinking skills	Definition
Sequence	A series of programming steps
Loop	Repetition of programming actions
Event	One programming action cause another thing to happen
Parallelism	Programming actions happening at the same time
Conditional	Decision on certain programming conditions
Operator	Programming involving mathematical expression
Data	Programming involving variables to store data

Bers [7] also proposed seven computational thinking skills for kids engaging in early coding curriculum: algorithms, modularity, control structures, representation, hardware/software, design process, and debugging. Of those skills, algorithms refer to the sequencing skill, which is similar to the sequence in Brennan and Resnick's definition.

Because the current study adopted ERWC approach, the basic robot training could not be used to evaluate those computational thinking skills discussed earlier. In addition, prior research [8] had shown that the sequence could be used to measure young children's basic computational thinking. Therefore, in the study, only sequence was considered for further analysis.

3 Research Method of the First Scenario

3.1 Research Design

A true experimental posttest with control group was used to fulfill the research question. The educational experiment lasted for two weeks. Figure 1 shows the research design of the study. Overall, after receiving the 3-h instruction, students needed to complete three computational thinking challenges (posttests).

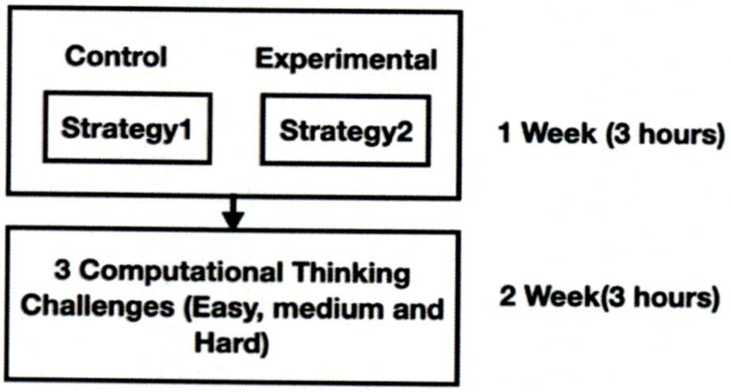

Fig. 1. The research design of the study.

3.2 Research Participant

18 first graders (male: 11; female: 7) from a public elementary school in Taiwan voluntarily participated in the study. Prior to the study, students had no experience of engaging in any ERWC learning activities. They were randomly assigned into two experimental groups (strategy 1: control group; strategy 2: experimental group). Two experimental groups had the equal number of students. Two teachers were responsible for delivering the instruction in two learning groups.

3.3 Technology Tool

A mouse-shape robot kit (Code & Go Robot Mouse) was an instructional tool in the first scenario. Green grid pieces and purple maze pieces formed different learning tasks. Students should click buttons on the mouse to control four movements: forward, backward, right turn, and left turn. A yellow cheese wedge was symbolized as a final destination on the mazes. When the robot mouse touched the cheese, a sound was produced in the mouse, which also represented that students completed the tasks. Figure 2 is a snapshot of the robot kit.

Fig. 2. Code & Go Robot Mouse.

3.4 Assessment Tool

The study adapted Bers' [9] 6-point computational thinking task scale to measure students' sequence concepts. Table 2 shows the definition of the scale.

Table 2. Definition of the scale.

Point	Definition
1	Did not complete the task
2	Very incomplete achievement of the task
3	Partially complete achievement of the task
4	Mostly complete achievement of the task
5	Complete achievement of the task

According to the complexity of the mazes, three levels of computational thinking challenges (Easy, medium and hard) were designed as the posttests in the second week of the experiment (see Table 3). Toward more hard challenges, students needed to complete more sequence tasks. Those sequence tasks were validated by two computer science teachers. During each posttest, students needed to independently complete the tasks

Table 3. Three levels of the tasks (Mouse).

Level	Sequence steps
Easy	10
Medium	20
Hard	30

within five minutes. When one student received a test, other students could not stand nearby to intervene in the testing process.

3.5 Instructional Strategy

Two instructional strategies were developed in the study:

1. Without visual aids (strategy 1: control group): After examining the mazes, students clicked the buttons on the robot mouse step-by-step. Students were not allowed to move the robot near the mazes to confirm the direction.
2. With visual aids (strategy 2: experimental group): While viewing the mazes, students put direction cards on the table to copy the maze path. Subsequently, students clicked the buttons on the robot mouse according to cards' sequences (See Fig. 3).

Fig. 3. With visual aid strategy (The first scenario).

4 Research Method of the Second Scenario

4.1 Research Design

The second scenario also adopted a true-experimental posttest with control group to investigate the research question. The research design process was the same as that in the first scenario.

4.2 Research Participant

18 first graders (male:10; female:8) from another public elementary school participated in the second research scenario. Students were randomly assigned into two groups (control:9 and experimental group:9). Different teachers led two learning groups. Prior to the study, students also had no experiences of using any programming tools.

4.3 Technology Tool

In the second research scenario, a car-shape robot kit (Botley Robot) served as an instructional tool to facilitate the instructional activities (see Fig. 4). Overall, the functions of the robot were similar to the one used in the first research scenario. However, when using Botley Robot, students needed to click the buttons (forward, backward, right turn, and left turn) on a remote controller. After receiving code messages, the robot performed the movements on the colorful cardboards, which formed different levels of learning tasks.

Fig. 4. The Botley Robot.

4.4 Assessment Tool

The assessment tool used in the second research scenario was the same as the one in the first research scenario. Three levels of computational thinking challenges were designed as the posttests. These tests were also validated by two computer science teachers (see Table 4). In the second week of the experiment, students needed to independently complete the tests within five minutes.

Table 4. Three levels of the tasks (Botley).

Level	Sequence steps
Easy	7
Medium	15
Hard	25

4.5 Instructional Strategy

Two instructional strategies adopted in the second research scenario was the same as those in the first research scenario:

1. Without visual aid (strategy 1: control group): While viewing the mazes on the cardboards, students clicked the buttons on the remote controller to input the programming codes. It was noted that students could not move the robot on the maze path to confirm the sequence.
2. With visual aid (strategy 2: experimental group): After examining the maze, students used the cards to record the sequences. Subsequently, students clicked the buttons on the remote controller by copying the cards' sequences (See Fig. 5).

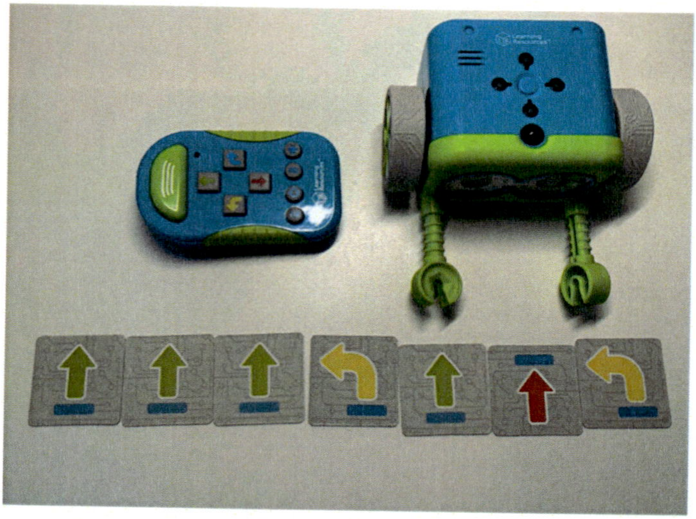

Fig. 5. With visual aid strategy (the second scenario).

5 Findings of the First Scenario

Table 5 reports the results of descriptive statistics. The findings showed that students in the experimental group performed better than students in the control group. Furthermore, regardless of the type of the groups, when students faced the hard challenges, their learning performances were lower than those in easy one.

Table 5. Results of descriptive statistics.

Test	Control Group (*M*/*SD*)	Experimental Group (*M*/*SD*)
Posttest1(easy)	3.44 (1.33)	4.33 (0.50)
Posttest2(medium)	3.56 (1.24)	4.33 (0.71)
Posttest3(hard)	3.11 (0.78)	4.22 (0.83)

Tables 6,7 and 8 summarize the results of one-way ANOVA. The findings indicated that no significant difference existed in the posttest 1 ($F = 3.51, p > 0.05$) and posttest 2 ($F = 2.69, p > 0.05$) between the control and experimental groups. However, a significant difference ($F = 8.51, p < 0.05$) was identified in the posttest 3 between the control and experimental groups.

Table 6. Results of one-way ANOVA for the first scenario (Posttest1).

Posttest1	Sum of Square	*df*	*Mean Square*	*F*	*p*
Between groups	3.56	1	3.56	3.51	0.08
Within groups	16.22	16	1.01		
Total	19.78	17			

Table 7. Results of one-way ANOVA for the first scenario (Posttest2).

Posttest2	Sum of Square	*df*	*Mean Square*	*F*	*p*
Between groups	2.72	1	2.72	2.69	0.12
Within groups	16.22	16	1.01		
Total	18.94	17			

Table 8. Results of one-way ANOVA for the first scenario (Posttest3).

Posttest3	Sum of Square	*df*	*Mean Square*	*F*	*p*
Between groups	5.56	1	5.56	8.51	0.01*
Within groups	10.44	16	0.65		
Total	16.00	17			

* $p < 0.05$

6 Findings of the Second Scenario

Table 9 shows the results of descriptive statistics. The findings indicated that students in the experimental group performed better than students in the control group. However, regardless of the type of the group, students' performances in the medium level of the test were better than those in other two tests.

Table 9. Results of descriptive statistics.

Test	Control group (*M*/*SD*)	Experimental group (*M*/*SD*)
Posttest1(easy)	3.11 (1.05)	4.00 (1.00)
Posttest2(medium)	3.67 (1.11)	4.11 (1.05)
Posttest3(hard)	3.11 (0.60)	4.00 (0.50)

Tables 10,11 and 12 summarize the results of one-way ANOVA. The findings reported that there was no significant difference in the posttest 1 ($F = 3.37, p > 0.05$) and posttest 2 ($F = 0.75, p > 0.05$) between two experimental groups. However, a significant difference ($F = 11.64$, $p < 0.01$) was shown in the posttest 3 between the control and experimental groups.

Table 10. Results of one-way ANOVA for the second scenario (Posttest1).

Posttest1	Sum of Square	*df*	*Mean Square*	*F*	*p*
Between Groups	3.56	1	3.56	3.37	0.09
Within Groups	16.89	16	1.06		
Total	20.44	17			

Table 11. Results of one-way ANOVA for the second scenario (Posttest2).

Posttest2	Sum of Square	*df*	*Mean Square*	*F*	*p*
Between Groups	0.89	1	0.89	0.75	0.40
Within Groups	18.89	16	1.18		
Total	19.78	17			

Table 12. Results of one-way ANOVA for the second scenario (Posttest3).

Posttest3	Sum of Square	*df*	*Mean Square*	*F*	*p*
Between Groups	3.56	1	3.56	11.64	0.00**
Within Groups	4.89	16	0.31		
Total	8.44	17			

* * $p < 0.01$

7 Conclusion

Although the instructional tools were different in two educational experiments, the findings from the two educational experiments confirmed that different types of instructional strategies only produced different learning outcomes for a hard learning task. One possible explanation was that students needed visual aids to support their learning process when solving higher-order thinking problems. In the lower-thinking challenges, visual aids were not necessary. However, overall, visual aids still could support student to engage in different levels of computational thinking tests. Because of the limited a sample size, the generalization of the findings of the study had a limitation. Future studies may increase sample size to verify the effect of varied instructional strategies on students' basic computational thinking skills.

References

1. Chou, P.-N.: Skill development and knowledge acquisition cultivated by maker education: evidence from Arduino-based educational robotics. EURASIA J. Math. Sci. Technol. Educ. **14**(10), em1600 (2018)
2. Chou, P.-N.: Little engineers: young children's learning patterns in an educational robotics project. Papers presented in World Engineering Education Forum, Albuquerque, NM (2018)
3. Chou, P.-N.: Using ScratchJr to foster young children's computational thinking competence: a case study in a third-grade computer class. J. Educ. Comput. Res. **58**(3), 570–595 (2020)
4. Lieto, M.C., et al.: Educational Robotics intervention on executive functions in preschool children: a pilot study. Comput. Hum. Behav. **71**, 16–23 (2017)
5. Sullivan, A., Bers, M.U.: Dancing robots: integrating art, music, and robotics in Singapore's early childhood centers. Int. J. Technol. Des. Educ. **28**(2), 325–346 (2017). https://doi.org/10.1007/s10798-017-9397-0

6. K. Brennan et al.: New frameworks for studying and assessing the development of computational thinking, Paper presented in 2002 AERA conference, Vancouver, Canada (2012)
7. Bers, M.U.: Coding as a playgroud: Programming and computational thinking in the early childhood classroom. Taylor & Francis, New York (2017)
8. Kazaoff, E.R., et al.: The effect of a classroom-based intensive robotics and programming workshop on sequencing ability in early childhood. Early Childhood Educ. J. **41**, 245–255 (2013)
9. Bers, M.U., et al.: Computational thinking and tinkering: exploration of an early childhood robotics curriculum. Comput. Educ. **72**, 145–157 (2014)

Design Framework and Model for Innovative Learning

The Validation of Constructivist Web-Based Learning Environment Model to Enhance Creativity Thinking for Undergraduate Student with Integration of Pedagogy and Neuroscience

Jetbordin Jitsopitanon[1](✉), Sumalee Chaijaroen[2], and Pornsawan Vongtathum[3]

[1] Doctor of Philosophy Student of Education Technology, Faculty of Education, Khon Kaen University, Khon Kaen, Thailand
j.jetbordin@kkumail.com

[2] Division of Education Technology, Faculty of Education, Khon Kaen University, Khon Kaen, Thailand
sumalee@kku.ac.tw

[3] Division of Computer Education, Faculty of Education, Khon Kaen University, Khon Kaen, Thailand

Abstract. This research was aimed to examine the internal and external validity of the design and development of constructivist web based-learning environment to enhance creativity thinking for undergraduate student with integration of pedagogy and neuroscience. The developmental Research Phase 2 Model Validation was employed. The sample groups consisted of 9 experts who each 3 examined the designing, media, and content, 27 students in Computer Education Program, Faculty of Education at Roi-Et Rajabhat University. The results from the model validation were revealed as follows. Firstly, the internal had 3 aspects of media, content and design models there is quality and appropriate in accordance with the theories and concepts in all elements. Secondly, for the external validation, In terms of comparing learners' creativity before and after learning with the web-based learning environment, 1) the learners had creative thinking according to Guilford principles [1] which are comprised of 4 areas: fluent thinking, flexible thinking, initiative thinking, and careful thinking. 2) The results of comparing learners' creativity before and after learning showed that the students had higher creative thinking after learning with statistical significance of .05. The results of the electroencephalogram and its occurrence position during creative thinking of the learners who used the web-based learning environment model showed the alpha waves at frequency 7–13 Hz in the frontal lope at AF3, AF4, F3, F4, F7, and F8 positions where creative thinking occurred. The results of different the academic achievement between before and after learning showed that the learners had a higher average score of academic achievement than before with statistical significance of .05.

Keywords: Constructivist · Learning environment model · Creative thinking

© Springer Nature Switzerland AG 2021
Y.-M. Huang et al. (Eds.): ICITL 2021, LNCS 13117, pp. 183–188, 2021.
https://doi.org/10.1007/978-3-030-91540-7_20

1 Introduction

At the present time, the university education focuses on teaching students who learn and develop themselves from classroom teaching from teachers. Students must learn a lot of information that changes all the time because knowledge of information technology has changed all the time the change towards an economic society based on knowledge and technology, along with epistemology that is believed that knowledge is unstable and changes all the time [9]. In addition, the constructivism was applied to this research. It focuses on building students' knowledge by way of interaction with information from various sources from the cognitive process linking the previous knowledge to the new one. Teachers can help students improve the intellectual structure by management of learning environments that enhances the students' knowledge building process by concordant merging the principle, theory and characteristic of technology media [2].

Aside from the constructivism, another key principle is promotes students tocreative. According to the context of the course "Database Systems in Database Design", the context of various organizations or the needs of users in various organizations are important, as the database can be designed to meet the needs of users. If an organization has a database and wants to improve the database system to be complete, responsive and efficient to use, the designer will have to redesign or modify the old database to improve it to meet the needs of that organization. If the designer is to design a database system in the context of the user's desire for novelty and uniqueness, originality in the design is important so that a new database that meets the needs of users can be created. It is noted that designing database systems requires knowledge and understanding with the focus on creative design to meet the needs of users in each context of the organization. Such design is consistent with the ability of creativity in 4 areas: fluency, flexibility, originality and elaboration [1].

Hence, this research aimed to develop Constructivist Web-based Learning Environment Model to Enhance Creativity Thinking for Undergraduate Student with Integration of Pedagogy and Neuroscience.

2 Research Purposes

2.1 To Study the Internal Validity of the Design Elements: Contents, Instructional Design, and Media

- The comparing learners' creativity before and after learning with the Constructivist Web-based Learning Environment Model.
- The comparing learners' creativity before and after learning.
- Electroencephalogram and its occurrence position during creative thinking.
- The comparing academic achievement between before and after learning.

3 Methodology

3.1 Research Design

The Model Research (phase 2: model Validation) [3] was employed in this study.

3.2 The Participantions

There were 3 experts for evaluation the quality of the simulation learning environment in 3 domains, contents, media, and instructional design. There were 27 students of ^{2th} years in computer education program, faculty of education at Roi-et Rajabhat university Thailand who are enrolled in the database system course of academic year 2020.

3.3 Research Instruments

For evaluation of constructivist web-based learning environment model to enhance creativity thinking for undergraduate student with integration of pedagogy and neuroscience was used the model evaluation form to evaluate the quality in 3 domains as follows: contents, instructional design, and media. For evaluation learner' creative thinking were used the learner' creativity interview form and creativity test. Emotive epoc + for electroencephalogram and its occurrence position during creative thinking of the learners who used the web-based learning environment model.

3.4 Data Collection and Analysis

Internal validation: data were collected from the experts interview to evaluate the quality of content, media and model designing. The interview combined interview questions and research questions in accordance with contexts, media and model designing from experts of measurement and assessment.

External validation was 1) to compare the creativity of students pre- and post-study with the learning environment model by conducting an interview with the students using a creative interview form. Data were analyzed by protocol analysis, summary, interpretation and description. The students' creativity was measured by data analysis using t-test dependent. 2) The students' EEG was measured at the position where it occurred while performing creative tasks. Data were analyzed by converting the time domain to the frequency domain using the fast fourier transform equation.

4 Results

4.1 The Result of Internal Validation

The result of internal validation showed that the seven components of constructivist web-based learning environment model have the consistency according to the synthesis of a theoretical framework and conceptual framework for designing and developing the constructivist web-based learning environment model. Due to the result of the evaluation, the constructivist web-based learning environment model had internal validity. From these internal results showed that internal validity of theoretical framework, designing framework and learning environment was consistent with the previous research.

4.2 The Result of External Validation Shows as Follows

According to the comparison of the students' creativity pre- and post-study with the learning environment model based on the creative thinking interview questionnaire, it was found that (1) in terms of fluency, the students were able to identify up to 8 data that should be stored in the library database system pre-study and up to 16 data post-study. Therefore, the students improved their creativity in thinking in terms of fluently post-study. (2) In terms of flexibility, the students were unable to come up with an answer in finding a relational database table structure to substitute for storing library data to achieve the goal pre-study. However, the students were unable to come up with an answer in finding a relational database table structure to substitute for storing library data to achieve the goal post-study. Therefore, the students improved their creativity in thinking in terms of flexibility post-study. (3) In terms of originality, the students had no ability to take initiative and were unable to design a new library database system to be unique pre-study. However, the students had ability to take initiative and were able to design a new library database system to be unique post-study. Therefore, the students improved their creativity in thinking in terms of originality post-study. (4) In terms of elaboration, the students were unable to improve the concept of the motorcycle rental shop database based on the existing database to be more complete pre-study. However, the students were unable to improve the concept of the motorcycle rental shop database based on the existing database to be more complete post-study. Therefore, the students improved their creativity in thinking in terms of elaboration post-study.comparative results of creative thinking obtained from the creativity assessment pre-and post-study.

Table 1. Comparison of creativity scores pre- and post-study

Group	*N*	$\overline{X}$	*S.D.*	*T*	*sig*
Pre	27	7.52	1.90	*12.20*	*.00*
Post	27	13.59	1.64		

According to Table 1, When comparing the creativity scores pre- and post-study, the pre-study score was $\overline{x} = 13.59$, S.D. = 1.64, and the post-study score was $\overline{x} = 7.52$, S.D. = 1.90. It can be concluded that the creativity scores post-study were higher that those pre-study with the statistical significance of .05.

4.3 Results of the Study of EEG and Its Position During the Students' Creative Tasks Performance

In the study of EEG and the position during the students' creative task performance following the constructivist web-based learning environment model, Even Related Potentials (ERP) was used as a stimulus that required cognitive processes in response to brain electrical signals in the form of digital signals which were then recorded into a computer with Emotiv EPOC +. The data from the time axis were converted to the frequency axis to see where and what frequency of the EEG was generated. The study found that while performing creative tasks, Alpha waves were formed in the frontal lope of the brain at the positions AF3, AF4, F3, F4, F7 and F8, which are the brain regions that control thinking, memory, intelligence, and problem solving, and creative thinking.

4.4 Students' Learning Achievement Pre- and Post-study

Table 2. Comparison of students' learning achievement pre- and post-study

Group	*N*	$\overline{X}$	*S.D.*	*T*	*sig*
Pre	27	7.63	1.90	*28.67*	*.00*
P ost	27	16.81	1.98		

According to Table 2, When comparing the students' learning achievement scores pre- and post-study, the post-study score was $\bar{x} = 16.81$, S.D. = 1.98, and the pre-study score was $\bar{x} = 7.63$, S.D. = 1.82. It can be concluded that the students' learning achievement scores post-study were higher that those pre-study with the statistical significance of .05.

5 Conclusion and Discussion

5.1 The Results of the Internal Validation

The results of the internal validation from the evaluation of the experts in media and model design found that the constructivist web-based learning environment model had the quality in every component of the model and were consistent with the theoretical framework and conceptual framework for designing and developing the constructivist web-based learning environment model.

5.2 The Results of the External Validation Are as Follows

The comparison of creative thinking pre- and post-study based on the creative thinking interview form showed that the students were more creative after learning than before because the after studying the students were able to modify, adjust and replace different functions, as well as creating novelty. In addition, they were able flexible and elaborate in improving the database. This result is consistent with the research by Jarunee Samat [4] which found that the students' creativity consisted of fluency, flexibility, originality and elaboration and that the learning environment could promote the students' creativity.

The results of comparing students' creativity before and after learning showed that the students had higher creative thinking after learning with statistical significance of .05. This is consistent with research by Sumalee Chaijaroen, Issara Kanjug and Charuni Samat [5] Jarunee Samat [4] which found that the target group in the study had higher creativity scores post-study with the statistical significance of .05.

The results of the electroencephalogram and its occurrence position during creative thinking of the students who used the web-based learning environment model showed the alpha waves at frequency 7–13 Hz in the frontal lope at AF3, AF4, F3, F4, F7, and F8 positions where creative thinking occurred. This is consistent with the research by Pornchai Duangthongsuk, Suchada Kornphetpanee and Prachya Kaewkaen [6] Saskia J., Andreas F., Marcus R. and Daniela S. [7] which studied the emergence of creativity with motivated success according to one's mind and found that the alpha waves (Alpha) were formed in the positions of AF3, AF4, F4, F7 and F8.

The results of different the academic achievement between before and after learning showed that the students had a higher average score of academic achievement than before with statistical significance of .05. This is consistent with the research by Sumalee Chaicharoen, Prama Khwaeng Muang, Prachya Kaewkaen and Jarunee Samat [8] which studied design and development of intellectual innovations that promoted information processing by integrating teaching science and neuroscience. They found that for the assessment of students' learning achievement, the Pratomsuksa 5 students of the school in the target group of 38 people had the score of $\overline{x} = 41.11$, S.D. = 2.78 post-study, which was more than pre-study $\overline{x} = 3.92$, S.D. = 2.56.

Acknowledgements. This research was supported by Ph.D. Program in Educational Technology, Faculty of Education, Khon Kaen University, and Research Group for Innovation and Cognitive Technology, Khon Kaen University which hereby giving the thankfulness all through this.

References

1. Guilford, J.P.: The Nature of Human Intelligence. McGraw-Hill Book Company, New York (1967)
2. Sumalee, C.: The learner's creative thinking learning with learning innovation to encourage human thinking. Eur. J. Soc. Sci. **28**, 213–218 (2012)
3. Richey, R.C., Klein, J.: Design and Developmental Research. Lawrence Erlbaum Associates, Hillsdale (2007)
4. Samat, C.: The development of constructivist web-based learning environment model to enhance creative thinking for higher education students. Doctor of Philosophy thesis in Education Technology, Graduate School, Khon Kaen University (2009)
5. Chaijaroen, S., Kanjug, I., Samat, C.: Learner's creative thinking learning with constructivist web-based learning environment model: integration between pedagogy and neuroscience. In: Rønningsbakk, L., Wu, T.-T., Sandnes, F.E., Huang, Y.-M. (eds.) ICITL 2019. LNCS, vol. 11937, pp. 663–671. Springer, Cham (2019). https://doi.org/10.1007/978-3-030-35343-8_70
6. Duangthongsuk, P., Kornphetpanee, S., Kaewkaen, P.: Thinking development program by stimulating the holistic nervous system for school administrators of Wittayakarn school. Research and Intellectual Science, Vol. 15, No. 1 (2017)
7. Fink, A., Schwab, D., Papousek, I.: Sensitivity of EEG upper alpha activity to cognitive and affective creativity interventions. Int. J. Psychophysiol. **82**, 233–239 (2011)
8. Chaijaroen, S., Kwanguang, P., Samat, C., Kanjug, I., Somabut, A.: The design and development of the cognitive innovation to enhance problem solving. In: The 24th International Conference on Computers in Education, India (2016)
9. Chaijaroen, S.: Instructional design: principles and theories to practices. Khon Kaen University, Department of Educational Technology (2015)

Resource Designing Framework of Constructivist Web-Based Learning Environment to Enhance the Problem-Solving for Robot Programming in Secondary Grade 3

Kriangsak Pongsuphan and Sumalee Chaijaroen(✉)

Khon Kaen University, Khon Kaen, Thailand
Kriangsak_p@kkumail.com, sumalee@kku.ac.th

Abstract. The purpose of this research is to synthesize the conceptual framework for designing learning resources in a learning environment based on Web-based of constructive Theory. To enhance the solution for robot programming in secondary grade 3. The Research is a documentary research And Survey Research. The qualitative data collection process is as follows. 1) The study of principles theories and related research. 2) The study relevant context. 3) The synthesis of theoretical and conceptual framework to design a learning environment in the learning network developed by the constructivist to enhance problem-solving of programming a robot for Students for secondary grade 3. On the basis of the Problem-solving (Jonassen 1997) with the following steps: Step 1 Problem Representation, Step 2 Search for Solutions and Step 3 Implement Solutions. This is consistent with the computer programming, (Thompson 1996a) which has the following steps. 1) Understand the problem. 2) Designing the program 3) Writing the program and 4) Looking back. The result of research is concept of design resources in a learning environment on web-based a constructivist that enhance problem solving, robot programming of consists. 1) Data bank 2) Experimental equipment 3) Robot Information Center.

Keywords: Resources · Constructivist · Problem-solving · Robot programming

1 Introduction

Teaching and learning in secondary grade 3. Emphasis on teaching students to learn and develop knowledge in the room by their teachers. Students need to learn the information a lot both the information they have changed at all. Because the knowledge of information technology is changing the progress all the time. The change to the socio-economic knowledge base and technology as well as philosophical knowledge (Epistemology). The belief that knowledge is not fixed.it can change at any time. And the theory applied in the design that corresponds to such characteristics. The Constructivist theory is focused on creating the knowledge of the students. Through interaction with information from different sources. Through the process of thinking (Cognitive Process). There is a mapping

© Springer Nature Switzerland AG 2021
Y.-M. Huang et al. (Eds.): ICITL 2021, LNCS 13117, pp. 189–195, 2021.
https://doi.org/10.1007/978-3-030-91540-7_21

between prior knowledge and new schema, then expanding the intellectual structure. There is a mapping prior knowledge to new knowledge and expanding schema. Teachers can help students adjust expand schema with the learning environment. To enhance the knowledge of the students by Integrating both theoretical principles and features of the media attribute technologies.

The reasons and importance of such. Therefore, Researcher the importance and the need to design the learning environment on web based the constructivist that enhance problem solving. Based on the development of theoretical frameworks, the principle of theory related to the cognitive theory and the theory of constructivist and the study of research related on problem solving Well-structure. To design and develop the learning environment on web-based Focus on the students to develop solutions that are problem solving well-structure. Enhancing teaching and learning management in line with 21st century learning. It responds to national research policy in creating intellectual capital and innovation. Encourage creative cooperation in society. Be Self-reliant To contribute to building the foundations of a new economic base for innovation. As well as developed in enhancing a problem solving.

The constructivist theory and important principles that enhance problem solving to learners to learn efficiently is to use the resources. The Instructional Design (ID) that allow students to take over their own learning transfer of knowledge from the teacher. Because the instructor will need to provide a learning environment to enhance problem solving about robot programming. And to facilitate the development of students. The learning environment of learning resources to enhance the problem solving of this student to create knowledge. By mapping the learner's prior knowledge and creating new knowledge from the learning task (Rachel 2002). The process to representation problems of the students. (Problem space) Find solutions to problems by searching through problem space that are cognitive processes (Jonassen 1997). So that students get the recommended strategic approach for the problem solving. And support the efforts of the learning environment with learning needs of learners (Hannafin 1999).

1.1 Problem Formulation

Students lack classification in the problem. They lack mapping to the sources of information. Lack of logical relationship they do not understand the task. They can distinguish problem from problem statement (Jonassen 1997). They lack the thought process to plan the solution. And cannot show how to solve the problem well.

1.2 The Purpose the Study

The study was designed resource learning environment on web-based constructivist to enhance Problem solving for robot programming in students Secondary grade 3.

1.3 Method

The research model in this study was a documentary research consisting of research, documents, principles and theories. Synthesis of the conceptual framework. It Show in the manner of models that mapping the relationship between theoretical principles and the elements of innovation. Designing a model of a learning environment based on constructivist Web-based that enhance problem solving. The Study related research Contextual of Problem Solving for Robot Programming and exploratory research to Used collect qualitative data.

Target Group. Target groups in the study consists of designers (Designers), developers (Developers) the assessors (Evaluators) researchers (Researchers) and students (Learners) are as follows: 1.) an expert inspection of the model include: 1) a content expert to verify the direct linear content 3 people. 2) The design professionals who use the theory as a basis (ID Theory) to examine the design and the development of the model 3 people. 3) Media experts to verify the quality of the media 3 people and 4) the expert assessment to verify the quality of the tools used to collect the data 3 people. 2.) The students secondary grade 3 in Hinlawungtor school and thairath84 of Khon Kaen Primary Educational Service Area Office 1 total 78 people and register in semester 1 of academic year 2562 To explore the context of teaching Characteristics of learners Contextual issues And attitude learner for checking features of designer. The modern developers 1 people to check the attributes of the Model Designer, environmental learning customer support. 5) Teacher in technology information communication subject 1 people for explore the features of the instructor.

Data Collection and Analysis. *Variable* Design and Development of a Constructivist Learning-Based Learning Environment Model that Enhance Problem Solving.

Benefits Expected

1. It is a design guideline based on ID Theory. Can be developed and adjusted to suit the student's needs to enhance problem solving in the context of students.
2. It is a guideline for designing a learning environment model based to enhance Students in problem solving.

Measurement Research. The tools in this study. It is a tool used to synthesize theoretical framework. Conceptual Framework Component Design Evaluation model for quality inspection. Include:

1. Synthesis documents, conceptual frameworks, learning resources in learning environment models that enhance problem solving for robot programming.
2. Assessment form for experts on the evaluation of conceptual frameworks, learning resources in learning environment models that enhance problem solving for Robot programming.

Data collection. The data collected in this study were collected from the tools used to synthesize theoretical frameworks. Conceptual Framework Component design Evaluation model for quality inspection. The following details.

1. Literature Review Analyses, theories, and research on the design of learning resources by studying the principles and theories related to learning theory.
2. Contextual Study of Problem Solving in Robot Programming. For students Secondary Grade 3. Study the context of instructional management in order to study the basics of problem solving of learners. This is the basis for designing the learning resources.
3. Synthesis of design conceptual framework based on literature review and contextual state of problem solving about robot programming for student secondary grade 3.
4. Conceptual Framework for Designing Learning Resources Offer expert review Correspondence between conceptual framework, learning resources Theory is based on the conceptual framework of the design criticizes and evaluates to suggests improvements. The suggestions that have been updated and corrected.

Data Analysis. Analysis of data from the instruments used in the synthesis of theoretical concepts. Concept design element model to determine the quality evaluation model. How to design and develop a model learning environment on the network. In this study, a design approach based on theory (ID theory) as detailed analysis of the following: (1) Theoretical framework. Methods Data were analysed using descriptive and analytical summary interpretation. Based on the theoretical principles involved. Research papers and from analysis of data from documents saved in the document. (2) The context of the teaching of students. Methods Data were analysed using descriptive and analytical summary interpretation. According to the poll for the students about the context of teaching (3) Frame design concept learning model learning environment on the network. Methods Data were analysed using descriptive analytical and abstract interpretation of data relating to the synthesis of the theoretical data recorded in the synthesis of the concept and context about teaching. (4) Design Resources the model learning environment on the network. Methods Data were analysed using descriptive analysis and interpretation of data in the summary record in the design and development of the model. (5) The characteristics of those involved with the design and development of a model's design, including the development of the learners and instructors. Data were analysed by means of a summary interpretation. From the data obtained from the survey design features of the development of the learner and the instructor. (6) The assessment of the experts about how to design a learning model learning environment on the network. Data were analysed by means of a summary interpretation data obtained from the assessment model learning environment on the network. Experts are of the content and media design model learning environment on the network (Fig. 1).

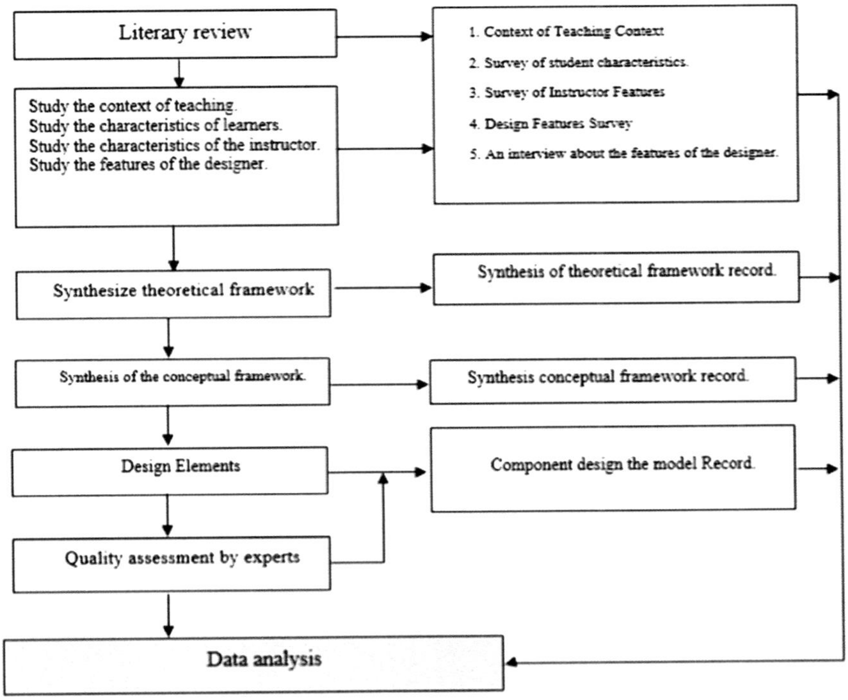

Fig. 1. Collection of data from tools used to synthesize theoretical frameworks.

1.4 Results

The Conceptual framework for designing learning resources in a learning environment based on a constructivist Web-based that enhance problem solving for robot programming in Secondary Grade 3 to consists.

1. Data bank. Consistency with design, such as intellectual treasure. Learning Resources, Knowledgebase, etc.
2. The equipment is experimental. Tools that help in the creation of knowledge, such as robotic experiments. Programming device simulation.
3. Information service robots (Robot Information Canter) is a collection. Information on the study will be used to solve problems in the classroom in the first place. In designing the learning is based on the principles, theories, including the theory of schema or cognitive structure.

The design of information in a manner that is a network concept. Menthol theoretical models are designed in such a way that the information is conceptual model theory of information processing. New theory of stable loads allowing the learner to record senses. Short-term memory Long-term memory and cognitive strategies (Cognitive strategies) (Figs. 2 and 3).

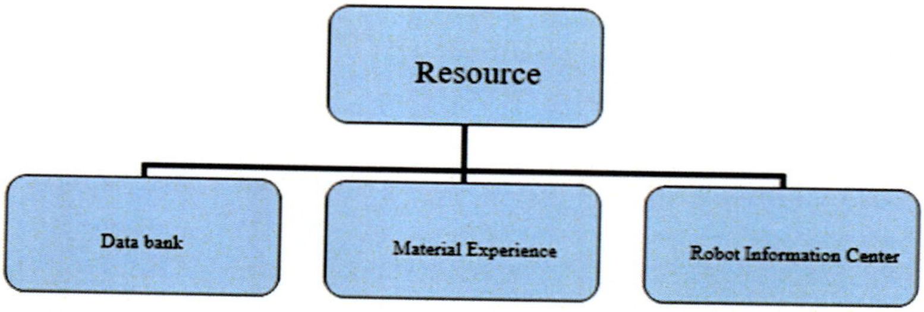

Fig. 2. Designing of resource synthesis framework of constructivist web-based learning environment to enhance the problem-solving for robot programming in secondary grade 3.

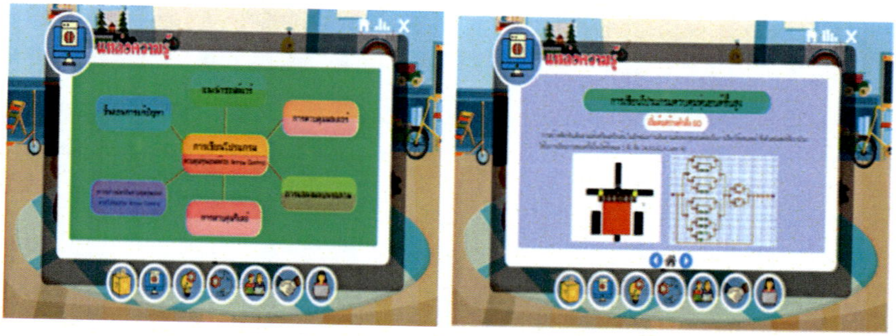

Fig. 3. Displays the knowledge resources screen on programming a robot controller.

1.5 Summary and Discussion

The design of learning resources in a constructivist learning environment to enhance the problem solving about robot programming For Secondary Grade 3. Students was found to consist of four basic elements: 1) Data bank 2) Experimental equipment and 3) Robot Information Center.

The theoretical foundations of constructivist theory include Cognitive Constructivist and Social Constructivist. Including a problem-solving framework about robot programming. This study uses document research methodology. Focused review Analytical Theory and the context is relevant and synthesized into a theoretical framework. This will be an important foundation for achieving the design goals. That can help both to create knowledge and to problems solving about robot programming and the principle of the theory.

Resources provide information to help learners find answers to use in a given problem situation. Information is presented with a mind map showing the relationship of all content understandable, work and support problem solving Graphics are used animation with appropriate content.

Acknowledgements. This research was supported by Ph.D. Program in Educational Technology, Faculty of Education, Research Group for Innovation and Cognitive Technology, Khon Kaen,

University, and Research and Technology Transfer Affairs Division, Khon Kaen University which hereby giving the thankfulness all through this.

References

Sundholm, H., Ramberg, R., Artman, H.: Learning conceptual design: activities with electronic whiteboards. In: Eriksen, M., Malmborg, L., Nilsen, J. (eds.) CADE2004 Web Proceedings of Computers in Art and Design Education (2004)

Hannafin, M.J.: Open-ended learning environment: Foundation, assumptions, and Implications for automated design. In: Tennyson, R. (ed.) Perspectives on Automating Instructional Design, pp. 101–129. Springer, New York (1999). https://doi.org/10.1007/978-3-642-57821-2_5

Jonassen, D.H.: Instructional design models for well-structured and ill-structured problem-solving learning outcomes. Educ. Technol. Res. Dev. **45**(1), 65–94 (1997). Conference, Copenhagen Business School, Denmark, and Malm University, Sweden, 29 June–1 July 2004

Thompson, S.: Haskell: The Craft of Functional Programming. Addison-Wesley (1996a)

Thompson, S.: Problem solving: recognising palindromes (1996b). http://www.ukc.ac.uk/computer_science/Haskellcraft/palindrome.html

Thompson, S.: Programming it in Haskell (1996c). http://www.ukc.ac.uk/computer_science/Haskell_craft/ProgInHaskell.html

Chaijaroen, S.: Education Technology: Theory, Practice, Education Technology: Principles Theories to Practices, 2nd edn. (2011)

Vygotsky, L.S.: Mind in Society: The Development of Higher Psychological Processes. Harvard University Press, Cambridge (1978)

AHP4Edu: An AHP-Based Assessment Model for Learning Effectiveness of Education

Yu-Lun Huang(✉) and Yu-Hsin Wu

Department of Electrical and Computer Engineering,
National Yang Ming Chiao Tung University, Hsinchu, Taiwan
yulun.huang@nycu.edu.tw

Abstract. The modern e-learning environment generates new types of students' learning records, including their operation records in the learning management system. Recently, wearable devices and a variety of sensors have become common in our daily life. By using these devices, we can access students' information such as heart rates and facial features. Previous studies [1, 2] have used the bioinformatics data mentioned above to analyze students' learning effectiveness. However, these approaches only utilize partial information and the diversity of data has not been put into consideration. This paper tries to better address this inefficiency by proposing an Analytic Hierarchy Process (AHP)-based model integrated with professional expertise in education. With this model, lecturers can customize the selection and importance of the criteria according to the used teaching strategy. Then, AHP4Edu can analyzes students' learning effectiveness scores from the sub-scores of the sub-criteria specified by an expert or a lecturer. We present simulations on assessing students' learning effectiveness for distance learning. We also demonstrate how AHP4Edu integrates heterogeneous data and provides a reliable learning effectiveness assessment for the lecturer.

Keywords: Learning effectiveness · Analytic hierarchy process · Multi-criteria decision-making approach

1 Introduction

When students feel lost in a learning process, they may not know what they learn nor how to apply what they've learned to actual cases. If a lecturer can manage how his/her students are learning in real-time, the lecturer can adjust his/her teaching strategy immediately. Thus, assessing students' learning effectiveness and reporting back to a lecturer is essential for promoting students' learning success.

In 2016, a Learning Analytics approach [3] was introduced by Khalil and Ebner to depict a life cycle for optimizing the learning effectiveness of students [4]. The cycle defines the measurement, collection, analysis, and reporting of data about students and their contexts so that students can leverage the analyzed results to understand how they

This work was supported in part by Ministry of Science and Technology of Taiwan (Grant No. 107-2511-H-009-005-MY3).

© Springer Nature Switzerland AG 2021
Y.-M. Huang et al. (Eds.): ICITL 2021, LNCS 13117, pp. 196–205, 2021.
https://doi.org/10.1007/978-3-030-91540-7_22

learn. With the feedback of students' learning effectiveness, a lecturer can discover students with learning difficulty at the earliest stage and figure out which parts of the lecture need more explanations. To analyze and report the learning effectiveness, we design an AHP-based student's learning effectiveness analysis model (AHP4Edu) to help lecturers manage students in the classroom.

The remaining sections of the paper are organized as follows. In Sect. 2, we introduce the structure of AHP4Edu. In Sect. 3, we apply AHP4Edu to distance learning and conduct several simulations to validate AHP4Edu. Then, we conclude the paper in Sect. 4.

2 AHP4Edu: An AHP-Based Learning Effectiveness Analysis Model for Education

AHP is a multi-criteria decision-making approach proposed by Thomas L. Saaty. The decision-making factors are arranged in a hierarchical structure. AHP lists all alternatives for evaluating the sub-criteria, criteria, and the final goal presented at different layers in the hierarchical structure to make a proper decision, as illustrated in Fig. 1. AHP is composed of three steps: hierarchy construction, pairwise comparison, and score determination.

Generally, a lecturer can assess student's learning effectiveness by giving quizzes, assigning homework, or offering one-on-one interviews. There are many complex factors when assessing a student's learning effectiveness. Giving a quiz or assigning homework cannot fully assess learning effectiveness because quizzes and assignments can only test the performance without considering other factors like engagement and motivation. Although interviewing each student can evaluate engagement and motivation, it takes much human work.

We design AHP4Edu to reduce human work and consider more factors upon assessing student's learning effectiveness. We divide the analysis of learning effectiveness into several independent sub-problems. For each sub-problem, lecturers can determine the corresponding criteria and their magnitudes through a pairwise comparison. With such, AHP4Edu can be dynamically adjusted to adapt to different teaching methods, like distance learning and blended learning.

2.1 Hierarchy

The hierarchy of AHP4Edu is composed of four layers (as shown in Fig. 1).

- Layer 1 is the goal, the Learning effectiveness.
- Layer 2 is the criteria for assessing the goal (Learning effectiveness). The criteria is recommended by educational experts.
- Layer 3 is the sub-criteria that may affect the criterion at Layer 2. The value of each sub-criterion may come from quizzes, homework, questionnaires, wearable sensors, camera, etc.
- Layer 4 represents the alternatives (i.e., the students to be assessed).

The weight of a link between a node and its parent node represents the relative importance between the two nodes. For a node with n ($n > 1$) children, the sum of the corresponding n links is 1. AHP4Edu evaluates every student represented at Layer 4 according to the sub-criteria at Layer 3. Then, AHP4Edu multiplies each score of the sub-criterion with the corresponding link weight and sums up the scores to derive the score of the criterion at Layer 2. The process repeats until AHP4Edu obtains the score of the final goal at Layer 1.

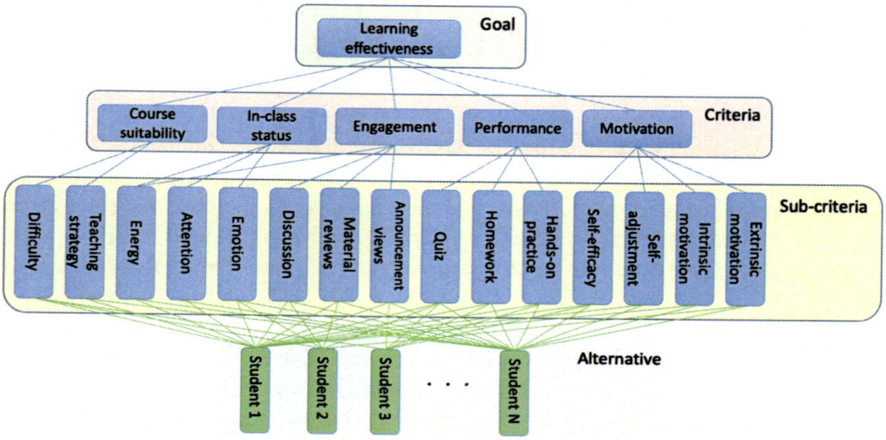

Fig. 1. Generic hierarchy of AHP4Edu

For evaluating the learning effectiveness of students, AHP4Edu considers the following criteria and the corresponding sub-criteria:

- Course suitability: This criterion evaluates the suitability of a course, a class, or an activity specified by a lecturer. The criterion can be assessed through several sub-criteria, such as the difficulty of course content and the teaching strategies.
  - Difficulty: AHP4Edu classifies the difficulty of the content as hard, moderate, and easy. The sub-criterion is either specified by the lecturer or self-evaluated by a student on a questionnaire.
  - Teaching strategies: Everyone has its own way of learning. When a student's learning style matches the lecturer's teaching strategies (such as direct instruction, flipped classroom, game-based learning, problem-based learning, etc.), the student can have better learning effectiveness. AHP4Edu assesses this criterion through questionnaires.
- In-class status: Experienced lecturers usually evaluate students' in-class physiological and mental status and adjust the teaching pace accordingly. Similarly, APH4Edu evaluates the criterion in terms of their energy, attention, and emotion.

- Energy: This sub-criterion classifies a student's energy levels into awake and sleepy. According to the research results presented by Jo et al. [5], AHP4Edu estimates the sub-criterion by measuring student's heart rates. The longer the time AHP4Edu detects a student as awake, the higher energy level the student obtains for this sub-criterion.
- Attention: The sub-criterion classifies a student's attention into concentrated and distracted. AHP4Edu evaluates student's attention by counting how long the student is "looking at" the lecturer, the blackboard, or the projection. If a student concentrates in a class, the student may swing his head just slightly. We infer the degree of head swing to the score of Attention.
- Emotion: AHP4Edu characterizes the emotions as independent dimensions, which includes arousal and valence. Arousal is the intensity level of emotion, ranging from calm (low) to excited (high), whereas valence is the pleasantness defined from negative to positive. Positive emotions have been correlated with more effective cognitive processing [6, 7], while negative emotions show otherwise. In AHP4Edu, students with the highest arousal and positive valence get the highest score in Emotion.

– Engagement: Learning engagement represents a student's voluntary participation in course activities. The more a student engages in a class, the more positive effects the student can obtain from the class. Such a criterion reveals students' willingness to engage and acquire more knowledge or skills. AHP4Edu estimates a student's engagement in terms of discussion, material reviews, announcement views, and energy (heart rate).

- Discussion: The more frequently a student asks questions, the more the student understands about the topic. AHP4Edu evaluates the sub-criterion by the frequency a student comments on a forum.
- Material reviews: The more time a student spends on the material, the more knowledge he/she can learn from it. AHP4Edu evaluates this sub-criterion by measuring how long and how frequently a student reviews the material.
- Announcement views: The sub-criterion represents the time and frequency a student spends on checking the announcements of a course. AHP4Edu evaluates this sub-criterion by counting how long and how frequently a student checks the announcements.
- Energy: In some teaching methods, like online teaching, energy may be considered a feature representing students' learning engagement [8]. We count the mental energy when estimating the learning engagement.

– Performance: The student's performance may reflect the success of his/her learning. AHP4Edu evaluates such a criterion in terms of the grades of quizzes, homework/assignments, and hands-on practice.

- Quiz: The grade of a quiz directly reflects how a student learns.

- Homework: The grade of homework or an assignment may reflect how much a student learns from the given lectures and how much a student understands for applying the learned concepts to a problem.
- Hands-on practice: The grade of hands-on practice (such as laboratory work and a term project) represents the ability to realize and implement what the student has learned.

– Motivation: Motivation gives essential supports to a student to help him/her overcome the barriers in learning. AHP4Edu estimates such a criterion in terms of self-efficacy, self-adjustment, extrinsic motivation, and intrinsic motivation.

- Self-efficacy: Self-efficacy represents the perception of a student's own ability to learn successfully in this course.
- Self-adjustment: This criterion represents how much a student can adjust himself/herself in response to the change of the learning environment.
- Extrinsic motivation: Extrinsic motivation represents explicit rewards offered by a lecturer to encourage students to participate in class activities or achieve better performances.
- Intrinsic motivation: Intrinsic motivation represents the internal rewards gained by the student by inspiring himself/herself to achieve better performances in class.

2.2 Pairwise Comparison

Apply AHP4Edu to assess students in class, a lecturer can choose some criteria and sub-criteria mentioned in Fig. 1. The lecturer can also change the link weights to emphasize some sub-criteria or criteria during the assessment. Figure 2(a) shows an example hierarchy of AHP4Edu. In the figure, G at Layer 1 is the goal of assessment and n criteria (C_i, $i = 1, 2, \ldots, n$) at Layer 2 are chosen for the assessment. Each criterion C_i has m sub-criteria $S_{i,j}$, where $j = 1, 2, \ldots, m$. The weights of C_i to the goal G are expressed as u_i, while the weights of $S_{i,j}$ are expressed as $w_{i,j}$ to its criteria C_i.

As mentioned in the previous section, the link weights are initialized by educational experts. Experts can assign the link weights to the sub-criteria and criteria by comparing the importance of any two criteria in AHP4Edu. We provide a guideline (Fig. 2(b)) for specifying the importance of criteria. If criterion C_1 is more important than C_2, then a_{12} in Fig. 2(c) will be assigned a value between 1 to 9, where the larger value represents greater importance. Otherwise, a_{12} should be assigned a value between $\frac{1}{9}$ to 1.

Unfortunately, inconsistency may occur if an expert assigns weights to too many criteria or sub-criteria. For example, inconsistency occurs if $C_2 : C_3 \neq \frac{a_{13}}{a_{12}}$. To ensure the consistency of the criteria and sub-criteria, AHP4Edu uses comparison matrix A to approximate the real weights. AHP4Edu gets the principle eigenvector $\boldsymbol{e}$ of A by solving $A\boldsymbol{e} = \lambda_{max}\boldsymbol{e}$, where the element e_i of $\boldsymbol{e}$ is proportional to weight u_i. Then, AHP4Edu normalizes $\boldsymbol{e}$ by making the summation of all elements 1. To achieve this, AHP4Edu divides each element of $\boldsymbol{e}$ by the summation of all elements and obtains the weight u_i ($u_i = \frac{e_i}{\sum_i e_i}$). The pairwise comparison is applied to the whole hierarchy of AHP4Edu to obtain the weights of criteria and sub-criteria, as shown in Fig. 2(d).

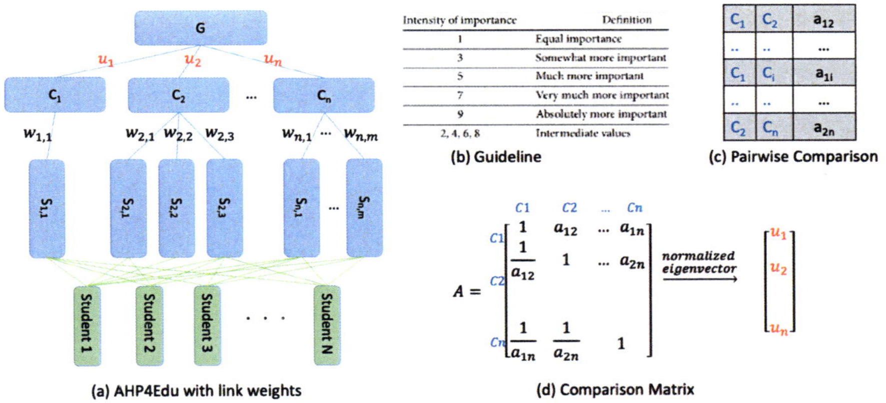

Fig. 2. Determination of link weights

2.3 Score Determination

AHP4Edu assesses students' learning effectiveness by assigning each student as an alternative at Layer 4. For every student, AHP4Edu estimates his/her learning effectiveness and derives the score of G by the following equation:

$$G = \sum_i \left(u_i \sum_j \left(w_{i,j} \times v_{i,j} \right) \right) \quad (1)$$

Equation (1) limits the final score in [0, 100] through two restrictions. The weight u_i and the value of inner summation follow Rule 1 and 2:

- Rule 1: $\sum_i u_i = 1$
- Rule 2: For all i, the value of $\sum_j \left(w_{i,j} \times v_{i,j} \right)$ are in range [0, 100].

3 Apply AHP4Edu to Distance Learning: Simulation

AHP4Edu can be adjusted to any teaching method (distance learning, online learning, blended learning, etc.) and customized according to the lecturer's needs. This section explains how to apply AHP4Edu to assess students taking a distance course.

Hierarchy Construction. Before constructing AHP4Edu for distance learning, we collect observations from educational experts to identify the criteria for assessing students' learning effectiveness and determine the relative importance of the criteria. Taking the following two observations for example, we identify 4 sub-criteria (under 3 criteria) in assessing learning effectiveness for distance learning: Teaching strategy, Emotion, Attention, and Discussion. Then, we build up the hierarchy for distance learning.

> *"Student A is taking Economics in his dormitory. The lecturer is giving direct instructions* **(Teaching strategy)**. *Since the explanations can be found in the course slides, Student A does not pay much attention to the lecture* **(Attention)**. *Student A spends some time on his comic books and smiles when reading something funny* **(Emotion)**. *Student A raises his head when there is a silent period or when the lecturer asks students to pay attention. Student A feels nervous when the lecturer asks a question* **(Emotion)**. *He may feel embarrassed if he cannot answer the question correctly.*
>
> *Student B loves the psychology online course. He pays attention to the lecture* **(Attention)** *and smiles when he learns something new* **(Emotion)**. *Student B always feels nervous when the lecturer is asking a question* **(Emotion)**, *and thus he is too shy to answer questions in class. He tries to answer questions by typing messages in the chat room* **(Discussion)**. *Student B is the one who left the most messages in the chat room* **(Discussion)**."

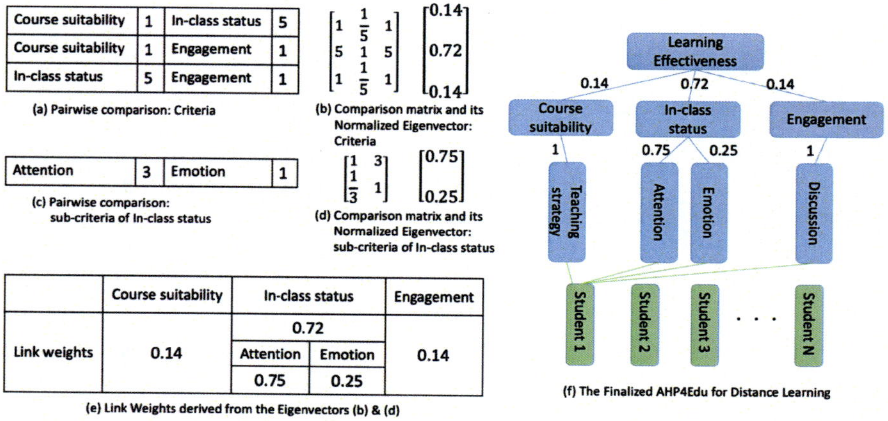

Fig. 3. A simplified AHP4Edu for distance learning

Pairwise Comparison. The second step is to compare the criteria and calculate their weights in pair. Again, we invite education experts to give the pairwise comparison for AHP4Edu for distance learning (see Fig. 3(a) and (c)).

In this case, the In-class status (5) is more critical than Course suitability (1), Course suitability (1) is equally vital to Engagement (1), while In-class status (5) is more critical than Engagement (1). Then, we can obtain the comparison matrix accordingly and derive the normalized eigenvector of the matrix (Fig. 3(b) and (d)). Finally, we get the weights of the criteria: Course suitability 0.14, In-class status 0.72, and Engagement 0.14. Similarly, we obtain the weights of the sub-criteria of In-class status, where Attention is 0.75 and Emotion is 0.25 (see Fig. 3(e)), and build up the simplified AHP4Edu for distance learning (Fig. 3(f)).

Score Determination. The final step is to determine the scores of the above criteria and sub-criteria. Taking the above observations of Student A and Student B as examples, 4 scores should be used to assess students' learning effectiveness: Teaching strategy, Attention, Emotion and Discussion.

- **Teaching Strategy & Discussion**: The lecturer gives questionnaires to both students to know if the teaching strategy meets students' learning styles. In this case, Student A thinks that direct instruction helps less for his learning because he can learn the contents from the lecturing slides. Student B shows high interest in the lectures. Suppose the lecturer estimates high interests as 100 and low interests as 33. Student A and Student B get 33 and 100 for Teaching strategy, respectively. Second, Student A feels bored during the lecture and is not active in the forum, while Student B likes to post messages on the forum. Hence, when analyzing the logs of the forum, Student A gets a score of fewer discussion (33), and Student B gets a score of more discussion (100).
- **Attention**: AHP4Edu evaluates Attention using students' facial angles [9]. DBSCAN (Density-based Spatial Clustering of Applications with Noise) is adopted to transform the facial angle to an attention score. In the case, we set the *eps* of DBSCAN to 3 and the *minPts* to the number of total points divided by 30. Then, we obtain the attention scores of 32.66 and 89.02 for Student A and Student B, respectively (see Fig. 4).

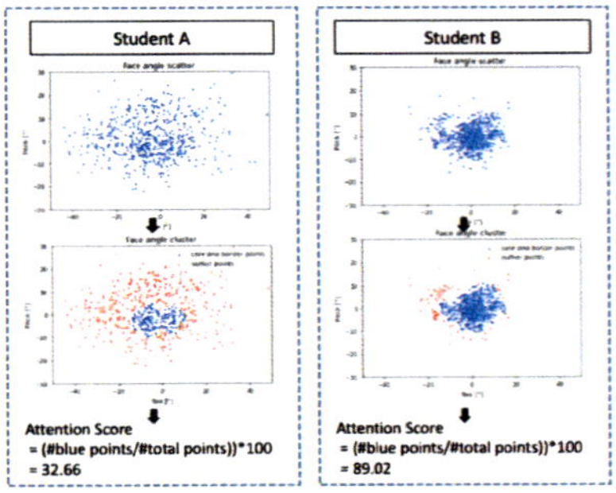

Fig. 4. Converting facial angles to attention scores

- **Emotion**: For analyzing the emotion, AHP4Edu converts facial images [9] to arousal and valence. We set the bounds of positive, neutral, and negative emotion to 0.25 (see Fig. 5). We define three parameters for converting arousal and valence (*ar*, *va*) to Emotion score: the base value of neutral emotion ($b_{neutral}$), amplifier of positive emotion (amp_p) and amplifier of negative emotion (amp_n). Then, we apply the following equation (Eq. (2)) to calculate the mean value of (*ar*, *va*)s as the Emotion score.

$$\text{Emotion score} = mean(m), \quad \text{where}$$

$$m = \begin{cases} b_{neutral} + \sqrt{va^2 + (ar+1)^2} \times amp_p, & \text{if } va > \delta \\ b_{neutral}, & \text{if } -\delta \le va \le \delta \\ b_{neutral} + \sqrt{va^2 + (ar+1)^2} \times amp_n, & \text{if } va < -\delta \end{cases} \tag{2}$$

Figure 5 shows the simulation results, where the blue points represent the positive emotion whose valence is greater than 0.25; the red points show the negative emotion whose valence is smaller than −0.25; and the green points represent the neutral emotion.

Obviously, Student B has more blue points and gets a higher score of 83.61, while Student A gets a smaller score of 42.33 for emotion.

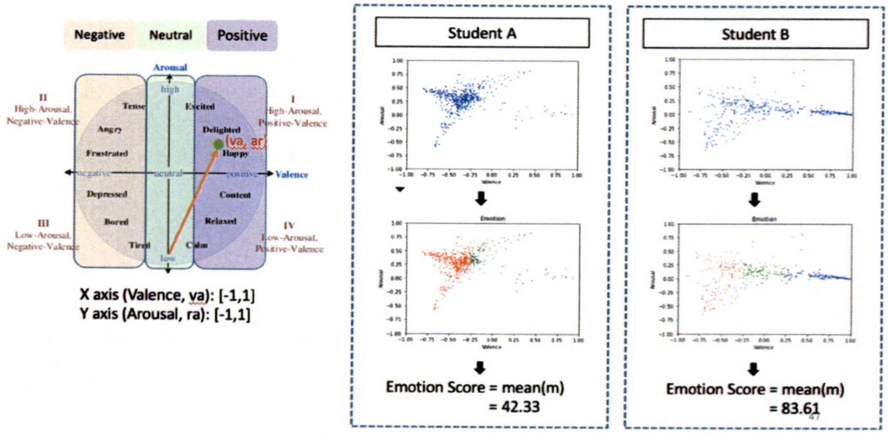

Fig. 5. Transforming valence and arousal of facial images to emotion scores (Color figure online)

After that, we can calculate the scores using Eq. (1) and obtain 35.08 and 94.42 as the scores of In-class status for Student A and B, respectively. If Student A receives a score of 33 on Teaching strategy and 77.78 on Discussion, Student B gets 100 and 94.70 on Teaching strategy and Discussion, we can come out with the final scores (learning effectiveness) for both students as 42.08 and 90.38.

4 Conclusion

We design a 4-layer AHP-based model, AHP4Edu, to evaluate the students' learning effectiveness. We invite several educational experts to brainstorm and determine the criteria required for evaluating students' learning effectiveness in different teaching methods. AHP4Edu provides a flexible framework to consider and hold complicated criteria for assessing learning effectiveness. A lecturer can customize the selection and weights (importance) of criteria according to the chosen teaching strategy. The customized weights can better estimate the learning effectiveness of students for the lecturer.

In the paper, we demonstrate how to apply AHP4Edu to distance learning and present simulations to prove the feasibility of AHP4Edu. Assessment results derived by our model can reflect the learning situation of students. The simulation results show that AHP4Edu can integrate heterogeneous data and provide lecturers with a reliable learning effectiveness assessment. For now, we only show the functionality of AHP4Eud with simulated data. We plan to apply AHP4Edu to an actual class in the next step.

AHP4Edu is the first step of our endeavor to decompose a complicated problem (assessing learning effectiveness) into measurable elements (heart rate, emotion, attention, teaching strategy, motivation, and engagement) and analyze them independently.

For the sub-problems or factors impacting each other, we can introduce neural networks or other analytical approaches as sub-models into AHP4Edu to make the assessment more complete.

References

1. Elbadrawy, A., Studham, R.S., Karypis, G.: Collaborative multi-regression models for predicting students' performance in course activities. In: LAK'15: Proceedings of the 5th International Conference on Learning Analytics and Knowledge, pp. 103–107. Association for Computing Machinery, New York (2015).
2. Monkaresi, H., Bosch, N., Calvo R.A., D'Mello, S.K.: Automated detection of engagement using video-based estimation of facial expressions and heart rate. In: IEEE Transactions on Affective Computing, pp. 15–25. IEEE (2016). https://ieeexplore.ieee.org/abstract/document/7373578
3. Society for Learning Analytics Research: "What is Learning Analytics?" https://www.solaresearch.org/about/what-is-learning-analytics/
4. Khalil, M., Ebner, M.: What is learning analytics about? A survey of different methods used in 2013–2015. (2016). https://arxiv.org/abs/1606.02878v1
5. Jo, S.-H., Kim, J.-M., Kim, D.K.: Heart rate change while drowsy driving. J. Korean Med. Sci. **34**(8), e56 (2019). https://doi.org/10.3346/jkms.2019.34.e56
6. Corradino, C., Fogarty, K.: Positive Emotions and Academic Achievement. (2016). https://wp.nyu.edu/steinhardt-appsychopus/positive-emotions-and-academic-achievement/
7. Hinton, C., Miyamoto, K., Della-Chiesa, B.: Brain research, learning and emotions: implications for education research, policy and practice (2008). https://doi.org/10.1111/j.1465-3435.2007.00336.x
8. Jung, Y., Lee, J.: Learning engagement and persistence in massive open online courses (MOOCS). Comput. Educ. **122**, 9–22 (2018). https://doi.org/10.1016/j.compedu.2018.02.013
9. Wu, B.F., Lin, C.H.: Adaptive feature mapping for customizing deep learning based facial expression recognition model. In: IEEE Access, vol. 6, pp. 12451–12461 (2018)

A Designing Framework for Flipped Classroom Learning Environment Model Combined with Augmented Reality to Enhance Creative Thinking in Product Design for High School Students

Sathaporn Wongchiranuwat[1], Charuni Samat[2](✉), Issara Kanjug[3], and Suchat Wattanachai[4]

[1] Doctor of Philosophy Student of Education Technology, Faculty of Education, Khon Kaen University, Khon Kaen, Thailand
[2] Division of Computer Education, Faculty of Education, Khon Kaen University, Khon Kaen, Thailand
[3] Division of Educational Technology, Faculty of Education, Khon Kaen University, Khon Kaen, Thailand
[4] Division of Surgery, Faculty of Veterinary Medicine, Khon Kaen University, Khon Kaen, Thailand

Abstract. The flipped learning model is a blend of digital technology solutions. To be used as a tool for learning design that focuses on enhancing knowledge construct, and creative thinking of students. This study was aimed to a designing framework for flipped classroom learning environment model. The target group consisted of 5 experts for this designing framework. This study employed phase 1 of model research, which was design process phase. Document analysis, survey methods were used to collect qualitative data and analyze data by interpreting and concluding. The results in 3 aspects revealed that 1) Synthesis of theoretical framework for flipped classroom learning environment model consists of 6 theoretical bases: psychology base, pedagogical base, creative thinking base, technology and media base, neuroscience base, and context of school base. 2) Synthesis of designing framework for flipped classroom learning environment model. There are 5 stages of the learning process which are separated into 2 stages Out-of-class activity and 3 stages of In-class activity. In the assessment of a designing framework for flipped classroom learning environment model by the experts, there is a correspondence between the theoretical principles that were used as the basis of creating the compositions, and the functions of the elements accounted for 84.68%. The elements of the Out-of-class were 82.5%, and the elements of the In-class were 86.87%. It is appropriate to enhance knowledge construction, creative thinking of learners.

Keywords: Flipped classroom · Creative thinking · Constructivist · Learning environment model

© Springer Nature Switzerland AG 2021
Y.-M. Huang et al. (Eds.): ICITL 2021, LNCS 13117, pp. 206–218, 2021.
https://doi.org/10.1007/978-3-030-91540-7_23

1 Introduction

Economic development based on the use of creative knowledge, and the integration of technology and innovation is an economic value-adding that emphasizes the competition of a creative economy. This competition has caused the need for creative workers, which is necessary for the 21st century [1]. The required competencies of the workers in the 21st century are the abilities of analytic thinking, creative thinking, communication, and cooperation. Education is a crucial way to enhance learners to have abilities and desired characteristics, which lead to a new paradigm of education [2]. According to epistemology, knowledge is changeable because the information is increased and changes all the time. Therefore, knowledge from teachers in classrooms may not be adequate.

However, the study revealed that learners were lack of creative thinking, inquiry, and knowledge construction, which were important thinking skills of learners. Flipped learning model is a learning form that is combined with the application of digital technology. Flipped learning model is also used as a tool to design appropriate learning for learners, which focuses on learners' differences and changeable styles of classroom teaching [3].

Furthermore, there is a relation with constructivist theory that promotes inquiry and knowledge construction, and learners' divergent thinking. Divergent thinking is multiple thinking; such as ways, aspects, and views, that can lead to a new invention and discover how to solve problem. There are four abilities of thinking, which are fluency, flexibility, originality, and elaboration [4, 5]. All four thinking abilities are involved in product design course that promotes learners' creative thinking and learning by doing in order to design innovative products that are able to use in daily life.

2 Literature Review

2.1 Flipped Learning Model

Flipped learning model is designed and developed by Jonathan Bergmann and Aron Sams [6]. It is a form of learning management emphasized on a shift of teachers' and learners' roles from being passive learners whom teachers explain and deliver everything in classrooms to be active learners who discover and inquire knowledge by themselves through learning technology materials provided by teachers. Moreover, the teachers will bring what the learners have learned outside classrooms to be classroom activities. For doing classroom activities, the teachers will be the coach to give learners. Consequently, the teachers and learners interact with one another and interact with various forms of effective and new technology, which encourage the learners to learn anywhere and anytime [7].

2.2 Creative Thinking

Creative thinking of Guilford [4]. The American psychologist believes that this is the development of the structure of Intellect by consisting of 3 thinking dimensions as operation categories, content categories, and product categories. Divergent thinking can lead to inventing or creating well as finding concepts or solutions to solve the problem successfully. Creative thinking is defined as fluency, flexibility, originality, and elaboration [2, 5].

2.3 Constructivist Theory

Constructivist theory is theory stated that learners discover and construct knowledge by themselves. This theory focuses on learner's schema by linking their prior knowledge to new experience, context, and also new information to construct new knowledge on their own. This is called cognitive structure constructivist theory also promotes social interaction among learners to share what they have learned with one another toward language, society, and culture. Constructivist theory is divided into 2 groups, which are Cognitive constructivism [8] and Social constructivism [9].

3 Purposes

This study was aimed to a designing framework for flipped classroom learning environment model combined with augmented reality to enhance creative thinking in product design for high school students.

4 Methodology

4.1 Scope of Research

The Model research was employed [10]. This is to intensively study the process of design and development model. In this study, research phrase 1 model development was implemented to present the results of the development process; synthesis of theoretical framework, synthesis of designing framework, and evaluate the efficiency of the designing framework of flipped classroom learning environment model [11].

4.2 Target Group of the Study

The target group used in this research is an expert in the designing framework for flipped classroom learning environment model. To check the quality of the learning environment model. Based on the theory (ID theory), 5 experts are professors in higher education institutions.

4.3 Research Design

Research Phrase 1 Model development was employed by survey research.

4.4 Research Instruments

The instruments in this study are as following details: 1) Document examination and analysis recoding form to synthesize of theoretical framework. 2) Recoding form to synthesize of designing framework of flipped classroom learning environment model. 3) Evaluation form for the experts used in the designing framework of flipped classroom learning environment model.

4.5 Data Collection and Analysis

The researchers collected the data as follows: 1) Synthesis of theoretical framework and elements of flipped classroom learning environment model. The data were collected by analyzing principles, theories, related research of the constructivism theory, cognitive theory, flipped learning model, pedagogy, technology and media, neuroscience, and context of school. 2) Synthesis of designing framework based on the theatrical framework was analyzed by data interpreting and using of descriptive analysis on the framework synthesis recording form. 3) Evaluate of flipped classroom learning environment model by experts. The analytical description, summarization, and interpretation were used to analyze the data.

5 Results

5.1 Synthesis of Theoretical Framework

The results show that the theoretical framework of flipped classroom learning environment model is comprised of 6 theoretical bases were as follows: 1) Psychology base. 2) Pedagogical base. 3) Creative thinking base. 4) Technology and media base. 5) Context of school base [12, 13]. (see Fig. 1).

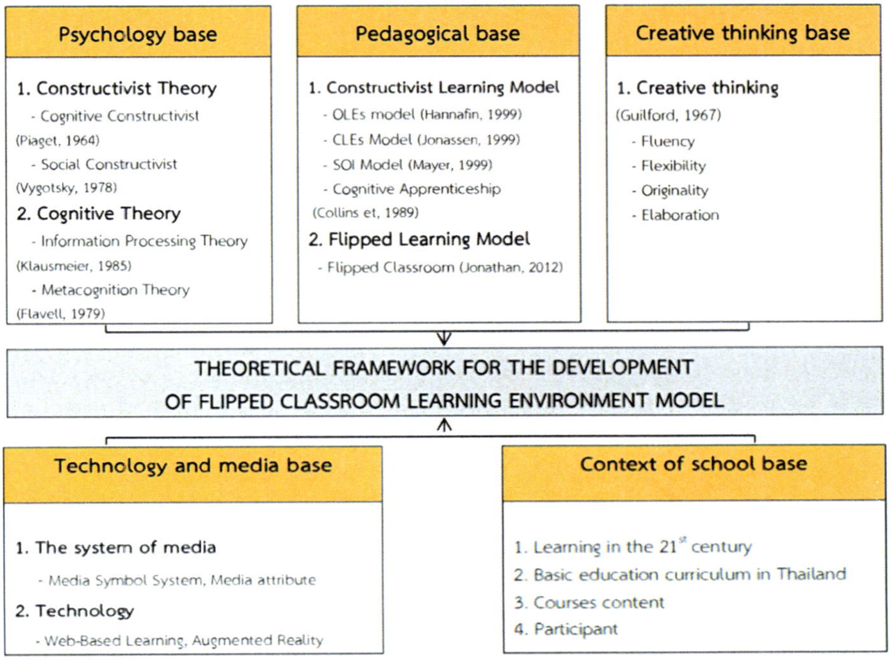

Fig. 1. Theoretical framework for flipped classroom learning environment model.

5.2 Synthesis of Designing Framework

The results show that the designing framework of flipped classroom learning environment model. There are 5 stages of the learning process which are separated into 2 stages Out-of-class learning following; Knowledge acquisition (Pre-class), Knowledge sharing (Post-class), and 3 stages of In-class learning following; Knowledge transfer, Knowledge construction, Knowledge reflection [14, 15] (see Fig. 2).

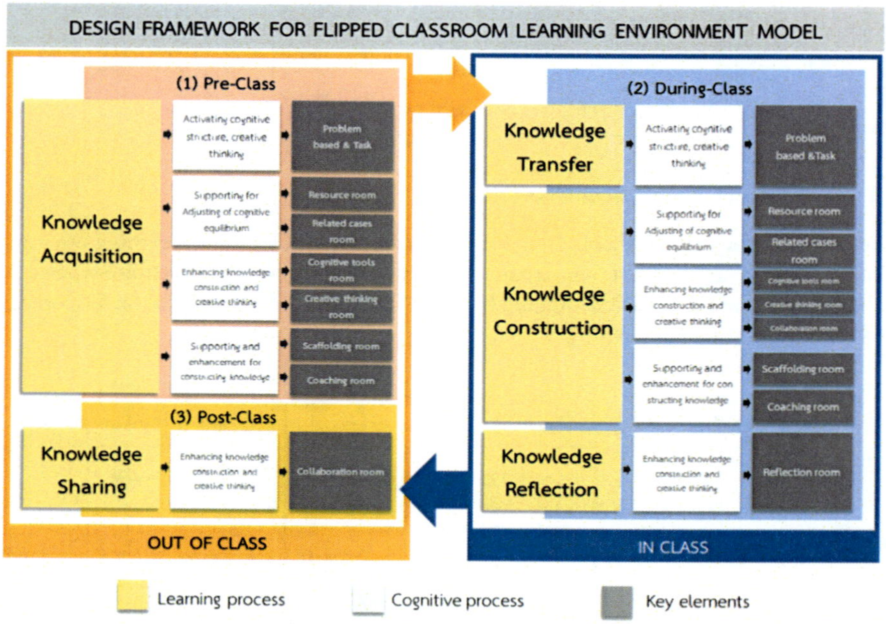

Fig. 2. Design framework for flipped classroom learning environment model.

Out-of-class learning having used to be the basis of a designing framework for flipped classroom learning environment model consists of 2 learning processes following; **1) Knowledge acquisition** is pre-class learning that aims to learn of individual learners in seeking knowledge and building self-knowledge which is a time for students who have studied knowledge about the subject matter learned and perform pre-learning tasks at flipped classroom learning environment model based on theoretical principles, consisting of (1) Activating of cognitive structure and creative thinking. (2) Supporting for adjusting of cognitive equilibrium. (3) Enhancing for knowledge construction and creative thinking. (4) Supporting and enhancement for constructing knowledge. **2) Knowledge sharing** is post-class learning that focuses on exchanging knowledge and social interaction with classmates after learners have learned in class learning, which is the creation of knowledge gained from reviewing knowledge of the subject matter from what has been learned with the flipped classroom learning environment model based on theoretical principles, consisting of Enhancing knowledge construction and creative thinking.

In-class learning having used to be the basis of a designing framework for flipped classroom learning environment model consists of 3 learning processes: **1) Knowledge transfer** is learning that occurs during the classroom that aims to previous knowledge before pre-class with new information which is a time for students to learn and doing learning tasks. It is group learning in a class together between learners and the teacher acts as a consultant (Coaching) based on theoretical principles consisting of Activating of cognitive structure and creative thinking. **2) Knowledge construction** is a search for additional information for learners. To use the solution from problem based during class, which is the nature of the pursuit and knowledge construction through learning with the Flipped classroom learning environment model based on theoretical principles consisting of (1) Supporting for adjusting of cognitive equilibrium. (2) Enhancing for knowledge construction and creative thinking. (3) Supporting and enhancement for constructing knowledge. **3) Knowledge reflection** is a reflection of knowledge understanding and summarizing the knowledge of learners during class leads to knowledge construction and creative thinking which is to control their own learning activities through learning with the Flipped Classroom Learning Environment Model based on theoretical principles consisting of enhancing for knowledge construction and creative thinking as shown in Table 1.

Table 1. Design framework for flipped classroom learning environment model.

Design framework for flipped classroom learning environment model			
Out of class	Cognitive process	Key elements	In-class
Pre-class 1. Knowledge acquisition	**– Activating cognitive structure, creative thinking.** Based on Cognitive constructivism [8], it is believed that "learners' knowledge construction through action." Knowledge arises from linking previous knowledge with new experiences. Which the problem-based aims to promote creativity based on the principles of Creative thinking [4]	**– Problem-based & Task.** It is an element that activating cognitive structure, creative thinking. **Pre-class** and **During-class** where the stories and problems are presented in an authentic context those students will face. Task, which promotes creative thinking	During-class **1.** Knowledge transfer

(continued)

Table 1. (*continued*)

Design framework for flipped classroom learning environment model			
Out of class	Cognitive process	Key elements	In-class
	– Supporting for adjusting of cognitive equilibrium, creative thinking. Based on the Information Processing theory [16], designed learning resources for learners. To use in the problem "Problem based & Task." It is based on CLEs Model [17] principles to design related cases in cases where students have insufficient experience in solving problems. To create a problem-solving thinking model and can link principles or knowledge in solving problems used for problem solving	**– Resource room.** It is an elements that supporting for adjusting of cognitive equilibrium, creative thinking. **Pre-class** and **During-class** were for search for relevant information in the form of text, concept, and learning videos for use in knowledge construct and answering learning tasks **– Related cases room.** It is an elements that supporting for adjusting of cognitive equilibrium, creative thinking. **Pre-class** and **During-class** were for learner's novice with insufficient, problem-solving experience	During-class 2. Knowledge construction
	– Enhancing knowledge construction, creative thinking. Based on OLEs model to design process tools [18]. That supports the cognitive processes of learners, which will lead to knowledge creation. It is based on Guilford's Principles of Creative Thinking [4], which is designed to encourage students' Creative thinking	**– Cognitive tools room.** It is an element that enhancing knowledge construction. **Pre-class** and **During-class** for collect tools used to support the knowledge building of learners. To use for searching data collection communication creation and integration **– Creative thinking room.** It is an element that promotes Creative thinking. Pre-class and During-class for students based on Creative thinking **– Collaboration room.** It is an element that enhancing knowledge construction, creative thinking. **During-class** for exchanging knowledge or opinions with friends, teachers, and experts to give multiple perspectives	

(*continued*)

Table 1. *(continued)*

Design framework for flipped classroom learning environment model			
Out of class	Cognitive process	Key elements	In-class
	– Supporting and enhancement for constructing knowledge. Based on Social constructivism [9], if learners are below the Zone of proximal development, they cannot learn on their own and need help. However, the design to help build knowledge of learners. Based on OLEs model [18], Scaffolds has been developed to design a support base for learners who need help related to learning. It is based on Cognitive apprenticeship [19], a method that helps novice learners become experts. In addition, intellectual internships while working will help develop problem-solving expertise	**– Scaffolding room.** It is an element that supporting and enhancement for constructing knowledge. **Pre-class** and **During-class** for construct knowledge. For helping students. When unable to solve problems or complete learning tasks by suggesting assistance that consists of four areas: conceptual scaffolding, metacognitive scaffolding, procedural scaffolding, and strategic scaffolding **– Coaching room.** It is an element that supporting and enhancement for construction knowledge. **Pre-class** and **During-class** for coaching before attending the class by giving advice, hinting, and directing in an online format	
	– Enhancing knowledge construction, creative thinking. It is a learning design that takes place During-class. That focuses on reflection, understanding, and summarizing the knowledge of learners based on Metacognition theory [20], believed that "learners are important to learning. Learners are in control of their learning activities. Self-regulation is a study of the control of cognitive activity that pays attention to the individual knowledge of what has been learned	**– Reflection room.** It is an element that enhancing knowledge construction, Creative thinking. **During-class** for controlling the learning activities of learners is a reflection of understanding and summarizing the knowledge of learners	During-class 3. Knowledge reflection

(continued)

Table 1. (*continued*)

Design framework for flipped classroom learning environment model			
Out of class	Cognitive process	Key elements	In-class
Post-class **2.** Knowledge sharing	**– Enhancing knowledge construction, creative thinking.** It is a Post-class learning design that focuses on exchanging knowledge. And social interaction with classmates After learners have learned In-class, which is the creation of knowledge gained from reviewing knowledge about the subject matter from what has been learned. It is based on Social constructivism [9], which places importance on social interaction in terms of language, society, and culture that contributes to the support of learners to express their opinions with others. For collaborating to solve problems while building knowledge. However, the design to help build knowledge of learners. It is based on OLEs model [18] principles to design communication tools. To communicate between learners and learners and teachers	**– Collaboration room.** It is an element that enhancing knowledge construction, creative thinking. Learning **Post-class** for exchanging knowledge or opinions with friends, teachers, and experts to create multiple perspectives. Leading to greater knowledge and understanding. From reviewing knowledge about the content from what was learned	

5.3 Evaluate the Efficiency of the Designing Framework

The results of experts on designing framework for flipped classroom learning environment model. It is a method of verification by an expert's reviewer, the design of the learning environment model the design of learning based on theoretical principles as the basis for design. This is appropriate and can promote knowledge based on the Flipped Classroom, Constructivist, and Creative thinking as shown in Table 2.

Table 2. The results of the assessment of the Designing Framework

No.	Lists of preconceptions towards The Flipped Classroom Learning Environment Model	Results of the experts (Percentage)
· **Out-of-class**: Elements of flipped classroom learning environmental model		
1. **Knowledge acquisition** (Pre-class)		
	1.1 Activating cognitive structure, creative thinking	
	• Problem based & Task	100
	1.2 Supporting for Adjusting of cognitive equilibrium, creative thinking)	
	• Resource room	100
	• Related cases room	80
	1.3 Enhancing knowledge construction, creative thinking	
	• Cognitive tools room	80
	• Creative thinking room	80
	1.4 Supporting and enhancement for constructing knowledge	
	• Scaffolding room	80
	• Coaching room	60
2. **Knowledge sharing** (Post-class)		
	2.1 Enhancing knowledge construction, creative thinking	
	• Collaboration room	80
	Total	**82.50**
· **In-class**: Elements of flipped classroom learning environmental model		
1. **Knowledge transfer** (During-class)		
	1.1 Activating cognitive structure, creative thinking	
	• Problem based & Task	100
2. **Knowledge construction** (During-class)		
	1.2 Supporting for adjusting of cognitive equilibrium, creative thinking	
	• Resource room	100
	• Related cases room	80
	2.2 Enhancing knowledge construction, creative thinking	

(continued)

Table 2. (*continued*)

No.	Lists of preconceptions towards The Flipped Classroom Learning Environment Model	Results of the experts (Percentage)
	• Cognitive tools room	60
	• Creative thinking room	80
	• Collaboration room	100
	2.3 Supporting and enhancement for constructing knowledge	
	• Scaffolding room	80
	• Coaching room	100
3. **Knowledge reflection** (During-class)		
	3.1 Enhancing knowledge construction, creative thinking	
	• Reflection room	80
	Total	**86.87**
	All Total (1 + 2)	84.68

According to Table 2, the assessment result of a designing framework for flipped classroom learning environment model, by the experts to check the consistency between the theoretical principles used as the basis for the composition. And the function of the elements of flipped classroom learning environment model, which consists of out of class and in class learning, It was found that the elements of the Out-of-class learning environment model consisted of 8 elements: 1) Problem based, 2) Resource room, 3) Related cases room, 4) Cognitive tools room, 5) Creative thinking room, 6) Scaffolding room, 7) Coaching room, 8) Collaboration room, And the elements of the In-class learning environment model consisted of 9 elements: 1) Problem based, 2) Resource room, 3) Related cases room, 4) Cognitive tools room, 5) Creative thinking room 6) Collaboration room, 7) Scaffolding room, 8) Coaching room, 9) Reflection room. There is a correspondence between the theoretical principles that are used as the basis for creating the composition and the functions of the elements accounted for 84.68%, the elements of the Out-of-class learning 82.5%, And the elements of the In-class learning 86.8%.

6 Conclusions

Consequently, the results of the study of synthesis of a designing framework for flipped classroom learning environment model. Based on the fundamental theory (ID theory), used as a basis for the synthesis of theoretical framework, designing framework of flipped classroom learning environment model. There are 5 stages of the learning process which are separated into 2 stages Out-of-class learning following; Knowledge acquisition (Pre-class), Knowledge sharing (Post-class), and 3 stages of In-class learning following;

Knowledge transfer, Knowledge construction, Knowledge reflection. This research result is consistent with a study of Issara kanjug [14]. Including the evaluation of the design of flipped classroom learning environmental model reviewed by expert reviewers. There is a correspondence between the theoretical principles that as the basis for creating the composition and the functions of the elements. It is appropriate to enhance knowledge construction, creative thinking of learners. This research result is consistent with a study of Charuni Samat, Sumalee Chaijaroen [2]. Moreover, it aligns with learning in the 21st century emphasizing flexible and various instructions. It is also assimilated with applied technology.

Acknowledgement. This research is supported by Graduate Development Scholarship 2021, National Research Council of Thailand, and The Innovation and Cognitive Technology Research Center, Faculty of Education, and the Research and Technology Transfers Affairs Division, Khon Kaen University supported this work.

References

1. Dede, C.: Comparing frameworks for 21st century skills. In: 21st Century Skills: Rethinking How Students Learn, vol. 20, pp. 51–76 (2010)
2. Samat, C., Chaijaroen, S.: Design and development of learning environment to enhance creative thinking and innovation skills for teacher training in the 21st century. In: ICCE, pp. 667–672 (2015)
3. Samat, C., Kampira, K.: Development of constructivist flipped classroom to enhance students' creative thinking for designing logo. In 24th: Think Global Act Local - Main Conference Proceedings, pp. 660–662 (2016)
4. Guilford, J.P.: The Nature of Human Intelligence. McGraw-Hill Book Company, New York (1967)
5. Sathanarugsawait, B., Samat, C., Wattanachai, S.: Survey results of learner context in the development of constructivist learning environment model. In: (MOOCS) for Higher Education ICITL 2020, Porto, Portugal, 23–25 November 2020, Proceedings, pp. 465–474 (2020)
6. Bergmann, J., Sams, A.: Flip Your Classroom: Reach Every Student in Every Class Every Day. International Society for Technology in Education; ASCD, Alexandria (2012)
7. Bergmann, J., Sams, A.: Before you flip, consider this. Phi Delta Kappan **94**(2), 25 (2014)
8. Piaget, J.: Part I: cognitive development in children: Piaget development and learning. J. Res. Sci. Teach. **2**, 176–186 (1964)
9. Vygotsky, L.S.: Mind in Society: The Development of Higher Psychological Processes. Harvard University Press, Cambridge (1978)
10. Richey, R.C., Klein, J.: Design and Developmental Research. Lawrence, New Jersey (2007)
11. Sathanarugsawait, B., Samat, C.: Synthesis of theoretical framework of constructivist creative thinking massive open online courses (MOOCs). In: First ICITL 2018, Portoroz, Slovenia, Proceedings. pp. 231–241 (2018)
12. Wongchiranuwat, S., Samat, C., Kanjug, I., Wattanachai, S.: The study of learner context for the development of constructivist learning environment model combined with augmented reality flipped classroom to enhance creative thinking. In: ICITL 2020, Porto, Portugal, Proceedings, pp. 338–348 (2020)

13. Sathanarugsawait, B., Samat, C., Wattanachai, S.: Survey results of learner context in the development of constructivist learning environment model. In: Third ICITL 2020, Porto, Portugal, Proceedings, pp. 465–474 (2020)
14. Kanjug, I., Wattanachai, S., Kanjug, P., Nangam, C.: SOCIALClassnet as an LMS for online flipped learning environment. In: 6th IIAI-AAI (2017)
15. Wongchiranuwat, S., Samat, C.: Synthesis of theoretical framework for augmented Reality learning environment to promote creative thinking. In: 24th ICCE Proceedings, pp. 639–641 (2016)
16. Klausmeier, H.J.: Educational Psychology, 5th edn. Harper & Row, New York (1985)
17. Jonassen, D.H.: Learning to Solve Problems A Handbook for Designing Problem-Solving Learning Environments. Routledge, New York (2011)
18. Hannafin, M., Land, S., Oliver, K.: Open learning environments: foundations, methods, and models. In: Reigeluth, C.M. (ed.) Instructional Design Theories and Models, vol. 2. Lawrence Erlbaum Associates, New Jersey (1999)
19. Brown, C.: Duguid. Situated cognition and the culture of learning. Educ. Res. **18**(1), 32–42 (1989)
20. Flavell, J.H.: Metacognitive aspects of problem solving. In: Resnick, L.B. (ed.) The Nature of Intelligence, pp. 231–236. Erlbaum, Hillsdale (1976)

Development of Constructivist Web-Based Learning Environment Model to Enhance Critical Thinking: Integration Between Pedagogy and Neuroscience Topic on Substance for Primary Students

Pimwarun Nunthaitaweekul(✉), Sumalee Chaijaroen, and Romwarin Gamlunglert

Department of Educational Technology, Khon Kaen University, Khon Kaen, Thailand
Pimwarun_n@kkumail.com

Abstract. The purpose of this research is to synthesize theoretical framework and designing framework for development of constructivist web-based learning environment model to enhance Critical Thinking subject on substance around using for Grade 6 students. Type I developmental research is the research design (Design and Development). The following were the procedures: 1) evaluate and analyze the principles and theories, 2) investigate the context of learners' knowledge creation and memory processes, and 3) synthesize the theoretical framework and design framework for a Constructivist web-based learning environment model to improve Critical thinking. The results of study that there are the designing framework has 8 elements as following: (1) Problem base, (2) resources center, (3) Related communities Center, (4) Collaboration center, (5) Cognitive tools, (6) Critical Thinking center, (7) Scaffolding center, and (8) Coaching center. Capable of critical thinking: 1) Elementary Clarification 2) Bases for a Decision 3) Inference 4) Advanced clarification 5) Supposition and integration.

Keywords: Constructivist web-based learning · Critical thinking · Constructivist theories

1 Introduction

Learning in the twenty - first century, in which we live in a knowledge-based society driven by the potential knowledge and thinking skills, plus the progress of technology, thus it will pursue knowledge continuously throughout life. This causes many people to develop themselves all the time. When the society is developing, the society will have to develop accordingly. Education is the important tool of the evolution of human knowledge, ability, and thinking skills, especially in the current society, the environment has changed dramatically over the years; therefore, this is necessary to develop them more increasingly. However, in today's educational management, the emphasis is on transferring and memorizing information. As a result, the learners' Critical Thinking skills are insufficient to develop thinking skills with critical thinking is one idea that could

© Springer Nature Switzerland AG 2021
Y.-M. Huang et al. (Eds.): ICITL 2021, LNCS 13117, pp. 219–227, 2021.
https://doi.org/10.1007/978-3-030-91540-7_24

help participants solving problems efficiently associated with the problems because most of the solution requires significant judgment thought [18].

For the reasons stated above, it is vital to modify learning to match the needs of 21st century learners. Researcher has realized the importance and the need for conducting the research in order to solve the problems which is entitled "Designing Framework for Development of Constructivist Web-Based Learning Environment Model to Enhance Critical Thinking". The study will apply the teaching and learning process and emphasize on the students Models for learning environments are being designed and developed. The model can be used as a medium to develop thinking skills and the selection of learners and use it as a method to manage learning, courses content in parallel with the development of critical thinking. The findings may lead to the development of the students in order to respond to the changes in the social world and the world today and it will be useful in applying knowledge to develop the researcher's profession and a guideline for further research. Therefore, Instead of passively receiving knowledge, teaching design must be adjusted to promote Critical Thinking abilities and knowledge construction. Instructional Design Theory was incorporated into the design. Theories used as Constructivist theories were employed as a foundation. Critical Thinking and Information Processing. These theories will aid learners in knowledge production and critical thinking, especially in science classes. Furthermore, the web-based media attribute and symbol system will aid knowledge production and critical thinking [5, 19].

Because of the aforementioned reason, this study aimed to design framework for development Primary kids' critical thinking skills are influenced by their learning surroundings. In the learning process, this could result in the learners acquiring cognitive abilities and critical thinking. The significance of synthesizing is recognized by researchers. The Designing Framework for Development of Constructivist Web-Based Learning Environment Model. This design framework may assist designers in creating a Constructivist web-based learning environment model that is effective. It will also assist in establishing credibility and providing useful guidelines for the creator of the constructivist web-based learning environment model [4–6, 11, 12, 17, 19].

2 Research Methodology

The Model research is first phase of research (Richey and Klein 2007) [16], with an emphasis on the design process, and model development. The procedure includes the following of Analyze associated ideas and Learning theory, constructivist theory, cognitive theory, critical thinking, media theory, and technology theory are examples of theories, and create a Constructivist web-based learning environment model to improve Critical thinking. Experts from diverse domains, Theorists, designers, developers, evaluators, researchers, and learners are just a few examples, took part in this phase. Model development is the first part of model research. Quantitative and qualitative methods were used to collect data. We used document analysis and a survey.

2.1 Research Objectives

The goal of this study is to create a framework for the development of a constructivist web-based learning environment model that will help elementary pupils improve their critical thinking skills.

2.2 Research Instruments

1. A form for document evaluation and analysis. The document analysis' breadth in relation to constructivist ideas, critical thinking, and media theory.
2. The synthesis record format of the designing framework of Constructivist Web-Based Learning Environment Model.
3. The expert review record form for the examination of the Designing framework. This instrument's framework consists of three primary issues: learning content, instructional design, and a multimedia learning environment.
4. The individuals' characteristics were adapted in an open-ended survey from Richey and Klein (2007).
5. The design and development processes on the learning environment model, For the designer and developer, there is an interview form, adapted from Richey and Klein (2007).

2.3 Data Collecting and Analysis

The information was gathered in the following format:

1. Synthesis of the Constructivist Web-Based Learning Environment Model's theoretical foundation for improving critical thinking in elementary students. The information was gathered by examining the constructivist theories, cognitive theories, critical thinking, pedagogy, multimedia learning, and media symbol system's principles, theories, associated research, and contextual studies.
2. Synthesis of the Constructivist Web-Based Learning Environment Model's Design Framework to Improve Primary Students' Critical Thinking. Constructivist theories, cognitive theories, critical thinking, pedagogy, multimedia learning, and the media symbol system were all highlighted and analyzed before being translated into the designing framework.
3. The above-mentioned investigation of connected materials and related researchers yielded the theoretical framework's synthesis and designing framework. Then, utilizing the synthesis of theoretical framework and designing framework record form, they were recorded.

3 Results of the Study

The following are the study's findings:

3.1 Designing Framework of Web-Based Learning Environment Model

The outcomes of this study's a theoretical framework that is synthesis that was utilized as a foundation in synthesizing the Constructivist Web-Based Learning Environment Model's designing framework to Enhance Critical Thinking for primary students discovered four important foundations for improving knowledge construction and critical thinking:

The Activation of Cognitive Structures and Enhance Critical Thinking. The relationship between different emphasized theories is presented, including Constructivist theories and Cognitive constructivist theory (Piaget 1964), Situated learning (Brown et al. 1989), and Critical thinking (Brown et al. 1989, Ennis 2011). As a component for Problem foundation, it was created with a complicated problem context in mind [2, 9, 15] (Fig. 1).

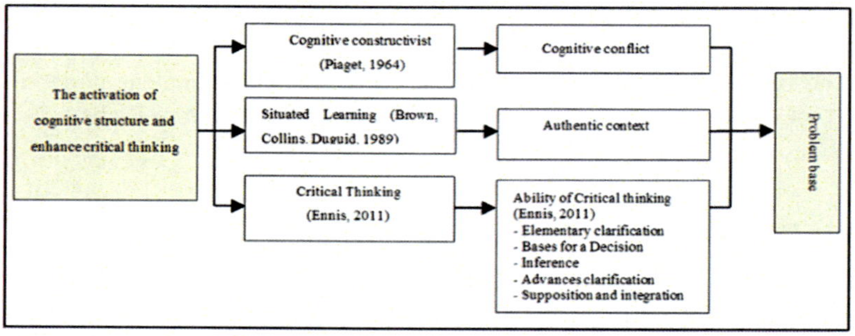

Fig. 1. The Theoretical framework designing to problem base.

The Enhancement for Cognitive Equilibrium. It is the following diagram depicts the relationship between the highlighted theories: Karlausmeier's Information Processing Theory (1985), Ausubel's Meaningful Learning Theory (1963), and the SOI Model (Mayer 1996). It was created as part of the Resources Center. In addition, CLEs (Jonassen 1999). It was created as a part of the Related Communities Center [1, 10, 13, 14] (Fig. 2).

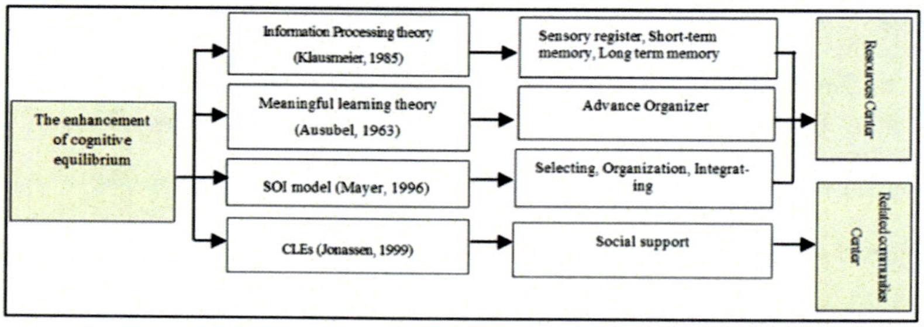

Fig. 2. The theoretical framework designing to Resources Center and Related communities Center.

The Support and Enhancement for Cognitive Structure and Critical Thinking. It is illustrated The following is the relationship between the highlighted theories: Social constructivism (Vygotsky 1978) was created as a component for the Collaboration-Center, OLEs (Hannafin et al. 1999) was created as a component for the Cognitive Tools, and critical thinking (Ennis 2011) was created as a component for the Critical Thinking Center [8, 9, 18] (Fig. 3).

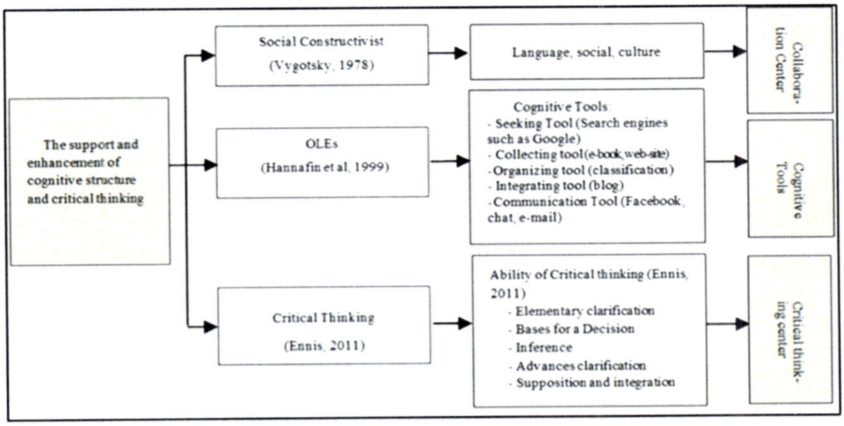

Fig. 3. The Theoretical framework designing to Collaboration Center, Cognitive Tools and Critical thinking Center.

Improving and Assisting Critical Thinking and Knowledge Construction. The relationship between the highlighted hypotheses is demonstrated as follows: Social constructivism (Vygotsky 1978), OLEs (Hannafin et al. 1999) designed as the component for Scaffolding Center (e.g., conceptual, metacognition, procedural, and strategic scaffolding), and Cognitive apprenticeship (Collin et al. 1991) designed as the component for Coaching-Center (e.g., (1) conceptual, (2) metacognition, (3) procedural, and (4) strategy scaffolding) [7, 8, 18] (Fig. 4).

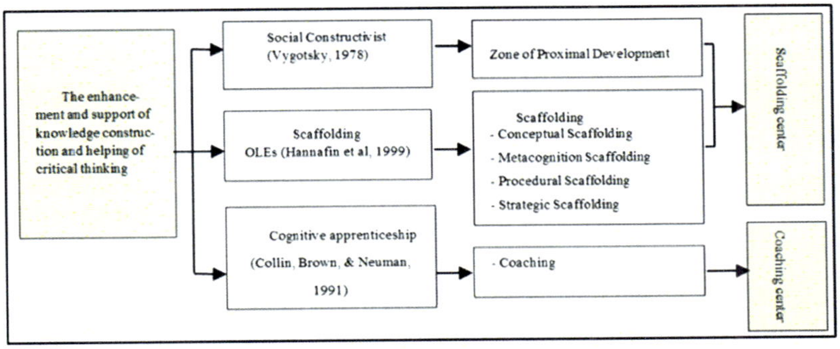

Fig. 4. The Theoretical framework designing to Scaffolding Center and Coaching Center.

According to the findings of the synthesis of the design framework based on theoretical framework and implemented in practice, the following are some examples of design aspects (see Figs. 5, 6, 7 and 8).

1. Problem based

   The purpose of the problem- base is to engage the cognitive structure by simulating the authentic setting. 1) Visual, 2) text, 3) audio, and 4) animation are used in the design to encourage students to recognize and pay attention by employing externally imposed stimuli to enable students identify with their own experiences.

Fig. 5. Design elements in the first page and problem base of the constructivist web-based learning environment model.

2. Resources Center and Related communities Center

   Resources Center is the gathering of data that should be made available to students during the procedure for resolving a problem. They use it to expand their knowledge by utilizing various information technologies. As a foundation, cognitive theories, particularly information processing theories that focus on memory processes, are used. In addition, the SOI model (Mayer 1996) is utilized to aid in the selection, organization, and integration of linked data.

Fig. 6. Design elements in resources center and related communities center of the constructivist web-based learning environment model.

3. Collaboration Center, Cognitive tools Center, Critical thinking Center

    Collaborative Center is used to utilized to provide students with the opportunity to learn norms for cooperating and developing a society of information sharing and collaborative problem solving. To answer the problem, the students will discuss various viewpoints. As a result, it was built to collaborate in issue solving via Face book, Line, and e-mail, allowing students to express their opinions and share information from anywhere, at any time, and in any place.

Fig. 7. Design elements in collaboration-center, cognitive tools-center and critical thinking-center of the constructivist web-based learning environment model.

4. Scaffolding Center and Coaching Center

    Scaffolding Center was created using the OLEs model (Hannafin 1999), since pupils have a time constraint on their growth called the zone of proximal development, which is focused on helping or scaffolding, and It was separated into four sections by scaffolding: 1) Conceptual Scaffolding, 2) Meta-cognitive Scaffolding, 3) Procedural Scaffolding, and 4) Strategic Scaffolding are the four types of scaffolding available.

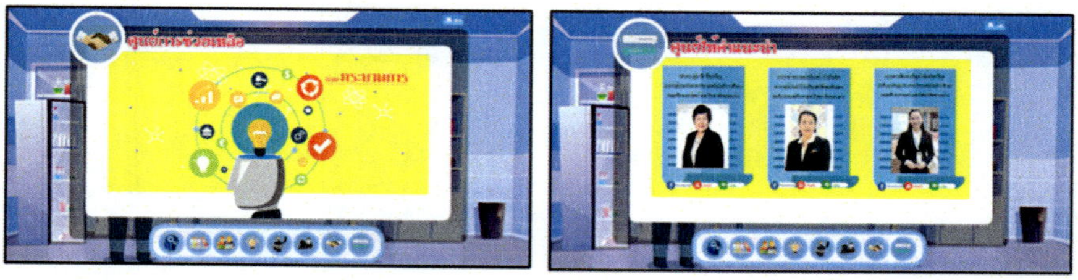

Fig. 8. Design elements in scaffolding center and coaching center of the constructivist web-based learning environment model.

4 Discussion and Conclusion

The theoretical framework of the Constructivist web-based learning environment to enhance Critical thinking There are three foundations: 1) psychological, 2) psychological, and 3) psychological. Pedagogical, pedagogical, pedagogical, pedagogical, pedagogical, pedagogical, it is in line with Kanjug Issara (2009), who investigated a theoretical framework for enhancing expert mental models in a learning context. The outcome of this investigation exemplifies the design framework of increase the constructivist web-based learning environment the foundations of critical thinking are essential. The results of study that there are the designing framework has 8 elements as following: (1) Problem base, (2) resources center, (3) Related communities Center, (4) Collaboration center, (5) Cognitive tools, (6) Critical Thinking center, (7) Scaffolding center, and (8) Coaching center. in addition to discovering: This model has built and developed quality models, as evidenced by the fact that the content is correct, up to date, and current, as determined by numerous specialists. Additionally, Design and media can motivate students to learn more and develop critical thinking skills. It's possible that this is because the learning environment model is different was developed utilizing a theoretical framework and instructional design theories that could be used to put the ideas into reality (e.g., Constructivist theory is used to construct knowledge). Encourage students to solve problems in order to reach a state of balance. It has also incorporated cognitive skills and critical thinking into its design.

Acknowledgements. This study was aided by a grant by the Ph.D. Program in Educational Technology, Faculty of Education, Khon Kaen University, and the Khon Kaen University Research Group for Innovation and Cognitive Technology, for which we are grateful.

References

1. Ausubel, D.: The Psychology of Meaningful Verbal Learning. Grune & Stratton, New York (1963)
2. Brown, J., Collins, A., Duguid, P.: Situated cognition and the culture of learning. Educ. Res. **18**(1), 32–42 (1989)

3. Centre for Education Research and Innovation: 21st Century Learning : Research, Innovation and Policy (2008)
4. Chaijaroen, S.: Development of knowledge construction using information technology. Department of Educational Technology, Khon Kaen University (2004)
5. Chaijaroen, S.: Educational Technology: Principles Theories to Practices. Khon Kaen University (2008)
6. Chaijaroen, S., Kanjug, I., Watkhawlam, W.: Synthesis of Learning Innovation Model Enhancing Learning's Learning Potential Using Brain-Based Learning. Faculty of Education, Khon Kaen University (2008)
7. Collins, A., Brown, J.S. Holum, A.: Cognitive apprenticeship: making thinking visible. Am. Educ. **15**(3), 6–11, 38–39 (1991)
8. Hanafin, M.: Open Learning Environment: Foundation, Methods, and Models. Instructional Designing Theories and Model: A New Paradigm of Instructional Theory Volume II (Charles M.). Lawrence Erlbaum Associates, Mahlway, N.J. (1999)
9. Illinois College of Education: https://education.illinois.edu/docs/default-source/faculty-documents/robert-ennis/thenatureofcriticalthinking_51711_000.pdf?sfvrsn=7bb51288_2. Accessed 11 July 2020
10. Jonassen, D.: Designing constructivist learning environments. In: Instructional Design Theories and Models: A New Paradigm of Instructional Theory, vol. II, pp. 215–239. Erlbaum, New Jersey (1999)
11. Kanjug, I.: Development of Learning Environments Model Enhancing Expertise Mental Model. Doctor of Philosophy Thesis in Educational Technology, Graduate School, Khon Kaen University (2009)
12. Kanjug, I., Chaijaroen, S.: The design of web-based learning environments enhancing mental model construction. Procedia. Soc. Behav. Sci. **46**, 3134–3140 (2012)
13. Klausmeier, H.J.: Educational Phycology, 6th edn. Harper & Row, New York (1985)
14. Mayer, R.E.: Designing instruction for constructivist learning. In: Instructional-Design Theories and Models: A New Paradigm of Instructional Theory, vol. II (1999)
15. Piaget, J.: Cognitive development in children: Piaget development and learning. J. Res. Sci. Teach. **2**(3), 176–186 (1964)
16. Richey, R.C., Klein, J.D.: Design and Development Research Methods, Strategies and Issues. Lawrence Erlbaum Associates (2007)
17. Charuni, S.: The development of constructivist web-based learning environment model to enhance creative thinking for higher education students. Doctor of Philosophy Thesis in Education Technology, Graduate School, Khon Kaen University (2009)
18. Vygotsky, L.S.: Mind in Society: The Development of Higher Psychological Processes. Harvard University Press, Cambridge (1978)
19. Wattanachai, S., Samat, C., Chaijaroen, S., Kanjug, I., Kong-im, K., Insorn, P.: Design and development of learning innovation enhancing the learner' thinking. Faculty of Education, Khon Kaen University (2005)

Using Design Patterns to Teach Conceptual Entity Relationship (ER) Data Modelling

Lizette Weilbach(✉), Marié Hattingh, and Komla Pillay

University of Pretoria, Private Bag X20, Hatfield 0028, UK
{lizette.weilbach,marie.hattingh,komla.pillay}@up.ac.za

Abstract. Relational databases are core to the development of information systems. Designing and presenting a quality conceptual Entity Relationship (ER) data schema to model the entities, attributes and relationships in such a database is equally important. Context and assumptions play an important role in the construction of these schemas. University students have limited real-world experience and typically struggle with the construction of database schemas. Case studies are used to provide students with functional details and context. Patterns are considered useful to transfer best practices and expert knowledge from experts to novice users. This paper proposes the use of patterns to teach ER data modelling to second year Systems Analysis and Design (SAD) students. An example ER pattern for a Point-of-Sales (POS) system is proposed with one possible context adjustment. Assumptions, functional requirements and business rules form part of the proposed pattern to explain the different contexts in which the pattern could be applied as well as the effect that these context adjustments will have on the ER data model. Guidelines are given to assist lectures with using the pattern to teach their students conceptual ER data modelling.

Keywords: Entity relationship diagram · Modelling · Systems Analysis and Design · Patterns

1 Introduction

Databases are core to the development of information systems [1]. Consequently, database design and modelling are considered important skills of industry ready Informatics graduates [2] and an essential student outcome required in an ABET accredited Information Systems programme [3]. It involves the generation of a quality model depicting the database on which the system will run. An ER data model, also referred to as an ER database schema is the most popular technique used for data modelling and taught in University data modules. Chen [4] first developed the ER conceptual data modelling technique. The model represents, in graphical format, the data needs of the business and requires problem solving skills, visualization of details, abstraction, expertise in determining the correct relationships, resolving M-M (many to many) relationships and correctly determining optional and mandatory semantics [5]. The construction of a physical data model progresses through a set of phases and starts off by discovering data entities and attributes and by identifying the binary relationships between these entities to

© Springer Nature Switzerland AG 2021
Y.-M. Huang et al. (Eds.): ICITL 2021, LNCS 13117, pp. 228–238, 2021.
https://doi.org/10.1007/978-3-030-91540-7_25

construct a logical data model. This logical model is then translated into a third normal form (3NF) relational model by applying normalization principles to exclude repeating groups, eliminate redundant data and eliminate transitive dependencies [4]. Finally, the relational model is converted into a physical database using the software intended for its implementation [6].

Novice learners find the task of drawing an ER model challenging due to its abstract nature [7]. In [1] it was indicated that there are four main issues with database design: (1) the skills to conduct proper requirement elicitation from the client; (2) the skills to conceive a database to meet the requirements; (3) the skills to convert the conceptual database design into a logical/technical design; and (4) the skills to contemplate their initial design. Another factor that influences the effectiveness of teaching ER modelling, is understanding the context within which the ER design needs to be applied [8]. The authors found, in their own teaching, that although students might have the requisite (theoretical) knowledge of ER modelling, they struggle to apply it in a specific context as they frequently make wrong or insufficient assumptions about the problem domain - which is not always explicitly stated in the case study (or mentioned by the client in the capstone project). In order to improve student learning and understanding of ER modelling, the authors, who are also lecturers responsible for teaching the capstone project, embarked on a new learning strategy in an attempt to improve the quality of the ER models which learners produce.

Kolfschoten et al. [9] showed that the use of design patterns can significantly reduce the cognitive load for computer-based teaching. Their study was conducted within the context of recognizing the dynamic nature of the engineering and technology domains. Within these domains they attempted to find a way that students can solve problems by "recognize(ing) the problem and apply(ing) readily applicable knowledge about solutions". They argue that the use of design patterns could assist novice learners to obtain expert knowledge in an effective and efficient way, and found these patterns to be very useful in transferring tacit best practices and expert knowledge.

The main objective of this conceptual paper is to propose the use of ER data model design patterns as a method which lecturers can use to teach students to construct ER data models for specific contexts, by reducing the cognitive load of novice learners. The research questions are as follows:

- What are the components of an ER data model pattern which educators can use to teach students ER modelling?
- In what way can educators make use of ER data model patterns to teach students ER Modelling?

To answer these questions, the authors propose an ER data model pattern for a Point-of-Sales (POS) system and illustrate the effect that different assumptions and context changes/adjustments have on the pattern. Application guidelines for teaching ER Modelling using these patterns are also stipulated. The research findings can therefore be valuable to both business practitioners and academics.

The paper is divided into five sections. Section two discusses literature on the problems with learning ER Modelling, using case studies and patterns to teach. Section three introduces the initial pattern with one context adjustment as illustration (due to page limitations the other seven context adjustments cannot be shown). Section four discusses the implementation with associated consequences and guidelines for implementation. Lastly, section five concludes the paper and provides the direction for future research.

2 Literature Review

The following two sections provide a brief summary of the challenges associated with teaching ER modelling and secondly the history of using patterns for learning.

2.1 Problems with Learning Entity Relationship (ER) Modelling

In [1] database analysis and design (within software engineering) was described as a process which is not precise, or well-defined. The task at hand is often open-ended and very dependent on the business processes and rules applicable in the organisation. This means no concise algorithms are available to derive the ER data model from for a particular set of requirements. ER modelling has often been described as a "wicked problem" [1, 10] because the correct (or suitable) solution often needs to be derived from partial, contradictory and constantly changing requirements and it in many cases contains multifaceted interdependencies. Armarego (in: [1]) describes the teaching of database modelling as an "educational dilemma" due to the following reasons: (1) further engagement with the problem leads to added complexity (as more elements are discovered); (2) learning strategies that students can utilise to make sense of the problem are vital to the process; (3) students need to have a firm understanding and intuition regarding the context in which a problem occurs in order to design an effective solution; (4) students need enough experience to assist them (the designers) in recognising similarities and differences which they can use to give them insight in the current scenario.

Connoley and Begg [1] indicated that the types of knowledge and understanding that are needed to accomplish database design and modelling include: background knowledge (which is subjective to each student), database concepts (relational model, SQL, ER modelling, normalisation), database analysis and design (fact-finding techniques, ER to relation mapping, relation to table mapping), database implementation (DBMS, architectures) and business and management (project management, business management, business environment, business processes professional, legal and ethical aspects). The latter aspect refers to the context in which the database will be implemented.

Understanding the context is important to allow all users (which include the designer) to have a common understanding on the meaning of the data that will be captured in the database [11]. Grimshaw et al. [11] stressed that even in teaching database design, context is important as the students, from a cultural context perspective, need to be able to relate to a familiar context when being taught database concepts. Therefore, the context in which students understand and interpret organisational knowledge of business processes and corresponding data, is key to teaching database design and modelling. As students need to rely on their own experience with real-world organisations (which is often still very limited in their second year) to identify and justify entity relationships and data integrities, they find the construction of ER models very challenging. Hussain's [8] research showed that the three main errors students made in database design which had a severe or moderate impact on the database schema were: wrong cardinality, wrong keys (which both had a severe impact on the database schema), and missing attributes (which had a moderate impact on the database schema). He investigated student data modelling errors, and uncovered four main reasons for these: (1) the student did not understand the ER concept or the problem domain; (2) the student is not conscientious in modelling, even though s/he might understand the ER concept; (3) the student made an incorrect assumption and (4) the student modelled additional concepts that were not part of the scope. The first and third errors are both related to the understanding (or the misunderstanding) of the context in which the database design needs to be applied.

2.2 Using Case Studies to Teach

Case studies are frequently used in SAD curricula to simulate a real-life situation, as described in Smuts and Hattingh [2]. Case studies in a SAD context usually sketch a problem scenario consisting of a number of business processes and associated business rules that need to be supported by designing an Information System. From the case study, students need to extract explicit and implicit functional requirements. According to Rosatelli and Self [12], the latter is very much a lecturer-led approach as students need to be explained the context, in order to understand the functional requirements. Rosatelli and Self [12] indicate that lecturers are key to facilitating learning from case studies by "asking the appropriate questions during the discussions". Winters and Mor [13] proposed case studies as a method to derive design patterns. They use patterns, derived from case studies, to develop more patterns that can be applied in practice.

2.3 Using Patterns to Teach

According to Eckstein et al. [14], the use of patterns provides a usable and accessible way to capture and communicate expert knowledge. The original concept of a pattern was described by Alexander et al. [15] as a re-usable solution which could address architectural problems that frequently occurred. In their own words they describe a pattern as follows [15]: "Each pattern describes a problem which occurs over and over again in our environment, and then describes the core of the solution to that problem, in such a way that you can use this solution a million times over, without ever doing it the same way twice." Their pattern concept has been widely accepted and used in the world of software engineering since Gamma et al. [16] published on its adoption and use in object-oriented software development. A pattern is not merely a recipe or a set of step-by-step instructions, but it is rather a solution to a problem which is represented in an abstract, instead of a concrete way.

In general, a pattern consists of the following four essential elements [16]:

1. The pattern name: this is the toughest part of designing a pattern. It describes a design problem, its solutions, and the consequences of applying the pattern in a word or two. This allows us to talk about our patterns with our colleagues and to refer to them

in our documentation. It makes it easier to think about designs and to communicate them and their trade-offs to others. Finding good names has been one of the hardest parts of developing our catalogue.
2. A description of the problem the pattern can be applied to: It is important to not only describe the problem, but also the context of the problem. It could include a list of assumptions made or conditions that must be met before it makes sense to apply the pattern.
3. The solution the pattern provides: this part of the pattern describes the elements of the design, their relationships, responsibilities, and collaborations. It should not describe a specific concrete design or implementation, as one needs to be able to apply it to different situations. It should rather provide an abstract description of the problem and how a general arrangement of elements can solve it.
4. The consequences of applying the pattern: These are the results of applying the pattern to the problem. They are important as they can assist the user to evaluate all the different design alternatives available to determine the best pattern for the problem at hand.

Eckstein et al. [14] explain that "patterns provide a method for capturing and communicating knowledge in a way that is most comfortable for you and most useful for your industry students". They further profess that patterns provide a "format and process for sharing successful practices in a way that allows each practice to be used by a variety of people in many different ways". This indicates that patterns provide students with solutions to a problem that they might encounter as well as the implications of such an implementation.

3 Pattern Development and Context

ER modelling is taught as a component of the Systems Analysis and Design (SAD) module in both first and second year at our institution. The concepts of ER modelling are introduced in the first year to SAD students. In the second year, the theoretical concepts of ERDs are taught in a separate module. Students are expected to model the data of the system in their SAD module by producing ER Diagrams (ERDs). They are provided with a case study and adopt the following steps when deriving their ERDs:

- Create new problem domain description based on the provided Information System application case study;
- Define functional requirements for the information system
- Define business rules for the problem domain;
- Identify entities, relationships, and semantics such as optional and mandatory;
- Resolve M-M relationships, and
- Define entity attributes.

Students struggle to produce ER data models based on the case studies they are provided with and consequently also struggle to produce the ER models required for their capstone projects. The authors have been teaching ER Modelling for 31 years (combined). They found the traditional in-class method of teaching ER modelling theory to be adequate for teaching the basic database concepts, but inadequate for teaching the application of these concepts to specific business contexts. To assist them with the latter, they developed three prominent ER patterns representing three types of systems which students typically encounter in their capstone projects: A Point-of-Sales (POS), Product manufacturing, and Scheduling System.

This conceptual paper provides, as an example, the ER pattern developed (with context adjustments) for a POS system. This particular pattern has eight context adjustments, but due to page limitation, only one can be illustrated. In line with Gamma et al. [16], the pattern starts off with a descriptive name; it discusses the general context in which the pattern could be implemented (by indicating the typical assumptions and functional requirements/use cases it addresses); it provides details on the business rules applicable to the pattern, as well as the consequences of applying the pattern. The POS ER pattern is presented in the following section.

Pattern Name: Entity Relationship (ER) Pattern for a Point-of-Sale System (POS).

Description of the context in which this pattern can be used:

This ERD pattern proposes a model of the data entities, attributes and relationships needed to represent the data of a POS System.

The assumptions made in the primary (initial) pattern are as follows:

- Information is kept about different types of employees (examples of employees include: store manager, cashier/sales person, packer, etc.)
- Employees (cashiers/sales people) conclude sales
- Products are bought from suppliers
- Products are sold to buyers/customers
- Buyers/customers make use of a payment type when they pay for their sales
- Product prices can change over time
- Products bought from suppliers are sold (as-is) to the buyers/customers
- The company doesn't keep information on the buyers/customers

Functional requirements/use cases supported by the primary (initial) pattern:

- The OWNER wants to:
  - Manage EMPLOYEES in the following way:
    1. Add employee type, Update employee type, Delete employee type, Add new employee, Update employee details, Delete employee (wrongly added and who never performed any activity on the system), View employee details (wrongly added and which was never assigned to an employee), View employee types
  - Manage PRODUCTS in the following way:

- Add new product type, Update product details, Delete product type (wrongly added and which was never assigned to a product), View product type, Add new product, Update product details, Delete product wrongly added/never sold, View product details,
- Manage SUPPLIERS in the following way:

  2. Add new supplier, Update supplier details, Delete supplier (wrongly added and from whom nothing was ever bought), View Supplier details

- Manage SALES in the following way:

  3. View sales, Generate sales report

- The CUSTOMER wants to:

  4. Buy products

Business rules to consider for the primary (initial) pattern: (Entities are shown in CAPITAL LETTERS and important attributes are underlined)

- PRODUCTS are bought from SUPPLIERS and re-sold (as-is) to CUSTOMERS
- A CUSTOMER ORDER has a status of "Ordered" or "Received"
- PRODUCTS have specified PRODUCT TYPE(S)
- The PRODUCT PRICE indicates the selling price
- The PRODUCT PRICE can change overtime
- PRODUCTS don't have SIZE(S)
- EMPLOYEES are linked to the SALES they capture
- SALES are paid using a specific PAYMENT METHOD
- A PRODUCT's QtyOnHand is decreased when a SALE is made
- CUSTOMER details are not captured
- CUSTOMERS cannot return PRODUCTS
- CUSTOMERS cannot buy more PRODUCTS than the available QtyOnHand

ER data model for primary/initial pattern is presented in Fig. 1 (due to page limitations the context adjustment is indicated with the purple entity).

Context adjustments for this pattern:

- Context adjustment 1 (Capture data on the CUSTOMER who makes the SALE):
  - The assumptions made in this adjustment are as follows:

    1. Customers are linked to sales, Customer details are captured

  - Added functional requirements/use cases:

    2. The OWNER wants to:

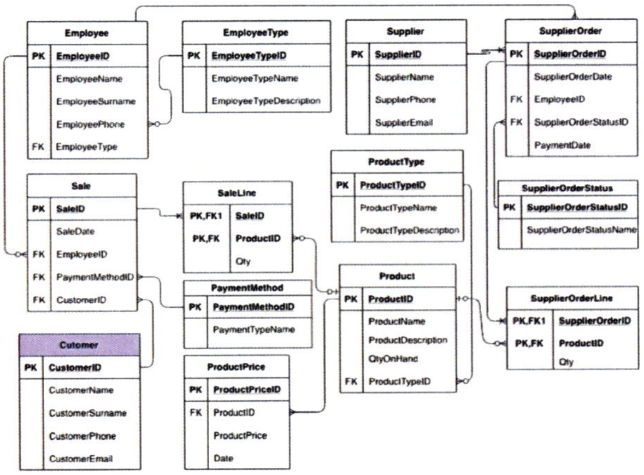

Fig. 1. Initial ER Model with context adjustment 1 (indicated in purple)

3. View customer details, View details on customer sales preferences (what does a customer typically buy?)

– Adjusted business rules:

4. CUSTOMER details are captured for SALES made

ER data model for Context adjustment 1 is presented in Fig. 1.

4 Discussion

Pattern learning is a proposed way of teaching [14] and is suggested in this paper as a means of teaching ER Modelling. Teaching ER Modelling is complex [1, 10] and it's imperative that context is considered when applying the pattern. In this study we propose an initial pattern (with context adjustments) for a POS system with the associated assumptions, functional requirements and business rules. Formally defining a pattern in such a way, addresses the "wrong assumption" issue Hussain [8] has uncovered as well as the correct functional requirements needed to develop a conceptual model which [1] cited as data modelling issues.

4.1 The Consequences of Applying This Pattern

The following needs to be kept in mind when using the proposed pattern:

1. The proposed pattern offers a solution for the ER model of a typical POS system but could be adapted to make allowances for programming efficiency.
2. The solution must be implemented within the context of the organisation's specific functional requirements/use cases and business rules.

3. Students need to understand the implication of the relationships, for example:

- The implication of the relationship between the order and the refund is that a customer will only be able to receive a refund for a product that formed part of the original order.
- If a product such as a pizza (which has toppings as components and a price linked to the product size) is refunded, the product (pizza) cannot be resold, therefore the quantity of the product will not be increased, but if a product such as a computer (which is made up of different hardware and software components) is returned, for a reason that allows it to be resold (e.g. not damaged or malfunctioning), the quantity of the product and or the components needs to increase again. The designed solution should support the specific business processes.

4.2 Guidelines for Lecturers to Use Patterns to Teach ERDs

In addition to following the four elements of developing a pattern as detailed in Sect. 2 above, lecturers need to consider the following guidelines when using ERD patterns to teach SAD students:

1. Establish different patterns and make sure to generalise them i.e. cater for all possibilities on a high level. These base patterns need to be thoroughly explained or reasoned so students don't simply replicate the given patterns but are able to adapt based on the adjusted context sections.
2. Delve into the pattern - highlight the things that make patterns unique or the same. Patterns support the holistic approach to systems thinking [17]. Consider the database design with "other" models, such as which use cases will be needed to add information to the database, what type of data will flow into the system when the use case is executed (data flow diagram or sequence diagram), which data store will store the data, or retrieve the data from (data store or objects).
3. Teach students how to apply the pattern in different case scenarios by offering them exercises based on different case studies - Students need to be taught how to recognise patterns. Coplien [17] warned that patterns are often misused or misunderstood. As a pattern is a "solution to a problem in a context" [15] the patterns need to be explained in the context of how it can be used, where it can be used and the implications of using it.
4. Show them how the pattern will be adjusted for a different context by providing complete memos for each case study e.g. what it would look like if you sell products without components, products with components, or products with different sizes.
5. Pull the specific ER Model through to the actual database design and programming. In the second year this can be achieved by coordinating tutorials or exercises between the database and programming modules. Both these modules should for example implement exercises based on a POS system.
6. Consider the output of the system versus the database design (for completeness of the design). Students often struggle with creating reports that are an integral part of a useful system. Reports can only be generated based on the data captured by the system and stored in the database.

5 Conclusion and Future Research

The study set out to establish what the components of an ER data pattern should be and how patterns can be used by educators to improve the teaching of ER modelling. This conceptual paper presented one of the ER patterns (with context adjustments) which the authors developed, namely the Entity Relationship (ER) Pattern for a POS System. Consequently, the authors also provided some guidelines for lecturers to use when implementing such a pattern.

This pattern (and the other two which have already been developed) will be employed to teach ER modelling in the second year SAD module. After implementation, these patterns will be updated/modified, based on the students' understanding and the effectiveness of their implementation thereof. More patterns will accordingly be developed, to also account for other scenarios that students might encounter in their capstone projects.

References

1. Connoly, T.M., Begg, C.E.: A constructivist-based approach to teaching database analysis and design. J. Inf. Syst. Educ. **17**, 43 (2006)
2. Smuts, H., Hattingh, M.J.: Towards a knowledge conversion model enabling programme design in higher education for shaping industry-ready graduates. In: Kabanda, S., Suleman, H., Gruner, S. (eds.) SACLA 2018. CCIS, vol. 963, pp. 124–139. Springer, Cham (2019). https://doi.org/10.1007/978-3-030-05813-5_9
3. ABET: ABET Accreditation (2021). https://www.abet.org/. Accessed 29 July 2021
4. Chen, P.P.-S.: The entity-relationship model—toward a unified view of data. ACM Trans. Database Syst. **1**, 9–36 (1976). https://doi.org/10.1145/320434.320440
5. Eid, I.: A learning system for entity relationship modeling. In: PACIS 2012 Proceedings (2012)
6. Hingorani, K., Gittens, D., Edwards, N.: Reinforcing database concepts using entity relationship diagrams (ERD) and normalization together for designing robust databases. IIS **18**, 202–209 (2017). https://doi.org/10.48009/1_iis_2017_148-155
7. Yang, L., Cao, L.: The effect of MySQL workbench in Teaching Entity-Relationship Diagram (ERD) to relational schema mapping. Int. J. Mod. Educ. Comput. Sci. **8**(7), 1–12 (2016). https://doi.org/10.5815/ijmecs.2016.07.01
8. Hussain, T.: Teaching entity-relationship models effectively. In: 2016 International Conference on Computational Science and Computational Intelligence (CSCI), pp 264–269 (2016)
9. Kolfschoten, G.L., de Vreede, G.-J.: A design approach for collaboration processes: a multi-method design science study in collaboration engineering. J. Manage. Inf. Syst. **26**, 225–256 (2009)
10. Douglas, L., Pamela, S., Katie, D., Jim, B.: Deconstructing the Education-Industrial Complex in the Digital Age. IGI Global (2017)
11. Grimshaw, D.J., Mott, P.L., Roberts, S.A.: The role of context in decision making: some implications for database design. Eur. J. Inf. Syst. **6**(2), 122–128 (1997)
12. Rosatelli, M.C., Self, J.: A collaborative case study system for distance learning. Int. J. Artif. Intell. Educ. **14**, 97–125 (2004)
13. Winters, N., Mor, Y.: Dealing with abstraction: case study generalisation as a method for eliciting design patterns. Comput. Hum. Behav. **25**, 1079–1088 (2009)

14. Eckstein, J.: Pedagogical patterns: capturing best practices in teaching object technology. Softw. Focus **2**, 9–12 (2001). https://doi.org/10.1002/swf.19
15. Alexander, C., Ishikawa, S., Silverstein, M., et al.: A Pattern Language: Towns, Buildings, Construction. Oxford University Press, New York (1977)
16. Gamma, E., Helm, R., Johnson, R., et al.: Design Patterns: Elements of Reusable Object-Oriented Software, 1st edn. Addison-Wesley Professional, Reading (1994)
17. Coplien, J.: Idioms and patterns as architectural literature. IEEE Softw. **14**, 36–42 (1997)

Education Practice Issues and Trends

Conceptualising a Model for Meaningful Digital Pedagogy

Janne Väätäjä and Satu-Maarit Frangou(✉)

University of Lapland, 96300 Rovaniemi, Finland
{janne.vaataja,satu-maarit.frangou}@ulapland.fi

Abstract. This action research aims to develop practices for the teacher education practicum that can support and encourage the collaborative planning of digital technology integration in teaching by university teacher educators and student teachers and supervising in-service teachers. More specifically, this study seeks to identify the features that make the pedagogical use of digital technologies meaningful. The background arises from the need to find ways to develop technology-enhanced pedagogy that encourages student teachers to engage in lifelong collaborative learning. We use the technology integrated matrix (TIM) as a theoretical frame-work and in the content analysis. The data collection took place during a primary school teacher education practicum period and involved teacher educators (N = 5), student teachers (N = 10), and classroom teachers (N = 5) in Finland. The results indicate that the pedagogical use of digital technologies needs to be considered throughout the teaching process: in the planning phase, action phase, and evaluation phase. Based on the results, we identify the key features of meaningful digital pedagogy to form a model that supports the codevelopment of digital pedagogical solutions.

Keywords: Primary school teacher education practicum · Meaningful · Learning community · Digital pedagogy

1 Introduction

There has been great interest in and the need to integrate digital technologies in Finnish primary education over the last decade and, hence, also in teacher training [16]. The latest cause for this has been the COVID-19 pandemic, which forced Finnish schools to transfer their teaching mostly to distance teaching in the spring of 2020. Contact teaching was arranged with restrictions; there was a shift back to contact teaching two weeks before the end of the semester, and the unstable situation has remained ever since. Therefore, teachers have had to prepare for sudden distance teaching if the risk of spreading the COVID-19 virus rises [6].

In teacher training, the integration of digital technology has been slow [14], and development projects in Finland have called for teacher education to better combine practical competences with scientific knowledge. Here, the supervision of in-service teachers' existing classroom practices and principles is highly influential during student

© Springer Nature Switzerland AG 2021
Y.-M. Huang et al. (Eds.): ICITL 2021, LNCS 13117, pp. 241–251, 2021.
https://doi.org/10.1007/978-3-030-91540-7_26

teachers' practicum periods. Therefore, continuous cooperation with university teacher training and in-service and student teachers is focal in enhancing student teachers' learning during practicums, helping all the actors become aware of the developed classroom practices and beliefs and knowledge affecting them [11]. This cooperation is supported by the Finnish National Core Curriculum, which promotes schools as learning communities, where the members of the community can learn with and from each other. The schools are also expected to interact with the surrounding society. Therefore, the schools should provide possibilities for their members to work on projects and collaborate with different actors outside the school community [7].

The idea of the learning community is implemented as part of the guided advanced practicum, which is part of the teacher education program at the University of Lapland. The idea of a learning community aims to support student teachers in developing colleague-based collaboration with the in-service teacher, teacher educators, and fellow students throughout the practicum [17]. Therefore, the interest is not in a certain group of members of the learning community but rather attempts to acknowledge and facilitate the development of all its members. The idea of reciprocity in learning communities is also promoted in the Guide on Policies to Improve Initial Teacher Education [5]. Furthermore, learning by doing with a more experienced colleague raises the possibility of getting positive experiences when integrating digital technologies in one's own teaching [11].

The use of digital tools in teaching cannot automatically be considered as enhancing the learning process. Self-directed learning practices and the frequent use of digital learning materials may be related to students' weaker learning outcomes at 15 years of age [18]. Thus, teacher-directed practices may be sometimes more efficient for achieving higher learning outcomes. Indeed, learning with digital tools is not necessarily enhanced [22]. Therefore, digital tools must be used in a pedagogically appropriate way, and pedagogical practices must be well structured to promote meaningful learning and meet learning goals.

The current research aims to contribute to the scientific debate on meaningful learning with and through digital technologies in a learning community context by considering and investigating its multisidedness, thereby developing a model for meaningful digital pedagogy. The principal aim of the study was to better understand the features of pedagogical solutions that are experienced as meaningful. Hence, the overarching question is as follows: "What features make the pedagogical use of digital technologies meaningful?" This will be investigated through the following subquestions:

1. How are the characteristics of meaningful learning considered in the planning phase?
2. How are the characteristics of meaningful learning considered in the action phase?
3. How are the characteristics of meaningful learning considered in the evaluation phase?

2 Technology Integration Matrix in the Context of Meaningful Digital Pedagogy

The concept of meaningful learning provides a framework through which meaningfulness can be evaluated. Meaningful learning can be understood as a concept describing personally valued, rich, and worthwhile learning experiences [1, 9]. Therefore, this approach toward learning experiences is associated with socioconstructivist and sociocultural learning theories [20]. Meaningful learning is likely to occur when learners are engaged in constructive, active, intentional, relational, and authentic learning processes [1, 9, 12, 13].

Meaningful learning processes involving digital technologies need to be planned in advance. Thus, the teacher should consider the pedagogical, which comprises the teacher's belief in what the learning situations should look like and the teacher's and learner's roles. Digital pedagogy often takes a socioconstructivist approach to teaching [19, 21, 22]. This fits well with the ideas from meaningful learning [1].

In the current study, digital pedagogy is understood as the meaningful integration of digital technologies into teaching practices. The integration of digital technologies is meaningful when they are used to enhance the learning process [15, 19]. However, we use the technology integrated matrix (TIM) as a theoretical framework and for theorizing the meaningfulness of technology integration because it provides an aspect of what kind of pedagogy different technologies can be utilized with [8, 10, 23]. The TIM framework also provides a more focused aspect, specifically on meaningful technology integration. The TIM was created by the Florida Center for Instructional Technology and comprises five characteristics of meaningful learning: active, constructive, authentic, collaborative, and goal directed. "Active" refers to the students' engagement in using technology as a tool rather than receiving information from the technology. The characteristic "constructive" means that the students are using technology to connect the new information with the information they already possess. "Authentic" refers to the students using technological tools to link the learning activities to real-life settings. "Collaborative" refers to students using technological tools to collaborate rather than working alone. Finally, "goal directed" means that technological tools are used to set goals, plan activities, and reflect on the entire learning process [10].

Furthermore, TIM includes five levels of technology integration: entry, adoption, adaptation, infusion, and transformation. In the "entry" level, teachers begin to use technologies for delivering curriculum content to pupils. In the "adoption" level, pupils are directed by the teacher in the conventional and procedural use of technological tools or applications. The "adaptation" level is achieved when the teacher is becoming a facilitator of pupils' independent use of technologies. In the "infusion" level, the teacher merely provides a learning context, and the pupils choose the technologies they want to use. The "transformation" level is achieved when the teacher encourages the pupils for innovative use of technologies to facilitate higher-order learning activities, which may not be possible without the use of technology. In all, the TIM provides a descriptive tool to plan and evaluate technology integration in the classroom [10, 15].

3 Research Methodology

Action research [2] aims to understand and improve the world by changing it. In the present study, the action research process [2] progressed as follows: 1) Analyze situation, 2) Generate new theories of change, 3) Plan action, 4) Take action and 5) Evaluate impact.

Action research approach [2] was chosen as the research methodology because it supported the ideas drawn from the learning community, which should provide a space for its members to align around shared goals. Aligning around shared goals makes it possible for members of the learning community to share results and learn from each other, thus improving their progress toward the set goals. In action research, the problems are usually practical, being directly or indirectly experienced by the research practitioner, and the participants are actively involved during the whole research process, not only during the data collection stage [4].

3.1 Participants

The collaborative research project lasted from 7 September 2020 to 9 October 2020, and it involved the researcher, five teacher educators, ten student teachers, and five in-service teachers participating in the guided advanced practicum. The guided advanced practicum is part of the Primary School Teacher Education Curriculum of the University of Lapland and is worth seven European Credit Transfer and Accumulation System (ECTS) credits. Student teachers are expected to deepen their knowledge concerning personal, pedagogical, and practical theory while learning to reflect on their developing teacher identities. During the project, the participants (N = 20) were divided into four individual groups based on the classroom grades. The four groups were comprised of different-aged pupils:

- *Group 1*: Second grade: two in-service teachers, four student teachers, and two teacher educators.
- *Group 2*: Third grade: one in-service teacher, two student teachers, and a teacher educator.
- *Group 3*: Fourth grade: one in-service teacher, two student teachers, and a teacher educator.
- *Group 4*: Sixth grade: one in-service teacher, two student teachers, and a teacher educator.

The common codevelopment goal of digital pedagogies was contextualized in each of the groups to meet the classroom's situated needs. The groups were encouraged to design and take responsibility as developers of their own work.

3.2 Data Collection

Data were drawn from common meetings, group meetings, planning reports, and an end survey for the research participants. Figure 1 represents the different meetings organized to engage the participants in the research process.

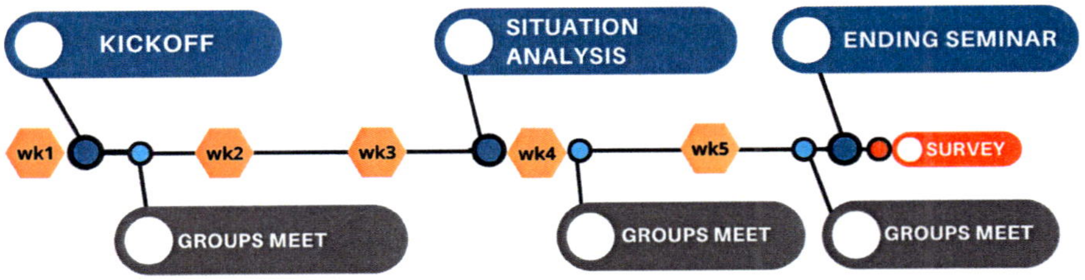

Fig. 1. Research process

All four groups attended the common meetings (CMs), which were a place for general discussion of the learning community. The CMs were arranged in Microsoft Teams and each of them lasted 1–2 h. Kickoff was a place for situation analysis, in which the learning community's common objective was set, and all the members could take part. The kickoff's agenda was to provide the groups with information about the learning community's common goal and help them contextualize the common objective in each group's context. A situation analysis was arranged halfway during the practicum to discuss how the process was proceeding. The end seminar was arranged to reflect on the results of the development process of the learning community. The CMs provided information about the participants' perceptions about the codevelopment of digital pedagogies. The first author observed the ongoing discussions in the CM and took field notes that provided the first set of data. The second author was the teacher educator of the second group.

Group meetings (GMs) were places where individual groups could discuss the objectives of the practicum and reflect on their achievement. The GMs were recorded, and each of the groups filled out a planning report, in which they wrote down their plans to reach their goals. The first meeting was arranged to set the main objective for the group. In the second meeting, they reflected on their process toward the objective and readjusted their actions, if necessary. The last GM was arranged to reflect on their success in meeting the set objectives.

Altogether, four datasets were collected. The first dataset consists of the planning reports (PR), which provide information about the groups' goals and practical solutions for reaching their goals. The first dataset is used to answer the first subquestion.

The second dataset consists of CM field notes, which provide information about the learning community's common objective. The third dataset consists of the recorded individual GMs, where the groups discussed how to contextualize the common goal in their classrooms. Each of the groups had their own contextualized goal for the codevelopment of digital pedagogies. The group members could decide among themselves how they would arrange the meetings. The second and third datasets are used to answer the second subquestion.

The fourth dataset consists of the survey answers provided by the participants. The survey provided an opportunity for the participants to anonymously share their thoughts about the research. The survey is referred to as "Survey." The fourth dataset is used to answer the third subquestion.

3.3 Data Analysis

The qualitative data were analyzed using the thematic analysis [3], which consists of generating initial coding, recognizing themes, and naming the main categories (Table 1). Generating initial codes means transforming the raw data into manageable forms.

Table 1. Codes, themes, and categories of the analysis

Generating initial codes	Recognizing themes	Naming main categories
Learner preparedness Activation Collaboration	Purposeful use of digital technologies	Planning phase
Adaptability Easy to use Learning objective related	Technology characteristics	
Searching for digital tools Sharing information with colleagues	Choosing the proper digital technology	
Instruction Supervision	Teacher-related activities	Action phase
Finding information Producing own materials Sharing information	Learner-related activities	
Technological knowledge Self-efficacy	Digital pedagogical competences	Evaluation phase
Motivating Adapting to changing situations	Evaluation of the teaching process	

Fifteen initial codes were generated from the collected data, and the codes were divided into six different themes. The six themes were placed under three categories: planning phase, action phase, and evaluation phase.

The planning phase includes three themes consisting of features to be considered before the actual pedagogical activities. The first theme, "Purposeful use of digital technologies," had three codes: pupil preparedness, activation, and collaboration.

The action phase consists of two themes—teacher- and learner-related activities that occurred in the actual learning situations after the planning phase. The teacher-related activities had two codes: instruction and supervision. Pupil-related activities had three codes: finding information, producing own materials, and sharing information.

The evaluation phase consists of two themes related to the participants' perceptions about their enhanced digital pedagogical competencies and evaluation of the teaching process. The first theme, "Digital pedagogical competences," had two codes: technological knowledge and self-efficacy. The second theme, "Evaluation of the teaching process," also had two codes: motivating and adapting to changing situations.

4 Results

How are the characteristics of meaningful learning considered in the planning phase? In the planning phase, the first recognized theme was the purposeful use of digital technologies. Pupil preparedness, activation, and collaboration were mentioned as goals that the pedagogical use of different digital technologies could help achieve.

Activating the pupils was found to be an important part of the lessons. The pedagogical use of digital technologies could provide them with ways to activate the pupils, letting them take more responsibility for their own learning. The participants also mentioned that they wanted pupils to collaborate with each other. Collaboration and activation are closely related to the TIM framework because the aim is to move toward learner-centered teaching practices [cf. 10, 15].

One aim was to raise learners' preparedness for studying with different digital technologies while giving teachers the opportunity to practice their pedagogical use. The participants wanted the learners to be prepared and comfortable using the same digital tools in distance teaching, for example. All the groups named some technologies, such as Google Classroom and Padlet, they wanted to learn to use as part of their teaching.

The second theme was technology characteristics. The groups raised the fact that digital technologies should possess some characteristics that could improve their meaningful pedagogical use: adaptability, ease of use, and learning objective related. Adaptability would make it possible to use the same digital technology on several different occasions. Ease of use concerns teachers and pupils. Learning objective relatedness was mentioned as the meaningful use of digital technology. According to the participants, the use of digital technology should always be connected to predetermined learning objectives. The TIM framework considers the context and learning objectives when integrating technologies in teaching. The TIM does not, however, provide any characteristics for usable technologies [cf. 8]. The defined characteristics for purposeful technologies may seem restrictive, but they can also help someone who is not confident in finding the proper technologies to use in their teaching.

Choosing the proper digital technology was the third theme in the planning phase. This was mentioned as one challenge in integrating digital technologies in teaching. The participants mentioned independent searching of the internet as one way to find the proper digital technology to use. Sharing information about digital technologies with colleagues was mentioned as an effective way to find the proper tools to use.

How are the characteristics of meaningful learning considered in the action phase?

In the action phase, the teacher-related activities consist of instructing the pupils how to use the digital technology and supervising the learning activities. Instructing the pupils to use digital technology was mentioned as a teacher-related activity; the instruction needs to provide pupils with information on how to log in to the digital application, navigate, and complete the assignments. Supervision was mentioned as a teacher's activity when pupils are working independently. Learner-related learning activities involved finding information, producing one's own materials, and sharing information. In the learning activities the learners' own phones and school computers were used.

Activating the learners and giving them responsibility for their own learning fits well with the characteristics of meaningful learning [cf. 1, 9]. Finding information was mentioned as an activity in which pupils should search for information about the phenomenon from the internet independently or in small groups. After finding information, the pupils should produce their materials and presentations based on their findings. Materials were produced using different digital platforms in different groups. Both the learner- and teacher-related activities during the action phase support the ideas drawn from the socioconstructivist learning theory [cf. 20]. Reflecting on the TIM [9], the integration of technologies should provide a means for the teacher to transform lessons toward more student-centered teaching. Therefore, the TIM framework emphasizes learners' activeness in the learning process, which is focal in the model's action phase [8].

How are the characteristics of meaningful learning considered in the evaluation phase? These features occurred after the action phase. The participants noted that their technological knowledge had been enhanced and that they felt their self-efficacy had increased toward the pedagogical use of digital technologies. The teachers did not raise any issues regarding their ability to learn to use digital technologies. However, they acknowledged that learning requires time and energy, which they do not always have sufficiently. The use of digital technologies was seen as a way to adapt to changing situations caused, for example, by the COVID-19 restrictions toward educational practices. Using and trying different technologies was seen as motivating for the pupils by the student teachers and in-service teachers. The TIM framework introduced five levels of technology integration: entry, adoption, adaptation, infusion, and transformation. The participants did not give a lot of freedom for the pupils regarding the choice of the tools used, but their own roles were emphasized as facilitators, and they provided students with various collaborative learning activities using technologies. Therefore, they were at the entry level of technology integration [cf. 8, 15, 23].

Reflecting on these findings, we answer the overarching research question: What features make the pedagogical use of digital technologies meaningful? Here, the participants saw many opportunities in using digital tools in the classroom environments and they shared similar views with each other even though they worked with different aged pupils. The key features characterizing meaningful pedagogical use of digital technologies are purposeful fitting for the context and well-thought-out choice of the digital tool that is activating and fitting for multiple uses. Figure 2 represents the model for meaningful pedagogy developed as part of the current study.

Overall, the model for meaningful digital pedagogy introduces ideas for socioconstructivist learning methods, such as active knowledge construction [cf. 20], when integrating digital technologies. In the model, the planning phase takes a socioconstructivist approach to learning, which affects the whole model [cf. 20, 23]. The action phase consists of the tasks that the teacher and pupils are expected to complete during learning activities. The teacher's role is a facilitator, whereas learners take more responsibility for their learning [19]. The evaluation phase consists of the reflection of digital pedagogical competences and evaluation of the teaching process. Meaningful technology integration is considered as a reflective process throughout the phases so that conscious choices are made that can be changed during the process if necessary. To make digital pedagogy meaningful, it is crucial to consider the learning objectives, context, curriculum, and available resources in all phases.

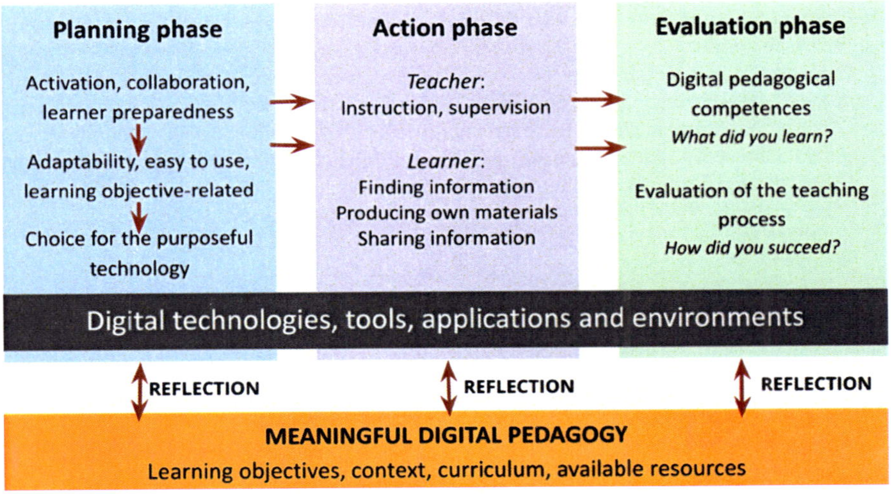

Fig. 2. Model of meaningful digital pedagogy

5 Discussion and Conclusion

The current paper set out to identify the features that make the pedagogical use of digital technologies meaningful. We applied the TIM to theorize the meaningfulness of technology integration in learning activities. The findings revealed that technologies provide possibilities to adapt to changing situations. The COVID-19 pandemic caused schools across the glove to move from contact teaching to distance teaching. This change made teachers change their teaching practices and use various digital tools to teach and stay in contact with their pupils. Based on the learning community concept, we found that collaboration between different actors was seen as beneficial, and the participants encouraged the development of these kinds of practices for codevelopment.

The main contribution lies in the developed model of meaningful digital pedagogy, which can extend the existing pedagogical models by guiding educators to a continuously reflective process of meaningful technology-assisted teaching and learning. The study has some shortfalls, such as the small number of participants, their baseline for performance comparison and the missing aspect from the TIM of the highest level of technology use, where learners choose their digital tools independently, hence indicating a direction for future research.

References

1. Ausubel, D.: The Psychology of Meaningful Verbal Learning. Grune and Stratton, New York (1963)
2. Burns, D.: Assessing Impact in Dynamic and Complex Environments: Systemic Action Research and Participatory Systemic Inquiry. CDI Practice Paper 8. IDS, Brighton (2014)
3. Braun, V., Clarke, V.: Using thematic analysis in psychology. Qual. Res. Psychol. **3**(2), 77–101 (2006). https://doi.org/10.1191/1478088706qp063oa

4. Craig, D.V.: Introduction to Action Research. Action Research Essentials, Jossey-Bass, San Francisco (2009)
5. European Commission ET2020 Working Group on Schools Policy, Shaping career-long perspectives on teaching: a guide on policies to improve initial teacher education, Publications Office of the European Union, Luxembourg (2015). http://ec.europa.eu/education/library/reports/initial-teacher-education_en.pdf. Accessed 09 Jul 2021
6. Finnish National Agency for Education: Distance education in Finland during the COVID-19 crisis Finland (2020). https://www.oph.fi/sites/default/files/documents/distance-education-in-finland-during-covid19initial-observations.pdf. Accessed 09 Jul 2021
7. Finnish National Board of Education: National Core Curriculum for Basic Education 2014. Next Print Oy (2016)
8. Florida Center for Instructional Technology: Technology Integration Matrix (2019). https://fcit.usf.edu/matrix/matrix/. Accessed 1 June 2019
9. Hakkarainen, P., Saarelainen, T., Ruokamo, H.: Towards meaningful learning through digital video supported, case based teaching. Aust. J. Educ. Technol. **23**(1), 87–109 (2007). https://doi.org/10.14742/ajet.1275
10. Harmes, J.C., Welsh, J.L., Winkelman, R.J.: A framework for defining and evaluating technology integration in the instruction of real-world skills. In: Ferrara, S., Rosen, Y., Tager, M. (eds.) Handbook of Research on Technology Tools for Real-world Skill Development, pp. 137–162. IGI Global, Hershey (2016)
11. Heikonen, L., Toom, A., Pyhältö, K., Pietarinen, J., Soini, T.: Student-teachers' strategies in classroom interaction in the context of the teaching practicum. J. Educ. Teach. **43**(5), 534–549 (2017). https://doi.org/10.1080/02607476.2017.1355080
12. Jonassen, D.H., Strobel, J.: Modeling for meaningful learning. In: Hung, D., Khine, M.S. (eds.) Engaged Learning with Emerging Technologies. Springer, Dordrecht (2006). https://doi.org/10.1007/1-4020-3669-8_1
13. Keskitalo, T., Pyykkö, E., Ruokamo, H.: Exploring the meaningful learning of students in second life. Educ. Technol. Soc. **14**(1), 16–26 (2011)
14. Kimav, A.U., Aydin, B.: A blueprint for in-service teacher training program in technology integration. J. Educ. Technol. Online Learn. **3**(3), 224–244 (2020)
15. Ledford, D.M.: Development of a Professional Learning Framework to Improve Teacher Practice in Technology Integration. Boise State University Theses and Dissertations (2016)
16. Lähdesmäki, S., Valli, P.: Bridging authentic learning task into technology supported transformative pedagogy in Finnish teacher training. In: Chova, L.G., Martínez, A.L., Torres, I.C. (eds.) EDULEARN18 Proceedings. 10th International Conference on Education and New Learning Technologies, pp. 5857–5863. IATED Academy (2018). https://doi.org/10.21125/edulearn.2018.1409
17. Næsheim-Bjørkvik, G., Helgevold, N., Østrem, S.: Lesson study as a professional tool to strengthen collaborative enquiry in mentoring sessions in initial teacher education. Eur. J. Teach. Educ. **42**(5), 557–573 (2019). https://doi.org/10.1080/02619768.2019.1641487
18. Saarinen, A.: Equality in Cognitive Learning Outcomes: The Roles of Educational Practices. University of Helsinki, Faculty of Educational Sciences, Helsinki Studies in Education, number 97 (2020)
19. Sailin, S., Mahmor, N.: Improving student teachers' digital pedagogy through meaningful learning activities. Malays. J. Learn. Instr. **15**(2), 143–173 (2018)
20. Vygotsky, L.S.: Mind in Society: The Development of Higher Psychological Processes. Harvard University Press, Cambridge (1978)
21. Väätäjä, J.O., Ruokamo, H.: Conceptualizing dimensions and a model for digital pedagogy. J. Pac. Rim Psychol. (2021). https://doi.org/10.1177/1834490921995395

22. Wadmany, R., Kliachko, S.: The significance of digital pedagogy: teachers' perceptions and the factors influencing their abilities as digital pedagogues. J. Educ. Technol. **11**(3), 22–33 (2014)
23. Welsh, J., Harmes, J.C., Winkelman, R.: Florida's technology integration matrix. Princ. Leadersh. **12**(2), 69–71 (2011)

Check for updates

Research on the Data Literacy Index System of Pre-service Teachers Under the Background of Big Data

Peiyao Su, Huimin Chen, Xiaoying Deng, Han Lin, and Zhe Li(✉)

Faculty of Education, Fujian Normal University, Fuzhou, China

Abstract. The arrival of the big data era has brought new challenges to the teaching methods and professional development of the teachers in the field of education. As a group that is about to become a teacher, pre-service teachers are also one of the necessary qualities of their way to the teacher's road. Based on the literature analysis and case study, this paper constructs a preliminary index system of the data literacy of the pre-service teachers, and carries out the pre-investigation. The research data is analyzed by using the SPSS25.0 software, and the index system is repaired according to the analysis results. In the end, the index system of the data literacy of the pre-service teachers is divided into three levels: attitude and awareness, knowledge and skill, morality and law. There are 8 secondary indicators, a total of 19 projects.

Keywords: Big data · Pre-service teachers · Data literacy · Index system

1 Introduction

As the carrier of information and the source of knowledge, data is of great significance to human beings. In the context of the era of big data, the amount of data is growing exponentially. The proliferation of data means that the range of human record, measurement and analysis is constantly expanding, and the boundary of knowledge is constantly extending. From the technical level to the application level, the mining and research on the hidden value of big data at home and abroad have set off a wave of upsurge in various fields in recent years, and the attention on big data in education is also rising continuously. Through the regular application of big data system, the school encourages teachers to move from experiential teaching to precise teaching, and students to precise positioning from fuzzy learning.

Teachers can obtain, analyze and apply data from teaching practice, and then guide teaching practice in turn, which can not only meet students' personalized learning needs, but also ultimately improve teaching performance. In other words, whether there is a certain amount of data literacy consistent with the educational needs in the era of big data will largely determine the level of teaching efficiency. It is very important for pre-service teachers to organize relevant courses and pay attention to the training of their data literacy, so that they can meet the data literacy index of future teaching needs, which is also the starting point and goal of this research.

© Springer Nature Switzerland AG 2021
Y.-M. Huang et al. (Eds.): ICITL 2021, LNCS 13117, pp. 252–261, 2021.
https://doi.org/10.1007/978-3-030-91540-7_27

2 Concept Definition

2.1 Data Quality

As an emerging research field, data literacy was first introduced abroad. In 2007, Stephenson and Caravello proposed the meaning of data literacy, that is, the awareness and ability to effectively and appropriately discover, evaluate and use information and data [1]. Carlson indicated that data literacy should include understanding the meaning of data, correctly understanding graphs and drawing correct conclusions based on data, and being able to judge when data is incorrectly or improperly used [2]. Mandinach and Gummer defined the ability to constitute data literacy indicates that data literacy refers to the ability to understand data and make effective use of data to make decisions, including the ability to distinguish, collect, analyze and summarize organizational data and optimize data [3].

2.2 Teachers' Data Literacy

At present, there is no unified definition of the concept of teachers' data literacy. The Data Quality Campaign in the United States defines teachers' data literacy as the continuous, effective, reasonable and legal acquisition, interpretation, application and exchange of data from various sources and different types of data according to their professional roles and responsibilities. Finally, the ability to improve students' learning effect [4]. Mandinach believed that teachers' data literacy refers to the ability of teachers to transform data into information and finally become operational knowledge to improve scientific decision-making and students' performance [3]. Athanases, from the perspective of teaching practice, believed that teachers' data literacy means that teachers collect and analyze students' homework and performance purposefully, reflect on and process these learning data, so as to promote teachers to improve teaching practice and improve students' performance [5].

Although different researchers at home and abroad have different understandings on the connotation and extension of data literacy, and no unified definition of data literacy has been formed at present, it is not difficult to find that the definitions of data literacy given by different researchers have many similarities and commonalities. It can be seen that the academic circle has reached a preliminary consensus on the definition of data literacy, which has laid a theoretical foundation for further in-depth research. The core connotation of teachers' data literacy is the basic skills of data acquisition, processing and analysis, as well as the ability and awareness of using data to optimize teaching management and decision-making.

2.3 Pre-service Teachers' Data Literacy

This study accepts the viewpoints of "pre-service teachers are future teachers" and "the training of pre-service teachers should be based on the standard of qualified teachers". As the reserve force of future teachers, it is very important for pre-service teachers to organize relevant courses and pay attention to the training of their data literacy, so that they can meet the data literacy index of future teaching needs. "The data literacy ability of pre-service teachers should be based on the standard of becoming a qualified teacher, that is, the data literacy ability of pre-service teachers can be referenced by the data literacy ability of teachers", which is also the starting point and logical starting point of this research.

Throughout the research at home and abroad, the definition of data literacy of pre-service teachers is still unclear. Pre-service teachers, whether in learning life or in the process of education, teaching and training, should use the standard of teachers to request themselves.

2.4 Data Literacy Ability Structure

There are few researches on the structural model and evaluation index system of data literacy ability. Prado divided data literacy into five areas: understanding data, finding and/or obtaining data, reading, interpreting and evaluating data, reading, using data [6]. Carlson proposed the framework system of data literacy, including database and data format introduction, data discovery and acquisition, data management and organization, data conversion, data quality assurance, metadata, data processing and reuse, data practice specification, data storage, data analysis, data visualization, data ethics [7].

In terms of the data literacy ability of teachers and pre-service teachers, many studies mainly start from the needs of teachers' professional development, and demand teachers' ability to use data to teach, which is used as the evaluation basis of teachers' data literacy ability. Such as the Danielson framework, from planning and preparation, classroom environment, teaching and professional evaluation of four aspects [8]. Light et al.'s data-driven decision model applied data to teaching, which can be summarized into six steps: data collection, organization, summary, analysis, data conversion into information, and decision-making assistance [9]. From the perspective of teaching process, Mandinach et al. summarized the ability of teaching data literacy into five domains: identify problems and frame questions, use data, transform data into information, transform information into a decision, and evaluate outcomes [10].

3 Study Design

3.1 Research Methodology

Through literature research, the main contents of data literacy of pre-service teachers were extracted. Then, based on case studies, relevant data of data literacy of pre-service teachers were improved to construct a comprehensive index system of data literacy of pre-service teachers. On the basis of literature research, analysis of data quality research situation at home and abroad, and determine the main dimensions of the normal data quality index system, through the typical case interviews, builded up the preliminary data quality index system of teachers and student, index system, based on the preliminary establishment of normal data literacy questionnaire, through the data analysis, in the process of the research topic for repairs. Finally, a formal index system was formed.

3.2 The Preliminary Construction of Data Literacy Index System

Firstly, the typical case study was used to study the data literacy of pre-service teachers, so as to improve the index system of data literacy of pre-service teachers. In this study, 5 typical cases of pre-service teachers with teaching experience and data processing experience were selected for the study.

Based on the research and elaboration of relevant connotation and index system of data literacy in domestic and foreign literatures, and combined with the results of the above typical case studies, this study constructed a preliminary index system of data literacy of pre-service teachers from three levels: attitude and awareness, knowledge and skills, morality and law.

The data literacy index system of pre-service teachers in this study consists of three first-level indicators, namely attitude and awareness, knowledge and skills, and morality and law. These three first-level indicators are composed of nine second-level indicators, which correspond to attitude and awareness respectively, including data attitude and data awareness. Knowledge and skills include data acquisition, data storage and management, data processing, data analysis, data expression and use, and data evaluation; Ethics and law include data ethics and law. These 9 secondary indicators are divided into 23 tertiary indicators.

3.3 Repair of Data Literacy Index System of Pre-service Teachers

Compile and Issue the Questionnaire. The respondents of the questionnaire were pre-service teachers who had some teaching experience. The three-level indicators of the data literacy index system of pre-service teachers that have been preliminarily constructed constitute the questionnaire, with a total of 23 items. The degree of conformity or attainment was taken as the evaluation standard and represented by Likert five-component scale: Very no – 1, no – 2, partially yes – 3, yes – 4, very yes – 5. The lowest score is 23 and the highest score is 115. The higher the score is, the higher the data literacy level of the respondents is.

In this study, "Questionnaire Star" professional questionnaire survey platform was used to release the questionnaire online, so that respondents could use computers and mobile terminals to enter the questionnaire through the link to fill in the questionnaire.

Recycling and Analysis of Questionnaire Results. A total of 60 valid questionnaires were collected in this questionnaire release and the data were input into SPSS25.0 statistical software for project analysis and reliability testing analysis. The 23 questions are numbered as Q1–Q23, a total of 23 questions.

The first is item analysis. In this study, the critical ratio method was used to calculate the decision value of each item in the questionnaire, that was, the CR value. In the classification of high and low groups, the grouping proportion was 27%, namely 16 groups. After grouping, independent sample T test was performed. When conducting independent sample T test, first check whether the square difference of the two groups is homogeneous according to the column of "Levene's test of variance equation". If $P > 0.05$, it indicates that the difference of variance does not reach the significant level of 0.05, namely homogeneity of variance. In this case, nihility hypothesis was accepted (i.e. the assumption that the square difference of the two groups is equal). At this point, the t-test data should refer to the value in the first column "Assume Equal Variances". If $P > 0.05$, it indicates that the significant level is not reached, then this item will be deleted. If the T-value statistic is less than 3, it indicates that the question item has poor discrimination (even if it reaches a significant level), which can be considered to be deleted. According to the t-test results of independent samples, P in the column of "Levene's test of variance equation" is greater than 0.05, indicating homogeneity of variance. Check the corresponding t-value and p-value in the column of "Assume equal variance". The T value statistics of all items are greater than 3, and the significance probability value P will be 0.05. Therefore, all items will be retained.

Followed by the reliability test, this study adopts the clone Bach alpha coefficient method to analyze the questionnaire reliability, by measuring the have 23 question about normal data quality, with alpha said based on standardization of reliability coefficient is 0.944, the questionnaire of overall reliability reached a higher level, if any one item to be deleted, Will reduce the overall reliability of the questionnaire, indicating that the questionnaire has a high reliability.

Modification and Improvement of Data Literacy Index System for Pre-service Teachers. After item analysis and reliability analysis of the questionnaire results, the results indicated that the questionnaire topics were well set. Now the validity analysis of the questionnaire results is carried out to modify and improve the preliminarily established data literacy index system for pre-service teachers. In this study, KMO and Bartlett spherical tests were performed on the data. The results showed that the KMO value was 0.811, greater than 0.8, indicating that the correlation between the variables of the item was good. This questionnaire had structural validity and was suitable for factor analysis. The Sig of Bartlett's sphericity test was 0.000, which was less than 0.05, indicating that the value of significance test was small, and the difference in statistics was also small. It showed that the relative independence of the data was small, the data was spherical distribution, which could be used for factor analysis. Therefore, the SPSS25.0 software tool was used to conduct factor analysis on the data. In this study, the principal component analysis method was adopted and the maximum variance method was used to rotate the factor load matrix.

Firstly, factor analysis was conducted on the dimensions of attitude and awareness. The KMO value was 0.705, which was suitable for factor analysis. As this study preset two secondary indicators under the first-level indicators of attitude and awareness, the parameters of factor extraction process were controlled when the principal component analysis method was used for factor analysis of questionnaire results. The initial eigenvalue describes the solution of the initial factor. The eigenvalue of the first factor is 3.373, explaining 67.454% of the total variance of the original variable, and the contribution rate of accumulated variance is 67.454%.The eigenvalue of the second factor is 0.633, which explains 12.663% of the total variance of the original variable, and the contribution rate of accumulated variance is 80.118%. By rotating square and load the data item knowable to the rotation factors, to reallocate the various factor to explain the variance of original variables, changed the variance contribution of each factor, can explain the total variance of 80.118%, more than 50%, so you can think the index of attitude and awareness the class is divided into two secondary index is practicable. In order to further analyze which secondary index under the conception the different factors mainly come from and whether the corresponding distribution is consistent with the initial index, this study further obtains the load table after the rotation of the factors, as shown in Table 1. According to the data shown in Table 1, the following factor analysis can be carried out: except Q1, which does not fall into the conceived index system, other factors are consistent with the conceived index system, so it is considered to delete the item Q1.

Table 1. Attitude and awareness dimensional questions and factor loads table

Factors	Questions	Factor loading
The data of awareness (Factor 1)	Q2 I am able to maintain a certain sensitivity to data in education and teaching	0.783
	Q3 I can consciously use data to assist teaching and evaluate the teaching effect	0.916
Data attitude (Factor 2)	Q4 I can be responsible for the data used in education and teaching	0.733
	Q5 I am able to treat the data generated in education and teaching with a rigorous and serious attitude	0.805
Factor 2	Q1 I can recognize the role of data in education and teaching	0.867

Principal component analysis is carried out on the dimension of knowledge and skills, and six factors are extracted according to the conceived index system. The KMO value is 0.857, which is very suitable for factor analysis and can explain 80.626% of the original questionnaire, which is greater than 50%. Therefore, it is feasible to divide the first-level indicator of knowledge and skills into six second-level indicators. From the load table after factor rotation (see Table 2), it can be seen that items Q6, Q7 and Q8 are included in factor 1, and they all belong to the first-level and second-level indicators of data acquisition. Q13 and Q14 fall into factor 2 and belong to the first-level and second-level indicators of data analysis. Q15, Q16 and Q17 belong to factor 3, and all belong to the first-level and second-level indicators of data expression and use. Q18 and Q19 fall into factor 5, both of which belong to the first-level and second-level indicators of data evaluation. Q9, Q11 this two item in the idea of the index system is belong to data storage and management and data processing respectively two different secondary indexes, but also fall into the factor 4, therefore, this study to adjust idea of index system, incorporating the above two secondary indexes for data management and processing the new secondary indicators, And delete data storage and management, data processing two secondary indicators. In addition, since Q10, Q12 and Q20 did not fall into the preset index system, they were considered to be deleted.

Principal component analysis was conducted on morality and law, and the KMO value was 0.726, which was suitable for factor analysis. One factor with eigenvalue greater than 1 was extracted, which could explain 78.696% of the original questionnaire. Therefore, the first-level index of morality and law was directly divided into the first-level index

Table 2. Knowledge and skill dimension questions and factor load table

Factors	Questions	Factor loading
Data acquisition (Factor 1)	Q6 I can master the methods and tools of data collection	0.494
	Q7 I can identify different types of data and record the data consciously	0.739
	Q8 I can accurately identify, locate, and access data sources	0.653
Data processing and management (Factor 4)	Q9 I can classify and manage the data acquired in education and teaching	0.763
	Q11 I can master the software tools for data processing	0.633
Data analysis (Factor 2)	Q13 I can reasonably analyze data from the perspective of education and teaching	0.632
	Q14 I am able to see the connections between data and data	0.699
Data expression and use (Factor 3)	Q15 I can visualize the data or generate reports	0.671
	Q16 I am able to use data properly in communication to communicate ideas and make sense	0.747
	Q17 I can effectively make use of data-driven teaching decision making to improve the teaching effect	0.752
Data evaluation (Factor 5)	Q18 I can evaluate the accuracy of the data	0.516
	Q19 I can use the scale with high reliability and validity to evaluate the teaching effect	0.806
Factor 1	Q10 I can update the data in the archive according to its life cycle	0.865
Factor 6	Q12 I am able to filter and filter the data appropriately	0.833
Factor 2	Q20 I can critically evaluate data in context	0.815

of data morality and law. Since only one factor is extracted for this dimension, there is no corresponding rotation factor loading table. The secondary indicators and topics corresponding to the moral and legal dimensions are listed here (see Table 3).

Table 3. Moral and legal dimension questions

Factors	Questions
Data ethics and law	Q21 I can understand the relevant laws and regulations, and do not create or disseminate data that endangers public information security or infringes on the interests of others
	Q22 I am able to use data accurately and responsibly, consistent with discipline or industry norms
	Q23 I can respect others and effectively protect the privacy of my own data during data collection, use and sharing

4 Conclusion

Based on the results of literature analysis and case studies, this study constructed a preliminary data literacy indicator system for pre-service teachers, which was compiled into a questionnaire for pre-investigation. For the pre-survey data, using SPSS25.0 software for CR project analysis, reliability testing and factor analysis, deleting some redundant items and making relevant changes to the secondary indicators, it has high reliability and structural validity. More in line with expectations. Therefore, this study finally determined 3 first-level indicators, 8 s-level indicators, a total of 19 items, and finally formed a formal data literacy indicator system for pre-service teachers (see Table 4).

The data literacy index system of pre-service teachers is a multi-level complex system. This study closely related to the connotation of data literacy of pre-service teachers, determined a relatively comprehensive and reasonable index system, and modified and improved the index system through data analysis, so as to ensure the scientific nature of the index system.

Table 4. The final version of the data literacy index system for pre-service teachers

Level 1 indicators	Level 2 indicators	Level 3 indicators
Attitude and awareness	Data awareness	I am able to maintain a certain sensitivity to data in education and teaching
		I can consciously use data to assist teaching and evaluate the teaching effect
	Data attitude	I can be responsible for the data used in education and teaching
		I am able to treat the data generated in education and teaching with a rigorous and serious attitude
Knowledge with skills	Data acquisition	I can master the methods and tools of data collection
		I can identify different types of data and record the data consciously

(*continued*)

Table 4. (*continued*)

Level 1 indicators	Level 2 indicators	Level 3 indicators
		I can accurately identify, locate, and access data sources
	Data processing and management	I can classify and manage the data acquired in education and teaching
		I can update the data in the archive according to its life cycle
	Data analysis	I can reasonably analyze data from the perspective of education and teaching
		I was able to see the connections between data and data
	Data expression and use	I can visualize the data or generate reports
		I am able to use data properly in communication to communicate ideas and make sense
		I can effectively make use of data-driven teaching decision making to improve the teaching effect
	Data evaluation	I can evaluate the accuracy of the data
		I can use the scale with high reliability and validity to evaluate the teaching effect
		I can critically evaluate data in context
Morality with law	Data ethics and law	I can understand the relevant laws and regulations, and do not create or disseminate data that endangers public information security or infringes on the interests of others
		I am able to use data accurately and responsibly, consistent with discipline or industry norms
		I can respect others and effectively protect the privacy of my own data during data collection, use and sharing

In addition, this study is aimed at pre-service teachers who are about to become teachers. Therefore, on the basis of reflecting the connotation of data literacy, this study highlights the professional characteristics of pre-service teachers who are about to become teachers and emphasizes more on the standards of data literacy that pre-service teachers should achieve in the teaching field. Therefore, the construction of this index system has a certain reference significance for normal universities in determining the cultivation strategy of pre-service teachers.

References

1. Stephenson, E., Caravello, P.: Incorporating data literacy into undergraduate information literacy programs in the social sciences. A pilot project. Ref. Serv. Rev. **35**(4), 525–540 (2007)
2. Carlson, J., Fosmire, M., Miller, C.C., Nelson, M.S.: Determining data information literacy needs: a study of students and research faculty. Portal-Libr. Acad. **11**(2), 629–657 (2011)
3. Mandinach, E.B., Gummer, E.S.: A systemic view of implementing data literacy in educator preparation. Educ. Res. **42**(1), 30–37 (2012)
4. Data Quality Campaign. Teacher data literacy: It's about time. https://dataqualitycampaign.org/resource/teacher-data-literacy-time. Accessed 10 Mar 2019
5. Athanases, S.Z., Bennett, L.H., Wahleithner, J.M.: Fostering data literacy through preservice teacher inquiry in English language arts. Teach. Educ. Q. **48**(1), 8–28 (2013)
6. Prado, J.C., Marzal, M.A.: Incorporating data literacy into information literacy programs: core competencies and contents. Libri-Int. J. Libr. Inf. Stud. **63**(2), 123–134 (2013)
7. Carlson, J., Bracke, M.S.: Planting the seeds for data literacy: lessons learned from a student-centered education program. Int. J. Digit. Curation **10**(1), 95–110 (2015)
8. Michelle, E.A., Corrine, A.K.: Danielson's framework for teaching. Child. Sch. **33**(1), 61–63 (2011)
9. Light, D., Wexler, D.H., Heinze, J.: Keeping Teachers in the Center: A Framework of Data-Driven Decision-Making. Education Development Center Inc, p. 6 (2005)
10. Mandinach, E.B., Gummer, E.S.: What does it mean for teachers to be data literate: laying out the skills, knowledge, and dispositions. Teach. Teach. Educ. **60**, 366–376 (2016)

Check for updates

An Integrated Conceptual Framework to Assess Small and Rural Municipalities' Readiness for Smart City Implementation: A Systematic Literature Review

Nkhangweni Lawrence Mashau[1](✉), Jan H. Kroeze[2], and Grant R. Howard[2]

[1] University of Venda, Thohoyandou, South Africa
lawrence.mashau@univen.ac.za
[2] School of Computing, University of South Africa, Pretoria, South Africa

Abstract. The term *smart city* is commonly used to describe the use of various types of digital infrastructure and technologies to collect data in order to provide information that can be used to manage resources efficiently and provide a better standard of living for citizens. Smart city technology could be also used to solve the education challenges of continuous urbanization, thereby facilitating the international sustainable development goal of quality education and lifelong learning opportunities for all communities (cf. https://sdgs.un.org/goals). Many cities have used information and communication technologies (ICTs) to enable smart city concepts. Most small and rural municipalities struggle to manage their resources, which results in service delivery problems. A smart city intervention may help small and rural municipalities to curb these problems, but there is slow implementation of this concept in these municipalities due to the lack of an integrated framework focusing on the assessment of small and rural municipalities' readiness for smart city implementation. The aim of this research is to address this gap in information systems (IS) knowledge. A systematic literature review is employed to provide an in-depth and critical summary of existing research relevant to the research question. Various concepts are synthesized into a holistic, integrated conceptual framework to assess small and rural municipalities' readiness towards smart city implementation. The framework can be used to assess small and rural municipalities to gauge their readiness level towards smart city implementation of a smart city initiative. In addition, municipal authorities can use this framework to identify the required components and key stakeholders for any smart city initiatives. This paper provides the foundation from which future empirical research can progress.

Keywords: Smart city · Small and rural municipalities' readiness · Literature review · Framework · Conceptual search · Education

1 Introduction

Urbanization is a reality in municipalities because more than 50% of the world population were living in urban areas by the year 2010 [1]. This number is expected to rise to 70%

© Springer Nature Switzerland AG 2021
Y.-M. Huang et al. (Eds.): ICITL 2021, LNCS 13117, pp. 262–273, 2021.
https://doi.org/10.1007/978-3-030-91540-7_28

by the year 2050 [2, 3]. The increase will present many challenges "such as providing housing, health, education, welfare, security as well as transport for its citizens" for municipalities, especially in small and rural municipalities [4, 6]. This exponential influx will affect service delivery greatly [3].

The term "smart city concept" is not new, it has been around for years now [7, 8]. It was coined around 1991 [9, 10]. Small and rural municipalities can improve service delivery through collection of real-time data, analyzing it, and sharing real-time information for decision makers to deal with service delivery issues [11]. Municipalities that share information using Information and Communication Technology (ICT) and physical devices that are connected through the Internet of Things (IoT) to collect and analyze digital data to improve citizens' standard of living, city operations, government services and the utilization of resources, are known as smart cities [12]. In other words, small and rural municipalities can use ICTs to enable smart city concepts to manage their infrastructure efficiently. The notion of a smart city is, therefore, considered as an economic driver for city development [9, 10, 13]. However, there is a low level of implementation [1] of the smart city concept in small and rural municipalities.

The literature on the smart city field presents numerous readiness frameworks [14, 15]. Most of the existing frameworks look at the global context [16–19]. The frameworks that are used to assess smart city readiness in a global context use technology, institution, economy, environment, social and legal factors as indicators. Despite the availability of these frameworks, small and rural municipalities are failing to implement smart city concepts successfully because the existing frameworks do not expose sufficient indicators that may be used to assess small and rural environments' readiness [14]. Literature indicates that a framework should be focused, otherwise it will be difficult for organizations to use it correctly [6, 14]. Cities or municipalities are unlikely to use a framework that does not address their specific issues because it would be difficult to follow [14, 20].

The few studies that do look at local contexts [7, 20] use technological, institutional and environmental factors as indicators to assess small and rural municipalities' readiness towards smart city implementation [1, 21], while other scholars suggest that there is a need for a framework that will look at human, cultural and societal factors to help cities to conduct a comprehensive assessment to measure small and rural municipalities' readiness towards smart city implementation [6, 22]. There is a lack of a single framework [8] that uses technological, institutional, environmental, cultural, human and societal factors as indicators to help small and rural municipalities to conduct comprehensive assessments to measure their readiness.

Therefore, there is a need to integrate and amend existing readiness assessment frameworks with a specific focus on small and rural environments. This paper develops an integrated conceptual framework to assess small and rural municipalities' readiness for smart city implementation. The factors that are identified as important indicators may help small and rural municipalities to conduct comprehensive assessments to measure their readiness level towards the implementation of a smart city concept. Therefore, the main aim of this paper is to propose an integrated conceptual framework to assess small and rural municipalities' readiness for smart city implementation. This framework is intended to help municipality leaders who are charged with the responsibility of implementing a smart city concept to gauge their readiness level before they engage in a smart city project [2]. This is critical because there is no framework that integrates existing frameworks to help small and rural municipalities to assess their readiness level.

2 Literature Review

2.1 Smart City Definitions

There is a serious debate in the literature on the definition of the smart city concept. The smart city concept has many definitions with no consensus on a specific definition [23]. The smart city concept has been defined differently by different scholars (see Table 1).

Table 1. Smart city definitions.

No	Author	Definition
1	[18]	The smart city concept refers to the connection of modern technologies that promote the usage of city infrastructure and resources efficiently
2	[16, 24]	A smart city is a city that monitors its resources through the integration of all critical digital infrastructure and technology
3	[25]	The smart city concept pertains to the connection of information and communications technology (ICT) systems to manage and improve efficiency and enhance citizens' quality of life, whereby promoting sustainable improvement in urban operations
4	[26]	A smart city is defined as a city that focuses on its essential ICT infrastructure to deliver improved services to citizens
5	[23, 27]	A smart city is a city that digitally integrates all key infrastructure elements such as railways, roads, tunnels, bridges, water, communications, main buildings, energy and harbors to optimize its resources and to increase services offered to the citizens

After the identification of various definitions in Table 1, this study has derived the following definition for a smart city concept: A smart city concept is a digital integration of information systems components to collect digital data and analyse it in real-time to monitor and manage city infrastructure and to allocate resources effectively, thereby improving service delivery and the quality of life of the citizens.

2.2 Aspects of Small and Rural Municipalities

Small and rural municipalities normally form part of local, district and national government. In South Africa, most people live within small and rural municipalities [29]. These municipalities are significant to the national economy [5]. Most cities could use smart city concepts to manage their resources effectively and to improve their economy. That is why most municipalities are engaging in smart city initiatives [30]. It is important for municipalities to gauge their readiness or preparedness level before they engage in smart city initiatives, in order to address significant aspects and to avoid preventable mistakes [1].

Literature postulates that a city or municipality should look at the stakeholders, budget, policies, population size and economy when assessing small and rural municipalities' readiness towards smart city implementation. In a municipality, a stakeholder can be any role player that contributes in one way or another towards a sustainable smart city. Stakeholders can be municipalities themselves, staff, government departments, state-owned entities, private companies, citizens, tourists, research communities, universities, application developers and software companies [31]. These stakeholders should understand the objectives behind implementing smart city concepts and provide the necessary support for a smart city project [5] because they are an important part of ensuring that a smart city concept becomes a reality in a city or municipality [15].

Stakeholders depend on municipality or city budgets to execute their duties properly [7]. Budgeting is critical in the development of a smart city. This aspect is key because, for a city to improve its information technology infrastructure and to acquire the latest, innovative technologies, it needs an adequate budget [5]. Municipalities should budget for money to buy digital infrastructure and to pay any service provider who will take part in their smart city projects [32, 33].

As indicated previously, small and rural municipalities are significant to the national economy. It is important, as well, to consider municipal economy because it improves the standard of living of the citizens by unlocking opportunities such as high-quality infrastructure, new business opportunities, growing ecosystems and competitiveness, to name just a few [34, 35]. A strong economy promotes digital innovation, development and the management of a smart city [9, 36]. For a city to be smart, it needs a strong economy and this can be achieved through the use of information technology, social growth and sustainability [35].

Furthermore, policies are critical to guide a smart city initiative [13]. A well-defined policy should have clear expectations and action plans on how to address issues such as quality of life, mobility, accessibility, health [4], education, and overall urban operations and services [37, 38]. However, when crafting these policies, policymakers should reconsider the structure and rules that delay digital innovation and the implementation of a smart city concept [39, 40].

The next section of this paper presents an overview of the method used to identify relevant literature sources for this study. Section 4 discusses major factors that are important in assessing small and rural municipalities' readiness. Section 5 proposes an integrated conceptual framework to assess small and rural municipalities' readiness for smart city implementation. This holistic framework is a synthesis based on knowledge that is already available. The last section concludes the paper.

3 Method

The study identified literature on municipality readiness towards smart city implementation through a systematic literature review. This section starts by outlining the search criteria and then explains the inclusion and exclusion of particular literature.

The researchers followed a systematic strategy [41] to identify, assess and synthesize existing literature produced by other scholars [42]. To search the literature, the phrase "smart city AND readiness" was used as the keywords to search for relevant sources in various databases. These databases include Scopus, ScienceDirect or Elsevier, AIS eLibrary (AISeL), Proquest (ABI/INFORM collection), Ebscohost and JSTOR. These databases were selected because they focus on IS research. The search was limited to peer-reviewed papers published between 2015 and 2020 in English. The search retrieved 29 articles from the listed databases (see Table 2).

The retrieved records were screened by examining the keywords, titles and abstracts to check their relevancy. Three records were excluded during this phase because the studies did not address smart city issues. After reading the full texts of the remaining sources, five more records were excluded because it transpired on this close reading that the content was not relevant – these sources dealt with different topics. A total of 21 sources remained.

Table 2. Search results.

Databases	Initial search results	Final reviewed results
Scopus	0	0
ScienceDirect	14	11
AIS eLibrary (AISeL)	2	2
Proquest (ABI/INFORM collection)	12	7
Ebscohost	1	1
JSTOR	0	0
Reviewed results from forward and backward search	0	24
Total	29	45

To identify additional sources relevant to this study, the researcher used forward searches (citation searches) to find later publications referencing the sources that had been identified during the initial sifting, as well as backward searches (reference searches) to identify older salient citations in the original list of 21 sources. During this phase, 24 new records with relevant topics, keywords and abstracts were identified and included. Therefore, 45 papers were included for review in this study (cf. Fig. 1).

A systematic literature review research method was used to identify literature with the objective of answering the research question. The research question was used to identify literature relevant to the research topic. The question for this study is as follows: *What are the important factors that can be used as indicators to assess small and rural municipalities' readiness towards smart city implementation?* The answer to the research question was obtained through an examination of the literature, using a critical, analytic and synthetic approach.

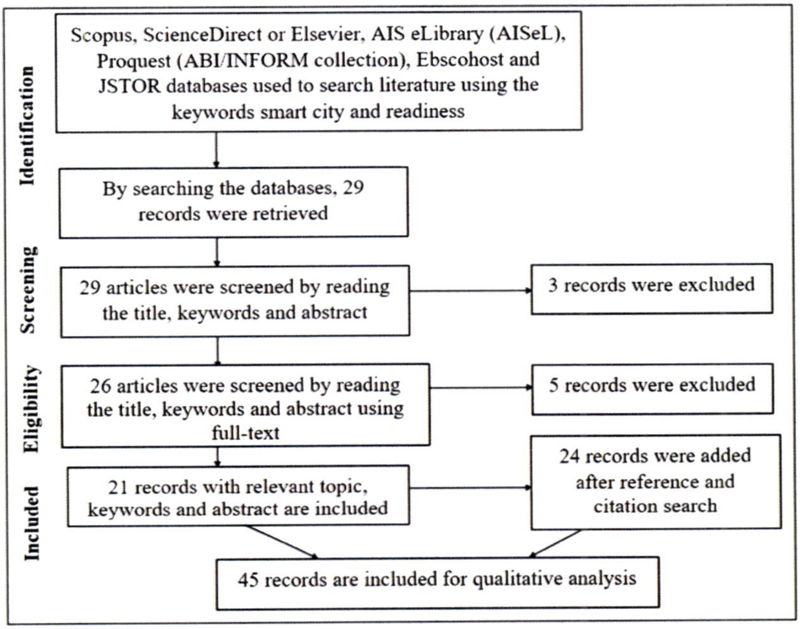

Fig. 1. Literature identification diagram.

4 Discussion

A systematic literature review provides insight into important factors that can be used to assess small and rural municipalities' readiness for smart city implementation [42]. This paper analyzed literature in the information systems field from the databases listed in Sect. 3. There are few studies that investigate the assessment of small and rural municipalities' readiness towards smart city implementation.

Therefore, this paper identified institutional factors, technological factors, human factors [14, 16], environmental factors [1], societal factors and cultural factors [16, 43] as essential factors that can be used to assess small and rural municipalities' readiness.

This paper identified **environmental factors** as one of the significant components when assessing small and rural municipalities' readiness [2]. To implement a smart city concept successfully, the environment should be ready [44]. When measuring environmental readiness, population size, stakeholders, policies, budget, economy, buildings, resources, social issues and cultural issues are important. Evaluating each of these will provide a municipality with an in-depth understanding of what should be improved before engaging in a smart city initiative [30].

According to the literature, population size is linked with policies, budget, buildings, economy, resources, social issues and cultural issues. When the population increases, it affects these aspects [1, 44]. For example, if the population increases, it affects existing resources and the budget, which will lead to poor service delivery. Assessing these factors will help the municipality to plan and sequence its smart city initiatives properly [1].

The **technological factor** is seen as a main factor for assessing small and rural municipalities' readiness because it plays a significant role in the implementation of a smart city [7, 45]. The development of a smart city is not the adoption of information technologies alone [16]. It also encompasses information systems drivers for a smart city development, which are smart technologies, technology infrastructure, data, innovation and IoT [1, 12].

Literature indicates that smart city projects should start with a physical infrastructure, since this is the foundation for the innovation of ecosystems [22]. Small and rural municipalities should assess their technological factor readiness level before engaging in a smart city initiative [1]. If a city's technological factor needs attention, the municipality can invest in the infrastructure, data, innovation and IoT to prepare for the smooth implementation of the project [1, 11].

Even though technology is regarded as a pillar in the implementation of smart city concept, it has some barriers that should be addressed [28]. Technology needs skilled human resources. Providing technology or information technology skills training or educating these human resources might pose challenges emanating from other factors. For example, a city should have a budget to train people [45]. If it does not have enough funds, this implies that its environmental element is not ready and that the human element will also not be ready [1].

Humans are regarded as enabling factors in different studies [46]. **Human factors** focus on the evaluation of human characteristics such as education level, experience and creativity [7]. These characteristics are important in the implementation of a smart city concept, because humans are agents of innovation during a smart city initiative [30]. People who do not have a certain level of education and experience with technology tend to find it difficult to participate in the project and smart city itself. In Africa, the inclusion of human and environment factors are especially important to facilitate the Africanisation of information systems within local cultures on the continent, thereby promoting optimism about smart city endeavors.

In a smart city, decision makers rely on the data produced by people to generate the trends, patterns, measures and indicators used to set their targets to monitor performance, assess risk and to make decisions [9, 40]. A city should assess its human factor readiness level before engaging in a smart city initiative [5]. This will assist cities to organize workshops to familiarize their citizens on how to use particular technologies.

Institutional factors are also known as organizational factors. These factors focus on the organizational executives, staff and partnership with other organizations. Organizations have a significant role to play by promoting the smart city concept as an innovation to transform a city [1, 47]. When pursuing a smart city project, organizations are supposed to be one hundred per cent involved throughout the smart city project process, with some among them providing a variety of forms of help while others contribute by sponsoring smart city initiatives and donating resources [5, 26]. Among the companies involved may be service providers that render system design, development and maintenance services to ensure successful implementation [5].

5 Conceptual Framework

The proposed integrated conceptual framework to assess small and rural municipalities' readiness for smart city implementation – which forms the context for this study – was developed by integrating 27 components from the Technology, Organization and Environment (TOE) framework; Delone and McLean model; Technology Readiness Index (TRI) and Diffusion of Innovation (DOI) theory. Figure 2 shows these components.

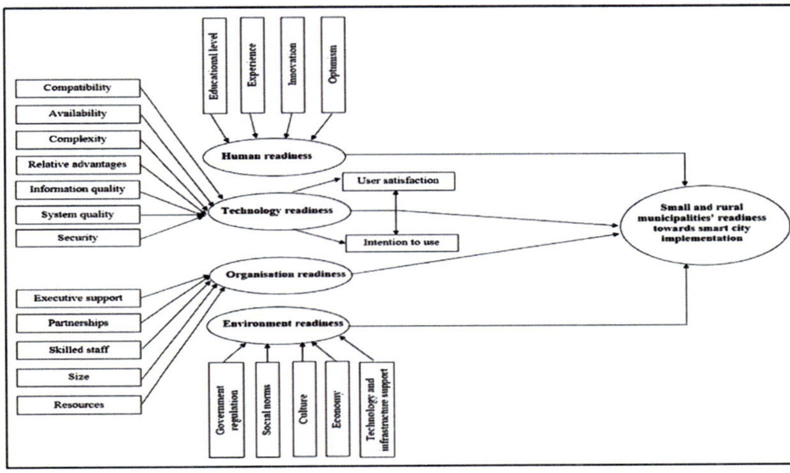

Fig. 2. Proposed integrated framework to assess small and rural municipalities' readiness for smart city implementation.

The proposed framework shows that human readiness, organization readiness, technology readiness [16] and environment readiness [1] are significant for small and rural municipalities' readiness towards smart city implementation. Once these four dimensions are ready, a city can be considered ready to implement a smart city concept. Human readiness is influenced by education level, experience [44], innovation and optimism, while organization readiness is influenced by executive support, partnerships, skilled staff, size and resources. Most scholars have identified technology readiness as key in collecting and analysing digital data. When collecting data for a smart city, data security is a major concern [13]. However, open data and big data pose some concerns for a smart city initiative. Therefore, when assessing a city's readiness level, a municipality should certify that the security and privacy requirements of their systems and data are satisfied [18, 48]. Compatibility, availability, complexity, relative advantages, information quality and system quality play a significant role in assessing technology readiness [13, 18]. Lastly, environment readiness is influenced by government regulation, social norms, culture, economy and technology support infrastructure [11]. If all human, technological, environmental and organizational aspects are ready, a city may implement a smart city initiative with minimal challenges.

Integrating human, technological, organizational and environmental factors in one framework will enable small and rural municipalities to conduct comprehensive assessments of their readiness for smart city implementation. Furthermore, the element of culture, social norms and size are especially important for small and rural municipalities.

6 Conclusion

This paper proposes an integrated conceptual framework (Fig. 2) that has been developed to assist small and rural municipalities to gauge their readiness level towards smart city implementation. It was created through analyzing various readiness frameworks in the smart city domain from previous studies to identify important factors that could be used. The rationale for this is to synthesize key factors and present an integrated framework that could be used to conduct a comprehensive assessment of small and rural municipalities' readiness towards smart city implementation.

The proposed framework gives broad principles and does not prescribe specific technologies, infrastructure, data and partnerships. The proposed framework could assist small and rural municipalities to measure their readiness level in a holistic way before embarking on a smart city initiative, thus enabling them to allocate and manage their resources effectively.

The integrated framework's indicators may also assist municipalities that are not yet ready for a smart city implementation to identify suitable hardware, software and other related concepts during strategic planning of smart city endeavors. Therefore, this framework might also be important for decision makers who are charged with the responsibility of smart city implementation in order to ensure that all essential aspects are addressed during planning and implementation.

The implementation of smart city technologies will enable smart education [49]. Smart education can improve citizens and learners' quality of learning using smart technologies that support education and training, thereby facilitating the international sustainable development goal of quality education and lifelong learning opportunities for all communities (cf. https://sdgs.un.org/goals). Smart city technologies will enable citizens and learners to learn effectively and comfortably [49, 50]. Citizens who are knowledgeable will be thoughtful, responsible and productive [50].

A limitation of the paper is the lack of empirical evidence to support the proposed framework. However, the integrated conceptual framework proposed in this paper provides the foundation from which future empirical research can proceed to validate, improve and implement the theoretical construct.

Acknowledgments. The work is based on research supported in part by the National Research Foundation (NRF) of South Africa (Grant Number 132180) and the University of South Africa's Research Professor Support Programme. The grant holder acknowledges that opinions, findings and conclusions or recommendations expressed are that of the authors and that the NRF/Unisa accepts no liability whatsoever in this regard. We would like to thank the editors, programme chairs and reviewers for their feedback that guided us to improve the article.

References

1. Dewi, M.A.A., Hidayanto, A.N., Purwandari, B., Kosandi, M., Budi, N.F.A.: Smart city readiness model based on technology-organization-environment (TOE) framework and its effect on adoption decision. In: 22nd Pacific Asia Conference on Information Systems (PACIS 2018), pp. 1–15. Association for Information Systems, Yokohama (2018)
2. Ibrahim, M., El-Zaart, A., Adams, C.: Smart sustainable cities roadmap: readiness for transformation towards urban sustainability. Sustain. Cities Soc. **60**(1), 530–540 (2018)
3. Smith, M.: Industry, government & academia - a relationship paradigm fit for the future of transport infrastructure assets. In: International High-Performance Built Environment Conference, pp. 1705–1715. Procedia Engineering (2017)
4. Shokeir, R.G., Yahia, I.B.: Moving toward smart cities: insights from the MENA region. Int. J. Web Based Communities **16**(1), 92–108 (2020)
5. Bashynska, I., Dyskina, A.: The overview-analytical document of the international experience of building smart city. Bus.: Theory Pract. **19**(1), 241–288 (2018)
6. Berst, J., Enbysk, L., Ebi, K., Cooley, D., Peeples, D.: Smart cities readiness guide: the planning manual for building tomorrow's cities today. Smart Cities Council, USA (2015). https://smartcitiescouncil.com/resources/smart-cities-readiness-guide. Accessed 17 Feb 2021
7. Yu, J., Wen, Y., Jin, J., Zhang, Y.: Towards a service-dominant platform for public value co-creation in a smart city: evidence from two metropolitan cities in China. Technol. Forecast. Soc. Chang. **142**(1), 168–182 (2019)
8. Moravcova-Skoludova, J., Chocholousova, M.: Contemporary technologies and smart city concept systems in the Czech Republic. In: 45th International Scientific Conference on Economic and Social Development: XIX International Social Congress (ISC 2019), pp. 177–185, Moscow (2019)
9. Alawadhi, S., et al.: Building understanding of smart city initiatives. In: Scholl, H.J., Janssen, M., Wimmer, M.A., Moe, C.E., Flak, L.S. (eds.) EGOV 2012. LNCS, vol. 7443, pp. 40–53. Springer, Heidelberg (2012). https://doi.org/10.1007/978-3-642-33489-4_4
10. Dameri, R.P., Dameri, R.P.: Searching for smart city definition: a comprehensive proposal. Int. J. Comput. Technol. **11**(1), 2544–2551 (2013)
11. Barham, H., Daim, T.: The use of readiness assessment for big data projects. Sustain. Cities Soc. **60**(1), 1–12 (2020)
12. Eremia, M., Toma, L., Sanduleac, M.: The smart city concept in the 21st century. In: 10th International Conference Interdisciplinarity in Engineering 2016, pp. 12–19. Procedia Engineering (2017)
13. Mahesa, R., Yudoko, G., Anggoro, Y.: Dataset on the sustainable smart city development in Indonesia. Data Brief **25**(1), 1–6 (2019)
14. Desdemoustier, J., Crutzen, N., Giffinger, R.: Municipalities' understanding of the smart city concept: an exploratory analysis in Belgium. Technol. Forecast. Soc. Chang. **142**, 129–141 (2019)
15. Staletić, N., Labus, A., Bogdanović, Z., Despotović-Zrakić, M., Radenković, B.: Citizens' readiness to crowdsource smart city services: a developing country perspective. Cities **107**(1), 1–11 (2020)
16. Nam, T., Pardo, T.A.: Conceptualizing smart city with dimensions of technology, people, and institutions. In: The Proceedings of the 12th Annual International Conference on Digital Government Research, p. 282. Association for Computing Machinery, Maryland (2011)
17. Monzon, A.: Smart cities concept and challenges: bases for the assessment of smart city projects. In: 2015 International Conference on Smart Cities and Green ICT Systems (SMARTGREENS), pp. 1–11. IEEE, Lisbon (2015)

18. Cilliers, L., Flowerday, S.: Information privacy concerns in a participatory crowdsourcing smart city project. J. Internet Technol. Secur. Trans. **3**(3), 280–287 (2014)
19. Das, D., Emuze, F., Das, D.: Smart city perspectives of Bloemfontein, South Africa. J. Constr. Proj. Manag. Innov. **4**(2), 930–949 (2014)
20. Aljowder, T., Ali, M., Kurnia, S.: Systematic literature review of the smart city maturity model. In: 2019 International Conference on Innovation and Intelligence for Informatics, Computing, and Technologies, 3ICT 2019, pp. 1–9. IEEE, Bahrain (2019)
21. Arief, A., Abbas, M.Y., Wahab, I.H.A., Latif, L.A., Abdullah, S.D., Sensuse, D.I.: The smart islands vision: towards smart city readiness in local government of Archipelagos. In: International Conference on Science and Technology, pp. 1–8. Journal of Physics: Conference Series, Surabaya, Indonesia (2019)
22. Appio, F.P., Lima, M., Paroutis, S.: Understanding Hangwi smart cities: innovation ecosystems, technological advancements, and societal challenges. Technol. Forecast. Soc. Chang. **14**(1), 1–14 (2019)
23. Neagu, I.-M.: Sustainable smart cities: a fog computing framework for a smart urban transport network. Studia Universitatis "Vasile Goldis" Arad – Econ. Ser. **28**(4), 68–80 (2018)
24. Szabo, R., et al.: Framework for smart city applications based on participatory sensing. In: 2013 IEEE 4th International Conference on Cognitive Infocommunications (CogInfoCom), pp. 295–300. IEEE, Budapest (2013)
25. Akhtar, N.: US city decision maker survey – a collaborative project run by HIS Markit the US conference of mayors: US smart cities – 2018. Cities of the 21st century (2018)
26. Farago, P.: A conceptual model for smart city evaluation: attributes and rules. In: 37th International Scientific Conference on Economic and Social Development – "Socio Economic Problems of Sustainable Development", pp. 1407–1415, Baku (2019)
27. Nagy, Z., Tóth, G., Szendi, D., Dóra, S., Tóth, G.: Opportunities for adaptation of the smart city concept - a regional approach. Theory Methodol. Pract. **12**(1), 87–93 (2016)
28. Dixon, T., Eames, M., Britnell, J., Watson, G.B., Hunt, M.: Urban retrofitting: identifying disruptive and sustaining technologies using performative and foresight techniques. Technol. Forecast. Soc. Chang. **89**(1), 131–144 (2014)
29. Walravens, N., Breuer, J., Ballon, P.: Open data as a catalyst for the smart city as a local innovation platform. Digiworld Econ. J. **4**(96), 15 (2014)
30. Vu, K., Hartley, K.: Promoting smart cities in developing countries: policy insights from Vietnam. Telecommun. Policy **42**(1), 845–859 (2018)
31. Veselitskaya, N., Karasev, O., Beloshitskiy, A.: Drivers and barriers for smart cities development. Theor. Empir. Res. Urban Manag. **14**(1), 85–110 (2019)
32. Hartley, M.K.: An analysis of business intelligence for improved public service delivery. Master's thesis. University of Cape Town, Cape Town, South Africa (2015). http://hdl.handle.net/11427/15534. Accessed 17 Feb 2021
33. Hartley, K., Seymour, L.F.L.: Towards a framework for the adoption of business intelligence in public sector organisations: the case of South Africa. In: Proceedings of the South African Institute of Computer Scientists and Information Technologists Conference on Knowledge, pp. 116–122 (2011)
34. Mora, L., Deakin, M., Reid, A.: Combining co-citation clustering and text-based analysis to reveal the main development paths of smart cities. Technol. Forecast. Soc. Chang. **142**(1), 56–69 (2019)
35. Ojasalo, J., Kauppinen, H.: Collaborative innovation with external actors: an empirical study on open innovation platforms in smart cities. Technol. Innov. Manag. Rev. **6**(12), 49–60 (2016)
36. Chourabi, H., et al.: Understanding smart cities: an integrative framework. In: Proceedings of the Annual Hawaii International Conference on System Sciences, pp. 2289–2297. IEEE, Hawaii (2012)

37. Prendeville, S., Cherim, E., Bocken, N.: Circular cities: mapping six cities in transition. Environ. Innov. Soc. Trans. **26**(1), 171–194 (2018)
38. Yigitcanlar, T., Kamruzzaman, M., Foth, M., Sabatini-Marques, J., da Costa, E., Ioppolo, G.: Can cities become smart without being sustainable? A systematic review of the literature. Sustain. Cities Soc. **45**(1), 348–365 (2019)
39. Oomens, I.M.F., Sadowski, B.M.: The importance of internal alignment in smart city initiatives: an ecosystem approach. Telecommun. Policy **1**(1), 1–16 (2019)
40. Schiavone, F., Paolone, F., Mancini, D.: Business model innovation for urban smartization. Technol. Forecast. Soc. Chang. **142**(1), 210–219 (2019)
41. Kitchenham, B.: Procedures for performing systematic reviews (Keele University Technical Report No. TR/SE-0401; NICTA Technical Report No. 0400011T.1). Keele University, Keele (2004). http://www.elizabete.com.br/rs/Tutrial_IHC_2012_files/Conceitos_RevisaoSistematica_kitchenham_2004.pdf. Accessed 09 July 2021
42. Okoli, C., Schabram, K.: A guide to conducting a systematic literature review of information systems research. SSRN Electron. J. **10**(26), 10–26 (2012)
43. Patrick, A.: Trends in smart cities: implications for research and practice in developing economies. In: AMCIS 2020 TREOs, vol. 71 (2020). https://aisel.aisnet.org/treos_amcis2020/71
44. Chichernea, V.: Smart cities communities and smart ICT platform. J. Inf. Syst. Oper. Manag. **1**(1), 1–11 (2015)
45. Joshi, S., Saxena, S., Godbole, T., Shreya: Developing smart cities: an integrated framework. In: 6th International Conference on Advances on Computing & Communications, ICACC 2016, pp. 902–909. Procedia Computer Science, Cochin (2016)
46. Supangkat, S.H., Arman, A.A., Nugraha, R.A., Fatimah, Y.A.: The implementation of Garuda smart city framework for smart city readiness mapping in Indonesia. J. Asia-Pac. Stud. **1**(28), 169–176 (2018)
47. Peto, R.: Security of smart city. Interdiscip. Descr. Complex Syst. **17**(1), 13–19 (2019)
48. Cilliers, L., Flowerday, S.: Factors that influence the usability of a participatory IVR crowdsourcing system in a smart city. S. Afr. Comput. J. **29**(3), 16–30 (2017)
49. Hoel, T., Mason, J.: Standards for smart education – towards a development framework. Smart Learn. Environ. **5**(1), 1–25 (2018). https://doi.org/10.1186/s40561-018-0052-3
50. Zhu, Z.-T., Yu, M.-H., Riezebos, P.: A research framework of smart education. Smart Learn. Environ. **3**(1), 1–17 (2016). https://doi.org/10.1186/s40561-016-0026-2

Check for updates

Digital Application Literacy

LeAnne J. Schmidt(✉)

Central Michigan University, Mt. Pleasant, MI 48859, USA
schmi61@cmich.edu

Abstract. After mixed results in emergency virtual and remote learning during the 2020 COVID pandemic, content assessment may have felt the greatest negative impacts. Even for in-person classroom settings, digital application literacy provides the opportunity for teachers to orient students to the nuances of digital applications so that novice experiences do not impact test performance. Digital Application Literacy (DAppLit) refers to the nimble use of a web-based app or software-based application for academic purposes, including assessment. Steps of DAppLit include: 1) Identifying goals and consequences outside the testing environment; 2) Modeling assessment to build digital application literacy skills; 3) Providing low-stakes experience before a high-stakes assessment; and 4) Reflecting and diagnosing the process for improvement. With impacts on assessment of virtual and remote learning, digital comprehension skills, and challenges to adaptive assessment, *digital application literacy* is a standard needed to properly equip all students for success in the assessment process.

Keywords: Assessment · Digital assessment literacy · Online assessment · Web-based assessment · Testing · Decision-making · DAppLit

1 Introduction

The pandemic school year of 2020–2021 under COVID-19 protocols has ended. What lies ahead in the 2021–2022 school year is currently undefined. The lessons of this dramatic and exhausting year were many and sometimes painful, but they were endured [1]. A leading question is "How well did students do in school this year?" [2]. Of course, it takes assessment to know the correct answer. For the most part, the answers are not forthcoming.

The flaw in this procedure is in the assessment avenue itself because 2020–2021 assessments, at least those which occurred, lack validity. States like Michigan enforced mandatory testing in the spring of 2021 for public school students. In cases in which the school district was conducting classes virtually, students were tested virtually. In school districts meeting in person, particularly ones which returned to school in early March due to government incentives, the state testing sessions were close on the heals of the return to school. Under state law, some third-grade students would not be promoted to the next grade level because of poor reading scores on these assessments, had it not been for a late-breaking bill in the State Congress to suspend the law for one year, due to COVID impacts [3]. The College Board cancelled significant components of the SAT testing

© Springer Nature Switzerland AG 2021
Y.-M. Huang et al. (Eds.): ICITL 2021, LNCS 13117, pp. 274–282, 2021.
https://doi.org/10.1007/978-3-030-91540-7_29

platform for 2021 as a result of complications with host locations and concerns for the validity of a virtual testing environment. Thus, the solution at hand is the cancellation of assessment and consequences, but when does this method end?

Classroom teachers faced similar challenges in managing ways to cope with assessing students who could have the textbook on the desk next to them during a testing session or a phone within reach to text a friend for an answer. Without assessment, class proved to be little more than a discussion or a lecture, often to blank screens with cameras in *off* mode. The main challenge occurred because the management methods of virtual courses were very different from those of in-person class meetings. For success to happen, a pivot to new methods of both formative and summative assessment was needed.

As teachers explored new technologies to enhance the classroom experience, they trod new pathways and navigated new challenges which few had been trained to manage. For teachers to learn the new online apps or computer applications themselves was the first concern. The next step was how to integrate them with the curriculum. Finally, it was necessary to teach the use of these new resources to students. Handling all three of these factors successfully was a Herculean task, particularly because it required new literacies, many of which had not yet been articulated. Digital Application Literacy is one such element.

Digital Application Literacy refers to the nimble use of an app (web-based) or application (computer-based) for education, including assessment. In order to reach a position of having Digital Application Literacy, students require proper orientation with new resources, guided practice, low-stakes experiences, and the opportunity to discuss the procedures in order to be fully successful in the new environment. While children may sometimes seem more computer savvy than their elders, that does not mean that they have adequately explored the depth and breadth of the options available to them. From this perspective, a "good enough" understanding is far from enough when students are being assessed, either formatively or summatively, by their interactions with the digital application.

1.1 To First-Timers, Doors Look Like Barriers

We don't come into this world knowing how to interpret our surroundings; we must be taught, by others with knowledge or by experience. To a toddler, the world is full of barriers, until he/she learns to circumvent them. To a first timer, a door looks like a barrier until one knows to turn the knob and push forward. This is the essential quality of literacy.

The same is true of all navigation features on a digital device. Blue words in the middle of a sentence do not inherently broadcast a message to click the portal to another web page; this must be learned through experience or education. The same is true of "user-friendly" icons in a toolbar, the magnifying glass which reveals a search bar, and the "X" to close a screen is not intuitive, especially when it occurs in one place on Windows and the opposite location on a Mac.

Teaching technology skills is essential. According to Chris Lehmann, Principal of Science Leadership Academy, "Technology must be like oxygen: ubiquitous, necessary, and invisible." [4]. In order to be ubiquitous, it must be available. With remote learning during the pandemic, school systems learned how necessary technology really is. To be invisible, it must be integrated as second nature to students, but first it must be taught through experience.

Technology alone is not a solution. As the TPACK framework expresses, teachers exist in multiple domains when operating in the classroom, specifically: technological knowledge, pedagogical knowledge, and content knowledge [5]. Digital Application Literacy is a pedagogical model for imparting technological knowledge to students, which is nuanced by choices informed by content knowledge, that is taught or assessed using the app/application.

The science of digital literacy (defined as reading in an online environment) plays a role which cannot be denied. Sahin [6] demonstrated that preference and experience impact the ability to read digital texts with the same expertise as printed ones. In a digital environment, reading speed and accuracy are inversely correlated to a greater degree than with print material [7]. The introduction of reading goals, initial browsing, and limited re-reading strongly correlate to improved comprehension in online texts [8]. When readers encounter difficult material to digest and interpret in a digital medium, they experience physical reactions, such as changes in skin conductance, increased heart rate, and a lowered volume of blood to the fingers [9]. On a digital page, type size, line spacing, presence of headings, and alignment impact comprehension to a greater degree than is true of text pages, whereas simple text enhancements like bold, underline, and italics do not [10]. Given the marked impact that these simple adjustments to a web page can make on comprehension, reason suggests the potential for even greater impacts when the method of initial contact with an app/application is augmented.

Apart from some simple enhancements like headings or the occasional image, printed pages have limited factors which compete for the reader's attention, whereas websites and individual pages represent an obstacle course of intrusions. Bland pages (entirely text-based) and overly interactive sites impede user facility, demonstrating moderate interactivity as the most successful approach [11]. Among pages of a website, contrasting complexity levels can be helpful though disorder and dissimilarity are not [12]. The linear task of reading on paper simply requires fewer decisions than digital navigation of a web page where page elements have power to change the experience [13]. When assessment is an outcome of the experience, these competing factors, user variables, and decision-making opportunities must be explored outside of the assessment framework in order to properly prepare learners to deliver their best work product.

An important conundrum can powerfully impact the results of digital assessment in the form of help availability. Many apps have built-in features to assist users in understanding the task, such as guided walkthroughs, tutorials, pop-up information when hovering, help bots, and companion help sites. When in a classroom-based assessment environment, getting help is most likely raising a hand to get the teacher's attention for a private question. In a digital assessment, the opportunity for help may be blurred by time limitations and fears of invalidating the assessment by clicking something "wrong." Self-diagnosis of the need for help is critical before students will seek help. High-level skills are required to reach the confidence to seek help, so the students who may need it most are those individuals least likely to utilize help features [14]. Proper preparedness in the availability of help features, the steps for reaching them, and the consequences of each step in both time and point deductions must be made clear to students outside the confines of an actual assessment.

Lest it seem like all digital assessment features are cautionary, the medium offers additional means for improving the opportunity of learners through methods which are not possible or are at least far more complex in the analog arena. The addition of color, for example, can add significant cost in the print medium, but does not have this drawback on a webpage. Thus, digital scaffolding, such as highlighting and color-coding of passages or page elements, are simply managed and yield benefits to reading comprehension and navigation [15]. Vocabulary terms can include hover text definitions to inform readers. Related topics when mentioned on a text page can be hyperlinked to improve the depth of knowledge and pursue a curiosity at the precise moment of greatest engagement. Even when such resources are not embedded as a feature of the app/application, working in a digital environment can empower students with the confidence to seek information in another browser window, an operation which would be far more complex with just paper and pencil. While this can cross ethical lines in assessment, such expectations should be made clear to students prior to the task, instead of becoming a quandary they must face in the middle of the assessment.

1.2 Digital Application Literacy

The model of Digital Application Literacy (DAppLit) focuses on equipping learners with skills to navigate, digest, and manage online applications effectively. It arose from the study of Digital Assessment Literacy theory, which was designed to equip teachers to target assessments so that they meet educational goals [16]. However, preparing assessments to meet the needs of students and the expectations of assigned curriculum does not solve the whole problem. The pedagogy of preparing learners for the task ahead of them is essential.

While it is true that Digital Assessment Literacy would guard against poorly written tests in favor of ideal assessment which properly evaluates each learning goal [17], some tenets of digital assessment are skill-based [18, 19]. For example, a fill-in-the-blank test engenders problems in scoring as a result of misspellings, unexpected capitalization or failure to do so, or the use of a synonym. These would be considered a *Digital Assessment Literacy* failing on the part of the teacher to account to the possible outcomes of the students. However, if the student must click "OK" to save each answer before moving on or before finishing the assessment, the matter can be solved by teaching principles to students. After all, a student who scores a zero on the assessment because his answers were not saved properly is different from a student who got the wrong answer to every assessment question. One is a failure of content knowledge, whereas the other is the result of a lack of technological acumen or experience with the assessment medium. Teaching with a DAppLit mindset can eliminate the failures of the latter issue.

2 Applying DAppLit

2.1 Identifying Goals and Consequences…Before It Counts

Classroom teachers, departments, schools, and districts have multiple purposes for choosing assessment. Students do not always understand those purposes, but look at every assessment as a "test" which translates to a high-stakes consequence with a permanent label affixed to them which limits their options in an on-going way. This is seldom the true story. Teachers may use formative assessment in each class session to collect data on student comprehension. Departments and districts may use assessment for alignment and calibration across multiple teachers or school buildings. Schools and districts may use assessment of students to evaluate teachers. Note that few of these are a means of direct pressure on student personal performance, but, for students, pressure comes with all tests. Students need to know who is really being assessed. They need to know if the assessment is intermittent. They need to know if it is reportable and fixable. Why? Overthinking and stressors can sabotage the outcome for a teacher seeking formative feedback. In formatives, feedback is the objective for teachers and for students. Undermining it with pressure invalidates the entire assessment. In summative assessment, students who know what is being tested and what the consequences will be for different performance levels are better equipped for optimal engagement of the task.

2.2 Modeling Assessment to Build Digital Application Literacy Skills

Hands-on learning has its place (and that will be part of 2.3), however, many young people have impulsive tendencies and others have issues with timidity, which impair the authenticity of responses. A practiced educator must take the time to explore features of the assessment medium with students. Modeling is often a missed step in the teaching process because it requires added time. Some features to include in modeling are sign-in procedures, such as using a Google SSO, reminding students to use their school email instead of a personal one, properly entering the class identification code so the teacher will have access via the app's teacher dashboard, and even whether they are allowed to sign in with a nickname or their given names. The rest depends on the app. Other considerations may include timing, features on the frame of the workspace, stages of the assessment, specifics on the topic, number of chances allowed, how to move from one question to another, types of answers, detail level of responses, and assumptions to make or avoid. However, this is not a matter of lecturing students about app use because this would significantly reduce engagement. Students should feel free to politely interrupt the process with pressing questions because the truth is that these spontaneous curiosities would be present when they are assessed independently. It benefits them to get answers outside the context of their own testing session to avoid impacts on assessment time limits and choice-making. An important feature to model is the help availability in the app or the use of "hints" which can sometimes impact the possible score with a slight reduction or a full cancellation of credit for the item/question.

2.3 Providing a Low-Stakes Experience Before a High-Stakes Assessment

Apart from pretesting a class to calibrate the level of fluency in a topic before any teaching lessons occur, educators are not in the practice of testing first and potentially teaching later…or so we think. However, failing to give students a real-time test environment experience in a digital medium prior to a summative assessment serves the same ends. Expectancy-Value Theory indicates that potential competing outcomes may impact the decision-making of students [20]. When an assessment medium was used through the course of a school year for multiple independent units, students improved 10% from the first assessment to one mid-year and an additional 15% by the end of the year [21]. When the content material is mutually exclusive the results indicate that students have learned how to use the assessment app/application up to 25% through the course of the year. However, many teachers would interpret the results as lower performance on the first assessment content and superior performance on the content topic of the last assessment. From a more comprehensive view, students are actually demonstrating better digital application literacy by the end of the school year, not greater content knowledge.

The danger in misapplying the improvement of students is corruption of the validity of assessment. While the later testing situation is more reflective of actual student knowledge, it is possible to eliminate DAppLit bias from all scores, by fully introducing the app/application to students in advance of an actual assessment. However, creativity is needed to find low-stakes methods which will simulate the real-time testing environment. With some apps, such as Google Forms, creating a beginning-of-the-year student questionnaire to gain personal profile information can serve as a preliminary experience for teachers who use Google Forms for weekly quizzes. Construction of the questionnaire should include test-like elements, such as the response validation feature which requires a date, time, or specifically formatted number, so that students face the possible anxiety of an error message. Another feature would be including some required and some optional questions so that students experience what to do or what messages they will encounter if they miss a required question. The same basic tenets apply with any quiz platform, including those which are part of a learning management system (LMS).

In other cases, it is necessary to create an assessment simulation in a more specifically targeted app. In this situation, an alternative version of the assessment can serve as the low-stakes practice for a later test. While more work is involved in creating two versions of the same content assessment and twice as many question prompts, the importance of valid summative assessment outweighs the short-term effort. One option to consider is using last year's assessment as a simulation and creating an updated version for the actual summative assessment. This provides a platform of incremental improvement which is also good pedagogy. The hidden benefit of these steps is that students can view the classroom environment as a safe place to make preliminary mistakes in order to learn and develop a classroom culture which serves as an *affinity space* [22]. While mistakes are not a desired goal, fixing them is suitable classwork.

2.4 Reflecting and Diagnosing the Process for Improvement

While reflection is often an undervalued step, utilizing it can serve as a means to share knowledge gained by one student with others in the class in a productive way. The reflection stage of teaching Digital Application Literacy is two-fold. It should occur after the low-stakes practice assessment, but it should also be implemented after the full-scale summative assessment. New situations and literacy challenges can arise in either setting, so capturing them as learning experiences will inform and empower students on subsequent assessments. Even if learners will not be using the same assessment medium in the class, transfer skills can apply this learning to other contexts.

Self-assessment or gauging performance can provide students with an invaluable skill. When teachers ask students how they performed on the assessment, answers shared with the classroom are likely to misrepresent the actual perception of students, so logging private responses, such as with test wrappers [23] can be a valuable tool. These allow learners to compare their initial perceptions with actual feedback from the assessment when it is available. Reconciling variations between perception and reality helps students to develop authentic perceptions in the future.

At least the first time the app/application is used for assessment, a dialogue should occur afterward to provide students with a forum for expressing frustrations and finding productive solutions before encountering the assessment platform again. While it is important to establish a judgment-free zone for discussion, responses from students may still be limited. Time for personal reflection is encouraged and permitting a private opportunity to explore alternative strategies may be helpful for students uncomfortable with sharing their mistakes and misinterpretations with the class.

3 Conclusions

The theory of Digital Application Literacy strikes at the heart of assessment literacy, but particularly Digital Assessment Literacy [16] which requires a diverse array of strategies and clear goal definition from teachers in order to accurately reveal the level of classroom learning that has occurred. Without digital application literacy, identifying the outcomes as the result of content learning is not possible. Too many other factors could corrupt the findings of the assessment. Since the assessment goal of the classroom teacher is presumably to determine how much the student knows about the content at the end of a lesson or unit, any corruption of those findings interferes with the entire process toward the educational goal.

The impact of an absence of digital application literacy among students can affect multiple aspects of classroom experience. Among those impacts are spending excess time teaching a concept that students already know well, but which does not display effectively in the assessment. Poorer scores among students impact them emotionally and can affect their academic standing. Classwide score impacts can label a class, a teacher, or a school as deficient, when that is merely the failure to adequately attending to digital application literacy.

Impacts are more profound in the arena of adaptive assessment. Because it is designed to pinpoint levels of understanding by posing questions across a wide range of levels and narrowing to specific areas to identify where knowledge gaps occur [24], inaccuracies in responses to questions during that narrowing phase could improperly limit the range for the rest of the assessment. Since the specifics of what a student knows and does not know are misrepresented by responses based on inadequate experience with the assessment medium [25], the resulting scores are more likely to underrepresent student knowledge levels.

Acknowledging the misalignments which can occur between assessing students adequately with and without preparation in the medium, the difference between content knowledge and digital application literacy, and the need for regular digital application literacy training of students and digital assessment literacy training of teachers paints an uncertain picture. Much like an optometric exam, educational experts must continue to ask the question: *Which is clearer – A or B?*, in order to reach the precise position that assessments are revealing what educators need to know. The ophthalmologist asks the question multiple times to gain precision in all aspects of measurement of the lens. Rushing the process of assessment could yield equally blurry results. Taking the time for appropriate digital application literacy yields not only clarity for teachers, but also the truest experience for students who can reflect on their actual knowledge and responses, minimizing anxieties and other emotional aspects related to the testing medium.

References

1. Tate, E.: As districts return to remote learning, are they any better prepared? EdSurge.com, 10 December 2020
2. Digital Learning Collaborative. Snapshot 2020: A review of K-12 online, blended, and digital learning, February 2020
3. Chambers, J.: Thousands of Michigan third graders flagged for retention under reading law. The Detroit News, 25 May 2021
4. Lehmann, C.: "School 2.0." Speech presented at National Association of Secondary School Principals conference, 28 February 2009
5. Mishra, P., Koehler, M.J.: Technological pedagogical content knowledge: a framework for teacher knowledge. Teach. Coll. Rec. **108**(6), 1017–1054 (2006)
6. Sahin, A.: Effects of linear texts in page scrolling and page-by-page reading forms on reading comprehension introduction. TOJET Turk. Online J. Educ. Technol. **10**(3), 94–100 (2011)
7. Miyata, H., Minagawa-Kawai, Y., Watanabe, S., Sasaki, T., Ueda, K.: Reading speed, comprehension and eye movements while reading Japanese novels: evidence from untrained readers and cases of speed-reading trainees. PloS One **7**(5), e36091 (2012)
8. Sung, Y.T., Wu, M.D., Chen, C.K., Chang, K.E.: Examining the online reading behavior and performance of fifth-graders: evidence from eye-movement data. Front. Psychol. **6**, 665 (2015)
9. Ward, R.D., Marsden, P.H.: Physiological responses to different webpage designs. Int. J. Hum.-Comput. Stud. **59**(1), 199–212 (2003)
10. Scaltritti, M., Miniukovich, A., Venuti, P., Job, R., De Angeli, A., Sulpizio, S.: Investigating effects of typographic variables on webpage reading through eye movements. Sci. Rep. **9**(1), 12711–12712 (2019)
11. Yung-Chin, T., Chia-Ho, T.: The research of dynamic images using effect in children webpage. Int. J. Organ. Innov. **9**(1), 97–106 (2016)
12. Deng, L., Poole, M.S.: Affect in web interfaces: a study of the impacts of web page visual complexity and order. MIS Q. **34**(4), 711–730 (2010)
13. Naumann, J., Salmerón, L.: Does navigation always predict performance? Effects of navigation on digital reading are moderated by comprehension skills. Int. Rev. Res. Open Distrib. Learn. **17**(1), 42–59 (2016)
14. Aleven, V., Stahl, E., Schworm, S.: Help seeking and help design in interactive learning environments. Rev. Educ. Res. **73**(3), 277–320 (2003)
15. Fernando, W.: Show me your true colours: scaffolding formative academic literacy assessment through an online learning platform. Assess. Writ. **36**, 63–76 (2018)
16. Eyal, L.: Digital assessment—the core role of the teacher in a digital environment. Educ. Technol. Soc. **15**(2), 37–49 (2012)
17. Horton, W.: E-Learning by Design, 2nd edn. Wiley, Hoboken (2012)
18. Sutherland-Smith, W.: Weavin the literacy Web: changes in reading from page to screen; "Web literacy" requires a rethinking of skills. More and different strategies are needed for decoding meaning. Read. Teach. **55**(7), 662 (2002)

19. Mery, Y., Newby, J., Peng, K.: Performance-based assessment in an online course: comparing different types of information literacy instruction. Portal (Baltimore, Md.) **12**(3), 283–298 (2012)
20. Vroom, V.H.: Work and Motivation. Wiley, New York (1964)
21. Schmidt, L.J.: Quartile analysis of test answer patterns and persistence in digital applications. [Doctoral dissertation, Central Michigan University.] (2021)
22. Gee, J.P.: Affinity spaces: how young people live and learn online and out of school. Phi Delta Kappan **99**(6), 8–13 (2018)
23. Lovett, M.: "Exam Wrappers." Eberly Center for Teaching Excellent & Educational Innovation. Carnegie Mellon University (2021)
24. Greiff, S., Wüstenberg, S., Holt, D.V., Goldhammer, F., Funke, J.: Computer-based assessment of complex problem solving. Educ. Tech. Res. Dev. **61**(3), 407–421 (2013)
25. Reckase, M., Ju, U., Kim, S.: How adaptive is an adaptive test: are all adaptive tests adaptive? J. Comput. Adapt. Test. **7**(1), 1–14 (2019)

Big Data in the Innovation Process - A Bibliometric Analysis

Zornitsa Yordanova(✉)

University of National and World Economy, 8mi dekemvri 23, Sofia, Bulgaria
zornitsayordanova@unwe.bg

Abstract. Big Data is widely used in a growing number of business processes to open up new spaces for optimizing, improving and adapting the decision making to the changing environment. Businesses and universities are forced by the competition to engage various and, until recently external, elements in their internal innovation efforts. Examples of such openness of the innovation process and innovation practices are the involvement of customers, students, competitors, living laboratories, external collaborators and often external data. Data plays a crucial role in innovation development. Big data has the ability to open up the innovation process of enterprises and to link the developed innovations with knowledge, information and lessons learned from many external sources. This study introduces a bibliometric analysis of the application of Big Data in the innovation process to analyse the current research on the topic. The analysis scrutinizingly examines the science literature by: keyword analysis, word and trend analysis, coupling clustering, source and authors' review to reveal the path of the research development in the field and to provide insight to innovation management professionals and scholars.

Keywords: Innovation process · Big Data · Innovation management · Data management · Bibliometric analysis

1 Introduction

It is widely discussed in the scientific literature that digitalization provides new opportunities for process improvement in industries and enables process innovation. [1]. Digitalization rely on data and technologies to automate and introduce novel advantages of data to optimize processes [2]. Data can also motivate and facilitate new value-creation and revenue-generation of opportunities [3]. Opening up to new and external data can make enterprises' innovation more adjusted and adapted to the constant changes of the market and customers' needs [3]. Data is reckoned to be crucial also in innovation management in times of crises and multidisciplinary or cross-sectional innovations [4]. Data and business intelligence solutions are acknowledged as an impetus for organizations of any size sector [5].

Big Data can ensure optimal use of resources, reduce decision-making time and introduce insights into product development [6] and is even seen as a tool for the firm's innovation competence [7].

© Springer Nature Switzerland AG 2021
Y.-M. Huang et al. (Eds.): ICITL 2021, LNCS 13117, pp. 283–292, 2021.
https://doi.org/10.1007/978-3-030-91540-7_30

The motivation for this research was provoked by the call for urgent research in the field of economic value of data and in particular big data [5] and the launch of a research project on the gaps and lags in the digitalization of the company's innovation process. The structure of the research is organized, emphasizing the results of the bibliometric analysis with a brief theoretical background on the research topic: innovation process and big data in business processes and innovation. The results may be of interest to scientists and practitioners dealing with management issues in terms of digitization and optimization of innovation management.

2 Theoretical Background

2.1 Innovation Process

Innovation process is usually seen as a means of development innovation and innovation management across organizations. Over the years, it has been intensively analysed for its development and progress. The enterprise innovation process (often mentioned as a firm's innovation process or internal innovation process) has attracted the interest of researchers since the 1950s and still is a subject of research because of its constantly developing nature. Generally, the innovation process is a chain of activities and strategic and organizational vision related to the development and commercialization of innovative products, processes, organizational setups or marketing initiatives. Its evolution has gone through different concepts and theories starting from more general and industry-based theories to more-internal-to firm's models, systematized holistically from Rothwell [8] into 5 categories: The Technology Push Theory - 1950s, The Market Pull Theory - 1960s, The Coupling Innovation Process Theory - 1970s-1980s, The Functional Integrated Innovation Process Theory (Imai, 1985) - 1980s, The Systems Integration and Networking Innovation Process Theory - 1990s.

This study steps on the simple innovation process presented by Tidd and Pavitt [9], containing the following phases for innovation development: search, select, implement and capture and the simple process-based version of Dziallas, Knut Blind [10]: strategy, definition, conceptualization, testing and validation, production and final market launch.

2.2 Big Data in Business Processes and Innovation

Data is simple raw facts that reflect the characteristics of an object or event [11]. Data and Big Data in specific can bring immense benefit for businesses by providing insights from analysing large sizes of various data [12]. Data-driven insights are crucial for business processes and innovations in general [13]. New digital business models related to Big Data and incorporated into the business processes can reduce costs, generate additional revenue from digital solutions, optimize customer interaction and improve customer service by studying their experience [14]. Business process management field has been already engaged with big data concepts and the science literature provides several models for big data use in order to guide, optimize and forecast business processes [15].

3 Research Design

The research design is based on criteria for inclusion and exclusion of data extraction and conducted bibliometric analyses for research of the complex topic from the multidisciplinary areas of innovation and technology management and business process management.

3.1 Data Extraction and Scope Definition

The data for conducting the analysis was extracted from Scopus database and offers science articles, conference papers and reviews, published in journals or conference papers indexed by Scopus. The Boolean search used for obtaining the science pieces of research was:

TITLE−ABS−KEY ("innovation process" AND "big data")

As a result, we achieved 59 research pieces. We excluded from our data set conference reviews and notes and the source that we based our research contains 54. We keep: articles (26), book chapters (3), conference papers (21) and reviews (4). The timespan of the publications was from 2013 to 2021 (extracted in April 2021) from 48 sources. Figure 1 presents the science production meeting our inclusion and exclusion criteria which seems to be highly under-researched (it is expected to immensely increase in the next few years with the advancements of Big Data application in business processes). The extraction was conducted in April 2021 which explains the decrease for this year on the figure.

Fig. 1. Science production on Big Data in innovation process

3.2 Bibliometric Analysis

The bibliometric analysis in this study was performed using the open source application Bibliometrix, the R package, and its Biblioshiny tool. It was chosen because Bibliometrix contains a wider range of techniques than all other bibliometric software and is suitable for non-coders through Biblioshiny [16].

The applied bibliometric analyses were:

- Keywords analysis (unigram, bigram and trigram analysis)
- Citation analysis
- Three fields plot analyses based on journals, keywords, countries, authors
- A thematic map (based on keywords, titles, abstracts)
- Clustering by coupling.

4 Results and Discussion

The results of the bibliometric analysis are presented sequentially according to their conduct. A discussion takes place after each presentation of results. The first analysis presents through three fields plot the top 10 countries researching the topic, keywords associated with these publications and the authors.

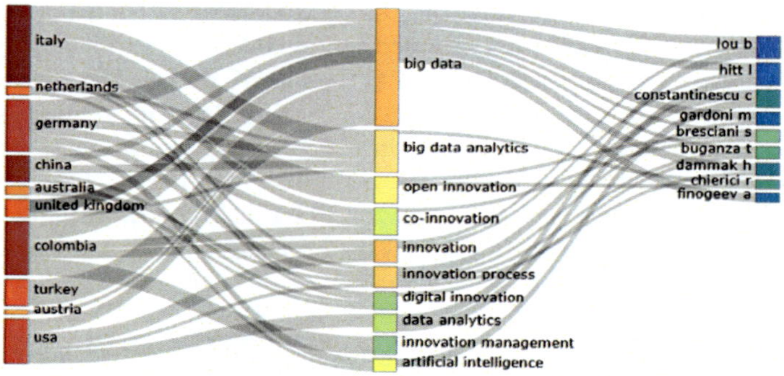

Fig. 2. Three plot analysis for top 10 countries, keywords and authors

The illustration of the analysed three elements on Fig. 2 are linked through their relationships which display the scale of each research stream. Thereby, it is clear that big data and big data analysis are amongst the central terms around the research in the area of innovation processes with big data use. The countries most interested in the topic are Germany and Italy. Authors from Italy specifically emphasized on research related to open innovation as part of their research on innovation process and big data utilization. The top 10 words encountered among the author's keywords are: big data, big data analytics, open innovation, co-innovation, innovation, innovation process, digital innovation, data analytics, innovation management and artificial intelligence. On Fig. 3 is presented a cross analysis of keywords, sources and affiliation of authors.

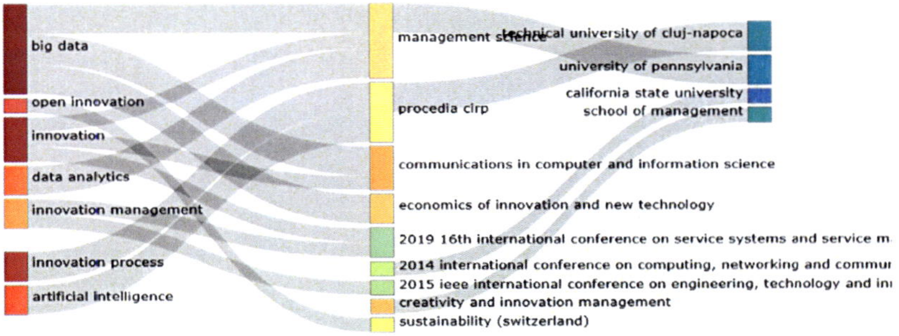

Fig. 3. Three plot analysis on author's keywords, sources and affiliation

The presented results provide insight on the sources publishing mostly on the topic. These are: Management Science, Procedia CIRP, Communications in computer and information science, Economics of innovation and new technology, Creativity and Innovation management and Sustainability as well as a few conference proceedings focusing on technology management.

Clarifying the focal point, the following figure provides information on the number of times the most common keywords are mentioned: big data (20), innovation (7) and innovation process (7) (Fig. 4).

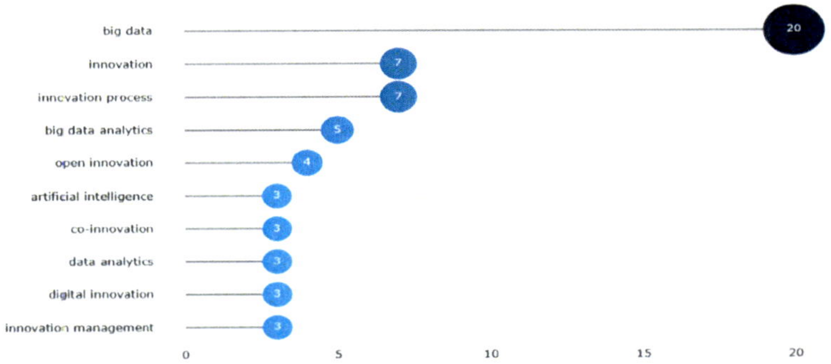

Fig. 4. Most relevant keywords (unigram)

The most represented words within titles using the approach of a single word (unigram) are presented on Fig. 5 through a tree mapping. Titles, opposed to author's keywords, are more insightful for the words-by topics in the scope of the research. Out of the words 'innovation' met in 23% of the titles and 'data' with 16% frequency, comprehension has been brought by words across the titles such as: analytics, social, framework, health, smart, technology, digital, capability, etc.

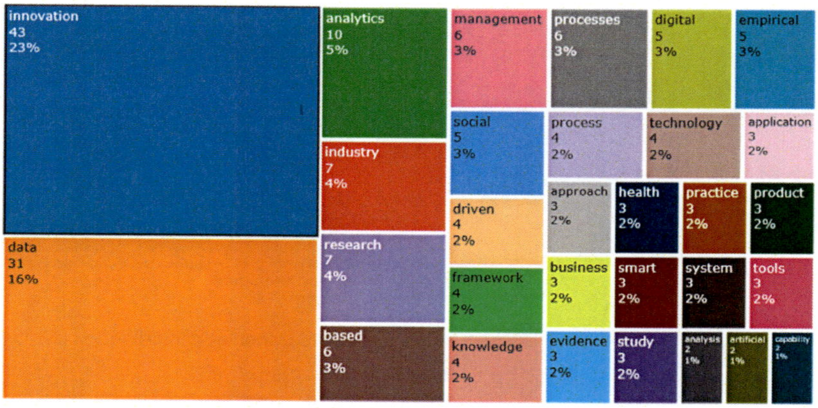

Fig. 5. Most relevant words within titles (unigram – one word)

Adding a value to the previous graph, in Fig. 6 is presents information on the phrases (bigram approach in word analysis) used in the titles as part of the scope of the study. Data analytics has been found in 16% of the titles and innovation process(es) itself in 16%. Data drive (7%), artificial intelligence (4%), driven innovation (4%), citizen observation (4%), content management (4%) and knowledge management (4%) complete the picture.

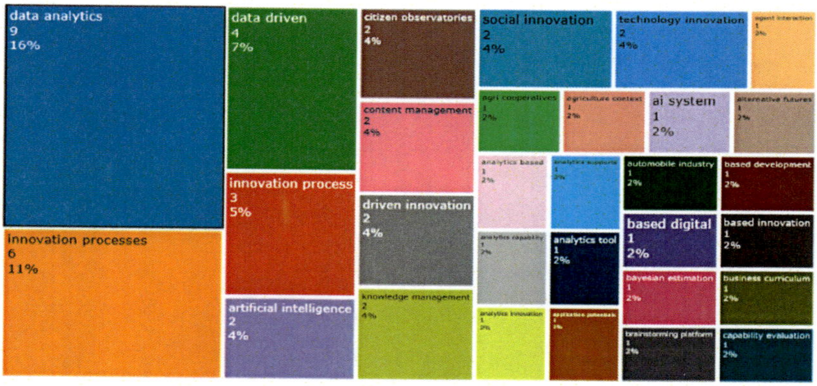

Fig. 6. Most relevant words within titles (bigrams – two words phases)

The next three figures (Fig. 7, Fig. 8 and Fig. 9) present consecutively the most frequently used words in abstracts using word analysis unigram, bigram and trigram methods. This is the most relevant word analysis as abstract concentrates the key information of a research. With this clear picture of the most focused part of a research publication as the abstract is, we pursue a holistic perspective on the most commonly met terms on this theme.

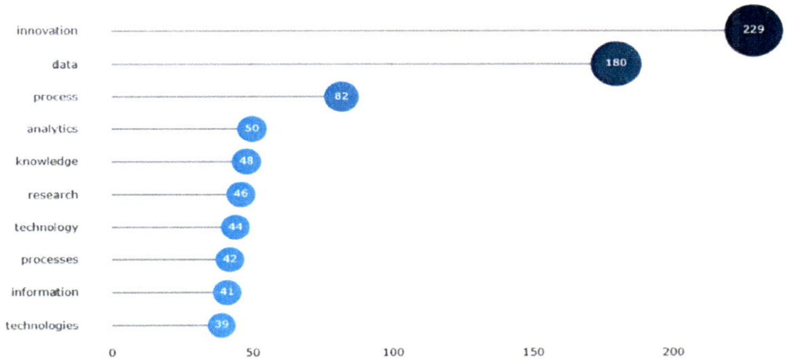

Fig. 7. Most relevant words in abstracts (single word analysis)

Word analysis by a single word in abstracts revealed that innovation, data, process and analytics were the most frequently used ones.

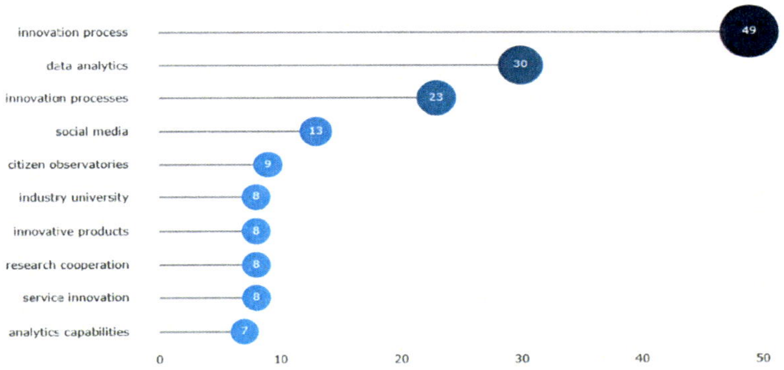

Fig. 8. Most relevant words within abstracts (bigrams – two words in a phrase)

In bigrams word analysis, the innovation process and data analytics are amongst the leading terms. Interesting insights on this matter are industry-university, social media, service innovation and analysis capabilities which all are still under-research topics within the central focal point of the research.

The trigrams word analysis provides insight on the main three words in sequence which are most frequently met in the abstracts of the analysed research publications. These are industry university research/cooperation, information/data rich environment/capabilities, flood risk management, etc. These results might be of possible direction for further research. The trend topics based on titles and across the years of research in the last 2–3 years has been focused on analytics, industry, data and processes which words give additional arguments and motivation for this research (focused on data as a driving change for the innovation process). The same analysis has been conducted but from bigrams perspective. This analysis discloses that in recent years,

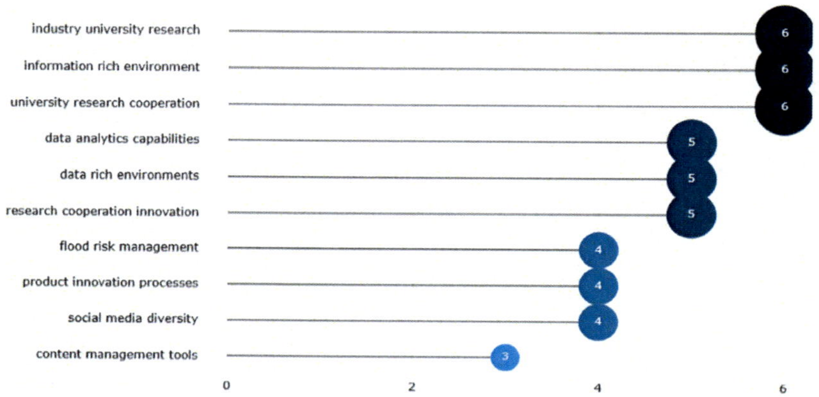

Fig. 9. Most relevant words within abstracts (trigrams – three words terms)

research on technology innovation, product design, data analytics, social media and research (industry/university) cooperation were the most debating points.

Figure 10 extends our perception on main clusters dealing with big data as part of the innovation process. Innovation, data and management were the central focal points of research, clustered by the Coupling method. An obvious differentiation is observed when we are examining topics through the prism of their impact rate and not their centrality. The level of impact intensity is displayed on the left side of the graph which suggests that data is the most impactful word within the research and not innovation itself. This might be reasoned by the multidisciplinarity of the research on the topic and still the strong engineering focus on such a technological managerial function as introducing Big Data in the firm's innovation process.

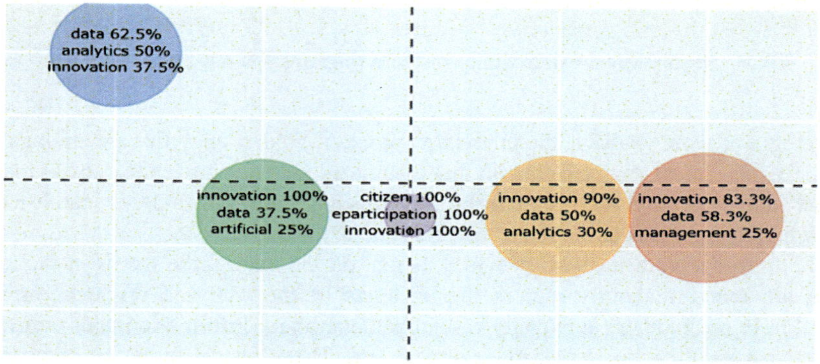

Fig. 10. Clusters by documents coupling

Figure 10 brings insight on the impact (y-vertical axis and x-horizontal line – the centrality of the research. The measures used for this analysis were: unit of analysis – documents, coupling measured by author's keywords; local measure – local citation score; cluster labelling by title terms. We use unigrams (single word analysis).

5 Conclusion

A painstaking analysis has taken place in this bibliometric research in order to reveal the clear picture of the extant research on Big Data applied in the enterprise innovation process. We defined the scope of this research to be with science publications, indexed in Scopus containing both terms of innovation process and big data. Thus, we based the bibliometric analysis on 54 high-quality publications. Several analyses have been conducted such as word analyses (unigram, bigram and trigram) on titles, keywords and abstracts of the scoped research, cluster analysis, trending topic analysis, analyses on the changing centrality of topics in the last years. The results of this study present a holistic and full picture of the existing knowledge and application of big data in the innovation process which directly impacts the firm' innovation performance. The findings of the study contribute to the innovation process theory and also call for further research on the ways by which the enterprise innovation process might be straightened through the use of big data into its phases. We identified that the most trending topics when it comes to big data in the innovation process for the last years 2018–2021 are topics related to technology innovation, product design, and analytics. Obviously, the theme is still under-researched and there are plenty of areas for further exploration such as integrating the concept of big data into firm-to-user collaboration, continuous innovation, validation of ideas, selecting innovative projects for portfolio management, etc. As some studies outlined that less than 50% of the SMEs are not innovative [17], BD should be analyzed in the light of overcoming the usual barriers for such firms which do not have innovation competence by their own.

Acknowledgements. This work was supported by the UNWE Research Programme (Research Grant No. 09/2021).

References

1. Chirumalla, K.: Building digitally-enabled process innovation in the process industries: a dynamic capabilities approach. Technovation **105**, 102256 (2021)
2. Buer, S.-V., Fragapane, G.I., Strandhagen, J.O.: The data-driven process improvement cycle: using digitalization for continuous improvement. IFAC-PapersOnLine **51**, 1035–1040 (2018)
3. Lager, T., Chirumalla, K.: Innovation and production management in the process industries: an extended editorial viewpoint and a way forward for future research. J. Bus. Chem. **17**, 1–16 (2020)
4. Naidoo, V.: Firm survival through a crisis: the influence of market orientation, marketing innovation and business strategy. Ind. Mark. Manag. **39**, 1311–1320 (2010)
5. Rotella, P.: Is data the new oil? Forbes (2012)

6. Zhan, Y., Tan, K.H., Li, Y., Tse, Y.K.: Unlocking the power of big data in new product development. Ann. Oper. Res. **270**, 577–595 (2018)
7. Ghasemaghaei, M., Calic, G.: Does big data enhance firm innovation competency? The mediating role of data-driven insights. J. Bus. Res. **104**, 69–84 (2019)
8. Rothwell, R.: Industrial innovation: success, strategy, trends. Chapters (1995)
9. Tidd, J., Bessant, J.R.: Managing Innovation: Integrating Technological Market and Organizational Change. Wiley, Hoboken (2011)
10. Dziallas, M., Blind, K.: Innovation indicators throughout the innovation process: an extensive literature analysis. Technovation **80**, 3–29 (2019)
11. Detlor, B., Hupfer, M.E., Ruhi, U., Zhao, L.: Information quality and community municipal portal use. Gov. Inf. Q. **30**, 23–32 (2013)
12. Gunasekaran, A., et al.: Big data and predictive analytics for supply chain and organizational performance. J. Bus. Res. **70**, 308–317 (2017)
13. Marcinkowski, B., Gawin, B.: Data-driven business model development–insights from the facility management industry. J. Facil. Manag. **19**, 129–149 (2020)
14. Vertakova, Y.V., Golovina, T.A., Polyanin, A.V.: Synergy of blockchain technologies and "big data" in business process management of economic systems. In: Popkova, E.G., Sergi, B.S. (eds.) ISC 2019. LNNS, vol. 87, pp. 856–865. Springer, Cham (2020). https://doi.org/10.1007/978-3-030-29586-8_97
15. Li, T., Xiong, L., Dong, A., Liu, Z.-S., Tan, W.: Optimization method based on big data in business process management. Clust. Comput. **22**, 5357–5365 (2019)
16. Moral Muñoz, J.A., Herrera Viedma, E., Santisteban Espejo, A., Cobo, M.J.: Software tools for conducting bibliometric analysis in science: an up-to-date review. El profesional de la información **29**(1), 4 (2020)
17. Carvalho, N., Yordanova, Z.: Why say no to innovation? Evidence from industrial SMEs in European Union. J. Technol. Manag. Innov. **13**(2), 43–56 (2018). https://doi.org/10.4067/S0718-27242018000200043. ISSN 0718-2724

The Student Role in Technology Supported Learning

Lisbet Rønningsbakk(✉)

UiT the Arctic University of Norway, Box 6050, Langnes N-9037 Tromsø, Norway
Lisbet.ronningsbakk@uit.no

Abstract. When technology enters classroom, it affects students' work in various ways. Students' learning strategies are challenged within the variety of new possibilities and opportunities that technologies offer in learning work. Technology supported learning bring more openness and flexibility into the assignments which is good for well-performing students but challenging for those with less developed learning strategies. They tend to be more vulnerable when the complexity increases and need more support to master the tasks. Or else they will drop out of the learning activity. Motivation also increases when students are offered technology supported work. Collaboration is also something that signifies learning work with technology. Technology supported learning therefore require collaborative skills; the ability to ask critical questions, to negotiate between different meanings, and to evaluate collaborative work.

Keywords: Learning strategies · Technology supported teaching · Profession oriented digital competence · Didactics · Student role behaviour

1 Introduction

When technologies enter the classroom, it transforms the activities in different ways. This paper presents how the student role is affected by using technologies. It is based on a pdh study that aimed to identify how technology change the way students work when learning. The data is based on observations of a 10th grade class which had not used technology in learning work before and therefore contributed with significant data on the changes that occurred in the student role.

First, the paper takes a closer look at what happened to the student role when the 10th grade students switched to using digital technology. Furthermore, some specific factors are pointed out that seemed to have an impact on the student role: increased complexity in the learning process, students with special needs for adapted teaching, and more emphasis on collaboration.

2 Method

The empirical basis of this study is a multi-case study at two schools in the North of Norway with 25 students in 4th (9–10 years old) and 10th grade (15–16 years old). The

© Springer Nature Switzerland AG 2021
Y.-M. Huang et al. (Eds.): ICITL 2021, LNCS 13117, pp. 293–302, 2021.
https://doi.org/10.1007/978-3-030-91540-7_31

data mainly build on reflection notes from participating observations, students' products, notes from meetings and other documents. The cases were selected on the background of teachers' specific interest and engagement for using technology.

The case study strategy fits well when investigating a phenomenon thoroughly through different sources of information [1, 2]. Generalizing knowledge from a few-unit study is challenging but still literature documents the relevance when applied to a similar situation [3, 4].

The main source of empirical data were five weeks of participating observations through one academic year. I observed teaching and learning situations where students worked both with and without technology to identify the changes that use of technology brought about. The data occurred through observation notes and reflections that were shared with the collaborating teachers who could respond and suggest changes. My experience as a previous teacher probably made me able to interact with the empirical field in a way they experienced as relevant. I also came with extra hands in the classrooms which granted me good relations and open access to the empirical field [5].

Being a researcher in a well-known field, challenge the need of a critical distance to the practice I took part in. I therefore needed a hermeneutic approach to avoid biased perceptions of the observed [6]. Several precautions were taken to be sure that my conceptions were relevant to the study's participants. The teachers and the school leaders were involved through discussing and sharing texts. I also reported all data about the students to their parents to assure their informed consent [5].

All data analyzing took place in the digital tool NVivo[1] where the materials were repeatedly coded to refine constructs and develop theoretical categories. The empirical data were finally presented in narratives, which has been the source of analyses and theorizing about the significant findings in the study [5].

2.1 Theory and Concepts

The theoretical framework has been collected within theory of learning and didactics, with a glance towards perspectives that emerges when technology challenge the traditional perception of teaching and learning. It is not room for a full review of the theoretical framework here but a presentation of some basic concepts that were used.

Danish Mads Hermansen has developed a concept of learning as a dynamic process within three processes: *feed forward – feedback*, *habitus – reflection*, and *toil – exuberance* [7, 8]. The dynamics between feed forward and feedback relates to the content or the objectives of the learning work. When starting the learning process, a zone of proximal development must be established, using the feedback on previous knowledge and the feed forward to expectations of the new content. The student retrieves previous knowledge and sets aims according to what the new content will contribute to the existing. When the work is in process the cognition shifts between habitus and reflection meaning that both reflective and non-reflective knowledge are activated in the process. Habitus stands for be haviour that is activated automatically because it is internalized, while reflection is needed to change the previous knowledge to the new added. Habitus

[1] NVivo is a well-known tool for qualitative data analysis: Qualitative Data Analysis Software | NVivo (qsrinternational.com).

enables automatic responses that are habituated from earlier learning and will offload the short time memory which is important for reflection. The third dynamics, toil – exuberance, is of vital importance since real learning also require some resistance to overcome and that the flow and easy mastering is important for building the strength needed to endure struggles [7, 8]. These perspectives can be useful when understanding student's role behaviour.

3 The Change of the Student Role

The changes that occur when adding technologies to the learning environment are substantial [5]. That this also affects the student role became particularly clear in the observations from Northwick school when the students switched to technology-supported learning in 10th grade. They had no experience in using technologies for learning supporting purposes before and this was therefore a significant change for them.

When 10th grader Belinda in my first visit said that using technology in school is unnecessary, it might be because the new practice breaks with her perception of what students should do at school. Hauge and Lund operate with the concept of «institutionalized student» [11]. The institutionalized student is delimited by the school's structure and culture which makes it difficult for the student to act outside what is expected. There are clear limits on how students (and teachers) can act without coming into conflict with the expected role behaviour and technologies challenged these expectations as the next paragraph will show.

3.1 The Adaptation to Technology Supported Learning for the Students in 10th Grade

The 10th graders were new to technology use in school when I first met them. They had just started using Moodle[2] to submit homework and other learning work for assessment [5]. Belinda's feedback that the work in Moodle involved unnecessary extra work was clearly linked to a student role adapted to teaching without technology support. She was used to draft by hand before submitting her work and continued doing so when writing on her computer. Habits are to be regarded as automatic actions that are situated within a specific situation which facilitates the work by controlling the course of action without having to think about what is to be done [7]. Belinda had established her work habits through nine years of schooling where the technology had been absent. In the new situation this habit pattern which had previously worked to release cognitive capacity [7], was not functional anymore. This may explain why she experienced the computer as a disruptive element in the learning process. When Belinda tried to adapt the new technology to old work habits it just increased the workload.

The physical environment was also not facilitated to use a computer in the classroom. It was very cramped on the desk for both the laptop and the textbooks. The students solved the need for space by storing the books on the floor and picking them up when they needed

[2] Moodle is an open-source learning platform that Northwick school implemented on every level of the school.

it. Neither the students' work habits nor the physical conditions in the classroom were able to support the changes that the technology brought about.

A couple of the other girls also said that they used a lot of technologies in their free time and that it might be okay to drop this at school. However, this view changed rapidly. A few months later, the students had changed their work habits. They had new ways of dealing with the practical challenges, such as working out in the hallway at a table where there was better space than at the classroom desk. They had adapted the use the learning platform Moodle, which provided access to the information and resources they needed to do the schoolwork. They wrote texts on computers and submitted them digitally, and they used Mind Maps[3] for teaching science. The feedback after the school year [5] showed that the students did not have major challenges in adjusting their roles in the encounter with the new technology. The only objection they made was about the quality of the internet connection. Not being able to deliver the assignments on time was a stress factor and a functioning internet is thus a prerequisite for the students[4].

The students quickly adapted to the new conditions for the learning work and adjusted their student roles to the new situation. This can perhaps be explained by the fact that we humans have an enormous capacity when it comes to forming new habits that are adapted to the challenges we face [7]. The skepticism that could be detected at the beginning of the year can be explained by the fact that all changes automatically activate resistance [7].

However, it may seem that the resistance is counteracted by the benefits that the use of technology can provide. During the school year more students began to bring their own portable equipment to school and there were also several who acquired new laptops during the period. This can perhaps be explained by the fact that they experienced the use of technology as useful in many ways. The fact that the students' involvement led them to use their own equipment at school may indicate that their role behaviour as students was expanded to include competencies and activities they had previously associated with their free time. If the use of technology in leisure time and at school complements and overlaps, it is possible to suggest that students also experience schoolwork as relevant to what they are interested in outside school. Such relevance will strengthen what Tiller and Tiller say is of vital importance: meaning and connection between students' lives at school and in their free time [9, 10]. When the student role is expanded to include competencies and resources the student has developed outside of school, the learning work is also given new life through increased relevance for the students outside school.

3.2 Increasing Complexity in the Learning Work

When the classes worked on larger projects it was clear that the learning work increased in complexity when using technologies. This was obvious when they worked with digital

[3] They used a specific application that was designed for students' own construction of knowledge, called Mind Map in the study. The designer was a local learning technology firm which collaborated with the school. Due to the anonymization of the school the brand therefore cannot be named properly.

[4] Most of the students answered a survey at the end of the school year with questions about their experience with technology in their learning work.

network resources, multimodal forms of presentation and other web-based tools, which also has been emphasized by other researchers [12]. For some students, the use of digital technology presented challenges while others seemed to handle this well.

A good example of how the learning work increased in complexity was a podcast project in 10th grade, using Audacity[5]. They assignment involved several steps. First, they had to draft a text and get response from the teachers. Then they had to record their own reading of the text and choose music to go with it before producing mp3-files. The assignment seemed very good fitted to the variation of the class since most students welcomed the assignment and showed great enthusiasm for it and they worked hard together in pairs.

With increasing complexity in the learning process, students face greater demands to their learning strategies and their beliefs to succeed. To meet the demands of the role in technology supported learning work, students therefore need more and better learning strategies and a belief that they will succeed, which must be learned in school. New expectations bring forward the need to revise the habituated learning patterns. The feedforward-feedback loop, which is thus forced from habitus to reflection [7] involving a shift from an automatic to a conscious pattern of action. Through awareness of the automatic action responses, students can assess whether the habitual responses are appropriate or whether they need to be changed [7]. Such awareness-raising has a positive effect on students' meta learning and self-regulation. This is also in line with the new overarching part of the Norwegian curriculum from 2020: students who learn to formulate questions, seek answers, and express their understanding in different ways will gradually be able to take an active role in their own learning and development [13], a role description that in many ways agrees well with the descriptions of a self-regulated student [14, 15]. The study showed that most students in 10th grade performed well and showed great enthusiasm for the task, which can indicate that they had the necessary learning strategies to succeed.

3.3 The Student Role When Having Special Needs

At the same time, it turned out that some students, and perhaps especially Ben, Christian and Daniel in 10th grade, seemed to benefit less from the transition to technology supported learning. In the light of the theory of self-regulated learning [15–17], students must have sufficient basic skills to succeed in the learning process. Neither Ben, Christian nor Daniel had the skills and competencies they needed to succeed, nor did they have the resilience needed to master the new challenges. It may thus appear that students who have special adaptation needs also have the greatest challenges in adapting their student role to use of technology.

How digital tools can help support students' learning can be linked to how the tools can work for scaffolding for the student's thinking, learning strategies and motivation during the learning process. Hermansen points to the dynamics between toil and exuberance as an important learning-driving force [7]. The feedforward feedback processes are dependent on the students being able to engage in learning work that requires effort, otherwise the progression will suffer. When the student starts with an assignment, he can

[5] A sound recording app.

be motivated and willing to learn, and assesses his possibilities positively. During the work, challenges may arise that require re-evaluations, which he must overcome to stay on the learning track [18]. The teacher or another support must then be present and help the student to progress, to bring them forward [19]. Boekaerts [20] explains how students develop avoidance strategies when they do not master the learning process. However, it is important to emphasize the close connection between students' experiences of mastering learning work in general and the role behaviours they develop. The teacher faces new challenges regarding adapting technology-supported teaching to the students, especially for those students who already have special adaptation needs. Salomon & Perkins believes that students' ability to take advantage of the opportunities that digital tools provide must be seen in the context of their ability to self-regulate learning [21]. This means that the student can assess and regulate the expectations and efforts in line with the experiences gained during the learning process [22]. When teaching is technology-supported, it must take care of the students with a need for adapted teaching so that they develop the necessary prerequisites to be self-regulated.

The 4th graders were generally more positive about all learning work than the tenth graders, and the use of technology did not there seem to make a difference for students with and without the need for special adaptation. This can have several causes. The PISA and TIMMS survey in 2000 and 2003 showed that Norwegian primary and lower secondary school students overestimate their own prerequisites and opportunities to succeed in academic performance. This may be due to the primary school's formative assessment which can be so positive and general that the students do not gain thorough enough insight into their own academic strengths and challenges [23]. Boekaerts says that students develop towards more and more performance orientation from the age of 10, which means that the older students are more concerned with being assessed by other students than the younger ones [18]. Possibly some of the 10th graders had accumulated negative experiences that had led to lack of commitment and desire to learn at school. Such negative experiences are situated in the teaching situation and are aroused when students encounter similar experiences [18].

3.4 The Student Role in Collaborations

The study shows that students had high motivation to collaborate on learning work where technology was included. Whether it was the technology or the actual design of the assignments that was decisive, it is not possible to determine from the data. But collaboration seemed to characterize the work in both classes when they worked with technology. This is well known from classrooms where students use technology [12].

The 4th graders Vivian and Thor were learning peers in a project about the planets. The collaboration between the two became important for the way they processed content from the web to prepare their presentation. Their good friendship helped them to actively adapt to each other even if their general level of performance in theoretical assignments were different. Their discussions showed student role behaviors that involved actively meeting each other's needs in the collaboration [5]. The learning work establishes a social zone for proximal development [12] and the collaboration takes on an active role as a scaffold for both students' learning. This can be challenging. Collaboration requires different strategies than individual work. Among other things students must master learning-promoting communication such as asking critical questions and giving constructive feedback. Vivian and Thor mastered this well [5].

Another situation occurred when Vivian was collaborating with Maria and Theresa in another assignment about legends. It did not go smoothly. The first part of the assignment involved searching for suitable pictures from the internet to illustrate the legend. They started with writing down search terms and made searches but did not agree about anything to use. Vivian then made one last attempt to search but the others accused her for not trusting them. It was the start of a conflict which revealed relational challenges that prevented the students from engaging in fruitful dialogues that could stimulate everyone's feedforward-feedback processes [5]. This also showed that relational relationships between students seem to matter when they collaborate. Hermansen points out that learning is a vital, existential process for the learners, which includes both emotional energy and cognitive patterns [7], which is strongly linked to the habitus of the student role. Students have developed habitual ways of dealing with learning work, which act as automatic impulses when they face new challenges. As this ability for automatic adaptation is so strong, Hermansen believes that it constitutes a *basic flow* in our lives [7]. When two or more people collaborate, there is a good chance that they will react differently in the encounter with the collaboration tasks, because they have developed different habits. This can create challenges when they together define the learning object or create a plan for the collaborative tasks. Vivian's attempt was probably only an expression of habits that were automatized in her student role, but in the collaboration with the other two, this was perceived as disloyalty because it broke with what the group had agreed on. Vivian's habitual student behavior was thus the subject of critical reflection from the others.

The individual's automatic responses will be linked to emotional energy, and it will arouse resistance if they do not work as intended. To move forward, students must be able to meta communicate about the learning work, to raise automatized behavioral patterns to a reflexive level, which can be very demanding [7]. The student role is thus challenged when the students collaborate, and it requires that they develop meta reflexive skills to understand how their own automatic skills will work or not work in a collaboration, and metacommunicative skills that make it possible to talk about this with their learning partners.

There may also be social challenges associated with the collaboration that led to the students not daring to invest too much in the learning work. If the social context is not perceived as safe, the students can choose to avoid the learning work because they fear being negatively assessed by the other students [16, 24]. To counteract this, teaching must facilitate the development of a student role that promotes the competencies and qualities needed to become resilient and withstand the resistance required to succeed in collaborative learning. It is important to focus on understanding and procedures rather than having the right answer [16], and to promote a safe learning environment where students dare to show what they are struggling with and can learn from their mistakes [25].

4 Conclusion

The development of the student role can be understood from Hermansen's model for feedback and feedforward [7, 8]. When students face challenges at school, their response is based on past experiences. New situations are interpreted according to the models or scripts that have previously solved similar situations, and the learning behaviour are governed by these. In other words, the assessments of what is required in new situations are made by thinking back on how they previously acted in similar situations.

In the study, it is first and foremost the 10th grade's response to introducing technology that sheds light on the changes in the student role. It was clear that the students acted on habits when they encountered the technology for the first time. But they adapted quickly to the new situation, which shows that for most students, the use of technology is easy to adapt. Most students were motivated to work with technology-supported teaching, which both observations and the student survey showed.

To exploit the potential for learning and teaching, the new technology requires adjustments for both teachers and students. The goal is for students to become self-regulated in their learning work. Independence requires competencies for them to be able to assess opportunities and make decisions in relation to their collaborative or individual work. Teachers must take this into account in their design for teaching and learning.

As the complexity of the learning process increases, the student role can be perceived as more demanding. Students need strategies that are fruitful and make it possible to carry out a learning process that develops and changes continuously during the work. Technology supported learning requires a broader repertoire of learning strategies because the assignments are more open and complex. Also, collaborative work requires communication skills that enables students to take advantage of the social learning situations.

When students are encouraged to develop new strategies and greater independence in the encounter with the learning work, this can be positive for students who master the student role well. But students who have challenges with poor basic skills and learning strategies can have these reinforced, something the teachers must pay special attention to in their teaching. After all, self-regulated learning requires the student to act independently based on reflection on their own prerequisites and competencies, their strategies, and the expectation of success in the learning process. The student role in a technology-rich learning environment is characterized by independence, self-awareness, activity, competence, and expectations of one's own learning outcome. Such a role will also fit well with the lifelong learning process where everyone is exposed to ever-changing demands for adjustment and development of new competencies, and which more than anything else emphasizes learning to learn. At the same time, such a student role is more demanding than a more traditional student role where the room for manoeuvre is not so extensive. Students who are vulnerable in a traditional teaching context may become more vulnerable when the room for manoeuvre becomes larger and the requirements for the student role are tightened.

References

1. Yin, R.K.: Case Study Research: Design and Methods, 3rd edn. Sage publications, Thousand Oaks, California, USA (2003)
2. Blaikie, N.: Designing Social Research. Cambridge Polity Press, Cambridge (2000)
3. de Vaus, D.: Comparative and cross-national designs. In: Alasuutari, P., Bickman, L., Brannen, J. (eds.) The Sage Handbook of Social Research Methods. Sage publications Los Angeles, USA (2008)
4. Flyvebjerg, B.: Five Misunderstandings about case study research. In: Seale, C., Gobo, G., Gubrium, J.F., Silverman, D. (eds.) Qualitative Research Practice. Sage Publications, London (2007)
5. Rønningsbakk, L.: Når didaktikken møter de digitalt innfødte: teknologistøttet læringsarbeid i skolen i lys av tradisjonell og nyskapende undervisning. UiT Norges arktiske universitet, Tromsø (2019)
6. Gilje, N., Grimen, H.: Samfunnsvitenskapenes forutsetninger. Universitetsforlaget, Oslo (1993)
7. Hermansen, M.: Omlæring. Klim forlag, Århus (2003)
8. Hermansen, M.: Motivasjon og den gode læring. In: Postholm, M.B., Tiller, T. (eds.) Profesjonsrettet pedagogikk 8–13. Cappelen Damm akademisk, Oslo (2014)
9. Tiller, T., Tiller, R.: Den andre dagen: det nye læringsrommet. Høyskoleforlaget, Kristiansand (2002)
10. Tiller, T.: Når skolen skulker sin omverden. In: Jentoft, S., Nergård, J.I., Røvik, K.A. (eds.) Hvor går Nord-Norge? Et institusjonelt perspektiv på folk og landsdel, pp. 127–136. Orkana akademisk, Stamsund (2012)
11. Hauge, T.E., Lund, A., Vestøl, J.M. (Red.): Undervisning i endring. IKT, aktivitet, design. Abstrakt forlag, Oslo (2007)
12. Lund, A., Hauge, T.E.: Designs for teaching and learning in technology-rich learning environments. In: Nordic Journal of Digital Literacy, 6 (2011, nr 4), pp. 258–272. Universitetsforlaget, Oslo (2011)
13. Utdanningsdirektoratet: Overordnet del av læreplanverket. Retrieved from 2.4 Å lære å lære (udir.no) Sist lest 18.07.21. Utdanningsdirektoratet, Oslo (2018)
14. Moos, D.C.: The role of Goal Structure in Undergraduates' Use of Sel-Regulatory Variables in Two Hypermedia Learning Tasks. (Master's of Arts), University of Maryland, USA (2004)
15. Zimmermann, B.J.: Self-regulated learning and academic achievement: an overview. In: Educational Psychologist, vol. 25/1990 (1). Taylor & Francis Online, London (1990)
16. Boekaerts, M.: Motivation to Learn. International Academy of Education in cooperation with International Bureau of Education (UNESCO), Geneva. Switzerland (2002)
17. Valle, A., Cabanach, R.G., Núñez, J., Gonzalez-Pienda, J., Rodríguez, S., Piñeiro, I.: Cognitive, motivational, and volitional dimensions of learning: an empirical test of a hypothetical model. In: Research in Higher Education, vol. 44(5), pp. 23. Springer Nature, Switzerland (2003). https://doi.org/10.1023/A:1025443325499
18. Boekaerts, M.: Understanding students' affective processes in the classroom. In: Schutz, P., Pekrun, R. (eds.) Emotion in Education. Elsevier Academic Press, San Diego, California, USA (2007)
19. Haugerud, T., Sand, K.E.: Nå vet jeg hvordan jeg fortsetter! I: L. Sand (red.) Den unike kompetansen (DUK) - et læringsprosjekt. Tyrili skriftserie nr. 4. Tyrili forskning og utvikling, Oslo (2002)
20. Boekaerts, M., Seegers, G., Vermeer, H.: Solving math problems: where and why does the solution process go astray? In: Educational Studies in Mathematics, Volume 28/1995. Springer Nature, Switzerland (1995)

21. Salomon, G., Perkins, D.: Learning in wonderland. What do computers really offer education? In: Kerr, S.T. (ed.) Technology and the Future of Schooling. Ninety-Fifth Yearbook of the National Society for the Study of Education. Part II. University of Chicago Press, Chicago (1996)
22. Boekaerts, M., Zeidner, M., Pintric, P.R.: Handbook of Self-Regulation. Elsevier, Academic press (1999)
23. Turmo, A.: Norske skoleelevers selvregulerte læring. I Raabe, M. (Red.): Utdanning 2007-muligheter, mål og mestring. Statistisk sentralbyrå (SSB), Oslo/Kongsvinger (2007)
24. Hundeide, K.: Det intersubjektive rommet. I: Dysthe, O. (red.) Dialog, samspel og læring (ss. 151–172). Abstrakt forlag, Oslo (2001)
25. Meyer, D.K., Turner, J.C.: Scaffolding emotions in classrooms. In: Schutz, P., Pekrun, R. (eds.) Emotions in Education. Elsevier Academic press, San Diego (2007)

Effects of E-recruitment Interface Attributes on the Attractiveness of Taiwanese Job Seekers

Judy F. Chen[1](✉), Clyde A. Warden[2], and Jia-Wen Liou[3]

[1] Business Administration Department, Overseas Chinese University, Taichung, Taiwan
jfc@ocu.edu.tw

[2] Marketing Department, National Chung Hsing University, Taichung, Taiwan
warden@dragon.nchu.edu.tw

[3] College of Intelligence, National Taichung University of Science and Technology, Taichung, Taiwan
daisy716@nutc.edu.tw

Abstract. The advancement of technology and the popularity of the Internet have significantly improved the operation of the human resources department. Understanding e-recruitment interface attributes will enable recruiters to better attract potential job seekers to apply for jobs online. Accordingly, this research employed an experimental design method with a questionnaire approach to explore and evaluate the effects of aesthetic forms, recruitment information, interactive functions, and information fitness interface attributes on job applicants. Research results indicate that the average related importance for high aesthetic, specific information, high interaction, and high fit is: 19.720%, 33.134%, 24.417%, and 22.729%, respectively. The most important attribute in determining preference is specific information, followed by high interaction. Moreover, there is a significant level of differences across educational levels toward high interaction. Results of this research can provide a reference to recruiters for designing the optimal e-recruitment interface to attract the desired candidates to apply for the position.

Keywords: E-recruitment · Recruiting information · Interface design · Attribute preference · E-training

1 Introduction

According to the Manpower Group's 2018 Talent Shortage Survey Results, 78% of employers in Taiwan face a talent shortage. Furthermore, the wide adoption of the Internet has had a profound impact on human resource management, especially in the field of talent recruitment. When the labor market is short of manpower, how to use the E-recruitment interface to attract outstanding talents to apply for jobs is an important issue. The popularization of the Internet has had a profound impact on human resource management, especially in the field of talent recruitment (Chapman and Webster 2003). Lee (2005) conducted content analysis on the e-recruitment webpages of Fortune 100 companies and concluded that most companies still need to further develop the e-recruitment system to improve their recruitment performance. Lang et al. (2011) analyzed 23 papers

© Springer Nature Switzerland AG 2021
Y.-M. Huang et al. (Eds.): ICITL 2021, LNCS 13117, pp. 303–309, 2021.
https://doi.org/10.1007/978-3-030-91540-7_32

discussing the driving factors, challenges and consequences of e-recruitment. The analysis results show that e-recruitment reduces the cost of recruitment and selection, increases the number of suitable job applicants, and provides organizations and job seekers with convenience, saves time and improves corporate image. Challenges encountered by the e-job recruitment include excluding potential job applicants, defrauding job applicants in the electronic evaluation process, security of job applicant data, and low qualifications of job applicants. Holm (2012) investigated the influence of e-recruitment on the design of the recruitment process, and results show e-recruitment transforms the traditional recruitment process into a collaborative recruitment process that has overcomes time and space. In addition, maintaining the company's e-recruitment webpage is an ongoing task of the new recruitment process. The design of the e-Job recruitment interface is critical to whether it can attract high-quality job seekers to apply for a job. At present, there has been little research on the e-job recruitment interfaces for Taiwan's job market. Therefore, this study intends to examine the effects of e-job web design attributes on the attractiveness of Taiwanese job seekers.

2 Literature Review

We review literature related to e-recruitment and four interface attributes (aesthetic form, recruitment information, interactive function and information fitness) in order to construct the framework of this research.

2.1 E-recruitment

The advancement of technology and the popularity of the Internet have significantly improved the operation of the human resources department. As a result, new professional terms have emerged, such as e-human resource management (E-HRM) (Dhamija 2012). E-recruitment is also a new term used to distinguish from the traditional recruitment method. E-recruitment refers to the company's own website or other online human websites, such as 104, 1111, Yes123, LinkedIn, Monster, etc., to post job vacancies. E-recruitment integrates and uses Internet technology to improve the efficiency and effectiveness of the recruitment process to identify and attract high-quality potential employees, which can help organizations to be innovative, flexible and competitive (Swart 2008).

The e-recruitment method can effectively achieve a large number of recruitment resources at a lower cost (Lee 2005a). Talent recruitment activities have become one of the most successful commercial applications on the Internet (Cober et al. 2004; Harrington 2002). In addition, in traditional recruitment methods (such as advertisements in newspapers and magazines), employers are usually limited to providing job applicants with information about their vacant positions. In contrast, e-recruitment can provide more information and space for communication (Van Birgelen et al. 2008). The goal of e-recruitment is basically the same as that of traditional recruitment, that is, to attract job seekers, maintain their interest and ultimately influence their job choices (Chapman and Gödöllei 2017). Hafeez and Farooq (2016) found that e-recruitment has a positive impact on job seekers and also increases the organization's attractiveness among competitors. Moreover, e-recruitment is easier to use and saves work costs.

The company's e-recruitment page is usually the main place for job seekers to initially collect information about the job opening in order to understand the job and then apply for the job (Williamson et al. 2003). In addition, the organization should evaluate the applicant's response to its web page since it is related to the organization's perceptions and attitudes. The company's e-recruitment page has become a key tool for employers to recruit job applicants, especially now that it is difficult for big companies to recruit talents. Understanding e-recruitment interface attributes will increase the ability to attract potential job seekers to apply for jobs. Four attributes (aesthetic form, recruitment information, interactive function, and information fitness) are being reviewed as follows.

2.2 Aesthetic Form

Cappelli (2001) pointed out that the design of the company's e-recruitment should take consideration of potential job applicants to attract their initial interest. When designing the e-recruitment page, the interface attributes can be distinguished from the surrounding environment, such as the visual layout (colors, images, workplace rewards and animations on the page) (Swart 2008). Cober et al. (2004) argued that the most visible way for employers to distinguish employment opportunities is to manipulate aesthetics on the recruitment web page. The form of the recruitment webpage, especially the pictures, colors, animations and videos on the webpage, will affect the user's perception of information and subsequent attractiveness. Dineen et al. (2007) studied the viewing time, information recall and attractiveness of e-recruitment information, and the results showed that with good aesthetics, customized information makes less qualified individuals less attracted the customized e-recruitment information, which can avoid recruiting unsuitable people. It can be seen that the aesthetic form is an important independent variable.

2.3 Recruitment Information

During job hunting, job seekers often lack information about organizational types (Breaugh and Starke 2000). Feldman and Klaas (2002) found that the most important factor for job seekers who are dissatisfied with online searches is lack of relevant employment information. Maurer and Liu (2007) suggested that employers should meet the informational needs of the target job seeker market while job seekers earnestly seek job opportunities. Job seekers can find the information they need while minimizing the search time of the job seeker; the employer can develop the employment information, emphasizing the central route clues of e-recruitment page of. In addition, job seekers believe that missing e-recruitment is a reminder that the employer is careless or not interested in recruiting high-quality job seekers (Barber and Roehling 1993). Highhouse and Hoffman (2001) argued that the amount of content available for review and the type of content available play a significant role in determining the applicant's interest in employment. Feldman et al. (2006) surveyed the content of job advertisements and found that providing potential job seekers to receive more specific employment information can increase the attractiveness of the job. Specific information plays an important role in the effectiveness of e-recruitment and the ability of job seekers to easily find the information they need (Van Birgelen et al. 2008). More and more research results show that corporate social performance may also affect its attractiveness as an employer, but the basic process of its impact has not been established in the research (Jones et al. 2014).

2.4 Interactive Function

Functions on the recruitment webpage affect the success of the recruitment mechanism of the webpage. The most widely used interactive tool is the navigation menu (Cober et al. 2004). The navigation menu guides job seekers to specific areas of information. Such a menu can be constructed to facilitate deeper processing of specific information areas, depending on the motivation of job seekers to increase their employer's knowledge. Interactivity may be affected by other tools, which can conduct real-time conversations to increase user participation and interest. Although the interactions that the website can provide may arouse the interest of potential job seekers (Cober et al. 2000), the functionality of the website as an application process is also important. Organizing the recruitment webpage can make the application process of job seekers easier and shorten the cycle of the recruitment process. In order to further facilitate the application, employers can provide job applicants with information about the application process, which may affect people's beliefs about the effectiveness of online job applications and the security of personal data submitted in response to positions. Some job seekers may hesitate to fill in and submit an online application because they do not understand the time required to fill in and submit online to obtain a job interview (Cober et al. 2004).

2.5 Information Fitness

Due to less space constraints, the e-recruitment webpage allows employers to clearly direct recruitment information to different groups of applicants. This is important because job applicants' perceptions of individual organizations will positively influence their job search behavior and will influence their self-selection decision to find a job with a particular employer (Cable and Judge 1996). On the e-recruitment webpage, organizations can convey information about recruitment through employee testimonials, which can also enable job seekers to understand the types of people they may encounter and deal with. Cober et al. (2003) examined how the perception (salary, organizational culture and training opportunities) and style (aesthetics and usability) of the organization's website content affect the attractiveness of the organization and found that the e-recruitment webpage's content and style are precursors in organizational attractiveness. Alsultanny and Alotaibi (2015) used a questionnaire survey method to survey 360 job seekers who have used e-recruitment methods to investigate their attitudes and willingness to use e-recruitment webpages. Results show the e-recruitment interface's entertainment, practicality, and ease of use are significantly related to their attitudes, and attitudes are significantly related to willingness to use.

3 Method

This research employs an experimental design method through a survey to explore and evaluate the influence of aesthetic forms, recruitment information, interactive functions, and information fitness interface attributes on attracting potential job applicants. This research designed e-recruitment pages for 4 types of job openings. The e-recruitment page for each position has two levels of e-recruitment pages with four attributes. For this experimental design, there are a total of 16 possible combinations (2 × 2). × 2 × 2), as shown in Table 1.

Table 1. Attributes and levels used in this study

No	Attribute	Level
1	Aesthetic form	High
		Low
2	Employment information	Specific
		General
3	Interactive function	High
		Low
4	Information fitness	High
		Low

Since the focus of this research is on the design of the employment website interface, this research recruited online job seekers as the research respondents. This research placed recruitment advertisements on the top three human resource banks in Taiwan (104, 1111, and Yes123). A slogan marked with this experimental advertisement was placed on the job search page. Along with the implementation of the experiment, this study conducted a questionnaire survey of participants in the experiment to understand the preferences of online job applicants for 16 e-recruitment interface attributes. We employed the 5 point Likert scale for the questionnaire.

4 Results

Total of 315 (109 males and 206 females) people participated in this experiment. All four designed attributes have positive part-worth values and significant difference between the high and the low of attributes. The average related importance for high aesthetic, specific information, high interaction and high fit is: 19.720%, 33.134%, 24.417% and 22.729%, respectively. Among them, the most important attribute in determining preference was specific information. The second most important attribute is high interaction.

As shown in Table 2, the ANOVA analysis shows that there is a significant level of differences among different educational levels (Table 3).

Participants with graduate degree prefer more specific employment information and higher interactive functions, comparing to other educational levels.

Table 2. Exhibits the ANOVA analysis.

Foster interest	*df*	High aesthetic	Specific information	High interaction	High fit
Gender	1	1.173	1.100	0.179	0.068
Marital status	2	0.002	0.188	1.081	0.064
Age	4	0.896	1.368	1.697	0.938
Education	5	2.464	1.064	3.391*	1.168
Experience	6	0.747	0.420	0.669	0.838
Sector	14	0.572	1.138	0.933	0.792
Job type	9	0.539	1.468	1.293	1.271

*$p < 0.05$

Table 3. Educational level of participants

Educational level	No	%
High school	30	9.5
Junior college	35	11.1
College	200	63.5

5 Conclusion

The findings of this study provides an insight about the attribute preferences of job applicants. When designing e-job opening interface, specific information is the most important attribute to pay attention to, followed by high interaction, then high information fitness, and high aesthetic last. Moreover, different educational background may affect the attribute preference. Different emphasis on mixing the interface attributes for different required educational job openings may work better.

The results of this research provide practical applications for system designers, recruiters and human resources managers who are in charge of designing e-job interface messages. Also, the research results will be able to help increase the knowledge of e-training the human resources field and in turn improve the effectiveness of e-training.

Acknowledgment. The authors are grateful to the Ministry of Science and Technology of the Republic of China, Taiwan, for financially supporting this research under Contract No. MOST 110-2511-H-240 -001 -.

References

Alsultanny, Y.A., Alotaibi, M.F.: Evaluating the factors affecting on intension to use of e-recruitment. Am. J. Inf. Sci. Comp. Eng. **1**(5), 324–331 (2015)

Barber, A.E., Roehling, M.V.: Job postings and the decision to interview: a verbal protocol analysis. J. Appl. Psychol. **78**(5), 845 (1993)
Breaugh, J.A., Starke, M.: Research on employee recruitment: so many studies, so many remaining questions. J. Manag. **26**(3), 405–434 (2000)
Cable, D.M., Judge, T.A.: Person–organization fit, job choice decisions, and organizational entry. Organ. Behav. Hum. Decis. Process. **67**(3), 294–311 (1996)
Chapman, D.S., Gödöllei, A.F.: E-recruiting: using technology to attract job applicants. In: The Wiley Blackwell Handbook of the Psychology of the Internet at Work, pp. 211–230. Wiley, Chichester (2017)
Chapman, D.S., Webster, J.: The use of technologies in the recruiting, screening, and selection processes for job candidates. Int. J. Sel. Assess. **11**(2–3), 113–120 (2003)
Cober, R.T., Brown, D.J., Blumental, A.J., Doverspike, D., Levy, P.: The quest for the qualified job surfer: it's time the public sector catches the wave. Publ. Person. Manag. **29**(4), 479–496 (2000)
Cober, R.T., Brown, D.J., Levy, P.E., Cober, A.B., Keeping, L.M.: Organizational web sites: web site content and style as determinants of organizational attraction. Int. J. Sel. Assess. **11**(2–3), 158–169 (2003)
Cober, R.T., Brown, D.J., Levy, P.E.: Form, content, and function: an evaluative methodology for corporate employment web sites. Hum. Resour. Manag. **43**(2–3), 201–218 (2004)
Dhamija, P.: E-recruitment: a roadmap towards e-human resource management. Res. World **3**(3), 33 (2012)
Feldman, D.C., Klaas, B.S.: Internet job hunting: a field study of applicant experiences with on-line recruiting. Hum. Resour. Manag. **41**(2), 175–192 (2002)
Feldman, D.C., Bearden, W.O., Hardesty, D.M.: Varying the content of job advertisements: the effects of message specificity. J. Advert. **35**(1), 123–141 (2006)
Hafeez, M., Farooq, U.: Exploring the association of e-recruitment with organizational attraction and mediating role of cost effectiveness and easy to use. Sci. Int. (Lahore) **28**(2), 1651–1657 (2016)
Harrington, A.: Can anyone build a better Monster? Fortune **145**(10), 189–191 (2002)
Holm, A.B.: E-recruitment: towards an ubiquitous recruitment process and candidate relationship management. German J. Hum. Resour. Manag. **26**(3), 241–259 (2012)
Jones, D.A., Willness, C.R., Madey, S.: Why are job seekers attracted by corporate social performance? Experimental and field tests of three signal-based mechanisms. Acad. Manag. J. **57**(2), 383–404 (2014)
Lang, S., Laumer, S., Maier, C., Eckhardt, A.: Drivers, challenges and consequences of E-recruiting: a literature review. In: Proceedings of the 49th SIGMIS Annual Conference on Computer Personnel Research, May 2011, pp. 26–35 (2011)
Maurer, S.D., Liu, Y.: Developing effective e-recruiting websites: Insights for managers from marketers. Bus. Horiz. **50**(4), 305–314 (2007)
Williamson, I.O., Lepak, D.P., King, J.: The effect of company recruitment web site orientation on individuals' perceptions of organizational attractiveness. J. Vocat. Behav. **63**(2), 242–263 (2003)
van Birgelen, M.J.H., Wetzels, M.G.M., van Dolen, W.M.: Effectiveness of corporate employment web sites: how content and form influence intentions to apply. Int. J. Manpow. **29**(8), 731–751 (2008)

Check for updates

Evolution of Lean Startup over the Years – A Bibliometric Analysis

Zornitsa Yordanova(✉)

University of National and World Economy, 8mi dekemvri 23, Sofia, Bulgaria
zornitsayordanova@unwe.bg

Abstract. Lean startup has just turned 10 years after its conceptualization by Eric Ries and it has been used in huge number of companies to boost innovation development since 2011. However, the divergent application of the method has often provoked conflicts and misunderstanding because of its varieties according to the type of organization it is used in: SMEs, startups, banks, government institutions and even universities. Several questions have been raised about its application and deployment in the literature during the years. This study aims at conducting a bibliometric analysis to find out what are the main applications, changes and curves of the concept during the years and to identify some knowledge gaps for future research agenda as well as to point out the main trends of Lean Startup use lately according to the science literature. The results, based on 369 publications, show practical insights for the diverse use of Lean Startup as a model of an enterprise functioning. The research also proposes a discussion on the means of digital transformation of Lean Startup concept integrated as an organizational model for managing science and innovation projects.

Keywords: Lean Startup · Innovation Management · Science projects · Innovation process · Digital transformation · Digitalization

1 Introduction

Enterprises have warmly embraced Lean Startup (LS) as a practical model for organization of innovation processes [1], product development [2], business model [3], operations, production, customer services, opportunity exploration [4] or organizational transformation [1] at reduced costs and higher efficiency in comparison to other alternative management approaches. In the last 10 years since the concept was conceptualized by Eric Rees in 2011 [5] and with the modernized version of the method in 2017 [6], which also adopted it for application in corporations, LS has received immerse attention from many scientists. Thus, the current study aims at revealing the accumulated insights of the last 10 years on Lean Startup research though conducting a bibliometric analysis.

Lean Startup has started to appear in the literature since 2000 [7] as a framework helping in reducing the risk of launching new products, however its official birth was in 2011 when the book The Lean Startup: How Today's Entrepreneurs Use Continuous Innovation to Create Radically Successful Businesses of Eric Ries [5] was published.

© Springer Nature Switzerland AG 2021
Y.-M. Huang et al. (Eds.): ICITL 2021, LNCS 13117, pp. 310–319, 2021.
https://doi.org/10.1007/978-3-030-91540-7_33

Lean Startup is seen as a business model for fast, lean and risk mitigating framework for development new products, innovations and change management. Because of its fast and exponential success, it had been also applied in many corporates as a means for product development and innovation which has led to the publication of the second book of Eric Ries in 2017: The Startup Way: How Modern Companies Use Entrepreneurial Management to Transform Culture and Drive Long-Term Growth [6].

In this study, we are revealing the global application of LS in diverse sectors and organizations' types, the changes and curves occurred in its implementation and use and the major trends for its development according to the science literature. Pursuing this, we conduct a bibliometric analysis on 369 publications extracted from the Scopus database. The results are of the interest of management professionals, startupers and scholars in the field of management and innovation and technology management in particular.

2 Theoretical Background: Lean Startup

LS has been largely researched in the literature. It proposes a framework for systematic and circular activities for achieving sustainable and continuous innovation/product development. The main elements, methods and characteristics of the method provide a broad roadmap for what the direction and activities of companies to be in their innovation development [8]. The minimum viable product (MVP) has been identified among the main advantages of the method over the years. It is a first and cost-optimal version of a product, introducing the core customer values and not any additional nice-to-have features that are not central to the customer and would contribute to the costs [9]. The purpose of it is to enroll the circle learning process for proving the hypotheses made for the potential of the product for the targeted customer [10]. LS and MVP in specific, emerged to reduce uncertainties concerning innovation-based projects, and to contribute to business model validation for any industry and type of organization [11]. It is generally based on experimentations as a systematic way for entrepreneurial endeavors and product development, essential for innovation development [12]. For this reason, it is also defined as 'a learning-by-doing methodology for iteration of early-stage business ideas' [13] as well as 'a pedagogical process to refine a new business venture by constructing and testing assumptions' [14]. It has been largely used also as project management method for innovative projects [15].

The literature has already provided some knowledge gaps such as strategic fit, international entrepreneurship, management tools and digitalization [16]. There are also authors who criticize the blind followers of the method as it could hamper the innovativeness and creativity of teams and companies with specific characteristics that do not fit to the assumptions and hypothesis of LS [8].

LS has evolved its role over the years in terms of application in different sectors such as information technologies [17], healthcare [18], construction [19], education and science [20] and many others and has been applied in different organization types [21]. We are exploring in this research the evolution of LS over the last 10 years after its official introduction using a 'bird' viewpoint to catch the comprehensive general direction of this evolution and we did this by conducting a bibliometric analysis to cover the whole research area on the topic.

3 Research Design: A Bibliometric Analysis

3.1 Data Selection

Data used for the bibliometric analysis is extracted from Scopus database since this source has been recognized as high-quality source in the field of Technology and Innovation Management and highly appropriate for conducting bibliometric analysis [22]. We used Boolean search with diverse term wording in order to not miss any one of the research done on the topic of Lean Startup. For achieving a dataset for analysis, we performed a search with the use of the following formula in Scopus database:

TITLE-ABS-KEY ("lean startup" OR "Lean-startup" OR "lean start-up")

We received 369 publications meeting the search criteria shown on Table 1.

Table 1. Science publications dealing with Lean Startup.

Timespan	2010:2021
Sources (Journals, Books, etc.)	220
Documents	369
Average years from publication	3.26
Average citations per documents	8.217
Average citations per year per doc	1.687
References	12460
Article	127
Book	4
Book chapter	31
Conference paper	180
Conference review	18
Others	9

For achieving focus and relevancy on the analysis, we removed conference reviews and other publications (notes, review, short survey). Thus, 342 publications remained as the scope of the study. Figure 1 shows the increasing interest on the topic which is still new for the management science (the data extraction was done in June 2021, which explained the low-levels of publication in 2021).

The most relevant and cited publications were sourced by the following to-tier journals presented on Fig. 2.

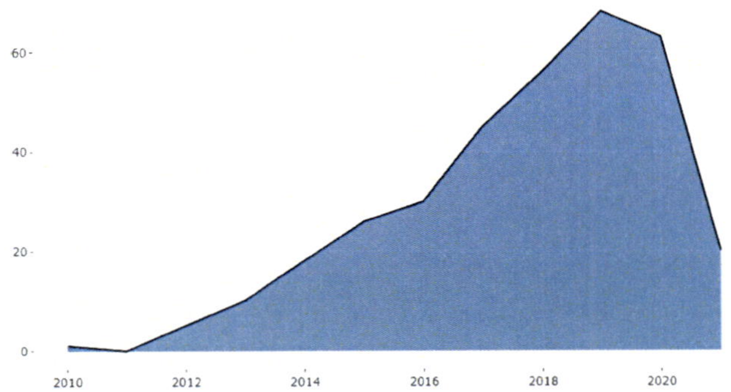

Fig. 1. Publications on Lean Startup over the years.

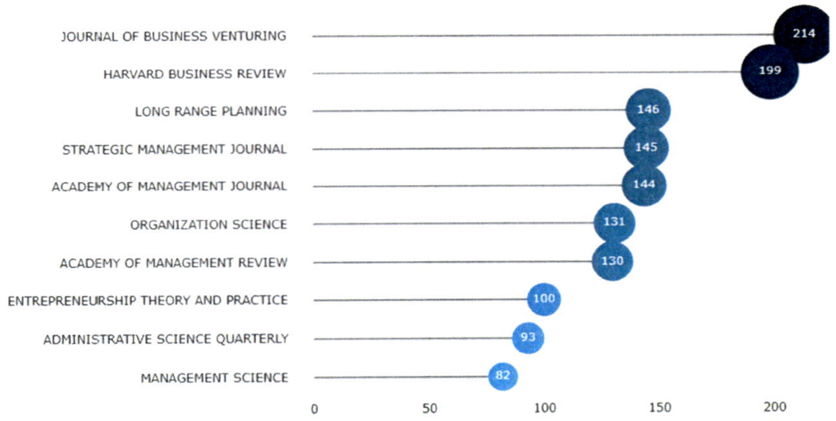

Fig. 2. Most cited sources.

3.2 Bibliometric Analysis Performed

A bibliometric analysis was conduct to trace the evolution of Lean Startup application over the years and in the different context of its employment. In this paper, Biblioshiny, a product of RStudio has been employed in which we uploaded the set from Scopus database containing 369 publications.

The main focus of this study is exploring the evolution of Lean Startup concept over the years. This is why, the thematic evolution analysis has been used as a tool. In this research, we experiment with basing thematic evolution analysis on author keywords, keywords plus, titles and abstracts. Minimum cluster frequency was set to 5 per thousand documents, minimum weight index 0,1 and three cutting points over the last 11 years: cutting year 1: 2016; cutting year 2: 2018; cutting year 3: 2019.

Using the visualization technique proposed by Cobo et al. [23] for each of the time slices researched, we present four quadrants (clusters of keywords) including Motor, Transversal, Niche, and Peripheral themes according to their centrality and density rank values along two axes. The centrality measures the degree of interaction and the density measures the internal strength of the network and identifies the degree of development of a theme [23].

4 Results and Discussion: Lean Startup Evolution over the Years and Trends of Development

The thematic evolution of Lean Startup is presented within four time slices for most of the analysis in this study. Since the youth of the concept, they cover only few years each but the dynamics in the evolution of Lean Startup and its application has reasoned this deeper analysis over the years. The used time slices are: 2010–2016; 2017–2018; 2019; 2020–2021. The third time slice reflects one year only because of the bigger number of publications then. The first graph presents the thematic evolution according to the words used in author keywords of the analyzed 342 publications between 2010 and 2021 (Fig. 3).

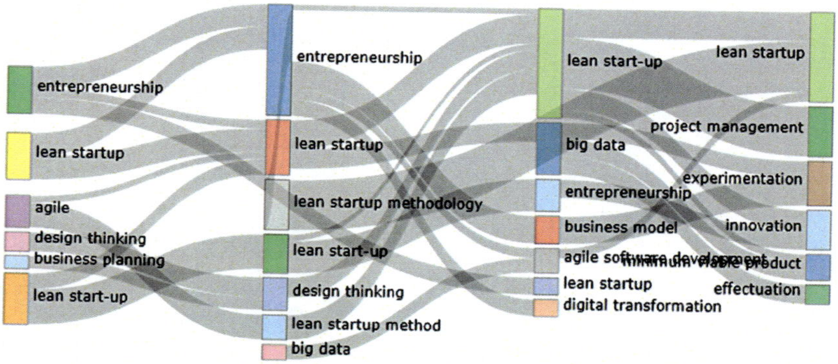

Fig. 3. Thematic evolution of Lean Startup – author keywords.

As Fig. 4 demonstrates, in the beginning of LS research, it was all related to entrepreneurship, agile, design thinking and business planning. In the second time period, some methodological aspects started to been analyzed as well as big data. In 2019 more technological shades of LS application have started to be on focus such as digital transformation, big data and agile software. In the last analyzed period project management, experimentation, effectuation and product development have evaluated to the emphasis of the research. This would mean that LS has only at its beginning of evolution since many of its potential benefits are just now starting to be researched (for ex. experimentation and project management).

In the next figure, the same perspective but according to the keywords plus is presented in order to conceptualize more generic outcome of the research done in the last 10 years.

In this viewpoint, the insightful sub-areas of research of LS may be summarized into: 1.) application of LS in other than software development companies (commerce); 2.)

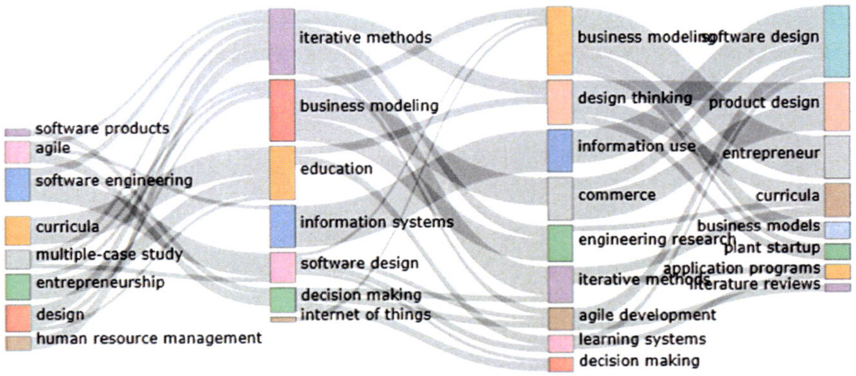

Fig. 4. Thematic evolution of LS – keywords plus.

application of LS for other than product and business development (human resources) 3.) education (curriculum).

The next figures present the thematic evolution in deeper details by period. In the first time slice from 2010 till 2016, LS has been mostly researched in the science literature entrepreneurship and agile which have not been highly researched in this context and were categorized as niche themes (well developed and very specialized themes, but marginal in the overall field). An insightful observation is the lack of Motor themes which fact usually accompanies novel topics such as LS for the management science. No Peripheral (declining) themes in this first time span have been identified. Software and engineering techniques were not still developed in their link to LS in this very first period (Fig. 5).

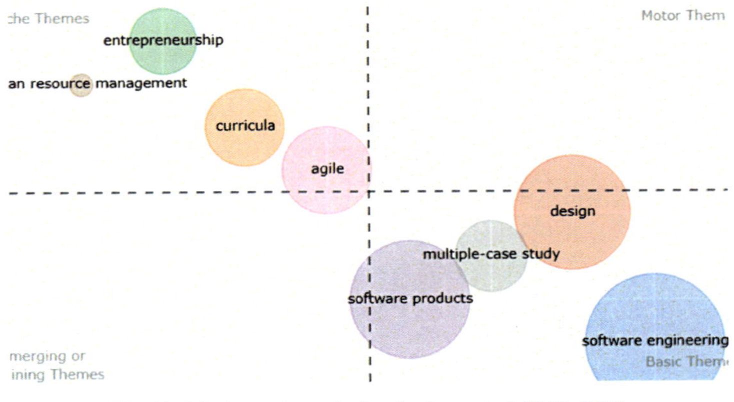

Fig. 5. LS thematic evolution in the period 2010–2016.

In the period of 2017–2018 when LS has started to become a hot topic for both science and business audiences, business modelling has become a motor theme (a well-developed theme that is a key to the structure of the research field, and is characterized by high centrality and high density). Still no declining topics have been identified which fact proved again the increasing interest in LS. Niche themes were starting to introduce more technical-related topics such as internet of things and information systems (Fig. 6).

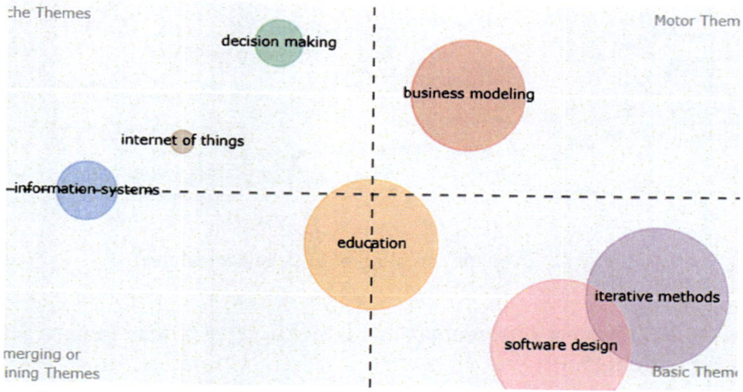

Fig. 6. LS thematic evolution in the period 2017–2018.

The pick of the LS research so far was 2019 when a basic for the conceptual method topic became agile development (because of the common features between agile and LS). Well researched themes that shaped the LS concept in this period were: business modelling, design thinking, learning systems and iterative methods (Fig. 7).

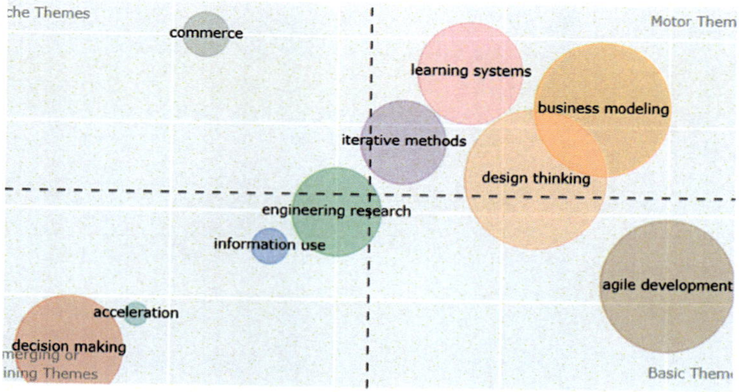

Fig. 7. LS thematic evolution in 2019.

During the last analyzed period of research (2020–2021), an interesting remark is the increasing interest in literature reviews on LS. An assumption for this would be the increasing application of the concept with case studies introduced which at this point have been accumulated a huge dataset for analysis (Fig. 8).

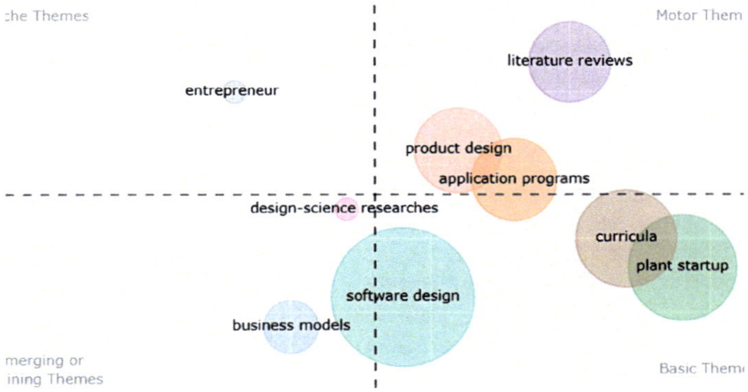

Fig. 8. LS thematic evolution in the period 2020–2021.

The evolution of LS has been marked by some clearly-pointed phases through which LS changed its core towards business modelling and education, starting from more tech-businesses towards diverse kinds of application. The increasing application of LS gives promises also for further changes and evolution as well as new borders of the model and its elements use.

5 Conclusion

The paper provides a unique historical analysis on the LS method over the years from its birth 10 years ago in 2011. In this paper, several bibliometric analyses and perspectives are employed in order to elicit the evolutionary trends of LS in four different sub-periods of its development for only ten years. Generally, LS has gone through a product development method in software development to a business modelling framework for diverse industries. The method's evolution has helped the transformation of small startups, large corporations, and government organizations. It has been increasingly incorporated into businesses, education, healthcare, and technology development. It is not bold to conclude that it has become part of human progress in the last 10 years by being applied practically in all areas of mankind's activity. With this paper, we call for further research on the evolution and changing role of Lean Startup's elements and core concepts over time, the changing role of users as part of the innovation development, and LS application for boosting innovation performance in non-innovative organizations [24].

Acknowledgement. The paper is supported by the BG NSF Grant No KP-06 OPR01/3-2018.

References

1. Hwang, S., Shin, J.: Using lean startup to power organizational transformation. Res. Technol. Manag. **62**(5), 40–49 (2019)
2. Abrahamsson, P., Oza, N. (eds.): LESS 2010. LNBIP, vol. 65. Springer, Heidelberg (2010). https://doi.org/10.1007/978-3-642-16416-3

3. Bortolini, R.F., Nogueira Cortimiglia, M., Danilevicz, A.d.M.F., Ghezzi, A.: Lean Startup: a comprehensive historical review. Manag. Dec. (2018). https://doi.org/10.1108/MD-07-2017-0663. Vol. ahead-of-print No. ahead-of-print.
4. Bakker, R.M., Shepherd, D.A.: Pull the plug or take the plunge? Multiple opportunities and the speed of venturing decisions in the Australian mining industry. Acad. Manag. J. **60**(1), 130–155 (2017). https://doi.org/10.5465/amj.2013.1165
5. Ries, E.: The Lean Startup: How Today's Entrepreneurs Use Continuous Innovation to Create Radically Successful Businesses. Crown Business, New York (2011)
6. Ries, E.: The Startup Way: How Modern Companies Use Entrepreneurial Management to Transform Culture and Drive Long-Term Growth, Currency (2017)
7. Rasmussen, E.S., Stoyan, T.: 3 - Lean startup. In: Pacheco-Torgal, F., Rasmussen, E., Granqvist, C.-G., Ivanov, V., Kaklauskas, A., Makonin, S. (eds.) In Woodhead Publishing Series in Civil and Structural Engineering, Start-Up Creation (Second Edition), Woodhead Publishing, pp. 41–58 (2020). https://doi.org/10.1016/B978-0-12-819946-6.00003-5. ISBN 9780128199466,
8. Yordanova, Z.: Lean Startup method hampers breakthrough innovations and company's innovativeness. Int. J. Innov. Technol. Manage. **15**(02), 1850012 (2018)
9. Maurya, A.: Running Lean: Iterate from Plan A to a Plan That Works. O'Reilly, Sebastopol, CA (2012)
10. Pease, J.F., Dean, J.H., Van Bossuyt, D.L.: lean design for the developing world: making design decisions through the use of validated learning techniques in the developing world. In: Proc. ASME 2014 Int. Mech. Eng. Congr. Expo. pp. 1–11 (2014). https://doi.org/10.1115/IMECE2014-36612
11. Silva, D.S., Ghezzi, A., Aguiar, R.B.d., Cortimiglia, M.N. and ten Caten, C.S.: Lean startup, agile methodologies and customer development for business model innovation: A systematic review and research agenda. Int. J. Entrepreneurial Behav. Res. **26**(4), 595–628 (2020). https://doi.org/10.1108/IJEBR-07-2019-0425
12. Hampel, C., Perkmann, M., Phillips, N.: Beyond the lean start-up: experimentation in corporate entrepreneurship and innovation. Innovation **22**(1), 1–11 (2020). https://doi.org/10.1080/14479338.2019.1632713
13. Leatherbee, M., Katila, R.: The lean startup method: early-stage teams and hypothesis-based probing of business ideas. Strateg. Entrep. J. **14**, 570–593 (2020). https://doi.org/10.1002/sej.1373
14. Ladd, T., Kendall, L.: Entrepreneurial cognition in the lean startup method. Proc. **2017**(1), (2017). https://doi.org/10.5465/AMBPP.2017.10753abstract
15. Yordanova, Z.: Knowledge transfer from lean startup method to project management for boosting innovation projects' performance. Int. J. Technol. Learn. Innov. Dev. (IJTLID), **9**(4), 293–309 (2017)
16. Harms, R., Schwery, M.: Lean startup: operationalizing lean startup capability and testing its performance implications. J. Small Bus. Manage. **58**(1), 200–223 (2020). https://doi.org/10.1080/00472778.2019.1659677
17. Werwath, M.: Lean startup and the challenges with "hard tech" startups. IEEE Eng. Manage. Rev. **47**(1), 22–23 (2019). https://doi.org/10.1109/EMR.2019.2903705
18. Sandra, E.P., Silva, R.D.C., Silva, M.B., Nascimento, M.A.: Lean startup applied in healthcare: a viable methodology for continuous improvement in the development of new products and services. IFAC Proc. Vol. **46**(24), 295–299 (2013). https://doi.org/10.3182/20130911-3-BR-3021.00054
19. Jung, J., Kim, S.-A.: Digital fabrication integrated architectural design process applying lean startup method. Proc. Korean BIM Soc. **8**(4), 23–33 (2018). https://doi.org/10.13161/KIBIM.2018.8.4.023

20. Yordanova, Z.: Digitalization of a systematic literature review process – lean startup and data analytics solution for scholars. In: Huang, T.-C., Wu, T.-T., Barroso, J., Sandnes, F.E., Martins, P., Huang, Y.-M. (eds.) ICITL 2020. LNCS, vol. 12555, pp. 236–244. Springer, Cham (2020). https://doi.org/10.1007/978-3-030-63885-6_27
21. Bortolini, R.F., Cortimiglia, M.N., de Moura, A., Danilevicz, F., Ghezzi, A.: Lean Startup: a comprehensive historical review. Manage. Dec. **59**(8), 1765–1783 (2018). https://doi.org/10.1108/MD-07-2017-0663
22. Baas, J., Schotten, M., Plume, A., Côté, G., Karimi, R.: Scopus as a curated, high-quality bibliometric data source for academic research in quantitative science studies. Quant. Sci. Stud. **1**(1), 377–386 (2020). https://doi.org/10.1162/qss_a_00019
23. Cobo, M.J., López-Herrera, A.G., Herrera-Viedma, E., Herrera, F.: An approach for detecting, quantifying, and visualizing the evolution of a research field: a practical application to the fuzzy sets theory field. J. Informetrics. **5**(1), 146–166 (2011)
24. Carvalho, N., Yordanova, Z.: Why say no to innovation? Evidence from industrial SMEs in European Union. J. Technol. Manag. Innov. **13**(2), 43–56 (2018). https://doi.org/10.4067/S0718-27242018000200043

Educational Gamification and Game-Based Learning

Effect of Game Elements on Game-Based Learning for Computer Programming Using Task-Technology Fit

Wei-Tsong Wang[1] and Mega Kartika Sari[2](✉)

[1] Department of Industrial and Information Management, National Cheng Kung University, Tainan City, Taiwan

[2] Institute of Information Management, National Cheng Kung University, Tainan City, Taiwan

Abstract. Several studies on game-based learning (GBL) examine the impact of using GBL on student achievement. In contrast, this study examines the game elements that differentiate existing GBLs (reward mechanism, visual programming environment, and flexible learning environment). In addition, this study reveals a comparison between two GBLs that apply the same game elements but have different variations. The purpose of this study was to determine whether the variations of the game elements that were applied even though both had applied the same game elements would give different results to the students' perspective in using GBL. We use Task-Technology Fit (TTF) theory to determine the effect of game elements on GBL suitability. The total participants in this experiment were 252 students majoring in informatics engineering. Statistical results indicate that the effect of the combination of the three variables on TTF is 87.7%. It implies that the combination of the application of game elements has a significant impact on the suitability of a system in helping students learn using GBL.

Keywords: Game-based learning · Task-Technology Fit · Computer programming

1 Introduction

The popularity of GBL makes researchers and developers provide a variety of innovations to support learning needs [1]. The popularity of GBL is due to the many benefits of GBL, such as increasing student achievement, motivation, and the positive influence of GBL [2]. GBL has been widely used for technical learning such as computer programming. It was recorded in the research of [3] from 3083 studies of gamification in education, 1104 studies in the field of engineering and computing, which made up the largest proportion of participants in their research. Several studies have discussed the success of GBL in computer programming learning [4, 5].

Many studies only focus on learning outcomes, computational thinking, and motivation alone [6, 7]. Therefore, this study focuses on designing a good fit in GBL, which also has an essential role in achieving success in GBL. As revealed by [8], "design may help bring together the various perspectives that have already been applied to games."

© Springer Nature Switzerland AG 2021
Y.-M. Huang et al. (Eds.): ICITL 2021, LNCS 13117, pp. 323–332, 2021.
https://doi.org/10.1007/978-3-030-91540-7_34

More importantly, the unsuitable design of the GBL can diminish the entertainment and the educational benefit [9]. Therefore, it is crucial to describe suitable design integration. Seeing the problems that exist in describing suitable design, this study uses Task-technology Fit (TTF) theory to determine what factors play an essential role in achieving the fit of a GBL.

Previous studies showed that TTF could measure a good fit of an information system to increase employee performance while using the system [10, 11]. Although TTF is widely used to measure system compatibility between tasks and technology, TTF has never been used to measure the compatibility of a GBL, especially for learning computer programming. In addition, previous studies have claimed the importance of sorting out the different design elements to determine which elements make the most significant difference to learning [12–15]. However, they have not discussed the suitability of integrating design elements into the GBL. Therefore, this study wanted to reveal the effect size of the game element on TTF and whether there are differences in students' perspectives who use different GBL for computer learning. Thus, the research questions of this study are as follows:

1. What factors from game elements affect the suitability of GBL in terms of computer learning?
2. What is the effect size of the game element's influence on TTF?
3. Are there differences in students' perspectives if each GBL has applied the same game elements with different variations?

2 Theoretical Background

2.1 Task-Technology Fit

[16] introduced TTF in 1995 and has been used to find a suitable technology design to complete a task [17–19]. Indeed, if technology provides users with good-fit features, it will positively impact their performance [20]. The more tasks or achievements a technology accomplishes, the higher the individual's perception of TTF [21].

In e-learning, TTF is still rarely used, and it is not known yet if a good TTF can affect student adoption of online learning [22]. Therefore, [23] examine the factors influencing student adoption of the Massive Open Online Course (MOOC) by integrating the TTF model, social motivation, and self-determination theory. The results support the theory that task, and technology positively impact TTF and that fit affects behavioral intention. In contrast to previous research, this study wants to know the factors that affect GBL's good-fit. Specifically, we focus on game element design as a technology used to help students learn computer programming.

2.2 GBL for Learning Computer Programming

In computer programming, many GBLs studies examined different game elements for the same purpose. For instance, [24] and [25] examined the GBL, which uses different gamification techniques for learning computer programming. [24] developed an online puzzle-based game learning whereas [25] examined the differences between classical and enriched courses with Scratch through real-life problem-based games. Although the two GBLs studied are different, these two GBLs aim to achieve student effectiveness in understanding programming algorithms. In addition, the results of both studies have a positive impact on student performance. Nevertheless, many studies show that the failure of GBL design can reduce the benefits of GBL itself [26]. However, the design of GBL, which is suitable for learning computer programming, has never been studied before. Therefore, from the most popular GBLs used to learn computer programming such as HackerRank, Codewars, Grasshopper, Programming Hub, and Solo Learn, we chose 2 GBLs with significant differences in implementation of game elements.

HackerRank and Grasshopper have significantly different characteristics in designing game elements from those five popular GBL. The different characteristics of game elements in Hackerrank and Grasshopper have represented other GBL's. We describe the differences in the two GBLs in Table 1 by categorizing the characteristics based on game elements' differences.

Table 1. Difference of HackerRank vs. Grasshopper

Differentiating factors	HackerRank	Grasshopper
Reward mechanism (RM)	Badge, leaderboard	Track progress
Visual programming environment (VP)	Text-based	Puzzle-based
Flexible learning environment (FL)	Daily challenge	Continuously

2.3 Differentiating factors

Reward Mechanism

Reward mechanisms such as points, badges, and leaderboards are the most common designs applied to GBL and increase students' motivation in their learning process [27–29]. However, [30] showed that leaderboards and badges failed to improve student's motivation and performance in the final exam. Their research emphasizes the importance of design principles in GBL to enable users to achieve desired learning outcomes. From the comparison of the two GBLs, HackerRank and Grasshopper implement different reward mechanisms. HackerRank uses a badge and leaderboard system, meanwhile, Grasshopper implements a progress track and animation that will appear every time students complete a challenge. In addition to examining the effect size of the reward mechanism, this study wants to determine whether there are differences in student perspectives regarding the different designs applied in the GBL for learning computer programming.

Visual Programming Learning Environment
Implementing a visual programming learning environment can provide more benefits for students in understanding programming concepts quickly [31, 32]. If the visual programming learning environment is unsuitable, GBL fails to provide educational benefits for the students [33]. Therefore, the growth of the programming environment is increasingly being developed [34] and creates variations in the design of the visual programming environment, such as text-based, block-based, and puzzle-based. These different visual programming environments aim to reduce the complexity of learning computer programming [35]. Several studies have examined visual programming language by comparing textual and block-based programming learning [36, 37]. [34] examined the differences between text-based and block-based and found that their learning outcomes had no difference except in their learning progress which had different paths while using the GBL. In comparison, puzzle-based success improved students' programming skills in previous studies [24]. From the comparison of the two GBLs, Grasshopper applies fun learning using puzzle-based learning while HackerRank applies text-based game learning. Both have the same goal of helping students more easily recognize and get used to the actual programming. From that difference, this study wants to explore whether there are differences from the learner's perspective on the visual learning environment and the effect size of the visual learning environment on the TTF to achieve a good fit for a GBL.

Flexible Learning Environment
Flexible learning is the ability of the GBL to provide freedom of choice, time, place, and how learning occurs [38]. The GBL provides this flexible learning can affect student performance [39] and student satisfaction [40]. Therefore, the flexible learning environment also has an essential role in implementing GBL. It is crucial to know the appropriate flexibility design for GBL since it can affect student performance and satisfaction. Due to this difference in flexible learning, Grasshopper gives learners the freedom to complete as many challenges as they want by simplifying the learning material into several small sub-sections or several simple test quizzes for each material. However, learners must complete the challenge in order. Meanwhile, HackerRank implements one daily challenge sorted from the difficulty level and gives the learner the freedom to complete the material randomly. From the difference between the two GBL, we want to compare the differences between the two GBL in providing the flexible learning environment to understand the effect size of flexibility and determine whether there are differences from the user's perspective on the flexible learning environment offered by GBL.

3 Method

3.1 Participants

Participants are undergraduate students majoring in informatics engineering from two universities in Yogyakarta, Indonesia. The total participants are volunteers consisting of 252 students who have taken early-level computer language learning courses. The participants were randomly divided into two groups to differentiate HackerRank and Grasshopper (136 HackerRank, 137 Grasshopper).

3.2 Experimental Design

In order to make both groups in this experiment equal, both groups must complete four fundamental challenges on the GBL that they had to use and fill out a questionnaire according to their experience in using GBL within ten days. The fundamental challenges, namely arithmetic operators, if statements, arrays, and loops, exist in each GBL. The researcher will verify the validity of the data based on the evidence sent by the participants that they have completed all the fundamental challenges.

This study adopts instruments from a similar previous study and uses a 5 Likert scale to measure the four variables. First, we modified the measurement for TTF from [16], which is then also used by [41] and [42]. The instrument for the reward system was adopted from [43]. Next, this study adopted item questionnaires from [44] for the visual programming environment. For the flexible learning environment, we adapted from [45].

3.3 Data Analysis

The data collected were analyzed using multiple regression to determine the effect of game elements on TTF. Then, we used an independent t-test to test whether there were differences in the user's perspective on the differences in GBL variations. The confidence level of this study is 95%.

As a test of validity and reliability, we used Pearson and Cronbach's alpha. The results of the factor analysis test can be seen in Table 2, where Pearson's standard validation uses r table < r count, where r table for this study 0.123 and Cronbach's alpha is above 0.7. Overall test results with Kaiser-Meyer-Olkin are 0.96, above the recommended standard value of 0.7. Therefore, the validity and reliability of each item that indicates the model we used are valid.

We conducted a preliminary analysis to ensure no violations of assumptions with normality, multicollinearity, heteroscedasticity, and autocorrelation. The results of the Kolmogorov-Smirnov test data show that the data is a normal distribution with the Kolmogorov-Smirnov Z test result of 0.99 and a significant value of 0.29, which is greater than 0.05. Furthermore, Table 2 displays the results of VIF and tolerance for the multicollinearity test. It indicates no multicollinearity with standard tolerance is more than 0.10, and VIF is less than 10. Next, the standard heteroscedasticity test used Glejser. The data does not have heteroscedasticity if the significant value in the coefficient is more than 0.05. The results of the heteroscedasticity test are 0.52, which is greater than 0.50. For autocorrelation using Durbin-Watson, the result condition for the calculated du value must be between du and 4-du in the Durbin-Watson table. The calculation results are d = 1.85 and are between two critical values of $1.81 < d < 2.19$. Thus indicating there was no violation of the assumption in this construct.

Table 2. Validity and Reliability

Construct	Item	Pearson correlation	Cronbach's alpha	Tolerance	VIF
TTF	TTF1	0.45*	0.93		
	TTF2	0.50*			
	TTF3	0.54*			
	TTF4	0.53*			
	TTF5	0.45*			
	TTF6	0.47*			
	TTF7	0.48*			
	TTF8	0.48*			
	TTF9	0.51*			
RM	RM1	0.86*	0.77	0.37	2.67
	RM2	0.81*			
	RM3	0.82*			
VP	VP1	0.86*	0.86	0.38	2.64
	VP2	0.86*			
	VP3	0.87*			
	VP4	0.86*			
	VP5	0.85*			
	VP6	0.38*			
FL	FL1	0.79*	0.87	0.28	3.58
	FL2	0.85*			
	FL3	0.87*			
	FL4	0.87*			

*p = 0.00, significant

4 Results and Discussion

We use multiple regression test results, which show that the three-game elements as independent variables have a significant linear correlation on TTF simultaneously and partially. The three variables are reward mechanism, visual programming environment, and flexible learning environment.

The results of the multiple regression from the F test showed that the effect of the game element on TTF was simultaneously significant, that is, 87.7% with F = 588.82 and probability equal to 0.00. Correspondingly, the three independent variables partially also show a significant positive linear correlation to TTF. The results of this test are shown in Table 3 with a correlation value of 0.76 for the reward mechanism variable, 0.86 for the visual programming environment variable, and 0.90 for the flexible learning environment variable. All three significantly have a positive linear correlation with a p-value equal to 0.00. Therefore, these three variables are also stated to have a significant positive effect on TTF with the following equations:

$$y = -0.49 + 0.23(\text{RM}) + 0.61(\text{VP}) + 1.23(\text{PE}) \tag{1}$$

Table 3 also shows the average difference between the two GBLs using independent t-test. The results show that differences in variations in implementing the same game element affect the user's perspective regarding the reward mechanism, visual programming environment, flexible learning environment, and even TTF with a significant value equal to 0.00 for the four variables.

Table 3. Summary of the results

Multiple linear regression				Independent t-test	
Construct/Predictors	Correllation	B	t-value	Mean difference	t-value
(Constant)		−0.49	−0.55		
TTF				0.57	5.45*
RM	0.76*	0.23	2.04**	0.42	3.96*
VP	0.86*	0.61	10.48*	0.70	7.38*
FL	0.90*	1.23	13.00*	0.40	3.71*

*p = 0.00; ** p < 0.05

We conclude that the flexible learning environment has the most significant influence from the results of simultaneous and partial tests. However, the other two variables are as important as the flexible learning environment variable considering these three variables affect 87.7% of TTF when combined. Meanwhile, from the results of the independent t-test, we conclude that although the two GBLs have applied the three characteristics of the game elements with the application of different variations, it can affect students' perspectives in using GBL. Therefore, it is essential to know which game element type is suitable for the GBL of the three game elements in implementing the game element.

5 Conclusion

This study focuses on GBL for beginner computer programming learning. The results of this study re-emphasize that the game element's design is a matter to achieve GBL fit to assist the student learning process effectively [46]. In terms of the use of game elements, the three of the game element in this study play an essential role in achieving the fit of the GBL. Although the most frequently used in GBL is the reward mechanism [47, 48], this study reveals that the reward mechanism has the smallest effect compared to the other game elements.

Moreover, given the different perspectives of students who use different GBL indicates that applying game elements without paying attention to the type of game elements is not enough. Therefore, further research needs to review the types of game elements that are suitable to be applied to GBL. The application of the correct type of game elements will undoubtedly help developers to design GBL easily. On the other hand, future research should examine the effect of TTF on learning performance to find out whether achieving a better fit can affect student performance apart from effectively completing the task.

References

1. Vahldick, A., Farah, P.R., Marcelino, M.J., Mendes, A.J.: A blocks-based serious game to support introductory computer programming in undergraduate education. Comput. Hum. Behav. Rep. **2**, 100037 (2020)
2. Chang, C.Y., Hwang, G.J.: Trends in digital game-based learning in the mobile era: a systematic review of journal publications from 2007 to 2016. Int. J. Mob. Learn. Org. **13**(1), 68–90 (2019)
3. Huang, R., et al.: The impact of gamification in educational settings on student learning outcomes: a meta-analysis. Educ. Tech. Res. Dev. **68**(4), 1875–1901 (2020)
4. Vaca-Cárdenas, L.A., et al.: Coding with Scratch: The design of an educational setting for Elementary pre-service teachers. In: 2015 International Conference on Interactive Collaborative Learning (ICL), pp. 1171–1177. IEEE, Italy (2015)
5. Hooshyar, D., Malva, L., Yang, Y., Pedaste, M., Wang, M., Lim, H.: An adaptive educational computer game: Effects on students' knowledge and learning attitude in computational thinking. Comput. Hum. Behav. **114**, 106575 (2021)
6. Zhao, W., Shute, V.J.: Can playing a video game foster computational thinking skills? Comput. Educ. **141**, 103633 (2019)
7. Hooshyar, D., Lim, H., Pedaste, M., Yang, K., Fathi, M., Yang, Y.: AutoThinking: an adaptive computational thinking game. In: Rønningsbakk, L., Wu, T.-T., Sandnes, F.E., Huang, Y.-M. (eds.) ICITL 2019. LNCS, vol. 11937, pp. 381–391. Springer, Cham (2019). https://doi.org/10.1007/978-3-030-35343-8_41
8. Gaydos, M.: Seriously considering design in educational games. Educ. Res. **44**(9), 478–483 (2015)
9. Park, J., Kim, S., Kim, A., Mun, Y.Y.: Learning to be better at the game: Performance vs. completion contingent reward for game-based learning. Comput. Educ. **139**, 1–15 (2019)
10. Vongjaturapat, S.: Application of the task-technology fit model to structure and evaluation of the adoption of smartphones for online library systems. Sci. Technol. Asia **23**(1), 39–56 (2018)
11. Isaac, O., Abdullah, Z., Ramayah, T., Mutahar, A.M.: Internet usage, user satisfaction, task-technology fit, and performance impact among public sector employees in Yemen. Int. J. Inf. Learn. Technol. **34**(3), 210–241 (2017)
12. Filsecker, M., Hickey, D.T.: A multilevel analysis of the effects of external rewards on elementary students' motivation, engagement and learning in an educational game. Comput. Educ. **75**, 136–148 (2014)
13. Sailer, M., Hense, J.U., Mayr, S.K., Mandl, H.: How gamification motivates: an experimental study of the effects of specific game design elements on psychological need satisfaction. Comput. Hum. Behav. **69**, 371–380 (2017)
14. Aldemir, T., Celik, B., Kaplan, G.: A qualitative investigation of student perceptions of game elements in a gamified course. Comput. Hum. Behav. **78**, 235–254 (2018)
15. Chen, C.-H., Shih, C.-C., Law, V.: The effects of competition in digital game-based learning (DGBL): a meta-analysis. Educ. Tech. Research Dev. **68**(4), 1855–1873 (2020). https://doi.org/10.1007/s11423-020-09794-1

16. Goodhue, D.L., Thompson, R.L.: Task-technology fit and individual performance. MIS Q. **19**(2), 213–236 (1995)
17. Zigurs, I., Buckland, B.K.: A theory of task/technology fit and group support systems effectiveness. MIS Q. **22**(3), 313–334 (1998)
18. Lu, H.P., Yang, Y.W.: Toward an understanding of the behavioral intention to use a social networking site: an extension of task-technology fit to social-technology fit. Comput. Hum. Behav. **34**, 323–332 (2014)
19. Omotayo, F.O., Haliru, A.: Perception of task-technology fit of digital library among undergraduates in selected universities in Nigeria. J. Acad. Librar. **46**(1), 102097 (2020)
20. Cane, S., McCarthy, R.: Analyzing the factors that affect information systems use: a task-technology fit meta-analysis. J. Comput. Inf. Syst. **50**(1), 108–123 (2009)
21. Ling, H.C., Chen, H.R., Ho, K.K., Hsiao, K.L.: Exploring the factors affecting customers' intention to purchase a smart speaker. J. Retail. Consum. Serv. **59**, 102331 (2021)
22. Wu, B., Chen, X.: Continuance intention to use MOOCs: integrating the technology acceptance model (TAM) and task technology fit (TTF) model. Comput. Hum. Behav. **67**, 221–232 (2017)
23. Khan, I.U., Hameed, Z., Yu, Y., Islam, T., Sheikh, Z., Khan, S.U.: Predicting the acceptance of MOOCs in a developing country: application of task-technology fit model, social motivation, and self-determination theory. Telematics Inform. **35**(4), 964–978 (2018)
24. Hsu, C.C., Wang, T.I.: Applying game mechanics and student-generated questions to an online puzzle-based game learning system to promote algorithmic thinking skills. Comput. Educ. **121**, 73–88 (2018)
25. Topalli, D., Cagiltay, N.E.: Improving programming skills in engineering education through problem-based game projects with scratch. Comput. Educ. **120**, 64–74 (2018)
26. Gallego-Durán, F.J., Villagrá-Arnedo, C.J., Satorre-Cuerda, R., Compañ-Rosique, P., Molina-Carmona, R., Llorens-Largo, F.: A guide for game-design-based gamification. Informatics **6**(4), 49 (2019)
27. Subhash, S., Cudney, E.A.: Gamified learning in higher education: a systematic review of the literature. Comput. Hum. Behav. **87**, 192–206 (2018)
28. van der Lubbe, L.M., Gerritsen, C., Klein, M.C.A., Hindriks, K.V.: Empowering vulnerable target groups with serious games and gamification. Entertain. Comput. **38**, 100402 (2021)
29. Nadolny, L., Valai, A., Cherrez, N.J., Elrick, D., Lovett, A., Nowatzke, M.: Examining the characteristics of game-based learning: a content analysis and design framework. Comput. Educ. **156**, 103936 (2020)
30. Hanus, M.D., Fox, J.: Assessing the effects of gamification in the classroom: a longitudinal study on intrinsic motivation, social comparison, satisfaction, effort, and academic performance. Comput. Educ. **80**, 152–161 (2015)
31. Uysal, M.P.: Evaluation of learning environments for object-oriented programming: measuring cognitive load with a novel measurement technique. Interact. Learn. Environ. **24**(7), 1590–1609 (2016)
32. Bak, N., Chang, B.M., Choi, K.: Smart Block: A visual block language and its programming environment for IoT. J. Comput. Lang. **60**, 100999 (2020)
33. Lavoué, E., Monterrat, B., Desmarais, M., George, S.: Adaptive gamification for learning environments. IEEE Trans. Learn. Technol. **12**(1), 16–28 (2018)
34. Weintrop, D., Wilensky, U.: Transitioning from introductory block-based and text-based environments to professional programming languages in high school computer science classrooms. Comput. Educ. **142**, 103646 (2019)
35. Broll, B., et al.: A visual programming environment for introducing distributed computing to secondary education. J. Parallel Distrib. Comput. **118**(1), 189–200 (2018)

36. Noone, M., Mooney, A.: Visual and textual programming languages: a systematic review of the literature. J. Comput. Educ. **5**(2), 149–174 (2018). https://doi.org/10.1007/s40692-018-0101-5
37. Weintrop, D., Wilensky, U.: To block or not to block, that is the question: students' perceptions of blocks-based programming. In: Proceedings of the 14th International Conference on Interaction Design and Children, pp. 199–208. Association for Computing Machinery, United States (2015)
38. Jiang, Z., Wu, H., Cheng, H., Wang, W., Xie, A.N., Fitzgerald, S.R.: Twelve tips for teaching medical students online under COVID-19. Med. Educ. Online **26**(1), 1854066 (2021)
39. Li, K.C., Wong, B.Y.Y.: Revisiting the definitions and implementation of flexible learning. In: Li, K.C., Yuen, K.S., Wong, B.T.M. (eds.) Innovations in Open and Flexible Education. EIS, pp. 3–13. Springer, Singapore (2018). https://doi.org/10.1007/978-981-10-7995-5_1
40. Sun, P.C., Tsai, R.J., Finger, G., Chen, Y.Y., Yeh, D.: What drives a successful e-Learning? An empirical investigation of the critical factors influencing learner satisfaction. Comput. Educ. **50**(4), 1183–1202 (2008)
41. Isaac, O., Aldholay, A., Abdullah, Z., Ramayah, T.: Online learning usage within Yemeni higher education: the role of compatibility and task-technology fit as mediating variables in the IS success model. Comput. Educ. **136**, 113–129 (2019)
42. McGill, T.J., Klobas, J.E.: A task–technology fit view of learning management system impact. Comput. Educ. **52**(2), 496–508 (2009)
43. McKernan, B., et al.: We don't need no stinkin'badges: the impact of reward features and feeling rewarded in educational games. Comput. Hum. Behav. **45**, 299–306 (2015)
44. Moons, J., De Backer, C.: The design and pilot evaluation of an interactive learning environment for introductory programming influenced by cognitive load theory and constructivism. Comput. Educ. **60**(1), 368–384 (2013)
45. Drennan, J., Kennedy, J., Pisarski, A.: Factors affecting student attitudes toward flexible online learning in management education. J. Educ. Res. **98**(6), 331–338 (2005)
46. Jost, N.S., Jossen, S.L., Rothen, N., Martarelli, C.S.: The advantage of distributed practice in a blended learning setting. Educ. Inf. Technol. **26**(3), 3097–3113 (2021). https://doi.org/10.1007/s10639-020-10424-9
47. Klock, A.C.T., Gasparini, I., Pimenta, M.S., Hamari, J.: Tailored gamification: a review of literature. Int. J. Hum. Comput. Stud. **144**, 102495 (2020)
48. Koivisto, J., Hamari, J.: The rise of motivational information systems: a review of gamification research. Int. J. Inf. Manage. **45**, 191–210 (2019)

A Development of Smart Coding Creative Kit to Enhance Creative Problem Solving Thinking for Children

Pornsawan Vongtathum[1(✉)], Charuni Samat[1], and Suchat Wattanachai[2]

[1] Faculty of Education, Khon Kaen University, Khon Kaen, Thailand
pornin@kku.ac.th
[2] Faculty of Veterinary Medicine, Khon Kaen University, Khon Kaen, Thailand

Abstract. This study aims to develop the board game- Smart Coding Creative Kit to enhance creative problem-solving thinking for children based on 4 processes of Youth Scotland's framework [9]. The target groups consisted of 1) 3 experts of media and innovation and 2) 30 grade 1–3 students by purposive sampling method. Statistics used to analyze quantitative data were average ($\overline{X}$) and standard deviation (*S.D.*) while interpreting and descriptive analysis were for qualitative data. Research results revealed efficiency of the evaluated Smart Coding Creative Kit that was in highest level ($\overline{X} = 4.50$, $S.D. = 0.58$) and opinion of the subjects who had board game trial was in high level as ($\overline{X} = 4.40$, $S.D. = 0.55$). This can illustrate the board game efficiency that can be used with children in according with the analysis results that found its suitability with a group of ages 5 with small members as 3.

Keywords: Board game · Creative problem solving thinking · Children

1 Introduction

Living in the 21st century has noticeably changed from the 19th and 20th. The partnership for 21st Century Skills (P21), this agency concerns that youth must have the necessary skills. Therefore, the vision and framework for learning in the 21st century have been developed by integrating knowledge, specialized skills, expertise, and knowledge in various fields together in order to be successful in both work and life. This framework for learning is the beginning for developing the new future skills for Thailand. To be successful, students have to learn these necessary skills such as critical thinking, problem solving, creativity, communication, and collaboration. In addition, Thailand will have to face the significant changes externally and internally that are rapidly and elaborately changing. It is both opportunity and risk to develop the country. Especially, the commitment to become an ASEAN in 2015 has resulted 11th National Economic and Social Development plan (2012–2016) [4] to be set as a guideline for improving the quality of people's immunity to changes and has intervened in human development through a

© Springer Nature Switzerland AG 2021
Y.-M. Huang et al. (Eds.): ICITL 2021, LNCS 13117, pp. 333–342, 2021.
https://doi.org/10.1007/978-3-030-91540-7_35

learning process that fosters culture supporting. Develop the people's ability to have a continuous learning life, and to continue to invent innovation practically and creatively. As it might be seen that developing learners to be adapt themselves to a learning society in the creative economic era potentially as those of other countries, it must develop problem solving skills to keep up with the changing situation of the world. And it is important to possess creativity for preparing of learners to work in the 21th century.

However, in various studies, it is found that there are some disadvantages for thinking process of problem solving and creativity especially the problem in teaching and learning that the learner's learning method requires to wait and think accordingly to teachers and others rather than thinking by themselves at first. And creative knowledge which is new to society will not be very noticeable. World Economic Forum (WEF) has recently stated the Global Competitiveness Report, it is pointed out that the education in both secondary and higher education in Thailand is at the lowest level according to many countries of ASEAN, using the term of "Abnormally low quality". This reflects the unreliability of the overall quality of Thai education, and it will affect the confidence of Thailand in other way in the future as well. The thinking process of Thai children also undergoes the deteriorating and delayed education which critically affects the country development. There are many critics mentioned their thoughts about this problem of Thai children. In the article of Srathongniam [7], his opinion says that the result of the management of Thai education in the past was still low according to assessment results of the Office of Educational Standard and Quality Assessment (ONESQA). The analytical thinking process of Thai children is mostly at fair level, it is dramatically different compared to the other countries. As resulted in PISA's assessment of knowledge and scientific skill, it appears that Thai children ranked below average which affects the quality of education and life to be dragging down.

From this point, it is only the result of the analysis of thinking skills from the test in upper elementary and high school levels. It will be beneficial in the long term if the teaching and learning process focuses more on thinking skills from the beginning, which is consistent with Piaget's theory of cognitive and development being said that the development of thinking in children in each age is related. It means that children at an older age are more successful in thinking due to the ability to develop in thinking from the previous step [5]. Especially in the course of computational science, which Thailand currently focuses on problem solving to lead to systematic thinking only for children. This may not be enough to extend the knowledge to design and develop programs at the high level as set. From an article of NSTDA [3], it is discussed about programming and developing thinking skills that computer programming is a skill that requires a lot of practice to become proficient which depends on analytical thinking skills, reasonably and orderly problem solving, including the use of algorithm. Conveying ideas in such systematic way will lead to effective programming. Therefore, creative problem solving is the key concept ability that can develop learners to be able to solve computer problems that efficiently lead to systematic program design and development. It must design the teaching method which develops on the basis of problem solving as the core. And this thinking skill should be cultivated from the elementary school according to Piaget's theory of intelligence.

The researcher team thus develop the board game innovation- Smart Coding Creative Kit to enhance creative problem-solving thinking for elementary students in which to be basis of their efficiency to advanced program in the future. The innovation is the integration of an application for teachers and students. In student interface of each task, they can learn from an animation with creating more interesting without having difficulties of reading fluency. The application is also able to evaluate their answers. Similarly, in teacher interface, the teacher can use all functions same as students but beneficially to create a group to collect and check students' answers. This can solve the traditional problem that collecting the answers in paper- based. In consequence, the data that stored in application database can be used and analyzed then in the future.

2 Research Objectives

To develop the board game- Smart Coding Creative Kit to enhance creative problem-solving thinking for children.

3 Research Scopes

3.1 Target Groups

In this research phase, to examine the efficiency of the evaluated Smart Coding Creative Kit, purposive sampling method was implemented for the target groups that comprised 1) 3 experts of media and innovation and 2) 30 grade 1–3 elementary students.

3.2 Research Design

Developmental Research Type I [6] was employed and purposed to design and develop by the following 3 phases: 1) Design process 2) Development process and 3) Evaluation process. However, this study was employed during phase 2 in developing Smart Coding Creative Kit to enhance creative problem-solving thinking for children, testing, and evaluating its use. The stakeholders comprised developers, evaluators, researchers, teacher, and learners.

3.3 Research Tools

Experimental instrument - The instrument used was the Smart Coding Creative Kit Board game. To develop the board game prototype, research results from phase 1- Design process were applied and generated as the designed board game components as 1) Problem-based and Tasks 2) Thinker- Companion 3) Task Notes and 4) Play Group. Furthermore, in prototype developing process, the researcher team had developed the board game on the basis of Youth Scotland's framework [9] that having 4 major and 6 minor processes as the following.

Design Phase

- Set objectives. This board game- Smart Coding Creative Kit was aimed to enhance children creative problem-solving thinking for algorithm design. The researcher synthesized 4 steps of problem-solving thinking for algorithm design as: 1) Analyze problem 2) Generating creative ideas 3) Preparing 4) Review the algorithm through problem-solving content to design an algorithm, which is the basic content that leads to future programming.
- Content Analysis. Algorithm Design was the content used in the board game development which the researchers hence analyzed it into the following table: 1) Sequential Algorithm 2) Decision Algorithm and 3) Loop Algorithm.
- Board Game Component Design.
  - Players. The game is played by 2–4 players, ages 5 and up.
  - Objective. The player can solve a problem by using a card correctly and fast which ones who award most golden coins can be the winner.
  - Rules. Gameplays requires to have 4 tasks or 4 stages according to the analyzed results of creative problem-solving thinking framework for algorithm design. In each procedure, each player group is provided 5 equipment types as 1) Command Cards 2) Special Cards 3) Loop Command Sheets 4) Dice and 5) Bug Coins. The main objective of the game is to allow the player to correctly place the command that directs Barry to collect the carrots safely and fast on the Golden Island. They can place the card in front of their own group while the teacher corrects the placed command that can run the game. At the end of the game, a group that is awarded most gold medals wins.
- Procedures. There are 3 game processes as 1) Goal Assignment 2) Board Settling and 3) Marching.
- Pieces. Game pieces can be explained as the following (Fig. 1).
- Prizes. A prize condition in this game is "Gold Coins" by stipulating conditions for awarding gold coins in each task. At the end of the game, the group with the most gold coins wins.

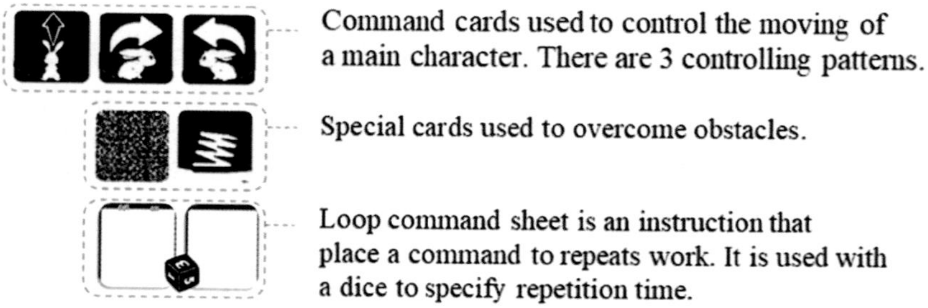

Fig. 1. Game pieces

Game Prototype Phase

The further step is to discover the components and internal structures based on the content that the researcher requested and applied it into the game structure. In the second step of game development, there are 3 sub-steps as:

- Aligning

  During this step, the content structure must be analyzed and designed in accordance with the game structure without conflict.
- Drafting

  Besides designing the possible game elements, the next step is to draft a game board and game pieces.
- Test with a focus group

  After the board game prototype was constructed, it was tested twice by the researcher team which later improved by using feedback and recommendations. Then, the prototype was tested with a group of 30 students who had the similarity to the research target group and bring their opinions to improve its quality again (Fig. 2).

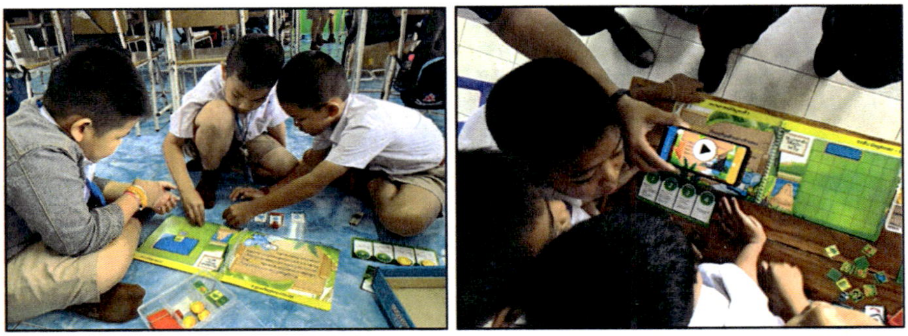

Fig. 2. Using of board game with the elementary students.

Development of Final Board Game Version

The final version was developed by the board game prototype for collecting data in the next research phase. The final version consists of two elements as board games and application development which detailed in the following.

- Board games elements

  From the Fig. 3 is the element of Smart Coding Creative Kit consist of: 1) Problem- based Book 2) Commands Card 3) Special Card 4) Loop Command Sheets 5) Character 6) Task sheet 7) Thinker- Companion Sheet.

Fig. 3. Element of smart coding creative kit.

- Application Development

AR Board Game application comprised both a mobile application on Android operating system for a user and database management in web application through API and web services for a system manager. To be able to retrieve and analyze results effectively, the various usage data is collected with Relational Database system. The application development processes are detailed below.

– Database Architecture

The 3- tier architecture was used in the design of AR Board Game application as shown in Figure 3.

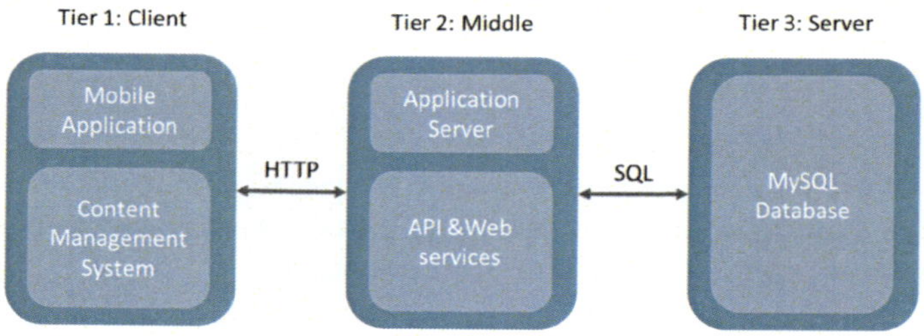

Fig. 4. Architecture of AR board game application

From Fig. 4, Tier 1 is a part of a user interface consisting of two parts: a Mobile Application for users and Content Management System for system managers. Tier 1 communicates with Tier 2 to exchange data via HTTP protocol. In Tier 2 architecture, it comprises 2 parts as one is Application Server and another one is APIs and Webservices which process the requested data from Tier 1 by retrieving it via SQL in MySQL database system in Tier 3.

– AR Board Game Application

See Fig. 5

Fig. 5. User interface of the smart coding creative kit

4 Data Collection

4.1 The Evaluation of Media and Innovation – The Experts

The experts evaluated the developed media and innovations by using the form which was developed by the following processes 1) Identify topics for media and innovation assessment 2) develop a form that based on the specified issues 3) examine and assess the form quality by 3 experts. A closed-ended question form was constructed to let the experts specify Item Objective Congruence with reasons or suggestions to improve its quality. This must be relevant to a principle and theory used as basis in a conceptual framework.

4.2 Interview Form of Board Game Use

The form used in interviews with students who had a similar context and background to the research target group. Their opinions were thus applied in board game developing to finalize the final version. The interview form was created by 1) defining the issues in the interview 2) identifying questions related to the topics or key words that requires needed information 3) examining its content validity by experts in measurement and evaluation 4) testing the examined interview form with students who were similar to the target group and 5) improving the form quality based on recommendations in which to be consistent with the interview issues.

5 Data Analyses

- To examine the efficiency of board game, 5-Point Rating Scale form was used by 3 experts to evaluate and shared opinions towards 3 aspects as 1) content and AR storytelling 2) presentation and 3) graphic as fonts and colors. They were then analyzed by basic statistics as average ($\overline{X}$) and standard deviation (S.D.)
- To study the students' opinion toward board game learning, student opinion survey and a semi-structured interview form were employed to collect and analyze data by interpreting with basic statistics as average ($\overline{X}$) and standard deviation (S.D.).

6 Results

The experts in media and innovation clarified evaluation results in according with 11. Chaijaroen [1]'s framework of all 3 domains as detailed here.

- Production. The opinion toward Smart Coding Creative Kit of 3 experts was found that the overall was at the highest level ($\overline{X}$ = 4.50, S.D. = 0.58) which the efficiency of AR Board Game was assessed at the highest level (Table 1).

Table 1. Rating average of smart coding creative kit quality

Evaluation item	Average of expert rating			Average of Expert evaluation results	Quality level
	1	2	3		
1. Content and AR Sorytelling	5.00	4.40	5.00	4.80	Highest
2.Presentations Styles	4.90	4.50	4.25	4.55	Highest
3. Graphic: Fonts ad Colors	4.15	4.15	4.15	4.15	High
Mean	**4.68**	**4.35**	**4.47**	**4.50**	**Highest**

- Context of Use. It was found that the most effective number of students per group is 3, and this game is suitable for students aged 5 and over.
- Opinions of students who used the innovation. It revealed their opinions that were at high level ($\overline{X}$ = 4.40, S.D. = 0.55). The results of the interviews with the sample groups showed the following issues: the problem situation is too long, the problem situation unclearly indicates the position of the pieces, the task is unclear, the reward is not motivating, the special card is too few and should be increased to make a variety, and the used card number should be presented in each stage (Table 2).

Table 2. Rating average of students' opinions after playing the smart coding creative kit

Evaluation domains	$\overline{X}$	S.D	Quality level
1. Content	4.40	0.58	High
2. Player	4.40	0.55	High
3. Board game and AR Application	4.55	0.57	Highest
4. Learning Activities	4.25	0.50	High
Mean	**4.40**	**0.55**	**High**

With regards to the evaluation of 3 domains, it was found that the developed Smart Coding Creative Kit can be used for further research data collection.

7 Discussion

The results of the evaluation of the Smart Coding Creative Kit by experts found that overall opinion was at the highest level ($\overline{X} = 4.50$, S.D. = 0.58) which the efficiency evaluation result of AR Board Game was at the highest level as well. This is consistent with the research of Eiamwilai [2] who developed board games based on principles of critical thinking which its quality evaluation results of the games by experts were at high level. Consequently, the board game was designed in accordance with Tinsman [8] principles that makes a quality and attractive board game in terms of playing time, player's alternatives, balanced rules and regulations, etc.

8 Recommendations for Further Research

- Develop board game application in online platforms that can be accessible to download, install, and ready to use.
- Develop a digital board game for real-time processing to attract more players' attention especially with exceptional children who may have a short attention span. The integration of technology may be possible to help them to have more attention.

Acknowledgements. We would like to express appreciation to Thai Media Fund for research grant. Also, we gratefully thank Faculty of Education, Khon Kaen University for supporting the research.

References

1. Chaijaroen, S.: Educational Technology: Principles Theories to Practices. Khon Kaen, Klungnanawittaya (2008)

2. Eiamwilai, W.: The Development of Board Game Based on Critical Thinking to Enhanced Digital Citizenship of 7th Grade Students. Graduate School, Srinakharinwirot University, Thesis towards the Degree of master of education (2020)
3. Institute for the Promotion of Science and Technology. http://oho.ipst.ac.th/ipst-course-description-primary-science/
4. Office of the National Economics and Social Development Board. http://www.nesdb.go.th/Portals/0/news/plan/p11/plan11
5. Piaget, J.: The Moral Judgment of the Child. Illinois, The Free Press (1960)
6. Richey, R.C., Klein, J.: Design and Developmental Research. Lawrence Erlbaum Associates, New Jersey (2007)
7. Sathongniam, K. http://www.dailynews.co.th/Content.do?contentId=50718
8. Tinsman, B.: The Game Inventer's Guidebook. Morgan James Publishing, LLC, Garden City, NY (2008)
9. Youth Scotland. http://www.spen.org.uk/mymedia/files/resource_pdfs/Youth%20Scotland%20-%20Board%20Game%20Toolkit.pdf

Board Game and Family Involvement Motivate Target Language Learning

Yingling Chen(✉)

Center for General Education, Asia Eastern University of Science and Technology, New Taipei City, Taiwan
cil0226@mail.aeust.edu.tw

Abstract. In this action research, the author encouraged the students created and designed L2 board games and examined how this approach (L2 board game design) could facilitate L2 learning and increase family interaction and bond. Fewer studies yet relatively providing routes of how family members and language teachers assist L2 students grasp knowledge by applying self-designed L2 board games. Therefore, this study investigated whether the application of self-designed L2 board game and family involvement assist improving L2 students' learning attitude and motivation. 58 freshmen participated in the action research. After 18-week courses, the use of semi-structure interview, class observation, and field recording methods were applied to be the main technique collecting research data. 15 Participants were randomly selected and asked to reflect on how self-designed L2 board games create the interactive learning opportunities and how family involvement developed the motivation in L2 learning. The results indicated that applying L2 board game and family involvement were successful strategies for improving family bonds and producing creative L2 learners.

Keywords: Board game · Second language learning · Creative learner

1 Introduction

When learning is composed of pleasure and ease in the educational field, instructors immigrate the students to operate material and process them into the long-term memory. Students engaged in learning without getting bored, anxious, and distracted. During the game play, participants learn to feel interesting about school and gain the enjoyment. Many influential researchers have found evidence that individuals pick up learning targets better when they have solid optimistic emotions [1–3]. When participants are involved and motivated and feel less pressure, L2 learning functions and absorbs easily. Learning through the affective filter in the brain and students grow better cognition, receive comprehension, and experience "aha" moments [4]. Therefore, a traditional quiet classroom does not produce such learning outcomes but from classrooms with creative activities. Generally speaking, board game provides players with valuable access toward L2 learning. The gamification of language learning is a new method for effectiveness.

© Springer Nature Switzerland AG 2021
Y.-M. Huang et al. (Eds.): ICITL 2021, LNCS 13117, pp. 343–351, 2021.
https://doi.org/10.1007/978-3-030-91540-7_36

1.1 Board Game, Family Involvement and L2 Learning

Boardgame is a media that strengthens to various language learning elements which allows L2 learners receive new information from whatever they are participating. Teaching L2 students in a joyful and motivated way requires collaboration in the combination of materials. Implementing multimedia language learning practices for students apply their target language produces a student-centered learning environment [5]. Classroom lecture is the traditional way of obtaining L2. Students require opportunities of language input and output in order to develop their target language. In addition, using board game and family involvement strategies for English course progresses potentials in developing learners' achievement and motivation. Gamification is using game-based mechanics and game story to attract people, provoke action, motivate learning, and overcome tasks [6] Effectively designed games are able to develop potential in efficiency and creativity among participants [7]. Board games have been applied positively as educational aids. The use of boardgames enhances teaching and learning especially in the understanding and processing the concepts of the kind. In particular, board games have been confirmed as operative learning tools [8].

Board Game is full of possibility to provide practical L2 content, on-site learning opportunities and unexpected exploration and discovery of the connected content of target material in the daily life. In other words, participating in board games and designing board games develop a new learning strategy to help language learners obtain target language without limited classroom lecture. Board games are used to recall essential concepts, deliver new knowledge creatively, and increase teamwork while making learning more entertaining [9]. L2 students in the assigned groups, incorporating the subject matters, given a complex instruction technique to solve, improve, and be familiar with the grammar rules. The creativeness and innovation of L2 board game design from learners' learning experiences have opened a new world to satisfy the needs of learners' exposure to their target language. Families are highly valued in education and are committed to students' educational success [10]. Suitable designed family involvement is able to develop positive learning environment and family bond. As a result, quality of the family relationship and L2 learning motivation increases after board game participation. The effectiveness of families and school's connection, family intervention increases well-being students, family involvement, and positive effects on learning outcomes [11]. Game based learning is an exploration of using a game as a media to achieve necessary learning goals. Knowledge and skills development enhance through the design and content of the game. The fundamentals of critical thinking skills as one of the must have learning skills can be cultivated by using game-based learning [12]. While the L2 learners tend to create and design their own board games and to be played by the learners, the researcher guided the learners create their own games for knowledge in an active setting and designed an experiential gaming approach to promote critical thinkers among the L2 students. The most importantly, making them apply cooperative learning method with their peers. Board game provides immediate reading practices and offers L2 input and output training, thus assisting L2 learners enhance the language learning experience. Language learning and family involvement provide a motivated platform for learners to do practical language training in and after class in a joyful way. Board game could be used for any sorts of listening, speaking, reading and writing L2 activities. The positive influence of game-based learning on language education is full of potential and valued.

2 The Research Methodology

This action research process helped the researcher understand what had happened in the English classroom and categorized changes that improved teaching and learning. The researcher collected meaningful data from the records of attendance logs, grade reports, industrial expert's comments, board game feedback, and students' designed board game. Samples of students' designed board games are also performances for the researcher to evaluate and estimate if the goal was being met.

2.1 Design of the Research

The author used students' designed board games to create a dynamic learning environment. A fun and interactive gaming strategy was incorporated to provide a creative dissimilarity on the target language learning. Students' designed L2 board games are carried out as a media to offer participants essential target curriculum. Second language learners are anticipated to incorporated classroom content into real life situation in order to make language learning meaningful. Action research identifies the strength and weakness, management, and practice needed to make the changes for better instruction. Action research is a rotation of investigation and reflection [13]. During the cycle, the researcher will discover the purpose, the goal, and how to reach the goal. The process of this action research is presented in Fig. 1.

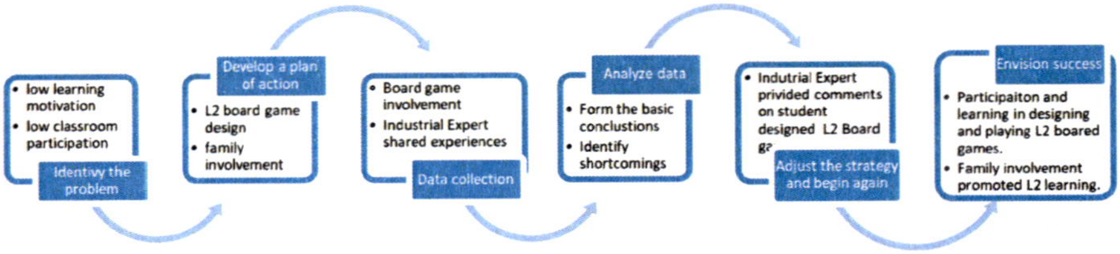

Fig. 1. The action research cycle in this study

Period of 18-week courses, students attended the program offered by the university. Students started to design their L2 board games from week 4 to week 15. In week 4, students experienced all kinds of board games such as speed competition, advantage token, acting, mystery, investigation, cooperative game, connection, event, ownership, and educational games. Therefore, student designers developed basic understanding of the mechanism. Then, they were able to create their own games. In week 5, industrial experts were invited to introduce a variety of interesting, fun, and attractive board games to students. In week 6, student designers combined and implemented more than two mechanisms in their designed board game for developing more attractive and interactive

Table 1. The process of the 18-week course.

W1	Introduction of the course	Form groups	W10	Design and Start a L2 board game from the scratch 3 Mechanism	
W2	The benefit of fun learning	Reading and vocabulary development	W11	Design and Start a L2 board game from the scratch 4 Obstacles and smoothness	
W3	The benefit of learning English through board games	Reading and vocabulary development	W12	Demonstrations in the class. Advantage and disadvantage were provided after the demonstrations.	
W4	Board game experience		W13	**Industrial Expert** evaluates students' L2 designed board games	
W5	**Industrial Expert** introduced a variety of Interesting, fun, and attractive board games and design		W14	Modify the L2 board games	
W6	Understand and implement the board game mechanism		W15	Demonstrations in the class Self-designed board game feast	
W7	Design and Start a L2 board game from the scratch 1 Background story		W16	The importance of Family involvement	Reading and vocabulary development
W8	Design and Start a L2 board game from the scratch 2 Rules		W17	Students were asked to play board games with their families. At the meantime, teaching them speaking English.	Students were asked to record the interaction during the game.
W9	Midterm Exam Introduction of the board game design	Receiving feedback from others.	W18	Video sharing in the class and showed how family involvement enhanced L2 learning and family bond.	The importance of family involvement and family bond in learning.

activities. In week 7, design and start a L2 board game from the scratch, students constructed the background story. In week 8, game rules were made. In week 9, the midterm week, students orally introduced the design of the board game and received feedback from others for further modification. In week 10, mechanism was programmed. In week 11, obstacles and smoothness were set. In week 12, students' designed board games were demonstrated in the class, every group took turns playing and provided advantages and disadvantages for further adjustment. In week 13, industrial experts were invited again for evaluating students' L2 designed board games. In week 14, after receiving opinions from the experts, modification and demonstration of the L2 board games were carried out. In week 15, students were asked to participate and experience in their peers' designed board games and provided feedback. In week 16 and 17, the importance of family involvement was focused especially on reading and vocabulary development, students were also asked to play board games with their families. At the meantime, teaching their family members speaking English. Students were asked to record the family interaction during the game. The process of this course is presented in Table 1.

In week 18, each group shared their video in the class and showed how family involvement enhanced L2 learning and family bond Table 1. The results of the 18-week course (Table 2).

Table 2. Students' achievement

Introduction of students' designed board game

Sample 1: Have fun with the family

Sample 2: Family involvement record

Sample 3: Family involvement record

Students' designed board game 1.

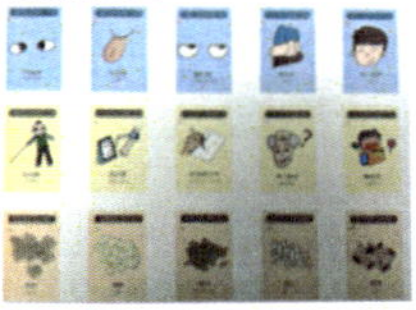

Students' designed board game 2.

2.2 Research Data Collection

Three open-ended questions were conducted in the semi-structured interview. Three experts in the educational field were sought in order to ensure the content validity. In addition, a preliminary interview was carried out for internal validity of the question items. Face-to-face interviews with participated college students were conducted and the answers given were recorded in writing forms by the researcher after certifying the validity of the semi-structured interview form. The purpose of this action research was to reveal the effectiveness of L2 board game application toward L2 learning motivation. L2 Students' actual experience of the board game play and design during and after the course is widely regarded as providing valuable insights into language learning and family interaction. Participation in the board game becomes a potent factor of a complete instructional strategy. After the interviews, a descriptive analysis approach was used for further data analysis, Step 1, themes was first formed. Consistency and coherence were confirmed by checking the relationship between the research questions. A code number was given to college students (S1, S2, S3...) codification and categorization are the methodologies in the qualitative data analysis. This ratio indicated that the analyses were reliable [14]. 15 randomly selected participants were asked to reflect on how student designed L2 board game functioned in their learning target and how family involvement increased the family bond and the model of collaborative learning scenarios.

3 Experimental Results and Discussions

3.1 Qualitative Data

Research Question 1. How are L2 Students' perceptions of self-designing L2 Board Game for enhancing target language learning?

The combination of self-designed L2 board game and English language learning did increase the learning motivation from the traditional classroom lecture. With the board game support, output in practical situations enable students became creative in the content material.

"I think L2 board game design is an interesting way to learn English. Board game is fun and creative and I like it very much. I never had the chance making a "board game". It is so fun and I was making a L2 board game! I learn English not only when I play it but also when I design it." (May, female student 2).

Regarding board game smooths English language learning and reduces the stress, freshmen articulated that learning should be associated with the real object. To use English and to produce English are important in learning.

"Playing the board game becomes a media for me to connect the curriculum. Boardgame provides motivating and practical instruction and allows me to adopt contentmaterial and develop my L2 ability. I think it is a practical strategy to use and learn L2for better learning outcomes." (May, male student 3)

When students design L2 board games for the curriculum, the content remains creative and logical opportunities to language learners. After experiencing their own designed board games, students preferred learning L2 through gaming activity over traditional didactic lectures in the classroom.

"Board game provides opportunities for me to learn the target language. This is my first-time playing board games. I experienced in class and then try to design another one with my team members. It is so much fun and creative. It is much better than just memorize and copy new vocabulary." (May, male student 1)

"I would definitely write a positive feedback for this class. My classmates and I enjoy designing the board game so much. Our major is Industrial and Commercial Design.

I think this is a good opportunity for me to put my actual learning in practice. The industrial expert likes our design of the mechanism, illustration, and colors. I learned new vocabulary and animal habitation from our game design." (June, female student 4).

Research Question 2. How are Students' motivation of learning L2 from their designed Board Game?

58 freshmen were engaged in designing L2 board games. 15 randomly selected participants in the qualitative data were well aware of achieving their positive learning outcome through the gaming activity. Low motivation in L2 learning was revealed from 3 participants. After participating the design activity, students presented different attitude in learning English.

"I don't like to take English test. I was always asked to memorize new vocabulary. The funny part is, I don't even remember the old vocabulary. I can I memorize the new one. The enthusiasm of using English is vital. I was bored in the past English class. After my teacher introduced me board games, it was so much fun. She invited two industrial experts to our class, and let the professional told us what are the attractive board games in the market. How can we design a new board game with interesting idea and creation? I did not know that I could learn English through participating and design a board game; English learning becomes motivated and meaningful." (May, male student 8).

"The teacher used a new way to motivate us learn English. Through making a new board game, my logical and critical thinking were trained. I wanted to show the peers how to play our designed board game and learn the target language from answering questions, getting puzzles, and collecting tokens. I was encouraged to learn English through this special course." (June, female student 5).

Making friends becomes another motivation in playing board games and learning the target language. Some students pointed out that designing a board game from scratch was not easy, it took time, cooperation, and brainstorming.

"I started to respect those board game designers on the market, I am sure that they must took a lot of time inventing and developing their board games. Our group used the poker cards as the inspiration and then we put more elements in the game. Each pattern represents a tribe, each number carries different tasks. The lowers number the easiest the task will be. Who earns the highest score become the chief of the tribe. I couldn't believe our group created the background story and obstacles by ourselves. I also thank my teacher's help for checking the English grammar of the rules and mechanism for our board game. I met new friends when making the game because we all from different majors. I enjoy making new friends and designing the board game."

"The day we took turns sharing our designed board games with others. I made a lot of new friends. The game designer introduced us how to play their board game. We shared and experienced at least three games. It was so much fun playing our own game. Although we couldn't speak fluent English, we tried hard during the game. We laughed a lot because we had funny pronunciation."

Research Question 3. How are the students' perceptions of how self-designed L2 board game and family involvement facilitates their target language learning?

The combination of self-designed L2 board game and family involvement facilitates English language learning and increases the learning motivation from the traditional classroom lecture. Students became more creative in the L2 board game design. At the meantime, family bond was also increased.

"This was my first time playing a board game with my grandmother, she was so cute when playing with my group members and me. We taught her to say "it's your turn to play", "please roll the dice", and "pick a card". My grandma was tong-tied. I bet board games can reduce the incidence of Alzheimer's disease. This is also the first time, I realized speaking English is fun and I wasn't shy using it."

"My hometown is in Kaohsiung, I went to my group members' home and played the board game with his grandfather. I was so surprised. Even though he is 76 years old, he had a very good rapid reaction. We needed to find out a kind of animal and said it out loud from multiple illustrations with very similar shape and color. He always beat us. I think I need to get a pair of presbyopia glasses. I envy and enjoy my friend's relationship with his grandpa. Maybe I should bring a board game and play with my family."

"After high school, I had less interaction with my families. I thank my teacher to assign this assignment to play a board game with my parents. When I started to use the smart phone, I seldom talked and spent time with them. I miss those days when I was little. I learned to create a board game, I was forced to speak English during the game. I never thought that my family and I will have so much fun in playing our designed board game. After the class, board game became the media of communication and provided me the bridge to reach my loved families." (June, male student 7).

4 Conclusions

Board games have been used effectively as instructive and informative tools in the learner centered settings. The researcher and students used self-designed board game to present L2 material on practical content and promote the curriculum in a stress-free way. A functional board game allows a language learning environment to turn on every student's learning motivation. Students' designed L2 educational board game strengthen their cooperation, creation, critical and logical thinking skills and also allow students become independent thinkers and learners. In addition, the lecture increased reinforcement of board game enhances learning and family bond. At the meantime, students realize a L2 board game increases their L2 knowledge and self-efficacy ability without experiencing any pressure, or receiving any orders from the instructor. The perceived fun feature of a board game would bring positive effect to a L2 learner and increase strong family bond among family members. The game should be fascinating by all the participants.

References

1. Dulay, H., Burt, M.: Remarks on creativity in language acquisition. In: Burt, M., Dulay, H., Finocchiaro, M. (eds.) Viewpoints on English as a second language. Regents, New York (1977)
2. Krashen, S.: Theory versus practice in language training. In: Blair, R.W. (ed.) Innovative Approaches to Language Teaching, pp. 25–27. Newbury House, Rowley (1982)

3. Kohn, A.: Feel-bad education. Educ. Week **24**(3), 44–45 (2004)
4. Willis, J.: The neuroscience of joyful education. Brain research tells us that when the fun stops, learning often stops too. Educ. Leadership **64**, 1–6 (2007)
5. Chen, Y.: Augmented reality technique assists target language learning. In: Rønningsbakk, L., Wu, T.-T., Sandnes, F.E., Huang, Y.-M. (eds.) ICITL 2019. LNCS, vol. 11937, pp. 558–567. Springer, Cham (2019). https://doi.org/10.1007/978-3-030-35343-8_59
6. Kapp, K.M.: The Gamification of Learning and Instruction: Game-Based Methods and Strategies for Training and Education. Pfeiffer, San Francisco (2012)
7. NMC (Ed.): Horizon Report 2014 Higher education edition, http://cdn.nmc.org/media/2014-nmc-horizon-report-he-EN-SC.pdf. Accessed 30 June 2021
8. Berland, M., Lee, V.R.: Collaborative strategic board games as a site for distributed computational thinking. Int. J. Game-Based Learn. **1**(2), 65–81 (2011). https://doi.org/10.4018/ijgbl.2011040105
9. Boctor, L.: Active-learning strategies: the use of a game to reinforce learning in nursing education. A case study. Nurse Educ. Pract. **13**(2), 96–100 (2013)
10. Henderson, A., Mapp, K.: A new wave of evidence: the impact of school, family, and community connections on student achievement. Southwest Educational Laboratory, Austin (2002)
11. Chrispeels, J.H. (ed.): Learning to Lead Together: the Promise and Challenge of Sharing Leadership. Sage, Thousand Oaks (2004)
12. Qian, M., et al.: Game-based learning and 21st century skills: a review of recent research. Comput. Hum. Behav. **63**, 50–58 (2016)
13. Sagor, R.: The Action Research Handbook. Corwin Press, Thousand Oaks (2005)
14. Miles, M.B., Huberman, A.M.: Qualitative Data Analysis: An Expanded Sourcebook, 2nd edn. Sage Publications, Inc., Thousand Oaks (1994)

Gamifying Digital Learning Platform for Information Security Awareness

Thanawat Rintanalert(✉) and Arthorn Luangsodsai

Department of Mathematics and Computer Science, Faculty of Science, Chulalongkorn University, 254 Phayathai Road, Wang Mai, Pathum Wan District, Bangkok 10330, Thailand
Arthorn.l@chula.ac.th

Abstract. Gamification, the process of integrating the "fun" aspect commonly found in a videogame to mundane processes like learning to make it more interesting. In this research, an undergraduate university student in Thailand is assigned into two separate groups: A and B. Group A designated as "Gamified Group" is to study the topic of information security via educational videogame. Group B designated as "Traditional Group" is to study the same topic via provided paper-based material. After that, both groups are to test their understanding of the topic by doing quizzes. We found that while gamified group expressed more interest and more actively participate in this experiment compared to the traditional group, the average test score from both groups is comparable to each other with further experiments shown that undergraduate students in their senior year from both groups achieved higher average score than first-year student likely due to their familiarity with information security from coursework they took during years of their study. This research proved that videogames can be used as a tool in a higher education environment, with the possibility of developing better education videogames with increasing efficiency and make them more appealing to the masses.

Keywords: Gamification · Information security · Videogame

1 Introduction

In the digitalization era, information has great importance and value. Thus arise the need for those who work in the information technology and banking field to equip themselves with appropriate knowledge and present-day extensive digital learning network has seen popularity as a platform to raise security awareness both for an individual and corporate environment. But learning can be monotonous especially when the lesson in question is not align with your current knowledge, experience, or interest. New learners could spend a long period just to acquire a basic glimpse and need a high degree of motivation to stay focused, many are discouraged by its tedious nature. Gamification has proven to improve learner's motivation and they are willing to participate in an activity. In this research, we provide the description of the experiment of using gamified learning platform as a tool to engage learners in the subject of information security awareness and compare the result of the experiment to those who learn the same subject via traditional paper-based

© Springer Nature Switzerland AG 2021
Y.-M. Huang et al. (Eds.): ICITL 2021, LNCS 13117, pp. 352–364, 2021.
https://doi.org/10.1007/978-3-030-91540-7_37

means. The hypothesis for this research is that gamifying learning process will improve the motivation of participants which will lead to improvement in test scores for security awareness tests comparing to those who study via traditional means.

1.1 Objectives

Steam customer purchased of videogame from 2020 onward highlight general public's interest in videogame and possibility for gamification to motivate user in a topic of information security. We are interested in two hypotheses: whether the gamified platform can complement traditional learning methods and whether the gamified platform is suitable for learning advance or complex topics.

1.2 Significance of the Study

First, there are several studies on gamification. However, our study of Thailand's context specifically focuses on university students in a computer science field. Second, the use of video games as a platform for academic purposes, while customary, is mostly concentrating on kid's education or elementary lessons. We hope to gain a better understanding of how gamification can help in a higher education environment.

1.3 On the Definition of Gamification

According to Wikipedia [1], Gamification is a strategic attempt to enhance activity to create a similar experience when playing a videogame with objectives to motivate and engage users, be the use of game design and principle in a non-game context so there might be an argument that the goal of gamification is not "having fun" but about value creation. However, in this research, we would like to provide a different perspective, in that "fun" is what makes a videogame a videogame. "Game can be fun to play, and fun alone is the approved reason for playing them" is a sentence that sociologist Erving Goffman uses in his essay "Fun in Game" [2] citing that we can include as many rules and design strategies we want but a "fun" videogame is what motivate and increase engagement while a "not fun" videogame does exact opposite. We agree with Goffman's argument based on our reasoning, personal experience in a lifetime of playing a videogame, and statistical proof between well-received game and badly-received game rest on one essence, Do you think your game is fun? And do those who play your game think so?

1.4 Difference Between Cyber Resilience, Cyber Security, and Information Security

While these three words seem to use interchangeably, they are different in perceived objectives. For cyber resilience and cyber security, both are related byword 'cyber' and are both forms of protection against cyber threats. However, cyber resilience recognizes the situation where the defensive line, cyber security, failed and focuses on how an organization can remain operational in a critical situation [3].

Information security can be described as the prevention of unauthorized access and modification of data in any given state of transferring and storing created to cover three objectives of confidentiality, integrity, and availability known as the CIA triad. Be those data be physical or digital, personal, or organizational data [4].

In conclusion, we can think of information security as the smallest parts of the three, perhaps most important as shown in Fig. 1, and related to the daily use of technology and how a person can prevent a situation where they are a target of cyber threats. If an attack does happen, cyber security acts as a defensive line to prevent further damage spread but if all else failed. Then, it will rely on cyber resilience as a fail-safe plan to survive the attack and recover to pre-attack state as much as possible. Fixing the system after the damage was done was counter-intuitive and the best approach is to prevent the attack from ever happening in the first place thus by raising awareness of individual people we can be certain that will reduce the incidents of cyber security breaches and cyber resilience must be used in the future.

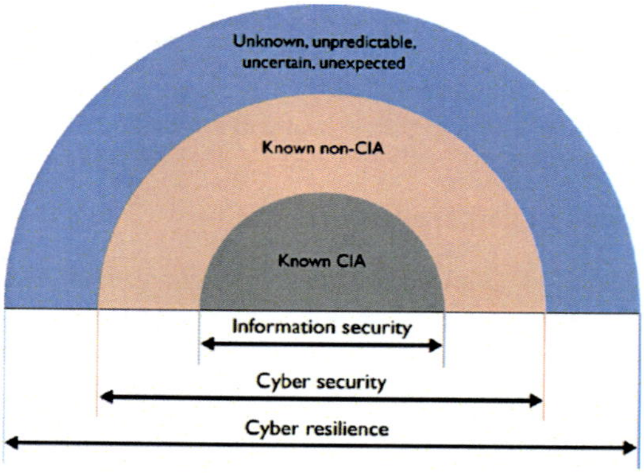

Fig. 1. Cyber security model

2 Literature Review

According to R.K. Dixit et al. (2008) [6] cybersecurity is the challenge of the digital era particularly when organizations want to comply with security policies such as Confidentiality, Integrity, and Availability also known as "CIA Triad". The paper quotes the integration of gamification with the traditional teaching model as means to help reach the learning objective, the experiment is carried out for university students in their final year. In the first part of an experiment, the lecturer would teach the subject about cryptography bound to the story/example concept. Using imaginative scenarios such as "Alice wants to prove to Bob that she solves the Rubik cube without actually solving. How can Alice convince Bob?" when students provided the answer for Alice, they also answer the key question of cryptography "How sender of cryptography prove that he/she is authorized sender without sending key?". The second part of the experiment is to use a riddle instead of a direct question with the sole objective to assess the student by creating more interest. In this case, the riddle is about how to cipher local language into a known language (e.g., English). The observation shows that students become interested in solving the riddle and finding a hidden answer. The process then linked to the coding lesson that the lecturer aimed to teach. The research concluded that gamification can be applied with traditional teaching with the result shown 80% of observed student participated in the experiment have increased engagement and attention span thus make the class more active.

In a journal by Ulrike Hammerschall (2019) [7], while agreed that gamification can be applied, pointed out that not all experiments in gamification ended successfully. Focusing on the motivation aspect of a participant, this research introduced a gamification framework for long-term engagement based on two theories: A Self Determination Theory (SDT) and Transtheoretical Model (TTM). The first theory, SDT, is an approach to human motivation and personality. It identifies three psychological "needs" that enhance motivation when satisfied, that is the need for competence, the need for relatedness, and the need for autonomy. Those three "needs" will determine how motivated the person is based on three stages: Intrinsic or highly motivated, Extrinsic or mildly motivated, and Amotivated or unmotivated. This research further clarifies that for someone to be interested or start a new activity, they need to be at least intrinsic about it and by using gamification, the aspect that makes videogame fun and engaging, will stimulate a person's motivation between intrinsic or extrinsic through reward, feedback, or fulfillment. The second theory, TTM, defines a model of behavior change developed by James O. Prochaska et al. (2005) [8] into 5 stages: Pre-Contemplation the stage with no intention to change; Contemplation the stage of thinking about change; Preparation the stage of preparing for change; Action the stage of changing and Maintenance the stage of keeping the changed behavior. The research notes that the first three-stage is the most important but using gamification in this period is useless, only during action and maintenance stages that the strength of gamification comes into play. The reason is that the player will have the autonomy to do the change and for that he/she needs to believe that one's effort is crucial for success.

Believing that, to complete the learning process, it is necessary to combine both scientific and everyday practices. Maciej Laskowski (2015) [9] experimented to find that students should learn by finding the practical solution to the problem instead of finding the answer in the textbook thus increasing students' involvement. Maciej also pointed out that the experiment is beneficial not only inside the education field as all "learners" regarding his or her professions, and lesson of intent are considered students. Gamification can split into two areas: 1.) Educational game and 2.) Gamified Classroom, Maciej chooses the latter to experiment on a group of IT students in their later year of bachelor's degree, called experiment A, and another group of master's degree students, called experiment B. The result has shown that, for experiment A, students who study in traditional class score better academically than students in the gamified classroom but have less participation rating. The student in the gamified classroom, where the leaderboard system is used, reported that a portion of students who ranked lower in the leaderboard has decrease motivation compared to the student at the top of the leaderboard. For experiment B, the gamified classroom has more participation rating and homework turned-in than traditional class but score lower academically than the student in the traditional classroom. It is theorized that because master's degree student only focuses on passing the class and generally do not mind about grading if they pass. A mentality that vastly different from bachelor's degree students. The journal ended with a conclusion that gamification in the academic field can improve attentiveness and participation of students but has almost no improvement academically.

Chee-Ken Wong and Chien-Sing Lee (2016) [10] developed a website that focused on the effect of gamification for learning Science, Technology, Mathematics, and Engineering (STEM). The participants of this experiment are diverse in their knowledge of the subject. As a means to find out that their gamified website succeeds, a survey was used to collect user's opinions on a website that would incorporate gamification as a base for future enhancement. The method of using a survey is what inspires to be used as one of the main features in this paper.

A dilemma of overspecialization is, according to Wikipedia (2020) [11], is when a person works in an excessively narrow occupation or field. Most time in a professional environment, specialization can be seen as beneficial as a person have in-depth knowledge and can handle more difficult tasks. The downside however is if a person is too narrowly over-specialized it can lead to poor training, unnecessary workflow, and risk their specialization become outdated as time went by, especially in information technology where technology advance rapidly. Marc E. Pratarelli (2007) [12] went into detail that as more and more innovation is created so need the specialist to maintain them leading to favor of specialization of specific IT field. Modern academics tend to prepare people to become specialists to satisfy job-market, companies and actively sought out a specialist for tasks/projects they currently handling but once those technologies are replaced by more advanced forms and become obsolete, thus lead to these specialists that have a harder time adjusting than their more flexible general-purpose counterpart. The research concluded that while specialist indeed is essential in the function of society, they are not to be replaced general-purpose workforces. Academics need to train these two types of workforces in equal ratios. And people who choose to become specialists need to realize their fatal weaknesses and dilemmas that one day, the knowledge they have mastered will be replaced and it is better to have a mindset of being flexible and ready for changes. For this paper, using a survey to gauge the understanding of participants on the topic of information security, we find this as an opportunity to discover how many university students suffered the same dilemmas which will grant us an understanding of the current academic situation in Thailand.

Yevgeniya Daineko et al. (2008) [13] has developed an educational software based on the game engine Unity 3D for studying physics. Believing that new technologies in education will have a significant effect on the process of interaction in the context of transferring knowledge. The author draws inspiration from various previous works that make use of virtual environments such as Virtual Star Laboratories by MIT, Project Eyes on Earth by NASA, A 3D model of a chocolate factory by FX Palo Alto, and Virtual Game Lab which is an experimental project by psychologist and engineer aims to study cognitive abilities and behavior of human to solve various mental diseases. The author outlined and went into detail of many potential game engines that are available such as Unity, UDK, Cry ENGINE, Torque 2D/3D, and HeroEngine, some engines are more specialized in developing genre of video game for example HeroEngine is commonly used by MMO (Massively Multiplayer Online) videogame developer. Unity is regarded as the game engine with a wide range of possibilities and an easier learning curve as well as its multiplatform allows for easy and quick porting of games into various mediums. Using game engines, the research conducted many scientific experiments inside virtual environments with the result showing that the execution is much easier and faster. It is also trivialized more dangerous experiments in which scientists can continue their work uninterrupted without fear of hazardous elements. We will go into more detail about the process of picking a game engine suitable for this paper.

Laura Alejandra Martinez-Tejada et al. (2020) [14] discussed many genres of videogames to choose for the experiment. It was decided that the game must be an easy game with flexibility for future development/improvement, a 2D platforming game was selected. The research also went into detail about the experiment of using various graphic aesthetics, game difficulty, sound, etc. to find out if any of those aspects affect the interest of the player and to keep them engaged. The result of this experiment concluded that what affects players' interest most is gameplay and difficulty, following by graphic aesthetic and game length, then the sound effect. Interestingly that while the aesthetic of the game affects the interest of players, a further experiment where players encounter repeatedly the same thing can considerably bore them, also many players reported feeling bored because intermission (between stages) is too long. The conclusion given is that for a game to keep players' interest it needs to have an adequate game length, balanced active game-time and idle time, do not repeat or reuse aesthetic which serves as a guideline for designing an engaging game for this paper.

In an article published by Venturebeat (2020) [15]. Steam, a video game digital distribution service by Valve, reported a 21.4% increase in games purchased by a customer in 2020 in comparison to 2019 with Valve summed up the growth in its blog post saying, "While Steam was already seeing significant growth in 2020 before COVID-19 lockdowns, video game playtime surged when people started staying home, dramatically increasing the number of customers buying and playing games,". While Steam has yet to disclose the purchased data of 2021, Analysts predict an increase in game purchased to continue rising with the current ongoing pandemic and recently announced Steam's 2021 Winter and Summer sales. Gameindustry.biz, United Kingdom videogame media, tracking digital download game sales from 16 major game companies across 50 European, Middle-East, African and Asian countries reported 4.3 million games were sold during March 16–22, 2020 [16] when the new pandemic first spread globally, a 63% increase compared to amount sold pre-pandemic. The report also points sharp increase in a country where pandemics hit the hardest and longest, Italy, which saw a 174.9% increase in digital game sales when the Italian government first announce a lockdown. Physical game sales also soar with about an 82% increase likely contributing to the abundance of logistic and delivery services born during the pandemic. This data is consistent with what other news media found such as CNBC, the Conversation, and TechSauce discussed below.

An article by TechSauce [17] cited an increase in gaming-related conversation on Twitter application by 97 percent in Thailand during pandemic ranking 4th after Japan, United States, and South Korea as countries that tweeting most about gaming. Twitter data analysts outline three key insights that are: Socialization, Leisure and stress relief, and Videogame popularity among Gen-Z and Millennial.

In a journal by Zhu Lin, with the release of Nintendo's "Animal Crossing: New Horizon" successfully get everyone's attention, the game's dreamland-like aesthetic and relaxing gameplay provide "temporarily escape" from harsh reality for many people who suffered anxiety and isolation during COVID lockdown. [18] The game's social platform is a perfect solution where people may meet up online. On the other side of the spectrum, id Software's action First Person shooter "Doom Eternal" released alongside Animal Crossing also gain an increase in popularity as a fun shoot-em-up game that provide "stress relieve" through the sheer amount of violence and gore presenting in-game with one videogame reviewer cited in the article that Doom Eternal help make them "less angry" [19].

3 Methodology

For this research, there are four stages of progression: First, Picking a target group. We choose Computer Science undergraduate students equally divided into two groups: Group A, "Gamified Group", and group B, "Traditional Group". As for experimentation. There are two tools in use:

- A paper-based document containing all the lessons the participant needs to learn about security awareness before the examination. This will give to the only participant of group B. (See Appendix)
- A gamified lesson in form of a simple videogame. The detailed lesson in-game is kept the same as the document given to group B with some alterations to suit the flow of gameplay. The game will be played only by the participant of group A.

The first group learns solely via the gamified platform and the second group solely via traditional paper-based means. Both groups are given approximately 30 min to study their assigned lesson. Once both groups finished studying, we will move to another stage, the Examination.

Second, Preparation for the gamified lesson. Taking lessons learned from an experiment by Laura Alejandra Martinez-Tejada et al. (2020) [14] it is safe to assume that one does not need to develop a complex videogame to complete the intended objective. Rather, the simpler the game the easier it to determine the effectiveness of gamification. Any result will be used for future research into more advance and complex videogames. We decided to choose Unity for developing our gamified platform as it is one of the most well-known game engines in the current market, due to its free-to-use and consumer-friendly policy, lower learning curve, versatility, low system requirement, the engine provides a vast library of materials and established online community. The finished gamified platform resembled a complication of minigame comprises into one single game.

Another notable mention is auxiliary applications, that may or may not be categorized as game engines like Torque, Blender, and Adobe may be used to help create models, artwork, or other functions needed in the finished game.

Unlike traditional learning methods that rely on repetition and memorization, Gamification can provide the student with an interactive lesson in similar manners to videogame use its storytelling and gameplay to captivate the player. For example, in one minigame, a student("player") assumes the role of "Mario" from the well-known classic platforming game "Super Mario Bros." shown in Fig. 2. We combined the story of Mario in his quest to save Princess Peach from the evil Bowser with a lesson we want a player to learn, in this case, about the common delivery method of computer viruses.

Fig. 2. A screen from the minigame resembled Super Mario Bros.

Another reason we choose to develop a minigame with Super Mario Bros. theme is that the game itself is an established videogame title, publicly well-known even to those who do not play videogame have heard of Mario. Thus, by role-playing as Mario, we created a sense of objective for the player. "To save the princess by choosing the correct answer for Mario". There, we continue into the gameplay section of minigame, to control Mario and hit one of the coin blocks that contain the correct answer shown in Fig. 3. In any case that, the student-controlled Mario chooses the wrong answer that coin block will become inactive with a message asking a player to choose another coin block. The process will repeat until the player finally chooses the correct answer.

However, the Mario character and the assets associated with the Mario series are the product of Nintendo and are protected by intellectual property law. An 'asset flip' or using copyright-free assets instead of Mario is considered. The change will only affect aesthetics and not the core gameplay of the game.

Another minigame example is a simple matching game, where the player assumes the role of an electrician to correctly connect all electrical wires shown in Fig. 4. The gameplay share similarity to choosing coin blocks in Mario minigame but different aesthetically. This is to prevent repetitive gameplay experiences and provide the player with something new to not bore them, a strategy often uses by many videogame developers to keep the gameplay loop fresh. Choosing the wrong wire resulted in that wire retracing

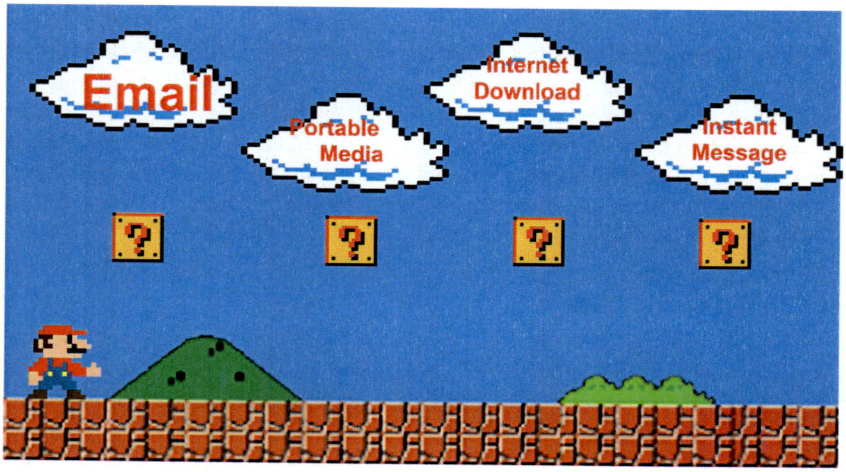

Fig. 3. Player-controlled Mario to hit one of the coin blocks that contain the correct answer. Choosing wrong coin blocks resulted in those blocks become inactive with the message "Wrong answer" shown to a player.

to the original position, letting the player know that their answer is incorrect and need to choose another answer.

As both students from groups A and B are given equal time of approximately 30 min to learn about information security. It is crucial to developed videogame based on this factor. Since, unlike reading material from texted paper, the playtime of each player can vary extensively and without reserving, some students might not be able to finish their game within the assigned 30 min. After both groups finished studying their assigned lesson, we then continue into the third phase. Taking quizzes.

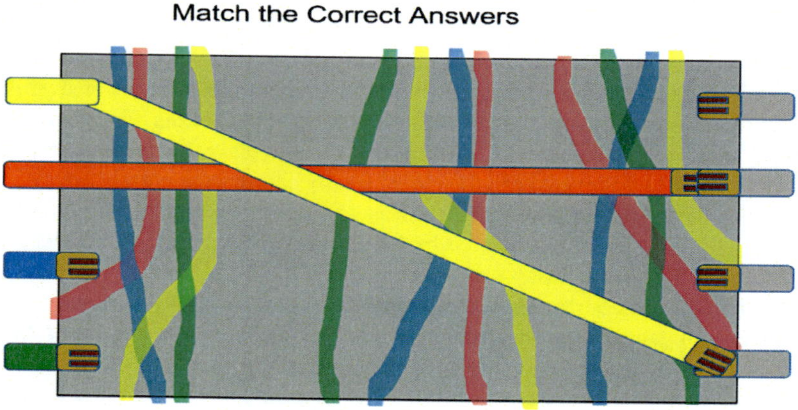

Fig. 4. An electric wiring minigame

Third, A Quiz. A test was given to participants of both Group A and B after they completed their respective lessons. The participants are instructed to complete the test within 30 min and are not allowed to use any means of assistance during this period. An exam has 3 parts with a gradually increase in difficultly starting from the most basic knowledge of information security in part 1 (easy), to intermediate in part 2 (normal), to advanced knowledge in information security in part 3 (hard), each part contains 10 questions with a total of 30 questions combined, each question uses a traditional 4 choices that participant must choose the only one which they think is most true. The basis for questions in the exam based on ISACA CISM's information security tests (2020–2021) [20, 21]. Once all participant from both groups completes their test. We will analyze the score of each group to compare the following:

- Which groups fare better academically in terms of scoring the most correct answers out of 30 questions.
- Comparing how many students from each group pass the easy difficulty.
- Comparing how many students from each group pass the easy and normal difficulty.
- Comparing how many students from each group pass all the difficulties in the exam, scoring a minimum of 18 scores with a minimum of 6 scores for each difficulty.

As the test using a linear progression of questions becoming gradually more difficult every 10 questions. It is an opportunity to see whether student from each group has the adequate knowledge to progress into more advance subject or they only specialized at parts of the exam. For example, one student might have intensive knowledge of advanced information technology but lack a basic understanding of information security. Another student, on the other hand, might have knowledge in basic and intermediate information technology but lack understanding in advanced knowledge. The passing line is more than 60% correction rate (6 out of 10) for the student to pass each part.

Forth, Result Analysis. The test result of both group A and B will be totaled and compared to prove that the hypothesis of this research that is: "By gamifying learning process will improve the motivation of participant which will lead to improvement in test score for security awareness exam comparing to the test score of those who study by traditional means" holds true. From there, depending on which hypothesis held true or not, we will analyze the factor that contributed to the result of the experiment, examining possible improvement(s), and reach the conclusion of this experiment.

Due to the ongoing COVID-19 pandemic and subsequent lockdown mandate, we made a backup plan in case the original plan to conduct experiments with a gathering of people together may not be possible. Paper examination and reading material will be provided via online form and file transferring. The videogame will be played by sharing the application and played in a limited timeframe as planned. Additionally, the target group may change to those with Computer Science knowledge or related fields with at least a bachelor's degree and similar age.

4 Result

The test was conducted on two separate occasions, both tests divided participants equally into two groups: A and B.

In the first test, with a student from the same coursework and academic years as a participant. Observation of students from Group A ("Gamified") showed a positive response and overall interest toward gamification platform with approximately a third of the group express the idea of binding difficult topic with videogame interesting. Nevertheless, the average scores of both groups shown in Fig. 5 are comparatively similar with students from both groups achieved passing scores (more than 60%) on Part I and Part II of the test, while retaining between 40–60% average score on Part III of the test. Both groups have shown great understanding of the material covered in Part I with an average score of 75% with a declining score continue Part II of 60% and III of 40%.

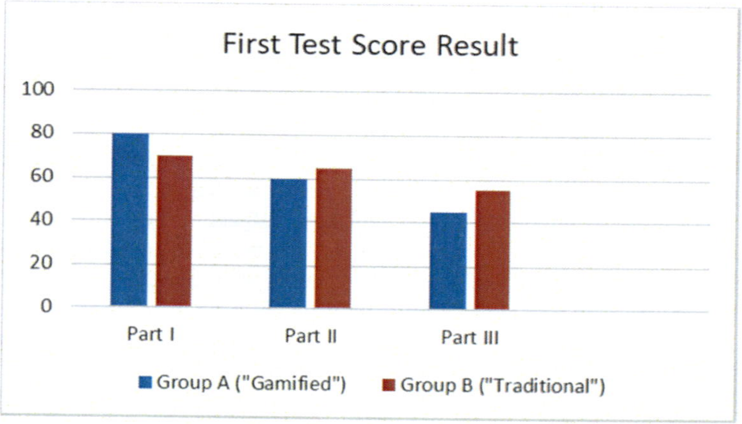

Fig. 5. An average test score of both groups in the first test

In the second test, a student from the same coursework but varied academic years as a participant. Observation of students from Group A ("Gamified") showed an identical positive response and overall interest as the first test although about half of the group express the binding of a difficult topic as interesting with other half commented that the gamified platform might not be able to provide enough material to an otherwise elaborate topic as information security. As a matter of score, the average scoring of both groups shown in Fig. 6 is comparatively similar, in the same manner as the first test. However, both groups showed an increase in average score across all three parts, with an average score of 80% on Part I and around 60% on Part II and III. The reason likely contributed toward the presence of the senior student in both groups who potentially have a prior lesson in topics covered in this test.

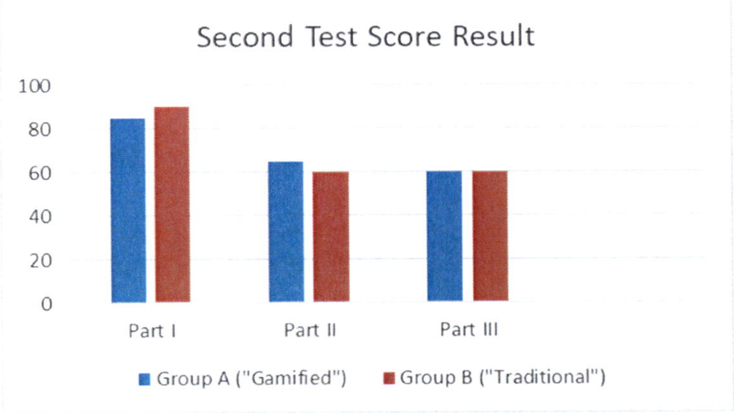

Fig. 6. An average test score of both groups in the second test

5 Conclusion

Through this experiment, it is observed that while most students found using the gamified platform as a great and interesting learning tool for information security, it offers limited benefits in terms of improving student scores when compared to traditional teaching. Mayhap due to the style of the game used in this research did not reflex all participant fondness and are more streamlined than lessons found in paper-based materials, which called for future research into developing more generally accepted gameplay and how to integrate more lessons into videogame while at the same time balancing the fun aspect. However, if we take into consideration other factors such as enjoyment and attentiveness. The gamified platform has achieved much more compared to the traditional learning method in both educational and fun. Overall, the result has shown that gamified platforms can be applied and use as an effective tool in a higher education environment to increases student engagement and study efficiency.

References

1. Wikipedia, Gamification. https://en.wikipedia.org/wiki/Gamification. Accessed 22 Aug 2021
2. Goffman, E.: Encounters: Two Studies in the Sociology of Interaction. Bobbs-Merrill Company Inc., Oxford (1961)
3. ASCENTOR, What's the difference between cyber security and cyber resilience – and why does resilience matter? https://insights.ascentor.co.uk/blog/2019/05/whats-the-difference-between-cyber-security-and-cyber-resilience-and-why-does-resilience-matter. Accessed 1 Aug 2021
4. Analyticsindiamag, Difference Between Cybersecurity & Information Security, 3 May 2020. Available: https://analyticsindiamag.com/difference-between-cybersecurity-information-security/. Accessed 1 Aug 2021
5. Huex Online, Cyber threats and how to maintain cyber integrity and security (2020). Available: http://huexonline.com/knowledge/28/557/. Accessed 20 Aug 2021

6. Dixit, R.K., Nirgude, M.A., Yalagi, P.S.: Gamification: An Instructional Strategy to Engage Laerners, pp. 138–141. IEEE (2018)
7. Hammerschall, U.: A gamification framework for long-term engagment in education based on self determination theory and the transtheoretical model of change. In: IEEE Global Engineering Education Conference (EDUCON) (2019)
8. Prochaska, J.O., Di Clemente, C.: The transtheoretical approach. In: Oxford Series in Clinical Psychology, pp. 147–171, Oxford (2005)
9. Laskowski, M.: Implementing gamification techniques into university study path - a case study. In: IEEE Global Engineering Education Conference (EDUCON) (2015)
10. Wong, C.-K., Lee, C.-S.: A better understanding of how gamification can help improve digital lifestyles. In: 22nd International Conference on Virtual System & Multimedia (VSMM) (2016)
11. Wikipedia, Overspecialization, 31 December 2020. https://en.wikipedia.org/wiki/Overspecialization. Accessed 15 May 2021
12. Pratarelli, M.E.: Extinction and overspecialization: the dark side of human innovation. Mankind Q. **48**, 83–98 (2007)
13. Daineko, Y., Ipalakova, M., Tsoy, D., Bolaov, Z., Yelgondy, Y., Shaipiten, A.: Development of the educational software based on a game engine. In: 2018 IEEE 12th International Conference on Application of Information and Communication Technologies (AICT) (2018)
14. Martinez-Tejada, L.A., Gonzalez, A.P., Yoshimura, N., Koike, Y.: Videogame design as a elicit tool for emotion recognition experiments. In: 2020 IEEE International Conference, pp. 4320–4326 (2020)
15. S. c. p. 2. m. g. i. 2. t. i. 2019, Venture Beat, 13 January 2020. https://venturebeat.com/2021/01/13/steam-2020-review/. Accessed 15 May 2021
16. Game industry biz, What is happening with video game sales during coronavirus, 20 March 2020. gamesindustry.biz/articles/2020–03–28-what-is-happening-with-video-game-sales-during-coronavirus. Accessed 1 Aug 2021
17. TechSauce, Gaming conversations increase 97% on Twitter in Thailand, 3 August 2020. https://techsauce.co/en/pr-news/gaming-conversations-increase-97-twitter-in-thailand. Accessed 1 Aug 2021
18. Zhu, L.: The psychology behind video games during COVID-19 pandemic: a case study of animal crossing: new horizons. Hum. Behav. Emerging Technol. **3**, 157–159 (2020)
19. Foreman, A.: Glory kill by glory kill, 'Doom Eternal' is helping me feel less angry, Mashable, 21 March 2020. https://mashable.com/article/doom-eternal-review. Accessed 1 Aug 2021
20. Information Systems Audit and Control Association (ISACA), Cybersecurity Fundamental. https://www.isaca.org/-/media/info/csxf-practice-quiz/index.html. Accessed 15 May 2021
21. Sprahil, User Information Security Awareness! Trivia Quiz, 5 January 2021. https://www.proprofs.com/quiz-school/story.php?title=user-information-security-awareness. Accessed 15 May 2021

A Study on the Application of Collaborative Learning by Using Moment Cam to Improve Mathematics Acceptability

Ting-Sheng Weng[1], Mu-Fen Chao[2], and Chien-Kuo Li[3](✉)

[1] Department of Business Administration, National Chiayi University, Chiayi City 600, Taiwan
[2] Department of Business Administration, Tamkang University, New Taipei City 251, Taiwan
[3] Department of Information Technology and Management, Shih Chien University, Taipei City, Taiwan
ckli@mail.usc.edu.tw

Abstract. In the workplace, mathematics is a fundamental skill. Mathematics is very important to business management students, and it is used as a tool in almost all four-year college courses. However, the number of students who can truly enjoy mathematics should be very small among business management students. The integration of information software into teaching has become an important trend, and the charm of anime for young people should not be underestimated. Therefore, in this study, the university students were given the opportunity to create a digital textbook for Grade 12 mathematics in which they were transformed into anime characters. In addition, the students were able to learn how to use the new software to create digital teaching materials by using group work and peer-to-peer collaboration. The study was conducted with a valid population of 36 students, and a focus group and questionnaire were used to collect information. It was found that by searching, developing the content, designing the questions and solutions, and explaining the origin of the formulae, the participating students were given the opportunity to learn the mathematics of Grade 12 again, gaining positive thoughts about mathematics and increasing their enthusiasm and willingness to learn mathematics. In addition, the study used the app "Moment Cam", which none of the study participants had experience with, for peer-to-peer collaborative learning. It was found that collaborative learning is also a good way to learn to use new tools.

Keywords: Moment cam · Mathematics · Collaborative learning · App

1 Introduction

In the workplace, mathematics is a basic capability and an auxiliary tool used in services, finance, and other industries [1]. Many occupations apply mathematics knowledge, and more than half of high-paid workers use mathematics that is more advanced than basic arithmetic in their daily routine work; 1/10 workers with lower income need to use higher arithmetic abilities when working [2, 3]. Thus, the importance of mathematics cannot be ignored in the development of work abilities.

© Springer Nature Switzerland AG 2021
Y.-M. Huang et al. (Eds.): ICITL 2021, LNCS 13117, pp. 365–376, 2021.
https://doi.org/10.1007/978-3-030-91540-7_38

Mathematics is of great significance to the students of Business Management Colleges as it is used as a tool in almost all four-year college courses, and the Department of Finance is one of the departments that rely most on mathematical tools. The junior-grade courses of the Department of Finance include basic business management subjects, such as Economics, Accounting, and Statistics, while the middle and senior-grade courses include courses about the advanced application of mathematics, such as Money Management and Banking, Fixed Income Securities, Equity Securities, Futures, and Option Pricing, thus, mathematical ability is necessary for junior to senior grades.

For graduates of the Department of Finance, their future employment industries may include futures and securities, investment consulting, banking, and insurance, thus, whether at school or work, mathematics will always be an important tool for them. As the graduates of the Department of Finance are in great demand in the job market, their incomes are above the average, and some students are guided by their parents in high school to choose to study in the Department of Finance. However, among the junior-grade students of the Department of Finance, there are still many students whose mathematics scores are below their average in high school, and after being admitted to the Department of Finance, they still lack interest in learning subjects that use mathematics. This study aimed at exploring whether the use of animated elements to compile digital teaching materials can increase such students' interest in mathematics learning and whether collaborative learning through group work is conducive to improving their learning effect when compiling digital teaching materials.

2 Literature Review

2.1 Impact of Anime and Manga on Learning

As they are diversified and interesting, comics have become a popular art form all over the world [4]. Comics show characters and their facial features in an extremely exaggerated and distorted way [5]. With the development of science and technology, an easy-to-operate photorealistic comics generation system was created, which enables the public to generate personalized photorealistic comics through simple operations. This system shortens the time and reduces the complicated process of hand painting, and can also be used in TV programs, cartoons, the internet, newspapers, magazines, digital entertainment, teaching, and other fields. By simply inputting photos into EnforManga's interactive system, photos can be converted into comics, and multiple photos can even be input at the same time to form a comic book [6, 7]. NPR (Non-Photorealistic Rendering) technology has gained more attention in recent years, and is used to make photorealistic photos into images in the style of hand painting [8]. Compared with real imaging, NPR mainly shows aesthetic feeling and artistic quality.

Learning interest is a key in the learning process, and if learners' interest can be stimulated in the learning process, it will help to improve their problem-solving abilities [9–11]. When learning mathematics, complex narration or problem-solving steps often seem unintelligible, which makes students perplexed, confused, or even give up, and lessens their interest in learning mathematics. Anime and manga can bring better illustrations and explanations than words for the complicated and unintelligible steps presented in a narration, which not only provides learners with more information, it also make it easier for people to understand [12, 13]. A growing number of peer-reviewed articles across the disciplines report that activities involving manga, graphic novels, and cartoons stimulate engagement and enjoyment in learning, helps students to memorize and clarify key concepts, and stimulates critical thinking [14]. As anime and manga-assisted instruction can make course content more lively and interesting, it makes students more interested in learning. As they are not limited by time or place, students whose scores are below the average can practice repeatedly with anime and manga-assisted teaching materials, which can help them improve their learning effects and understand concepts [13].

2.2 Specify Assignments for Collaborative Learning

School assignments are indispensable in the learning process, an essential part of teaching activities, and important to help students learn and grow [15]. According to [16], if school assignments are properly planned and executed, they can effectively enable students to take the initiative to arrange their time, cultivate their sense of responsibility, and increase their independent decision-making skills [17]. In addition, school assignments can bring many benefits. For students, school assignments can verify their achievements and understanding of course content, deepen their impression of the course, guide their learning direction, and highlight the focus of the course, meaning that students can learn by themselves, develop their interest in learning, and find suitable learning methods. For teachers, assigning some courses as homework enables teachers to interpret the course content more efficiently, and identify the areas that students need to strengthen [18]. Interesting and creative assignments will allow students to experience the fun of seeking knowledge while enhancing their capabilities [19].

In addition to traditional paper-based homework, with the progress of science and technology, electronic homework is becoming more and more popular. Tan and Liu [20] discussed the effect of electronic homework, and found that it can help students deepen their learning impression and transform the core scientific concepts of the teaching materials into knowledge of their own. The best advantages of electronic assignments include convenience, variety, and making students learn independently.

"Collaborative learning" is an umbrella term for a variety of educational approaches that involve joint intellectual efforts by students, or students and teachers together. Usually, students work in groups of two or more, mutually search for understanding, solutions, or meanings, or create a product. While collaborative learning activities vary widely, most center on students' exploration or application of course material, and not simply the teacher's presentation or explication of it [21]. Collaborative learning includes two types: learning together with peers and learning together with teachers and students. Some scholars have put forward relevant arguments for learning with peers. During the process of learning by observing peers, people with high, average, and low skills have dual roles as instructors and learners: people with high achievements and skills teach those with average and low knowledge and skills [22]. Also, during this time, the learning situation of those with average and low achievements can be known. Peers can grow up synchronously by observing and helping each other [23]. In the process of peers working together to complete group works, whether through interpersonal interaction or observing and learning, they can achieve the goal of learning while also developing social skills, such as cooperation with others, listening, communication, and compromise [23–26].

Comics and anime are good memories for many people from their childhood. According to relevant literature, integrating anime and manga into teaching, and letting learners enter interesting and meaningful visual learning scenes, should help to improve their learning interest and effect. Collaborative learning can enrich participants' knowledge synchronously and improve their learning effect. This study introduced anime and manga to the teaching materials of junior-grade students in the Department of Finance, and used interesting and electronic multimedia group work to conduct collaborative learning and observe its influence on students learning interest and effect.

3 Research Process

This study applied peer-to-peer collaborative learning through group assignments, and evaluated the learning method. The purpose of the evaluation was not only to check assignments, but to understand students' learning conditions, promptly motivate students, increase their enthusiasm and confidence in learning, and cultivate their self-awareness, reflection, and progress [27]. The research subjects and related steps are described as follows.

3.1 Research Subjects

This study took a total of 40 freshmen from the Department of Finance of a national university in mid-south part of Taiwan as the subjects, and divided them into 13 groups, including one group of 4 people and the remaining groups of 3 people per group. However, during the study, the group of 4 people quit, thus, there were 36 valid subjects, divided into 12 groups.

3.2 Research Method

Focus groups interviews and a questionnaire survey were conducted to explore the learning experience of the participants. When deciding the contents of the group work, the focus group method was used to collect opinions. The questionnaire survey was conducted in Week 4 and Week 9 of this study, and open-ended questions were designed to understand the participants' experience and self-assessment in the study.

3.3 Research Assignment

Before using digital teaching materials, it is necessary to know more about the influence of employing electronic teaching materials on teaching and learning [28–30]. As the subjects had little contact with calculus, statistics, economics, or accounting, they may not be able to compile the digital teaching materials. Therefore, it was decided to take senior high school mathematics as the theme of the designated assignment.

This study collected opinions from the subjects through focus groups, and after discussions, it was decided that the theme of group work was to let students make digital teaching materials for "Mathematics of Grade 12". During the discussion of the focus groups, many mentioned and agreed that "Mathematics of Grade 12 is a basic course that connects with college courses, and is the foundation of mathematics for college students, thus, its importance cannot be ignored" and "Mathematics of Grade 12 is still familiar to me, but it is a challenging task to present mathematics with comics, which is worth thinking about." Among the 40 subjects, as based on the self-assessment, 29 believed that they did not perform well on mathematics in Grade 12, accounting for 72.5%; 33 thought that they did not like mathematics in high school, accounting for 82.5%; 23 believed that they did not perform well and did not like mathematics in Grade 12, accounting for 57.5%. All the subjects studied "Mathematics of Grade 12" in high school, and most of them considered it a subject that would make students feel stress.

Each group had 9 weeks to complete the assignment, and the content of their report must include digital photorealistic anime and manga teaching materials covering all chapters of "Mathematics of Grade 12". During these 9 weeks, each group was required to discuss their works with their professor every week, where the professor could raise suggestions for modification, and share the progress and content of the groups, but was not permitted to evaluate the contents until the students had finished. Figure 1 shows the flow chart of discussing the assignment with the subjects.

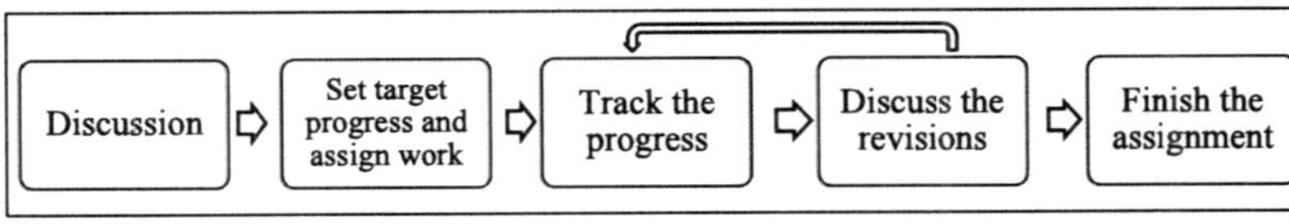

Fig. 1. Flow chart of discussion with students.

The once a week homework review and evaluation allowed the professor to observe the students' understanding and mastery of the content, as well as detect any changes in their mood and attitudes. Weekly evaluations were intended to understand the differences in each student's personality and protect students' self-confidence and self-esteem. By giving such regular evaluations, students could understand the direction of their progress through constant revisions, and then, make more complete works.

When making the digital photorealistic anime and manga teaching material for the "Mathematics of Grade 12" group assignment, the subjects used free downloadable App "Moment Cam", "Color Manga Camera", and "Comic Sketch Camera", as these APPs can deform, exaggerate, and make photos into manga, which are effects evolved from photo retouching software. According to [31], "photo retouching" refers to using digital tools on computers or mobile devices to retouch and edit digital photos to improve the shooting effect, such as adjusting the light and tone, removing defects, etc. In the past, retouching skills required professional knowledge, which limited the application to celebrities, advertisements, modelling, etc. However, with the development of the digital age and the progress of science and technology, it has gradually spread to the general public, and contemporary software, such as "Moment Cam", which turns users into cartoon characters, has become popular social software. Ren, the founder of the "Moment Cam" App, believed that it is so simple to operate the App that users can easily make cartoon images and share them with others, which can help people show humor and personality, become closer to each other, and create more happiness in life [32].

The "Moment Cam", "Comic Sketch Camera", and "Color Comics Camera" Apps used in this study can be downloaded and used for free, thus, it is very convenient for students, and with no economic burden. In terms of functions, in addition to having cartoon presentations in color or black and white, an image can be matched with words and sound effects to increase its liveliness and diversity, just like the original presentation of photorealistic comics. Table 1 shows the progress of making photorealistic anime and manga mathematics teaching materials.

Table 1. Progress of making photorealistic anime and manga mathematics teaching materials.

Work	Week 1–2	Week 3	Week 4	Week 5	Week 6	Week 7	Week 8	Week 9
Project execution	Select the math teaching materials of Grade 12, and collect relevant contents and design topics	Design teaching materials, including formulas and principle descriptions	Edit example questions	Shoot the classroom scene	Design actions in different scenes	Discuss the revision	Discussion of details of the revision	Make the final revision and submit the report
Making cartoon characters	Try to make personal cartoon character	Try to make a variety of lively and funny expressions of personal cartoon characters	Peer observation of personal cartoon characters	Place cartoon characters in the real-life tables and chairs in the classroom scene	Background processing	Special effects integration		
Software application and Peer observation			Put cartoon characters into the digital teaching material	Peer observation of each group's progress	Peer observation of each group's progress	Peer observation of each group's progress	Peer observation of each group's progress	

The Apps, such as Color Manga Camera and Moment Cam, as well as the making steps and technologies of the software, were provided to the participating students. After each group selected their Grade 12 teaching material, they started creating their personal cartoon characters, as shown in Table 1. The students first took their photos with smartphones, and then, applied the abovementioned Apps to make the photos into static and live personal cartoon images with different styles, which were then input into their digital mathematics homework as characters. The photos of the teaching material authors were produced only with the consent of the parties concerned, as shown in Fig. 2.

When making their personal cartoon characters, members of the same group did not have to take group photos at the same time or place, instead, members were encouraged to take their selfies, make them into cartoon characters with distinct personal styles, and then, uniformly upload the characters to Facebook and place them in the same classroom scene, as shown in Fig. 3. As "Moment Cam" is a customized App with many facial expressions to choose from, each group member could choose various facial expressions, such as joy or confusion, and match the plot developments with vivid character movements according to their preference, as shown in Fig. 4. Finally, the cartoon characters, playing the role of students, were placed into the classroom scenes, and integrated through PowerPoint to make the digital photorealistic anime and manga mathematics teaching materials.

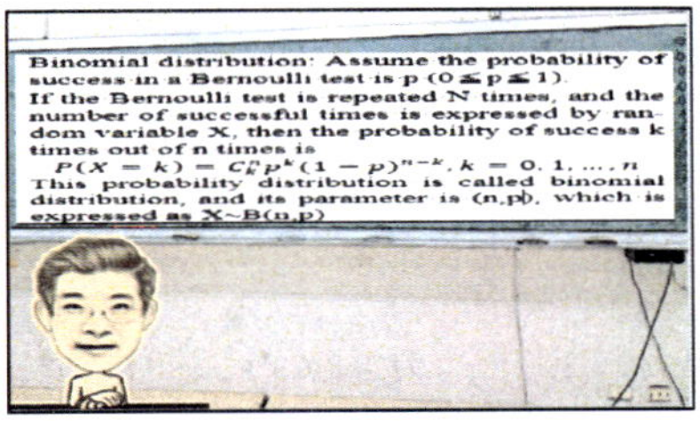

Fig. 2. Photorealistic cartoon characters placed into classroom scenes.

Fig. 3. Photorealistic cartoon characters placed into classroom scenes.

Fig. 4. Various possible reactions, facial expressions, and movements of students.

The duration of this study was 9 weeks. At the end of Week 4, each group presented a draft of their digital teaching materials. At that time, the first questionnaire survey was conducted to collect the subjects' participation experience with open questions. From Week 5, each group watched the digital teaching materials designed by other groups, and then, revised their work. In Week 9, when the assignment was submitted for presentation, the second questionnaire survey was conducted to collect the subjects' participation experience with open questions.

4 Results

In the first questionnaire survey in Week 4, regarding the subjects who originally disliked mathematics and believed that their mathematics performance in Grade 12 was poor, the experience of making the digital Grade 12 teaching material using photorealistic anime and manga was summarized, as follows:

1. We could think about how to make boring mathematics attractive from different angles, which can train students to think in many ways.
2. Presenting the results in a way that I had thought about not only made me know more about the application of the whole mathematical formula, but also greatly interested me to learn more.
3. The basic application of mathematics is wide in daily life. If we can learn it easily, we can reduce our aversion to it.
4. I like drawing, but I usually can't draw the feeling I want. With these Apps, I can make the pictures I want.
5. I like reading comics, and I can draw pictures myself. I can express my desired results more vividly through these Apps.
6. Comics can present the message with very simple images, and combining them with mathematics can make boring mathematics easier to understand.
7. I am not interested in static comics or hand painting, but the presentation of anime and manga can arouse my great interest.
8. I am not good at drawing, but I can make different effects through the Apps, which is a method that can get twice the result with half the effort.

Their experiences of group collaborative learning, individual learning, and using new technology to make digital teaching materials are, as follows:

1. At the beginning, only simple technical modifications were made, and the finished draft was relatively rough, so I began to study the software. Although it was hard, it also made me learn one more software.
2. For both work and the report, we must have certain steps and processes, or we will mess up our plans and thoughts, and fail to present the best report.
3. It helped me learn to stand in the position of others, think for others, respect their opinions, and know how to communicate and coordinate with group members.
4. By absorbing the teacher's advice and revising each assignment, I found more production techniques in the process.
5. When doing group work, I felt imbalanced because of the uneven division of labor, but I also realized that able people can do more work, and there is no right or wrong.

From Week 5, each group provided works for their peers to observe and learn from each other. Each group communicated autonomously and conducted peer-to-peer collaborative learning. In Week 9, the assignment was submitted and a questionnaire survey was conducted to learn about the experiences of the students that participated in the research. The general reactions are, as follows:

1. By observing the works of other groups, I could see the relative deficiencies in my group, and I also humbly asked others for their production methods, and members of other groups lent a helping hand.
2. The teacher once said, “A successful report is to attract the attention of the audience”, so we aimed at it. Our peers’ focus gave us the greatest affirmation.
3. Through the report, I not only learned the knowledge of mathematics, but also learned how to cooperate with my peers, and realized that the report was not just for homework submission, but also for myself.
4. This report allowed me to learn the importance of taking suggestions, and the revised works were more complete. Teachers were added to the contents of the report and became the main role, which also added interest to the report.
5. Integrating photorealistic anime and manga, and comics into mathematics teaching materials gives boring mathematics a brand-new and avant-garde interpretation. If mathematics can be taught in this way in the future, it will surely get many positive responses and reduce the gap between students and mathematics.

5 Conclusions and Suggestions

5.1 Conclusions

With the coming of the digital age, teaching models are also changing, and with the continuous development and innovation of information technology, textbooks will gradually develop from the original paper to the electronic version [20]. Mathematics is an important subject that is recognized as the foundation of science, technology, and social development, and closely connected with life. However, it is also the subject students feel most afraid of, which may be because of its boring and complex content. Students often start to dislike mathematics in Grade 4 or 5 of elementary school, and mathematics in junior high school is more difficult, which makes students even less confident in their abilities. Many students in senior high school even choose an art class to avoid mathematics, and finally, give up mathematics completely after the college entrance examination [33, 34].

This study aimed at Grade 12 mathematics, and combined mathematics with digitalization to allow junior college students to compile the digital mathematics teaching materials of Grade 12. Through this assignment, the subjects learned how to apply new software together through peer-to-peer collaborative learning, and compiled the digital photorealistic anime and manga mathematics teaching materials.

In the nine-week research process, through findings and compiling teaching materials, designing questions and solutions, and explaining the origin of formulas, the participating students who disliked or believed that they did not learn mathematics well in Grade 12 had the opportunity to study it again, and they became more positive about mathematics, thus, enhancing their enthusiasm and interest in mathematics.

This study applied new Apps to carry out peer-to-peer collaborative learning. In order to understand the functions of “Moment Cam” and its effects, group members carried out collaborative learning within groups and explored together in the early stage by learning from each other. After 4 weeks, the members of each group gradually developed similar abilities and thinking, and then, peer observations were available to each group for the students to learn and communicate, thus, each group learned skills they lacked, drew inspiration, and learned from each other to pursue results with better quality. Moreover, it also stimulated students' innovation and positivity and improved the learning effect. For learning how to apply new tools, apart from one-way interpretation, collaborative learning is a good learning method.

5.2 Suggestions

Regarding the complicated steps presented in mathematics narration problems, the effect of anime and manga can bring better illustration and explanation than words, and provide learners with more information that is easier to understand [12, 13]. This study compiled the digital anime and manga teaching materials of "Mathematics of Grade 12". After peer evaluation and observation, it was considered that anime and manga helped to clarify the concepts that were difficult to understand in the past. Perhaps physics and chemistry courses, which are also difficult for students to understand, can compile digital photorealistic anime and manga teaching materials to facilitate course learning.

Anime and manga are attractive even to children. While this study produced only digital photorealistic anime and manga teaching materials to motivate Grade 12 students to learn mathematics, it proposed expanding the range to Grade 11, Grade 10, Junior High School, and Elementary School, to help students learn and develop their interest in mathematics.

Acknowledgments. The authors appreciate the comments of the review committee. This research was financially supported by the Ministry of Science and Technology under grant no. MOST 108-2511-H-415-0017-MY2.

References

1. Ma, H.L.: A study on mathematics knowledge required by students of business studies in university of science and technology for employment. In: Proceedings of Symposium on External Connection of Mathematics, pp. 1–33 (2012)
2. Stein, S.K.: Strength in Numbers: Discovering the Joy and Power of Mathematics in Everyday Life. Wiley, New York (1996)
3. Ma, H.L., Wu, D.B., Lee, Y.S., Lee, J.R.: External connection of mathematics: Mathematics and attitude to the vocation of service. National Science Council project, NSC100-2511-S275-001-MY3, pp. 1–13 (2013)
4. Lai, Y.C.: Automatic multilingual manga processing framework. National Science Council project, MOST109-2221-E011-129-MY3, p. 1 (2021)
5. Feng, X.F., Pan, X.: Generating algorithm of portrait cartoon based on feature deformation. J. Zhejiang Univ. Technol. **3**, 278–281 (2010)
6. Tobita, H., Shibasaki K.: EnforManga: interactive comic creation using drag-and-drop and deformation. In: Proceedings of 11th IEEE International Symposium on Multimedia, pp. 269–274 (2010)
7. Way, D.L., Chiang, C.C.: Real-time portrait manga video rendering from facial tracking. National Science Council Project, NSC 100-2221-E-119-001, pp. 1–17 (2012)

8. Way, D. L.: The synthesis of realistic comic characters. National Science Council Project, NSC 99-2221-E-119-001, pp. 1–21 (2011)
9. Lin, L., Atkinson, R.K.: Using animations and visual cueing to support learning of scientific concepts and processes. Comput. Educ. **56**(3), 650–658 (2011)
10. Mayer, K.: Addressing students' misconceptions about gases, mass, and composition. J. Chem. Educ. **88**(1), 111–115 (2011)
11. Tsai, M.R., Su, K.D.: Visual media integrated into nutrition and health to assess students' learning performances. J. Technol. Eng. Educ. **47**(2), 58–84 (2014)
12. Baecker, R., Small, I.: Animation at the Interface. In: Laurel, B. (ed.) The Art of Human-Computer Interface Design, pp. 251–267. Addison-Wesley Publishing Company (1990)
13. Lu, S.Y., Lin, T.W.: Learning effects through the multimedia animation in teaching origami. J. Natl. Taichung Univ. Humanities Arts **27**(1), 111–130 (2013)
14. Van der Sluis, H.: Manga, graphic novels, and comics in higher education? New Vistas **7**(1), 24–30 (2021)
15. Shyu, M.L.: Extension of creative teaching-homework assigned by students. Educ. Monthly **276**, 40–41 (1990)
16. Connors, N.A.: Homework: a new direction. National Middle School Association, Columbus (1991)
17. Cheng, Y.L.: Use creative strategies to solve problems: the study about elementary students' homework problems. In: Theory and Practice Forum on Enhancing the Effectiveness of Remedial Teaching in Primary and Secondary Schools, pp. 121–140 (2012)
18. Chen, K.L.: Common memory in study-homework. Educ. Monthly **511**, 94–96 (2010)
19. Chou, L.W.: Based on textbooks, design colorful homework-development and research on homework resources of mathematics textbooks. Daguan Zhoukan **12**, 242–243 (2012)
20. Tan, H.T., Liu, Y.C.: Effects of electronic workbooks on students' learning attitude and learning achievement. Educ. Technol. Learn. **1**(1), 13–38 (2013)
21. Smith, B.L., MacGregor, J.T.: What is collaborative learning? In: Goodsell, A., Maher, M., Tinto, V., Smith, B.L., MacGregor J.T. (eds.) Collaborative Learning: A Sourcebook for Higher Education, Pennsylvania State University, USA, National Center on Postsecondary Teaching, Learning, and Assessment Publishing (1992)
22. Verba, M., Winnykamen, F.: Expert-novice interactions: Influence of partner status. Eur. J. Psychol. Educ. **7**(1), 61–71 (1992)
23. Fan, T.Y.: A study of the implementation of peer mentoring methodology in university of technology. J. Chihlee Inst. Technol. **35**, 259–290 (2015)
24. Cohen, E.G.: Restructuring the classroom: conditions for productive small groups. Rev. Educ. Res. **64**(1), 1–35 (1994)
25. Johnson, D.W., Johnson, R.: Leading the Cooperative School, 2nd edn. Interaction Book Company, Edina (1994)
26. Slavin, R. E.: Cooperative Learning, 2nd edn. A Simon & Schuster Company, Needham Heights (1995)
27. Pu, H.L.: A study on the evaluation of students' mathematics homework under the background of new curriculum. Kaoshi Zhoukan **48**, 87 (2010)
28. Connell, C., Bayliss, L., Farmer, W.: Effects of e-book readers and tablet computers on reading comprehension. Int. J. Instr. Media **39**(2), 131–140 (2012)
29. Kim, J.-H., Jung, H.: South Korean digital textbook project. Comput. Sch. **27**(3–4), 247–265 (2010)
30. Woody, W.D., Daniel, D.B., Baker, C.A.: E-books or textbooks: Students prefer textbooks. Comput. Educ. **55**(3), 945–948 (2010)
31. Chen, I. A., Huang, W. Y.: More than beauty – The relationship between selfie editing and pleasure. In: Papers of the 2016 Annual Meeting of China Communication Society, 05C1, pp. 1–21 (2016)

32. Shen, L.L.: Moment cam: the business model behind the hottest app. China Small Medium Enterprises **4**, 35–37 (2014)
33. Huang, M.H.: The spirit of the new curriculum of mathematics in elementary schools. In: New Curriculum of Mathematics in Elementary Schools (Junior Grade), Teachers' Seminar of Taiwan Province National Schools of the Ministry of Education, pp. 1–17 (1994)
34. Yang, K.H., Chang, C.E.: Development and evaluation of a situated math game with mastery learning strategy. Educ. Technol. Learn. **4**(2), 95–118 (2016)

Developing an Application for Teaching Mathematics to Children with Dyscalculia: A Pilot Case Study

Diana Carvalho[1,2], Tânia Rocha[1,2](✉), Paulo Martins[1,2], and João Barroso[1,2]

[1] UTAD - University of Trás-os-Montes e Alto Douro, Quinta de Prados, 5001-801 Vila Real, Portugal
{dianac,trocha,pmartins,jbarroso}@utad.pt
[2] INESC TEC, Rua Dr. Roberto Frias, 4200-465 Porto, Portugal

Abstract. Dyscalculia is a specific neurological affliction that disrupts a person's ability to understand and manipulate numbers. We intend to develop a serious game for children who attend primary school (up to 4th grade) and whose purpose is making the learning of basic mathematics (simple arithmetic) easier, by introducing specific mathematical problems and educational games that stimulate memory, among other aspects. To that end, we undertook a straightforward and preliminary evaluation of the serious game developed and present its results. Indeed, we believe that the findings of our pilot case study can be useful to determine some perceptions that may be vital to understanding the problems with teaching mathematics and the issues students face in this regard.

Keywords: Dyscalculia · Basic education · Mathematics · Serious games · Learning disability · Developmental disorders · Multimedia interfaces

1 Introduction

1.1 Dyscalculia

A child with dyscalculia can exhibit several symptoms, such as difficulty in recognizing numbers, in correlating numeric symbols ("5") with their corresponding word ("five"), or even in recognizing patterns and putting things in order. Furthermore, dyscalculia not only affects children in a school environment, but also in day-to-day activities, like struggling to remember distinct numbers (e.g. postal codes or telephone numbers), issues concerning money, distinguishing left from right, watching the clock and telling the time [1].

Developmental Dyscalculia (DD) in children is relatively common, with a prevalence of 3 to 6% in the school population and with high rates of comorbidities such as ADHD and dyslexia [1, 8]. In point of fact, there is a relevant correlation between mathematical challenges and the inability to read: it is estimated that 40% of dyslexics also have a mathematical disability [5].

© Springer Nature Switzerland AG 2021
Y.-M. Huang et al. (Eds.): ICITL 2021, LNCS 13117, pp. 377–386, 2021.
https://doi.org/10.1007/978-3-030-91540-7_39

Furthermore, children with dyscalculia exhibit general deficits in number processing, including access to verbal and semantic numerical information, counting points, reciting number sequences and writing numbers [6]. Despite this, children with dyscalculia but no reading disabilities presented average, and even above average, results in tasks involving phonological working memory, access to non-numerical verbal information, non-verbal intelligence, language skills and psychomotor skills [10].

In this paper, we explore the impact of an application created with the purpose of teaching mathematic with students from different school years. After briefly presenting the related work and discussing the importance of such an application, we describe the methodology used for this case study and its results. By reporting our observations, we throw some light on how children of different school years may take advantage of an application purposefully created to help teach mathematics and, as such, how these types of applications could help children with developmental dyscalculia.

1.2 Related Work

In this section, we briefly outline scientific background related to developmental dyscalculia and the importance of creating interfaces that can help children with these disorders.

Research showed that children with arithmetic difficulties performed poorly on a task that required the memorization of dynamic visual information [11]. These results are consistent with other findings [4], that report lower performance in children with arithmetic disabilities regarding the memory game Corsi Block Tapping test. Thus, deficits in working memory systems have contributed substantially to specific deficiencies in the construction of a number's cognitive representations, in the formation of concepts and procedures, and in the retrieval of arithmetic facts in children with DD [2, 3].

In another study [7], the aim was to assess the differences between strategy selection and information processing in children with and without mathematical disabilities, of the first and second school year. The chosen strategies and the time needed for the problem solving were recorded on an experimental basis and each was classified according to the association's strategy choice model. Based on performance, indexed by achievement test scores, the sample group with the learning disability (LD) was then subdivided and reclassified into two groups: an LD-enhanced group and an LD-no-change group (a group that did not show a great ability to work around problems). Nevertheless, there appeared to be no substantial differences between the two groups. The performance characteristics of the LD-no-change group, compared to the remaining group, included frequent errors in memory counting and retrieval, frequent use of an immature computational strategy, poor strategy choices, and a variable rate of information processing. These performance aspects were taken into account in terms of the strategy choice model and in terms of potential long-term memory deficits and working memory capacity.

During the research carried out, multiple applications were taken into account and analysed (Table 1) [12–14]. We concluded that none of the applications mentioned met all the necessary requirements for an improved learning by our target audience.

Hence, we want to create an easy-to-use application that tackles two challenges: (1) does not require constant adult supervision, but rather expects only assistance if needed;

Table 1. Comparison of several applications already in the market.

Application	Ease of use	Mathematical problems	Logical reasoning	Memorization	Daily activities	Portuguese language
Socratic	No	Yes	No	No	No	Yes
Photomath	No	Yes	No	No	No	Yes
Mental Math Practice	No	Yes	Yes	No	No	No
Flow Free	Yes	No	Yes	No	No	Yes*
Lumosity	No	Yes	Yes	No	No	Yes
NeuroNation***	No	No	No	Yes	Yes	Yes
Prodigy math game	-	-	-	-	No	**
Know abacus	Yes	Yes	No	No	No	Yes
Math & Logic - Brain Games: Preschoolers to age 10	No	Yes	Yes	No	No	Yes

Legend:
* Brazilian Portuguese,
** Not available in Portugal,
*** Not suitable for the age group (up to the fourth school year)

(2) has a simple and easy-to-understand vocabulary in which a child can understand any and all mathematical problems with no difficulty.

Also, as already mentioned, there are some situations where dyscalculia is associated with dyslexia, so we also intend to implement a reading function in order to simplify the problem's interpretation. Indeed, our research shows that the only application with this feature is NeuroNation. However, it is not suitable for our target audience.

For all the described reasons, and considering the ultimate reality of the applications currently available on the market, we intend to develop an application that meets all of the following requirements for an improved learning experience: be ease of use; support the Portuguese language; provide mathematical problems, logical reasoning, memorization exercises and daily activities.

2 Case Study

We divided the case study into two different phases: (1) usability evaluation of the interface developed; (2) accessibility assessment of the application. The adopted methodology consists of a quasi-experimental design with a qualitative focus. A non-probabilistic convenience sampling technique was used.

2.1 Participants

In order to carry out the usability testing, we contacted the Augusto Moreno School Group, located in Bragança, Portugal. As such, the functional prototype was tested at the Santa Comba de Rossas primary school. Fourteen students participated: two from the first grade, six from the second, one from the third and five from the fourth grade. We assessed if the participants were used to using a computer and a computer mouse for study purposes through a questionnaire with closed-ended questions, at the beginning of each test. Indeed, only one first grader was not used to using the computer to study. However, he was used to working with the computer on a general basis and, as such, that fact would not skew our results in terms of performance. Out of all of the participants, ten of them had not yet used a computer to specifically study mathematics.

2.2 Apparatus

The activities were performed individually, in a controlled environment, with a participant observer (which oriented the user in the task's fulfillment). All tasks were displayed on the computer screen. The following material resources were used: a computer monitor displaying the application, a computer mouse for interaction.

2.3 Application

The application was developed with precise requirements, which we describe next. Furthermore, a series of graphical assets were created for the branding of the application, such as a logo, icons and its graphical user interface.

Functional Requirements. In the application's homepage (see Fig. 1), the user has access to the main menu, where he/she can select the intended option: either "Challenges" or "Teaching Games".

On one hand, if the user selects the menu "Challenges", the following steps will take place: (1) a new screen will appear, in which the user can choose their school year (see Fig. 2), and thus corresponding level of difficulty ("1st grade", "2nd grade", "3rd grade", "4th grade"); (2) after selecting the intended option, the challenge begins, consisting of 5 multiple choice math problems related to the subject taught in the corresponding year (see Fig. 3); (3) at the end of each challenge, the application displays how many questions the user has answered correctly. Here, the user will have the option to repeat the challenge or exit to the homepage.

Fig. 1. Homepage featuring the main menu.

Fig. 2. Screen of the second level of the application, when selecting the option "Challenges".

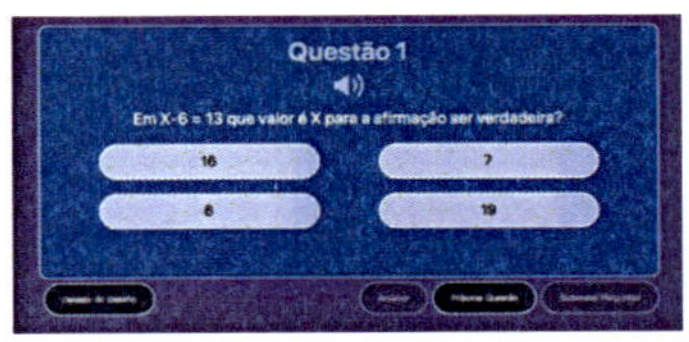

Fig. 3. Screen of the first question of the "Challenges" section, featuring multiple choice questions according to the level of difficulty selected.

On the other hand, if the user selects the menu "Teaching Games", the following steps will take place: (1) a new screen will appear in which the user can choose the educational game they want to play, either "Memory game", "Quick Calculation", "Association" (see Fig. 4); (2) after selecting one of the three games proposed, the game begins. The rules will depend on each educational game.

Fig. 4. Screen of the second level of the application, when selecting the option "Teaching Games" in the main menu.

When the user selects "Memory game", he/she can then choose the game's difficulty level (see Fig. 5), between easy (numbers between 1 and 8), medium (numbers between 1 and 16), and difficult (numbers between 1 and 20). Each difficulty level works by the same principle: the user has to find the corresponding pairs of all the numbers displayed, using memory as the main element and exercising it. Similarly, if the user selects "Quick Calculation", a new screen will display a sum and four possible answers (see Fig. 6). There is a time limit of 30 s for the game, but if the user correctly hits five questions in a row, this time will be extended. The game's difficulty also progressively increases each time the user hits a correct answer.

Fig. 5. Screen displaying the memory game's difficulty level.

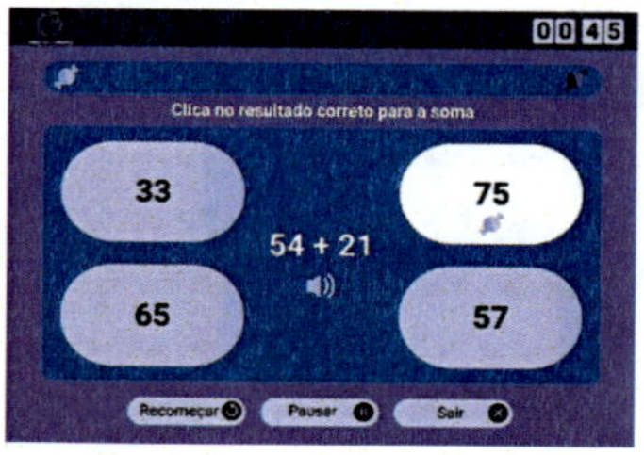

Fig. 6. Example of the quick calculation game layout.

Finally, if the user selects "Association", he /she will be asked to answer 10 problems following the same principle: associate cardinal numbers written in numerical form to their textual form and vice versa (see Fig. 7). Each question grants four answers, some of which are very similar to the right answer and others are quite different. At the end, the user submits the answers and the results obtained are displayed, as well as a motivating qualitative rating (see Fig. 8).

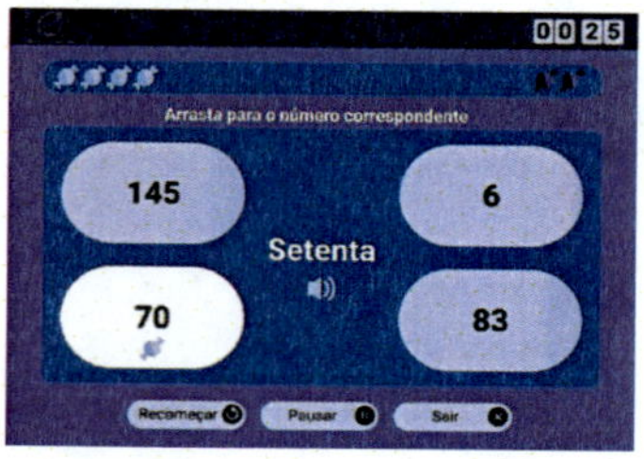

Fig. 7. Example of the association game layout.

Furthermore, throughout the application there must be a text-to-speech feature, where the user is provided with the possibility to hover the mouse over the words and hear them out loud.

Non-functional Requirements. The application was developed the specific non-functional requirements that dictated its correct use: (1) it must be in Portuguese; (2) it

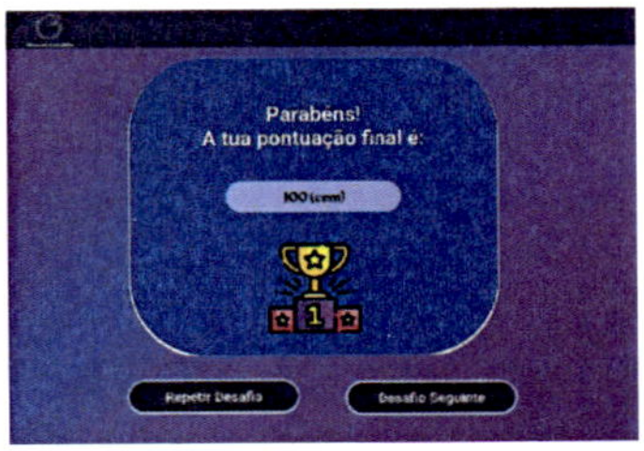

Fig. 8. Final screen with the results obtained by the user.

must have a responsive design; (3) it must only contain mathematical problems appropriate to the target audience's age group; and (4) it must have a simple and straightforward language.

2.4 Experimental Design

The experiment made use of a within-participant design. The methods of data collection used are directly related to the research methods adopted.

At the beginning and end of each test, a specific questionnaire suitable for each age group was completed. During the test, direct observation and text annotations were very important to register all observation data and oral comments made by the users. Additionally, we performed interviews after the tests to better understand the users' different attitudes and behaviors throughout interaction.

2.5 Procedures

We were given the opportunity to carry out the experiment for two hours during the school time. As such, due to the time constraints of having to perform the experiment with fourteen participants during only two hours, we decided to prioritize the application's challenges section, instead of the teaching games. Each task was explained before the participant initiated it. The users were asked to: (1) select the intended option on the main menu of the application; (2) complete the corresponding tasks.

2.6 Results and Discussion

As previously explained, a final questionnaire was delivered to the participants, in order to assess their opinion on the application. Indeed, most of the participants acknowledged their positive feedback on the matter, saying they really enjoyed using the application. Out of all of the participants, only two had a negative feedback on the application, as they did not like operating it. Similarly, when asked if the interface was easy to use, one participant reported it was not easy, two said that it was roughly easy, and the rest stated it was easy to use.

Furthermore, when inquired about the understanding of the questions and the text in general, only three participants had issues with the text comprehension. However, all of the participants acknowledged that the use of the application could, indeed, help them with the study of mathematics if used on a regular basis. Also, only three participants were not sure if they would use the application again in the future. Contrarily, the rest of the students would definitely use the application again if the opportunity was provided. Regarding completion times, students completed their challenge within 4 to 8 min total.

Post-test Analysis. After reviewing the results of the questionnaire, we can conclude that most of the students asserted that the application would be of great help for the study of mathematics, both inside and outside of the classroom context, regardless of the difficulties they may have experienced in their first use of the application.

Observations During the Test. During the experiment, there were some observations worth mentioning: most students had difficulties in realizing that it was mandatory to click the "Next Question" button in order to move on to the next question; most students had difficulty identifying the "submit answers" final button as mandatory for the challenge submission; a significant number of students needed an explanation about the exercises to be able to answer correctly. Even though the application's text was straightforward, the participants were not yet comfortable with the subjects.

Suggestions Provided by Students. At the end of each test, we felt it was imperative to ask students for their suggestions, in order to improve the application. Overall, 1st, 2nd and 4th graders said that the challenges' questions were too difficult and thus it would be good to have some easier queries, as the school subjects they had been taught so far were not sufficiently comprehensive. A 3rd grader felt that the questions for his grade should be more diversified and a 4th grader suggested that the application should allow some calculations to be executed, in order to facilitate the reasoning for the answer. As for the calculation game, a student suggested increasing the game time, as the 30-second limit was too short.

Accessibility Testing. Regarding accessibility, during the development of the application we resorted to the "Wave platform" (Web Accessibility Evaluation Tool) for testing. It has a set of assessment tools that identify errors and warnings, in order to perfect the accessibility for individuals with disabilities. Thus, several tests were carried out and changes were made at the programming level, in order to rectify any errors. The last tests performed in Wave for our application did not show any errors. "Warnings" were presented; however, they did not alter the application's functioning. Also, as the final prototype had already been evaluated in the Usability Test whilst still manifesting these warnings, we decided not to make any changes in terms of programming. They should be, nevertheless, resolved later when continuing with our research.

Final Remarks. Taking into account all the data collected from testing the prototype, we consider that there are some usability errors worth correcting, namely the buttons "Next Question" and "Submit Answers". Indeed, only one of the fourteen students automatically inferred their use without any help. This problem could be solved by changing the design of the buttons (from text to arrows), thus rendering the buttons more intuitive, or by making sure the application automatically heads over to the following questions after the user clicks on the correct answer. As for the remaining pages (homepage, challenge choice, etc.), all students understood their content and there were no issues using the buttons. Therefore, we can consider that there is no usability error in them. With regard to colours and text, there were no negative observations reported by the students. In fact, the students who had some sort of difficulty with the text had, in general, difficulty in reading. This problem was easily overcome with the application's text-to-speech feature.

3 Conclusions and Future Work

This exploratory investigation was intended to understand if an application developed for teaching mathematics could bring advantages to the students' daily study. Although it is not possible to assume the benefits of the application for children with dyscalculia, as it was not possible to carry out a usability test in this context, we can state that the application would be an asset in both individual or supervised study for basic education students. Indeed, the results obtained suggest that these types of applications have a lot of potential as a driving force in the struggle against developmental dyscalculia.

Regarding usability, although there were some problems when testing the functional prototype, it fulfills our initial expectations. Furthermore, with minor adjustments we could improve its usability and overcome specific issues on this subject. On the other hand, regarding accessibility, tested using Wave, we believe that in time it would also be possible to correct the found "warnings", thus achieving an even more accessible platform.

It is also important to report the suggestions and feedback provided by the school teacher. In this case, the teacher showed great interest in the application and even considered using it during classes or for home study. She pointed out that many of the problems encountered with regard to the questions' difficulty stemmed from the COVID-19 obligation for confinement, causing a delay in teaching the corresponding subjects during the first 4 months of the calendar year. She explained that, perhaps, if the experiment was performed at the end of the school year, the aforementioned problems would not be so significant.

For future work, we consider correcting the interface's design problems and perform a new, and complete, usability test, more focused on quantitative results. Also, the COVID-19 pandemic may become more controlled and allow for a school year completely on-site, minimizing the problems found due to the lack of these conditions.

Indeed, this pilot case study presents preliminary perceptions that may be vital to understanding the problems with teaching mathematics and the issues students face in this regard. Overall, we may infer that with some changes and a future testing of the prototype, the application would achieve a better outcome. Undeniably, the application created could be favorable to basic education students after the suggested changes.

Acknowledgments. We thank all people who directly or indirectly helped in this study, namely Santa Comba de Rossas primary school, Ana Dias, Ana Vale, Diana Alves, Diana Ferreira, José Ribeiro, Márcia Pires and Rui Vaz.

References

1. Koumoula, A., Tsironi, V., Stamouli, V., Bardani, I., Siapati, S., Annika, G., et al: An epidemiological study of number processing and mental calculation in Greek schoolchildren. J. Learn Disabil. **37**, 377–388 (2004)
2. Shalev, R. S., Auerbach, J., Manor, O., Gross-Tsur, V.: Developmental dyscalculia: prevalence and prognosis. Eur. Child Adolesc. Psychiatry **9**, S2–S58 (2000)
3. Geary, D.C.: Mathematical disabilities: cognitive, neuropsychological, and genetic components. Psychol. Bull. **114**(2), 345 (1993)
4. McLean, J.F., Hitch, G.J.: Working memory impairments in children with specific arithmetic learning difficulties. J. Exp. Child Psychol. **74**(3), 240–260 (1999)
5. Lewis, C., Hitch, G., Walker, P.: The prevalence of specific arithmetic difficulties and specific reading difficulties in 9- and 10-year old boys and girls. J. Child Psychol. Psychiatry **35**, 283–292 (1994)
6. De Smedt, B.; Gilmore, C.K.: Defective number module or impaired access? Numerical magnitude processing in first graders with mathematical difficulties. J. Exper. Child Psychol. **108**(2), 278–292 (2011)
7. Mussolin, C., De Volder, A., Grandin, C., Schlögel, X., Nassogne, M.C., Noël, M.P.: Neural correlates of symbolic number comparison in developmental dyscalculia. J. Cogn. Neurosci. **22**(5), 860–874 (2010)
8. Shalev, R: Developmental Dyscalculia. J. Child Neurol. **19**(10), 765–771 (2004)
9. Hannel, G.: Dyscalculia Action Plans For Successful Learning in Mathematics, 2nd edn. Routledge, New York (2013)
10. American Psychiatric Association: Diagnostic and Statistical Manual of Mental Disorders, DSM-5, 5th edn. American Psychiatric Publishing, Washington D.C. (2013)
11. Haberstroh, S., Schulte-Körne, G.: The diagnosis and treatment of Dyscalculia. Dtsch. Arztebl. Int. **2019**(116), 107–114 (2019). https://doi.org/10.3238/arztebl.2019.0107
12. Singh, M.: Top 10 must-have free apps for Dyscalculia. NumberDyslexia (2019)
13. Rohizan, R.: MathFun: A Mobile App for Dyscalculia Children. IOP Publishing (2020)
14. Torres-Carrión, P., Sarmiento-Guerrero, C., Torres-Diaz, J.C., Barba-Guamán, L.: Educational math game for stimulation of children with Dyscalculia. In: Rocha, Á., Guarda, T. (eds.) ICITS 2018. AISC, vol. 721, pp. 614–623. Springer, Cham (2018). https://doi.org/10.1007/978-3-319-73450-7_58

Innovative Technologies and Pedagogies Enhanced Learning

Analytical Skills in Statistical Applications Based on End-of-Term Students' Self-evaluations

Jane Lu Hsu(✉) and Melchior Antoine

National Chung Hsing University, Taichung 402202, Taiwan
jlu@dragon.nchu.edu.tw

Abstract. With big data and crowd computing in the contemporary business environment, the minimum requirement for a business graduate to locate a job includes the ability to work on data and delivering some meaningful preliminary results for decision making in management. The objectives of this study are as follows: (1) reveal students' end-of-term self-evaluations of statistical methods they feel comfortable in application; (2) categorize statistical models into various levels and then link students' end-of-term self-evaluations to understand students' confidence in statistical applications; and (3) evaluate the effects of problem-based learning (PBL) on student outcomes for the various subjects. Three courses are included in data generation: (1) Statistics (I) and (II), (2) Regression Analysis, and (3) Business Forecasting. In both Regression Analysis and Business Forecasting, PBL was applied, and term projects were required for students to practice their analytical skills in PBL exercises and projects. Results indicated that the more advanced the statistical courses students took, the more they perceive learning statistics as important. Moreover, students valued the importance of using statistical applications at work in the future higher if a more advanced course had been taken. Suggestions based on findings in this study are provided for instructors to enhance students' analytical skills in undergraduate statistical courses.

Keywords: Analytical skills · Statistical applications · Self-evaluations

1 Introduction

Fundamental analytical skills need to be provided by instructors in statistical courses in undergraduate business education. In conventional introductory statistical courses for business students, analytical skills are not emphasized in course materials, and generally the layout of textbooks in sequential order includes probabilities, discounted and continuous distributions, population parameters, point and interval estimates, hypothesis testing, analysis of variance, regression analysis, nonparametric analysis, and business forecasting [1]. Statistical concepts are built on theorems and formulae, and memorization and problem-solving using hand-held calculators are the standard learning process in introductory statistics [1].

© Springer Nature Switzerland AG 2021
Y.-M. Huang et al. (Eds.): ICITL 2021, LNCS 13117, pp. 389–396, 2021.
https://doi.org/10.1007/978-3-030-91540-7_40

In evaluating students' learning performance, instructor grading has been the most commonly applied method. Quizzes, assignments, participation, mid-term and final examinations are typical evaluation measures to account for students' final grades. In conventional teaching of statistical courses, it is understandable that students may not be trained to deal with empirical data using business analytical skills, which could be far reaching. However, we still do not know how wide that gap is.

With big data and crowd computing in the contemporary business environment, the minimum requirement for a business graduate to locate a job includes the ability to work on data and delivering some meaningful preliminary results for decision making in management. Conventional statistical courses are not able to equip students in fulfilling this goal due to (1) examples in statistical courses being over-simplified to ease the burden of teaching within a limited timeframe; (2) students not having the advantage to handle real data without learning how to practice the basics at first; (3) solving real-world issues using real data has not been the core objective of undergraduate statistical courses.

Therefore, in this study we sought to make use of problem-based learning (PBL) methods to improve student outcomes for three statistics-related courses.

2 Literature Review

There have been a number of studies on statistical education competencies/performance and attitudes in non-specialist students for students in courses such as business and the social sciences [2, 3]. It is believed that if students view statistics as important that it would lead to more positive attitudes and to greater competency [4]. Often statistics is seen by students as being too abstract and too impractical in their everyday lives [5]. However, business and management courses presumably provide an opportunity to demonstrate the practicality of statistical courses in the world of work. The courses taught in introductory business statistics if taught well may assist students in being competent in future employment.

It is also useful to measure how important students see statistical courses alongside their actual performance. Another interesting comparison is between students self-evaluated competencies in various statistical courses and their actual reported grades. Some research has demonstrated that students' attitude toward statistical courses may improve after the course [4].

Problem-Based Learning. PBL has been promoted as an effective method to improve student performance in higher education courses, including statistics-related courses [6–8]. PBL and associated teaching methods have grown in popularity as a result of advances in understanding how students learn, and it seeks to make students the central focus in learning approaches. In particular, PBL approaches tend to promote the idea that students should be seen as actively participating in their own learning as opposed to being passive receivers of knowledge [9]. The four principles of PBL include the following: constructiveness, self-directedness, collaboration, and contextuality [10]. Moreover, PBL approaches seek to focus learning within appropriate social contexts: Learning is seen as a communal activity, and teaching methods are designed in a manner that relies on real-world experience, examples, or contexts to teach students. This often means that student rely on prior experience or work-related experience, making this pedagogical approach ideal for adult learners preparing for the professional world [9].

PBL approaches, within this context, are seen as potentially effective for teaching statistics-related courses. One on the most common complaints or issues with teaching statistics is its abstract nature: Students often find it difficult to see the value of concepts learned in the world of statistics and how it applies to real-word situations [11]. PBL methods, by making use of scenarios or problems that are familiar to students, may help improve attitudes toward statistics and help ameliorate the "unapproachableness" of statistics [6, 7, 12]. For example, Yuliana and Firmansah demonstrated the effectiveness of PBL in improving the students' understanding toward statistics [13]. A number of studies have also demonstrated the effectiveness of PBL methods in improving students' performance [8, 12] or perception of the importance [14] of statistics.

In this study, we examine the outcomes of PBL methods for three statistics-related courses: namely, Statistics (I) and (II), Regression Analysis, and Business Forecasting.

2.1 Research Objectives

Based on the preceding literature review, the objectives of this study are as follows: (1) reveal students' end-of-term self-evaluations of statistical methods they feel comfortable in application; (2) categorize statistical models into various levels and then link students' end-of-term self-evaluations to understand students' confidence in statistical applications; and (3) evaluate the effects of PBL on student outcomes for the various subjects.

3 Research Methodology

This study is in the exploratory phase of utilizing students' end-of-term evaluations to reveal their confidence in applying statistical methods in practice. Three courses are included in data generation: (1) Statistics (I) and (II), (2) Regression Analysis, and (3) Business Forecasting.

Statistics (I) and (II) are core courses required for business students. Regression Analysis and Business Forecasting are elective courses for senior students. Statistics (I) and (II) are prerequisites for those taking Regression Analysis and Business Forecasting. Among all of these courses, Business Forecasting is the most advanced course in statistical training before students' graduation.

PBL was applied during the class. This included using cases and problems to teach students how to apply statistical models in a highly practical manner to solve an issue. In classes such as introductory statistics and regression analysis 1 h was allocated for each session to work on PBL training, which included computer lab assignments and other cases.

Students were asked to fill out a questionnaire in the last session before final examinations. The purpose of the study was thoroughly explained to students before handing out questionnaires. The questionnaire sought to acquire information on students' perception of the importance of learning statistics and the importance of using statistical implications at work. A scale ranked from 1 to 10 was used, with 10 representing the most important. Furthermore, students were asked to name the statistical methods they would feel comfortable with in application using an open-ended question. The questionnaires were filled out after the semester of each class.

Students were asked to rate the importance of analytical skills in the workplace on a Likert-type scale of 1–10. They were also asked to rate on a scale of 1–10 their future competitiveness in the workplace in terms of skills such as "the ability to think logically," the ability to solve problems," "analytical ability," and so on. Students were also asked to rate their current level of knowledge and skills in solving and understanding statistical problems, applying statistics in practice, inspecting peers work and providing feedback, and so on. Moreover, the questionnaire allowed students the opportunity to rank a number of statements about the likelihood of statistics being relevant to their life and career. The questionnaire is available upon request.

4 Results

In a class of more than 90 students, less than 5% refused to participate in the survey. Since there were no bonus points for filling out the questionnaire, the main reason for refusal was lack of interest in the survey. The total number of valid samples included 89 students from Statistics (I), 71 from Statistics (II), 18 from Regression Analysis, and 16 from Business Forecasting.

The PBL-based term projects used in the study are depicted in Table 1. They included subjects such as "Impulse Purchase of Sports Shoes and Its Linkage to Purchasing Channels," "Influences of Weather on Fruit Trading Prices and Quantities," and "Factors Influencing Popularities of YouTube Videos – Using Marvel." As can be seen, an effort was made to include subjects that students would typically express interest in.

Table 1. Models used in term projects in PBL

Course	Term projects	Models used
Regression analysis	Impulse Purchase of Sports Shoes and Its Linkage to Purchasing Channels	Multiple Regression
	Factors Influencing 30-Day Commercial Paper Rate in Secondary Financial Market in Taiwan	Stepwise Regression Autoregressive Model
	Death Caused by Vehicle Accidents Due to Road Conditions	Logistic Regression
	Influences of Weather on Fruit Trading Prices and Quantities	Stepwise Regression Multiple Regression
	Monthly Differences in Credit Card Charges for Target Customers	Multiple Regression
	Factors Influencing Airline Delays Using Regression Models	Multiple Regression

(*continued*)

Table 1. *(continued)*

Course	Term projects	Models used
Business forecasting	Forecasting Copper Prices in International Markets	ARIMA Seasonal ARIMA
	Hospitality Development in Taiwan	Exponential Smoothing ARIMA
	Factors Influencing Vehicle Accidents in Taichung City	Logistic Regression
	Factors Influencing Birth Rate in Taiwan	Stepwise Regression Exponential Smoothing
	Factors Influencing Popularities of YouTube Videos – Using Marvel Entertainment as an Example	Multiple Regression
	Forecasting NBA Championship in Playoffs	Logistic Regression

4.1 Evaluation of the Importance of Statistics-Related Subjects

In the questionnaire, students were asked to rank the importance of learning statistics and the importance of using statistical applications at work in the future using a scale that ranged from 1 to 10, with 10 being the most important. Results indicated that the more advanced the statistical courses students took, the more they perceive learning statistics as important. Moreover, students valued the importance of using statistical applications at work in the future higher if a more advanced course, such as Business Forecasting had been taken (Table 2). In short, there was a positive relationship between the level of advancement in a course and the Importance of Learning Statistics and the Importance of Using Statistical Applications at Work in the Future.

Table 2. Students' end-of-term importance evaluation

Courses	Importance of learning statistics	Importance of using statistical applications at work in the future
Statistics (I) & II	8.58	9.00
Regression analysis	8.78	9.28
Business forecasting	9.06	9.31

Note. Measured on a scale from 1 to 10, with 10 being the most important

4.2 Statistical Methods Students Feel Comfortable with in Application

As mentioned previously, in the questionnaire, students were asked to name the statistical methods they would feel comfortable with in application using open-ended questions.

In Statistics (I) and (II), the statistical methods named by students ranged from basic to mid-level. Analysis of variance and hypothesis testing were among the areas listed as options for students' responses. It should be mentioned that PBL learning methods were not employed in Statistics (I) and (II). Therefore, it was explained to students that they could fill out the relevant questions with the chapter/section titles for which they had a better understanding of the materials or for which they scored higher in examinations.

In both Regression Analysis and Business Forecasting, PBL was applied, and term projects were required for students to practice their analytical skills in PBL exercises and projects.

Students had opportunities to practice what they had learned in applications. Hence, statistical methods they provided as answers in the questionnaire were more specific. Some advanced analytical models, such as Holt-Winters Method and Seasonal ARIMA, were listed in the questionnaire as possible options (see Table 3). Table 3 reveals that for Statistics (I) and (II), students felt comfortable with random sampling, normal distribution, binomial distribution, and confidence interval at the basic level and analysis of variance and hypothesis testing at the mid-level. For Regression Analysis, they were comfortable with analysis of variance, t-test, F-test, regression analysis, and stepwise regression (Mid-level). For Business Forecasting, students indicated being comfortable with regression analysis and stepwise regression at the mid-level and with exponential smoothing, Holt-Winters method, ARIMA, and seasonal ARIMA at the high-level.

Table 3. Statistical Methods Students' Feel Comfortable with in Application

Courses		Statistical methods
Statistics (I) & (II)	Basic	Random sampling Normal distribution Binomial Distribution Confidence interval
	Mid-level	Analysis of variance Hypothesis testing
Regression analysis	Mid-level	Analysis of variance t-Test F-Test Regression analysis Stepwise regression
Business forecasting	Mid-level	Regression analysis Stepwise regression
	High-level	Exponential smoothing Holt-winters method ARIMA Seasonal ARIMA

5 Conclusion and Implications

In this study, we sought to determine the effectiveness of PBL learning approaches on students' outcomes in terms of the perception of the importance of three statistics-related courses. Students appeared to believe that the most advanced course—Forecasting in Business—was the most important in terms of both Importance of Learning Statistics and Importance of Using Statistical Applications at Work in the Future. However, all the other courses had higher ratings in terms of perceived levels of importance (>8.5).

The prominence of Forecasting in Business in terms of importance may be explained by the fact that this course is practical in the sense that it prepares students for the world of work or for their desired professions in business. Such a course would better serve the purposes of PBL approaches, as PBL seeks to contextualize education in the real world, including professional contexts [9, 10]. This means that even basic introductory courses should seek to make their content and teaching methods more relatable to students in terms of practicality and usefulness in work.

The study had a few limitations. The study is exploratory and ongoing. Therefore, a number of results have not been included, such as the self-evaluation of students in terms of performance, as compared to their actual results. Furthermore, there was a lack of a control group. A more ideal study would include an experimental control group that experienced PBL methods and a control group that did not experience PBL methods. Additionally, a longitudinal approach, comparing past student performance in the absence of PBL methods versus current student performance with PBL methods would also be useful. We plan to incorporate such approaches in the future aspects of this ongoing study.

Research Funding. This research is supported by Ministry of Science and Technology (MOST-110-2511-H-005-001) in Taiwan.

References

1. Groebner, D.F., Shannon, P.W., Fry, P.C.: Business Statistics: A Decision-Making Approach, 10th edn. Pearson Education Inc., Hoboken (2018)
2. Esnard, T.R., Alladin, F.M., Samlal, K.C.: Prior mathematics performance, statistics anxiety, self-efficacy and expectations for performance in statistics: a survey of social sciences students in a Caribbean institution of higher education. Stat. Educ. Res. J. **20**(1), 4 (2021)
3. Sharma, A.M., Srivastav, A.: Study to assess attitudes towards statistics of business school students: an application of the SATS-36 in India. Int. J. Instr. **14**(3), 207–222 (2021)
4. Acee, T.W., Weinstein, C.E.: Effects of a value-reappraisal intervention on statistics students' motivation and performance. Int. J. Exp. Educ. **78**(4), 487–512 (2010)
5. Gould, R.: Statistics and the modern student. Int. Stat. Rev. **78**(2), 297–315 (2010)
6. Karpiak, C.P.: Assessment of problem-based learning in the undergraduate statistics course. Teach. Psychol. **38**(4), 251–254 (2011)
7. de Jong, N., Verstegen, D.M., Tan, F.E., O'connor, S.J.: A comparison of classroom and online asynchronous problem-based learning for students undertaking statistics training as part of a Public Health Master's degree. Adv. Health Sci. Eeuc. **18**(2), 245–264 (2013)
8. Leppink, J., Broers, N.J., Imbos, T., van der Vleuten, C.P., Berger, M.P.: The effect of guidance in problem-based learning of statistics. Int. J. Exp. Educ. **82**(3), 391–407 (2014)

9. Hung, W., Jonassen, D.H., Liu, R.: Problem-based learning. In: Hung, W., Jonassen, D.H., Liu, R. (eds.) Handbook of Research On Educational Communications and Technology, vol. 3(1), pp. 485–506, Routledge, UK (2008)
10. Dolmans, D.H., De Grave, W., Wolfhagen, I.H., Van Der Vleuten, C.P.: Problem-based learning: future challenges for educational practice and research. Med. Educ. **39**(7), 732–741 (2005)
11. D'Andrea, J., Wooten, R.: Improving performance and enhancing introductory statistics using projects. Am. J. Comput. Math. **7**(1), 21–28 (2017)
12. Jamshidi, H., Maslakpak, M.H., Parizad, N.: Does problem-based learning education improve knowledge, attitude, and perception toward patient safety among nursing students? Randomized controlled trial. BMC Nursing **20**(1), 1–9 (2021)
13. Yuliana, Y., Firmansah, F.: The effectiveness of problem-based learning with social media assistance to improve students' understanding toward statistics. Inf. J. **7**(2), 97–108 (2018)
14. Lawton, S., Taylor, L.: Student perceptions of engagement in an introductory statistics course. J. Educ. Stat. **28**(1), 45–55 (2020)

Exploring Affordances and Student Perceptions of MALL in Familiar Environments

Rustam Shadiev[1(✉)], Taoying Liu[1], Narzikul Shadiev[2], Mirzaali Fayziev[2], Elena Gaevskaya[3], Roza Zhussupova[4], and Olimboy Otajonov[5]

[1] Nanjing Normal University, No. 122, Ninghai road, Nanjing 210097, China
[2] Samarkand State University, No. 15, University Blv., Samarkand 140104, Uzbekistan
[3] St Petersburg State University, No. 7/9, University Embankment, St Petersburg 199034, Russia
[4] L.N. Gumilyov Eurasian National University, No. 2, Satpayev Street, Nur-Sultan, 010008 Astana, Kazakhstan
[5] Urgench State University, No. 14, Kh.Alimdjan Street, Urgench 220100, Uzbekistan

Abstract. This study aimed to explore affordances and student perceptions of mobile-assisted language learning (MALL) in familiar environments to facilitate English as a foreign language (EFL) learning. Twenty-five undergraduate students participated in this study. Students learned EFL in class and then they worked on learning tasks in familiar learning environments outside of classroom. The students used resources from learning environments such as objects, people, situations, and scenarios to complete assigned tasks by describing them. They used a mobile learning system installed on Tablet PCs during learning process. We explored affordances and student perceptions of MALL in familiar environments to facilitate English as a foreign language (EFL) learning. The results showed that personal, specific, innovate, familiar, predictable, and meaningful were affordances of familiar environments for EFL learning. The students had positive perceptions of technology. Based on our results, several implications along with practical suggestions were prepared for EFL teachers and researchers.

Keywords: MALL · Familiarity · Affordances · Perceptions

1 Introduction

Harmer [1] suggested that a balance should be kept between meaningful language input and output in foreign language acquisition. However, in Asian regions, some scholars pay less attention to language output but more to language input [2]. This study aimed to address this issue by exposing language learners to equal language input and output. That is, students received language input in class and produced language output in the real world outside of class [3].

When students learn in the real world they are able to explore, discuss, and meaningfully construct knowledge in contexts that involve real-world problems relevant to learners [4, 5]. Such contexts are rich with resources (e.g. objects, people, situations,

© Springer Nature Switzerland AG 2021
Y.-M. Huang et al. (Eds.): ICITL 2021, LNCS 13117, pp. 397–412, 2021.
https://doi.org/10.1007/978-3-030-91540-7_41

and scenarios) so that students are able to use them for learning and practice opportunities [6]. Scholars mentioned that familiarity with learning environments is beneficial for learning [7] because familiarity helps cognitive processes, e.g. information processing [8]. The cultural schema theory [9] explains why familiarity with learning environments can be beneficial for learning. According to this theory, we gain knowledge from our surroundings or environments; such knowledge would be organized and stored in our brain as cultural schemata. After we enter the environment many times, these schemata are constantly updated. Finally, information and experiences related to these environments are stored in our brains as background knowledge, thus, we become familiar with the environments. In familiar environments, our experiences and existing information (stored schemata) about the environments could become good learning inspiration and facilitate generation of various learning ideas. More importantly, when we enter such environments, the stored schemata can guide our behavior and we can even predict what is going to happen next. So, we do not need to spend extra cognitive resources to deal with information processing caused by surrounding environments such as getting to know it or locating required resources for learning. Familiar environments help direct our attention to more important tasks. In familiar environments, learners will be involved in learning more, because they can associate their daily encounters with what they learn and make learning process more meaningful for them.

If familiar environments really help learning, then we aimed to investigate what potential or affordances of familiar environments are to facilitate language learning. According to Yamanobe et al. [10], affordance is defined as action possibilities offered to a human by its environments. Bower and Sturman [11] suggested that an affordance exists as long as the person can take the necessary actions to utilize it. Limited studies on familiarity with contexts and their effect on language learning may indicate that potential of familiar environments is not being fully harnessed for educational purpose. One reason is because educators and researchers in the field do not fully understand potentials or affordances of familiar environments. As such, they struggle to make appropriate and innovative use of affordances and as a result the effectiveness of teaching and learning is compromised. Therefore, in this present study, we aimed to fill in this gap in the literature.

Language learning in the real world can be supported by mobile learning technology [12]. For example, learners can use technology to apply knowledge to the real world and practice their skills [13]. Learners can create written or verbal content and share it with peers and the instructor for further discussion and reflection using technology [14] In this study we developed a mobile learning system to assist students' English learning in the real world. In order to determine whether our mobile learning system is useful for learning and can be accepted by students, we aimed to explore their perceptions of the mobile learning system.

The following research questions were addressed in this study: 1. What are affordances of familiar environments for learning? 2. How do learners perceive the mobile learning system?

2 Method

Twenty-five undergraduate students from China participated in this study. The students had more than 10 years of English as a foreign language (EFL) learning experience. All students learned EFL in class and then outside of classroom they worked on five learning tasks with such topics as environmental matters, healthy lifestyle, transportation, dinning, and interesting place. All students were surveyed after the learning activity.

To assist students' EFL learning, we designed a mobile learning system (Fig. 1). The platform was installed on tablet PCs. It included the following functions: (1) digital textbook (to provide learning material which the students learned in class and outside), learning tasks (to provide topics, task, and instruction; the students had to complete learning tasks during the learning activity), learning map (to share location, upload created content, and give comments; the students had to show location of learning sites on the map where their learning content was created), online dictionary (to translate unfamiliar vocabulary), communication tool (to support communication among students).

Fig. 1. Mobile learning system

To explore contextual affordances of familiar contexts for learning, researchers coded created content. Two researchers discussed any confrontations until they reached a consistent point of view. After several discussions, final codes were produced.

To explore perceptions of the system, students were surveyed at the end of the study. We used Technology Acceptance Model (TAM) developed by Davis (1989) to guide the design of our questionnaire. TAM is one of the most commonly used models for measuring the information system acceptance [15]. The following dimensions were included in our survey: perceived ease of the system use to investigate whether it is easy for students to use the mobile learning system; perceived usefulness of the system to explore whether our system is useful for students; perceived satisfaction to study students' satisfaction with our system; behavioral intention to use the system to investigate whether students would like to use the mobile learning system in the future.

Finally, to support our research findings related to two research questions ten students were interviewed by researchers of this study. Every student was interviewed for about twenty minutes. They were asked about their learning experiences in familiar environments using our mobile learning system.

3 Results and Discussion

Contextual Affordances of Familiar Environment

The results are presented in Appendix A. According to the data, contextual affordances of familiar environment included the following categories: personal specific, innovate, familiar, predictable, and meaningful.

Personal. In terms of personal, students who learned in familiar environments were more inclined to describe from personal perspective. For example, most students mentioned about their past experiences, feelings, daily observations or habits. Thus, these students tend to write more.

Specific. As for affordance specific, students who learned in familiar environments tend to add more specific details. Because they had previous experiences in familiar environments, so they could elaborate more specific details in their written content. Most of students described many specific issues which cannot be easily found at first and tried to describe them in specific details. For example, what environmental issue bothers them most, what are reasons for this issue and how it can be solved in that specific context.

Innovate. In terms of innovate, students who learned in familiar environments could use their imagination and association to enrich their writing. Several of them envisioned something that could be achieved in the future.

Familiar. Familiar included the following coding: time, location, latest news, people, people's routine, special provision, route, related story, history, special service, problem duration, inner information and tradition. We found that the writing of students who learned in familiar environments showed their familiarity with the learning site. For example, because they were familiar with the place, so they knew the opening time and closing time of a shop; they knew people and what people usually do in the learning site; they knew the special service of a restaurant; they knew related story or history or special provision or inner information of the site; they knew how long issues existed; even more, one student mentioned about a tradition of the local place, because he/she grew up there. So, a familiar environment provided richer learning resources and the students tended to write more.

Predictable. As for affordance predictable, a familiar environment involves relevant and predictable situations from students' background as well as previous experiences (Skehan, 1998). Students could predict what will happen because they were familiar with the environment. So, they felt more confident and relaxed when they conducted tasks without too much concern related to surroundings.

Meaningful. In terms of affordance meaningful, what students wrote was relevant to them, all scenarios, acts and items of the environment were meaningful. This could promote their understanding and application of knowledge. For example, a student mentioned that she always went to school playground for a walk after finishing her classes to relieve learning pressure and relax.

From interviews we found two extra advantages of learning in familiar environments. First, for the students who learned in familiar environments, it was easier to learn and easier to participant in activities, because they did not need to spend extra time and energy to explore the learning environment before tasks as they were familiar with the environment. Second, the students who learned in familiar environments felt more relaxed and confident during tasks. For example, one student even interviewed a foreigner to get more information.

Students' Perceptions Towards the Mobile Learning System. According to the survey results, most students highly valued the system. In general, they agreed that the system was easy to use ($M = 4.26$; $SD = 0.58$) and useful for learning ($M = 4.04$, $SD = 0.57$). Most students were satisfied with their learning in the real world using the system ($M = 4.03$, $SD = 0.70$), and they intend to use the system for learning in the future ($M = 3.73$, $SD = 0.44$). The students said that the learning system enabled them to check the task instructions at anywhere and anytime. They could also check their own and peers' content and give comments. In addition, during collaborative tasks, they often shared their own ideas and confusions with their partners using the communication tool.

In the interview, most students said they usually first learn related vocabulary and sentence in the "digital textbook", and then checked the task instructions in the "learning tasks". Most of them thought the "online dictionary" was very useful, using which they could look up difficult words. When they forgot how to spell some words, they could check the dictionary. Most students were satisfied with the "learning map". All content created by students were shown there. Students could check their own writing and also other students' writing. Thus, they could find their writing deficiencies and learn from other students. The map also helped students know where content of their peers was created because created content was tagged on the map. Knowing locations where content was created helped understand context of the location. Otherwise, it will not be easy to know context and learn from it or help others to improve their own content. Several students mentioned that sometimes they had no idea about one specific topic, they would refer to other student's writing on the system, then they could get good inspiration. About the "communication tool", most of the students said they usually used it in collaborative tasks. Students in the same collaborative group would ask their partners those questions: "have you finished this task?", "where did you go on this task?", "I have no idea about this task, any good suggestion?". Sometimes they said like "your writing is so good! Help me!", "oh, you all finished the task, I think I should start!" Through such communication, students could urge each other to study and make progress together.

But several students mentioned that there are more functions needed in the system. For example, they liked to have more learning resources on the system so that they could look up more information. In addition, they hoped to have the function that could monitor students' learning progress. Because the students were in a free learning environment without too many constraints, some students were not so self-motivated and could not be involved in learning. They usually spend much time on unrelated things.

Suggestions for Educators and Researchers in the Field. Based on the results, we suggest that when designing learning activities outside of classroom, it is better that efl teachers ask students to learn in places which are familiar and comfortable to them. In this case, students will be exposed to environments with more useful learning resources and students will know what resources are available to them and where. We suggest that teachers need to understand potential or affordances of familiar environments for language learning. If this goal is achieved, teachers may fully harness those potentials for educational purpose. They need to introduce affordances to students to make their learning more efficient. Being aware of affordances of familiar environments students can make their content more innovative, meaningful and personal as well as to add more specific details to describe learning resources from the learning sites. In terms of the learning system, we suggest that the students need to have more time to get acquainted with it and to know how to use it for learning. This will help them focus on the learning tasks during learning activity instead of studying how to operate the system. Map function of the system was found to be useful to identify learning context and then learn from others or give appropriate comments. Therefore, researchers and educators may consider incorporating this function into their learning system if learning process is going to be shared among students and it takes place outside of classroom. Learning progress function can also be considered in future learning systems as to help students monitor their progress on tasks.

Appendix A

Content data coding: affordances of familiar learning environments.

Category	Coding	Definition	Example
Personal	Experience	Describe daily encounters or special memory	*Before, I've met couples in the library several times who have talked wildly or acted inappropriately, but now I don't have that problem because I avoid their usual seats and sit with my roommate on different side. The funny thing is, when I sit in the same position, I see the same face every day even if I don't know her name. I checked her books and they are on taking the postgraduate entrance exam. After I see her study so hard, she becomes a stimulus to my daily learning*
	Feeling	Express personal feeling based on personal experience	*Compared with the library, I prefer to study in the classroom. I am used to studying in an environment that is not particularly quiet, and it is better to have some sound, certainly not noise. It may seem strange, but my attention tends to be more focus in such environment. Just like now, I can hear the voice of the teacher in the next classroom, footsteps and birds outside the window, which makes me feel relaxed*

(*continued*)

(*continued*)

Category	Coding	Definition	Example
	Evaluation	Express personal opinion based on personal experience	*I often go to the second restaurant in the school canteen for three reasons. Firstly, my monthly living expenses are limited and the dishes of the school canteen are cheap relatively, so I can afford eating here. Secondly, there are three school canteens in our school, compared with other two canteens, I think the environment and food in the second canteen are the better than those of the other two, most dishes here are very delicious. Last but not least, usually there are relatively few people here and it's easy to find the right place*
	Daily Observation	Describe phenomenon observed in daily life	*If you arrive at the library before 8 o 'clock, you will see many students open the door in front of the library. This phenomenon is most common in review week. There would be two or three lines, one above and one below the stairs, and each line would be long and spectacular enough to show the students' love for learning*
	Daily routine	Describe something they do on a regular basis	*I usually walk or run here at night, almost every day, because there is plenty of time in the evening. I can go to the dormitory to take a bath and sleep directly after exercise. It's very comfortable to do exercise on the playground*
	Habit	Describe something that they are used to doing	

(*continued*)

(*continued*)

Category	Coding	Definition	Example
	Impression	Describe deepest or first impression	*When I went there first time, there was a waitress with warm smile standing at the door to greet guests and invite guests to come in. I've been there many times, Every time the waiter keeps very polite and friendly. It gives me a fantastic impression so I prefer to go there for eating*
	Interest	Describe personal interest	*My favorite thing is to write code and run programs in my computer. It's really interesting to see that lines of numeric letters can run different pictures*
Specific	Solution /Suggestion	Put forward specific solutions /suggestions based on personal need or experience	*First, I need to buy some receipt boxes and prepare labels so that I can organize my dormitory more effectively. Secondly, I'd better reduce the frequency of cooking in the dormitory in summer and choose food that doesn't need oil for cooking. Finally, I need to train myself to put things back where I get them, so that I don't have to tidy my dormitory every day*
	Issue	Put forward specific issues which they observed in daily life	*My room's window faces the east, so our clothes hanging on the bars usually don't get enough sunshine to dry quickly, especially in the winter, it takes more than 3 days. Besides, the bars outside the window is not suitable to hang the bigger sheets and quilts*

(*continued*)

(*continued*)

Category	Coding	Definition	Example
Innovate	Imagination	Describe the scenario they envision or expect to see	*First of all, I think can set up an automatic glass roof. When it rains, the roof closed automatically, when sunny, will automatically open*
Familiar	Time	Describe the specified time requirements, such as opening time, closing time etc	*It opens on 7:00 a.m. and closes on 18:30 p.m, providing breakfast, lunch and supper. But the canteen will be closed from 9:00 to 11:00 in the morning and from 2:00 to 4:00 in the afternoon. So if you want to have a meal here, you have to avoid these times*
	Location	Describe the location in detail	*It's very convenient to eat here because the first canteen is close to the graduate apartment building*
	Latest news	Describe recently released messages	*In fact, the library has implemented the function of Internet seat selection, but many people don't use it. Firstly, library should continue to promote network seat selection and standardize regulations. Secondly, the library can set up seat selection service volunteers to supervise students to select seats before using them. What's more, the library can also improve the function of seat selection system. Students' study time can be counted according to seat selection system, the ranking can be published, and even rewards can be given to in the top rank*

(*continued*)

(*continued*)

Category	Coding	Definition	Example
	People	Describe people they see often	*A lot of people exercise here every day, not just college students, but many residents near college town. Beside the playground are the gymnasium and the dormitory, so many students like running after class and then straight back to the dormitory*
	People's Routine	Describe other people's daily routine	*First, Older people in nearby neighborhoods come to the playground in the morning or at night. They almost come everyday, especially the dancing women. These old people will walk on the playground. Secondly, there are some middle-aged people outside school who often bring their children to the playground. Because of restricted working time, they often come on weekends or after work in the evening. Finally, quite a large group of students come to the playground every day and every time. They often come in the morning or evening. At noon, a few student will take a walk on the playground*

(*continued*)

(*continued*)

Category	Coding	Definition	Example
	Special provision	Describe special requirements of one place	*Our library is accessible by swiping a student card. I guess this is to ensure the learning environment for students. The library doesn't open until eight in the morning, and because the library forbit eating, so you can always see people standing in line at the door, breakfast in hand, just before eight in the morning. Of course, students will be more conscious, they will eat at the door and then go in. Some people will take some food to go in,but the meal is no smell, so it will not affect others*
	Route	Describe in detail of the route from one place to another place	*I often go there to eat barbecue with my friends. Every time I go there by walking because it is closed to my college. after going out, turn right then go straight about three minutes, turn left and cross the road then go straight about ten minutes, finally take the elevator to the third floor to get there*

(*continued*)

(*continued*)

Category	Coding	Definition	Example
	Related story	Describe story or information related to one place	*There was an interesting story that a handsome school leader named Ma jiadong, is good at playing football very much and has football skills. It is said that he represented our college to attend provincial football match and won the great prize. Besides, he majored in Mathematics rather than a sports student. Thus it can be seen that he is fond of playing football and it is pity that I have no chance to meet him*
	History	Describe in detail of the history of one place	*The Library of Nanjing Normal University was set up in 1952 on the basis of the former library of Jinling Women's College of Arts and Sciences, and collected the collection and publications of the former Nanjing Normal University and Jinling University. After more than half a century of development, it has become a large comprehensive academic library*
	Special service	Describe the special service for specific people in specific time	*Every Friday, Saturday, Sunday evening after 9 o'clock, the bar will give each table a dozen beer free of charge, so it is also a very affordable place for consumption*

(*continued*)

(*continued*)

Category	Coding	Definition	Example
	Problem duration	Describe the problem duration they observed	*The facility problems are the most serious problems on the playground, such as broken plastic runway and dirty seats in the auditorium. Since I entered school in the fall of 2018, the playground has been like this. Maybe the problems is old question, for Suiyuan is an old campus with a long history*
	Inner information	Describe in detail of the inner information of one place. For example, what type of books are available in a library and how are they displayed	*Suiyuan Library mainly provides the required Chinese and foreign books and magazines for undergraduates, postgraduates and teachers. Its collection focuses on literature and history, including ancient books, reference books, samples, documents and Dissertations of the Master's degree*
	Tradition	Describe special tradition of one place	*In my hometown, no one is unfamiliar with Jiuhua Mountain. Our traditional custom is to go to Mount Jiuhua on the second day of the year to worship, in order to bless the year's peace, smoothness and benefit*
Predictable	Regular scenarios	Predict what will happen generally	*Besides, as there are nearly 10 school buses running within 12 a.m. and 14 p.m., the great noise will appear every ten or fifteen minutes and I can hardly have a nap during lunch time*
	Consequences	Predict possible good/bad consequences	

(*continued*)

(*continued*)

Category	Coding	Definition	Example
Meaningful	Happy/relax/relieve pressure	Describe daily scenarios that could make them happy or relax or relieve pressure	*There was a time when I was under great academic pressure. Faced with all kinds of difficulties, I feel unable to calm down. So I began to come to the playground. Walking when it rained, and running when it didn't rain. In this way, after a period of time, I feel much better. Academic pressures are also gradually diminishing. The playground is such a place where you can lie down, run, and, more importantly, see more people who are positive about life*
	trigger thinking	Describe daily scenarios that could trigger thinking	*I can observe many small details of parent-child interaction through walking, which will trigger my professional thinking*
	Relieve physical discomfort	Describe daily scenarios that could relieve physical discomfort	*For me, I always prefer to take a walk around the playground, as I mentioned, doing so to help relieve my digestion problem and also enjoy myself* *Usually, when I'm not feeling good of my stomach, I choose to take a walk on the playground, and after walking for about half an hour I always feel better*

References

1. Harmer, J.: The Practice of English Language Teaching. London/New York, pp. 401–405 (2001)
2. Meyer, D.: Broadening language learning strategies for Asian EFL students. Lang. Educ. Asia **3**(2), 243–251 (2012)

3. Huang, Y.-M., Shadiev, R., Sun, A., Hwang, W.-Y., Liu, T.-Y.: A study of the cognitive diffusion model: facilitating students' high level cognitive processes with authentic support. Educ. Tech. Res. Dev. **65**, 505–531 (2017)
4. Council, N.R.: How people learn: Bridging research and practice. National Academies Press (1999)
5. Hwang, W.-Y., Shih, T.K., Ma, Z.-H., Shadiev, R., Chen, S.-Y.: Evaluating listening and speaking skills in a mobile game-based learning environment with situational contexts. Comput. Assist. Lang. Learn. **29**, 639–657 (2016)
6. Shadiev, R., Liu, T., Hwang, W.Y.: Review of research on mobile-assisted language learning in familiar, authentic environments. Br. J. Edu. Technol. **51**, 709–720 (2020)
7. Skehan, P.: A cognitive approach to language learning. Oxford University Press (1998)
8. Shadiev, R., Hwang, W.-Y., Liu, T.-Y.: A study of the use of wearable devices for healthy and enjoyable English as a foreign language learning in authentic contexts. J. Educ. Technol. Soc. **21**, 217–231 (2018)
9. Nishida, H.: A cognitive approach to intercultural communication based on schema theory. Int. J. Intercult. Relat. **23**, 753–777 (1999)
10. Yamanobe, N., et al.: A brief review of affordance in robotic manipulation research. Adv. Robot. **31**, 1086–1101 (2017)
11. Bower, M., Sturman, D.: What are the educational affordances of wearable technologies? Comput. Educ. **88**, 343–353 (2015)
12. Shadiev, R., Hwang, W.Y., Liu, T.Y.: Facilitating cognitive processes during EFL smartwatch-supported learning activities in authentic contexts. Br. J. Educ. Technol. (2021)
13. Cavus, N., Ibrahim, D.: Learning English using children's stories in mobile devices. Br. J. Edu. Technol. **48**, 625–641 (2017)
14. Tingir, S., Cavlazoglu, B., Caliskan, O., Koklu, O., Intepe-Tingir, S.: Effects of mobile devices on K–12 students' achievement: a meta-analysis. J. Comput. Assist. Learn. **33**, 355–369 (2017)
15. Al-Emran, M., Mezhuyev, V., Kamaludin, A.: Technology acceptance model in M-learning context: a systematic review. Comput. Educ. **125**, 389–412 (2018)

The Study of Smart Coding Creative Kit to Enhance Creative Problem Solving Thinking for Children

Pornsawan Vongtathum[1](✉), Charuni Samat[1], and Pinyarat Singha[2]

[1] Faculty of Education, Khon Kaen University, Khon Kaen, Thailand
pornin@kku.ac.th
[2] Anubannakaephadungratchakitcharoen School, Nakae District, Nakhon Pathom, Thailand

Abstract. This study was aimed to designing and developing the Smart Coding Creative Kit to enhance Creative Problem Solving Thinking for Children. This study was aimed to 1) to study the Creative Problem Solving Thinking of children using the Smart Coding Creative Kit, 2) to study relationships between Creative Problem Solving Thinking and learner's achievement of children using the Smart Coding Creative Kit and 3) study learner's attitudes learning with Smart Coding Creative Kit. The developmental research (phase I) was employed in this study. The procedures were as following: 1) design process 2) development process 3) evaluation process. The target group is students studying in Grade 1, 2 and 3 in Khonkaen Primary Educational Service Area Office 25, consisting of 2 schools (Khon Kaen University Demonstration Elementary School (Modindang) and Bannonmuang School) and Nakhon Phanom Primary Educational Service Area Office 1, consisting of 2 schools (Anubannakaepadungratchakitcharoen School and Bannongbor School). The result revealed that: 1) The Creative Problem Solving Thinking of the children was found that the creative problem-solving of children ($N = 257$) was at a 100% better overall. When analyzed individually, it was found that the concept Accounted for 100%. Accounted for 98.75%. Problem analysis Accounted for 77.50%, and creating a variety of options Accounting for 74.59%, respectively. 2) The learning achievement was significantly and positively related to Creative Problem Solving Thinking a very high level of positive correlation. 3) The learners' attitude of leaners towards learning with the Smart Coding Creative Kit was at the highest level ($\overline{X} = 4.33$, $S.D. = 0.88$).

Keywords: Board game · Creative problem solving thinking · Children

1 Introduction

Learners development in the 21th century is totally different from the previous centuries due to the changes in such ways especially in technology that has been rapidly growing which affects the management of education to be changed from tradition paradigm to a new paradigm. It emphasizes on the learners as the center of learning by developing learners to realize the process of creating knowledge on their own. Based on complicated

© Springer Nature Switzerland AG 2021
Y.-M. Huang et al. (Eds.): ICITL 2021, LNCS 13117, pp. 413–421, 2021.
https://doi.org/10.1007/978-3-030-91540-7_42

problems from world change, which is an innovative world that focuses on creativity, novelty, and unique. Therefore, the world of education has changed quite a lot over the past few years. Education that is recognized as creating knowledge, abilities, and developing of human's potential is the education that focuses on the learners as the center of learning. It means that giving every learners chance to know, and gain both knowledge and experience and develop each learner's potential as much as possible without restrictions in intellectual level, and ability to perceive, etc. It is also hoped that learners are able to learn without time and place restrictions. Another important thing is that it gives learners chances to think analytically and synthetically to solve problems in all levels [6]. Thus, thinking skills should be developed for learners in the 21st century who will face many complex situations combined with the exponential growth of technology. Lastly, the target of today's education is to enable learners to creatively solve problems with the effectively use of technology.

According to framework of learning skills in 21st century, it shows that learning and innovation skills have to do something with the learners. These abilities are necessary to prepare learners for the work in real life in order to be good problem solvers especially in 21st century which the problems are more complex in every way than the previous eras [7]. Basic important abilities that teachers must develop to prepare the learners to handle these situations are creative thinking, innovative thinking, critical thinking and problem solving thinking, communication and collaboration. As seen that the thinking skill is the most common for learning in 21st century. And important thought for learning in the 21st century are critical thinking, creative thinking, and problem solving thinking [7].

However, the assessment results of the Office of Educational Standards and Quality Assessment (ONESQA) shows that the analytical thinking process of Thai children is mostly at fair level, and this is a big difference compared to the other countries. Because the PISA's assessment of knowledge and scientific ability appears that Thai children obtained score below than average which affects their education and life quality.

In the era of technology and innovation, one of the important course is computational science course for learners in elementary school. If the teaching method aims to promote problem solving through algorithm design which is the basic for computer programming, this will lead to the advanced thinking process of learners. And from the development of Piaget's theory of intelligence, the design of learning will be developed according to the intellectual development of learners through playing board game that focuses on designing to be resemble to the learner's context promoting problem solving based on the design of algorithm which is related to the teaching of computer programming in the United States in term of "Unplug". It is a teaching method that focuses on problem solving without using computer, even though video games are being more and more used in learning development nowadays. Because videos games are designed not only for entertainment but also for developing the learning about what the video games designer need the players to learn. Video games help players to straightly gain experience and encourage learning by action, it also helps create a collaborative learning environment through interaction while playing [4] and an educational board game for learning that attempts to improve students' creative problem solving (CPS) skills [1]. Although, video games are mostly designed to be online in the present but the adoption of traditional games such as board games for the knowledge development on a particular subject is still very popular. This is all because that board games bring chance to the interaction between players and eliminate the problem of the internet access in some area [2]. In addition, the basics of elementary school children who just have just passed their childhood, their basics of using of technology may not be as proficient as it should be. Learning through board games is very necessary at this age and also the process of design checking of the learner's problem solving, with the help of virtual reality simulation (VR), it will potentially bring learner's attention. Virtual reality simulation is the development the technology which is combined between reality and virtual reality together through software and hardware such as webcam, or another related hardware which the virtual image will be displayed on the monitor, phone screen, projector, or even on other display devices. The virtual image that appears will interact with the users immediately both in the form of both 3D image and animation, or even media with sound effects. This depends on how the media is designed to be in order to entertain, and attract people. The research appreciates the importance of the innovation development by using computer technology to explicate the process of learning management that focuses on thinking process and the design on the basics of Piaget's theory of intelligence which supports the learners to create knowledge on their own through a small group process, and expand the knowledge through a large group process in class with the teachers. The teachers will change the teaching method from using simple lectures and slides in teaching to using board games instead, which focuses on the problem solving thinking of learners. And this gives learners a chance to make a process of problem solving thinking to meet the potential of each learner. Moreover, the current state of teaching and learning in the primary school level aims to the core subjects which are science, mathematics, and languages. By content, these subjects all focuses on advance thinking ability, so that the development of problem solving thinking will not be quite useful in only computer course. In the other hand, it can be the basis for the development of learning in core courses as well.

2 Research Objectives

- To study the creative problem-solving thinking of students who learned with the Smart Coding Creative Kit.
- To study the correlation of creative problem-solving thinking and learning achievement of students who learned with the Smart Coding Creative Kit.
- To study the satisfaction of students who learned with the Smart Coding Creative Kit.

3 Research Scopes

3.1 Target Groups

The 257 students were selected by Purposive sampling who studying in grades 1, 2 and 3 of 2 primary schools in Khon Kaen Primary Education Service Area Office 25 as Khon Kaen University Demonstration Elementary School (Modindang) and Baan Non Mueang school; and 2 primary schools in Nakhon Phanom Primary Education Service Area Office 1 which are Anuban Nakae Phadungratchakitcharoen school and Baan Nong Bo school.

3.2 Research Design

Developmental Research Type I [5] was employed. This research type emphasizes on designing and developing with 3 stages as Design process, Development process, and Evaluation process. In according to this, this study was conducted during research phase 3 to study the results of Smart Coding Creative Kit to enhance creative problem-solving thinking for children. The stakeholder in this phase comprised researchers, teacher, and learners.

3.3 Research Tools

- Evaluation form of creative problem-solving thinking. Based on the researcher synthesized creative problem- solving framework for algorithm design [8], it was constructed in a form of a subjective test used to measure problem-solving thinking of post-learning with the Smart Coding Creative Kit board game. There are 4 stages of creative problem- solving as 1) Analyze problem 2) Generate creative ideas 3) Prepare: choose concepts and prepare and 4) Review the algorithm.
- Learning achievement test. It was formed as an objective test that used to examine elementary students' learning achievement in the topic of problem solving and algorithm.
- Evaluation form of students' satisfaction. The 5-rating scale form was to evaluate their satisfaction toward Smart Coding Creative Kit board game in the following 3 domains as board game design, board game play process, and students' knowledge.

4 Data Collection

- After improved the quality of Smart Coding Creative Kit to enhance creative problem solving thinking for children, it was thus used with the 257 grade 1–3 students in all 4 subject schools.
- Each 3 members were then randomly grouped in each group and allowed them to play the board game in total 15 task levels starting from level 1–15 respectively.
- In the next process, evaluation form of creative problem-solving thinking, learning achievement test, and evaluation form of students' satisfaction were assigned to students after they have learned with Smart Coding Creative Kit board game.

5 Data Analyses

- The evaluation form of creative problem-solving thinking was used to evaluate the performance of creative problem solving thinking of the students who learned with the Creative Problem Solving Thinking to Enhance Creative Problem Solving Thinking for Children. The statistics used to analyze the data was percentage.
- The correlation of creative problem solving thinking and students' learning achievement using Smart Coding Creative Kit was measured by Spearman Rank Correlation Coefficient and Pearson Correlation Coefficient methods.
- Students' satisfaction toward Smart Coding Creative Kit learning was post- learning evaluated by evaluation form of students' satisfaction based on basic statistics as average ($\overline{X}$) and standard deviation (*S.D.*).

6 Results

6.1 To Study the Creative Problem-Solving Thinking of Students

The study results were from creative problem-solving thinking of 257 elementary students from 4 schools who learning with Smart Coding Creative Kit. The 3 group members implemented the experimenting by playing with 15 levels of board games through a group process. After that, their creative problem-solving process was studied by using the developed subjective evaluation form based on researcher's synthesized creative problem solving framework [8]. The statistic used to analyze data was percentage as shown on Table 1.

Table 1. Overall analysis results of creative problem solving of students learning with smart coding creative kit.

Creative problem solving										
Criteria	Problem analysis		Generating of creative ideas		Preparing		Reviewing of algorithm		Sum	
	Student (n)	%	Student (n)	%	Student (n)	%	Student (n)	%	Student (n)	%
Excellent	98	40.84	105	43.75	221	92.09	256	99.58	156	62.08
Good	88	36.67	74	30.84	16	6.67	1	0.42	97	36.25
Pass	54	22.50	61	25.27	3	1.25	0	0.00	4	1.67
Failed	0	0.00	0	0.00	0	0.00	0	0.00	0	0.00
Good level and above	186	77.50	179	74.59	237	98.75	257	100	257	100

The results from Table 1 shows the students' creative problem solving that is in good level and above or overall as 100% of 257 students ($N = 257$). In according to the results of each stage as Reviewing of Algorithm, Preparing, Problem Analysis, and Generating of Creative Ideas show 100%, 98.75%, 77.50%, and 74.59% respectively.

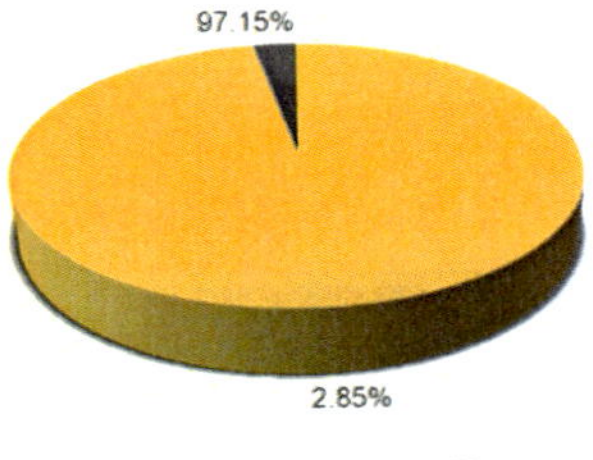

Fig. 1. Results of 4 stages of creative problem solving of students learning with smart coding creative kit.

From the data in Fig. 1 that shows of creative problem solving of 257 students learning with the Smart Coding Creative Kit by the learning achievement test, it was found that 97.15% or 247 students of them got 12 out of 20 scores. This indicates that the average of the students achieved the required 60%.

The study results of the creative problem solving of students in all 4 schools (I = 257), it revealed their efficiency in Review the algorithm, Preparing, Problem Analysis, and Generating Creative Ideas as 100%, 98.75%, 77.50%, and 74.59% respectively, as shown in Fig. 2.

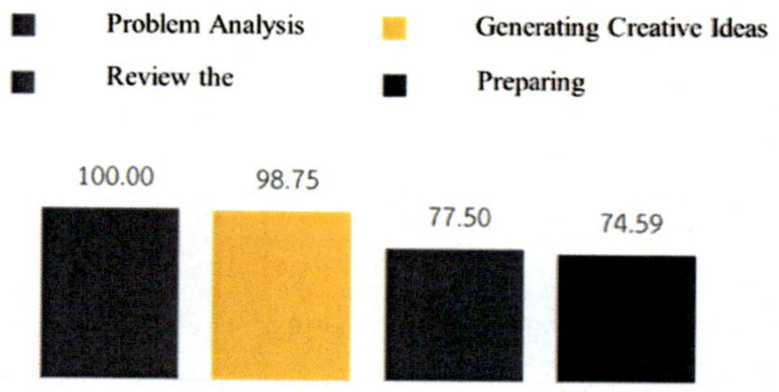

Fig. 2. Results of 4 stages of creative problem solving of students learning with smart coding creative kit

6.2 To Study the Correlation of Creative Problem-Solving Thinking and Learning Achievement of Students

The study results of the correlation of creative problem-solving thinking and student learning achievement learning with the Smart Coding Creative Kit innovations in overall showed a high positive correlation (0.71). In addition, the correlation of Khon Kaen University Demonstration Elementary School (Modindang) a high level of positive correlation (r = 0.66), Baan Non Muang School had a moderate positive correlation (r = 0.59), Anuban Nakae Phadungratchakitcharoen school had a moderate positive correlation (r = 0.60), and Baan Nong Bo School had a moderately positive correlation (r = 0.55) (Table 2).

6.3 To Study the Satisfaction of Students

The satisfaction of the students learning with Smart Coding Creative Kit to Enhance Creative Problem-Solving Thinking for Children in overall 4 schools, it was found that at a high level ($\overline{X}$ = 4.33, *S.D.* = 0.88). In terms of board game design, the students had the highest satisfaction at a high level ($\overline{X}$ = 4.46, *S.D.* = 0.78), followed by the process of game playing at a high level ($\overline{X}$ = 4.30, *S.D.* = 0.90) and the knowledge gained at a high level ($\overline{X}$ = 4.27, *S.D.* = 0.92) (Table 3).

Table 2. Results of the correlation analysis of learning achievement to creative problem-solving thinking of target groups by Pearson Correlation coefficient

Group		Correlation
Khon Kaen University Demonstration Elementary School (Modindang)	Person Correlation	0.66**
	Sig. (2-tailed)	0.00
Baan Non Muang School	Person Correlation	0.59**
	Sig. (2-tailed)	0.00
Anuban Nakae Phadungratchakitcharoen school	Person Correlation	0.60**
	Sig. (2-tailed)	0.00
Baan Nong Bo School	Person Correlation	0.55**
	Sig. (2-tailed)	0.00

** Statistical significance level of .01

Table 3. Satisfaction results of the students learning with smart coding creative kit to enhance creative problem-solving thinking for children

Evaluation item	$\overline{X}$	*S.D.*	Quality level
1. Board Game Design	4.46	0.78	High
2. Process of Game Playing	4.30	0.90	High
3. Knowledge Gained	4.27	0.92	High
Total average	**4.33**	**0.88**	**High**

7 Discussion

The results of the study of creative problem-solving thinking of the students who learned with the Smart Coding Creative Kit was in good level and above (100%), the correlation of creative problem-solving thinking and student learning achievement learning with the Smart Coding Creative Kit innovations in overall showed a high positive correlation (0.71) which consistent with Waraporn and Kantaphon [8] who studied board game behavior and affected factor elements among adolescents in Bangkok. The study found that the board games can enhance thinking process as creative thinking, better problem solving, have more concentration on studying in terms of emotions and feelings. It furthermore makes students have fun and feel relaxed from stress which hence control emotions better.

It is also consistent with study results of Elizabeth N. Treher [3] on Learning with Board Game: Play for Performance that board games is beneficial to education and learning. This can be even more valuable if the board games are properly designed for learning. In conclusion, the Smart Coding Creative Kit board game is a learning material that is analyzed and designed in according with the context of learners and constructivist theory as the basis for design. integrated with the framework design that mainly emphasizes on creative problem solving. As a result, learning with this board game can enhance creative problem solving thinking and resulted in a significantly higher learner's achievement.

8 Recommendations for Further Research

The findings of the target group that relates 10 students with special needs or learning disabilities, they are rather quiet and keep observing, rarely provide opinions due to their behaviors that slow to learn and take more time to play than general students. To solve this problem, the teacher should regularly give guidelines and might bring them to explain the rules in advance to prepare them or to increase their confidence. Alternatively, teachers may separate groups to play. If they refuse to join the group, they can be allowed to play alone.

9 Discussion

The results of the evaluation of the Smart Coding Creative Kit by experts found that overall opinion was at the highest level ($\overline{X} = 4.50$, $S.D. = 0.58$) which the efficiency evaluation result of AR Board Game was at the highest level as well. This is consistent with the research of Eiamwilai [2] who developed board games based on principles of critical thinking which its quality evaluation results of the games by experts were at high level. Consequently, the board game was designed in accordance with Tinsman [8] principles that makes a quality and attractive board game in terms of playing time, player's alternatives, balanced rules and regulations, etc.

Acknowledgements. We would like to express appreciation to Thai Media Fund for research grant. Also, we gratefully thank Faculty of Education, Khon Kaen University for supporting the research.

References

1. Chen, S.-Y., Tsai, J.-C., Liu, S.-Y., Chang, C.-Y.: The effect of a scientific board game on improving creative problem solving skills. Think. Skill. Creativ. **41**, 100921 (2021). https://doi.org/10.1016/j.tsc.2021.100921
2. Clerveaux, V., Spence, B., Katada, T.: Using game technique as a strategy in promoting disaster awareness in Caribbean multicultural societies: the disaster awareness game. J. Disaster Res. **3**(5), 1–13 (2008)
3. Treher, E.N.: Learning with Board Games: Play for Performance. The Learning Key, Inc. (2011). www.thelearningkey.com
4. Ferdig, R.: Handbook of Research on Effective Electronic Gaming in Education. Information Science Reference, Hershey (2008)
5. Richey, R.C., Klein, J.: Design and Developmental Research. Lawrence Erlbaum Associates, New Jersey (2007)
6. Suthipon, J.: http://hu.swu.ac.th/hu/km/Files/2_Changes_in_the_world21.pdf
7. Treffinger, D.J.: Creative Problem Solving: An Introduction. Prufrock Press, Waco (2005)

8. Vongtathum, P., et al.: Designing of smart coding creative kit to enhance creative problem solving thinking for children. J. Arts Sci. Chaiyaphum Rajabhat Univ. **8**(2) (2021)
9. Waraporn, L., Kantaphon, T.: Board game behavior and composition of the factors affecting the game play among adolescents in Bangkok. Soc. Res. J. **40**(2), 107–132 (2020)

Learner's Ill- Structures Problem Solving with a Constructivist Web-Based Learning Environment Model

Chan Singkaew and Sumalee Chaijaroen(✉)

Education Technology Major, Faculty of Education, KhonKaen University, Khonkaen, Thailand
Sumalee@kku.ac.th

Abstract. The purposes of this research were: 1) To study the process of problem-solving with a complex structure of learners using the learning environment model. 2) To study the EEG and the position of the learners while performing the problem-solving task. The Model Research Phase II: model validation was employed in this research. The sample for phase II: external validation were 30 diploma students of Rajamangala University of Technology Isan, Khon Kaen campus. 2.The results of the comparison of solving problems between before and after learning with the model revealed that Before learning, students cannot solve the problem by using ill-structured problem solving process. After learning, students can solve the problem by using ill-structure problem-solving process as follow: 1) Articulate problem space 2) Identify and clarify problem 3) Generate possible problem solutions 4) Assess and select alternative solutions 5) Monitor the problem space and solution options 6) Implement and monitor the solution and 7) adapt the solution and the problem solving after was significantly higher than before at 0.05 level. The learners' Bain electric wave as perform ill-structured problem solving task in laboratory revealed that while learner performed ill-structured problem solving task found Alpha (7–13 Hz) in all area such that AF3, AF4, F3, F4, F7, F8. This result may believe that the learner had cognitive process, problem solving.

Keywords: Ill- structures problems solving · Learning environment model · Bain electric wave

1 Introduction

Due to the change of technology and information technology, information has continuously and rapidly increased. Such changes have resulted in a shift in cultural, economic, social, and political problems. The problem to be more intense and ill- structures problems in life and that arise in the operation, especially in the electrical and electronic professions in the design and installation of electrical systems, which are complex of subject matter and the impact of design and installation, there will be a nature of impact problems, for example, if the design is incorrect and the equipment is used may cause damage such as a short circuit, fire. Cause damage to life, property. There must be problem-solving skills in operation. It is necessary to promote skills in seeking knowledge. Solving problems to solve problems for efficiency and safety. From the above

© Springer Nature Switzerland AG 2021
Y.-M. Huang et al. (Eds.): ICITL 2021, LNCS 13117, pp. 422–429, 2021.
https://doi.org/10.1007/978-3-030-91540-7_43

reasons, the researcher is aware of the importance of learning design and management that focuses on providing learners with skills to seek knowledge and construct knowledge to solve ill structure problems in electrical and electronic work, Therefore, to be able to create knowledge to keep up with changes information and can apply knowledge to solve problems effectively create safety in life and property, as well as apply previous knowledge and experience to solve problems in the future.

2 Research Purpose

1. To study the process of problem-solving with a complex structure of learners using the learning environment model.
2. To study the EEG and the position of the learners while performing the problem-solving task.

3 Research Methodology

This research uses the Model Research in Phase 2, Model Validation.

4 Research Instruments

1. The learning environment Constructivism that promotes problem-solving and learning transfer with improvements in the study, Phase 1, model development
2. The problem-solving measure used for studying problem-solving of learners Built base on Jonassen (1997) and the content of home electrical installations. There are 5 which are: 1) A measure to solve the problem of a problem situation of installing electrical equipment in the house 2) A measure to solve the problem of a problem situation of choosing the electric wire by calculation. 3) A measure to solve the problem of a problem situation of choosing the protective equipment with calculations 4) A measure to solve the problem of a problem situation choosing the electricity meter with calculations 5) A measure to solve the problem of a problem situation of the electrical equipment connection
3. The problem-solving interview used for studying the problem-solving of learners is built base on Jonassen (1997)
4. Emotive EPOC+ consists of 14 probe connectors arranged by International 10–20 or International 10–20 Systems standards: AF3, AF4, F3, F4, F7, F8, FC5, FC6, P7, P8, T7, T8, O1, O2

5 Data Collection

The learning environment Constructivism promotes problem-solving and learning transfer with improvements in the study, Phase 1 model development to manage learning with learners to study the effects of using the model by studying Problem-solving process before and after learning, study methods as follows (Fig. 1).

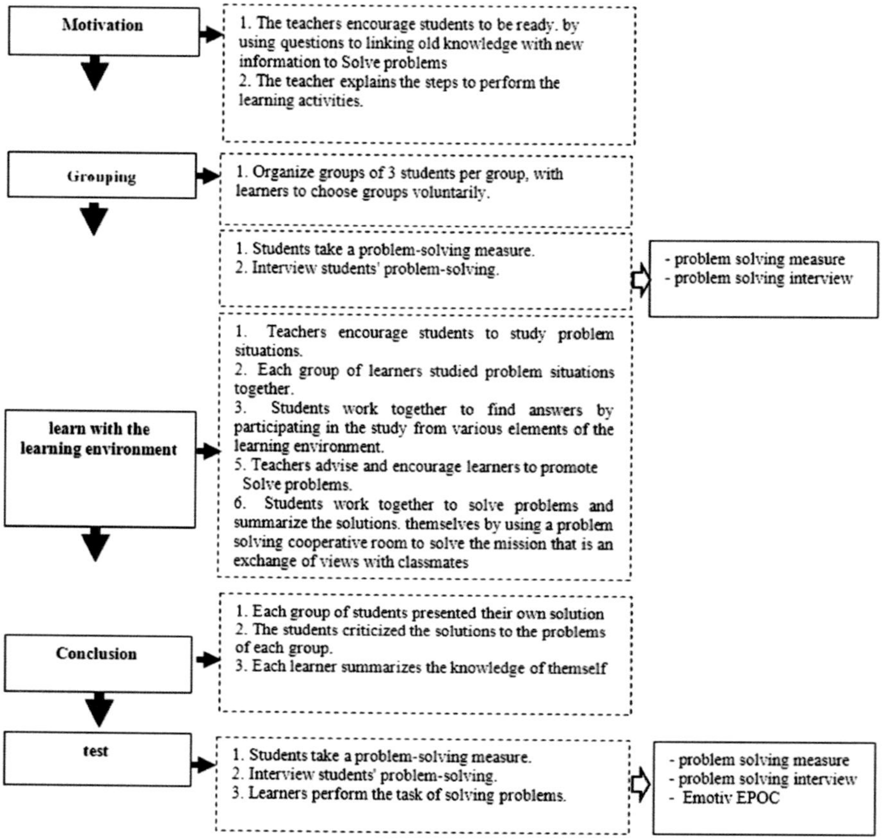

Fig. 1. A data collection process

6 Result

6.1 Result of Comparison of the Students' Problem Solving from the Interview

The students' problem-solving before and after learning was different. The learners have a three-step problem-solving process: Step 1: Finding the Problem, Step 2:Finding the Cause of the Problem, and Step 3: Solving the Problem. And after learning, it was found that the students used the problem-solving process in order of complex problem-solving processes in 7 steps as follows: 1) Articulate problem space 2) Identify and clarify problem 3) Creating a solution. Step 4) Assess and select alternative solutions Step 5 identifying gaps in problems and solutions) Monitor the problem space and solution options 6) Implement and monitor the solution and 7) adapt the solution as the following details.

Problem-solving of learners before learning, it found that students did not have complex problem-solving processes, according to Jonassen's problem-solving process (1997), but the students had a 3 step problem-solving process. Step 1 Finding the problem, the students can found the problem by looking the problem by the electrical appliances or the result of the electric pan not working, smelly meat Fridge not cold, the light bulb. Step 2 Identify the cause of the problem. Learners can find the cause by analyzing the results of electrical appliances. What can be the cause? what is involved? and then check for any reason for example, the result of the problem of the electric pan not working Related things include: Electrical wires to be connected and plugs and the body of the electric pan. The students checked by trying to connect the pan to a plug outside the house. If normal, check whether the wires are broken or the size of the wires is too small by calculating the electricity consumption of electrical appliances and comparing them with the size of the wires that are suitable or not. If the wires are normal, check the plug using a multimeter to test if the voltage is normal. Step 3 Problem Solving Learners can solve problems by applying the solutions from previous experiences or try the methods that have been used to solve problems such as the problem of the electric pan not working, the cause of the problem is that the electric wire is small. Learners solved the problem by changing the wires to a larger size.

Problem-solving with ill structures of learners after class, that the students had a ill structure problem-solving process in 7 steps:

Step 1: Articulate problem space, Learners can identify gaps in problems is specified The current problem condition, the refrigerator does not work, the meat smells, the water is not cold. The light in the room is less bright than usual, the lamp flashes when several appliances are turned on at the same time. The electrical cable connected to the plug generates smoke. The electric pan connected to the plug does not work. The desired condition after troubleshooting, the refrigerator is working, odorless meat, chilled water, normal room lighting, the lamp does not flash when several electrical appliances turn on at the same time, the electrical cable connected to the plug does not produce smoke, the electric pan works normally and the limitation to solve the problem is that there is only 1 day to install appliances and electrical equipment and the budget is limited to only 1,500 baht.

Step 2: Identifying the Real Problem, Learners can identify real and pseudo-problems. The real problems learners identified from the goals of the stakeholders were: 1) Chanchai's sister, whose goal is to make Chanchai's home appliances is work normal. 2) Chanchai wants the electrical appliances to work, such as refrigerators, light bulbs, electric pans, and water heaters. Electrical appliances can works when enabled at the same time. and 3) Technicians want to install electrical equipment and electrical appliances successfully and work within the specified time and budget. The goals of stakeholders were common, electrical appliances to work. Therefore, the students Identify Electrical appliances malfunction. It's a real problem.

Step 3: Identify and clarify problem, Learners can create solutions that could reduce or alleviate the root cause by analyzing the cause of problems that cause electrical malfunctions. which is caused by The electrical cable is small, not suitable for electrical appliances. and create a solution to the problem that makes the electric wire to be the right size for electrical appliances. There are 3 ways: 1) Replace every new electrical wire 2) Change some new electrical wires, only the wires connected to the plug for the refrigerator coffee machine electric pan and in case of other types of electrical appliances and 3) change new electrical appliances to suit the old electrical wires.

Step 4: Assess and select alternative solutions, Learners can assess alternatives and choose solutions, assessing and choosing a solution from the problem constraint sush as the cost and time and then choose the most feasible solution. The students evaluate the approach to problem-solving from the following limitations. 1) Time constraints The quickest way is to replace appliances with new ones. The second is replacing some new electrical wires and the slowest is changing all the new electrical wires. 2) Cost Limitation The cheapest way is to Change some new electrical wires, followed by replacing all new electrical wires and the costliest way is to replace the new electrical appliances to suit the old electrical wires. When considering time and cost constraints, learners evaluate the solution of replacing electrical wires as the most feasible solution. Because it doesn't take much time and the price is not high within the time limit and the price set. Therefore, learners choose a solution to the problem. Remove the old power cable and replace some of the power cables in the next solution.

Step 5: Monitor the problem space and solution options, Students will be able to identify gaps in problems and solutions by examining the solution of removing the old wires and replacing some new electrical wires only those that are connected to electrical appliances that use a lot of electricity to be larger can solve the current problem is electrical malfunctions. Because the electric cable is small, it is not suitable for electrical appliances. to the desired condition is that the electrical appliances can work within the limitation of problem-solving, which is limited to 1-day installation time and budget is only 1500 baht and learners formulate strategies for solving problems: 1) Strategies for purchasing electrical equipment are made by contacting multiple stores to compare prices. Promotion and check the model of wires and plugs including rails for wiring. Then consider the store with the lowest prices at The distance that must be purchased to the nearest because it reduces the cost and travel time. to reduce constraints in solving budget problems 2) Wiring strategy by students choosing in-wall wiring in order to reduce the time constraints and for the aesthetics of wiring instead of clip-on and wall-mounted wiring and to be able to improve and repair Therefore, the chosen solution is within the budget and time specified within 1 day and within the budget of 1500 baht.

Step 6: Implement and monitor the solution, The Learners can apply a problem-solving approach, remove the old wires and change some new electrical, which students will start by purchasing electrical equipment according to the calculation and buy it for a price of not more than 1,500 baht. The Learner checks prices, promotions, and distances from many stores. When receive electrical equipment and remove the original equipment first then bring the new device to install in place of the original location but change the wiring from a clip to a walk in the rails on the wall which makes wiring faster. The power socket is floating on the wall instead of the original. it makes it possible to control the installation time not to exceed 1 day and found that learners were able to reflect the results of solving problems. The students indicated that they could buy the sky equipment in a budget of not more than 1500 because of the survey of both prices. Promotion and distance of the shop that sells and choose the shop that sells the cheapest and closest This makes it possible to buy sky equipment at a price that is within the specified budget.

Installing electrical equipment and appliances takes less than a day because choosing the equipment from the nearest store gives you more time to install and choose a way to install the cable in the rail. Floating wall socket Makes it work fast, so it can install within 1 day. Electrical appliances can work because the electrical equipment to be connected has the appropriate size, which calculates and the quality is according to TIS standards. The homeowner is satisfied with the installation and pays the specified wage because the electrical appliances are working and the electrical wiring on the rails. Make the connection beautiful and safe.

Step 7: adapt the solution, Learners can adjust the approach for solving the problem by adjusting the way from removing the old wires and replacing some new electrical wires to removing all the old wires and replacing all new electrical wires. when found that after replacing some new electrical wires, there are still malfunctioning electrical appliances. And to make the solution effective under the limitations of solving problems, students change the way of connecting wires by changing from walking in rails to clipping on the wall because it is cheaper than walking in rails. (Compensation for the purchase of additional electrical equipment to stay within the specified budget) and the distance of the clip will be beaten further to reduce the wiring time but still, maintain strength and beautiful prayer.

6.2 Result of Comparison of the Students' Problem Solving from the Problem Solving Measure

Before and after the class the students took a problem-solving measure, after which the scores of both were taken to find the mean and standard deviation. The hypothesis was tested by comparing the mean scores of problem-solving between before and after school with t-test dependent statistics. Comparative results are shown in Table 1.

Table 1. Comparison of average problem-solving scores between before and after

Problem solving	*n*	*x*	*S.D*	*t*	*df*	*sig*
Pre-test	30	7.86	1.59	−32.91	29	.000
Post-test	30	15.96	1.44			

From the table in the study of problem-solving of learners from the problem-solving measure, the results showed that the students' problem-solving scores averaged higher after studying than before. (before = 7.86 and after = 15.96) at the statistical significance level of .05 showed that the learning environment model promote problem-solving of learners.

EEG and the location while Learners perform complex problem-solving tasks in the laboratory while taking EEG measurements as perform problem-solving tasks. The results showed that *Delta* (1–4 Hz), *Theta* (4–7 Hz), *Alpha* (7–13 Hz), and *Beta* (13–30 Hz) wavelengths were present at all measurement locations: AF3, AF4, F3, F4. F7 and F8, which are the waves that correspond to problem-solving.

7 Discuss

The students' problem-solving before and after learning was different. The learners have a three-step problem-solving process: Step 1: Finding the Problem, Step 2: Finding the Cause of the Problem, and Step 3: Solving the Problem. And after learning, it was found that the students used the problem-solving process in order of complex problem-solving processes in 7 steps as follows: Step 1: Identifying gaps in the problem Step 2: Identifying the real problem Step 2: Creating a solution. Step 4: Evaluating alternatives and choosing a solution, Step 5 identifying gaps in problems and solutions, Step 6 implementing the solution, and Step 7 adjusting the solution as the following Step 1: Identifying the gaps in the problem, the students were able to identify the gaps in the problem by can identify the current problem situation, the after the problem is solved, and the problem constraint. Step 2: Identifying Real Problems, that learners can identify real problems from stakeholder's goal. Step 3 Creating a solution to the problem, that students can create solutions to problems. The students have a process of creating a solution to the problem by analyzing the cause of the problem. and create solutions to reduce or mitigate the root cause of the problem. Step 4: Assessing alternatives and choosing a solution to the problem, learners can assess alternatives and choose a solution by asses the problem constrain and choose the most feasible solution. Step 5, Problem Solving Problems and Ways to Solve Problems, the learners can direct the gaps in the problems. and directing alternative solutions by identifying strategies that can be used for the solution. Step 6 Implementing the problem-solving approach, the students were able to apply the problem-solvingapproach and reflect the results of applying the approach. Step 7: Adjusting theproblem-solving approach, the learners can adjust the problem-solving approach if the problem was not solved. The comparison of the students' problem solving between before and after learning with the model. Obtained from the problem-solving scale, it was found that problem-solving after school was significantly higher than before school at the 0.05 level, consistent with the study of Sumalee et al. (2020), Charuni et al. (2019), Pinyarat Singha and Sumalee Chaicharoen (2019), Seksan Yampinit (2011), Suchart Wattanachai (2010), Chia and Chang et al. (2017), HaeRan and Yeoungsuk (2016), Connie and Charlene (2006) studied complex problem-solving base on complex problem solving (Jonassen 1997). Learners have a complex problem-solving process adapted from (Jonassen 1997) because learners are encouraged by the task of learning through situational intelligence. Start from the analysis of the gap in the problem. Identify the real problem Then create all possible solutions. and evaluating alternatives and choosing a solution. Addressing gaps in problems and solutions Implement a problem-solving approach and adjust the approach to problem-solving. In addition to promoting problem-solving processes through learning missions, Students also practice problem-solving with complex structures through the Problem Solving Center. which allows learners to practice the problem-solving process by solving each step by dragging the text or typing in the answers that can be checked. The fact that students have complex problem-solving processes may be a result of learning through the learning environment. created by the researcher.

8 Suggestion

1. Should be studied the relationship of complex problem solving with other advanced thinking.
2. Should be studied the brain areas involved in other advanced thinking

References

Richey, R.C., Klein, J.: Design and Developmental Research. Mahwah, New Jersey (2007)

Jonassen, D.H.: Instructional design model for well-structured and ill-structured problem solving learning outcomes. Educ. Tech. Res. Dev. **45**(1), 65–95 (1997)

Chaijaroen, S., Kanjug, I., Samat, C.: Learner's creative thinking learning with constructivist web-based learning environment model: integration between pedagogy and neuroscience. In: Rønningsbakk, L., Wu, T.-T., Sandnes, F.E., Huang, Y.-M. (eds.) ICITL 2019. LNCS, vol. 11937, pp. 663–671. Springer, Cham (2019). https://doi.org/10.1007/978-3-030-35343-8_70

Chaijaroen, S., Kanjug, I., Samat, C., Wonganu, P.: Outcomes of problem-solving using constructivist learning environment to enhance learners' problem solving. In: Huang, T.-C., Wu, T.-T., Barroso, J., Sandnes, F.E., Martins, P., Huang, Y.-M. (eds.) ICITL 2020. LNCS, vol. 12555, pp. 591–597. Springer, Cham (2020). https://doi.org/10.1007/978-3-030-63885-6_64

Check for updates

The Development of Internet of Things Learning Kit to Enhancing Programming Skills for High School Students

Nutthakarn Moeikao[1], Non Jarungsirawat[1], Issara Kanjug[2](✉), and Charuni Samat[2]

[1] Faculty of Education, Demonstration School of Khon Kaen University, Kaen University, Khon Kaen, Thailand
[2] Educational Technology, Faculty of Education, Khon Kaen University, Khon Kaen, Thailand
issaraka@kku.ac.th

Abstract. The purpose of this research was the development of internet of things learning kit to enhancing programming skills for high school students. The research methodology is pre-experimental design. The research participants consisted of 9 experts in 3 domains – 3 experts in content in computer programming content, 3 experts in learning media designer, 3 experts in designing constructivist learning environments, and 68 students in high school of Demonstration School of Khon Kaen University Secondary School. The research instruments are the expert review recording for examining the quality in 3 domains as follows: learning contents, learning media, and instructional design and the questionnaire form to studying learner's preference learning experience about the internet of things learning kit to enhancing programming skills. The results revealed that: The internet of things learning kit to enhancing programming skills for high school students were 8 elements as follows: 1) Problem base, 2) Resource, 3) Cognitive tools, 4) Collaboration, 5) Programming Problem Solving Center, 6) Scaffolding, 7) Programmer Community, and 8) Programming Coaching Room. The result of experts' reviews the efficiency of internet of things learning kit to enhancing programming skills was 81.20% and the results of the learner's preference about learning experience using the internet of things learning kit to enhancing programming skills was 75.96% with were higher than the specified criterion as 70%.

Keywords: Internet of Things · Programming skills · Instructional design · Constructivist · Learning environments

1 Introduction

In the digital world, there are a lot of smart technologies emerging around us and they are expanding rapidly in a very short period. Human resources preparation for such growth is essential today. Programming skills [1] are one of the most important skills that learners should be encouraged. Programming requires a combination of skills, especially problem-solving skills [5] that require a systematic approach. Most of the smart technologies are developed based on the Internet of Things (IoT) which includes engineering design concepts [10, 11], problem solving and programming. As the researcher

© Springer Nature Switzerland AG 2021
Y.-M. Huang et al. (Eds.): ICITL 2021, LNCS 13117, pp. 430–438, 2021.
https://doi.org/10.1007/978-3-030-91540-7_44

is educational personnel in the Computer and Programming Department. The studying the context of teaching and learning programming in Thailand, it was found that most of the students' learning still focused on the pattern of memorizing information that the teachers directly conveyed through lectures and assign tasks for students [13]. More than 80 percent of the students commented that although such a learning method could allow him to answer mission questions, it did not provide a deep understanding. As a result, they are unable to apply the knowledge gained to develop innovations for solving problems around them because they are not encouraged to develop the skills necessary for programming, especially problem-solving skills to systematic programming [1, 13].

From the information. Therefore, the researcher has an idea to develop an Internet of Things learning kit that focuses on enhancing learners' programming skills by bringing the fundamentals of problem-solving and programming are designed as a learning environment in the form of Web-based learning and packed into IoT boards. In this studying the researcher uses a Raspberry Pi, which has a built-in web server feature. It also organizes various devices used for learning IoT programming content, including Raspberry Pi, Relay Module, LED, DHT22 temperature and humidity sensor, etc.

2 Methodology

This study was aimed to the development of internet of things learning kit to enhancing programming skills for high school students. Research methodology is pre-experimental design the procedures were as following: (1) Studying principles, learning context, and theories, (2) Synthesizing the theoretical framework and designing framework, (3) Develop the internet of things learning kit to enhancing programming skills, (4) Evaluating the efficiency of the internet of things learning kit to enhancing programming skills [9], and (5) Study the learner's preference learning experience [9] about the internet of things learning kit to enhancing programming skills.

2.1 Research Participants

The research participants consisted of 9 experts in 3 domains – 3 experts in content selected by specialist in computer programming content, 3 experts in learning media designer selected by specialist in leaning media design, 3 experts in designing constructivist learning environments selected by specialist in constructivist learning environment design [7, 9], and 68 students in high school of Demonstration School of Khon Kaen University Secondary School.

2.2 Research Instruments

The instruments in this study as following details: 1) the expert review recording for examining the quality in 3 domains as follows [7, 9]: learning contents, learning media, and instructional design, 2) the questionnaire form to studying learner's preference learning experience about the internet of things learning kit to enhancing programming skills.

2.3 Data Collecting and Analysis

The researchers collected data as follows: 1) Synthesis of theoretical framework and components of the learning environment. The data were collected by analyzing principles, theories, related research, and contextual study. 2) Synthesis of designing framework: The above synthesized theoretical framework was taken into this process. 3) Develop the learning environments of internet of things learning kit follow the elements of designing framework. 4) Evaluate of the learning environments in the dimension of learning contests, learning media, and instructional design [7, 9] by experts in 3 domains as follows: learning contents, learning media, and instructional design and adjust according to the suggestions. 5) Collected learner's preference learning experience about the internet of things learning kit to enhancing programming skills by using a questionnaire form, and were data analyzed by using summarization, interpretation description (see Fig. 1).

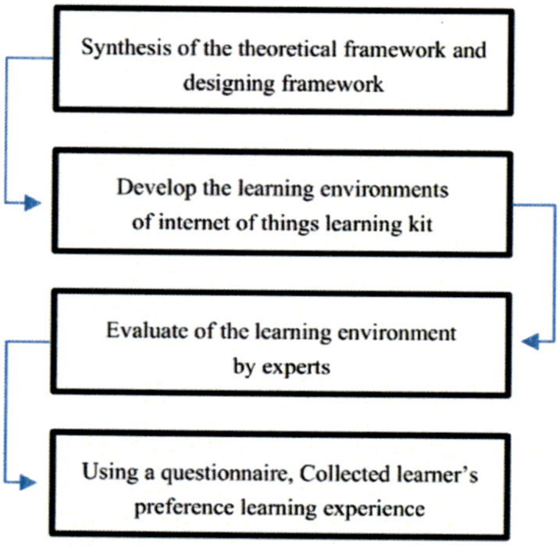

Fig. 1. Process of data collection

3 Results

3.1 The Development of Internet of Things Learning Kit to Enhancing Programming Skills for High School Students

The designing learning environments to enhancing programming skills. The learning environments of internet of things learning kit to enhancing programming skills was produced based on synthesis of theoretical framework in 6 crucial based include [13]: Learning context base [12], Psychology base, Pedagogy base [4, 6], Technology and media base [7], Problem solving base [5] and Programming base [1] and synthesis of designing framework based on theoretical framework. Therefore, the internet of things learning kit to enhancing programming skills comprised of 8 components as follows: (1) Problem base, (2) Resources, (3) Cognitive Tools, (4) Collaboration, (5) Programming Problem Solving Center, (6) Scaffolding, (7) Programmer Community, and (8) Programming Coaching Room. The description of each key element is shown in Table 1.

Table 1. The key elements and descriptions of learning environments of internet of things learning kit to enhancing programming skills.

No.	Key elements	Descriptions
1	Problem base	It was shown Problem base and learning task [2] to activating cognitive structure, programming skills [7, 9, 13]. (Ex. Fig. 2(b))
2	Resources	It was shown Resources [6] to supporting cognitive equilibrium [2] to provide information designed based on information processing theory [3], SOI Model [3], and OLEs [4]. (Ex. Fig.4(a))
3	Cognitive tools	It was shown Cognitive Tools as tools to supporting information comprehensive and programming problem solving designed based on cognitive tools concept of OLEs model [4]. (Ex. Fig. 4(b))
4	Collaboration	It was shown Collaboration to enhancing programming problem solving [1] by collaborative with their friends and experts for expanding multiple perspectives. (Ex. Fig. 4(c))
5	Programming problem solving center	It was shown Programming Problem Solving Center to enhancing programming skills by solve the problem designed based on programming and problem Solving 4 phases [1, 5]: Problem representation, Search for solutions, Implementation and Use and Maintenance [1, 13].(Ex. Fig. 4(d))
6	Scaffolding	It was shown Scaffolding to supporting and enhancement programming skills using 4 scaffolding [4] included Conceptual, Metacognition, Procedural, Strategic. (Ex. Fig. 5(a))
7	Programmer community	It was shown Programming Community to making communities of programmer for sharing and consulting [7] programming idea. (Ex. Fig. 5(b))
8	Programming coaching room	It was shown Programming Coaching Room to supporting learner's programming through coaching by teacher and experts [7, 9, 13]. (Ex. Fig. 5(c))

The learning environments of internet of things learning kit to enhancing programming skills was produced based on designing framework (see Fig. 2, 3, 4 and 5).

The component of internet of things learning kit. The internet of things learning kit are material boxset using for learning task included: Raspberry Pi, Relay module, LED, Resister 330 ohms, DHT22 humidity and temperature sensor, Servo motor, Ultrasonic sensor, Soil moisture sensor, Protoboard, and Jumper wire (see Fig. 6).

(a) (b)

Fig. 2. (a) Welcome screen (b) Problem base (see details in Table 1.)

(a) (b)

Fig. 3. (a)(b) Learning tasks (see details in Table 1.)

(a) (b)

(c) (d)

Fig. 4. (a) Resources (b) Cognitive tools (c) Collaboration (d) Programming Problem Solving Center (see details in Table 1.)

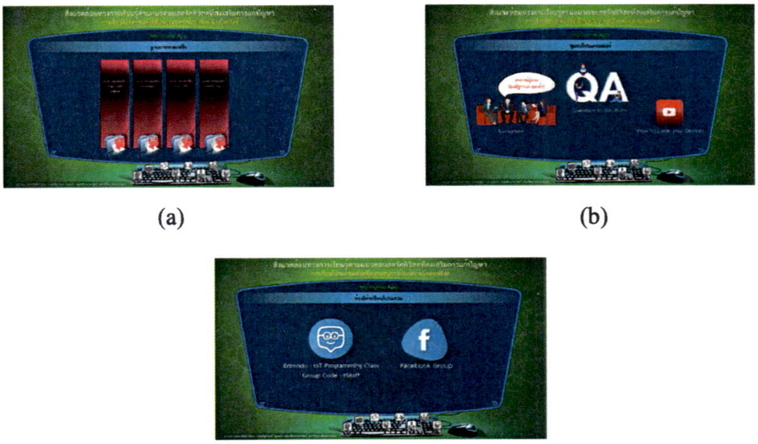

(a) (b) (c)

Fig. 5. (a) Scaffolding (b) Programmer Community (c) Programming Coaching Room (see details in Table 1.)

Fig. 6. Component of internet of things learning kit

3.2 The Efficiency of Internet of Things Learning Kit to Enhancing Programming Skills

The efficiency of IoT learning kit to enhancing programming skills as the following:

The experts' review. showed that the design of the learning environments was appropriate and congruent with underlined theories and principles as mentioned above see detailed in Table 2.

According to Table 2, the results of the assessment of the expert on the learning content was 84.67%, learning media was 80.0%, and the designing elements of the learning environments of IoT learning kit was 78.85% and the total of the assessment of the experts was 81.20% with were higher than the specified criterion as 70%. The experts' review was found that the elements of the learning environments of internet of things learning kit to enhancing programming skill are appropriate for supporting learner to solve problem for programming and leads learner to search for the solution for programming. The instructional design of learning environment exactly consistent with the principles and theories used as a basis for design overall, more appropriate.

Table 2. The efficiency of internet of things learning kit to enhancing programming skills

No.	List assessment	Results of the expert (Percentage)
Learning content		
1	Appropriate learning content	84.67
		84.67
Learning media		
2	Navigation	76.34
3	Composition	79.00
4	Image and video	83.46
5	Stability	81.57
		80.09
The designing elements of the learning environments of IoT learning kit		
6	Problem base	82.05
7	Resources	79.40
8	Cognitive Tools	75.78
9	Collaboration	78.84
10	Programming Problem Solving Center	81.59
11	Scaffolding	78.80
12	Programmer Community	77.65
13	Programming Coaching Room	76.70
		78.85
Total		81.20

3.3 The Learner's Preference Learning Experience Using the Internet of Things Learning Kit to Enhancing Programming Skills

The results of the learner's preference about learning experience using the internet of things learning kit to enhancing programming skills were follow detail in Table 3.

Table 3. The learner's preference learning experience using the IoT learning kit to enhancing programming skills

No.	List assessment	Results of learners (Percentage)
1	Appropriate of learning content	75.54
2	Appropriate of system navigation	78.70
3	Appropriate of screen composition	69.83
4	Appropriate of image and video	72.43
5	Stability	78.24
6	Using problem base	76.65
7	Using resources	74.54
8	Using cognitive tools	69.45
9	Using collaboration	81.12
10	Using programming problem solving center	82.67
11	Using scaffolding	70.01
12	Using programmer community	78.21
13	Using programming coaching room	80.12
		75.96
Total		75.96

4 Discussion and Future Work

This research focuses on the development of internet of things kit to enhancing programming skills for high school students. Based on principles of learning context, psychology base, pedagogical base, media and technology base, programming base, and problem-solving base to design the components of learning environments in Internet of Thing kit to enhancing programming skills including: (1) Problem base, (2) Resources, (3) Cognitive Tools, (4) Collaboration, (5) Programming Problem Solving Center, (6) Scaffolding, (7) Programmer Community, and (8) Programming Coaching Room. After study about learning context of learner using IoT learning kit found that some students learning task has been relatively slow because no prior knowledge about using IoT devices. Therefore, the researcher has made a using manual and explained for basic use. In the future work, the researcher has planned to study the programming process in-depth such as through in-depth interviews, study learning achievement compared with the learners' programming problem solving, etc.

References

1. Dale, N.B., Weems, C.: Programming and problem solving with Java. Jones and Bartlett Learning (2008)
2. Kamii, C.: The equilibration of cognitive structures: the central problem of intellectual development. JSTOR (1986)

3. Brown, J.S., Collins, A., Duguid, P.: Situated cognition and the culture of learning. Educ. Res. **18**, 32–42 (1989)
4. Hannafin, M., Land, S., Oliver, K.: Open learning environments: foundations, methods, and models. Instruct. Des. Theories Models New Paradigm Instruct. Theory **2**, 115–140 (1999)
5. Jonassen, D.H.: Instructional design models for well-structured and III-structured problem-solving learning outcomes. Educ. Tech. Res. Dev. **45**, 65–94 (1997)
6. Klausmeier, H.J.: (Information Processing Theory) (1985). http://www.oknation.net/blog/print.php?id=132965. Accessed 21 May 2016
7. Chijaroen, S.: Education technology: priciples, teories, and implementation. Khon Kaen: Anna Ofset (2014)
8. Mayer, R., Mayer, R.E.: The Cambridge handbook of multimedia learning. Cambridge University Press (2005)
9. Samat, C., Chaijaroen, S., Kanjug, I., Vongtathum, P.: Design and development of constructivist multimedia learning environment enhancing skills in computer programming. In: 2017 6th IIAI International Congress on Advanced Applied Informatics (IIAI-AAI), pp. 1023–1026. IEEE (2017)
10. Gubbi, J., Buyya, R., Marusic, S., Palaniswami, M.: Internet of Things (IoT): a vision, architectural elements, and future directions. Futur. Gener. Comput. Syst. **29**, 1645–1660 (2013)
11. Madakam, S., Lake, V., Lake, V., Lake, V.: Internet of Things (IoT): a literature review. J. Comput. Commun. **3**, 164 (2015)
12. Trilling, B., Fadel, C.: 21st century skills: learning for life in our times. John Wiley and Sons (2009)
13. Moeikao, N., Samat, C.: Synthesis of Designing Framework for Constructivist Learning Environments Model to Enhancing Programming Problem Solving for Connecting Internet of Thing Devices. In: Wu, T.-T., Huang, Y.-M., Shadieva, R., Lin, L., Starčič, A.I. (eds.) ICITL 2018. LNCS, vol. 11003, pp. 253–260. Springer, Cham (2018). https://doi.org/10.1007/978-3-319-99737-7_26

Computer Integrated Education Evaluation: A Case Study

Corlia Smuts[1] and Hanlie Smuts[2](✉)

[1] Department of Humanities Education, University of Pretoria, Pretoria, South Africa
corlia.smuts@up.ac.za
[2] Department of Informatics, University of Pretoria, Pretoria, South Africa
hanlie.smuts@up.ac.za

Abstract. The combination of digital technologies and the focus on student-centred learning, enable the integration of pedagogical methods with the effective use of technology. This integration required educators to meaningfully engage with educational technologies as it is deployed across all aspects of teaching and learning such as teaching techniques, delivery methods and learning solutions. Furthermore, mechanisms are required to establish priority for professional development for educators in order to increase efficacy of teaching and learning design. Therefore, the purpose of this interpretive case study was to identify the key considerations that educators think through in order to achieve computer integrated education design. In addition, to create a development priority and roadmap, the key considerations were mapped to the taxonomy of blended learning design. Data was collected via 13 semi-structured interviews from the case study institution, a private school operating in South Africa. Through an automated analysis process, 30 concepts and 12 themes were identified. The primary areas identified for the case study institution to attend to relate to two taxonomy areas, namely attitudes and beliefs (educator judgement relating to the use of technology by students/learners) and contextual determinants (policy, affordability, skills determinants).

Keywords: Educational technology · Blended learning · e-Learning · Taxonomy

1 Introduction

With the advent of new technology and access to countless information resources, the way we are being taught and the way we teach have never been so diverse [1]. From the traditional face-to-face classroom setting, technology has now made it possible to learn and teach using blended learning, distance learning and online platforms. Therefore, the use and expansion of technology has completely changed the quality of, and approach to, education [2]. These information technologies make a greater variety of educational practices possible and create more learning opportunities, while diversifying the approaches of both teachers and learners toward education [3]. The need for teachers and learners to adapt has therefore also become of utmost importance [4]. Educators now have the opportunity to use technology to enable learners to learn and practice language at

© Springer Nature Switzerland AG 2021
Y.-M. Huang et al. (Eds.): ICITL 2021, LNCS 13117, pp. 439–449, 2021.
https://doi.org/10.1007/978-3-030-91540-7_45

all levels of language input and -output (reading, listening, writing and speaking), while educators can also use technology to design specific learning components to enable the learning of language for set purposes and accommodating a variety of levels of fluency [4].

However, with these advances and all of the benefits and possibilities it brings, some challenges also occur and scholars have reported that these issues require more attention and further investigation [5]. These barriers include, but are not limited to; slow change, cultural/societal resistance, lack of support/resources for enablement/ the inability of educators and education systems to integrate technology and adjust to its demands, a lack of strategy and/or planning [6].

Therefore, this study aimed to establish the key considerations impacting computer integrated education. The primary research question that this study aimed to address was: "*What are the key considerations that educators think through for achieving computer integrated education design and how may it be measured?*". This was achieved by applying a single case study research strategy and collecting data through 13 semi-structured interviews. Particular themes were identified from the interviews and mapped to the taxonomy of blended learning design [7]. By evaluating the findings against the taxonomy of blended learning design, educators will be able to increase efficacy of teaching- and learning design, as well as understand where they need to focus their own skills improvement.

Section 2 of this paper provides the background to the study and presents an overview of blended learning, technology tools impact and challenges, as well as the influence on teaching practice. The approach to this study is discussed in Sect. 3, while Sect. 4 provides an overview of the data analysis of the study and report the findings derived from the semi-structured interviews. Section 5 illustrates measurement of the computer integrated design aspects and Sect. 6 concludes the paper.

2 Background

Based on the benefits of the use of technology as well as the barriers/challenges described, it is now apparent that there is a disparity between what technology could do for teachers and learners versus what it is currently doing/how it is used [8].

In the following sections, we consider this shift in teaching practice and blended learning, as well as the impact of computer integrated education.

2.1 E-learning and the Blended Classroom

Industry, the corporate sphere, the economy and the 'world of work' is constantly changing and through the increase in technology, innovation and automation the needs and pressure placed on the work force are also at an increase [9]. In order to adjust to these ever-changing demands, education systems are also constantly changing and adapting to produce an appropriately qualified work force [9]. Some of the most prominent innovations in education systems included electronic learning, games-based learning, technical skills development and subject-integration [10].

As technology has developed and now proliferates all areas of society, it is important to understand the definition of technology as it is used in education and e-learning [11]. Seeing as technology is developing continuously, the concept of e-learning is also ever changing and dynamic. E-learning consists of four different domains which must be considered when e-learning is conceptualised and implemented; type of technology, the system of delivery, educational- and communication paradigms [12]. Blended learning can therefore be defined as innovative and adaptable methods of education, teaching and learning which allows learning to be learner-centred and can improve a learners' interaction with the material [13]. Research has shown that a blended-learning approach can greatly benefit students seeing as it combines online teaching and learning with in-class teaching and classroom time [14]. This approach allows students to interact with the material comfortably at home while homework and more conventional schoolwork can be focused in the classroom [15].

In accordance with these global trends and the emergence of blended learning environs, and the consequential change of direction and shift in priority, teachers and educators have also been encouraged to assimilate learner-centeredness into their teaching style and classroom [11]. Additionally, educators also need to develop and acquire the skills necessary to introduce e-learning and other Information, Communication and Technology (ICT) tools into their classrooms keeping learner-centred learning in mind. In order for teachers to fully utilize the technology available to them, they would require the appropriate support in terms of new skills development, professional development and practical help as to the usage of ICT in the classroom and for the preparation of lessons [8].

In order to meet the challenge, it is important to investigate and understand the current level of educator ICT skills, where there is a gap in their knowledge and establish their current ICT needs and related teaching priorities in order to encourage teachers to adopt better ICT practices and methods in teaching which will in turn impact students and foster learning enrichment [8, 16].

2.2 Technology Tools and Teaching Practice

Taking the concepts of type of technology, the system of delivery, educational- and communication paradigms as previously discussed into account, the static use of an electronic device in a classroom does not automatically constitute e-learning [11, 12]. Therefore, in order for the device to be effectively used for e-learning as an ICT tool, it needs to play a core role in the learning process and provide support and stimulus for learners which cannot be substituted with traditional methods and materials [17]. Further studies have found that studies the usage of e-learning tools in classrooms had a positive impact on the improvement of the language ability and achievement of students in the English language classroom [8]. It can therefore be deduced that in order to bridge the gaps between ICT tool- and resource availability, e-learning and educator competence in a real-time classroom, teachers are required to develop new technical skill sets and be able to innovate new ways to use the available ICT resources in an integrated, blended manner [18]. According to Schneider and Stern [19], teachers are unable to use ICT tools effectively to create a blended teaching and learning environment without a clear understanding of the relationship between pedagogical knowledge and the role e-learning tools play as a medium for teaching and learning [19]. Therefore, if educators are expected to prepare learners for a technological saturated working environment after school, they too need to be well versed and able to use the appropriate ICT tools [11]. However, educators may find it difficult to use ICT tools if they are unable to see said tools as being part of their pedagogical frame of reference [19].

In order for the educator to properly instruct learners and convey the appropriate knowledge, they must themselves be in possession of the appropriate pedagogical knowledge related to what they are teaching [11]. Pedagogical knowledge does not simply refer to content knowledge but also a deep understanding of teaching, learning, the educational process and the values, purposes and aims thereof [20]. Additionally, pedagogical knowledge can also include an understanding of effective lesson conveyance, assessment, student- and classroom management and lesson planning [8].

2.3 Challenges of Integrating Technology Tools Teaching

In order for ICT tools to be used effectively and appropriately in the classroom to offer invaluable support to learner, both content knowledge and appropriate instructional methods need to be integrated appropriately into the blended environment [21]. It can also be concluded that educators need to know how to create an ICT enriched classroom by implementing blended learning in a flexible and creative manner and be guided by the curriculum, learning outcomes, experience and content knowledge [22]. Additionally, the students in our schools today are also exposed to a variety of technologies from a young age which created an ever-expanding cycle where educators and schools are forced to also embrace the changes brought to the education sector though the introduction of new technologies and the needs of learners to also adopt and acquire new technology-based skills [23].

According to Amin [24], the acquisition of ICT related skills have posed some difficulties for bother student- and veteran teachers [25]. In another study, Flanagan [26] investigated and contrasted the method used by beginner- and veteran teachers when it came to solving ICT related problems as they occur in the classroom. Additionally, Hedgcock and Ferris [27] also found that the greatest challenge faced by teachers is the lack of ICT-based skills and training and an inability to properly prepare for the use of technology in the classroom in order to foster a blended-learning environment [27]. This hesitance and doubt that teachers experience has been coined by Al-Alak and Ibrahim [28] as "computer anxiety" and has been shown to negatively affect the teachers' intentions and ability to use technology in the classroom [11, 28]. More recent research has suggested that the gap between what is expected of educators in terms of blended learning and that which they know they are actually able to achieve, has gone as far as causing "technophobia" among many teachers [29]. It was found that this "computer anxiety" and "technophobia" were primary a result of teachers not possessing the skills, knowledge, confidence or experience when it comes to using technology in the classroom [29].

In addition to the challenges teachers face as discussed above, educators must also focus on fulfilling their roles as teacher, meeting the standard of the curriculum and ensure that all of the learners' needs are met while keeping their individual ability and learning capacity in mind [11]. Therefore, it comes as no surprise that research shows that many educators are feeling overwhelmed and ill-equipped as they attempt to follow new educational trends and meet the standards [11].

3 Reseach Approach

The objective of this paper was to establish the key considerations that educators think through for realising computer integrated education design. In order to achieve the aim of the study, an interpretive, single case study research strategy was applied. The case study institution is a South African private school, primarily catering to foreign learners from diplomatic families. This school consists of 257 learners from Grade 0 to Grade 12 and employs 25 educators, as well as a support- and administrative team of 12 people. We designed a semi-structured interview guide that consisted of demographic questions, as well as questions pertaining to computer integrated education design and evaluation. Data was collected through 13 semi-structured interviews. The profile of the educators that were interviewed is shown in Table 1.

Table 1. Respondent profile.

Educators interviewed			Tenure as educator			Tenure at case study institution		
Elementary school	3	23%	< 5 yrs	5	38%	< 4 yrs	9	69%
Middle school	4	31%	5–7yrs	5	38%	4–7yrs	3	23%
High school	6	46%	>7yrs	3	24%	>7yrs	1	8%
Total	**13**	**100%**		**13**	**100%**		**13**	**100%**

The transcriptions of the interviews were analyzed using Leximancer [30] in order to identify and report patterns and themes within the data [31], emphasizing both organization and rich description of the data set and theoretically inform interpretation of meaning [32, 33]. Leximancer software (V5.0) is advanced natural language processing software utilizing Bayesian theory. Leximancer applies an unsupervised iterative process to determine the frequency of concepts and their relationships, and as such, has no preconception to extract the data. The final analysis is gleaned from the data itself [34]. Leximancer identified the main concepts in text reliably based on the interdependence of words in the text. Leximancer automatically infer concepts and themes from the data and provide clear, concise and accurate interpretations [35]. In the next section, we discuss the data analysis and findings of the study.

4 Data Analysis and Findings

The purpose of this study is to present the educator key considerations for computer integrated education design. The qualitative data collected through the 13 semi-structured interviews were analysed in order to identify the key considerations. The interview data was visualised through a concept map depicted in Fig. 1. Leximancer generated a total of 30 concepts and 12 themes from the interview data and shown in Table 2. Theme refers to a cluster of concepts that have commonalities reflected by their proximity in the concept map. The theme name is derived from the most prominent concept that appears in the group of interconnected concepts. The calculation of the number of hits informed the themes that were formed based on the interview text and fit each concept based on the Leximancer's machine learning capabilities [36].

In terms of the "tools" theme, when technology integration in the classroom is seamless and thoughtful, students not only become more engaged, they begin to take more control over their own learning. The choice of technology integration highlights the ability and capability of finding and evaluating the best tools and devices suited to the classroom situation and that may be applied across various contexts, The "students" theme highlighted the aspect that learners adapted well to the on-line environment and that they may be taught where ever they are and that the educator may share resources with them wherever he / she is. Special needs of learners may also be addressed in this manner. The "technology" theme impacts educator pedagogical knowledge as their own training often included very little technology training apart from using an overhead projector.

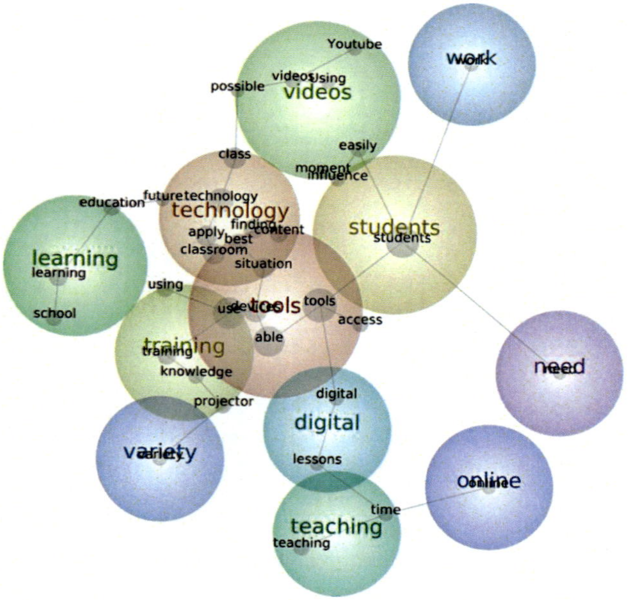

Fig. 1. Interview data concept map.

Tools make the content more attractive and accessible and also allow for learning to be more active and engaging such as making use of a gamified learning experience, building lesson plans using differentiated instruction and technology, build a class website, create a classroom blog and using social media as a training tool. The application of technology

Table 2. Themes and concepts from the interviews.

No	Theme	Hits	Concepts
1	Tools	65	Tools, use, able, devices, situation, training, content, using
2	Students	56	Sstudents, learners
3	Technology	46	Technology, class, classroom, apply, finding, best, content
4	Learning	29	Learning, education
5	Training	19	Training, using
6	Teaching	15	Teaching, time
7	Work	14	Work
8	Online	11	Online
9	Videos	11	Videos, Youtube
10	Digital	8	Digital
11	Need	7	Need
12	Variety	7	Variety

is not a one-size-fit-all approach and the best content, approach and application must be adopted for the particular context. The "learning", "training" and "teaching" themes consider the purpose and need of each activity or lesson in order to evaluate which tool would be best suited to the outcome. Learning is enabled through exposure to a wide variety of material, information, and it enables learners to practice and apply while they manage their own learning path. Collaborative learning is being utilised more and the material is adapted to make up for the lack of classroom contact. With regards to computer integrated education, time-management, punctuality and organisation of all concerned have become a top priority. "Work" and "online" refer to workload and was highlighted in the automated analysis as using technology as introduction for a lesson or by recording a lesson, the educator workload is impacted, and in some instances, reduced. Learners' work packs may be submitted online, changing the typical workflow experienced as opposed to when no technology is utilised. Furthermore, when learners present their work online to their peers, there is a completely new dynamic added to collaborative learning. There is a lot of simultaneous learning taking place. The "videos" and "digital" themes contributes in the classroom as learners seem to pay more attention to technology in the classroom and the teacher can be more creative in the class. YouTube has a vast collection of helpful tutorials, while online discussion boards are used to see how learners engage with the content. The "need" and "variety" themes are focused on the educators and what is required in terms of tool selection best supporting the learning outcomes. Educators reflected that their knowledge of a variety of tools are limited and that they seek the advice and guidance of colleagues.

In the next section we evaluated the findings obtained through the interviews against the taxonomy of blended learning design [37].

5 Computer Integrated Education Design Evaluation

The aim of this study was to present the key considerations that educators reflect on for computer integrated education design. The next step in this research study was to visualise a measurement of the computer integrated education application in the case study institution. For this purpose, we applied the taxonomy for effective blended learning design [37] as it is useful not only for describing key factors impacting blended learning design, but also as a professional development tool for educators to increase efficacy of teaching and learning design [37]. In order to visualise the findings and create a professional development roadmap for the case study institution, we used a basic red-amber-green status where the themes and concepts defined through the automated analysis were evaluated against the taxonomy dimensions and characteristics as depicted in Fig. 2.

One taxonomy dimension, "how student learning takes place" was well presented in the educator interviews, while 5 more taxonomy dimensions only contained green and amber characteristics. For "content knowledge" attention must be given to the content knowledge that the educator must have to adequately meet the needs of students, while making a variety of knowledge available to them. For "pedagogical knowledge", assessment and how technology means are used to achieve it, must be considered, while access and computer integrated education knowledge skill must be developed in the "technology knowledge" dimension. In terms of the "learner experience" dimension, one aspect requires development and this includes problem solving i.e. addressing the challenges students are facing when attempting to utilise computer integrated education material. Focus in the "educator skills" dimension must be on management and development. Educators must build their own capability to apply technology in computer integrated education while educator development need to develop a dynamic understanding of technology, as well as learn how to interact fluidly therewith during instruction. In the "beliefs and attitudes" dimension one characteristic i.e. educator judgement regarding the use of technology by a learner, requires urgent development attention. The same applies to policy, skills determinants and affordability in the final taxonomy dimension, "contextual determinants". Judgement regarding the thoughts and beliefs of others when it comes to using technology tools for teaching and learning, must be based on the application of technology as an information source. Affordability is driven by the technology architecture that the school subscribes to and the associated cost of ownership. Policy, especially as it relates to privacy and protection of personal information must be clearly defined and applied consistently. Finally, educators must focus on different capabilities of computer integrated education and the adjustment to a digital environment, designing revised curricula.

This computer integrated education evaluation may be utilised to create a professional development plan for educators in the case study institution or to create individual educator profiles for targeted individual professional development.

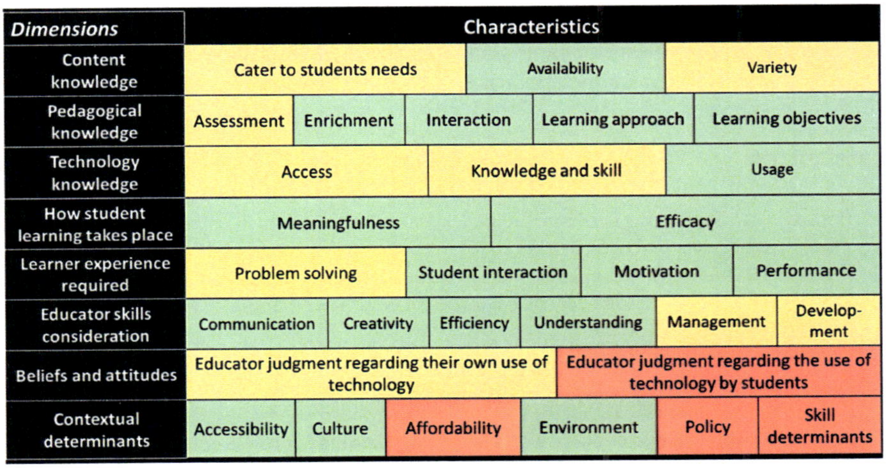

Fig. 2. Computer integrated education evaluation for the case study institution.

6 Conclusion

In 21st century teaching, educators are expected to integrate traditional pedagogical methods with the effective use of technology in computer integrated education. These increasingly sophisticated technologies, create a requirement for educators to gain new skills to meaningfully engage with these technology tools. In this study we presented a computer integrated education evaluation case study where data was collected through 13 semi-structured interviews. The taxonomy of blended learning [7] was used to map the findings from the interviews to with the aim to develop a professional development agenda for the case study institution.

Thirteen educators across elementary, middle and high school were identified with varying years of experience as well as varying tenures at the case study institution. The data from the semi-structured interviews were analysed with automated natural language processing software, Leximancer 5.0. Through the analysis process, 30 concepts related to 12 themes were identified. These concepts and themes described the educators' key considerations when applying computer integrated education design. The four most prominent themes identified included tools, students, technology and learning.

In order to create a measurement of the case study institution's computer integrated education capability, the taxonomy of blended learning, consisting of 8 dimensions and 31 characteristics, were utilised. Similar themes between the taxonomy and interview analysis were identified and visualised with a green status. Where themes overlapped somewhat and minor issues were mentioned in the interviews, an amber visualisation was applied. Where taxonomy characteristics could not be matched to a prominent theme in the interview data, a red visualisation was used. Based on this evaluation, the case study institution may design a professional development plan for its educators.

This study was based on an interpretive paradigm and a basic red-amber-green mechanism was used to inform the evaluation and consequent professional development plan. As such, for future research, the development of a quantitative measurement tool based on the taxonomy of blended learning may be designed and evaluated. Furthermore, the suggested professional development plan may be tested with the case study institution as the next research step for the application of the findings of this study.

References

1. Bergman, L.: Supporting academic literacies: university teachers in collaboration for change. Teach. High. Educ. **21**(5), 516–531 (2016)
2. Enakrire Rexwhite, T., Ocholla Dennis, N.: Information and communication technologies for knowledge management in academic libraries in Nigeria and South Africa. South African J. Inf. Manage. **19**(1), 1–9 (2017)
3. Chawinga Winner, D. Zinn, S.: Use of Web 2.0 by students in the faculty of information science and communications at mzuzu university, Malawi : original research. South African J. Inf. Manage. **18**(1), 1–12 (2016)
4. Pop, C., Brink, R.: Repositioning work-integrated learning in diverse communities. In: Work-Integrated Learning in the 21st Century, Emerald Publishing Limited, pp.115–128 (2017)
5. Shulman, L.S.: Those who understand: knowledge growth in teaching. Educ. Res. **15**(2), 4–14 (1986)
6. Salloum, S.A., Al-Emran, M., Shaalan, K., Tarhini, A.: Factors affecting the E-learning acceptance: a case study from UAE. Educ. Inf. Technol. **24**(1), 509–530 (2018). https://doi.org/10.1007/s10639-018-9786-3
7. Smuts, H., Smuts, C.: effective blended learning – a taxonomy of key factors impacting design decisions. In: Innovative Technologies and Learning, Huang, T.-C., et al., (Eds.), pp. 428–441. Springer International Publishing Cham (2020)
8. Adegbenro, B.J., Gumbo, T.M.: Exploring the conceptual relationship between teachers' procedural functional knowledge and pedagogical content knowledge. South African J. Higher Educ. **29**(5), 29–47 (2015)
9. Maree, K.: How to fix the gap between school and work in south africa. retrieved from the conversation (2020). https://theconversation.com/how-to-fix-the-gap-between-school-and-work-in-south-africa-130077
10. Newton, D.: Education innovations that could change the world (2019). https://www.forbes.com/sites/dereknewton/2019/11/15/a-hundred-education-innovations-that-could-change-the-world/#2209e3dc634c
11. Gibson, R.T.: The experiences of high school English Home Language educators in preparing and delivering e- learning lessons to Further Education and Training (FET) learners: a qualitative study. University of KwaZulu Natal, Pietermaritzburg (2019)
12. Sangrà, A., Vlachopoulos, D., Cabrera, N.: Building an inclusive definition of e-learning: an approach to the conceptual framework. Int. Rev. Res. Open Distrib. Learn. **13**(2), 145–159 (2012)
13. Protsiv, M., Atkins, S.: The experiences of lecturers in African, Asian and European universities in preparing and delivering blended health research methods courses: a qualitative study. Glob. Health Action **9**(1), 20–49 (2016)
14. Garrison, D.R., Kanuka, H.: Blended learning: uncovering its transformative potential in higher education. Internet Higher Educ. **7**(2), 95–105 (2004)
15. Basal, A.: The implementation of a flipped classroom in foreign language teaching. J. Dist. Educ. **16**(4), 28–38 (2015)
16. Conole, G.: E-Learning: the Hype and the Reality. J. Interact. Media Educ. **2**(21), 1–18 (2004)
17. Tavangarian, D., et al.: Is e-Learning the solution for individual learning?. Electron. J. e-Learn. **2**(2), 273–280

18. Gedik, N., Kiraz, E., Ozden, M.: The optimum blend: affordances and challenges of blended learning for students. Turkish Online J. Qual. Inquiry **3**, 102–117 (2012)
19. Schneider, M., Stern, E.: The developmental relations between conceptual and procedural knowledge: a multimethod approach. American Psychol. Assoc. **46**(1), 178–192 (2010)
20. Mishra, P., Koehler, M.J.: Technological pedagogical content knowledge: a framework for teacher knowledge. Teach. Coll. Rec. **108**(6), 1017–1054 (2006)
21. Ma, X., et al.: The teaching of Chinese as a second or foreign language: a systematic review of the literature 2005–2015. J. Multiling. Multicult. Dev. **38**(9), 815–830 (2017)
22. McGrail, E.: Laptop technology and pedagogy in the english language arts classroom. J. Technol. Teach. Educ. **15**(1), 59–85 (2007)
23. Lambert, J., Cuper, P.: Multimedia technologies and familiar spaces: 21st century teaching for 21st century learners. Contemp. Issues Technol. Teacher Educ. **8**(3), 264–276 (2008)
24. Amin, S.: An effective use of ICT for education and learning by drawing on worldwide knowledge, research and experience: ICT as a change agent for education (A Literature review). Schol. J. Educ. **2**(4), 38–45, **42**, 38–45 (2013)
25. Hennessy, S., Harrison, D., Wamakote, L.: Teacher factors influencing classroom use of ICT in sub-Saharan Africa. Itupale Online J. African Stud. **2**, 39–54 (2010)
26. Flanagan, S.: Two teachers' technology use: recommendations for english teacher preparation, in society for information technology and teacher education. In: International Conference 2011, Koehler, M., Mishra, P. (Eds.). Association for the Advancement of Computing in Education (AACE): Nashville, pp. 3727–3735. Tennessee, USA (2011)
27. Hedgcock, J., Ferris, D.: Teaching readers of english: students, texts, and contexts. Routledge (2018)
28. Al-alak, B.A., Ibrahim, A.M.A.: Measuring the acceptance and adoption of e-learning by academic staff. Knowl. Manage. E-Learn. **3**(2), 201–221 (2011)
29. Azarfam, A.Y., Jabbari, Y.: Dealing with teachers' technophobia in classroom. Adv. Asian Soc. Sci. **2**(2), 452–455 (2012)
30. Leximancer. Leximancer User Guide. 2020 (2021). https://info.leximancer.com/. Accessed on 2 Jul 2021
31. Vaismoradi, M., Turunen, H., Bondas, T.: Content analysis and thematic analysis: implications for conducting a qualitative descriptive study. Nurs. Health Sci. **15**(3), 398–405 (2013)
32. Alhojailan, M.I.: Thematic Analysis: A Critical Review of its Process and Evaluation. West East Journal of Social Sciences **1**(1), 39–47 (2012)
33. Leedy, P.D., Ormrod, J.E.: Practical research: planning and design. 12th (Edn) (ed.) Pearson (2018)
34. Smith, A.E., Humphreys, M.S.: Evaluation of unsupervised semantic mapping of natural language with Leximancer concept mapping. Behav. Res. Methods **38**(2), 262–279 (2006)
35. Wilk, V., Soutar, G.N., Harrigan, P.: Tackling social media data analysis. J. Cetacean Res. Manag. **22**(2), 94–113 (2019)
36. Kim, D., Kim, S.: Sustainable Supply Chain Based on News Articles and Sustainability Reports: Text Mining with Leximancer and DICTION. Sustainability **9**(6), 1008 (2017)
37. Smuts, H., Smuts, C.: Effective Blended Learning – A Taxonomy of Key Factors Impacting Design Decisions. In: Huang, T.-C., Wu, T.-T., Barroso, J., Sandnes, F.E., Martins, P., Huang, Y.-M. (eds.) ICITL 2020. LNCS, vol. 12555, pp. 428–441. Springer, Cham (2020). https://doi.org/10.1007/978-3-030-63885-6_48

Check for updates

Impact of the IRS Idiom Teaching on Elementary Students' Learning Achievement and Motivation

Mei-Jie Lai[1], Hong-Ren Chen[1](✉), and Sen-Chi Yu[2]

[1] Department of Digital Content and Technology, National Taichung University of Education, Taichung 403, Taiwan
hrchen@mail.ntcu.edu.tw

[2] Department of Counseling and Applied Psychology, National Taichung University of Education, Taichung 403, Taiwan

Abstract. Idiom learning is an essential part in Chinese education. Some scholars discovered that there's a general lack of motivation in learning Chinese idioms among elementary students; hence it is an important issue to increase learners' learning motivation and improve their application of idioms. With the advances of information technology, Interactive Response Strategy (IRS) used into the classroom has already become popular. The study used a quasi-experimental design and randomly select two classes of 49 students of grade 3 from an elementary school in Taichung city of Taiwan as subjects. Each class as experimental and control group respectively. The experimental group will be taught using IRS integrated into Chinese Idiom learning, while the control group follows traditional lecture style. The results show the following findings after statistical analysis: (1) In terms of learning efficiency, IRS integrated into grade 3 Chinese idiom learning is superior to traditional lecture style. (2) In terms of learning motivation, IRS integrated into grade 3 Chinese idiom learning is superior to traditional lecture style.

Keywords: Idiom learning · Interactive response system · Learning efficiency · Learning motivation

1 Introduction

The flexible use of Chinese idioms can make writing and language expression play the icing on the cake. Learning idioms can diversify one's vocabulary, increase articulation and writing ability, achieving a general improvement in language ability. Some scholars discover the lack of motivation of learners in learning idioms, which leads to idioms only being memorized for a short period of time just for tests and exams. Learners also seldom use idioms in daily writing, lacking the proper application of this knowledge [1]. Learners have low learning motivation in regards to learning idioms, which leads to their inability to store them as long term memory [2]. Learning motivation is an intrinsic psychological progression, when instructors enable learners to become invested into

© Springer Nature Switzerland AG 2021
Y.-M. Huang et al. (Eds.): ICITL 2021, LNCS 13117, pp. 450–457, 2021.
https://doi.org/10.1007/978-3-030-91540-7_46

the course, sustain the learning activity and reach the teaching goals [3]. The present research seek to focus on increasing learners' learning motivation in in learning idioms and gain feedback on learners' situations through IRS. The study hopes to invigorate learners' interests in learning idioms, enabling them to apply this knowledge to real life, improve oral and writing abilities while improving conciseness.

Technology integration into education has become more diversified in recent years. Through the integration of information technology into the classroom, the learning atmosphere becomes more alive and allows a two-way communication between instructors and learners, increasing both learning motivation and interest. Interactive Response Systems (IRS) such as Zuvio, Plickers and Kahoot! Can assist instructors in managing learners' learning progress and make teaching adjustments accordingly. IRS can increase learners' class participation rates [4]. Should game-like elements be introduced while using IRS, not only can the system increase learners' learning motivation, but also learning concentration. Integrating information technology into Chinese idiom education can have significant increase in learner's learning motivation and learning efficiency [1].

The present study used Kahoot! IRS integrated into Chinese idiom teaching due to its ease in use and ability to increase interactivity and entertainment in teaching. The study hopes to analyze the impact of IRS integrated into Chinese idiom teaching have on third grade learners' learning motivation and efficiency. Through this strategy, instructors can immediately gain insight on learners' situation and manage their progress. The study's research motivation sprouted from learners' low learning motivation and lack of real-time feedback mechanics.

2 Literature Review

2.1 Interactive Response System (IRS)

IRS can assist instructors in managing learners' learning situations in class, rapidly gaining insight on their learning evaluation and enable instructors to make immediate teaching adjustments. Educators can increase earners' learning interest, interactivity and entertainment value in class. IRS's advantages [5, 6], as listed in Fig. 1, can diversify teaching styles and increase learners' learning motivation, reversing the passive role of learners. It can also increase teaching efficiency and learning interest, which in turn increases learner/teacher interaction and offers convenience in evaluation. Through a digitized evaluation system, educators can quickly understand learners' learning situation and provide immediate strategic adjustment; learners' progression can also be recorded through the statistics graph, allowing educators to find weaknesses in learners' situation and provide remedy.

Huang [7] proposed the concept of integrating information technology into education. By involving information technology into education, educators can transform the diverse IT tools into tools that facilitate learning while providing learners a more active response and give meaning to learning itself. Further enhancing learning efficiency while gradually building learners' learning interest. Such examples include: integrating IRS into classes, gaining an immediate insight on learners' situation, educators are able to use this system as a reference to adjust pacing.

Fig. 1. IRS advantages and characteristic

Kahoot! is a game-based learning system. Learners can use different electronic devices to conduct interactive learning through an internet-enabled environment. The feature of this system is allowing competitiveness while answering questions. Not only can the students answer immediately, but the instructors will have a better understanding of the learners' learning situation, and adjust teaching strategies accordingly. This system can enhance the interactivity and entertainment value, further increasing learners' initiative and increase learner efficiency, even beyond the goals set by the instructors. Wang [8] found that Kahoot! IRS have the effect of increasing initiative. Graham [9] proposed that Kahoot! Allows teachers to quickly and easily create question-based learning games which can be use to evaluate learning situation, review knowledge and teach new learning content or facilitate learning discussion.

2.2 Chinese Idiom Learning

Language is the foundation of learning. Under the influence of various electronics, most children lack writing abilities nowadays. Huang [10] thought that if elementary learners are to increase their writing abilities, the proficiency in Chinese idioms is a definite requirement. Adequate Chinese idiom usage can make writings and spoken words more concise, causing them to become more vivid. He [11] thought that Chinese idiom teaching should follow four main principles: Vivification, a diverse teaching style and interesting teaching materials is a guarantee to successful Chinese idiom teaching, educators should use more word games to inspire interest in learners; Integration, Chinese idiom teaching should incorporate speaking, reading and writing activities, possibly even interdisciplinary studies such as mathematics. Practicality, idiom learning should combine writing education; Diversify, flexible teaching materials and innovative methods can be used in tandem with plentiful teaching resources. A diversified approach can aid learners in learning idioms. Following the advancements of the tech era, integrating information technology into education can make idiom learning more diversified. Liu [1] according to a mobile learning strategy applied in the research of sixth grade elementary idiom learning, learners prefer digital learning platforms over pen and paper tests. Through a mobile learning strategy, a significant increase in learners scores was observed.

2.3 Learning Motivation Theory

Learning motivation is a integral part in learning, it is the driving force behind learning. Learning motivation is learner's motivation for achievement, a mental need for seeking individual success, which is one of the main reason that affects academic achievements [12]. Keller proposed the ARCS model in 1983, which stands for: Attention, Relevance, Confidence and Satisfaction. In the classroom, learning efficiency degrades because during the learning process, instructors are unable to inspire interest an increase concentration [13]. In teaching design, ways of understanding and increasing learning motivation is very important, since learners' active participation and pursuit of knowledge stems from learning motivation [14]. In designing a teaching strategy, instructors can follow the ARCS strategy to inspire learners' learning motivation, which would help immensely during teaching. Cultivating abilities that children can use is our main goal, the driving force of which is learning motivation.

3 Research Method

The study utilized a quasi-experimental pretest-posttest design. The subject of the research focused on the impact of IRS integrated grade 3 Chinese idiom learning have on learning motivation and learning efficiency. Separating test subjects into experimental and control group, both groups of learners were required to take learning efficiency pre/post-tests in order to determine the differences in learning performance. Prior to the experiment, both groups of learners would take learing efficiency pretest, then each group will be taught with their respective styles and methods. After the experiment, both groups will then take learning efficiency posttest and learning motivation scale.

3.1 Research Design

Prior to the experiment, the study will explain the learning activity and how to operate Kahoot! IRS, which will last a total of 20 min. Before entering the system, learners will be instructed to take learning efficiency pretest for 40 min. Experimental and control group will each begin their learning activities; Experimental group will be taught using IRS integrated Chinese idiom learning while control group will use traditional lecture style. The experiment lasted 200 min, spreading across 5 lessons of 40 min each. After the lesson ended, learners will take learning efficiency posttest, which lasts 40 min and then fill out the learning motivation scale, which lasted 20 min. The experiment structure is shown as Fig. 2.

3.2 Research Tools

Using Keller's ARCS model and designed with Likert's 5 point scale in mind, the total score will be taken as an indicator of personal learning motivation, the lower the score, the more passive one's learning motivation is. The scale's internal consistency is .95 [15]. Kahoot! is a game-based test platform. Instructors can design questions on said platform, which will then be displayed in a game-like fashion. While answering, a

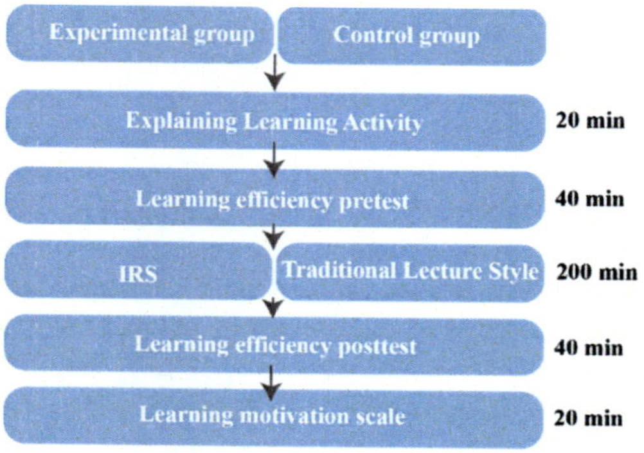

Fig. 2. Experiment structure

countdown feature will appear, accompanied by music. Learners can use smart phones, tablets or computers to answer questions. After the quiz, learners can see their own ranking and scores, instructors can also see learners' scores and question analysis.

Before using Kahoot! Insructors will need to ensure both Wi-Fi connection and the necessary hardware is present in the area. First of all, instructors will need to distribute one tablet to each learner, connect teaching terminal to the Kahoot! IRS while also display questions through the touchscreen tv. The study will then explain learning activities, process and how to operate the system to learners. Learners can interact with the instructor after turning on the tablet and enter the platform's homepage, entering PIN and connecting to the game (see Fig. 3).

Fig. 3. Test subjects' learning progress

4 Experimental Analysis and Results

4.1 Discuss the Difference in "Chinese Idiom Learning Efficiency" Between Experimental and Control Group

Perform ANOVA tests on both groups of learners using different teaching methods, and discuss the differences in learning efficiency. Both groups of learners averaged higher in posttest scores than pretest ones. Among them, experimental group's posttest average (89.16) is higher than control group learners' scores (77.24). Before conducting ANOVA, a test of homogeneity of regression must be performed in order to test whether the regression is homogenous. The test reported no significance, $F = 1.543, p = .221 > .05$. Both groups are homogenous, ANOVA can continue.

Table 1. ANOVA summary table of different teaching styles' learning efficiencies

Source	Type III *SS*	*df*	Avg *SS*	*F*	Significance
Pretest	6209.657	1	6209.257	26.289	.000***
Groups	1706.272	1	1706.272	7.224	.010*
Error	10864.636	46	236.188		

*$p < .05$, **$p < .01$, ***$p < .000$

It can be seen from Table 1 that both groups exhibited significance, $F = 7.224$, $p = .010 < .05$. The data meant that learners' posttest scores will have significant differences depending on the teaching styles. In Chinese Idiom teaching, IRS method is superior to traditional lecture style. It can be known from Table 2, the adjusted mean of experimental group is 89.104, while the control group is 77.300. Experimental group had higher adjusted mean than those of the control group, learners' posttest scores also exhibited significance after receiving different teaching styles, which indicated that IRS method is superior to traditional lecture style.

Table 2. Adjusted mean of posttest scores of different learning methods

Group	Avg	*SD*	95% *CI*	
			Upper bound	Lower bound
Experimental	89.104a	3.137	82.709	95.419
Control	77.300a	3.074	71.113	83.487

Covariate: Pretest scores = 44.6939.

4.2 Discuss the Differences Between Experimental and Control Group on "Chinese Idiom Learning Motivation"

After receiving different teaching methods, both group of learners will be analyzed via the four dimensions (Attention, Relevance, Confidence and Satisfaction) to determine the influences on their learning motivation.

It can be indicated form Table 3 that both groups' general learning motivation scores exhibited significance after the test, $p = .000 < .05$. This can be interpreted as the IRS method is superior to traditional lecture style.

Table 3. Independent sample t test of both groups of learners' learning motivation scale

Group	Number	Avg	*SD*	Avg *SD*	*t* value	Significance
Experimental	24	69.00	6.672	1.362	4.128	.000***
Control	25	60.52	7.649	1.529		

$^{*}p < .05$, $^{**}p < .01$, $^{***}p < .001$

Table 4. Independent sample t tests of learning motivation scale dimensions of both groups

Dimension	Group	amount	Avg.	*SD.*	Avg. *SD.*	*t* value	Significance
Attention	Experimental	24	4.46	.581	.118	3.881	.000***
	Control	25	3.77	.672	.134		
Relevance	Experimental	24	4.44	.585	.119	2.683	.010*
	Control	25	3.89	.841	.168		
Confidence	Experimental	24	3.67	.325	.066	2.397	.021*
	Control	25	3.36	.564	.112		
Satisfaction	Experimental	24	4.65	.434	.088	3.602	.001**
	Control	25	4.11	.608	.121		

$^{*}p < .05$, $^{**}p < .01$, $^{***}p < .001$

It can be seen from Table 4 that both groups of learners that all four dimensions of attention aspect ($t = 3.881$, $p = .000 < .05$), relevance ($t = 2.683$, $p = .010 < .05$), confidence ($t = 2.397$, $p = .021 < .05$) and satisfaction ($t = 3.602$, $p = .001 < .05$) reached significance. This indicated that learners underwent IRS method was more active in learning motivation than those of traditional lecture style.

5 Conclusions

Through analyzing the IRS method, learners generally exhibit significant differences and increased averages. It can be inferred that using the IRS method is superior to traditional lecture style in teaching Chinese Idioms. This result proved Lin's [16] thoughts about educators should incorporate information technology into teaching in order to increase learners' learning efficiency using a diversified approach. After integrating IRS into classes, learners' learning achievements were higher than those of the traditional lecture style [17, 18]. There have been quite a number of studies on utilizing Kahoot, the results of which confirmed that integrating Kahoot into teaching activities can increase learners learning efficiency [19, 20].

References

1. Liu, Y.-L.: Using Mobile Learning on Chinese Idioms for the Sixth Grader of Elementary School. Asia University, Taichung (2019)

2. Liu, W.-S.: Design Idiom Teaching App for Primary School. Huafan University, New Taipei (2015)
3. Chang, C.-H.: Educational Psychology. Tung Hua, Taiwan (2007)
4. Huang, C.W.: A study of integrating rewarding mechanism into the classroom interactive system and its instructional applications. Master thesis, National Tsing Hua University, Hsinchu, Taiwan (2013)
5. Huang, T.-S.: A study on the assisted instruction enhance the effectiveness of teacher-student interaction and learning – use the IRS as an example. J. Comput. Sci. Technol. **4**(1), 24–38 (2014)
6. Chang, C.S., Chen, T.S., Hsu, H.L.: The implications of learning cloud for education: from the perspectives of learners. In: Proceeding of Seventh IEEE International Conference on Wireless, Mobile and Ubiquitous Technology in Education, pp. 157–161 (2012)
7. Huang, J.-S.: Talking about the strategy of applying IRS instant feedback system to university course teaching. Taiwan Educ. Rev. Monthly **6**(10), 81–87 (2017)
8. Wang, C.-W.: The Design and Implementation of Team-Game-Tournament with Instant Feedback System into a University Course. Tamkang University, New Taipai (2016)
9. Graham, K.: TechMatters: getting into Kahoot! (s): exploring a game-based learning system to enhance student learning. LOEX Quart. **42**(3), 6–7 (2015)
10. Huang, R.-L.: Improve compositional ability from a systematic perspective. Educ. Monthly **480**, 80–83 (2005)
11. Ho, Y.-C.: A study on Chinese idioms in the viewpoint of grammar and rhetoric with it's teaching methods. J. Taipei Municip. Teach. Coll. **36**(1), 1–24 (2005)
12. Stipek, D.: Effects of different instructional approaches on Young Chidren's achievement and motivation. Child Dev. **66**(1), 209–223 (1995)
13. Yang, T.-H.: Using ARCS Motivational Model to Promote Technical and Vocational College Students' Motivation to Learn and Achievement: A Quasi-Experiment Study. National Sun Yat-sen University, Kaohsiung (2010)
14. Keller, J.M.: Strategies for stimulating the motivation to learn. Perform. Instr. **26**(8), 1–7 (1987)
15. Keller, J.M.: Motivation by design. Unpublished manuscript. Florida State University, Tallahassee, FL (1999)
16. Lin, Y.-H.: A Study of Phonics and IWB-Assisted English Remedial Instruction in an Elementary School. National Chung Cheng University, Chiayi (2013)
17. Su, W.-R.: The Study of Interactive Response System Integrating the Fifth Grade Mathematics Teaching-Decimal Conceptions as the Example. National Pingtung University, Pingtung (2010)
18. Wang, Y.-C.: Effectiveness in Teaching Decimal Multiplication Using Multimedia Instructions with IRS Systems for the Fifth Graders. Asia University, Taichung (2012)
19. Chou, Y.-R.: Effects of Paper-Based Test and Kahoot Test on Students' English Reading Performance and Attitude Based on Students' Question-Posing. Unpublished Master Thesis, National Formosa University, Yunlin (2015)
20. Tsai, S.-H.: A Study on the Influence of Kahoot on Junior High School Students' Learning Achievement with Different Learning Styles. Unpublished Master thesis, National Chinan International University, Nantou (2017)

Multimedia Technology Enhanced Learning

On the Convenience of Speeding Up Lecture Recordings: Increased Playback Speed Reduces Learning

Ida Ness[1], Kathinka Opdal[1], and Frode Eika Sandnes[1,2](✉)

[1] Oslo Metropolitan University, 0130 Oslo, Norway
{s187533,frodes}@oslomet.no
[2] Kristiania University College, 0153 Oslo, Norway

Abstract. Audio and video lectures give students much freedom to study where and when they like. These digital media formats usually also give students flexibility to choose the playback speed. In this study we conducted a simple experiment to assess the effects of the playback speed on learning. A total of 20 participants were recruited using convenience sampling. The participants were divided into two groups, one half listening to a podcast at normal speed and the other at double speed, and thereafter completed a multiple-choice test. The results showed that the test scores were significantly lower at double playback speed. These results may have implications for teachers and students.

Keywords: Playback speed · Time-compression audio lectures · Video lectures · Recall · Learning · Accessibility · Personalization

1 Introduction

Audio and specifically video-based lecture content has become widely available to students especially during the COVID-19 pandemic. Pre-recorded content gives students much freedom and flexibility in when they study, where they study and how they study. Another benefit of pre-recorded audio and video material is that students usually have the flexibility of adjusting the playback speed as well as going back and repeating specific segments [1]. Recordings are also believed to be beneficial for students with certain disabilities such as reduced vision [1] as one does not have to consider challenges associated with visual presentation [2] such as legibility of text [3, 4] but rather rely on non-visual cues [5, 6].

In a traditional physical lecture, students are bound to a time and place as well as following the pace of the lecturer. During course evaluations it is not uncommon for teachers to receive contradicting feedback indicating that the lectures are too slow, or too fast. Students who are unfamiliar with a topic or have a different language background may prefer a slow pace, while other students who already are familiar with the topic may want the lectures to move at a more rapid pace. Lecturers are therefore faced with the dilemma of diverging student needs. If they more slowly, all may comprehend the

© Springer Nature Switzerland AG 2021
Y.-M. Huang et al. (Eds.): ICITL 2021, LNCS 13117, pp. 461–469, 2021.
https://doi.org/10.1007/978-3-030-91540-7_47

content, but one may risk losing the interest of the more advanced students. If one decides to move at a faster pace one risk losing the students that need a slower pace. With personal playback of pre-recorded contents, the students can select their preferred pace.

Much of the literature distinguishes between playback speed and time-compression or time-stretching [7]. Simply speeding up a recording will also increase the pitch and make spoken dialogue sound unnatural. This is the effect that can be heard if playing back a magnetic tape at a different speed than the original. Therefore, such applications typically employ some time-compression or time-stretching algorithm [8] so that the playback speed can be altered without affecting the pitch. For simplicity time-compression will be implied when referring to increased playback speed herein.

Informal dialogues with students reveal that some students indeed make use of this possibility, usually speeding up lectures that are too slow. There are also reports of an emerging trend where audiobook listeners listen to audiobooks at faster speeds. Users of screen readers with synthetic text-to-speech output typically speed up the speaking rate to cover more material per time unit. One may also imagine the opposite, that is, to decrease the playback speed when learning how to conduct certain tasks in detail, for instance when learning to play musical instruments or perform certain vocation-oriented tasks.

Playback speed is not the sole factor, also the actual speaking rate needs to be considered. A universal measure of speaking rate is words per minute (wpm), which is also used to measure text entry rates [9–11]. "Normal" speaking rate is believed to be around 150 words per minute, although individual variations can be large. In contrast, reading speeds are believed to be nearly twice that, namely 200–300 words per minute. One must also keep in mind that there are different types of reading such as skimming and careful (deep) reading. Obviously, the reading mode affects the reading speed.

We therefore wanted to explore to what degree an altered playback speed affects learning, in particular increased playback speed. We wanted to explore if playback speed can be comprehended when played at typical reading speeds. Our hypothesis was that increased playback speed will negatively affect learning. A controlled between groups experiment was designed where half of the participants listened to a podcast at normal speed and the other half listened to the same podcast at double speed upon which they completed a questionnaire. Although several similar experiments have been conducted in the past, we believe that it is important to replicate such experiments in the current technological context as the technology has advanced much since the early studies 50 years ago, both in terms of general accessibility, familiarity among end-users and audio quality.

This paper is organized as follows. The next section reviews related work. Section 3 presents the methodology. Results are presented in Sect. 4 followed by a discussion in Sect. 5. The paper is closed with concluding remarks in Sect. 6.

2 Related Works

Several studies have explored the effects of speech rate on learning and some studies go back more than 50 years [12]. Barabasz [12] performed an experiment with more than

100 participants at graduate level by adjusting the playback speed of speech recorded on magnetic tape. The two conditions included normal speed and a second condition with the speed increased by 30%. The listening experiment was followed up with a test. The author found no effect of playback speed on recall.

King [13] conducted an experiment using time-compressed speech and found that the short-term listening performance started to deteriorate at 60% compression rate.

Ritzhaupt et al. [14] assessed performance with speech compressed at 40% and 80%. They found no effects on performance but did observe a significant effect on participants preference for the 40% compression rate.

Ritzhaupt and Barron [15] also conducted a large-scale study involving 300 participants with four conditions, namely normal playback speed, 50% increase, 100% increase and 150% increase. The results show a significant decrease in performance with 150% increase in playback speed compared to the other conditions.

Playback speed in conjunction with visual stimuli has also been investigated. A study involving 150 participants showed that increased playback speed combined with visual cues improved the recall but not the performance [16]. Goldhaber [17] found that both the playback speed and academic level of the listener were influential factors.

Speech rate has also been studied in context of screen reader users [18, 19]. Generally, experienced text-to-speech screen reader users configure the synthetic speech rate to twice, or three times, the normal rate, making it nearly intelligible for non-trained listeners. Also, screen-reader users often "skim-read" by skipping words, sentences and paragraphs using dedicated screen-reader controls. This allows screen reader users to cover more ground in a shorter time and hence more flexibility and freedom.

Speaking rate is also of interest to broadcasters [20]. For instance, for newscasts, it is important to employ a speaking rate that is comprehensible to the broad range of listeners which may have diverse backgrounds in terms of education and language proficiency.

3 Method

3.1 Experimental Design

A between-groups experiment was chosen to ensure that each participant only was exposed to one of the two conditions. Playback speed was the independent variable with the two levels normal (original) speed and double speed. Success (recall) rate was the dependent variable.

3.2 Participants

A total of 20 participants were recruited using convenience sampling, of which 12 were female and 8 were male. All the participants were native Norwegian language users. Their mean age was 33.7 years of age ($SD = 11.90$). The youngest participant was 24 years old and the oldest 59 years old. A Mann-Whitney U test shows that the age of the males ($M = 35.3$, $SD = 13.8$) and the females ($M = 32.7$, $SD = 11.1$) were not significantly different ($W = 45$, $p = .846$). A non-parametric test was used as a Shapiro-Wilk test revealed that the age distributions were not normally distributed.

An attempt was made to divide the participants into two balanced groups using stratified sampling. The 20 participants were therefore split into two groups of 10 participants with 4 males and 6 females in each group. A Mann-Whitney U test confirmed that there were no significant differences in age across the two groups ($W = 58.5, p = .542$).

3.3 Material

For the listening experiment a professional Norwegian language podcast by Selda Ekiz published by the National Broadcasting Corporation in Norway (NRK) was used. The theme of this 8 min and 50 s podcast is Why are fungi important to us? (Smartere på 10 minutter: Hvorfor er soppen viktig for oss?). This podcast was chosen as it was relatively short and thus suitable for the experiment. Moreover, the podcast is on a general topic which most participants could relate to. The podcast was professionally produced and therefore believed to be engaging to listeners.

Based on the content of the podcast a 24-question multiple choice test was designed with four alternatives for each question, in which only one option was correct. The questions addressed various information provided in the podcast. Google Forms was used to implement the questionnaire.

3.4 Procedure

The experiment was conducted remotely and electronically due to the COVID-19 pandemic. The participants were sent links to the podcast and questionnaire. It was not possible to adjust the playback speed on the podcast in the player on the website of the Norwegian Broadcasting Corporation. Therefore, the participants were asked to use the default podcast app available on their smartphones. This app is available on all smartphones and all the participants had smartphones.

Half of the participants played the podcast at its original speed according to its original duration of 8:50 min, while the other half of the participants listened to the podcast at double speed, namely 4:25 s. The participants who were assigned to listen to the podcast at double speed were instructed how to configure the podcast app.

The participants were asked to sit in a room without others present, and switch off any music, radio, television, or other potentially disturbing elements. They were instructed not to take notes or listen to the podcast, or parts of the podcast, several times, nor search for answers on the Internet. The experimenters pointed out that it was not their comprehension that was tested but the podcast.

The experiment was anonymous as it was conducted within a single session requiring no linking of observations [21].

3.5 Analysis

The success rate for each person was found by tallying all the correct answers and dividing these by the number of questions. The success rates for the participants were analyzed statistically using the open-source statistical analysis software JASP version 0.13.1.0 [22].

4 Results

Figure 1 shows the result of the experiment. Clearly, those who listened to the podcast at normal speed achieved a nearly twice as high recall rate ($M = 75.0\%$, $SD = 13.0\%$) than those who listened to the podcast at double speed ($M = 45.8\%$, $SD = 10.8\%$). An independent sample t-test shows that this difference was statistically significant ($t(18) = 3.46$, $p < .001$, Cohen's $d = 2.441$). The large effect size confirms this difference.

We also assessed the participants for bias. A Welch t-test confirmed that there were no effects of gender ($t(10.270) = 0.354$, $p = .731$). A Welch test was used since a Levene's test revealed a deviation from the assumption of equal variances ($F(1) = 6.910$, $p = .017$). Moreover, age did not correlate with the correct rate ($r_s(20) = 0.021$, $p = .929$).

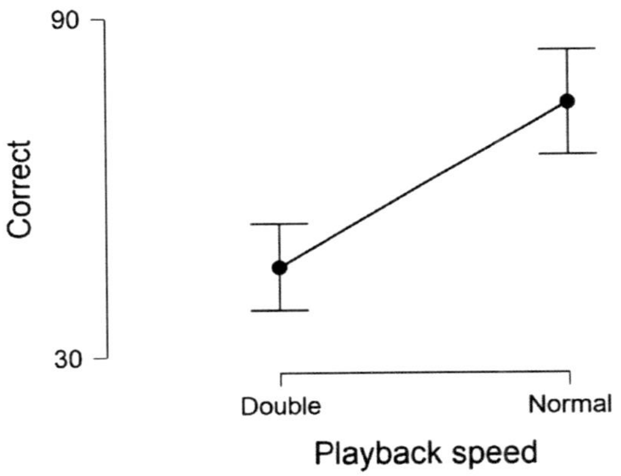

Fig. 1. Recall rates of normal and double playback speed (percentages). Error bars show 95% confidence intervals.

5 Discussion

The results support the hypothesis that reading speed affects recall, that is, if the audio playback speed is increased the recall is reduced. One possible explanation for this is that the audio played back at a higher speed is harder to comprehend. Another explanation is that the participants were given half the time to absorb the material. Perhaps the normal playback rate gives the participants sufficient space to process and briefly reflect over the information provided, while at half speed the participants were unable to do much apart from listening. On the other hand, there was obviously a longer time delay between the presentation of the information and the time to give the response for the participants who listened at normal speed, which could also have contributed to participants forgetting some of the contents, while those who listened to the podcast in half the time had a comparatively smaller chance of forgetting the content. The experiment was not designed to distinguish between the root cause, whether it is the legibility of the audio or other factors that results in the lower recall rates.

The results agree with previous findings such as results reported by King [13] and Ritzhaupt and Barron [15], while they disagree with the results of other studies such as Barabasz [12], Ritzhaupt et al. [14]. One possible explanation for the diverging results could be the quality of the audio technology used in the studies, as well as the degree of playback speed change. Clearly, studies with a large change in playback speed are probably more likely to trigger effects on recall than small playback speed changes. However, one should be careful when contrasting the results from these different studies since the experimental setups were not standardized.

6 Limitations

There are several weaknesses with the current experiment. First, the sample was relatively small with a comparatively wide spread of participants. It would be relevant to repeat the experiment with a larger sample and perhaps more focused cohorts of pupils (up to and including secondary school level) and students (at university level).

We did not probe the background of the participants and in this instance participants with a background in biology would have found the questionnaire easier than those without explicit training in biology. In hindsight we should have also asked about this, even with narrow cohorts, as participants may have diverse backgrounds with a myriad of study combinations or personal interests and hobbies. Moreover, we did not probe if any of the participants had reduced cognitive function such as reduced memory, as this could also have impacted the recall rates [23]. We should also have asked participants if they had any hearing.

The experiment was conducted remotely, and we were therefore unable to control the environment in which the experiment took place. It is therefore possible that some participants had background noise or other disturbances that may have affected the results [24–26].

Another aspect which was not addressed herein was the difficulty of the message. As the readability of written language affects comprehension [27–29], it is also possible that the language used in the podcast could have impacted the results. One way to check for this would be to assess the theoretical readability of the content by applying readability indices to a transcript of the podcast contents. However, the podcast was produced by the Norwegian natural broadcaster and presumably has gone through certain quality assurance procedures. Moreover, all the participants listened to the same content and there would thus be no bias across the two groups.

In hindsight it would have been relevant to probe the participants preferred playback speed. Preferred playback speed is highly personal and depends on factors such as listening context and training in listening to fast audio.

7 Conclusion

A study exploring audio lecture playback speed on learning was reported. The results showed that audio content played back at double speed led to reduced recall rate during a multiple-choice post-test. The results thus confirm our hypothesis that playback speed affects learning. These results may have implications for teachers who deliver pre-recorded audio or video lecture material. In this between groups experiment the participants had to listen to the audio in the designated speed category. In a real pedagogical setting the student will have a choice of speeding the audio or not, with the default being normal playback speed. Students who are more comfortable with speeding up the playback speed may do so permanently or during parts of a recording. However, it is likely that this may compromise comprehension and the students should be made aware of this. On the other hand, speeding up the content may help retain students' interest in the topic. It may be worthwhile to compromise the comprehension of some details, as it is probably better to have some learning outcome than no learning outcome. In any case, the freedom for students to choose their preferred playback speed is most likely a benefit to the learning process. Teachers should take explicit steps to ensure that students are aware of such functionality. This study did not address the degree with which students are aware of playback speed controls. Future work could explore students' perceptions of, and experience with, such speed control mechanisms. Another avenue of exploration is playback speed of videos where audio stimuli are accompanied by visual stimuli, both in textual format and as teachers' facial cues and gesticulations [30].

References

1. Junor, L.: Teaching by tape: some benefits, problems, and solutions. Dist. Educ. **13**(1), 93–107 (1992). https://doi.org/10.1080/0158791920130108
2. Sandnes, F.E.: What do low-vision users really want from smart glasses? Faces, text and perhaps no glasses at all. In: Miesenberger, K., Bühler, C., Penaz, P. (eds.) ICCHP 2016. LNCS, vol. 9758, pp. 187–194. Springer, Cham (2016). https://doi.org/10.1007/978-3-319-41264-1_25
3. Sandnes, F.E., Zhao, A.: An interactive color picker that ensures WCAG2.0 compliant color contrast levels. Procedia Comput. Sci. **67**, 87–94 (2015). https://doi.org/10.1016/j.procs.2015.09.252
4. Sandnes, F.E.: Understanding WCAG2.0 color contrast requirements through 3D color space visualization. Stud. Health Technol. Inform **229**, 366–375 (2016). https://doi.org/10.3233/978-1-61499-684-2-366
5. dos Santos, A.D.P., Medola, F.O., Cinelli, M.J., Garcia Ramirez, A.R., Sandnes, F.E.: Are electronic white canes better than traditional canes? A comparative study with blind and blindfolded participants. Univ. Access Inf. Soc. **20**(1), 93–103 (2020). https://doi.org/10.1007/s10209-020-00712-z
6. Lin, M.W., Cheng, Y.M., Yu, W., Sandnes, F.E.: Investigation into the feasibility of using tactons to provide navigation cues in pedestrian situations. In: Proceedings of the 20th Australasian Conference on Computer-Human Interaction: Designing for Habitus and Habitat, pp. 299–302 (2008). https://doi.org/10.1145/1517744.1517794
7. Pastore, R., Ritzhaupt, A.D.: Using time-compression to make multimedia learning more efficient: current research and practice. TechTrends **59**(2), 66–74 (2015). https://doi.org/10.1007/s11528-015-0841-2
8. Omoigui, N., He, L., Gupta, A., Grudin, J., Sanocki, E.: Time-compression: systems concerns, usage, and benefits. In: Proceedings of the SIGCHI Conference on Human Factors in Computing Systems, pp. 136–143. ACM (1999). https://doi.org/10.1145/302979.303017
9. Sandnes, F.E., Thorkildssen, H.W., Arvei, A., Buverad, J.O.: Techniques for fast and easy mobile text-entry with three-keys. In: Proceedings of the 37th Annual Hawaii International Conference on System Sciences 2004. IEEE (2004). https://doi.org/10.1109/HICSS.2004.1265675

10. Sandnes, F.E.: Evaluating mobile text entry strategies with finite state automata. In: Proceedings of the 7th International Conference on Human Computer Interaction with Mobile Devices and Services, pp. 115–121. ACM (2005). https://doi.org/10.1145/1085777.1085797
11. Aschim, T.B., Gjerstad, J.L., Lien, L.V., Tahsin, R., Sandnes, F.E.: Are split tablet keyboards better? A study of soft keyboard layout and hand posture. In: Lamas, D., Loizides, F., Nacke, L., Petrie, H., Winckler, M., Zaphiris, P. (eds.) INTERACT 2019. LNCS, vol. 11748, pp. 647–655. Springer, Cham (2019). https://doi.org/10.1007/978-3-030-29387-1_37
12. Barabasz, A.F.: A study of recall and retention of accelerated lecture presentation. J. Commun. **18**(3), 283–287 (1968). https://doi.org/10.1111/j.1460-2466.1968.tb00077.x
13. King, P.E., Behnke, R.R.: The effect of time-compressed speech on comprehensive, interpretive, and short-term listening. Hum. Commun. Res. **15**(3), 428–443 (1989). https://doi.org/10.1111/j.1468-2958.1989.tb00192.x
14. Ritzhaupt, A.D., Gomes, N.D., Barron, A.E.: The effects of time-compressed audio and verbal redundancy on learner performance and satisfaction. Comput. Hum. Behav. **24**(5), 2434–2445 (2008). https://doi.org/10.1016/j.chb.2008.02.017
15. Ritzhaupt, A.D., Barron, A.: Effects of time-compressed narration and representational adjunct images on cued-recall, content recognition, and learner satisfaction. J. Educ. Comput. Res. **39**(2), 161–184 (2008). https://doi.org/10.2190/EC.39.2.d
16. Ritzhaupt, A.D., Barron, A.E., Kealy, W.A.: Conjoint processing of time-compressed narration in multimedia instruction: the effects on recall, but not recognition. J. Educ. Comput. Res. **44**(2), 203–217 (2011). https://doi.org/10.2190/EC.44.2.d
17. Goldhaber, G.M.: Listener comprehension of compressed speech as a function of the academic grade level of the subjects. J. Commun. **20**(2), 167–173 (1970). https://doi.org/10.1111/j.1460-2466.1970.tb00874.x
18. Borodin, Y., Bigham, J.P., Dausch, G., Ramakrishnan, I.V.: More than meets the eye: a survey of screen-reader browsing strategies. In: Proceedings of the 2010 International Cross Disciplinary Conference on Web Accessibility. ACM (2010). https://doi.org/10.1145/1805986.1806005
19. Lee, H., Jang, Y., Hong, K.-H.: A comparison of the listening speed of the Korean TTS for the blind: based on their screen reader experiences. In: Miesenberger, K., Fels, D., Archambault, D., Peňáz, P., Zagler, W. (eds.) ICCHP 2014. LNCS, vol. 8547, pp. 49–52. Springer, Cham (2014). https://doi.org/10.1007/978-3-319-08596-8_8
20. Smith, J.R., McEwen, W.J.: Effect of newscast delivery rate on recall and judgment of sources. J. Broadcast. Electron. Media **18**(1), 73–78 (1973). https://doi.org/10.1080/08838157309363721
21. Sandnes, F.E.: HIDE: short IDs for robust and anonymous linking of users across multiple sessions in small HCI experiments. In: CHI 2021 Conference on Human Factors in Computing Systems Extended Abstracts Proceedings. ACM (2021). https://doi.org/10.1145/3411763.3451794
22. JASP Team. JASP (Version 0.14.1) [Computer software] (2020)
23. Sandnes, F.E., Lundh, M.V.: Calendars for individuals with cognitive disabilities: a comparison of table view and list view. In: Proceedings of the 17th International ACM SIGACCESS Conference on Computers and Accessibility, pp. 329–330. ACM (2015). https://doi.org/10.1145/2700648.2811363
24. Vasilev, M.R., Kirkby, J.A., Angele, B.: Auditory distraction during reading: a Bayesian meta-analysis of a continuing controversy. Perspect. Psychol. Sci. **13**(5), 567–597 (2018). https://doi.org/10.1177/1745691617747398
25. Thompson, W.F., Glenn Schellenberg, E., Letnic, A.K.: Fast and loud background music disrupts reading comprehension. Psychol. Music **40**(6), 700–708 (2011). https://doi.org/10.1177/0305735611400173

26. Halin, N.: Distracted while reading? Changing to a hard-to-read font shields against the effects of environmental noise and speech on text memory. Front. Psychol. **7**, 1196 (2016). https://doi.org/10.3389/fpsyg.2016.01196
27. Kaushik, H.M., Eika, E., Sandnes, F.E.: Towards universal accessibility on the web: do grammar checking tools improve text readability? In: Antona, M., Stephanidis, C. (eds.) HCII 2020. LNCS, vol. 12188, pp. 272–288. Springer, Cham (2020). https://doi.org/10.1007/978-3-030-49282-3_19
28. Eika, E., Sandnes, F.E.: Authoring WCAG2.0-compliant texts for the web through text readability visualization. In: Antona, M., Stephanidis, C. (eds.) UAHCI 2016. LNCS, vol. 9737, pp. 49–58. Springer, Cham (2016). https://doi.org/10.1007/978-3-319-40250-5_5
29. Eika, E., Sandnes, F.E.: Assessing the reading level of web texts for WCAG2.0 compliance—can it be done automatically? In: Di Bucchianico, G., Kercher, P. (eds.) Advances in Design for Inclusion, pp. 361–371. Springer International Publishing, Cham (2016). https://doi.org/10.1007/978-3-319-41962-6_32
30. Sandnes, F.E.: Absence and presence of faces in videos during the COVID19 lockdown. In: 9th International Conference on Software Development and Technologies for Enhancing Accessibility and Fighting Info-exclusion, pp. 189–193. ACM (2020). https://doi.org/10.1145/3439231.3439235t

My Morning Routine: An Interactive UDL Compliant E-Book on Health and Hygiene for Learners with Visual Difficulties

Azka Rizwan(✉), Mohsina Abid, Noor Us Subah Quidwai, and Midhat Noor Kiyani

National University of Sciences and Technology (NUST), Islamabad, Pakistan
arizwan.msitl20seecs@seecs.edu.pk

Abstract. Health instruction assembles students' information, abilities, and positive perspectives about wellbeing. However, 40% of the children in Pakistan are visually impaired and 38% have some cognitive disability due to malnutrition and poor hygiene practices. Despite COVID-19 putting the focus on the significance of hand cleanliness to forestall the spread of illness, reports from different countries have shown that the hand hygiene compliance rate has been estimated at only 40%. Using a Universal Design of Learning (UDL) approach, this research developed and produced a UDL compliant interactive android e-book that teaches young minds about the importance of staying clean and sanitization, especially to those learners who respond better when materials are paired with lights, sounds and/or movement. The scripting, story layout, design, and development were implemented using the seven stages of action and Nielson's design heuristics. Drawing upon the cyclic process of developing prototypes and then learners providing feedback upon each version, this e-book was designed to optimize learning by minimizing the cognitive load on the learners, providing ease for learners with visual or cognitive learning disabilities. Results showed that the visually challenged learners responded well to the minimal design interface and graphics. Major impact of the research was students developing the habits of handwashing and following healthy morning routines, as indicated in the interviews and surveys conducted from the learners.

Keywords: Universal design of learning · UDL · Health · Hygiene · Interactive · E-book · Visually impaired · Hand washing · Morning routine · COVID-19

1 Introduction

Instructing young children about good habits regarding personal health and hygiene is critically important as a lot of life-long habits form in the early life stages [1]. This research is aimed at creating and designing an interactive e-book that helps learners in developing the personal hygiene habits via a gamified, storytelling method. It is targeted for young learners within the age range of 3 to 5 years who have some visual difficulties and visually attend better when materials are paired with light, movement and/or sound.

© Springer Nature Switzerland AG 2021
Y.-M. Huang et al. (Eds.): ICITL 2021, LNCS 13117, pp. 470–482, 2021.
https://doi.org/10.1007/978-3-030-91540-7_48

1.1 Literature Survey

To identify the research gap, a comprehensive study was carried out to investigate the problem under study and the current relevant work on health and hygiene practices.

Significance of Hygiene Awareness and Sanitation Practices. Health instruction assembles students' information, abilities, and positive perspectives about wellbeing. It instructs about physical, mental, emotional, and social wellbeing and inspires students to improve and sustain their wellbeing, preempt infection, and decrease unsafe practices, while likewise advancing learning in different subjects [2]. Studies from CDC [3] have shown that the reading and math scores of students who received extensive health instruction were effectively better than the individuals who did not. Healthy students have higher participation, have better assessments, and perform better on tests.

Despite COVID-19 putting the focus on the significance of hand cleanliness to forestall the spread of illness, three billion individuals around the world, including countless school-going children, do not have access to hand washing amenities with soap [4]. Moreover, individuals living in provincial regions, metropolitan ghettos, disaster inclined regions, and low-income countries are the most powerless and the most affected [5]. According to a situational analysis of children in Pakistan, 44% of the children under 5 years of age are stunted, of which an alarming 52% are physically deficit, 40% are visually impaired and 38% have some cognitive learning disability due to malnutrition, insufficient maternal, infant, and neonatal health care, immunization, and poor sanitary practices [6].

Multiple reports from different countries amidst the onset of the Covid-19 pandemic have shown that the hand hygiene compliance rate has been estimated at only 40% [7], while the rate of adherence in critical care units is only 46.25% [8]. Although this is a simple and lifesaving task, it is not, regrettably, always undertaken [9]. The current pandemic has made handwashing the focus of attention. The next practical research works should make sure that this continues [10].

Hygiene Awareness Through Digital Game-Based Learning & Storytelling. Although the significance and potential outcomes of hand washing have been reported in all the studies cited, it is also reported that a very small percentage of people follow these good hygiene practices, especially in developing countries [11, 12]. Hence, a developing country like Pakistan needs to double down on its endeavors in advancing health and hygiene awareness and effectively executing United Nations' Sustainable Development Goal (SDG) 3 and 6 identified with wellbeing and WASH, respectively.

To guarantee better advancement, a methodology known as game-based learning can be used. Kebritchi and Hirumi [13] surveyed various papers and games and referred to the connection between students' inspiration and computerized game-based learning. However, they did not address the connection between computerized game-based learning and hygiene games, and specifically their importance in developing countries. Hence, to reinforce the advancement on SDG 3 (health) in Pakistan, imaginative methodologies like game-based learning are the need of today as the focal point of focused case studies. Kostkova et al. [14, 15] featured and stressed the potential of hygiene games by introducing the investigation on e-Bug games that spotlight hand and respiratory hygiene and microorganisms for junior and senior school students. The authors concluded that the game taught the basics of hand and respiratory hygiene. However, this research did not establish how much actual learning was accomplished after playing the game as learners did have some pre-requisite knowledge about this theme. In another research, Soler et al. [16] explored the design and evaluation of Molarcropolis, a mobile game that uses persuasive techniques to raise oral health and dental hygiene awareness in adolescents. While the research showed clear implications for effectiveness in the long run, it was targeted at 14–25 year-olds and did not conclude any real impact on the habits of the targeted audience. Molner et al. [17] developed a mobile game 'Edugames4all MicrobeQuest!' targeted at 9–12 year-olds that creates awareness about important health issues and teaches microbiology. However, this game was not developed with a universal design approach, and the results showed that the younger audience of the spectrum got tired of reading the text/instructions. Therefore, it is important to do research on and develop games (targeting this topic) that deploy a universal design for better engagement, representation and providing multiple means of action and expression.

Significance of Current Study. As Piagetian theory of cognitive development states, children start learning from the moment they are born [1] and key to their emotional and physical development is health and hygiene. Considering the risk at which children under the age of 7 are, the aim of this research is to develop this mobile application for learners with low vision in the range of 3–5 years, particularly students with visual difficulties, and to educate them on the importance of health and hygiene to ensure that every child inculcates healthy habits in their lifestyle.

There are some similar paid and free versions of 'Read to Me' story apps available to download on the iPad. Some examples include: an interactive UDL friendly book 'Big Cat in the Garden Story Creator' [18]; 'Hop on Pop' [19] with read-to-me, text highlighting and automatic page turning features; 'The Monster at the End of This Book' [20] with an interactive gamified story-telling approach; 'One Fish, Two Fish' [21]; 'Foot Book' [22]; 'The Boy Giant' [23] and 'The Smelly Sprout' [24].

Only 12.5% of the world's population can afford an iPad/iPhone while 86.8% of global smartphone users have Android devices [25]. Considering that this application is being designed specifically for Pakistani children, it will be designed on the Android platform using an interactive storytelling format to accommodate the learners facing visual difficulties.

2 Methodology

This section highlights design process of our interactive e-book and the underlying research methodology, data collection tools and analysis to get learners' feedback.

2.1 E-Book Design and Development

The design of this e-book was guided by Universal Design of Learning (UDL) approach [26] and Neilson's Design Heuristics [27].

UDL Guided Design. To account for the variability in the learning needs of diverse learners, UDL guidelines and checklists were used for the design of the application [28]. Using these guidelines and checklists, the interactive e-book was developed to ensure its inclusivity and options for variability for multiple types of learners, as summarized in Table 1.

Table 1. UDL guided design of e-book

Guideline	Checkpoint	Example
Engagement	Recruiting interest	Relevant to every learner; fast or slow. Especially helpful for low vision students. Distractions (animations) were minimized
	Sustaining effort & persistence	Goal-directed; clear and easily understandable
	Self-regulation	Promotes healthy expectations from every learner
Representation	Perception	For visual learners, audio with text on the screen is provided; for auditory learners, narration of story and instructions are available as well
	Language & Symbols	Simple and clear vocabulary is used. More languages can be added to make it inclusive
	Comprehension	Provides a connection by highlighting the importance of a healthy morning routine
Action & Expression	Physical action	Utilizes a touch-based system, provides haptic feedback. Playable on any Android phone or tablet (version 4.0.0/above)
	Expression & Communication	Multiple kids following the same routine in the story encourage all kids to follow
	Executive functions	Learners reflect upon routine(s) they are following; and new things they can add in their morning routine or improve upon

Neilson's Design Heuristics. This interactive e-book was designed, developed, and produced in multiple stages based on Nielson's design heuristics [29], see Fig. 1.

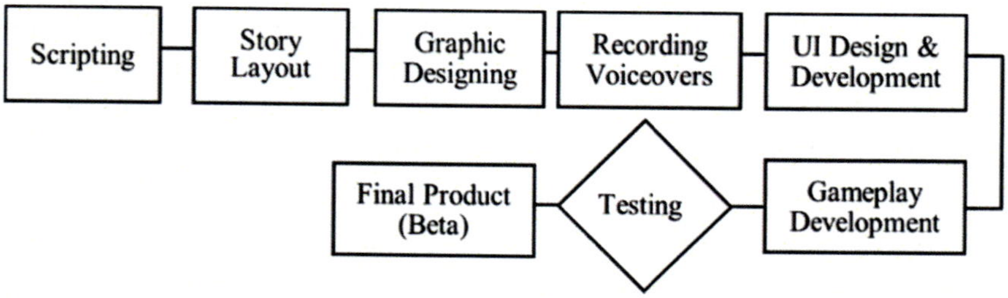

Fig. 1. The e-book design, development & production process

Scripting and Story Layout. First up was the scripting stage, which involved creating the characters, their narratives, and the story progression. Once the characters were developed, the layout of the story was created, and health and hygiene elements were incorporated into it.

Graphic Designing and Voiceovers. Using Canva and Adobe Photoshop, the characters and story setting were created, see Fig. 2. Then, voice actors were used to record voiceovers for the characters and the music was licensed from Electronic Arts (EA).

Fig. 2. Graphical design of e-book on Canva & Adobe

Interface Design and Gameplay Development. Using MIT app inventor, the application interface and story elements were coded. The development of the e-book was initially planned to utilize the Kotobee Author application [30]. However, the production of the e-book on Kotobee proved to be difficult as Kotobee is a paid service and it allowed only three application builds for the free version. Since the development of any application requires production of multiple test files, the option of using Kotobee was complex, time consuming, and cost prohibitive. Hence, the development and production plan changed to using MIT app inventor [31]; a free online tool that utilizes block-coding to create Android applications (code available online [32]).

Final Product. An e-book application with an interactive UDL design, with a main screen, settings' screen, five story/gameplay screens and three interactive question screens, see Fig. 3. Additional resources including demo video of the final product are available online [33].

Fig. 3. Glimpse of the final product

Testing and Evaluation. The e-book application was created and tested using the android emulator, visual studio, and a wireless internet connection on a phone. The application was tested multiple times using real-time processing to see the changes taking effect. The final beta version was evaluated on an honor 8x android phone.

2.2 Research Methodology

To collect the learners' feedback and rich explanations with their experience using the application, qualitative research was conducted for recording their comprehensive responses [34].

Research Participants. The focus group participants for the analysis of the prototypes were chosen via convenient and voluntary response sampling [35]. Initial surveys were conducted to select participants for the target group which involved learners who were 3–5 years old and had some visual impairment(s). The reason for focusing on this specific age group was because of the risk for health issues at which the children in this age group are – especially in Pakistan, as the literature survey indicates [6]. Since children in this age group learn through emulation of the actions of their peers and environmental contacts, they inculcate habits and from their teachers, classmates, and family, which becomes an essential part of their lives [36]. This survey was for the parents/guardians of the prospective target group in which they were asked to fill in the form if they had kids meeting research participants' requirements (3–5 years old and diagnosed with a visual impairment). Through these surveys, a focus group of 10 was chosen in accordance with privacy, willingness, and consent. To eliminate bias in the study, only the participant's age and visual impairment were factored into account. Other factors related to gender, education, financial background, race, ethnicity, religion, political views, and personal beliefs were disregarded.

2.3 Data Collection Tools and Analysis

To collect learners' feedback on their interactive experiences with the developed application, online focus group surveys and one-on-one semi-structured video interviews were employed as central data collection methods (see Table 2). Throughout the study, data was collected online due to the restrictions imposed by the pandemic. Research ethics were given the priority, and supervisors of the participants were asked about informed consent to avoid any misunderstandings or possible risk [37].

Ten focus group surveys and five one-on-one video interviews with children were conducted. The data was collected using video conferencing tools: MS Teams & Zoom (for the interviews), Google forms (for the surveys) were used, and responses were stored and analyzed using MS Excel. Analysis involved a review of videos, surveys, and transcribed records of the interviews to assess the quality of interactions of the learners with the application [38].

Table 2. Summary of data collection tools and analysis

Participants group	Number of participants	Analysis techniques	Conduct/design
Focus group application use	10	Retrospective testing online	Online (audio, video), screen recording
Focus group questionnaire	10	MS excel	Google forms
One-on-one semi-structured interviews	5	Audio-visual recordings/Interviews (online)	MS teams Zoom

There were two sessions conducted with each of the ten participants.

Session 1. In the first session, we employed two techniques to collect data from the participants. First, their interaction with the application was recorded with a mic and face camera with the learner's consent. Secondly, an online survey questionnaire (available online at [39]), was used *that* participant had to fill out after using the application.

Session 2. The second session was a semi-structured online interview to which only half of the focus group consented. The interview lasted approximately 20 min and was conducted *with* retrospective testing techniques [40], where the learners were questioned on their interactive e-book experiences, their actions, and the thought processes behind them.

The interviews were transcribed, and a deductive thematic analysis [41] was conducted to identify key elements from the interviews. This involved coding all the data before identifying and reviewing four key themes. Each theme was examined to gain an understanding of participants' perceptions and motivations.

3 Results

The results from the participant usage of the 10 focus group surveys and the 5 one-on-one interviews are discussed here.

3.1 Focus Group Surveys

The results from the focus group surveys were stored and analyzed using MS Excel. The surveys were divided into two parts. The first part was the experience with the application itself that was recorded with a mic and face camera with the learner's consent. The results of the first analysis are shown in Table 3.

Table 3. Results of the application testing.

Participant	Age	Total time taken (~minutes)	Face-cam	Audio	Visual difficulty
One	3	10	On	On	Low visual acuity
Two	3	9	On	On	Low visual acuity
Three	3	9	On	On	Low visual acuity
Four	4	10	Off	On	Low visual acuity
Five	4	7	On	On	Low visual acuity
Six	4	7	Off	On	Low visual acuity
Seven	5	8	On	On	Dyslexia
Eight	5	3	On	On	Low visual acuity
Nine	5	4	On	On	Low visual acuity
Ten	5	3	On	On	Loss of peripheral vision

The second part of the focus group surveys was filling out the questionnaire after using the application. The learners were allowed to fill this out under supervision if help was required. The results of the questionnaire were recorded and stored in MS Excel (detailed responses available online [42]).

The results of the questionnaire and surveys showed that most of the learners enjoyed the interactive e-book experience. The youngest age group took the longest to finish the entire story, and the oldest age group finished the fastest except for learner 7. Upon analysis, we found out that learner 7 was a student who faced difficulties due to dyslexia as they required extra time to parse the direction of text in the interactive activity. Learner 4 had the severest case of low visual acuity (hazy vision) and required the most time out of everyone in that age group. Learner 10, despite having loss of peripheral vision, finished the fastest (due to having intact central vision, despite being unable to see below eye level). Learners 1–3, 5, 6, 8 and 9 had near visual acuity within the range of N.40 to N.80 at 25cm [43, 44].

It was quite surprising to note that only two of the learners turned off the cameras. This showed that most of the students were quite engaged in the story book and were actively interacting and participating in the study.

The results of the questionnaire showed that all the learners found the e-book interface easy to use. The instructions were simple for them to understand, with the verbal pacing at a comfortable level. However, some of them found the accent of the verbal instructions slightly difficult to comprehend due to not being native English speakers. The e-book text was also clearly visible for almost all the learners, except for learner 4 and 7. All of them responded positively about the e-book's graphics, background music and the story progression. Learner 7, however, had moderate difficulties with the graphics, colors, the on-screen text, and level of background music (due to dyslexia). Also, most of the learners finished the questionnaire without adult intervention. This shows that the UDL compliant e-book developed in the study optimized relevance (age-relevant content).

3.2 One-on-One Interviews

The one-on-one interviews were conducted with only five of the 10 original participants as only half of them expressed consent and willingness to participate in interviews. The interviews were audio-visually recorded and discussed recorded application testing with the learners. Learners were questioned on why they performed certain actions and what was their thought process while interacting with the e-book (e.g., opinion about interface design). From the interviews, four key thematic elements were deduced and coded.

Thematic Element One: Interface Design. Since the targeted audience was learners with visual impairments, specifically low vision, they were satisfied with the minimal interface design. An initial prototype implemented animations into the interface design. However, based on the learners' testing and suggestions, they were removed due to increased cognitive load. It is in accordance with the research [45] which suggests that some learners have cognitive difficulties with their visual impairments, and they cannot handle splitting their attention between too many competing elements like animations. One of the learners with severe near visual acuity said: "I cannot enjoy cartoons because of the movement and voices, but I could easily read this e-book because the characters were stationary". Another learner with dyslexia commented: "The simple interface and directions helped me follow the story without having to worry all the time about [which] buttons to press". This principle aligned with Nielson's Seven Principles of interface design [29].

Thematic Element Two: Graphic Design. In this study, the choice of graphic design was complex and posed various challenges. Since the target learners were catered for their low visual acuities (among other visual impairments), the design had to be simple, but also colorful because children respond better to bright and vivid colors and images. The learners were very satisfied with the graphics used. Most of them enjoyed the bright colors and patterns as well. A learner said: "I really liked the colorful rooms and characters in the story. Colors and pictures help me learn faster and understand what is being said." A few exceptions were there who answered that the colors were too 'loud' for them. They felt that the graphics were distracting them from the main point of the story. The learner with dyslexia commented: "The graphics were too bright and colorful, and it was like they were shouting loudly at me, 'look at me!', which made it difficult to follow the narration of the story simultaneously."

Thematic Element Three: Alternatives to Visual Design. Audio instructions and audio & haptic feedback was provided to the learners. All of them, especially the ones with low peripheral vision answered that it helped them out a lot. A learner said: "The vibrations helped me a lot. I knew I had pressed the correct interaction on the screen when I felt the vibrations." Learners respond well to auditory/haptic stimulus when their visual senses are dulled [16]. This played a key factor in determining the total playback time of the individual learners (separate from the age factor). Another learner said: "The verbal instructions helped me focus on the story without worrying about reading the text correctly. I could focus on the characters and answering the questions easily." However, the learners expressed that all instructions, including the options for the interactive questions, should have been audibly presented. The learner with severe near visual acuity commented: "I cannot read anything clearly because of the hazy vision. It would help me more if the answer options were verbally instructed as well."

Thematic Element Four: Thematic Design (Health & Hygiene). The theme of the e-book, health & hygiene, was clearly apparent from the title page of the e-book. One learner said: "I liked the title page. It showed pictures of what I do every morning after I wake up. I follow a healthy routine!" They related to the routine that they themselves follow every morning. Another learner said: "I understood that Kayla was going to talk about healthy habits like brushing teeth, washing hands, etc., with her friends."

Some learners were even encouraged to inculcate the habit of having a healthy breakfast every morning and question the validity of health in their existing routines, and explicitly expressed so in the interviews. One learner commented: "I eat chips for breakfast every morning. But I saw [Sam] enjoying his cereal. Are chips not healthy? I will also have an apple in the morning now." Another learner was encouraged to share the healthy habits with others as well and commented: "My [little] sister cries every morning before going to school. I will read this book to her, and it will make her happy too!".

4 Conclusions

In this study, we discussed the importance of health and hygiene, particularly highlighted for a post-pandemic learning scenario by designing an interactive, UDL compliant e-book on health and hygiene practices. This interactive e-book catered to learners who have visual impairment(s) including low visual acuity, dyslexia, and loss of peripheral vision. Due to technical and time constraints, the sample size of the study was kept small to ensure that the quality of study is not compromised. However, even amidst these challenges, the study was able to produce some key results and outcomes [46]. The interactive experiences engaged learners on multiple levels of interest, by providing variability in the design of the e-book. This study concludes that information about important topics, such as health and hygiene, can be inculcated into the minds of young learners by utilizing techniques like game-based learning and digital storytelling for better motivation and expediency. Moreover, if learners are provided a rationale and modelling for these behaviors, they are inspired to learn even better. This interactive e-book will help teachers, schools, and parents to guide kids about importance of health and hygiene. Based on the positive feedback and interactive experiences of students, more chapters like importance of physical exercise and healthy lifestyle will be added in this e-book in the future study while improving the interface design and gameplay.

References

1. Brainerd, C.J.: Jean Piaget, learning research, and American education. In: Zimmerman, B.J., Schunk, D.H. (eds.) Educational psychology: A century of contributions, pp. 251–287. Lawrence Erlbaum Associates Publishers (2003)
2. School Health. http://www.education.nh.gov/instruction/school_health/health_coord_education.htm#health_ed/. Accessed 21 May 2021
3. CDC Healthy Schools. https://www.cdc.gov/healthyschools/sher/characteristics/index.htm. Accessed 11 May 2021
4. Hutton, G., Chase, C.: The knowledge base for achieving the sustainable development goal targets on water supply, sanitation and hygiene. Int. J. Environ. Res. Public Health **13**(6), 536 (2016)
5. UNICEF: Pakistan Annual Report, 13–17 (2016)
6. The situation analysis of children in Pakistan. https://www.unicef.org/pakistan/reports/situation-analysis-children-pakistan. Accessed 21 May 2021
7. Erasmus, V., et al.: Systematic review of studies on compliance with hand hygiene guidelines in hospital care. Infect. Control Hosp. Epidemiol. **31**, 283–294 (2010)
8. Bezerra, T.B., Valim, M.D., Bortolini, J., Ribeiro, R.P., Marcon, S.R., Moura, M.E.B.: Adherence to hand hygiene in critical sectors: can we go on like this? J. Clin. Nurs. **29**(13–14), 2691–2698 (2020)
9. Doronina, O., Jones, D., Martello, M., Biron, A., Lavoie-Tremblay, M.: A systematic review on the effectiveness of interventions to improve hand hygiene compliance of nurses in the hospital setting. J. Nurs. Scholarsh. **49**, 143 (2017)
10. Alzyood, M., Jackson, D., Aveyard, H., Brooke, J.: COVID-19 reinforces the importance of handwashing. J. Clin. Nurs. **29**(15–16), 2760–2761 (2020)
11. Fewtrell, L., Kaufmann, R.B., Kay, D., Enanoria, W., Haller, L., Colford, J.M.: Water, sanitation, and hygiene interventions to reduce diarrhea in less developed countries: a systematic review and meta-analysis. Lancet. Infect. Dis **5**(1), 42–52 (2005)
12. Zahidie, A., Rabbani, F.: Impact of water and sanitation and health education interventions on health and hygiene behaviors: a study from a northern Pakistani village. Pakistan J. Public Health, **3**(1) (2013)
13. Kebritchi, M., Hirumi, A.: Examining the pedagogical foundations of modern educational computer games. Comp. Educ. **51**(4), 1729–1743 (2008)
14. Kostkova, P., Farrell, D., de Quincey, E., Weinberg, J.R., Lecky, D., McNulty, C.: eBug-teaching children hygiene principles using educational games. Stud. Health Technol. Inf. **160**(1), 600–604 (2010)
15. Farrell, D., et al.: Computer games to teach hygiene: an evaluation of the e-Bug junior game. J. Antimicrob. Chemother. **66**(5), v39-44 (2011)
16. Soler, C., Zacarías, A., Lucero, A.: Molarcropolis: a mobile persuasive game to raise oral health and dental hygiene awareness. In: Proceedings of the International Conference on Advances in Computer Entertainment Technology, pp. 388–391 (2009)
17. Molnar, A., Kostkova, P.: Learning about hygiene and antibiotic resistance through mobile games: evaluation of learning effectiveness, pp. 95–99 (2018)
18. Big Cat in the Garden (Collins). https://apps.apple.com/us/app/id499208536?ign-mpt=uo%3D4. Accessed 15 Apr 2021

19. Hop on Pop (Oceanhouse Media). https://apps.apple.com/us/app/hop-on-pop-by-dr-seuss/id1092652588. Accessed 15 Apr 2021
20. The Monster at the End of This Book (Sesame Street). https://apps.apple.com/us/app/the-monster-at-the-end/id409467802. Accessed 15 Apr 2021
21. One Fish, Two Fish (Oceanhouse Media). https://apps.apple.com/us/app/one-fish-two-fish-dr-seuss/id1092650486. Accessed 15 Apr 2021
22. Foot Book (Oceanhouse Media). https://apps.apple.com/us/app/the-foot-book-read-learn/id1275266549. Accessed 15 Apr 2021
23. The Boy Giant (Jason Stewart). https://apprecs.com/ios/491334739/the-boy-giant-hd. Accessed 15 Apr 2021
24. The Smelly Sprout (Allan Plenderleith). https://apps.apple.com/us/app/the-smelly-sprout/id485311259?ign-mpt=uo%3D4. Accessed 15 Apr 2021
25. IDC 2016: Interaction Design and Children: Association for Computing Machinery, New York, NY, United States (2016)
26. Meyer, A., Rose, D.H., Gordon, D.: Universal Design of Learning: Theory and Practice, 1st edn. CAST Professional Publishing, United States (2016)
27. Masmuzidin, M.Z., Aziz, N.A.: The adaptation of Shneiderman's golden rules and nielsen's heuristics on motivational augmented reality technology design for young children. In: IEEE 9th International Conference on System Engineering and Technology (ICSET), pp. 62–67. IEEE, Malaysia (2019). https://doi.org/10.1109/ICSEngT.2019.8906373
28. UDL Guidelines (Cast). https://udlguidelines.cast.org/. Accessed 2 Jul 2021
29. Norman, D.A.: The Design of Everyday Things. MIT Press (2013)
30. Kotobee Author: https://www.kotobee.com/en/products/author. Accessed 3 May 2021
31. MIT App Inventor: http://ai2.appinventor.mit.edu/#5008874028793856. Accessed 12 May 2021
32. Rizwan, A.: My morning routine.aia. Figshare. Software (2021). https://doi.org/10.6084/m9.figshare.14932374.v1
33. Rizwan, A.: My morning routine (application resources). Figshare. Media (2021). https://doi.org/10.6084/m9.figshare.14935350.v1
34. Kyngäs, H.: Qualitative research and content analysis. In: Kyngäs, H., Mikkonen, K., Kääriäinen, M. (eds.) The Application of Content Analysis in Nursing Science Research, pp. 3–11. Springer, Cham (2020). https://doi.org/10.1007/978-3-030-30199-6_1
35. Edgar, T.W., Manz, D.O.: Exploratory study. In: Research Methods for Cyber Security, pp. 95–130. Elsevier (2017). https://doi.org/10.1016/B978-0-12-805349-2.00004-2
36. Myers, D.G., DeWall, C.N.: Psychology, 12th edn. Worth Publishers Inc, New York (2018)
37. Miyan, M.Z., Baloch, H., Husnain, M.: Hygiene awareness through digital game-based learning. New Trends Issues Proc. Human. Soc. Sci. 4(8), 67–73 (2017)
38. Hollander, J.: The social contexts of focus groups. J. Contemp. Ethnogr. **33**, 602–637 (2004)
39. Rizwan, A.: Research questionnaire II. Figshare. Survey Questionnaire (2021). https://doi.org/10.6084/m9.figshare.16613836.v2
40. Gunawan, I., Indrawan, G., Sariyasa.: User experience evaluation of academic progress information systems using retrospective think aloud and user experience questionnaire. J. Phy. Conf. Ser. **1810**(1) (2021)
41. Kiger, M.E., Varpio, L.: Thematic analysis of qualitative data: AMEE Guide No. 131. Med. Teacher **42**(8), 846–854 (2020)
42. Rizwan, A.: Questionnaire responses. Figshare. Dataset (2021). https://doi.org/10.6084/m9.figshare.14935425.v1
43. Radner, W.: Reading charts in ophthalmology. Graefes Arch. Clin. Exp. Ophthalmol. **255**(8), 1465–1482 (2017). https://doi.org/10.1007/s00417-017-3659-0
44. WHO: Blindness and Vision Impairment. https://www.who.int/news-room/fact-sheets/detail/blindness-and-visual-impairment. Accessed 30 May 2021

45. Jan, J.E., Heaven, R.K.B., Matsuba, C., Langley, M.B., Roman-Lantzy, C., Anthony, T.L.: Windows into the visual brain: new discoveries about the visual system, its functions, and implications for practitioners. J. Vis. Impairment Blind. **107**(4), 251–261 (2013)
46. Kiyani, M.N., Haider, I., Javed, F.: Designing Freirean-inspired community relevant steam curriculum for underserved students in Pakistan using action research process. In: Huang, T.-C., Wu, T.-T., Barroso, J., Sandnes, F.E., Martins, P., Huang, Y.-M. (eds.) ICITL 2020. LNCS, vol. 12555, pp. 536–546. Springer, Cham (2020). https://doi.org/10.1007/978-3-030-63885-6_58

Applying E-Book System to Facilitate Student' Flipped Learning Performance in Software Engineering Courses

I-Chun Lin[1], Tz-Chi Wang[2], and Yen-Ting Lin[2](✉)

[1] Department of Information Management, R.O.C. Military Academy, No.1, Wei-Wu Rd., Fengshan Dist, Kaohsiung City 83059, Taiwan (R.O.C.)

[2] Department of Computer Science, National Pingtung University, No.4-18, Minsheng Rd., Pingtung County, Pingtung City 900391, Taiwan (R.O.C.)

Abstract. In recent years, many institutions have pointed out that software developments are important to nations, societies, and individuals. However, to develop quality software, students should not only possess programming skills, but also have to apply the knowledge and skills of software engineering. This entails the importance of software engineering education. Currently, most software engineering courses were conducted using the traditional teaching strategy. Most students can only recite and understand the pertinent knowledge with concerning software engineering after learning. As mentioned above, this study adopts a learner-centered pedagogy, named flipped classroom, to improve software engineering education. Moreover, in order to promote students' learning performance before the class in flipped classrooms, this study applies an e-book system, named BookRoll. By using the e-book system, students can learn at anytime and anywhere before the class. Simultaneously, their reading behaviors may be recorded by the system. Teachers can facilitate the student discussions and interactions with peers in the class by capturing and analyzing student reading status and further enhancing their learning performance. To explore students' learning performance in software engineering courses, students from two classes were invited to learn with different learning approaches (flipped learning approach and flipped learning with e-book system approach). The experimental results showed that the students who learned with the proposed approach outperformed those students who learned with traditional flipped learning approach.

Keywords: E-book · Software engineering · Flipped classroom · Learning performance

1 Introduction

Developing software with good infrastructure and robustness is not just a matter of students having programming and writing skills. Thus, students need to enhance knowledge and technology skills for software project development [1]. In other words, students have to learn how to use a scientific approach to define the criteria, methods, and procedures

© Springer Nature Switzerland AG 2021
Y.-M. Huang et al. (Eds.): ICITL 2021, LNCS 13117, pp. 483–490, 2021.
https://doi.org/10.1007/978-3-030-91540-7_49

required in the software development process so that they may efficiently develop robust software that meets the requirements of users. This also shows how important software engineering education is to students.

The ideal way to teach software engineering courses is to perform proper theoretical teaching, practical operations, and teacher-student interactions in a student-centered manner. However, in view of the constraints of the semester, most teachers can only use traditional classroom teaching strategies to teach theory in a unidirectional fashion [2]. Consequently, most students may not recall and understand the relevant knowledge after participating in the software engineering courses [3]. In other words, the students may not have the high-level reasoning capacity to use the knowledge gained in software engineering courses to solve practical problems.

In light of the above, the flipped classroom is an appropriate teaching strategy to support the teaching of software engineering. The flipped classroom is a student-centered learning strategy that aims to flip the learning activities inside and outside the classroom into a traditional classroom. In recent years, there have been several studies on the flipped classroom, and the results point out that the positive impacts of the flipped classroom on teachers and students at various educational levels and subjects [4, 5]. However, in order to successfully implement the flipped classroom strategy in courses, the effectiveness of student learning performance before the classroom becomes the key to effective instructional activities by teachers and students in the classroom [6].

As noted above, this study applied the flipped classroom teaching strategy to support software engineering courses. In order to promote the learning model, an e-book system, named BookRoll, was used to assist students in reading learning materials before the class. Moreover, an experiment was conducted to evaluate the effects of the proposed approach on students' learning performance in software engineering courses.

2 Literature Review

2.1 Software Engineering Education

In general, most software engineering courses are conducted by the teacher's lectures. Others are combined with practical software operations in the computer classroom [3]. However, regardless of the type of teaching method, it is mostly a teacher-centered teaching method, and most students always passively receive knowledge. Therefore, students may be unable to apply the software engineering knowledge in practical situations, and they may not be able to effectively apply what they have learned to address related problems going forward. In addition, literatures stated that software engineering courses should attach importance to students' discussion and thinking on practical cases, and create a student-centered learning environment to train students how to apply software engineering technology to solve problems in the software development life cycle [7–9]. Furthermore, with the help of external media, such as technology and digital resources, students can more efficiently acquire the ability to resolve software engineering problems, so that they can achieve the main goal of software engineering education [3, 10].

2.2 Flipped Classroom

Contrary to the learning activities in traditional classrooms, flipped classroom reverses the learning activities in and out of class in traditional classrooms. In the flipped classroom, teachers' lectures in class are replaced by videos or other multimedia resources, so that students can learn the materials outside the classroom. As a result, limited class time can be released and used for conducting practice, discussion, and problem solving activities. In this way, students are able to interact with teachers and their peers during class hours to stimulate critical thinking, problem solving skills, social cooperation and practical innovation [11, 12].

A key issue in the development of the flipped classroom is the effectiveness of student learning outside the classroom, which influences the status of teachers and students in classroom instructional activities [13]. In the out-of-class learning environment, students may not be able to fully comprehend whether their individual learning effectiveness has reached the level required for classroom instructional activities. This may prevent students from participating in instructional activities due to lack of sufficient prior knowledge when participating in classroom instructional activities [14].

2.3 E-Book

In recent years, with the popularity of reading technology, it has become a trend to use various devices (desktop, laptop, smart phones, or tablets) to carry and operate digital resources. E-books have also become one of the representative digital resources in the mobile generation [14]. The development of e-books shows the advantages of combining paper-books with computer technology, such as rich multimedia resources, multiple interactive mechanisms, convenient annotation functions, non-linear reading, and personalized analysis services.

Several studies have explored the influence of e-books integrated into teaching activities on students' learning performance. Korat [16] explored the impact of e-books on the language learning and literacy abilities of Israeli kindergarten and first grade children. The results of the study indicated that children who read e-books showed better literacy and reading skills. Li, Fan, Huang, & Chen [17] developed an e-book reading system that can effectively improve readers' reading effectiveness through the reading guide module and note reading. Liang & Huang [18] applied reading rate tracking technology to collect reading rate data for 24 sixth grade primary school students. The results of the analysis found that compared with paper-books, e-books can facilitate the students to capture the information in the books.

3 BookRoll E-Book System

This study applied flipped learning strategy to support software engineering courses. In order to promote the learning process, an e-book system, named BookRoll, was used to support students to read digital learning materials before the class. The BookRoll system is a web application that enable teachers and students to use it through web browsers. Students can use the system to read learning materials out of class for learning software

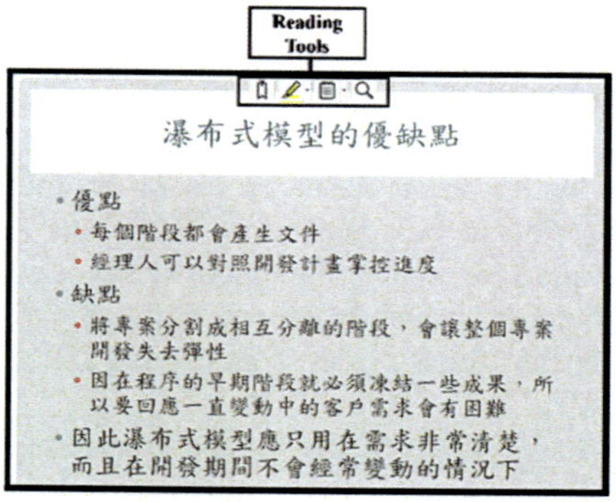

Fig. 1. BookRoll reading interface for students.

engineering prior knowledge, as show in Fig. 1. Moreover, teachers can use the system to obtain students' learning status and reading behaviors.

When students use the system to read learning materials, the system provides several functions such as bookmark function, highlight function, question mark function, note function, and search function to assist students in reading, as show in Fig. 2. At the same time, the system can automatically record students' reading behaviors, including reading time, reading completion, highlighting content, question mark content, and note content. In addition, the system provides a dashboard function for teachers to efficiently capture the reading status of students, including an overview of the status of all participating students, an overview of the reading status of individual students, real-time reading status, marker status, and so on, as show in Fig. 3.

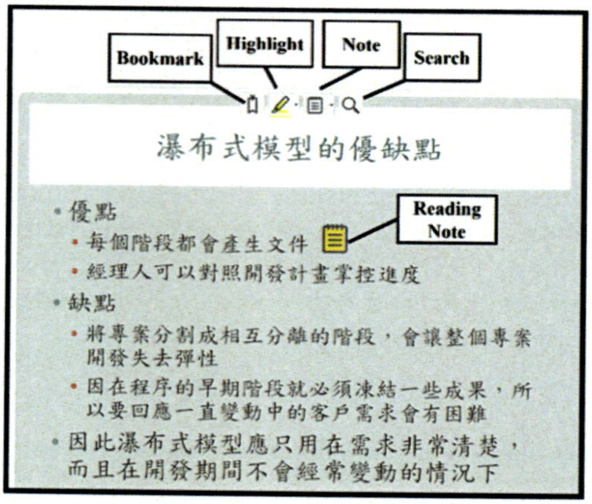

Fig. 2. BookRoll reading functions.

Fig. 3. BookRoll reading behavior dashboard.

4 Experiment

In order to evaluate the effects of the proposed learning approach for students participating in software engineering courses, a quasi-experimental was conducted in university software engineering courses. The duration of the experiment was 10 weeks (25 h). A total of 64 university students and an instructor participated in the study. The experimental group consisted of 37 students. The control group consisted of 27 students. The experimental group was supported by the flipped classroom learning approach with the e-book system to conduct the course. The control group was supported by the flipped classroom learning approach without the e-book system to conduct the course.

To evaluate the effectiveness of the proposed approach, various data sources were analyzed, including a prior knowledge test, a learning achievement test, and a learning motivation questionnaire results. The prior knowledge test was designed to assess the students' knowledge level with regard to software engineering before participating in the courses. The learning achievement test was designed to evaluate the students' learning results after the conclusion of the courses. The above two tests included 10 single-choice test items, and the maximum score was 100 points.

To measure students' goals and beliefs about the importance and interest of the teaching activities in the courses, the learning motivation questionnaire was used from the intrinsic scale of Motivated Strategies for Learning Questionnaire (MSLQ) [19]. The learning motivation questionnaire consisted of nine items with a seven-point Likert scale. For all students participated in this experiment, the pre-test and post-test Cronbach's alpha values of the learning motivation questionnaire were 0.919 and 0.948, respectively.

Before the formal course, students in the experimental group and control group were asked to take two pre-tests. One was the learning motivation questionnaire to measure the initial learning motivation. The other was the prior knowledge test to assess whether the students in the two groups had equal knowledge level with regard to software engineering. In addition, the instructor spent 30 min explaining the learning approaches adopted by each of the two groups, respectively. Additionally, the students in the experimental group obtained an additional 20 min of instruction with regard to the operations of the proposed system.

During the course, the instructor asked the students of the two groups to look at the lecture slides and videos to learn the relevant concepts of the subject outside the classroom. For this reason, this study planed 61 instructional videos, each about 5 to 8 min, and 10 slides for students to watch and learn anytime. Additionally, students in the experimental group were able to use the e-book system to read the slides outside the classroom. During class time, the instructor assigned case studies, discussions, and practice exercises to facilitate students' integration into teaching activities to promote their learning.

After completing the learning activities, the students from both groups received two post-tests, the learning motivation questionnaire and the learning achievement test, to complete the experiment conducted in this study.

5 Results

5.1 Analysis of Learning Achievement

A one-way independent sample analysis of covariance (ANCOVA) was used as the analysis method of learning achievement test results to exclude the difference between the prior knowledge of the two groups. Define the learning achievement test score as dependent variable and the prior knowledge test score as covariate.

The result confirmed the homogeneity of the regression coefficient ($F = 1038, p >$ .05). The adjusted means and standard deviations were 88.99 and 2.33 for the experimental group and 77.09 and 2.84 for the control group. The results of the analysis indicated that there was a statistically significant difference between the adjusted learning achievement test scores ($F(1,61) = 10.431$, $p = 0.002 < 0.05$). Moreover, the learning achievement of the experimental group was significantly higher than that of the control group. The results revealed that the proposed approach was more beneficial to students' learning achievement than the traditional flipped classroom learning approach in software engineering courses.

5.2 Analysis of Learning Motivation

To measure the effect of the proposed approach on students' learning motivation in software engineering courses. The one-way independent sample analysis of covariance (ANCOVA) was used as the analysis method of learning motivation questionnaire results to exclude the difference between the pretest of the learning motivation of the two groups. Define the post-test score of the learning motivation as dependent variable and the pre-test score as covariate. The result confirmed the homogeneity of the regression coefficient ($F = 1.127, p = 0.293 > 0.05$). The adjusted means and standard deviations were 6.07

and 0.12 for the experimental group and 5.66 and 0.15 for the control group. The results of the analysis indicated that there was a statistically significant difference between the adjusted learning motivation scores ($F(1,61) = 4.140, p = 0.046 < 0.05$). Moreover, the learning motivation of the experimental group was significantly higher than that of the control group. The results revealed that the proposed approach was more beneficial to students' learning motivation than the traditional flipped classroom learning approach in software engineering courses.

6 Conclusions

This study adopts the student-centered learning approach "flipped classroom" as the pedagogy and applies an e-book system in university software engineering courses. For students, they can view the videos recorded by the instructor during their learning activity outside the classroom, and use the e-book system to learn the slides produced by the instructor. For instructors, adopting the e-book system in the flipped classroom is a useful way to capture students' reading behaviors towards the slides, so that instructors can understand students' learning process through their reading behaviors. Based on this, instructors can design teaching activities to facilitate discussion and interaction between students, peers, and teachers in the classroom. The results indicated that the proposed approach was efficient in improving students' learning achievement and learning motivation in software engineering courses.

Overall, the primary contribution of this study is to advance the instruction of software engineering courses. However, the limitations of this study are that the scale of the experiment is insufficient and a random selection of participants is not used for the study. In addition, experimental groups with different conditions will be planned to conduct the courses in order to cover more samples and provide more analytical results. In the future, this study will conduct more multiple and in-depth analyses of reading behaviors for high learning motivation, low learning motivation, high learning achievement, and low learning achievement in order to investigate the impact of the proposed approach on various types of students.

References

1. Alhammad, M.M., Moreno, A.M.: Gamification in software engineering education: a systematic mapping. J. Syst. Softw. **141**, 131–150 (2018)
2. Lin, Y.T.: Effects of flipped learning approaches on students' learning performance in software engineering education. Sustainability **13**(17), 9849 (2021)
3. Lin, Y.T.: Impacts of a flipped classroom with a smart learning diagnosis system on students' learning performance, perception, and problem solving ability in a software engineering course. Comput. Hum. Behav. **95**, 187–196 (2019)
4. López Núñez, J.A., López-Belmonte, J., Moreno-Guerrero, A.-J., Marín-Marín, J.A.: Dietary Intervention through flipped learning as a techno pedagogy for the promotion of healthy eating in secondary education. Int. J. Environ. Res. Public Health **17**(9), 3007 (2020)
5. Pozo Sánchez, S., López-Belmonte, J., Moreno-Guerrero, A.-J., Sola Reche, J.M., Fuentes Cabrera, A.: Effect of bring-your-own-device program on flipped learning in higher education students. Sustainability **12**, 3729 (2020)

6. Lai, C.L., Hwang, G.J.: A self-regulated flipped classroom approach to improving students' learning performance in a mathematics course. Comput. Educ. **100**, 126–140 (2016)
7. Alok, G., Thiyagarajan, A., Condoor, S.: Effective approach towards development of idea through foundations to product design. J. Eng. Educ. Transform. **31**, 47–52 (2018)
8. Cico, O., Jaccheri, L., Nguyen-Duc, A., Zhang, H.: Exploring the intersection between software industry and software engineering education - a systematic mapping of software engineering trends. J. Syst. Softw. **172**, 110736 (2021)
9. Marijan, D., Gotlieb, A.: Industry-academia research collaboration in software engineering: the Certus model. Inf. Softw. Technol. **132**, 106473 (2021)
10. Salas-Morera, L., Arauzo-Azofra, A., García-Hernández, L., Palomo-Romero, J.M., Hervás-Martínez, C.: PpcProject: an educational tool for software project management. Comput. Educ. **69**, 181–188 (2013)
11. Alias, M., Iksan, Z., Karim, A., Nawawi, A., Nawawi, S.: A novel approach in problem-solving skills using flipped classroom technique. Creat. Educ. **11**, 38–53 (2020)
12. Awidi, I.T., Paynter, M.: The impact of a flipped classroom approach on student learning experience. Comput. Educ. **128**, 269–283 (2019)
13. Kim, M.K., Kim, S.M., Khera, O., Getman, J.: The experience of three flipped classrooms in an urban university: an exploration of design principles. Internet High. Educ. **22**, 37–50 (2014)
14. Zhu, X.: E-book ILL in academic libraries: a three-year trend report. J. Acad. Librariansh. **44**(3), 343–351 (2018)
15. Sage, K., Augustine, H., Shand, H., Bakner, K., Rayne, S.: Reading from print, computer, and tablet: equivalent learning in the digital age. Educ. Inf. Technol. **24**(4), 2477–2502 (2019). https://doi.org/10.1007/s10639-019-09887-2
16. Korat, O.: Reading electronic books as a support for vocabulary, story comprehension and word reading in kindergarten and first grade. Comput. Educ. **55**(1), 24–31 (2010)
17. Li, L.Y., Fan, C.Y., Huang, D.W., Chen, G.D.: The effects of the e-book system with the reading guidance and the annotation map on the reading performance of college students. Educ. Technol. Soc. **17**(1), 320–331 (2014)
18. Liang, T.H., Huang, Y.M.: An investigation of reading rate patterns and retrieval outcomes of elementary school students with e-books. Educ. Technol. Soc. **17**(1), 218–230 (2014)
19. Pintrich, P.R., De Groot, E.V.: Motivational and self-regulated learning components of classroom academic performance. J. Educ. Psychol. **82**(1), 33–40 (1990)

Effectiveness of Online Multimedia Courses for Improving Children's Self-regulation Through Social-Emotional Learning

Fu-Rung Yang[1], Mei-Hsin Wu[2], Jih-Hsin Tang[3](✉), and Chih-Fen Wei[4]

[1] Department of Education, University of Taipei, Taipei, Taiwan
[2] Taipei Municipal Guting Elementary School, Taipei, Taiwan
[3] Department of Information Management, National Taipei University of Business, Taipei, Taiwan
[4] Department of Psychology and Counseling, University of Taipei, Taipei, Taiwan

Abstract. This study determined the effectiveness of an online multimedia social-emotional learning (SEL) course through quantitative analyses (with respect to interaction, trust attachment, competitive hostility, and conflict dominance) and qualitative interviews. In total, 17 fourth-grade students from the same class participated. Their data were analyzed using nonparametric tests in SPSS 22.0, and the children were interviewed about how they regulated their emotions and interacted with their peers. According to the quantitative results, after the SEL course, students exhibited improvement in the positive aspects of their interpersonal relationships (with respect to interaction and trust attachment) but not the negative aspects (with respect to competitive hostility and conflict dominance). The interviews indicated that the students were more emotionally aware and had better relationships with their peers after the SEL course. In general, the results indicate the effectiveness of online multimedia SEL courses.

Keywords: Online multimedia course · Self-regulation · Social Emotional Learning · E-learning

1 Introduction

Social-emotional learning (SEL) is a process that involves the student's knowledge, attitudes, and skills; the aim in SEL is for the student to be able to manage their emotions, feel and demonstrate empathy toward others, establish and maintain supportive relationships, and achieve personal and collective goals. The Collaborative for Academic, Social, and Emotional Learning (CASEL) identifies five core competencies that SEL must develop [1]:

1. Self-awareness: The ability to understand one's own emotions, thoughts, and values and how they influence behavior across contexts.
2. Self-management: The ability to manage one's emotions, thoughts, and behaviors effectively in different situations and to achieve one's goals and aspirations.

© Springer Nature Switzerland AG 2021
Y.-M. Huang et al. (Eds.): ICITL 2021, LNCS 13117, pp. 491–497, 2021.
https://doi.org/10.1007/978-3-030-91540-7_50

3. Social awareness: The ability to understand the perspectives of and empathize with others, including those from diverse backgrounds, cultures, and contexts.
4. Relationship skills: The ability to establish and maintain healthy and supportive relationships and to effectively navigate settings involving diverse individuals and groups.
5. Responsible decision making: The ability to make caring and constructive choices about how one behaves and interacts with others in a variety of situations.

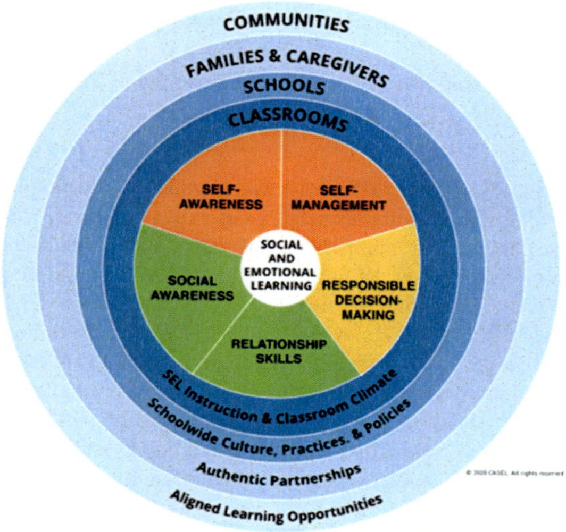

Fig. 1. CASEL (https://drc.casel.org/what-is-sel%20%20/).

The CASEL action framework also emphasizes that SEL occurs outside the classroom, in the family and community [2]. Durlak, Weissberg, Dymnicki, Taylor, and Schellinger [3] reported that relative to students who did not, students who participated in SEL courses had better academic performance and classroom behavior; were more capable of managing depression; and had a better attitude toward themselves, others, and their school. Taylor, Oberle, Durlak, and Weissberg [4] observed that the influence of SEL lasted long after students had attended classes on the subject. Specifically, at 18 years after their last SEL course, students who had taken SEL courses learned, behaved, and handled emotional distress better than their peers who had not; they were also less likely to abuse drugs.

Digital learning involves using the Internet to help students learn better [5]. E-learning allows students to freely choose when and where to engage in learning, and it can be flexibly adapted to any learning plan [6]. Bryant, Campbell, and Kerr [7] demonstrated that a technology-centric flexible learning course provided an effective learning environment for students. Dawson, Ven, and Gunter [8] investigated lower-grade students with emotional behavior disorder; they found that the students had better reading accuracy when reading from a computer and when the teacher read to them than when reading a physical book on their own. In general, computers helped these children with emotional behavior disorder learn better and afforded them the convenience to learn whenever they wished to, without the constraint of a timetable.

Considering the aforementioned context, in the present study, we evaluated how much an online multimedia teaching program improved self-regulation in children as part of SEL.

2 Method

In this study, we used two TV programs, "When We Are Together" [9] and "Children Together+" [10] from Da Ai TV Station in Taiwan, because they helped cultivate the five SEL competencies, doing so through games and discussion.

2.1 Participants

This study's participants were 17 fourth-grade students (5 boys and 12 girls, mean age = 10 years). They were in the same class and were enrolled in a music class for musically talented students.

2.2 Procedure

The study implemented a 40-min online multimedia SEL course over 8 weeks. In the course, students viewed videos online and teachers discussed with students about how to manage emotions.

3 Measurement

This study administered the Peer Adaptation Scale [11] before and after the 8-week course to analyze the effectiveness of the SEL course. The scale has 43 items over two dimensions: the positive relationship dimension, comprising the subscales interaction and trust attachment, and the negative relationship dimension, comprising the subscales competitive hostility and conflict dominance (four subscales in total).

4 Result

4.1 Quantitative Analysis

In this study, nonparametric tests were conducted to compare the pretest and posttest results with respect to the four subscales and two dimensions. The means and standard deviations of the data are reported in Table 1.

Table 1. Descriptive statistics of pretest and posttest results for the peer adaptation Scale (N = 17)

Subscale	Pretest M(SD)	Posttest M(SD)	Z-value
Interaction	41.94(6.35)	45.00(4.34)	−2.01*
Trust attachment	39.18(5.74)	42.00(5.40)	−2.16*
Positive relationship	**80.18(11.93)**	**87.00(9.37)**	**−2.36***
Competitive hostility	20.24(5.37)	20.35(5.44)	−0.23
Conflict dominance	16.88(3.52)	16.18(4.52)	−0.63
Negative relationship	**37.12(8.14)**	**36.53(8.47)**	**−0.06**

$^{*}p < .05$, $^{**}p < .01$

With respect to the subscales, students obtained higher scores for the interaction subscale at the posttest (mean [*M*] = 45.00, standard deviation [*SD*] = 4.34) than at the pretest (*M* = 41.84, *SD* = 6.35), and this difference was also present in a test of interaction ($Z = -2.01, p = 0.45$). Similarly, students obtained higher scores for the trust attachment subscale at the posttest (*M* = 42.00, *SD* = 5.40) than at the pretest (*M* = 39.18, *SD* = 5.74); this difference was significant ($Z = -2.16, p = 0.03$). However, the posttest and pretest scores did not significantly differ with respect to the competitive hostility subscale (posttest: *M* = 20.35, *SD* = 5.44; pretest: *M* = 20.24, *SD* = 5.37) or conflict dominance subscale (posttest: *M* = 16.18, *SD* = 4.52; pretest: *M* = 16.88, *SD* = 3.52).

With respect to the dimensions, students received higher scores for the positive relationship dimension at the posttest (*M* = 87.00, *SD* = 9.37) than at the pretest (*M* = 80.18, *SD* = 11.93); this difference was significant ($Z = -2.36, p = 0.018$). However, the posttest and pretest scores did not significantly differ with respect to the negative relationship dimension (posttest: *M* = 36.53, *SD* = 8.47; pretest: *M* = 37.12, *SD* = 8.14).

The Wilcoxon signed-rank test was conducted (Table 2). With respect to the interaction subscale, nine (*M* rank = 7.17) and three (*M* rank = 4.50) students scored higher and lower, respectively, at the posttest than at the pretest. Regarding the trust attachment subscale, 13 (*M* rank = 9.38) and 4 (*M* rank = 7.75) students scored higher and lower, respectively, at the posttest than at the pretest. Thus, with respect to the positive relationship dimension, 12 (*M* rank = 9.46) and 4 (*M* rank = 5.63) students scored higher and lower at the posttest, respectively, than at the pretest.

With respect to the competitive hostility subscale, eight (*M* rank = 6.69) and six (*M* rank = 8.58) students scored higher and lower, respectively, at the posttest than at the pretest. Regarding the conflict dominance subscale, nine (*M* rank = 7.89) and six (*M* rank = 8.17) students scored higher and lower, respectively, at the posttest than at the pretest. Thus, with respect to the negative relationship dimension, eight (*M* rank = 9.06) and eight (*M* rank = 7.94) students scored higher and lower, respectively, at the posttest than at the pretest.

Table 2. Wilcoxon signed-rank test ($N = 17$)

Subscale	Ranks	*N*	Mean rank	Sum of ranks
Interaction	Negative ranks	3	4.50	13.50
	Positive ranks	9	7.17	64.50
	Ties	5		
Trust attachment	Negative ranks	4	7.75	31.00
	Positive ranks	13	9.38	122.00
	Ties	0		
Positive relationship	**Negative ranks**	**4**	**5.63**	**22.50**
	Positive ranks	**12**	**9.46**	**113.50**
	Ties	**1**		
Competitive hostility	Negative ranks	6	8.58	51.50
	Positive ranks	8	6.69	53.50
	Ties	3		
Conflict dominance	Negative ranks	6	8.17	49.00
	Positive ranks	9	7.89	71.00
	Ties	2		
Negative relationship	**Negative ranks**	**8**	**7.94**	**63.50**
	Positive ranks	**8**	**9.06**	**72.50**
	Ties	**1**		

4.2 Qualitative Analysis

After they had undergone the online multimedia SEL course, the students were interviewed regarding how they manage their emotions and interact with others. The interview helped students reflect on the differences between various methods of emotional regulation and approaches to peer interaction.

The students stated the following regarding breathing deeply as a means to calmly regulate their emotions, which they learned in the SEL course.

- *Deep breathing is a good way, because it helps me regulate my emotions. Chatting is also a good method, because I can forget about bad things. (S01)*
- *I take a deep breath and calm myself down, and I focus on doing things that I like to do. (S08)*
- *When I get angry, I think about it for 6 s before doing something. (S17)*
- *The students also stated that they interacted more with their peers after attending the SEL course.*
- *I learned to use empathy to communicate with my classmates. Being able to empathize with others makes others feel better, and it also helps me have better interpersonal relationships. (S03)*

– *I learned how to be aware of the emotions of myself and others, which improves my relationships with others. (S05)*

In general, after the SEL course, the students had learned the emotional regulation technique of deep breathing and felt that they had better interpersonal relationships.

5 Discussion

This study explored the improvements in students' interpersonal relationships and emotional regulation ability after an online multimedia SEL course. According to the quantitative results, the course was associated with an improvement in the positive aspects of interpersonal relationships (specifically, interaction and trust attachment) but not with improvement in the negative aspects of interpersonal relationships (specifically, competitive hostility and conflict dominance). We surmise that this lack of improvement was due to the participants being musically talented students who had weekly music tests and who played in an orchestra; this resulted in a competitive environment.

According to the qualitative results, the students gradually became more aware of their emotions during the 8-week course. They acted less on impulse and learned how to breathe deeply and calm down when agitated. In the class, acts of reciprocal altruism became more frequent in addition to positive, empathetic interactions overall. Thus, the results indicate that the online multimedia SEL course is effective.

5.1 Theoretical Implications

This study used a novel, online multimedia approach to SEL courses. An online multimedia format enables students to construct ideas and provide feedback. This study focused on student-centered e-learning and emphasized self-directed emotional regulation and development.

5.2 Practical Implications

Teachers should adopt online multimedia approaches to SEL, especially considering how distance learning has become the norm during the COVID-19 pandemic and how it has the inherent advantages of being accessible anytime and anywhere. The online multimedia SEL course implemented in this study enhanced the positive aspects of the students' interpersonal relationships. However, the courses did not lessen the negative aspects of the students' interpersonal relationships. Future studies can devise approaches to address such an imbalance by, for example, implementing an SEL course over a longer period.

References

1. Collaborative for Academic, Social, and Emotional Learning (CASEL): What Is Social and Emotional Learning? (2020). https://drc.casel.org/what-is-sel%20%20/

2. Collaborative for Academic, Social, and Emotional Learning (CASEL): Key Implementation Insights from the Collaborating Districts Initiative. Chicago, IL, CASEL (2017)
3. Durlak, J.A., Weissberg, R.P., Dymnicki, A.B., Taylor, R.D., Schellinger, K.B.: The impact of enhancing students' social and emotional learning: a meta-analysis of school-based universal interventions. Child dev. **82**(1), 405–432 (2011). https://doi.org/10.1111/j.1467-8624.2010.01564.x
4. Taylor, R.D., Oberle, E., Durlak, J.A., Weissberg, R.P.: Promoting positive youth development through school-based social and emotional learning interventions: a meta-analysis of follow-up effects. Child Dev. **88**(4), 1156–1171 (2017). https://doi.org/10.1111/cdev.12864
5. Rosenberg, M.J., Foshay, R.: E-learning: strategies for delivering knowledge in the digital age. Perform. Improv. **41**(5), 50–51 (2002). https://doi.org/10.1002/pfi.4140410512
6. Institute for Information Industry: The best guide for digital learning. Taipei: Institute for Information Industry (2003)
7. Bryant, K., Campbell, J., Kerr, D.: Impact of web based flexible learning on academic performance in information systems. J. Inf. Syst. Educ. 14(1), 41 (2003). https://aisel.aisnet.org/jise/vol14/iss1/5
8. Dawson, L., Ven, M.L., Gunter, P.L.: The effects of teachers versus computer reading models. Behav. Disord. **25**, 105–1013 (2000). https://doi.org/10.1177/019874290002500202
9. Da Ai Television: When We Are Together (2017). http://daai.tv/search?q=%E7%95%B6%E6%88%91%E5%80%91%E7%AB%A5%E5%9C%A8%E4%B8%80%E8%B5%B7&target=Episode&dstart=&dend=
10. Da Ai Television: Children Together+ (2017). https://daai.tv/search?q=%E7%AB%A5%E5%9C%A8%E4%B8%80%E8%B5%B7+&target=Episode&dstart=&dend=
11. Lo, P.H., Chen, L.C.: Peer Adaptation Scale. Psychological Publishing, Taipei (2016)

Combining Flipped Learning and Formative Assessment to Enhance the Learning Performance of Students in Programming

Shu-Chen Cheng[1], Yu-Ping Cheng[2], Yueh-Min Huang[2](✉), and Yeongwook Yang[3]

[1] Department of Computer Science and Information Engineering, Southern Taiwan University of Science and Technology, Tainan, Taiwan
kittyc@stust.edu.tw

[2] Department of Engineering Science, National Cheng Kung University, Tainan, Taiwan
n98061513@gs.ncku.edu.tw, huang@mail.ncku.edu.tw

[3] Division of Computer Engineering, Hanshin University, Osan, Republic of Korea
ywkyung@hs.ac.kr

Abstract. Information technology is booming, students are no longer just acquiring knowledge through books, and their learning approaches are no longer limited to traditional lectures or classrooms. In recent years, flipped learning has become a novel instructional strategy, which allows meaningful learning by watching videos or reading materials before class in a student-oriented way. However, teachers cannot confirm whether students can learn new knowledge and concepts through flipped learning. Therefore, this study aims flipped learning combined with formative assessment to explore whether students can effectively improve their learning performance in programming. This study designed and recorded videos and developed an online formative assessment system to provide test items related to APP Inventor programming. These results show that compared with the control group, the experimental group can significantly improve their learning performance and learning progress in programming by combining flipped learning and the online formative assessment system. In addition, the teacher can examine each student's problems in the learning process through the proposed system by this study, and give them help and guidance in programming.

Keywords: Flipped learning · Formative assessment · Learning performance

1 Introduction

In traditional instructional strategies, most teachers teach students through lectures in the classroom, so students can only acquire knowledge from books. With the advancement of information technology, e-learning has become one of the sources of acquiring knowledge for students and they can improve their learning performance through digital materials and multimedia resources [1, 2]. Some studies combined wearable technologies with different experimental activities to explore the cognitive load of students in

© Springer Nature Switzerland AG 2021
Y.-M. Huang et al. (Eds.): ICITL 2021, LNCS 13117, pp. 498–507, 2021.
https://doi.org/10.1007/978-3-030-91540-7_51

the classroom [3–6]. In addition, teachers can combine information technology with the material to increase students' learning motivation in the classroom [7, 8]. Compared with general lectures, students can read massive open educational resources anytime and anywhere by combining online learning and digital learning tools to enhance their knowledge and concepts [9].

In higher education, flipped learning has attracted more and more attention [10]. Many researchers inferred that flipped learning was an instructional strategy to effectively enhance students' learning performance [11, 12], and can improve students' engagement in the classroom [13]. In addition, combining formative assessment with information technology in the classroom can improve students' learning performance [14]. Although many studies have confirmed that flipped learning and formative assessment can effectively improve students' learning performance. However, this research investigated that there are few studies discussing how to combine flipped learning and formative assessment to improve the learning performance of higher education students in programming. Therefore, this study developed an online formative assessment system and recorded 84 videos as learning materials for flipped learning. In addition, this study used the proposed system to explore whether students can effectively improve their learning performance in programming.

2 Literature Review

2.1 Flipped Learning

The vigorous development of information technology has become more and more common for teachers to use digital teaching materials or tools in the classroom. In order to effectively improve the learning performance or engagement of students in the classroom, researchers have developed many educational applications, multimedia resources, and online learning platforms to promote the development of flipped learning [13]. Related to research on flipped learning, Tütüncü and Aksu (2018) pointed out that flipped learning can effectively improve students' learning performance in the classroom [15]. Awidi and Paynter (2019) indicated that teachers can improve students' learning experience in the classroom through flipped learning [16].

Flipped learning can not only use multimedia videos as learning materials [11] but also can use a variety of digital resources or tools for flipped learning, such as game-based flipped learning approach [17] or MOOC-based flipped learning [18]. In addition, the learning materials provided by teachers to implement flipped learning should be kept as simple as possible, and they can also maintain good interaction with students in the classroom [19]. Although previous studies have proved that flipped learning can help to improve students' learning performance [20] and learning motivation [21], flipped learning also causes other problems. For instance, students need to spend a lot of time in flipped learning courses, which may increase their workload [22]. Therefore, this study aims to examine the problems encountered by students in flipped learning with a formative assessment.

2.2 Formative Assessment

In traditional assessment methods, teachers can only evaluate students' learning situations based on their test scores and homework scores. However, students may encounter certain problems in the learning process, which may cause students to learn wrong knowledge and concepts, and teachers cannot immediately solve these problems in the classroom. Therefore, formative assessment is an assessment method used by teachers to measure students' specific topics and skills [23]. Teachers can use formative assessment to evaluate students' learning performance on specific topics or units [24]. Many studies have confirmed that formative assessment can effectively improve students' learning performance in the classroom [25–27]. In addition, Elmahdi, Al-Hattami, and Fawzi (2018) pointed out that teachers' use of formative assessment in the classroom can help improve student engagement in the learning process [14].

As stated above, there have been related studies on flipped learning and formative assessment that have confirmed its effectiveness. However, there are few studies to explore that the flipped learning combines with formative assessment to improve higher education student's learning performance in programming. Therefore, this study provides videos based on the instructional strategy of flipped learning, so that students can understand the operation interface of APP Inventor and the functions and concepts of various programming blocks, and use the online formative assessment system to examine students' learning performance.

3 Research Method

This study is based on flipped learning to provide students with videos of the APP Inventor programming and develops an online formative assessment system to explore whether this system can improve the learning performance of the students in the experimental group in programming. Therefore, this study designed and recorded 84 videos as learning materials for flipped learning, and built 111 test items on an online formative assessment system to provide students in the experimental group for online tests.

3.1 Participants

This study investigated 73 students from the Department of Computer Science and Information Engineering, all of whom were from a university of science and technology in southern Taiwan. Among them, 32 were assigned to the experimental group and 41 were assigned to the control group. Before the experiment started, all students had not participated in the App Inventor course based on flipped learning.

3.2 Learning Material and Online Formative Assessment System

- Videos of App Inventor Programming based on Flipped Learning

The App Inventor course taught by the teacher has 12 units, and each unit contains a total of 7 videos. The teacher has recorded a total of 84 videos as learning materials for flipped learning. In addition, the length of each video varies from 5 to 20 min, and each video used English as the vocal language. The 7 videos included in each unit are introduced as follows (X is the unit number, there are 12 units in total):

- Unit X-1 Basic Operation (only demo without subtitles)
- Unit X-2 Advanced Operation (only demo without subtitles)
- Unit X-3 Basic Operation (only subtitles without a demo)
- Unit X-4 Advanced Operation (only subtitles without a demo)
- Unit X-5 Introduction of Basic Operation Block
- Unit X-6 Introduction of Advanced Operation Block
- Unit X-7 Summary of Unit X

Figure 1a and Fig. 1b are videos of the actual operation of App Inventor programming. Students can learn the relevant components and interfaces of App Inventor through Unit X-1 and Unit X-2. Since Unit X-1 and Unit X-2 do not show Chinese subtitles, students can watch the videos with Chinese and English subtitles provided by Unit X-3 and Unit X-4 (as shown in Fig. 1c) as Unit X-1 and Unit X-2 supplementary materials. Figure 1d shows the block assembly function of App Inventor. Students can learn the concepts between App Inventor's components and code through Unit X-5 and Unit X-6. In addition, students can review the key content of App Inventor in this unit through Unit X-7.

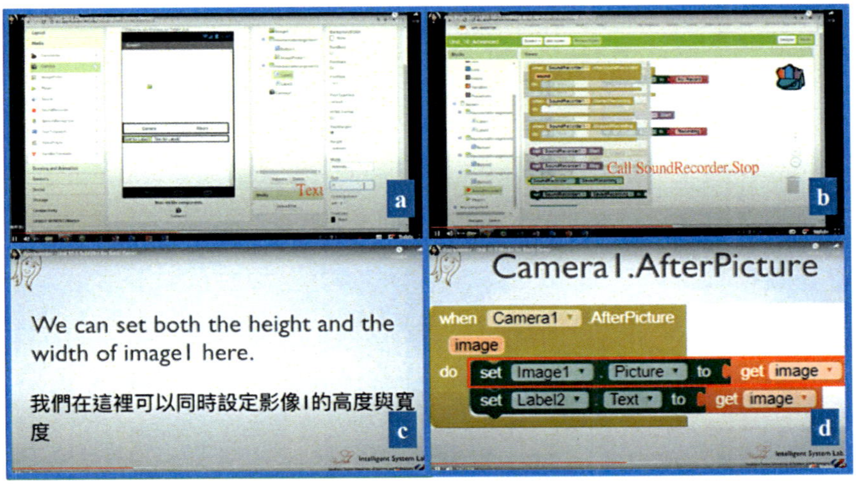

Fig. 1. Videos of App Inventor Programming based on flipped learning.

- Online Formative Assessment System

This study developed an online formative assessment system and released it on the server to provide students with online tests. The App Inventor course taught by the teacher has 12 units, and these materials are related to the components and objects of App Inventor, such as Button, CheckBox, Layout, Image, Label, TextBox, etc. In addition, this study proposed system contains 111 test items, of which Unit 1–6 has a total of 68 items, and Unit 7–12 has a total of 43 items. This study includes two test types, Unit 1–6 and Unit 7–12, and the test units are designated by the teacher. This system presets 10 test items each time, and it provides test items in random numbers. Figure 2 shows the example of test items in the online formative assessment system. Students need to judge whether the picture in the "Settings" is correct according to the picture in the "Question" and click the "Yes" or "No" options to submit the answer.

In addition, the test items also include a combination of block assembly functions of visual programming (as shown in Fig. 3). Therefore, students need to learn the knowledge and concepts of the components and objects in the video based on the flipped learning, and actually operate the APP Inventor to understand the program results of the components and object. After the students complete their answers, this system immediately displays the test results and uploads them to the server. Teachers can also adjust the video of the course based on the students' answer records.

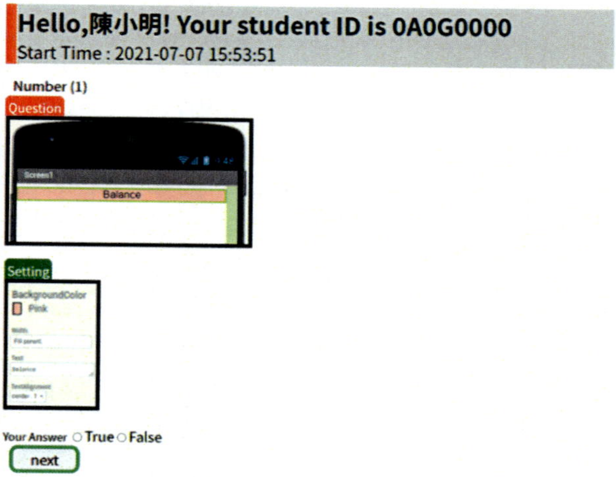

Fig. 2. The example of test items for component and object in the online formative assessment system.

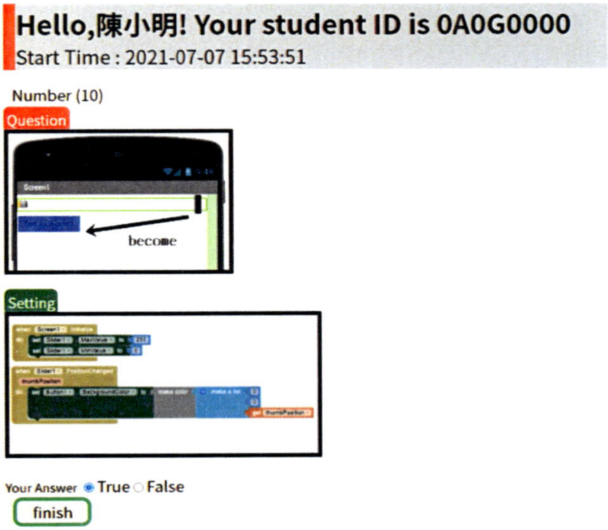

Fig. 3. The example of test items for block assembly functions in the online formative assessment system.

3.3 Experimental Process

This study investigated 73 students to implement a 13-week experimental activity. Figure 4 shows the experimental procedure of this study. Before the experimental activity, the teacher would introduce the experimental procedure and learning approach to all students. The two groups of students conducted the pre-test in the first week to measure their knowledge and concepts in programming. The students in the experimental group and the students in the control group are based on the instructional strategy of flipped learning to watch the videos of the App Inventor programming. Students in the two

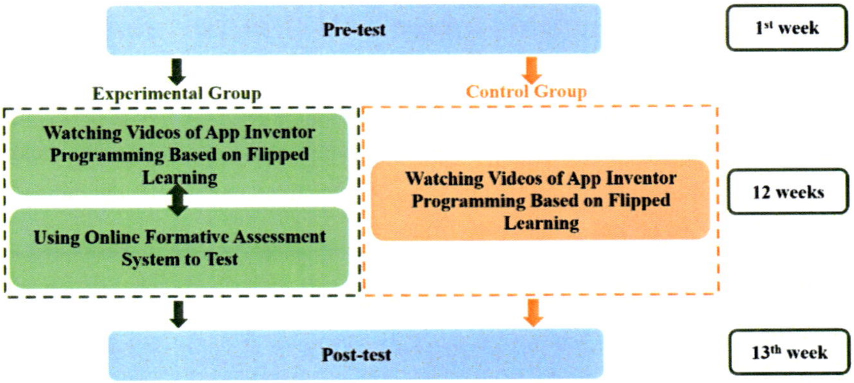

Fig. 4. The experimental procedure of this study.

groups watched a video of one unit each week and implemented a total of 12 weeks of flipped learning. In addition, students in the experimental group can use the online formative assessment system proposed by this study to conduct online tests. Finally, the two groups of students conducted a post-test in the 13th week to measure their learning performance in the programming.

4 Experimental Results

This study designed and recorded 84 videos as learning materials for flipped learning, and developed an online formative assessment system to explore whether this system can improve students' learning performance in programming. Table 1 shows the results of the independent sample *t*-test of the pre-test. The mean of the experimental group was 41.09 and the standard deviation was 8.58; the mean of the control group was 40.07, the standard deviation was 11.54, and the t value was 0.418 ($p > 0.05$). This result shows that before the experimental activity, there is no significant difference in the learning performance in programming between the two groups.

Table 1. The independent sample *t*-test of pre-test.

Group	*N*	Mean	Standard deviation	*t*
Experimental group	32	41.09	8.58	0.418
Control group	41	40.07	11.54	

Table 2 shows the independent sample *t*-test results of the post-test. The mean of the experimental group was 85.09 and the standard deviation was 14.8; the mean of the control group was 58.54, the standard deviation was 13.5, and the *t* value was 7.996 ($p < 0.001$). There are significant differences between the two groups. In addition, Table 3 shows the independent sample *t*-test results of learning progress. The mean of the experimental group was 44 and the standard deviation was 14.61; the mean of the control group was 18.46, the standard deviation was 16.21, and the *t* value was 6.969 ($p < 0.001$), There is a significant difference between the two groups.

According to these results, the experimental group can significantly improve their learning performance in the App Inventor course by combining flipped learning with the online formative assessment system, and it can also significantly improve their learning progress in programming.

Table 2. The independent sample *t*-test of post-test.

Group	*N*	Mean	Standard deviation	*t*
Experimental group	32	85.09	14.8	7.996***
Control group	41	58.54	13.5	

* $p < 0.05$, ** $p < 0.01$, *** $p < 0.001$.

Table 3. The independent sample *t*-test of learning progress.

Group	*N*	Mean	Standard deviation	*t*
Experimental group	32	44	14.61	6.969***
Control group	41	18.46	16.21	

* $p < 0.05$, ** $p < 0.01$, *** $p < 0.001$.

5 Conclusion

This study designed and recorded 84 videos of APP Inventor programming based on flipped learning, and developed an online formative assessment system to provide 111 test items related to APP Inventor programming to explore whether the combination of flipped learning and formative evaluation can be improved the learning performance of the experimental group in programming. According to the results, compared with the control group, the experimental group can significantly improve their learning performance and learning progress in programming by combining flipped learning and the online formative assessment system. In addition, through formative assessment, teachers can directly examine which steps students are prone to problems and errors, and then give corresponding guidance to each student.

References

1. Liu, R., Wang, L., Lei, J., Wang, Q., Ren, Y.: Effects of an immersive virtual reality-based classroom on students' learning performance in science lessons. Br. J. Edu. Technol. **51**(6), 2034–2049 (2020)
2. Hwang, G.J., Wu, P.H., Chen, C.C., Tu, N.T.: Effects of an augmented reality-based educational game on students' learning achievements and attitudes in real-world observations. Interact. Learn. Environ. **24**(8), 1895–1906 (2016)
3. Chen, M.P., Wang, L.C., Zou, D., Lin, S.Y., Xie, H., Tsai, C.C.: Effects of captions and English proficiency on learning effectiveness, motivation and attitude in augmented-reality-enhanced theme-based contextualized EFL learning. Comput. Assist. Lang. Learn. 1–31 (2020)
4. Huang, Y.M., Cheng, Y.P., Cheng, S.C., Chen, Y.Y.: Exploring the correlation between attention and cognitive load through association rule mining by using a brainwave sensing headband. IEEE Access **8**, 38880–38891 (2020)
5. Cheng, S.-C., Cheng, Y.-P., Huang, C.-H., Huang, Y.-M.: Exploring the correlation between attention and cognitive load of students when attending different classes. In: Wu, T.-T., Huang, Y.-M., Shadieva, R., Lin, L., Starčič, A.I. (eds.) ICITL 2018. LNCS, vol. 11003, pp. 205–214. Springer, Cham (2018). https://doi.org/10.1007/978-3-319-99737-7_21

6. Cheng, S.C., Cheng, Y.P., Chen, Y.L., Huang, Y.M.: Using brainwave to measure and explore the correlation between attention and cognitive load. In: 25th International Conference on Computers in Education: Technology and Innovation: Computer-Based Educational Systems for the 21st Century. ICCE 2017, pp. 258–265. Asia-Pacific Society for Computers in Education, New Zealand (2017)
7. Wu, C.-H., Tzeng, Y.-L., Huang, Y.-M.: Measuring performance in leaning process of digital game-based learning and static E-learning. Educ. Tech. Res. Dev. **68**(5), 2215–2237 (2020). https://doi.org/10.1007/s11423-020-09765-6
8. Hao, K.C., Lee, L.C.: The development and evaluation of an educational game integrating augmented reality, ARCS model, and types of games for English experiment learning: an analysis of learning. Interact. Learn. Environ. 1–14 (2019)
9. Cheng, S.-C., Cheng, Y.-P., Huang, Y.-M., Chiang, I.R.: Constructing an information search platform using data mining to improve student learning. In: Huang, T.-C., Wu, T.-T., Barroso, J., Sandnes, F.E., Martins, P., Huang, Y.-M. (eds.) ICITL 2020. LNCS, vol. 12555, pp. 227–235. Springer, Cham (2020). https://doi.org/10.1007/978-3-030-63885-6_26
10. Karabulut-Ilgu, A., Jaramillo Cherrez, N., Jahren, C.T.: A systematic review of research on the flipped learning method in engineering education. Br. J. Edu. Technol. **49**(3), 398–411 (2018)
11. van Alten, D.C., Phielix, C., Janssen, J., Kester, L.: Self-regulated learning support in flipped learning videos enhances learning outcomes. Comput. Educ. **158**, 104000 (2020)
12. van Alten, D.C., Phielix, C., Janssen, J., Kester, L.: Effects of flipping the classroom on learning outcomes and satisfaction: a meta-analysis. Educ. Res. Rev. **28**, 100281 (2019)
13. Bond, M.: Facilitating student engagement through the flipped learning approach in K-12: a systematic review. Comput. Educ. **151**, 103819 (2020)
14. Elmahdi, I., Al-Hattami, A., Fawzi, H.: Using technology for formative assessment to improve students' learning. Turk. Online J. Educ. Technol. TOJET **17**(2), 182–188 (2018)
15. Tütüncü, N., Aksu, M.: A systematic review of flipped classroom studies in Turkish education. Int. J. Soc. Sci. Educ. Res. **4**(2), 207–229 (2018)
16. Awidi, I.T., Paynter, M.: The impact of a flipped classroom approach on student learning experience. Comput. Educ. **128**, 269–283 (2019)
17. Hwang, G.J., Chang, C.Y.: Facilitating decision-making performances in nursing treatments: a contextual digital game-based flipped learning approach. Interact. Learn. Environ. 1–16 (2020)
18. Wang, K., Zhu, C.: MOOC-based flipped learning in higher education: students' participation, experience and learning performance. Int. J. Educ. Technol. High. Educ. **16**(1), 1–18 (2019). https://doi.org/10.1186/s41239-019-0163-0
19. Sharma, N., Lau, C.S., Doherty, I., Harbutt, D.: How we flipped the medical classroom. Med. Teach. **37**(4), 327–330 (2015)
20. Chen Hsieh, J.S., Wu, W.C.V., Marek, M.W.: Using the flipped classroom to enhance EFL learning. Comput. Assist. Lang. Learn. **30**(1–2), 1–21 (2017)
21. Lin, Y.N., Hsia, L.H., Hwang, G.J.: Promoting pre-class guidance and in-class reflection: a SQIRC-based mobile flipped learning approach to promoting students' billiards skills, strategies, motivation and self-efficacy. Comput. Educ. **160**, 104035 (2021)
22. Khanova, J., Roth, M.T., Rodgers, J.E., McLaughlin, J.E.: Student experiences across multiple flipped courses in a single curriculum. Med. Educ. **49**(10), 1038–1048 (2015)
23. Bell, B., Cowie, B.: The characteristics of formative assessment in science education. Sci. Educ. **85**(5), 536–553 (2001)
24. Dixson, D.D., Worrell, F.C.: Formative and summative assessment in the classroom. Theory Pract. **55**(2), 153–159 (2016)

25. Zainuddin, Z., Shujahat, M., Haruna, H., Chu, S.K.W.: The role of gamified e-quizzes on student learning and engagement: An interactive gamification solution for a formative assessment system. Comput. Educ. **145**, 103729 (2020)
26. Dalby, D., Swan, M.: Using digital technology to enhance formative assessment in mathematics classrooms. Br. J. Educ. Technol. **50**(2), 832–845 (2019)
27. Pailai, J., Wunnasri, W., Yoshida, K., Hayashi, Y., Hirashima, T.: The practical use of Kit-Build concept map on formative assessment. Res. Pract. Technol. Enhanc. Learn. **12**(1), 1–23 (2017). https://doi.org/10.1186/s41039-017-0060-x

Online Course and Web-Based Environment

The Framework for Development of the Constructivist Learning Environment Model to Enhance Ill-Structured Problem Solving in Industrial Automation System Supporting by Metacognition

Samrit Thima(✉) and Sumalee Chaijaroen

Department of Educational Technology, Khon Kaen University, Khon Kaen, Thailand
samrit.th@kkumail.com

Abstract. The objective of this research was to synthesize the theoretical framework and designing the framework of the constructivist learning environment model based on constructivist theory to enhance the ill-structured problem-solving skill. Model research [15] was used in this study, which focuses on processes of design and model development. The research procedure consists of three processes: The first one document analysis and examination of learning and teaching context. The second one, investigating and analyzing the related theories such as learning theories, constructivist theories, ill-structured problem solving, metacognition, media theory, and technology. The third one, synthesizing the theoretical framework and designing the framework for Constructivist learning environment model to enhance ill-structured problem solving based on the reviewed of theories. The participants of this research were experts from a variety of fields such as theorists, designer, developer, evaluators, and learners. The results of this research were shown that there are five components of the theoretical framework consists of (1) Psychological base, (2) Pedagogical base, (3) Contextual base, (4) Problem-solving base, and (5) Media Theory and Technology base. The designing framework has four processes of knowledge construction consists of (1) The activation of cognitive structure and problem-solving enhancement, (2) The enhancement of cognitive equilibrium, (3) The enhancing of cognitive structure and problem-solving, and (4) The enhancement and support of knowledge construction and helping of problem-solving, and the designing frameworks has seven components as following: (1) Problem base, (2) Sensor in industrial automation system resources center, (3) Cognitive tools, (4) Enhancing ill-structured problem-solving center, (5) Collaboration center, (6) Scaffolding and (7) Coaching.

Keywords: Constructivist learning environment model · Constructivist theories · Ill-structured problem-solving

© Springer Nature Switzerland AG 2021
Y.-M. Huang et al. (Eds.): ICITL 2021, LNCS 13117, pp. 511–520, 2021.
https://doi.org/10.1007/978-3-030-91540-7_52

1 Introduction

Nowadays, the development of the world's communication and information technology has transformed the world into a globalization era and affect the change of Thailand as well as other countries around the world. Therefore, education management is considered to be one of the most important foundations in developing people to have the ability to seek and apply information. "Student-centered learning" gives importance to learners Through the practice of self-acting, the development of thinking potential, problem-solving skill as well as the pursuit of self-knowledge by interacting with various learning sources that lead to knowledge construction [10]. The new conceptual framework for 21st-century learning focuses on providing a flexible, creative, challenging, and complex learning environment to accommodate the rapidly changing global society riddled with new challenges. 21st-century learning is about providing an environment where students face real-world problems. Learning is not limited to the classroom, but it connects students, experts, tutors, and communities to create diverse perspectives for entering a global knowledge community. The role of the teacher must change from the person who transmits knowledge to be a helper support and provide a learning environment for students to practice thinking solving problems can turn information into knowledge and bring knowledge as a tool to practice and to be useful in the context of the real encounter. Since the 4.0 era, the emergence of technology in Thailand has continued to increase especially in the industrial sector. Therefore, students are strongly encouraged to develop the skills necessary to solve complex problems and be able to solve real-world problems.

Overcoming the previous problem, the implementation of constructivist theory can be a solution which helps learner improving their complex problem-solving skill. This theory was focusing on creating new knowledge by believing that learners already have prior knowledge learning is a process that takes place within the learner. The learners create knowledge from the relationship between what they see and their prior knowledge. They try to use their understanding of events and phenomena they see to create a cognitive structure [3]. The learning environment was designed based on the constructivist theories: cognitive constructivist [14] and social constructivist [19], Cognitive theories: Information processing [11], Metacognition theory [5], ill-structured problem solving [7, 9]. These theories can be helping the learners to construction the knowledge and enhanced theirs problem-solving skill, especially in the course Industrial Automation System. Moreover, the ability of the Internet communication system in the form of media attribute and symbols system of the web base consist of hypertext and hyperlink also may support the learner too. [3, 12, 18].

Consequently, this paper purpose to design and develop the constructivist learning environment model that enhances ill-structured problem-solving in industrial automation system supporting by metacognition. This framework can be helping a designer to effectively design the constructivist learning environment model to encourage the learners to construct knowledge and enhance the problem-solving skill.

2 Research Methodology

2.1 Research Objectives

The objective of this research is to design and develop a Framework of Constructivist Learning Environment Model to Enhance Ill-Structured Problem-Solving in Industrial Automation System Supporting by Metacognition.

2.2 Target Group

The target groups consist of (1) experts to evaluate the model in the following areas: model content, media quality, model designing and collecting data instruments (2) a model designer (3) a model developer and (4) a instructor. They are also included 30 undergraduate learners of electrical engineering Faculty of Industrial Education Rajamangala University of Technology Isan, Khon Kaen Campus, who enrolled in a course of programmable logic control courses for the survey of learners' characteristics and opinion surveys for learners about the context of learning management.

2.3 Data Collecting and Research Instruments

- The data of context of learning and teaching in industrial automation system was collecting by document form.
- The data for synthesizing the theoretical framework, designing framework of the model was collecting by recording form.
- The data of quality assessment of the framework was collecting by the experts' assessment form.

2.4 Data Analysis

- The context of learning and teaching in industrial automation system were analyzed using summarization, interpretation, and analytical description.
- Synthesizing of the designing framework, which was developed based on the theoretical framework. The data was analyzed using summarization, interpretation, and analytical description.

3 Research Results

3.1 Theoretical Framework of Constructivist Learning Environment Model

The results of applying relevant principles, theories, related documented, and related researches were synthesized and analyzed by using summarization, interpretation, and analytical description. The theoretical framework has been developed which consists of 5 fundamentals: (1) Psychological base, (2) Pedagogies base, (3) Contextual base, (4) Media Theory and Technology base, and (5) Problem solving base (see Fig. 1).

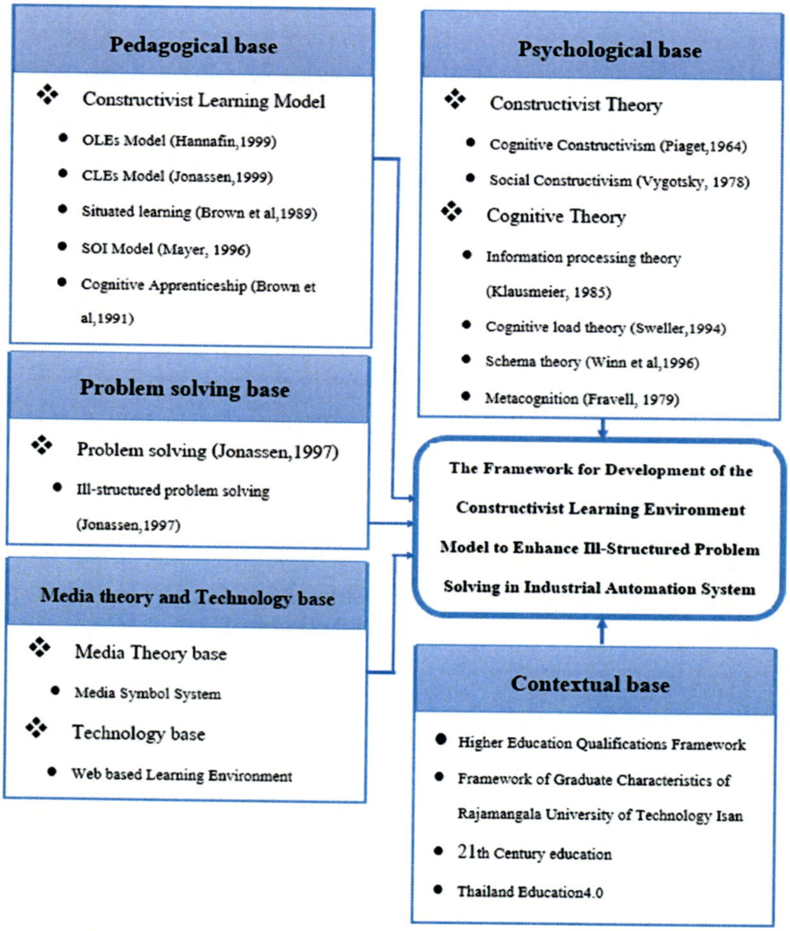

Fig. 1. Theoretical framework of the Constructivist Learning Environment Model to Enhance Ill-Structured Problem Solving in Industrial Automation System Supporting by Metacognition.

3.2 Designing Framework of Constructivist Learning Environment Model

Based on the theoretical framework, the designing framework was developed by using the recording form and then was analyzed using summarization, interpretation, and analytical description. The results showed that the designing framework consists of 4 columns: (1) Knowledge construction process (2) Core principle, theory applied in the design of the model (3) Sub principle, theory applied in the design of the model and (4) Elements of the model. The designing framework of the model showed the four processes of knowledge construction below:

1. The activation of cognitive structure and problem-solving enhancement: It acts as a gateway through which students enter the content. This process was designed based on cognitive constructivist [14] that believes that the learners should be activated by a problem and led to cognitive conflict; Situated learning [1] which focus on authentic situations that are consistent with industrial automation control system; Constructivist learning environments [8] which is useful for ill-structured problem-solving tasks by presenting in a question, case, or problem; Ill-structured problem solving [7, 9] which focuses on the cognitive process for ill-structured problem solving, especially in the work of automatic control systems, students will encounter a variety of problems; Metacognition theory [5] and Social constructivist [19] which to support cognitive process for ill-structured problem-solving because the researchers believe that having metacognition will help learners to solve problems better, and solving complex problems requires the perspectives of many involved parties. Therefore, having metacognition and collaborative problem-solving can enhance students' problem-solving skills. All of the above theories were designed as the component of the industrial automation system Problem base.
2. The enhancement of cognitive equilibrium: This process emphasizes supporting and enhance learners' knowledge construction comprised of two components: Sensor in industrial automation system resources center and Cognitive tools. The component of Sensor in industrial automation system resources center was designed by four theories include (1.) Cognitive Load Theory [16], the content of industrial sensors is quite complex, making it difficult for learners to information processing. Therefore, Cognitive Load Theory will make it easier for information to stay in the learner's long-term memory. (2.) Schema theory is to enhancement of cognitive equilibrium by presenting Learning resources center in schema as context. (3.) SOI Theory [13] focuses on three cognitive processes: (1) selecting, (2) organizing, and (3) integrating. (4.) Information Processing Theory [11], focuses on cognition and information processing which consists of three components: (1) sensory register, (2) Short term memory, and (3) long-term memory. Consequently, the design of industrial sensor learning resources is based on the above-mentioned theory. The component of Cognitive tools was designed by OLEs [6] as four cognitive tools include: (1) seeking Tool such as search engines, (2) organizing tool, (3) collecting tool, and (4) communication tool.

3. The enhancing of cognitive structure and problem solving: the researchers believe that having metacognition and collaboration can enhance students' problem-solving skills. Therefore, the following theories have been used. The cognitive process of ill-structured problem solving [7] focuses on the problem-solving step; Metacognition theory [5] which emphasizes metacognitive knowledge and metacognitive skill. The above theory has been designed as Enhancing ill-structured problem-solving center. Social Constructivist [19] has been used to design a Collaboration center, which emphasizes the learner's interaction with others. In solving complex industrial problems, the problems that students encounter may have different approaches to solving them; so, they can discuss their knowledge, experience, and their thinking to increase their cognitive structure.
4. The enhancement and support of knowledge construction and helping of problem-solving. There have three theories that have been considered in the design consist of OLEs [6], Social Constructivist [19], and Cognitive apprenticeship [1]. Social Constructivist [19] believe in Zone of Proximal Development (ZPD), when the learners are faced with problems that are too difficult to solve means that the learner need help. Especially in complex industrial applications, inexperienced learners are less likely to be successful in solving problems. Therefore, Social Constructivist: ZPD was used to design as scaffolding to support the learners. OLEs has been designed as scaffolding center, which consists of four elements: (1) conceptual scaffolding, (2) metacognition scaffolding, (3) procedural scaffolding (4) strategic Scaffolding. Cognitive apprenticeship, expert/coach has been designed as Coaching center to support the learners who cannot complete the learning tasks by themselves.

The designing framework of the Constructivist Learning Environment Model to Enhance Ill-Structured Problem Solving in Industrial Automation System Supporting by Metacognition was synthesized based on above mention four processes of knowledge construction can be illustrated in Fig. 2.

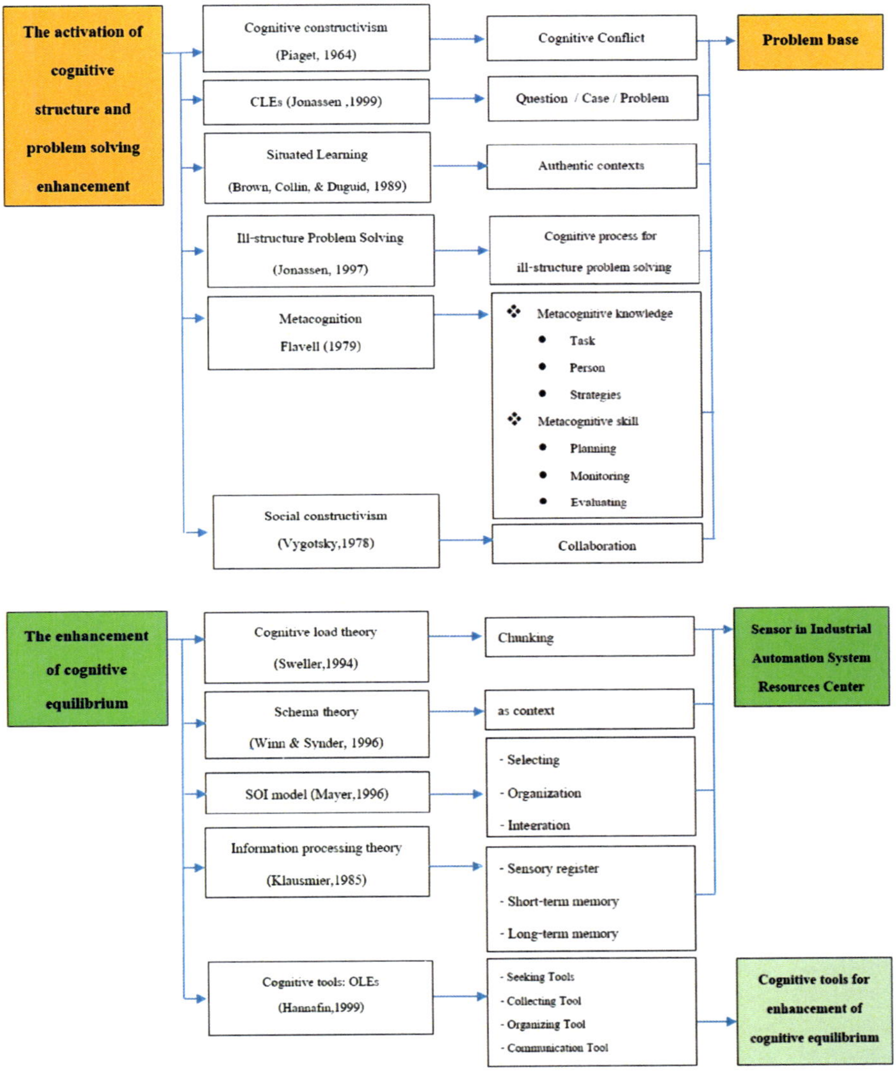

Fig. 2. Designing framework of the Constructivist Learning Environment Model to Enhance Ill-Structured Problem Solving in Industrial Automation System Supporting by Metacognition.

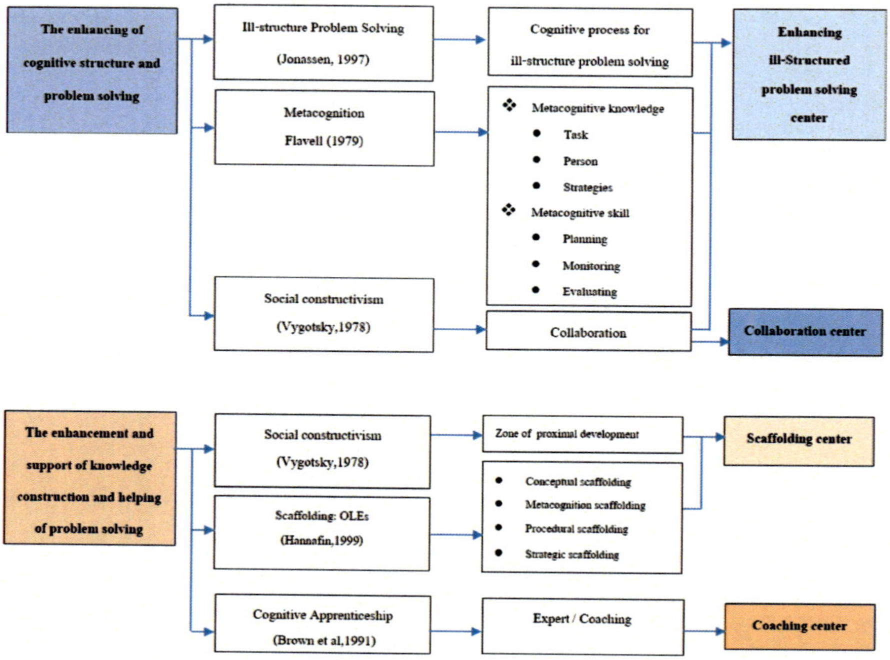

Fig. 2. continued

4 Discussion

The paradigm of educational management in the 21st century emphasizes learning management that promotes competence for lifelong learning. The results of this study are consistent with the methods of learning management mentioned above because this framework can help the learners build their knowledge by themselves. The results of the designing framework include seven components of the model as following: (1) industrial automation system Problem base, (2) Sensor in industrial automation system resources center, (3) Cognitive tools, (4) Enhancing ill-structured problem-solving center, (5) Collaboration center, (6) Scaffolding center and (7) Coaching center, that was provided to support the learners to construct their knowledge. Learning is not limited to the classroom, connecting learners with experts, coaches, and communities can also help learners build diverse perspectives and construct knowledge. This result was consistent with the studies of [4, 10, 17]. This model could be a benefit for instructors to designing a constructivist learning environment to effectively increase learners' cognitive process and enhance their problem-solving.

5 Conclusion

A new conceptual framework for learning in the 21st century focuses on providing a flexible, creative, challenging, and complex learning environment to support the changing global society. Teachers need to change the role and concept from the person who transmits the knowledge to be a helper, supporter and provide a learning environment for students to the practice of thinking, problem-solving, and turning on information into knowledge and bring knowledge as a tool to solving a problem in the context of the real encounter. The finding of this study is consistent with the methods of learning management mentioned above.

Acknowledgements. The researcher would like to thank all parties involved in making this research successful. Faculty of Education, Khon Kaen University which hereby giving thankfulness all through this.

References

1. Brown, J., Collins, A., Duguid, P.: John: Situated cognition and the culture of learning. Educ. Res. **18**(1), 32–42 (1989)
2. Chaijaroen, S.: Development of knowledge construction using information technology. Department of Educational Technology, Khon Kaen University (2004)
3. Chaijaroen, S.: Instructional design: principles and theories to practices. Department of Educational Technology, Khon Kaen University (2015)
4. Choi, H.J., Johnson, S.D.: The effect of context-based video instruction on learning and motivation in online courses. Am. J. Distance Educ. Am. **19**, 215–227 (2005)
5. Flavell, J.H.: Metacognition and cognitive monitoring: a new area of cognitive–developmental inquiry. Am. Psychol. **34**(10), 906–911 (1979)
6. Hanafin, M.: Open Learning Environment: Foundation, Methods, and Models. Instructional Designing Theories and Model: A New Paradigm of Instructional Theory Volume II. (Charles M.). Lawrence Erlbaum Associates, Mahlway (1999)
7. Jonassen, D.H.: Instructional design models for well-structured and Ill-structured problem-solving learning outcomes. Educ. Tech. Res. Dev. **45**(1), 65–94 (1997)
8. Jonassen, D.H.: Designing constructivist learning environments. In: Reigeluth, C., (Ed.). Instructional-Design Theories and Models: A New Paradigm of Instructional Theory, pp. 215–239. Pennsylvania State University, University Park (1999)
9. Jonassen, D.H.: Learning to Solve Problems a Handbook for Designing Problem-Solving Learning Environments. Routledge, New York (2011)
10. Kanjug, I., Chaijaroen, S.: The design of web-based learning environments enhancing mental model construction. Procedia - Soc. Behav. Sci. **46**, 3134–3140 (2012)
11. Klausmeier, H.J.: Educational Psychology, 5th edn. Harper & Row, New York (1985)
12. Kozma, R.B.: Learning with media. Rev. Educ. Res. **61**(2), 179–211 (1991)
13. Mayer, R.E.: Designing instruction for constructivist learning. In: Instructional-Design Theories and Models: A New Paradigm of Instructional Theory, vol. II (1999)
14. Piaget, J.: Part I: cognitive development in children: Piaget development and learning. J. Res. Sci. Teach. **2**, 176–186 (1964)
15. Richey, R.C., Klein, J.D.: Design and Development Research: Methods Strategies and Issues. Lawrence Erlbaum Associates, Mahlway (2007)

16. Sweller, J.: Cognitive load theory, learning difficulty, and instructional design. Learn. Instr. **4**, 295–312 (1994)
17. Wang, Q.: Designing a web-based constructivist learning environment. Interact. Learn. Environ. **17**(1), 1–13 (2009)
18. Wattanachai, S.: Development of constructivist web-based learning environment model to foster problems solving and transfer of learning. Doctor of Philosophy Thesis in Educational Technology, Graduate School, Khon Kaen University (2010)
19. Vygotsky, L.S.: Mind in Society: The Development of Higher Psychological Processes. Har

Using the Diffusion of Innovation Theory to Explain Foundation Phase Teachers' Perceptions of Online Zoom Classes During a Pandemic – A Case of a South African Private School

Komla Pillay(✉) and Tania Prinsloo

Informatics Department, University of Pretoria, Pretoria, South Africa
komla.pillay@up.ac.za

Abstract. In this paper, the emphasis is on teaching the foundation phases of school via the Zoom platform during the Covid-19 pandemic. Fifteen out of the eighteen teachers of a private school in South Africa completed the survey questions, and the questions were then analyzed using the Diffusion of Innovation Theory. Most teachers felt that they were able to use Zoom successfully, although they prefer face-to-face teaching. The paper's main contribution is the identification of six factors affecting the use of Zoom, namely the importance of being prepared, the role that the environment plays, the resources available, the ability of the student, the infrastructure in place, and lastly, the part that discipline plays. Future research will involve more grades in the study, not only grades 1 to 3, and survey other schools and their teachers using similar online teaching tools.

Keywords: Zoom · Diffusion of innovation theory · Foundation phase teachers · Pandemic

1 Introduction

Like many countries worldwide, South Africa had to stop physical school attendance due to the Covid-19 pandemic. The worldwide Covid-19 pandemic forced many schooling environments to look for Information Communication Technologies (ICT) to continue the academic program. Many resourced private schools in the South African schooling environment resorted to using online Google classrooms, online Zoom classes, and other such ICTs [1]. One such private school adopted Zoom classes to ensure the daily schedule was followed as much as possible. In this article, the foundation phase from Grade 1 to Grade 3 is explored to determine if teachers could teach successfully during the trying Covid-19 period.

© Springer Nature Switzerland AG 2021
Y.-M. Huang et al. (Eds.): ICITL 2021, LNCS 13117, pp. 521–532, 2021.
https://doi.org/10.1007/978-3-030-91540-7_53

2 Background of the Study

The case studied private school is located in a middle- to high-income area. The school established an online timetable that consisted of 40-min sessions, break times, and independent work time. Students were given this timetable before the day that classes started. Teachers provided students with their in-class workbooks to take home. Teachers also uploaded material onto the student portal; parents or guardians were expected to have the uploaded material printed before starting the Zoom classes.

The school offered primarily compulsory Zoom classes. Due to not having control over the student's resources at home, offline learning was also an option. Online Zoom class attendance was more than 85% at all times. It must be noted that the private school and its student cohort is much more resourced than the average South African public school. This research cannot be translated across the education system in South Africa – there can be inferences drawn to other similarly resourced private schools.

Foundation Phase classes in South Africa include grades R to 3 [2]. This study used grades 1 to 3 as Grade R does not exist in the case studied entity. The case studied school is a dual medium English and Afrikaans school. There are three English and 3 Afrikaans classes per grade. The sample for this study was eighteen teachers.

2.1 Zoom Classes

Zoom is a modern learning tool that enables students to learn online. Zoom can be used in many ways – online teaching and online meetings are two examples. Zoom enables video communication facilitating virtual tutoring, advising, career counselling, and mentoring, allowing the students to learn beyond the classroom [3]. Teaching online using Zoom enables synchronous class meetings that allow the teacher and all students to log in to a web conferencing system according to a predetermined scheduled.

The case studied school uses the web conferencing software Zoom, which limits each session to 40 min. Zoom can be used on laptops, desktops, and various other mobile devices (tablets or smartphones), allowing many different platforms for students to access the class sessions.

2.2 Diffusion of Innovation Theory

The diffusion of innovation theory explains how, why and how fast a particular technology or innovation will be adopted. Typically, new innovations have a small number of innovators that use an innovation, which grows progressively as the innovation proves successful [4]. Figure 1 demonstrates how innovation adopters are categorized.

There are five categories that adopters can be classified into: innovators, early adopters, early majority, late majority, and laggards. Roger's diffusion of innovation theory outlines how a potential adopter goes through collecting information, analyzing information, and then determining if the innovation deserves the investment. The potential adopter is concerned with the return being worth the investment [5]. An adopter follows this process before deciding when would be the best time for them to invest in the innovation, if at all.

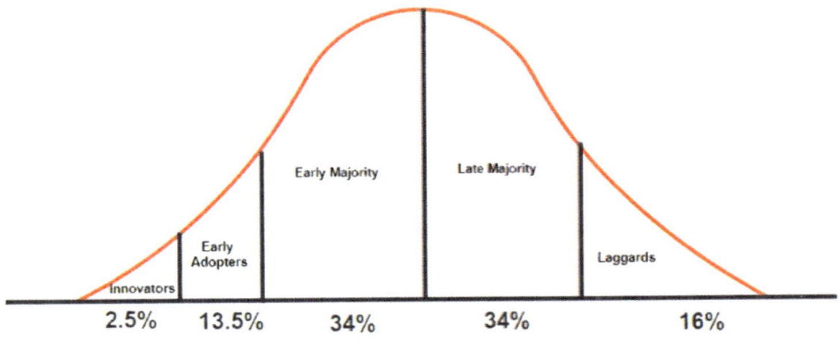

Fig. 1. Categorization of innovation adopters [5:281]

Adoption of a new innovation can be attained by considering five characteristics of the innovation. According to Rogers [5], these five characteristics from the innovator's perspective can determine the adoption of an innovation. The five characteristics are:

Relative advantage: This characteristic talks to the benefits that an individual would consider when adopting an innovation. The greater the relative advantage, the faster the rate of adoption.

- *Compatibility:* "The degree to which an innovation is perceived as consistent with the existing values, past experiences, and need of potential adopter." [5].
- *Trialability:* refers to the degree to which the innovation can be experimented on [5].
- *Observability*: if the innovators can see the value add of the innovation, the easier it is for an innovation to be adopted.
- *Ease of use:* innovations that are easy to understand and use are adopted at a faster rate.

3 Purpose of the Study

The purpose of this study was to explain the Foundation Phase teachers' use of Online Zoom Classes. The study uses Roger's innovation attributes to examine the Foundation Phase teachers' use of Zoom classes. Using Roger's diffusion of innovation, this study analyzed the Foundation Phase teachers' use of Zoom and their perceived attributes that affect their decision to adopt Zoom. The study also outlines factors that impact the use of Zoom by Foundation Phase teachers.

Three research questions helped in achieving the purpose of this study:

1. What are the Foundation Phase teachers' perceptions of Online Zoom classes?
2. How do Roger's (2003) major innovation attributes explain Foundation Phase teachers' perceptions of Online Zoom classes?
3. What factors impact the use of Zoom for teaching Foundation Phase classes?

4 Methodology

A case study approach was used to qualitatively investigate Foundation Phase teachers' use of Zoom and their perceptions regarding its' use in an urban private school in South

Africa. Qualitative research is the collection, organization, description, and interpretation of textual, verbal, and graphic data. Qualitative research typically takes place in a natural setting allowing the researcher to foster understanding from a high level of involvement in the "actual experiences" [6]. An identifier of qualitative research is the social phenomenon being investigated from the viewpoint of the participant. Creswell defines case study research as when a "researcher explores in depth a program, an event, an activity, a process, or one or more individuals" [7].

This study collected and interpreted data via a questionnaire. The questionnaire had both open and closed-ended questions. Thematic analysis and descriptive statistics were used to analyses the data. The sample for this study was the Foundation Phase teachers at an urban private school. There was a total of eighteen Foundation Phase teachers, fifteen of which completed the questionnaire. Data were collected anonymously, and no participant will be able to be identified by the presentation of data. Table 1 shows the teachers, number of years of experience teaching foundation phase, and age category.

Table 1. Age and number of years teaching Foundation Phase.

ID	Age category	Number of years teaching foundation phase
1	40–49	19
2	30–39	15
3	40–49	23
4	20–29	2,5
5	20-29	4
6	50–59	20
7	20–29	4
8	30–39	16
9	30–39	8
10	50–59	28
11	>60	38
12	40–49	18
13	30–39	10
14	30–39	15
15	40–49	21

Twelve of the fifteen participants have ten or more years of experience teaching the foundation phase. This demonstrates the high level of experience of the participants. The questions were taken from three other studies, diffusion of innovation study for the use of interactive whiteboards [8], a study for the perception of an individual adopting an Information Technology (IT) innovation [9] and Detailed Review Of Rogers' Diffusion Of Innovations Theory And Educational Technology [10]. The school management tested the questionnaire before they were finalized and distributed. The questionnaire was made up of open and close-ended questions. The close-ended questions were asked on a 5 point Likert scale – Strongly Disagree, Disagree, Neutral, Agree, and Strongly Agree. The open and close-ended questions are presented and discussed in the analysis and findings sections.

5 Analysis

The collected data were analyzed qualitatively by organizing responses according to themes in order to determine what factors impact the use of Zoom by Foundation Phase teachers. Descriptive statistics were used to present the data gathered in the close-ended questions.

The summarized response to the close-ended questions:

- 93% of respondents disagree with Zoom being better than physical classes, and 7% were neutral.
- 100% of respondents disagreed with the statement that Zoom works just as well as physical classes.
- 93% of respondents disagree that Zoom enables them to accomplish their daily tasks more quickly, and 7% were neutral.
- 93% of respondents disagree that Zoom makes it easier to do the task at hand, and 7% were neutral.
- 86% of respondents disagreed that Zoom enhanced their effectiveness to complete the task, with 7% being neutral and 7% agreeing.
- 80% of respondents disagreed that Zoom gave them greater control over the task, with 14% being neutral and 6% agreeing.
- 60% of the respondents disagree that using Zoom was compatible with the way they teach, with 33% being neutral and 7% agreeing.
- 93% of respondents agreed that experimenting with Zoom before adopting it, is very important, and 7% disagreed.
- 100% of respondents agreed that it is essential to ask questions about Zoom before acquiring it.
- 80% of respondents would have no difficulty telling others about the results of using Zoom, while 20% were neutral.
- 73% of respondents believe they could communicate to others the consequences of using Zoom, while 27% were neutral.
- 80% of respondents find Zoom clear and understandable, with 13% being neutral and 7% disagreeing.
- 100% of respondents agreed that learning to operate Zoom is easy for them.

The summarized response to the open-ended questions are outlined below:

- Do you consider the online Zoom class an effective tool for your students' learning? Give reasons.

Most respondents answered yes and no based on the circumstances. They indicated that Zoom was effective in giving students access but was less effective than the classroom. They further highlighted that Foundation Phase needs more hands-on interaction than Zoom allows. Teachers realize too late that a student does not understand the work being taught only when the work is handed-in. Whereas, in a physical environment, students' shortfalls are immediately picked-up on. Some students are shy, and some need one on one interaction to realize their potential fully. Respondents identified these characteristics that determine the success of the Zoom environment.

- Did you access online material or information from the Internet or Intranet during the online classes?

93% of respondents accessed online material from the Internet or Intranet.

- What are the advantages of using Online Zoom classes for instruction? Elaborate - you are welcome to provide reasons from both teacher and student perspectives?

Zoom allows continued teaching in times of a pandemic, illness, or crisis to ensure the health and safety of teachers and students. Allows easy interaction if the internet is stable. Can visually interact as the students and teacher can see each other. The teacher can also share their screen working through the content. Sessions can be recorded for students to catch up or for teachers to use to improve their teaching. Students can also use recordings to work at their own pace. It can be an affordable means of communication if all stakeholders have uncapped internet connectivity. Students have an opportunity to become familiar with technology and keep up to date with advancements. Zoom allows individuals to work from the comfort of their own homes. Zoom allows the curious nature of students to explore and have fun with technology. Zoom further allows teachers to have control of the class as they can mute students if required.

- What are the disadvantages or challenges of using Online Zoom classes for instruction? Elaborate - you are welcome to provide reasons from both teacher and student perspectives.

Technology can fail when least expected, leaving teachers stressed about reconnecting or leaving students feeling uncertain. Load shedding which a restriction of the country's electricity supply in order to keep the electricity grid stable. If Internet connectivity is not stable, teachers end up spending much time repeating instructions, and also students are lost when they do rejoin the session after losing connectivity. Zoom does not allow all the students to be viewed at once. Many siblings share devices which make it challenging for them to be online during the entire school day. Some students are not adequately seated to participate in the Zoom class and complete the associated physical worksheets or books. Foundation Phase learners sometimes need support to ensure that they are logged on at the right time and have the right resources on hand for the scheduled session – many parents are working and are unable to provide this support. The opposite of this also happens, "helicopter parents"; these parents get over-involved in the students learning and confuses the students. Teachers are unsure of what students understand and cannot adequately monitor what the students are doing. Students tend to suffer in silence as they do not want attention by asking questions or not communicating their difficulties. Teachers find it difficult to teach new concepts but find it easier to do revision using Zoom. Students take a lot of time to settle into class and also encounter many distractions while in the Zoom class. These distractions include eating, dogs barking, siblings crying, parents talking, and household appliances, to name a few. Teachers find the quality of students' work is inferior when taught on Zoom versus the physical classroom. Children can't maintain attention online, resulting in them being lost. They don't follow all the rules, and the computer literacy between the students differs. The school uses the free version of Zoom, so class sessions are limited to 40 min per session – this sometimes does not allow the teacher to complete their explanation or exercise. The momentum is lost if the session ends, and then the students and teacher must log back on to a new session. Students are sometimes poorly disciplined, attending class late, unmuting themselves, or eating during class. Not all Foundation Phase students can concentrate for long periods in an online environment. Students do not have all the required resources available on hand to complete a given task.

- Have you received any training (workshops, training sessions etc.) about the uses of Online Zoom classes?

20% of teachers indicated that they received no training on the use of Zoom. The other 80% of respondents received some informal training at the school. Mostly they shared information with colleagues or figured out things as they went along.

6 Findings

The findings of this study are outlined in response to each research question.

6.1 What Are the Foundation Phase Teachers' Perceptions of Online Zoom Classes?

A qualitative approach was used to explore the respondents' perceptions of Zoom. Therefore, they were asked these questions to answer this research question.

- What are the advantages of using Online Zoom classes for instruction? Elaborate – you are welcome to provide reasons from both teacher and student perspectives.
- What are the disadvantages of using Online Zoom classes for instruction? Elaborate – you are welcome to provide reasons from both teacher and student perspectives.
- What are the challenges that you face when using Online Zoom sessions for teaching?
- Have you received any training (workshops, training sessions etc.) in relation to the uses of Online Zoom classes?

From the analysis of these questions, we can conclude that the Foundation Phase teachers find value in using Zoom as a supporting rather than a primary medium of instruction. Although there are numerous advantages, the disadvantages outweigh the advantages of using Zoom in foundation phase teaching. The value lies in Zoom enabling a continued academic program for unexpected events like a pandemic and other environmental events that do not allow the physical gathering of teachers and students.

The biggest challenge is ensuring the internet infrastructure is stable for everyone. If the Internet connectivity is not stable, much time is wasted trying to get everyone to common ground. Student concentration and discipline are very challenging and sensitive to deal with in an online environment. Teachers are adequately trained and have systems in place at school to handle these sensitive matters. The other challenges have ways to counteract them, such as ensuring students have all the relevant resources. Teachers can communicate in advance the specific resource lists required for specific sessions. The limited duration of the Zoom sessions can be overcome by the school purchasing a Zoom license for unlimited use.

Although the training was not sufficiently provided, most disadvantages and challenges are not related to a lack of training. It appears that most teachers were okay with exploring Zoom and learning the tool as they progressed – it can be deduced that many aspects of Zoom are self-explanatory.

In summary, Foundation Phase teachers' perceptions of Zoom is that it is a tool to be used in an emergency or unexpected circumstances to support the continuity of the school's academic program. They do not in any way see Zoom in its' current form replacing traditional in-class teaching.

6.2 How Does Roger's (2003) Major Attributes of Innovation Explain Foundation Phase Teachers' Perceptions of Online Zoom Classes?

This research question was addressed by the close-ended questions that were analyzed descriptively. This was used to explore the respondents' use of Zoom and the factors that might affect their decision to use it. The Foundation Phase teachers' response to the questions helps address the five major attributes of innovation that affect the teacher's decision to use Zoom. Rogers' (2003) attributes of innovation are relative advantage, compatibility, trialability, demonstrability, and ease of use.

- Relative Advantage

These questions addressed this indicator:

- Zoom is better than physical classes.
- Zoom works just as well as physical classes.
- Zoom enables me to accomplish my daily tasks more quickly.
- Zoom makes it easier to do the task at hand.
- Zoom enhances my effectiveness in completing the task.
- Zoom gives me greater control over the task.

The soundest predictor of an innovation's rate of adoption is its perceived relative advantage. This indicator talks to the benefits that an individual would consider when adopting an innovation. From the analysis, it is evident that respondents mostly disagreed with these indicators. The respondents disagree with Zoom being better or working similarly to physical classes. The respondents do not see this innovation as being able to support their objectives better. Therefore, this indicator had a negative response.

- Compatibility

This question addressed this indicator:

- Using Zoom is compatible with the way I teach.

According to Rogers [5], compatibility refers to "the degree to which an innovation is perceived as consistent with the existing values, past experiences, and need of potential adopter." The process of adopting a particular innovation can be fast-tracked if the users of the innovation find it compatible with their experiences and expectations. Concerning Zoom classes, the teachers mainly had a negative perception. The teachers could not translate their regular, tried and tested approach to a fully online environment via the Zoom class. This indicator had a negative response.

- Trialability

These questions addressed this indicator:

- Experimenting with Zoom before adopting it is very important.
- It is essential to ask questions about Zoom before acquiring it.

Trialability refers to the degree to which the innovation can be experimented on [5]. Participants did not have a choice whether to use Zoom classes. This was compulsory for the teachers. Many of them saw the benefit of experimenting with Zoom before class. This facilitated their preparedness. They also felt that asking questions before implementing is better; however, it was mandatory in this instance, so they did not have the opportunity to question technology adoption. This indicator had a positive response.

- Observability/Demonstrability

These questions addressed this indicator:

- I would have no difficulty telling others about the results of using Zoom.
- I believe I could communicate to others the consequences of using Zoom.

This refers to the degree to which the results are visible to the affected community [5]. The respondents are mostly comfortable with telling others or communicating the results of using Zoom. This indicator had a positive response.

• Complexity/Ease of Use

These questions addressed this indicator:

- Zoom is clear and understandable.
- Learning to operate Zoom is easy for me.

This indicator refers to how innovation is easy to use and understand [5]. Respondents find Zoom both easy to use and understandable. This indicator had a positive response.

These five indicators played a role in motivating the respondents to use or plan to use Zoom for their teaching. Although three of the five characteristics received a positive response, the essential characteristic of relative advantage received a negative response. This again points to the respondents using this innovation under extenuating circumstances but not as an innovation that can replace the traditional classroom.

6.3 What Factors Impact the Use of Zoom for Teaching Foundation Phase Classes?

This question was answered by using thematic analysis. The advantages, disadvantages together with challenges were analyzed. Common findings were grouped into themes that are the factors that impact the use of Zoom for teaching Foundation Phase students.

Figure 2 depicts the factors that impact the use of Zoom for teaching Foundation Phase students. The aspects are described in no particular order.

• Being prepared

Both teachers and students must be adequately prepared. Teachers must have their electronic material prepared and uploaded to prevent wasting time getting ready. Students must have access to their virtual schedule to report timeously to the session.

Fig. 2. Factors that impact the use of zoom for teaching foundation phase students

- Environment

A conducive environment needs to be created. Teachers and students should ideally be in a room that can reduce environment sound like talking or dogs barking in the background. Adequate seating and correct furniture dimensions should be in place. There needs to be a "formal" area where students can work to foster the "feeling" of being in the classroom.

- Resources

Teachers must communicate to students and their guardians in advance of the resources that will be required. Teachers can also print and supply the resources (worksheets and class books). Students or guardians must ensure that all relevant material for a particular session is on hand and within reach. Ideally, each student must have an electronic device to work on independently, not a mobile phone. The device must enable good auditory and visual specifications

- Student ability

Arrange separate classes or schedules for students struggling with concentration or the ability to work independently. The school must be aware that this will mean more teaching resources.

- Infrastructure

Adequate infrastructure is crucial. Uncapped access to a stable Internet connectivity, with decent download speeds. Poor infrastructure results in lost time and missed communication.

- Discipline/rules

Setting and adopting rules is vital. No eating allowed during the session. No speaking unless asked to. No discussing non content-related concerns. Attend the session on time.

7 Conclusion

It is concluded that a private school in South Africa managed to transition to online Zoom classes during the Covid-19 pandemic successfully. Most teachers felt that Zoom was clear and understandable, and easy to communicate to others, although teachers still prefer face-to-face teaching. The Diffusion of Innovation Theory is used to explain the teachers' perceptions of Zoom classes, and it is discussed in terms of compatibility, trialability, observability, and complexity or ease of use. Six factors from the teachers' responses were identified as themes. Future research can include expanding the study to other schools as well as other grades to determine if Zoom is a suitable substitute for face-to-face teaching, as was deemed necessary in the case of Covid-19. Future research can also include the investigation of schools introducing a distance learning option using

Zoom as the tool of class dissemination. This could potentially improve the income of the school without too many additional resources being required.

References

1. Jantjies, M.: What South Africa's teachers brought to the virtual classroom during COVID-19 (2020) [online]. https://theconversation.com/what-south-africas-teachers-brought-to-the-virtual-classroom-during-Covid-19-147306
2. Schaffler, D., Mirna, N., Booyse, R.: Exploring South African Foundation Phase teachers' understanding, skills and training needs in the teaching of phonological awareness. Lang. Learn. J. (2019). https://doi.org/10.1080/09571736.2019.1655585
3. Mouton, M.: Using Zoom to Teach Synchronously Online. Open Library, Pressbooks (2020)
4. Robinson, L.: A Summary of Diffusion Innovation (2009) [online]. https://twut.nd.edu/PDF/Summary_Diffusion_Theory.pdf
5. Rogers, E.M.: Diffusion of Innovations. Free Press, New York (2003)
6. Creswell, J.W.: Research Design: Qualitative and Quantitative Approaches. Thousand Oaks, CA Sage (1994)
7. Creswell, J.W.: Research Design: Qualitative, Quantitative, and Mixed Methods Approaches, 2nd edn. Thousand Oaks, CA Sage (2003)
8. Jwaifell, M., Gasaymeh, A.: Using the diffusion of innovation theory to explain the degree of English teachers' adoption of interactive whiteboards in the modern systems School in Jordan: a case study. Contemp. Educ. Technol. **4**, 138–149 (2013)
9. Moore, G.C., Benbasat, I.: Development of an instrument to measure the perceptions of adopting an information technology innovation. Inf. Syst. Res. **2**(3), 192–222 (1991)
10. Sahin, I.: Detailed review of Rogers' diffusion of innovations theory and educational technology. Turkish Online J. Educ. Technol. **5**(2), 3 (2016)

Enhancing Learners' Creative Thinking in the Massive Open Online Course (Moocs) Learning Environment Model for Higher Education

Benjaporn Sathanarugsawait[1], Charuni Samat[2(✉)], and Suchat Wattanachai[3]

[1] Faculty of Education, Doctor of Philosophy Student of Education Technology, Khon Kaen University, Khon Kaen, Thailand

[2] Faculty of Education, Division of Computer Education, Khon Kaen University, Khon Kaen, Thailand

[3] Faculty of Veterinary Medicine, Division of Surgery, Khon Kaen University, Khon Kaen, Thailand

Abstract. This research was aimed to study the creative effect of the students who study with massive open online course (MOOCs) learning environment model for higher education. The target groups consisted of 20 juniors majored in Business Information Technology, Faculty of Information Technology, Sripatum University, Khon Kaen Campus, and 30 juniors Business Computer, Faculty of Business Administration, North Eastern University. Model Research consists of several types of research, including document research. Survey research and pre-experimental research one shot case study to examine the validity of the learning environment model and the success of using the learning environment model. The instruments used in the study consisted of experimental instruments and data collection tools. Perform quantitative data collection and qualitative. The data were analyzed using basic statistics such as percentage, mean, standard deviation. Protocol analysis Summary. Interpretation and analytical narrative. The results of the study found that the creative thinking of students studying with open online learning environment models (MOOCs) that promote creativity for higher education students. There are 60% of learners who pass the 60% criteria as specified. The students had average scores for creativity of 19.19, 20.76 and standard deviations of 0.54, 0.55.

Keywords: Creative thinking · Learning environment model · Massive open online course

1 Introduction

Currently, the labor market is quite affected by the global situation. Changes can happen at any time, according to a report from the World Economic Forum (WEF), predicting that in the next five years, workforces will face extreme conditions. Double-disruption Both from COVID and the use of automation, this impact could put workers with skills

© Springer Nature Switzerland AG 2021
Y.-M. Huang et al. (Eds.): ICITL 2021, LNCS 13117, pp. 533–541, 2021.
https://doi.org/10.1007/978-3-030-91540-7_54

that don't meet the changing market demands at risk of losing their jobs: Creativity, originality and initiative – Creativity and Innovative Skills, which is an important skill [1]. Consistent with the results of the study, the 21st Century skills were summarized, learning skills and innovation that students focused on creative thinking. Using a variety of thought-building techniques creates new ideas [2] to enhance creative thinking are fluency, flexibility, originality, and elaboration [3] this will prepare you for future work skills. Changing the world in teaching and learning management, teachers should focus on enabling learners to learn on their own. By teachers to support and a paradigm shift in how to create knowledge through cognitive processes that focus on students to create knowledge by taking action through their thought processes. Connect prior knowledge with new knowledge and expand the cognitive structure and provide a learning environment that fosters the learner's knowledge-building process [4]. Using technology that is appropriate to the context. Use Massive Open Online Courses, which are characterized by an unlimited number of participants, an "open" system that anyone can take. MOOCs are an educational experience for learners and also improve the results of the study develop learners' learning skills and implement effective communication with teachers [5]. As mentioned previously. To study the creative effect of the students who study with massive open online course (MOOCs) learning environment model for higher education.

2 Literature Review

2.1 Creative Thinking

Guilford's Creativity (1967) was the basis for the study of the multidirectional thinking abilities of the brain. Called creative thinking that focuses on divergent thinking, which is the idea that leads to inventing new things. Including thinking and discovering solutions to problems successfully, consisting of 1) Fluency that mean the ability to create ideas for answers Fluently, quickly, in large quantities in a limited time and such as keyword of word fluency and ideational fluency 2) Flexibility that mean the ability to create a wide variety of ideas in a useful way and such as keyword of spontaneous flexibility and adaptive flexibility. 3) Originality is an application of design thinking for creating new ideas and 4) Elaboration is to create a detailed idea by creating evaluation criteria and adding details. Improved to make it better [3, 6].

2.2 Learning Environment Model

Learning environment model is a learning management that promotes learning in accordance with the needs of the learners, and facilitate the learners to be able to learn on their own through various learning resources, media by a combination of various theories and computer technology. To create knowledge (Knowledge Construction) to help support students' enthusiasm, opt-in Analyze and synthesize data and the Web based learning environment is a form of application, use internet network services which educators are very interested in nowadays Used to support teaching and learning management for maximum efficiency [7].

2.3 Massive Open Online Course

Massively Open Online Courses, or MOOCs, are defined as open learning systems that emphasize participation and broad reach in an unlimited number of learners. To enroll in classes and learn through online platforms [8]. Students can learn through video lectures or video tutorial content. And forums. That supports the design of a learning environment to enhance creative thinking.

3 Purposes

To study the creative effect of the students who study with massive open online course (MOOCs) learning environment model for higher education.

4 Method and Result

4.1 Scope of Research

This research is a model research type II model research of Richey & Klein (2007) [9] focusing on the creative outcomes of learners studying with an open online learning environment model. The research is divided into 3 phases (Phase), which are: Phase 1, Model development, Phase 2, Model validation, Phase 3, Model use, this time In phase 2, model development and phase 3, model use will be the presentation of research results in the study period.

4.2 Target Group of the Study

The target groups consisted of 20 juniors majored in Business Information Technology, Faculty of Information Technology, Sripatum University, Khon Kaen campus, to study the external validity that is the study of impact on learners when applying the learning environment model, and 30 juniors Business Computer, Faculty of Business Administration, North Eastern University. To study the use of the learning environment model. This is a study of the results resulting from the use of the learner's learning environment model, including creative thinking.

4.3 Research Design

The research model of the study in Phase 2, Model validation and Phase 3, Model use, used a variety of study methods. It consists of several types of research, including document research, survey research and pre-experimental research One shot case study to examine the validity of the learning environment model and the success of using the learning environment model.

4.4 Research Instruments

In this study, the researcher has created tools for use in the study and data collection, consisting of the following tools:

The model research in the Phase 2 study was to examine the validity of the learning environment model. External directness study Use a pre-experimental research model (Pre-experimental design) one-shot case study a tool used to examine external validity by using the Creativity Measure to study the creativity of students studying with the Learning Environment Model. The target groups consisted of 20 juniors majored in Business Information Technology, Faculty of Information Technology, Sripatum University, Khon Kaen campus.

The success of using the learning environment model using the creative thinking model. To study the creativity of students studying with the learning environment model. The target groups consisted of 30 juniors Business Computer, Faculty of Business Administration, North Eastern University.

4.5 Data Collection and Analysis

Data were collected in the Phase 2 study. The external directness of the model. The study from the impact of learners when applying the learning environment model to be used in learning management is the creativity of students. The process is as follows: 1) the learning management process: (1) clarifying and introducing learners about learning the learning environment model; (2) bringing them into lessons by linking learners' prior knowledge, with the subject studied (3) divide 20 learners into subgroups, 3–4 students per group according to the results of the study context (4) let learners learn with the learning environment model 2) Data collection The researcher collects the data after the learners Learn with a learning environment model. Let learners do a measure of creativity. 3) Data analysis consists of quantitative data analysis. And qualitative the researcher will present the data analysis. Student creativity the data were analyzed using basic statistical values, i.e. mean, standard deviation, and percentage, from the data obtained from the Student Creativity Scale. And using data analysis methods by protocol analysis, summary, interpretation.

Data were collected in the Phase 3 study to study the success of using the learning environment model. The application of the learning environment model in learning management is the creativity of the learners. The process is as follows: 1) the learning management process: (1) clarifying and introducing learners about learning the learning environment model; (2) bringing them into lessons by linking learners' prior knowledge. With the subject studied (3) Divide, 30 learners, into subgroups, 3–4 students per group according to the results of the study context (4) let the learners learn with the learning environment model. 2) Collect the data after that learner learns with the learning environment model let learners do a measure of creativity. 3) Data analysis consists of quantitative data analysis. And qualitative the researcher will present the data analysis. Student creativity the data were analyzed using basic statistical values, i.e., mean, standard deviation, and percentage, from the data obtained from the Student Creativity Scale. And using data analysis methods by protocol analysis, summary, interpretation.

4.6 Research Results

The creative effect of the students who study with massive open online course (MOOCs) learning environment model for higher education. In this study, the following results are presented: The scores obtained from measuring the creativity of students studying with the learning environment model. Obtained from the students' creativity measurement [3]. Using it with the target group in phase 2 of 20 people, it was found that the overall creativity score of a full score of 30 showed that 20 students received a score of 18 or more, representing 80.00% of the students. Dear all The mean score was 19.19 and the standard deviation was 0.54 and the creativity score for each aspect found that the ability to Fluency thinking had the highest mean score of 7.10 and the standard deviation was 0.49. Accounted for 71.00%, followed by the ability to creative thinking in Flexibility, Originality, and Elaboration with average scores of 5.40, 4.00, and 3.40, respectively, which shows that the average score of the learners passed the 60 hundred criteria as specified. As in Table 1.

Table 1. Post-study creativity scores of students studying with the learning environment model phase 2 model validations.

No.	Fluency		Flexibility		Originality		Elaboration		Total	%
	Score	%	Score	%	Score	%	Score	%		
1	8	80.00	7	87.50	4	66.67	3	50.00	22	73.33
2	6	60.00	5	62.50	4	66.67	4	66.67	19	63.33
3	6	60.00	4	50.00	4	66.67	3	50.00	17	56.67
4	7	70.00	5	62.50	4	66.67	4	66.67	20	66.67
5	8	80.00	5	62.50	4	66.67	3	50.00	20	66.67
6	6	60.00	5	62.50	4	66.67	4	66.67	19	63.33
7	8	80.00	5	62.50	4	66.67	3	50.00	20	66.67
8	6	60.00	5	62.50	3	50.00	2	33.33	16	53.33
9	8	80.00	6	75.00	4	66.67	3	50.00	21	70.00
10	8	80.00	6	75.00	4	66.67	4	66.67	22	73.33
11	7	70.00	7	87.50	5	83.33	4	66.67	23	76.67
12	7	70.00	7	87.50	4	66.67	3	50.00	21	70.00
13	8	80.00	5	62.50	5	83.33	5	83.33	23	76.67
14	7	70.00	6	75.00	4	66.67	4	66.67	21	70.00
15	8	80.00	4	50.00	5	83.33	3	50.00	20	66.67
16	5	50.00	4	50.00	4	66.67	4	66.67	17	56.67
17	6	60.00	4	50.00	3	50.00	2	33.33	15	50.00
18	8	80.00	6	75.00	4	66.67	3	50.00	21	70.00

(continued)

Table 1. (*continued*)

No.	Fluency		Flexibility		Originality		Elaboration		Total	%
	Score	%	Score	%	Score	%	Score	%		
19	8	80.00	6	75.00	4	66.67	4	66.67	22	73.33
20	7	70.00	6	75.00	3	50.00	3	50.00	19	63.33
									Total results	
$\bar{x}$	7.10		5.40		4.00		3.40		19.19	
S.D.	490		550		570		510			
%	7100		6750		6667		5667		97.63	
	Total number of learners (number)								20	
	Number of students who have passed the percentage criteria 60 (number)								16	
	Percentage of learners with a passing score percentage 60 (18 score)								00.80	
	Average score of students ($\bar{x}$)								19.19	
	Standard deviation (S.D.)								54.0	

- The scores obtained from measuring the creativity of students studying with the learning environment model, obtained from the students' creativity measurement Using it with the target group in phase 3 of 30 people, it was found that the overall creativity score of a full score of 30 showed that there were 26 learners who received a score of 18 or more, representing 86.67% of the students. Dear all with a gray mean of 20.76 and a standard deviation of 0.55 and a score of creativity in each aspect found that the ability to think creatively (Fluency) had the highest mean score of 7.28. The standard deviation was 0.57, representing 72.80%, followed by the ability to Flexibility thinking on the Originality) and Elaboration with average scores of 5.67, 4.08 and 3.63, respectively, which shows that the average score of the learners passed the 60 hundred criteria as specified in Table 2.

Table 2. Post-study creativity scores of students learning with learning environment model phase 3 model use.

No.	Fluency		Flexibility		Originality		Elaboration		Total	%
	Score	%	Score	%	Score	%	Score	%		
1	8	80.00	5	62.50	4	66.67	3	50.00	20	66.67
2	6	60.00	7	87.50	5	83.33	4	66.67	22	73.33
3	8	80.00	5	62.50	4	66.67	4	66.67	21	70.00
4	6	60.00	7	87.50	3	50.00	3	50.00	19	63.33
5	6	60.00	7	87.50	3	50.00	3	50.00	19	63.33

(*continued*)

Table 2. (*continued*)

No.	Fluency		Flexibility		Originality		Elaboration		Total	%
	Score	%	Score	%	Score	%	Score	%		
6	8	80.00	7	87.50	4	66.67	4	66.67	23	76.67
7	6	60.00	5	62.50	3	50.00	3	50.00	17	56.67
8	6	60.00	4	50.00	4	66.67	3	50.00	17	56.67
9	7	70.00	5	62.50	4	66.67	4	66.67	20	66.67
10	8	80.00	5	62.50	4	66.67	3	50.00	20	66.67
11	6	60.00	5	62.50	4	66.67	4	66.67	19	63.33
12	8	80.00	5	62.50	4	66.67	3	50.00	20	66.67
13	7	70.00	6	75.00	3	50.00	3	50.00	19	63.33
14	8	80.00	6	75.00	4	66.67	3	50.00	21	70.00
15	7	70.00	7	87.50	4	66.67	3	50.00	21	70.00
16	8	80.00	5	62.50	5	83.33	5	83.33	23	76.67
17	7	70.00	6	75.00	4	66.67	4	66.67	21	70.00
18	8	80.00	6	75.00	5	83.33	4	66.67	23	76.67
19	8	80.00	6	75.00	4	66.67	4	66.67	22	73.33
20	7	70.00	7	87.50	5	83.33	4	66.67	23	76.67
21	7	70.00	7	87.50	4	66.67	3	50.00	21	70.00
22	8	80.00	6	75.00	5	83.33	5	83.33	24	80.00
23	7	70.00	6	75.00	4	66.67	4	66.67	21	70.00
24	8	80.00	4	50.00	5	83.33	3	50.00	20	66.67
25	5	50.00	4	50.00	4	66.67	4	66.67	17	56.67
26	6	60.00	5	62.50	3	50.00	3	50.00	17	56.67
27	8	80.00	6	75.00	4	66.67	3	50.00	21	70.00
28	8	80.00	6	75.00	4	66.67	4	66.67	22	73.33
29	8	80.00	7	87.50	4	66.67	4	66.67	23	76.67
30	8	80.00	6	75.00	5	83.33	5	83.33	24	80.00
									Total results	
$\bar{x}$	7.28		675		084		633		76.20	
S.D.	570		480		520		580			
%	8072		8370		0668		4260		20.69	
	Total number of learners (number)								30	
	Number of students who have passed the percentage criteria 60 (number)								26	
	Percentage of learners with a passing score percentage 60 (18 score)								67.86	
	Average score of students ($\bar{x}$)								76.20	
	Standard deviation (S.D.)								55.0	

5 Conclusions

Results of the student's creative thinking who learned with massive open online course (MOOCs) learning environment model for higher education. There are 2 phases, Phase 2 and Phase 3 in this study, the results will be presented as follows: Phase 2, the scores obtained from measuring the creativity of students studying with the learning environment model [10]. Obtained from the students' creativity measurement. Using it with the target group in phase 2 of 20 people, it was found that the overall creativity score of a full score of 30 showed that 20 students received a score of 18 or more, representing 80.00% of the students. Dear all The mean score was 19.19 and the standard deviation was 0.54 and the creativity score for each aspect found that the ability to Fluency thinking had the highest mean score of 7.10 and the standard deviation was 0.49. Accounted for 71.00%, followed by the ability to creative thinking in Flexibility, Originality, and Elaboration with average scores of 5.40, 4.00, and 3.40, respectively, which shows that the average score of the learners passed the 60% as specified. Phase 3, The scores were obtained from measuring the creativity of students studying with the learning environment model [11]. Obtained from the students' creativity measurement Using it with the target group in phase 3 of 30 people, it was found that the overall creativity score of a full score of 30 showed that 26 learners received a score of 18 or more, representing 86.67% of the students. Dear all with a gray mean of 20.76 and a standard deviation of 0.55 and a score of creativity in each aspect found that the ability to Fluency thinking had the highest mean score of 7.28. The standard deviation was 0.57, representing 72.80%, followed by the ability to Flexibility thinking. Originality and Elaboration with average scores of 5.67, 4.08, and 3.63, respectively, which shows that the average score of the learners passed 60%.

Results of the student's creative thinking that learned with model showed 60% of the target passed at 60% of learning standard by the evaluation outcomes in research phase 2 and 3. Their average creative thinking evaluation and S.D. values were 19.19, 20.76, and 0.54 and 0.55 respectively. In addition, the protocol analysis of the creativity in those 2 phases illustrated that the students had such ability in terms of 1) Fluency 2) Flexibility 3) Originality, and 4) Elaboration.

Acknowledgement. This work was supported by the Innovation and Cognitive Technology Research Center, Faculty of Education, and the Research and Technology Transfers Affairs Division, Khon Kaen University.

References

1. World Economic Forum: The Future of Jobs Report 2020, p. 36 (2020)
2. Samat, C., Chaijaroen, S.: Design and development of learning environment to enhance creative thinking and innovation skills for teacher training in the 21st century. In: ICCE, pp. 667–672 (2015)
3. Guilford, J.P.: The Nature of Human Intelligence. McGraw-Hill Book Company, New York (1967)
4. Piaget, J., Cook, M.T.: The Origins of Intelligence in Children. International University Press, New York (1952)

5. Sathanarugsawait, B., Samat, C., Wattanachai, S.: Survey Results of Learner Context in the Development of Constructivist Learning Environment Model to Enhance Creative Thinking with Massive Open Online Course (MOOCS) for Higher Education: Innovative Technologies and Learning, Third International Conference, ICITL 2020, Porto, Portugal, November 23–25, 2020, Proceedings, pp. 465–474 (2020). https://doi.org/10.1007/978-3-030-63885-6_51
6. Sathanarugsawait, B., Samat, C.: Synthesis of theoretical framework of constructivist creative thinking Massive Open Online Courses (MOOCs) for higher education. In: Wu, T.-T., Huang, Y.-M., Shadieva, R., Lin, L., Starčič, A.I. (eds.) ICITL 2018. LNCS, vol. 11003, pp. 146–150. Springer, Cham (2018). https://doi.org/10.1007/978-3-319-99737-7_14
7. Jonassen, D.H., Peck, K.L., Wilson, B.G.: Learning with Technology: A Constructive Perspective. Prentice Hall, Upper Saddle River (1999)
8. Kaplan, A.M., Haenlein, M.: Higher education and the digital revolution: about MOOCs, SPOCs, social media, and the Cookie Monster. Bus. Horiz. **59**(4), 441–450 (2016). https://doi.org/10.1016/j.bushor.2016.03.008
9. Richey, R.C., Klein, J.: Design and Developmental Research. Lawrence, New Jersey (2007)
10. Wongchiranuwat, S., Samat, C., Kanjug, I., Wattanachai, S.: The Study of Learner Context for The Development of Constructivist Learning Environment Model Combined with Mixed Reality Flipped Classroom to Enhance Creative Thinking, ICITL 2020, Porto, Portugal, Proceedings, pp. 348–338 (2020)
11. Wongchiranuwat, S., Samat, C.: Synthesis of theoretical framework for augmented Reality learning environment to promote creative thinking. In: 24th ICCE Proceedings, pp. 639–641 (2016)

Designing of Learning Environment Model to Enhance Student' Self Regulation by Using Massive Open Online Course

Benjaporn Sathanarugsawait[1](✉) and Charuni Samat[2]

[1] Division of Business Information Technology, School of Information Technology, Sripatum University, Khon Kaen, Thailand
Benjaporn.sa@spu.ac.th

[2] Faculty of Education, Division of Computer Education, Khon Kaen University, Khon Kaen, Thailand

Abstract. The purpose of this study was to study the design and development of a learning environment model to enhance student' self-regulation by using massive open online course. The target groups used in the research were 1) content experts. in design and media and technology, 3 people each, and 2) 80 high school students at Sri Kranuan Wittayakhom School, Kranuan District, Khon Kaen Province. The research model in this study is development research. It is research in many forms, including document research. Survey research and pre-experimental research there is a development process, namely the synthesis of theoretical frameworks and design conceptual framework Synthesis of models and creating a learning environment, and evaluating the effectiveness of the learning environment. The data were analyzed by using basic statistics and interpreting conclusions. The results revealed that the learning environment consisted of 7 components: Problem base, Resource room, Self-regulation room, Cognitive tool Room, Collaboration Room, Scaffolding Room, and Coaching room.

Keywords: Self regulation · Learning environment model · Massive open online course

1 Introduction

Continuous self-learning lifelong learning it is the process of change and development that occurs in the person. As a result of acquiring knowledge, skills, or experience from education, perception, knowledge, skills, and attitudes, which can be learned by systematic or non-systematic learning methods. causing that person to develop himself. The process of change and development that takes place in the person. As a result of acquiring knowledge, skills, or experience from education, perception, knowledge, skills, and attitudes can be learned through different learning methods. systematically or not systematically causing that person to develop himself which is the nature of the new era of higher education students. In teaching and learning management, teachers should focus on enabling learners to learn on their own. The teacher is a coach to help support and

© Springer Nature Switzerland AG 2021
Y.-M. Huang et al. (Eds.): ICITL 2021, LNCS 13117, pp. 542–547, 2021.
https://doi.org/10.1007/978-3-030-91540-7_55

promote the knowledge creation of learners. That encourages learners to build their own knowledge and a paradigm shift in how to create knowledge through cognitive processes that focus on students to create knowledge by taking action through their own thought processes. Connect prior knowledge with new knowledge and expand the cognitive structure and provide a learning environment that fosters the learner's knowledge-building process. including principles Theories and characteristics of media technology that are consistent Massive Open Online Courses will be open online teaching and learning management system. which is characterized by allowing an unlimited number of people to attend. It is an open system where everyone can attend. Free of charge and using online technology as a learning aid.

The researcher recognizes the importance of encouraging learners to develop self-regulation skills by using an open online teaching system. Therefore, the researcher has an idea to study the design and development of a learning environment model to enhance student' self-regulation by using massive open online course. Using an open online teaching system Based on the development of theoretical framework, related theories, and research studies on knowledge creation. Contextual Fundamentals Fundamentals of Learning Psychology Fundamentals of Pedagogical Sciences Fundamentals of media characteristics and media symbol system creative fundamentals to design and develop a learning environment that focuses on the learners to learn the subject matter while developing an emphasis on the cognitive process, where the findings will lead to the development of the quality of the learners.

2 Literature Review

2.1 Self-regulation

Self-Regulation refers to the way students become experts in their own learning process. Neither mental abilities nor acting skills Self-control, rather than the process of self-control, whereby learners transform their mental abilities into job-related skills in areas of work such as academics, sports, music, and health [2]. Learn with goal setting self-awareness Develop strategies for learning, controlling one's job satisfaction, and self-assessment to adjust the course of action to achieve goals. which consists of 1) Goal Setting is to record the goals of the learners in learning. 2) Self-efficacy is the perception of a learner's ability 3) Task strategies are strategies for planning learners' learning. 4) the satisfaction of learners from the assessment of the learners' own performance.

2.2 Learning Environment Model

The learning environment is the application of teaching methods based on the characteristics of media on the network known as Web-based learning environment is teaching in the classroom that takes advantage of the Internet as a medium of teaching in such a way that students can interact with the content to be learned and Teachers and learners use the properties of technology on the network to manage teaching that has the feature of hyper-linking. multidimensional text is a text or hypermedia link that is a media link with an important feature of the Internet. Presenting content that is text, static, audio, animated, or video Which is prepared in the form of hyperlinks that allow learners to choose to study as they wish. Communication on the Internet: Learners can communicate with each other or interact with each other either person-to-person, learner-to-group, or group-to-group. Information searching is a tool that allows learners to search for additional information [7].

2.3 Massive Open Online Course

Massive Open Online Courses, or MOOCs, are defined as an open learning system that emphasizes broad participation and accessibility in an unlimited number of learners. It is characterized by allowing access to an unlimited number of people. It is an "open" system that everyone who wants to study must learn. Without the cost of studying and use online technology as a tool Open education for lifelong learning [3] to enroll in classes and learn through online platforms [8]. That supports the design of a learning environment to enhance self-regulation.

3 Purposes

To design and develop a learning environment model to enhance student' self-regulation by using massive open online course.

4 Method and Result

4.1 Scope of Research

This research is a Type II model search research of Richey & Klein (2007) [7] focusing on the design and development of a learning environment model to enhance student' self-regulation by using massive open online course. It is a model development research in many forms, including document research. survey research and pre-experimental research.

4.2 Target Group of the Study

The target groups used in the research were 1) content experts. in design and media and technology, 3 people each, and 2) 80 high school students at Sri Kranuan Wittayakhom School, Kranuan District, Khon Kaen Province.

4.3 Research Design

This research Focus on the design and development process of the model. Based on the instructional design theory and using educational methods, consisting of (1) synthesis of theoretical framework, i.e. the study of theoretical principles; context studies and a synthesis of a theoretical framework. (2) synthesis of a designing framework for design a learning environment model. (3) synthesis of a learning environment model and evaluating the learning environment model. (4) The design and development of the learning environment.

4.4 Research Instruments

This study The tools used consisted of (1) tools used for collecting data on the synthesis of theoretical framework, i.e. audit log form and document analysis; Survey on the context of learners Teacher's Context Survey on context, environment and learning support Theoretical Conceptual Synthesis Record Form (2) The tool used for collecting the data of synthesis of a designing framework, i.e. the Record Synthesis of a designing framework for design a learning environment model (3) the instrument for collecting the Synthesis Data. The learning environment model is the record form of the learning environment model synthesis. Learning Environment Model Assessment Form (4) The tools used for collecting data on the design and development of the learning environment model are the learning environment design and development record form. Survey on characteristics of learning environment model designers and (5) the learning environment model survey and practitioners.

4.5 Data Collection and Analysis

Data Collection and Analysis Model development is as follows:

The synthesis of theoretical framework consists of 1) a study of theoretical principles; The researcher collects data on principles and theories. by recording various data in the audit log form and analyzing the document; 2) the study of the context The researcher collected the data by having the learners, tutors, survey the context and the information technology staff to survey the learning environment and support. The data were analyzed using basic statistical values such as mean, standard deviation, percentage, summary interpretation. and analytical lectures.

The synthesis of a designing framework for design a learning environment model. The researcher collected the data by recording various data in the Synthesis Record Form for the Learning Environment Model Design Concept. and analyze the data by summarizing and interpreting and analytical lectures.

The Synthesis a learning environment model. The researcher collected the model synthesis data by recording various data in the learning environment model synthesis record form. and analyze the data by summarizing and interpreting and analytical lectures. Then, the researchers assessed the learning environment model. Data were collected to assess the learning environment model by using the learning environment model assessment form. and analyze the data by summarizing and interpreting and analytical lectures.

Design and development of the learning environment model. The researcher collected data on the design and development of the learning environment. By recording various information in the learning environment design and development memorandum. and analyze the data by summarizing, interpreting, and analyzing narrative.

4.6 Research Results

Design and development of a learning environment model to enhance student' self regulation by using massive open online course. The researcher collected data on the design and development of the learning environment. In this study, the results are presented in three parts as follows:

The synthesis of theoretical framework of the learning environment model to enhance student' self-regulation by using massive open online course consists of 5 fundamentals: Context base, Psychology base, self-regulation base, Pedagogical base and Media and technology base (Fig. 1).

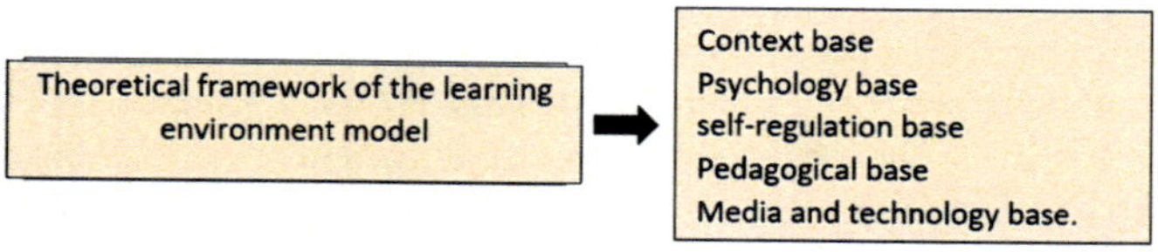

Fig. 1. Theoretical framework of the learning environment model.

The synthesis of a designing framework for design a learning environment model consist of Stimulation of cognitive structures and self-regulation, Cognitive balancing and self-regulation support, Promoting the expansion of intellectual structures and self-regulation, and helping and supporting knowledge creation.

The synthesis of the learning environment model consists of 7 components: Problem base, Resource room, Self-regulation room, Cognitive tool Room, Collaboration Room, Scaffolding Room, and Coaching room (Fig. 2).

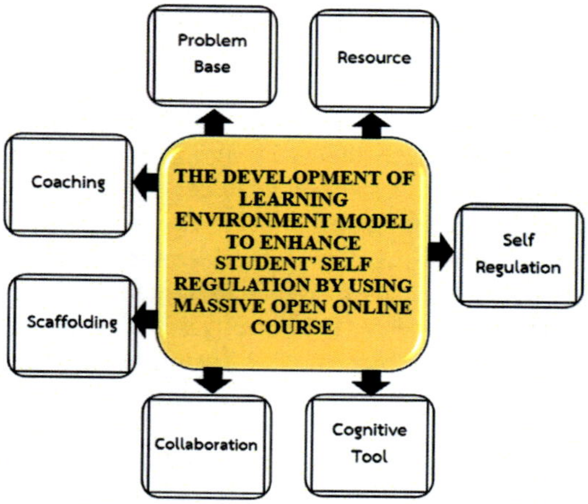

Fig. 2. A learning environment model synthesis to enhance student' self-regulation by using massive open online course.

5 Conclusions

The results of the design and development of a learning environment model to enhance student' self-regulation by using massive open online course. The researcher collected data for the design and development of the learning environment as follows: (1) The synthesis of theoretical framework of the learning environment model to enhance student' self-regulation by using massive open online course consists of 5 fundamentals: Context base, Psychology base, self-regulation base, Pedagogical base and Media and technology base. (2) The synthesis of a designing framework for design a learning environment model consist of Stimulation of cognitive structures and self-regulation, Cognitive balancing and self-regulation support, Promoting the expansion of intellectual structures and self-regulation, and helping and supporting knowledge creation. (3) The synthesis of the learning environment model consists of 7 components: Problem base, Resource room, Self-regulation room, Cognitive tool Room, Collaboration Room, Scaffolding Room, and Coaching room.

Acknowledgement. This research is supported by Sripatum University, Khon Kaen Campus, Thailand.

References

1. World Economic Forum: The Future of Jobs Report 2020, p. 36 (2020)
2. Samat, C., Chaijaroen, S.: Design and development of learning environment to enhance creative thinking and innovation skills for teacher training in the 21st century. In: ICCE, pp. 667–672 (2015)
3. Zimmerman, B.J.: Self-regulated learning: theories, measures, and outcomes. In: Wright, J.D. (ed.) International Encyclopedia of the Social and Behavioral Sciences, pp. 541–546. Elsevier, Oxford (2015)
4. Piagėt, J., Cook, M.T.: The Origins of Intelligence in Children. International University Press, New York (1952)
5. Sathanarugsawait, B., Samat, C., Wattanachai, S.: Survey Results of Learner Context in the Development of Constructivist Learning Environment Model to Enhance Creative Thinking with Massive Open Online Course (MOOCS) for Higher Education: Innovative Technologies and Learning, Third International Conference, ICITL 2020, Porto, Portugal, 23–25, November 2020, Proceedings, pp. 465–474 (2020). https://doi.org/10.1007/978-3-030-63885-6_51
6. Sathanarugsawait, B., Samat, C.: Synthesis of theoretical framework of constructivist creative thinking Massive Open Online Courses (MOOCs) for higher education. In: Wu, T.-T., Huang, Y.-M., Shadieva, R., Lin, L., Starčič, A.I. (eds.) ICITL 2018. LNCS, vol. 11003, pp. 146–150. Springer, Cham (2018). https://doi.org/10.1007/978-3-319-99737-7_14
7. Jonassen, D.H., Peck, K.L., Wilson, B.G.: Learning with Technology: A Constructive Perspective. Prentice Hall, Upper Saddle River (1999)
8. Kaplan, A.M., Haenlein, M.: Higher education and the digital revolution: about MOOCs, SPOCs, social media, and the Cookie Monster. Bus. Horiz. **59**(4), 441–450 (2016). https://doi.org/10.1016/j.bushor.2016.03.008
9. Richey, R.C., Klein, J.: Design and Developmental Research. Lawrence, New Jersey (2007)
10. Wongchiranuwat, S., Samat, C., Kanjug, I., Wattanachai, S.: The Study of Learner Context for the Development of Constructivist Learning Environment Model Combined with Mixed Reality Flipped Classroom to Enhance Creative Thinking, ICITL 2020, Porto, Portugal, Proceedings, pp. 348–338 (2020)
11. Wongchiranuwat, S., Samat, C.: Synthesis of theoretical framework for augmented reality learning environment to promote creative thinking. In: 24th ICCE Proceedings, pp. 639–641 (2016)

Higher Education Students' Perceptions Towards Using Facebook as a Learning Platform

Rdouan Faizi[1](✉) and Maria Rudneva[2]

[1] ENSIAS, Mohammed V University in Rabat, Rabat, Morocco
rdouan.faizi@um5.ac.ma
[2] RUDN University, Moscow, Russia
rudneva-ma@rudn.ru

Abstract. Given the ongoing debate among educators regarding the effect of social networks on education, our aim in this article is to explore the perceptions of students towards using Facebook as a learning environment. In this vein, on the basis of the survey we carried out among university students, it was revealed that 87.4% of the informants resort to this Web-based community to improve their learning. Facebook has, actually, been reported to provide students with an ideal opportunity to access a plethora of learning resources and all class-related information and activities. It also allows them to discuss different topics with classmates and peers and enables them to seek help on learning problems they encounter. Despite the significant role that Facebook plays in boosting students' learning experience, 72.3% of the subjects noted that no interaction occurs with teachers on this platform. Facebook might, thus, be considered to be more useful for informal rather than formal learning.

Keywords: Higher education · Facebook · Students · Survey · Perceptions

1 Introduction

Given the rapid advances in information and communication technologies over the past couple of years, the Internet has become a participatory and collaborative platform where users can interact and collaborate with each other as well as an open space where they create and share digital content. This evolution of the Web from a set of simple static pages to a more dynamic and collaborative web has been accelerated by the emergence and proliferation of a wide range of Web 2.0 applications, commonly known as social media. The latter includes a variety of applications, namely social networks, media sharing websites and discussion forums.

Today, these web-based communities are widely used by millions of people around the world for a variety of purposes. Given their ubiquity, they have influenced both our personal and professional lives. These online services and tools have impacted how people communicate and interact with each other. More importantly, they affected the way many processes and activities are carried out in diverse fields. The effect of social media is already felt in a variety of domains. Nevertheless, one of the fields in which

© Springer Nature Switzerland AG 2021
Y.-M. Huang et al. (Eds.): ICITL 2021, LNCS 13117, pp. 548–554, 2021.
https://doi.org/10.1007/978-3-030-91540-7_56

their use is likely to be beneficial is education [1–4]. This is primarily due to the fact that a large number of social media users are teenagers, most of whom are undoubtedly students. The latter are deeply immersed in these virtual spaces and have recourse to them not only for communication and entrainment, but for educational purposes as well [5–8]. Our purpose in this work is, therefore, to examine the usefulness of these digital tools in education. Nonetheless, analysis in the present work will be confined to examining the role that social networks (namely, Facebook) potentially play in enhancing students' learning.

2 Students' Views on Using Facebook as an Educational Platform

Given the students' immersion in social networks, there is an ongoing debate regarding the potential impact of these technologies on the learning experience and academic performance of students [9–11]. In fact, despite the numerous opportunities that these social media platforms offer to both students and teachers, many educators still question the usefulness and value of incorporating these web-based platforms in education. Concrete evidence that confirms or refutes these arguments are, thus, needed [12, 13]. The aim of the present section is, therefore, to examine the students' views on using Facebook as an educational tool.

2.1 Research Methodology

To investigate the potential effect of Facebook on education, a research study was undertaken to examine how students use this social network and how they view its role in fostering their learning experience. For this purpose, a web-based questionnaire was administered to students at Mohammed V University, Morocco. The target population for the present study was mainly engineering and master students, specialized in information and communications technologies. Their age varies between 20 and 25. The questionnaire was sent to both male and female students. However, no gender-based analysis in carried out in this work. The adoption of an online rather than a classical paper-based questionnaire was driven by the fact that online surveys enable us to reach the great majority of the participants and that data retrieval and analysis in such questionnaires is much easier and faster. The tool that was used for data collection and analysis is Google Forms.

Ethical approval for the study was obtained from all the subjects before the study. In fact, all the prospective participants were informed (via email and on the online form) about the purpose of the research study and were also notified that all their responses would be anonymous and that their participation is entirely voluntary.

The survey that was administered to the students was based on closed-ended questions, which can only be answered by selecting from a limited number of options. It consisted of two major parts. The first part was concerned with the subjects' usage patterns of Facebook while the second was devoted to collecting data about the informants' perceptions towards the use of this online network as a learning platform.

2.2 Data Processing

Analysis of the data that was retrieved from the survey showed that most of the interviewed students are deeply immersed in this social network. In fact, more than 94% of the surveyed 420 students are active members of Facebook. The students' immersion in this social networking site is clearly demonstrated by the usage frequency of this platform. The findings of the present study, actually, show that a considerable number of students who answered the questionnaire spend a huge amount of their time browsing this online network. Consult the illustration below.

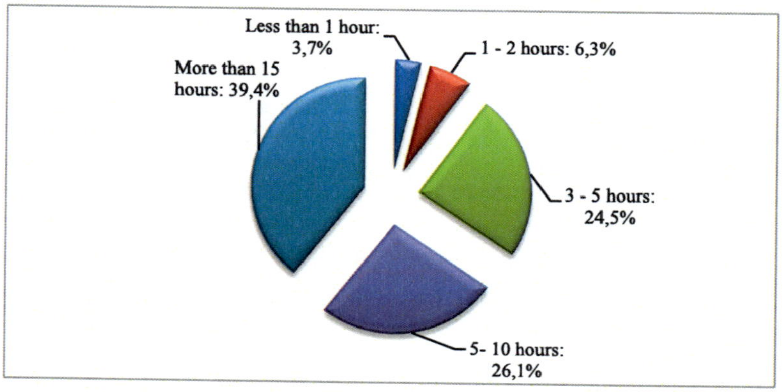

Fig. 1. Number of hours that students spend on Facebook per week.

As Fig. 1 explicitly exhibits, the great majority of respondents (90%) spend at least 3 h a week on Facebook while only 10% of these students get connected for no more than 2 h. This obviously demonstrates that using Facebook is a priority among higher education students.

When inquired about the main reasons for using Facebook, the informants noted that they resort to this social network for different reasons. Results of this study showed that the informants use Facebook to interact with friends and family, meet new people, be entertained as well as follow trends. But in addition to these purposes, the participants in the survey were found out to use Facebook more importantly for educational reasons. Indeed, 87.4% of the students who participated in the survey reported that they use this online community essentially to enrich their learning experience in different topics and subjects. In this respect, the subjects claimed that Facebook allows them to have access to a plethora of valuable learning materials (i.e. links to tutorials, assignments and other useful resources). It also enables to discuss distinct topics with classmates, seek feedback or help on problems that are having as well as check for class exercises and homework.

To get more concrete evidence on the reasons of using Facebook as a learning platform, the respondents were asked to indicate the people that they interact most with on this social networking website. The subjects were asked to rank three options (i.e. friends, classmates/peers and new people) from most to least important. The results are illustrated in the figure given below (Fig. 2).

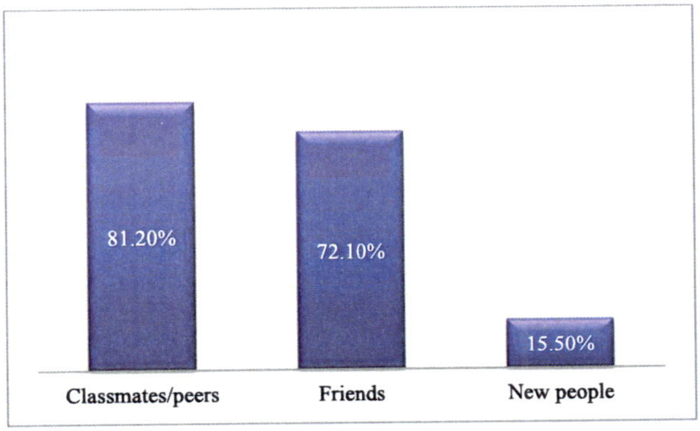

Fig. 2. Individuals with whom students interact on Facebook.

As the figure clearly displays, the people that the surveyed students communicate mostly with are classmates or peers (81.20%). As such, discussion on this online platform is likely to be around educational issues. This confirms the idea that Facebook can serve as a learning environment.

To back up more the assumption or idea that Facebook can be used for educational purposes, the subjects were particularly asked about their typical activities and contributions on this social media platform. In this context, the findings of the survey revealed that a considerable number of respondents are actively engaged in creating and publishing educational content. Among the most common contributions of students are making comments or providing feedback (53.3%), proposing links to learning resources (39.9%), making announcements of academic activities or events (35.3%). Nonetheless, about 30% of the informants admitted that they make no contributions on Facebook. Their use of this social is merely limited to following what other students or peers post.

Furthermore, since some educators have been questioning the validity of using Facebook in education settings and its effect on students' learning, the participants in the survey were also inquired about the impact that this online network might have on their academic performance. To this end, the informants were asked to select one of the following five options, namely "very positive", "positive", "neutral", "negative" or "very negative". The answers of the respondents are summarized in the figure given below (Fig. 3).

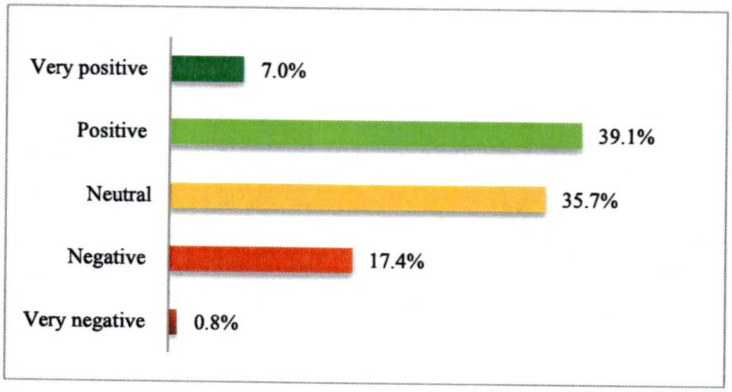

Fig. 3. Students' views on the impact of Facebook on their academic achievement.

Even if the informants diverge as to the kind of impact that Facebook has on their learning outcomes, almost half of the informants (i.e. 46.1%) converge on the fact that this social media platform positively impacts their learning experience. By contrast, 35.7% of the participants are still confused as they are not able to decide whether the effect is negative or positive.

Despite the fact that only the minority of the informants (i.e. 18.2%) believe that Facebook could have a negative impact on students' learning and despite the great educational opportunities of Facebook as a communication tool, it has been noted that interaction between students and teachers on this platform is minimal. In actual fact, when the respondents were asked whether they interact with faculty on this social platform, the great majority (72.3%) stipulated that no interaction seems to take place between them and instructors on Facebook. Moreover, of all those subjects who claimed to communicate with teachers (27.7%), only 13% stated they interact only with one single faculty member on this platform.

To get more information regarding the lack or scarcity of interaction between students and teachers on Facebook, the informants were further asked if they would accept teachers as members of their Facebook groups. In this context, it was found out that 58.3% of the subjects were for teacher-student interaction. However, 5.2% were against while the rest (i.e. 36.5%) were neutral. The absence of mutual interaction between students and teachers on social Facebook is, thus, likely to be due to the reluctance of faculty members to embrace such tools in education. Many studies have, actually, shown that many instructors tend to avoid using such platforms for fear that the boundary between teachers and students might quickly get blurred [14].

Bearing in mind the findings outlined above, it is clearly evident that Facebook supports education thanks to the advantages it offers to the major educational actors, namely end users and learning providers. Therefore, in contrast to the belief that this social network can have a negative effect on students' academic achievement, it has become clear that, via this online platform, students can interact with classmates and peers, easily access valuable learning materials and learn in social ways. On the other hand, teachers can use this social network to instantly interact and communicate in an efficient way with students and with the learning community. Furthermore, they can gain insights into what and how these students are learning. These findings are consistent with those of many preceding research works, namely [15–21], which all confirm the positive impact that Facebook can have on the learning experience of higher education students.

3 Conclusion

The main objective of this work was to examine the potential impact of using Facebook in education. For this purpose, a questionnaire was submitted to a group of Moroccan university students to identify their perceptions on the use this online social network as a learning/teaching platform. The findings of the present research work demonstrated that the majority of the surveyed students are greatly immersed in Facebook as they use it not only as a source of entrainment or as a communication channel but as learning tool as well. In this respect, they noted that this virtual community gives them easy access to a wide range of learning resources and to class-related information and activities. Moreover, it enables them to interact with their classmates and peers and to get feedback and help on problems that they encounter while learning. In spite of the considerable educational benefits that Facebook has, it was noticed that the number of faculty members who use this online community to interact with students is still insignificant. Nevertheless, given the growing popularity of Facebook and of many other social media platforms over the years, these social networking websites should be incorporated in education settings to support learning and teaching practices.

References

1. Bicen, H., Cavus, N.: Social network sites usage habits of undergraduate students: case study of Facebook. Procedia – Soc. Behav. Sci. **28**, 943–947 (2011)
2. Madge, C., Meek, J., Wellens, J., Hooley, T.: Facebook, social integration and informal learning at university: it is more for socialising and talking to friends about work than for actually doing work. Learn. Media Technol. **34**(2), 141–155 (2009)
3. Faizi, R., El Afia, A., Chiheb, R.: Social media: An optimal virtual environment for learning foreign languages. Int. J. Emerg. Technol. Learn. (iJET) **9**(5), 64–66 (2014)
4. Ukwishaka, M.C., Aghaee, N.: Using social media for peer interaction in higher education: students' perception of using Facebook to support peer learning. In: 14th IADIS International Conference e-Learning 2020, EL 2020, Part of the 14th Multi Conference on Computer Science and Information Systems, MCCSIS 2020, 21–23 July 2020, pp. 109–116. IADIS Press (2020)
5. Eteokleous-Grigoriou, N., Ktoridou, D.: Social networking for educational purposes: the development of social-cultural skills through special interest groups. In: Mallia, G. (ed.) The Social Classroom: Integrating Social Network Use in Education, pp. 394–416. Information Science Reference, Hershey (2014). https://doi.org/10.4018/978-1-4666-4904-0.ch020
6. Faizi, R., Chiheb, R., El Afia, A.: Students' perceptions towards using Web 2.0 technologies in education. Int. J. Emerg. Technol. Learn. (iJET), **10**(6), 32 (2015)
7. Moorthy, K., et al.: Is Facebook useful for learning? A study in private universities in Malaysia. Comput. Educ. **130**, 94–104 (2019)
8. Faizi, R., El Fkihi, S.: Analyzing students' perceptions towards using Facebook as a learning platform. In: Proceedings of IADIS International Conference e-Learning 2018, Madrid, Spain (2018)

9. Vázquez-Cano, E., Díez-Arcón, P.: Facebook or LMS in distance education? Why university students prefer to interact in Facebook groups. Int. Rev. Res. Open Distrib. Learn. **22**(3), 119–141 (2021)
10. Chen, Y.C.: The effect of using a Facebook group as a learning management system. ASEE Comput. Educ. (CoED) J. **5**(4), 42 (2014)
11. Feng, S., Wong, Y.K., Wong, L.Y., Hossain, L.: The Internet and Facebook usage on academic distraction of college students. Comput. Educ. **134**, 41–49 (2019)
12. Faizi, R., El Fkihi, S.: Could social media replace formal education? In: Proceedings of the 28th International Business Information Management Association Conference - Vision 2020: Innovation Management, Development Sustainability, and Competitive Economic Growth 2016, pp. 3380–3384. International Business Information Management Association (2016a)
13. Faizi, R.: Teachers' perceptions towards using Web 2.0 in language learning and teaching. Educ. Inf. Technol. **23**(3), 1219–1230 (2017). https://doi.org/10.1007/s10639-017-9661-7
14. Faizi, R., El Fkihi, S.: Incorporating Web 2.0 technologies in education: opportunities and challenges. In: Proceedings of the 28th International Business Information Management Association Conference - Vision 2020: Innovation Management, Development Sustainability, and Competitive Economic Growth, pp. 3242–3248 (2016b).
15. Staines, Z., Lauchs, M.: Students' engagement with Facebook in a university undergraduate policing unit. Aust. J. Educ. Technol. **29**(6) (2013)
16. Al-Oqily, I., Alkhatib, G., Al-Khasawneh, A., Alian, M.: Social networks impact: the case of Jordan youth. Int. J. Continuing Eng. Educ. Life-Long Learn. **23**(1), 100–114 (2013)
17. Faizi, R.: Moroccan higher education students' and teachers' perceptions towards using Web 2.0 technologies in language learning and teaching. Knowl. Manag. E-learning Int. J. (KM&EL), **10**(1), 86–96 (2018b)
18. Moghavvemi, S., Sulaiman, A., Aziz, A.A., Wai, P.S.: The impact of Facebook usage on academic performance. In: 2017 International Conference on Research and Innovation in Information Systems (ICRIIS), pp. 1–5. IEEE (2017)
19. Rice, A.: Students push their Facebook use further into course work. The Chronicle of Higher Education, pp. 1–3 (2011)
20. Jumaat, N.F., Ahmad, N., Samah, N.A., Ashari, Z.M., Ali, D.F., Abdullah, A.H.: Facebook as a platform of social interactions for meaningful learning. Int. J. Emerg. Technol. Learn. (iJET) **14**(04), 151–159 (2019)
21. Inpeng, S., Nomnian, S.: The use of Facebook in a TEFL program based on the TPACK framework. LEARN J. Lang. Educ. Acquisit. Res. Netw. **13**(2), 369–393 (2020)

STEAM Education

Gender Differences in Engineering Design Thinking in a Project-Based STEAM Course

Wan-Hsuan Yen[1](✉), Chi-Cheng Chang[1], and John Willliams[2]

[1] Department of Technology Application and Human Resource Development, National Taiwan Normal University, No. 162, Section 1, HePing E. Road, 106 Taipei, Taiwan

[2] Graduate Research STEM Education Research Group, School of Education, Curtin University, Perth, Australia

Abstract. The underrepresentation of women in science, technology, engineering, art, and mathematics (STEAM)-related fields remains a concern for educators and the engineering community. Females tend to need more social support and learn better within a group. Using Project-based Learning (PjBL) seems to provide a supportive approach for female students to engage with STEAM. We adopted IDEO's design process to evaluate the progress both female and male students made after participating in a PjBL-STEAM course. 137 high school students were recruited in this course to tackle the task to build a truss tower. Both female and male students evidenced significant progress in all constructs of engineering design thinking ability. In addition, there was no significant difference between female and male students' posttest result. Our research echoes earlier research that female students can benefit from group work and develop substantial learning outcomes from PjBL-STEAM course.

Keywords: STEAM · Science-technology-engineering-art-math · Project-based learning · Gender · Female engineer · Engineering design thinking

1 Introduction

The underrepresentation of women in science, technology, engineering, art, and mathematics (STEAM)-related fields remains a concern for educators and the engineering community [1]. Not only is this difference in gender considered an inequality issue, but the lack of numbers of capable STEAM workers also trigger researchers and policy makers to pay more attention to such imbalance [2]. Some cross-disciplinary researches have postulated why such a gender gap exists, although these reasons for the gender gap seem to be complex and contentious, the two major themes of ability and attitude emerge [1]. Generally speaking, female students may not receive adequate attention in STEAM courses, while community support has a strong influence on woman's selection of majors and retention in the classroom [2, 3]. Indications are that peer support and group oriented learning activities could benefit female students in STEAM learning.

Project-based Learning (PjBL) is a type of active learning that engages students to develop their own understanding of a domain by applying its methods and principles [4]

© Springer Nature Switzerland AG 2021
Y.-M. Huang et al. (Eds.): ICITL 2021, LNCS 13117, pp. 557–566, 2021.
https://doi.org/10.1007/978-3-030-91540-7_57

to the development of a project. A meta-analysis of 225 studies across STEAM disciplines (biology, chemistry, computer science, engineering, geology, math, physics, and psychology) showed a benefit of active learning approaches on outcomes such as exam performance [5]. Furthermore, PjBL-STEAM courses can enhance higher level abilities such as metacognition, reflection, and design thinking as well as subject knowledge (for example mathematics and science) [6].

Engineering design thinking is a complex, critical high level ability in the engineering discipline. It is identified as a cornerstone of interdisciplinary STEAM [7]. Throughout the engineering design process, design thinking approaches use solution-based methods to explore human-centered values. How a designer thinks can be defined as the cognitive process and strategies employed by a designer while working on a design problem.

Although it is clear that engagement in PjBL-STEAM courses benefits students, the influence on individual students varies by achievement level, ethnicity, and culture [8]. However, few studies exist on the perceived improvement in engineering design thinking and the possible influence by gender.

The thesis of this research is that studying the relationship between different genders and engineering design thinking ability could contribute to addressing this gap. This study may also identify the areas where a PjBL-STEAM course might be beneficial. Therefore, this study attempted to explore the influence of gender on engineering design thinking when engaged in STEAM through PjBL.

Based on previous literature, we developed a PjBL-STEAM course around a challenging engineering project that aimed to build a water tower using a truss that can withstand the most severe earthquakes. The goal of this task was to build a truss tower with minimum material (constraint) while withstanding maximum earthquake forces (function). Students learned elements of STEAM knowledge in their introductory classes, and integrated this when constructing the water tower. We tested students' engineering design thinking ability before and after the course. Finally, we analyzed the role of gender in engineering design thinking ability to determine whether gender is related engineering design thinking ability. In the following text, we will describe PjBL and its benefits in STEAM education, engineering design thinking, and the influence of gender.

2 Literature Review

2.1 PjBL and Its Benefit for STEAM Education

PjBL is a pedagogical approach that organizes learning around projects [8]. Blumenfeld et al. [9] considered PjBL to be a comprehensive perspective focused on teaching by students' pursuing solutions to nontrivial problems through asking and refining questions, debating ideas, making predictions, designing plans and/or experiments, collecting and analyzing data, drawing conclusions, communicating their ideas and findings to others, asking new questions, and creating artifacts.

PjBL has gained popularity compared to traditional lecturing methods, since PjBL allows students to gain broader and deeper understandings about a subject and also allows students to engage in more relevant and contemporary learning opportunities. Furthermore, it triggers higher-level skills such as exploring, creating, and constructing solutions, rather than lower-level cognitive learning, such as reading and memorizing which is usually associated with traditional lecturing [8].

Furthermore, PjBL serves as an ideal pedagogical approach for STEAM education, especially for engineering. Tseng et al. [10] found that PjBL activity significantly integrates STEAM and enhances students' attitudes toward engineering. Students also mentioned that this course was useful for their future careers. In addition, PjBL helps students gain conceptual and procedural knowledge. Fan and Yu [11], through a quasi-experimental study, also found that conceptual knowledge and higher-order thinking skills can be improved. Brears et al. [12] suggested that project-based curricula provide a natural approach to supporting the integration of STEAM disciplines, mirroring real-world processes used by engineers when solving problems or developing innovations.

2.2 Engineering Design Thinking

In recent years, engineering design has received substantial attention as an essential component of STEAM education. Some scholars believe that the PjBL-STEAM tenet that integrates engineering design principles can enhance real-world applicability [13]. Without emphasizing the practice of engineering design, STEAM education could be less meaningful.

Design thinking refers to the cognitive processes and strategies employed by designers when working on design problems [14]. Mentzer et al. [15] concluded that design thinking is a creative way of problem solving and promotes the development of diverse ideas, which are essential for innovation. In short, it includes analysis/synthesis, divergent/convergent thinking, visual analogy, overcoming fixation, and creativity [16]. A common empirical method to study design thinking is by excavating the thought processes that designers go through when performing design tasks [14].

In order to develop or evaluate student's design thinking ability, teachers often adopt IDEO's design thinking process [6]. The process consists of five phases (Fig. 1): Discovery, Interpretation, Ideation, Experimentation, and Evolution [17].

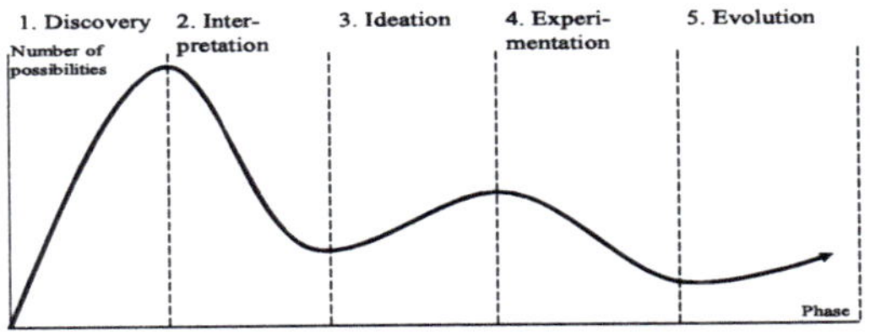

Fig. 1. IDEO design thinking process [17]

2.3 Gender's Difference in STEAM Learning

The underrepresentation of women in STEAM-related fields remains a concern for educators and the engineering community [1, 18, 19]. Not only is this difference in gender considered a justice issue, it is also political and economic issue [2]. Many people believe the recruiting and retaining of woman engineering students is an effective method to boost numbers in the engineering professions as well as stimulate the economy [1, 20].

Some cross-disciplinary researchers have discovered why such a gender gap exists [1]. First of all, there are gender differences in confidence, belongingness, and parental encouragement related to STEAM careers [1]. Furthermore, women also perceived themselves as less similar to the prototype of a STEAM professional, such as a scientist or an engineer, than men did [1]. While these reasons for the gender gap seem to be complex and contentious, the two major themes, ability and attitude, emerge [19].

However, these two factors are not independent from each other. For instance, attitude is heavily influenced by school achievement, and high-performing students are more likely to pursue well-paid careers, such as STEAM-based jobs. Although some studies found females tend to earn higher school grades than males, including in STEAM subjects, other studies show that males perform better than females in subjects like Math and Physics [3, 18–20]. Furthermore, the support of a community has a strong influence on woman's selection and retention in classrooms and workplaces [2]. The numbers of female peers and group oriented learning activities could benefit female students in STEAM learning [3].

As shown earlier, PjBL not only has students working on real life problems, but it is usually done in a group. It is also known as an effective method to develop student's high level abilities such as design thinking. Lou et al. [21] used a PjBL internet-based platform to allow female students to develop integrated STEAM knowledge by designing a solar car. They found that PjBL enhances students' attitudes toward future STEAM careers and also facilitates acquiring science and mathematics disciplinary knowledge.

Although PjBL-STEAM courses have been shown to benefit students, their influence on different students varies by achievement level, ethnicity, and culture [8]. However, few studies exist on the improvement in engineering design thinking and the possible influence of gender.

As shown here, studying the relationship between gender and engineering design thinking ability could contribute to addressing this gap. Therefore, this study attempted to explore the influence of gender on engineering design thinking when learning STEAM through PjBL. In our research, we explore the following questions:

1. What is the influence of gender on the learning outcomes of engineering design thinking from a PjBL-STEAM course?
2. Is there a gender difference in improvement of engineering design thinking ability after a PjBL-STEAM course?

3 Method

3.1 Participants and Procedures

A total of 137 high school students in 20 schools voluntarily participated the PjBL-STEAM class. 62 students are female (45.3%) and 75 students are male (54.7%). The goal of this course is to have students build a truss tower with minimum weight that withstands the maximum earthquake possible (Figs. 2 and 3). The course lasts 10 weeks and its activities include: the introduction of earthquake and building safety, the analysis of truss tower structure, using of CAD system (2D), using of CAD system (3D), using a 3D printer, truss tower structure manufacturing and assembly, strength test and analysis, re-design and re-test. Before the course began, each student needed to fill out the pre-test of IDEO (2012) engineering design thinking. After finishing the course, the students would fill out the post-test of the same questionnaire to evaluate their improvements.

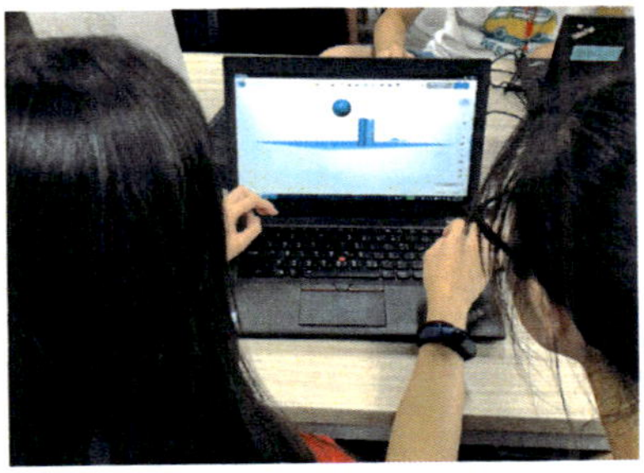

Fig. 2. Female students learn to design water tower in groups

Fig. 3. A female student analyzing the existing structure

3.2 Engineering Design Process Inventory

Due to the popularity of IDEO's design process [17] among STEAM teachers when designing courses [6], we adopted the process and modified the content to fit the engineering purpose to assess student's self perceived improvement in engineering design thinking. Matching five stages of the IDEO model, Engineering Design Thinking is measured by five constructs: Discovery, Interpretation, Ideation, Experimentation, and Evolution. The final questionnaire consisted of 30 items, such as "I know how to evaluate whether the designed product fits the constraint and requirement." and "I will consider as many varieties of engineering design in the beginning." Students rated their perceptions on a 5-point Likert scale. Cronbach's alpha was .73, .84, .82, .75, and .71, for each construct respectively.

3.3 Data Analysis

We used SPSS 23 to compute the descriptive statistics and paired t-test to examine whether male and female students' engineering design ability improves after the course. Furthermore, we used ANCOVA to examine the differences between male and female student's engineering thinking ability posttest when control the effect of pretest.

4 Results

4.1 Descriptive Analysis

The mean and standard deviation of pretest and posttest of each construct of engineering design thinking is listed in Tables 1 and 2. As shown in Table 1, the lowest and highest ability in pretest for female is Interpretation (3.98) and Ideation (4.36), separately. On the other hand, the lowest and highest ability in pre-test for male is Interpretation (3.92) and Discovery (4.27). In posttest, the lowest ability for female is still Interpretation (4.34), but the highest ability become Discovery and Experimentation (4.51). On the male side, the lowest ability remains Interpretation (4.32), and the highest changed to Experimentation (4.48).

Table 1. Mean and Standard Deviation of female and male students' pretest of each engineering design stage

Engineering design thinking	Female ($N = 62$)		Male ($N = 74$)	
	Mean of pretest	SD of pretest	Mean of pretest	SD of pretest
1. Discovery	4.35	.37	4.27	.42
2. Interpretation	3.98	.51	3.92	.62
3. Ideation	4.36	.46	4.19	.53
4. Experimentation	4.25	.43	4.21	.51
5. Evolution	4.15	.49	4.06	.59

$^{*}p < .05$, $^{**}p < .01$, $^{***}p < .001$

Table 2. Mean and Standard Deviation of female and male students' posttest of each engineering design stage

Engineering design thinking	Female ($N = 62$)		Male ($N = 74$)	
	Mean of posttest	SD of posttest	Mean of posttest	SD of posttest
1. Discovery	4.51	.41	4.46	.36
2. Interpretation	4.34	.49	4.32	.45
3. Ideation	4.49	.46	4.41	.40
4. Experimentation	4.51	.40	4.48	.41
5. Evolution	4.32	.48	4.37	.43

* $p < .05$, ** $p < .01$, *** $p < .001$

4.2 Progress Between Pretest and Posttest

The paired t-test result is shown in Tables 3 and 4. All constructs of both female and male show significant differences between pretest and posttest.

Table 3. Paired *t*-test for female pretest and posttest

Engineering design thinking	Post-pre mean diff.	*S.D*	*t*	*p*
1. Discovery	.16	.36	3.47***	.001
2. Interpretation	.35	.47	5.94***	< .001
3. Ideation	.13	.44	2.34*	.023
4. Experimentation	.26	.36	5.70***	< .001
5. Evolution	.16	.40	3.18***	.002

* $p < .05$, ** $p < .01$, *** $p < .001$

Table 4. Paired t-test for male pretest and posttest

Engineering design thinking	Post-pre mean diff.	*S.D*	*t*	*p*
1. Discovery	.17	.35	4.12***	< .001
2. Interpretation	.38	.52	6.24***	< .001
3. Ideation	.21	.46	3.86***	< .001
4. Experimentation	.25	.41	5.24***	< .001
5. Evolution	.30	.51	5.08***	< .001

* $p < .05$, ** $p < .01$, *** $p < .001$

4.3 Difference Between Female and Male

The ANCOVA result is shown in Table 5. When the pretest of engineering design thinking ability is controlled, we no interaction between gender and pretest of engineering design thinking nor gender and the engineering design thinking posttest.

Table 5. ANCOVA for female and male posttest

Source of variance	SS	df	MS	F	p	η_p^2
COV pretest	9.04	1	9.04	113.48	< .001	.46
Gender	.31	1	.31	3.85	.05	.03
Gender * COV	.30	1	.30	3.72	.06	.03
Error	10.44	131	.08			

$^{*}p < .05$, $^{**}p < .01$, $^{***}p < .001$

5 Discussion and Conclusion

Our research shows that, learning in a PjBL-STEAM course such as building and testing a truss tower, both male and female students' ability in engineering design thinking improved. All five constructs of engineering design thinking, for both males and females, also improved significantly after the class. Furthermore, there is no significant difference between male and female students in the posttest of engineering design thinking. This suggests female students and male students may have similar levels of learning effect from PjBL about STEAM.

Jagannathan and Komives [20] concluded that female students are less called upon in class than their male classmates, and they may lose confidence or consider themselves less fit for the roles of STEAM professionals. Not only did female students usually perform poorer but they needed more support to succeed in STEAM fields than their male peers. In our research, we found female students learnt as competently as male students when engaged in projects in a group. Such result shows that females may learn and perform at a similar level as males if an equal opportunity of learning and sufficient same gender peers appearance in the environment [3]. Although the total number of male students in the class was slightly higher than the total number of female students, we did ensure that each female student was accompanied by one or more same gender peers in their group.

In addition, we also echo earlier research that PjBL is an effective method to develop high level STEAM ability, such as design thinking. Through problem focused real world learning, students are more engaged as they feel they are able to make significant contributions. Furthermore, the social learning and construction allows them to self-reflect and monitor their own learning, which is critical in higher level ability [11]. As a result, STEAM based PjBL is suitable for female student development as well as high level ability development.

6 Limitations and Future Direction

There are several limitations of this research. First of all, the sample of high school students, both female and male, might be biased since only the self-registered and selected students enrolled in the course and completed the study. Since students who voluntarily participated in STEAM related courses may be more interested or confident in their STEAM ability than the general student population. To verify the external validity, in the future, this learning method should be extended to students with different intentions. Secondly, since the questionnaire is self-evaluated, it is possible that bias may have influenced reliability. For future research, it might be better if external evaluation, by teacher's or peer's can be included to avoid such bias. Last but not least, although female students had similar learning results as the male students, it may not be sufficient if we aim to enhance female student's interests and confidence. In future research, it would be enlightening if more pro-female mechanisms are in place, such as peer and teacher support, to verify the possible benefit to female students.

References

1. Ehrlinger, J., Plant, E., Hartwig, M.K., Vossen, J.J., Columb, C.J., Brewer, L.E.: Do gender differences in perceived prototypical computer scientists and engineers contribute to gender gaps in computer science and engineering? Sex Roles **78**(1–2), 40–51 (2017). https://doi.org/10.1007/s11199-017-0763-x
2. Mahajan, P., Suresh, G.: Engineering a woman: marketing opportunities and challenges in India. Am. J. Manag. Sci. Eng. **2**, 11–22 (2017). https://doi.org/10.11648/j.ajmse.20170201.12
3. Sagala, R., Umam, R., Thahir, A., Saregar, A., Wardani, I.: The effectiveness of STEM-based on gender differences: the impact of physics concept understanding. Eur. J. Educ. Res. **8**, 753–761 (2019)
4. Beier, M.E., Kim, M.H., Saterbak, A., Leautaud, V., Bishnoi, S., Gilberto, J.M.: The effect of authentic project-based learning on attitudes and career aspirations in STEM. J. Res. Sci. Teach. **56**, 3–23 (2019). https://doi.org/10.1002/tea.21465
5. Freeman, S., et al.: Active learning increases student performance in science, engineering, and mathematics. Proc. Natl. Acad. Sci. **111**, 8410–8415 (2014)
6. Falloon, G., Forbes, A., Stevenson, M., Bower, M., Hatzigianni, M.: STEM in the making? Investigating STEM learning in junior school makerspaces. Res. Sci. Educ. (2020). https://doi.org/10.1007/s11165-020-09949-3
7. Johns, G., Mentzer, N.: STEM integration through design and inquiry. Technol. Eng. Teach. **76**, 13–17 (2016)
8. Chen, C.-H., Yang, Y.-C.: Revisiting the effects of project-based learning on students' academic achievement: a meta-analysis investigating moderators. Educ. Res. Rev. **26**, 71–81 (2019). https://doi.org/10.1016/j.edurev.2018.11.001
9. Blumenfeld, P.C., Soloway, E., Marx, R.W., Krajcik, J.S., Guzdial, M., Palincsar, A.: Motivating project-based learning: sustaining the doing. Support. Learn. Educ. Psychol. **26**, 369–398 (1991). https://doi.org/10.1080/00461520.1991.9653139
10. Tseng, K.-H., Chang, C.-C., Lou, S.-J., Chen, W.-P.: Attitudes towards science, technology, engineering and mathematics (STEM) in a project-based learning (PjBL) environment. Int. J. Technol. Des. Educ. **23**, 87–102 (2013). https://doi.org/10.1007/s10798-011-9160-x

11. Fan, S.-C., Yu, K.-C.: How an integrative STEM curriculum can benefit students in engineering design practices. Int. J. Technol. Des. Educ. **27**(1), 107–129 (2015). https://doi.org/10.1007/s10798-015-9328-x
12. Brears, L., MacIntyre, B., O'Sullivan, G.: Preparing teachers for the 21st century using PBL as an integrating strategy in science and technology education. Des. Technol. Educ. Int. J. **16** (2011)
13. Capraro, R.M., Slough, Scott.W.: Why PBL? Why STEM? Why now? an Introduction to STEM Project-Based Learning. In: Capraro, R.M., Capraro, M.M., Morgan, J.R. (eds.) STEM Project-Based Learning: An Integrated Science, Technology, Engineering, and Mathematics (STEM) Approach, pp. 1–5. SensePublishers, Rotterdam (2013)
14. Dinar, M., et al.: Empirical studies of designer thinking: past, present, and future. J. Mech. Des. **137** (2015). https://doi.org/10.1115/1.4029025
15. Mentzer, N., Becker, K., Sutton, M.: Engineering design thinking: high school students' performance and knowledge. J. Eng. Educ. **104**, 417–432 (2015). https://doi.org/10.1002/jee.20105
16. Greene, M.T., Gonzalez, R., Papalambros, P.Y., McGowan, A.-M.: Design thinking vs. systems thinking for engineering design: what's the difference? In: Manuscript for 21st International Conference on Engineering Design. The University of British Columbia, Vancouver, Canada (2017)
17. IDEO: Design Thinking for Educators (2012)
18. O'Dea, R.E., Lagisz, M., Jennions, M.D., Nakagawa, S.: Gender differences in individual variation in academic grades fail to fit expected patterns for STEM. Nat. Commun. **9**, 3777 (2018). https://doi.org/10.1038/s41467-018-06292-0
19. Reilly, D., Neumann, D.L., Andrews, G.: Investigating gender differences in mathematics and science: results from the 2011 trends in mathematics and science survey. Res. Sci. Educ. **49**(1), 25–50 (2017). https://doi.org/10.1007/s11165-017-9630-6
20. Jagannathan, R.K., Komives, C.: Teaching by induction: project-based learning for Silicon Valley. J. Eng. Educ. Transform. **33**, 22–26 (2019). https://doi.org/10.16920/jeet/2019/v33i1/149003
21. Lou, S.J., Liu, Y.H., Shih, R.C., Tseng, K.H.: The senior high school students' learning behavioral model of STEM in PBL. Int. J. Technol. Des. Educ. **21**, 161–183 (2011). https://doi.org/10.1007/s10798-010-9112-x

STEM Learning in Digital Higher Education: Have It Your Way!

Margarida M. Pinheiro[1] (✉) and Vanda Santos[2]

[1] CIDTFF, ISCA-UA, University of Aveiro, Aveiro, Portugal
margarida.pinheiro@ua.pt
[2] CIDTFF, University of Aveiro, Aveiro, Portugal
vandasantos@ua.pt

Abstract. The academic community of the University of Aveiro (UA, Portugal) has been called to debate learning experiences, to prepare forward-looking training systems, and to share practices. To achieve this, UA outlined a pedagogical innovation Program that has been providing its teachers and students with different technological and methodological options, to help prepare the future of digital education. The objectives of the present paper are: (i) to present a dedicated Program designed to support teachers' professional development, and (ii) to report two learning contexts that make use of the Program proposals. The two practices involved Science, Technology, Engineering, and Mathematics (STEM) students. The first part of this study follows a descriptive methodology, given the interest in making the reasoning beyond the Program familiar to others. The second part makes use of the case study methodology, presenting two cases that directly derived from the application of the Program. The study provides insights regarding e-learning in STEM Education at the UA and the impact of transformational strategies on the community. To encourage active learning and transferability of the Program to real-life situations in a non-formal context, a short-term activity is proposed as a suggestion for future work.

Keywords: STEM education · E- learning · Digital education · Active learning · Pedagogical innovation · Teachers' professional development program

1 Introduction

Teaching is a hard job. Also is learning. We learn while teaching and we teach ourselves as we learn. So, whenever we speak about teaching, we also speak about learning and the other way around. To help this journey of teaching and learning be savored each step of the way, several resources can be combined, including a multiplicity of emerging innovative technologies and numerous active methodologies [4]. For this to happen globally and in an integrated way, it is essential to give Higher Education Institutions (HEIs) the power to engage academics and students, through the creation of shared moments of reflection within the university community. The last two years have been full of challenges that, in a very short time, compelled academics, students and institutions to tread new paths,

© Springer Nature Switzerland AG 2021
Y.-M. Huang et al. (Eds.): ICITL 2021, LNCS 13117, pp. 567–578, 2021.
https://doi.org/10.1007/978-3-030-91540-7_58

fueling the creation of diverse learning and teaching environments. The point is that trying to combine all of this with successful pedagogies capable of providing beneficial and optimized learning environments for all, requires assertive guidance from institutional policy representatives.

The academic community of the University of Aveiro (UA, Portugal) has been called to debate learning experiences, to prepare forward-looking training systems, and to share practices. To this end, UA has been providing its teachers and students with spaces for training and reflection on different technological and methodological options, to help prepare the future of digital education, with the "Docência+" Program being one of these spaces. The objectives of the present paper are: (i) to present a dedicated Program designed to support teachers' professional development, and (ii) to report two learning contexts that make use of the Program proposals. The two later practices involving Science, Technology, Engineering, and Mathematics (STEM) students, act as a framework for STEM Education, either at the level of each scientific area individually, or at the interconnection between them. To encourage active learning and transferability of the Program to real-life situations in a non-formal context, a short-term activity is proposed, as a suggestion for future work. Evidence from the Program's webpage and from the practices are used to explain the experience of the UA. Both descriptive and case study methodologies are used.

The topic is relevant because, by sharing tangible applications of learning technologies and methodologies, in the case of STEM's contexts, we hope to launch clues to create more effective learning environments or at least contribute to reflection on the theme. Furthermore, the increasing demand for STEM areas (where technology plays a central role), puts the issue of learning strategies and the development of students' skills to the point.

This paper is organized as follows: after the introduction, the second section address the "Docência+" program; the third section describes the methodology; the next section presents the two case studies; to conclude, the chapter includes study's limitations as well as some suggestions and roads for future research.

2 The "Docência+" Program

2.1 Objectives and Context

The growing need to pay attention to the "teaching" dimension of Higher Education was the basis of an initiative focused on the training and qualification of teachers [5]. This initiative, that was called "Docência+", came from the joint decision of the UA (through its Teaching and Learning Nucleus) and the University of Minho (UM) (through its Research Centre IDEA) [11].

The Teaching and Learning Nucleus of the UA, under the direct supervision of the Rector's Office, is an element to support the strategic definition of the institution. Among its competences, we highlight "Streamline curriculum and pedagogical innovation processes" and "Promote the training and pedagogical updating of teachers" [3]. The Centre IDEA, coordinated by the Pro-Rectorate for Student Affairs and Pedagogical Innovation, is conceived to promote, and value Innovation and the Development of Teaching and Learning at UM [5].

Being a top-down proposal, the Program brings together teaching staff, students, and higher management bodies of the institutions' government, though contributing to the creation of a prepared and active community that is attentive to the teaching dimension of the university work. The 1st edition of "Docência+" took place in July 2019 and took the form of a training retreat. In fact, during the two and a half days of the event, the participants were gathered in the same space (in a spirit of sharing and openness), had access to training in many dimensions of teaching, intervened in workshops and closely interacted with the responsible of the HEIs involved [5]. In the two editions of 2020 (July and September), capacity building for digital teaching and learning processes was reinforced and a special emphasis was given to the role of students as agents for the continuous improvement of institutions. Considering the pandemic context, the activities took place in an exclusively online format [5]. The program combined synchronous and asynchronous working times, for a total of about 20 h. As the result of the entire Program, the participants, organized in teams accompanied by two pairs of mentors from UA and UM (including teachers and students), were invited to develop a transformation plan for a course in which they were involved. This hands-on personalized work was particularly relevant in the context of preparing the 2020 academic year, in which many courses worked in a b-learning regime. As in the previous edition, the 2nd one focused on "How to prepare a course in a b-learning model", "How to use technologies and methodologies in a teaching context", "How to evaluate learning" and "How to evaluate the functioning of courses considering their continuous improvement" [5]. Following the same line of the previous editions, the 4th edition (July 2021) brings some news, such as IDP Journeys (Inter-institutional Pedagogical Development days), thus promoting greater diversity in sharing and discussion [5]. In all editions, enrollment was open to professors with assigned teaching service, and participation was free but limited to the existing vacancies,

All editions of the program (except the former) made use of a Padlet [1] that serves as a repository of content and a space for sharing among all participants.

2.2 "Docência+": Pack and Padlet

The topics covered by the different editions of the training, gave rise to a set of videos with concepts worked on in the program, that were compiled in what was called the "Docência+" Pack. These videos cover four big topics: blended learning, methodologies and technologies, assessment in learning, and evaluation of the transformation of a course [5]. All those videos are available at a dedicated YouTube channel [4].

To complement the Pack and create an interactive communication space, several Padlets were also used. A Padlet is a digital tool that, by including images, links, videos, or documents, can act both as a "mural" notice board and as an interactive space, enabling either students or teachers to post or comment there. Its accessibility is an added value as it is user-friendly and available just a click away. From a first initial mural, the user is guided to different Padlets, each one designed to each of the four working topics.

Blended-Learning. This module begins with an introduction to the principles of blended-learning, and then suggests different proposals for preparing a course within this model. A guiding question to this model invites academics to self-reflect on their teaching practices, namely, on "To what extent do you believe that b-learning is possible in your course?" [10].

Methodologies and Technologies. This module introduces and discusses some active methodologies and digital technologies that can be used both in person and virtually. Beginning with methodologies, the first part of this dedicated Padlet presents cross-disciplinary approaches designed to motivate students to apply their knowledge to real-world scenarios, thus promoting higher levels of cognition. In particular, Problem/Project Based Learning (PBL), Challenge Based Learning (CBL), Gamification and Game Based Learning (GBL), Team Based Learning (TBL), Flipped Classes, and Think-Pair-Share strategies. Regarding technologies, the second part also addresses different techniques, namely Perusall, Audience Response Systems (ARS), Team Collaborative Software (e.g., Miro, Trello), Mind Maps (e.g., Mindmup, Mindmeister), Padlet, and Videos (e.g., Loom, Powtoon). A guiding question to this model invites academics to self-reflect on their teaching practices, namely, on "How can I promote meaningful learning in order to engage students in my course?" [10].

Assessment in Learning. This module introduces and discusses different types of assessment for both face-to-face and virtual teaching. By going through this module, teachers are invited to consider not only feedback strategies, or students as partners in the assessment, but also to pay attention to the importance of soft skills, always without losing sight of all aspects related to humanization principles (e.g., equity, inclusion, transparency). A guiding question to this model invites academics to self-reflect on their teaching practices, namely, on "How can I develop and present assessment solutions considering the articulation between the learning objectives and the assessment elements, and the distribution of these in the space and in the environment?".

Evaluation of the Transformation of a Course. This module reflets on the evaluation of a course as a process of continuous improvement. This module represents the culmination of the whole program as it invites to the hands-on transformation, and to the continuous self-reflection on the design of the process.

3 Methodology

Based on the previous framework and with the purpose of collecting information about the "Docência+" program, a descriptive methodology was adopted, given the interest in making the reasoning beyond the program familiar to others. The second part makes use of the case study methodology, presenting two cases that directly derived from the application of the Program.

To clearly describe the Program, the data collection method was based on the information available on the websites related to the program. Regarding the two following case studies, data collection derived either from the webpage and documents made available for the cases or from the teachers' information on the design of the cases.

The investigation was carried out during the 2020/2021 academic year.

4 The Learning Contexts

A total of 55 graduate students and 49 undergraduate students were enrolled in this study. The next two sections present the two learning contexts.

4.1 The Research Methodologies for Social Sciences (RMSC) Course

Context. The RMSC is a mandatory course that integrates the curriculum of both the Master in Finance and the Master in Marketing (so, STEM students were enrolled), available at the Higher Institute for Accountancy and Administration of Aveiro University (ISCA-UA). It comprises 4 ECTS, with a 2-hour class once a week, and is placed in the first semester of the first year. The general objective of this course is to provide students with the necessary skills to write and present their master thesis, project work or final report of internship [12]. The course is taught in two classes, one for each Master's degree. Both Masters took place in an after-work period, with classes taking place every weekday, between 7 pm and 11 pm. The teacher responsible (TR) for this course has attended the first two editions of the "Docência+" Program, and only after that time, she decided to proceed with the transformation of the course. The case study we are now going to report refers to the first semester of the 2020/2021 academic year. This means that the course ran entirely in an e-learning mode, during the pandemic COVID-19 situation. A total of 55 students were enrolled: 25 in Finance plus 30 in Marketing. A total of 13 classes were given in Finance and 14 in Marketing. For both Masters, two teachers were addressed: the TR for the course (with a PhD in Social Sciences) and another one in the specific area of Finance or Marketing, for each Master, respectively.

Learning-Design. The e-learning modality in which the RMSC operated, together with the reflection and learning provided by the "Docência+" Program, challenged the TR to embrace a different learning design than in previous years. A first encouragement arose from the need to put into practice some of the learning that was achieved with the Program. A second incentive came from the need to address online classes. After considering different options, the TR decided to use only a small number of methodologies and technologies that, in some way, departed from the models more traditionally used in the classroom, at least in what was the practice of that course to date. Since the learning outcomes of the RMSC consisted of providing students with the basic knowledge of the process of developing a scientific research work, necessary for the preparation, planning, elaboration, and writing and oral presentation, it was considered essential to promote spaces for debate and reflection. The idea was to provide students with different tools so that they could respond to the expected outcomes, but, at the same time, to make them reflect on the concept of what scientific research is and how it can be achieved. So, it was our intention to make the RMSC a space for critical reflection that could involve feedback from everyone (teachers and peers). Therefore, our first choice was to use a Padlet, where interaction could take place, in an always up-to-date way. To this end, a common Padlet was built for the RMSC, as a whole (Table 1); from this point onwards, and when a more specific distinction was needed (namely for the works related to each Masters, Finance and Marketing), students were referred to a specific Padlet (Table 2).

Table 1. Common Padlet design.

Part	Narrative	Technology
About RMSC	Basics: TR presentation, ECTS, schedule, references	Documents TED-Ed videos YouTube videos Self-made Videos Survey QR codes Web links
Methodological script	The path proposed: the Manual of the Course, TBL, Think-Pair-Share, Flipped Classes, Padlet, ARS, TED-Ed Lessons, videos	
Exploring ideas	To know more about: Blended Learning, Feedback	
Assessment (What you should know about it)	Assessment: types, why do it, how to do it in the course	
Masters' Padlet's	Access to the Padlet in Finance and to the one in Marketing	
Evaluate the course	The course's evaluation: tools for the regular evaluation of the CU	
Workshops	Information on elective workshops to support the course	
Discussion forum	Place for discussion	
Contents and classes	Previous information on each class: the content, what to prepare before coming to class	
Extra information	Extra information to support the course: templates, open classes	

Table 2. Specific Padlet for each Master

Part	Narrative	Technology
Who am I?	Students' self-presentation	Documents Videos
Groups' creation	Group identification	
Groups outputs	A column for each group to display its outputs	
Models	Templates to be used for each Master, respectively	

To promote collaborative learning through group discussion and ideas' sharing, our second option was to use both a Think-Pair-Share or a TBL methodology. As a quickly and easy tool to stimulate students, Think-Pair-Share [6] enables students to think over a subject on their own for a minute, to discuss it with their neighbors for a couple of minutes (giving them the appropriate time to uncover what they already know about that subject), and to bring up questions and ideas to share with all the others. Besides promoting collaborative learning, "*TBL requires students to become active participants who are accountable and responsible for their learning"* [9, p.55]. In fact, classes were proposed as spaces for debate and critical reflection, with the teacher occasionally playing a guiding role in each group reasoning (by using real-time virtual rooms). To keep students' interaction and learning flowing, the methodology concluded with a discussion between-group.

The next challenge was then to get the students prepared for the synchronous sessions. To incentivize students' study before classes, a flipped methodology was used all along the semester. This means that contents were available in an asynchronous way (through Padlet within the Contents and Classes' Tab), allowing students to access it, (to go back, to read or play it again, and to raise questions) before they access synchronous classes. So, when they came to classes, not only were they prepared to discuss the subject of the class but also teacher had free up time to work with each group more individually.

To diversify the presentation of contents within the Padlet, several tools were introduced, with videos being the most used. As most of the videos presented at the RMSC were selected from the TED-Ed Lessons, the teacher not only saved time by not creating them, but also was given the opportunity to decide on the lesson that best meets hers objective.

To make the synchronous classes dynamics, less repetitive and increase interactivity, ARS were also used. This means that during classes, students were invited to access their smartphones to answer different questions, give their opinion on some issues or rate a statement. Mentimeter and VoxVote were the two apps used to get students' feedback in real time.

All these information was compiled in a booklet, entitled the Manual of the Course, where students could find all the information they may need, namely about contents, methodologies, assessment, or course's rules. Students had access to this Manual from their very first day in class.

Planification. To help students understanding the methodology of the Course, especially the one regarding the asynchronous work before the class, a plan of action was provided (Table 3).

Table 3. Course Plan.

Class	Syllabus	What to do before class	Methodologies & Technologies
1 [date]	The Course Energizers for online teambuilding	--	Manual Padlet ARS TBL
2 [date]	Why do I need to do a research project?	Access Padlet at Previous information on each class's tab	Manual Padlet TBL
...			

Occasionally and according to the feedback received, some minor adjustments were made.

4.2 The Didactics and Technology of Mathematics Course

Context. The course of Didactics and Technology of Mathematics (DTM) is a mandatory unit of the curriculum of the 1st cycle in Basic Education, available at UA. It consists of 4 ECTS, with a 3-hour class once a week, and is placed in the second semester of the third year. The general objective of this course is to mobilize and broaden knowledge and abilities related to elementary Mathematics, manage/handle Information Technology (IT) tools best suited for the exploration of the analyzed mathematical topics, organize meaningful Mathematical learning experiences which foster the use of information technologies, develop and evidence autonomy in the development of educational activities, promote team spirit in group work activities, and show pre-disposition for continuous self-education within the scope of Mathematics Education. The course was taught in two classes. The teacher (non-responsible) for this course attended the second edition of the "Docência+" Program. The case study that we are now going to report refers to the second semester of the 2020/2021 school year, in which this course DTM was part of a larger project aimed to train future teachers to teach children through CBL. The course ran in a b-learning mode during the COVID-19 pandemic situation. In total, 49 students were enrolled.

Learning-design. The DTM worked in the context of a project, in articulation with the course of Didactics of Natural and Social Sciences (DNSS). In this experience, students were challenged to develop CBL projects in accordance with a common motto for both courses. This motto was centered on the United Nations Sustainable Development Goals (SDG – 14 and 15) [9] using technological resources and technologies to support active learning. These projects allowed students to work with different areas in each topic, in a STEAM strand.

The aim of the project was to deepen the experience and skills developed by students in the CBL project, to challenge them to elaborate their projects more autonomously, and to present and discuss them in a dedicated Forum, open to the entire community. Several methodologies (e.g., CBL, Flipped Classes, Brainstorming, Mind Maps and Gamification), and technologies (e.g., Mentimeter, Kahoot!, Google forms, Google docs, Loom, Powtoon, Power Point, Padlet and videos) promoting active learning, were implemented in those projects, according to the nature of the content and type of activities. Within the Learning Management Systems (LMS) the option was to used Moodle and Padlet, the later integrating all the courses involved in the project. In the presentations given in the DTM course, the students used: Mind Maps, Kahoot!, videos (Fig. 1), Power Point, Padlet (Fig. 2).

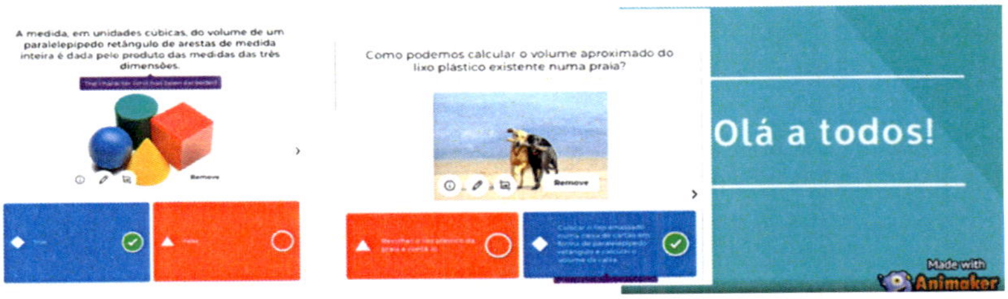

Fig. 1. Some images of Kahoot! and video.

Fig. 2. Some images of Padlets (teacher and students).

Students had also to develop the guiding questions within each CBL project, more specifically, for each of the scientific areas, DTM and DNSS. The work developed throughout the semester (e.g., experimental activity reports, reading sheets) either in class or in the context of autonomous work, was presented, in the form of a portfolio, in a Padlet. Each student made an individual reflection on one of the activity plans proposed by his CBL's group, theoretically justifying the methodological options adopted.

Planification. To help students understanding the detailed proposal of the Course, especially the one regarding the work for the semester, a plan of action was provided (Table 4).

Table 4. Course plan

Class	Syllabus	Methodologies & Technologies
1	General guidelines for teaching and learning processes in Mathematics	Mind Maps Padlet ARS Videos Padlet Kahoot!
2	Presentation and discussion of the basic ideas for the CBL project – general and mathematics	
3	Research in mathematics education involving technology	
4	Mathematical, curricular, didactic, and technological aspects of mathematical topics to be contemplated in the projects, in the logic of CBL	

Occasionally and according to the feedback received, some minor adjustments were made.

5 Final Remarks

Terms such as "co-creation of teaching and learning", "students as partners" or "collaborative learning" have been gaining increasing attention from the academic community (e.g., [2]). This growing interest has been motivating research to support practices, but also practices that can lead to greater knowledge about which methodologies are most appropriate to promote active learning and students' engagement. Alongside these issues, digital is also an unavoidable subject, given the growing use of blended or e-learning modalities [8]. To respond to these needs and support teachers' professional development, different support structures aimed to create more effective learning environments and communities of practice have been designed by HEIs.

The present paper provides an accurate and deep understanding of the power of a transformational strategy on academics' experiences at a Portuguese University, namely regarding e-learning in STEM Education. It was not our intention to emphasize how the "Docência+" approach affect each STEM area individually. Rather, we were interested to report two learning STEM contexts that make use of a dedicated Program designed to support teachers' professional development. The contribution of this pedagogical innovation Program to promote and disseminate innovative practices was essential for a different approach in classrooms. The methodologies and technologies presented allowed us to have a greater and better knowledge of a range of teaching tools available, contributing to having students in the classroom literally more involved, increasingly committed to their own learning and, thus, prepare the future of digital education among STEM students. The continuous supportive evaluation of the several editions of the Program, gives incentive to spread its reasoning, methodologies, and results of STEM practices with technology.

The main limitation of this study lies on the fact that the use of the methodological and technological proposals by "Docência+", still do not have a continuous focus on our practices. The exploratory nature of this research does not allow the generalization of results. However, the need to carry out four editions of the Program in just three years, somehow seems to validate the perception of interest of HEIs in the professional pedagogical development of their teachers. Findings need further validation and additional evidence should be collected in future studies. This does not imply that the conclusions are not valid, but rather that their universality cannot be assumed without further and more comprehensive studies being carried out.

Upcoming possibilities within this topic include considering other universities (namely universities with distinct profiles), other countries, or different research populations and samples. Another aspect to explore, would also be running the proposals in non-formal contexts [4], encouraging the transferability of the Program to real-life situations, as short-term activities.

Promoting and designing teaching and learning projects in various contexts, may be stimulated by a top-down vision, within co-constructed and collaborative networks focused on teaching practices and innovation. So, STEM learning in digital education? Yes, please. Engage yourself in more dialogue, create knowledge, and have it your way!

Acknowledgments. The authors were supported by National Funds through FCT– Fundação para a Ciência e a Tecnologia, I.P. under the project UIDB/00194/2020. Vanda Santos' work is supported in the scope of the framework contract foreseen in the numbers 4, 5 and 6 of the article 23, of the Decree-Law 57/2016, of August 29, changed by Law 57/2017, of July 19.

References

1. Beltrán-Martín, I.: Using Padlet for collaborative learning. In: HEAD'19. 5th International Conference on Higher Education Advances, pp. 201–211. Editorial Universitat Politècnica de València, July 2019
2. Bovill, C.: Co-creation in learning and teaching: the case for a whole-class approach in higher education. High. Educ. **79**(6), 1023–1037 (2019). https://doi.org/10.1007/s10734-019-00453-w
3. Despacho n.º 11565/2019 de Entidades administrativas independentes e Administração Autónoma. Diário da República: II série, no. 235, https://dre.pt/web/guest/home/-/dre/126959059/details/maximized?serie=II&parte_filter=33&dreId=126958976 (2019)
4. Docência+ Pack. Formação Docência+[Video]. YouTube. https://www.youtube.com/playlist?list=PLBdGO2pTpFBAxMrNvneWKpLHatBvmbJ-g. 24 Feb 2021
5. Freeman, S., et al.: Active learning increases student performance in science, engineering, and mathematics. Proc. Natl. Acad. Sci. **111**(23), 8410–8415 (2014)
6. Ginsburg, H.P., Choi, Y.E., Lopez, L.S., Netley, R., Chi, C.Y.: Happy birthday to you: Early mathematical thinking of Asian, South American and US children. Learning and teaching mathematics: An international perspective, pp. 163–207 (1997)
7. Hornink, G.G., Vieira, F., Costa, M.J.O.: Papel do Centro IDEA-UMinho na transição para o ensino online durante a pandemia COVID-19: enfrentar desafios e criar oportunidades (2020)
8. Kaddoura, M.: Think pair share: a teaching learning strategy to enhance students' critical thinking. Educ. Res. Q. **36**(4), 3–24 (2013)
9. Lane, D.: Teaching skills for facilitating team-based learning. New Dir. Teach. Learn. **116**, 55–68 (2008)

10. Lencastre, J.A., Coutinho, C.P.: Blended learning. In: Encyclopedia of Information Science and Technology, Third Edition, pp. 1360–1368. IGI Global (2015)
11. United Nations: The Sustainable Development Goals Report 2016. United Nations, New York (2016)
12. Universidade do Minho. Docência +. https://padlet.com/docencia_mais/blearning (2021)
13. Universidade de Aveiro. Inovação Pedagógica. https://www.ua.pt/pt/inovacaopedagogica/page/26714 (2021)
14. Universidade de Aveiro. Master in Finance. https://www.ua.pt/en/course/409 (2021)

Bilingual Instruction Model for a STEAM Course: A Preliminary Study

Fu-Rung Yang(✉)

Department of Education, University of Taipei, Taipei, Taiwan

Abstract. This study proposes a natural science course for elementary school students in Taiwan that combines the STEAM (science, technology, engineering, art, and math) and CLIL (content and language integrated learning) models. The course's lesson plan explains the teaching content and procedures for teachers who are interested in using English to teach STEAM-based natural science courses. Compared with the lesson plans applied in traditional natural science and English classes, the lesson plan of this STEAM–CLIL natural science course incorporates problem-based integrated learning and may be used to train teachers to teach natural sciences and to develop STEAM and bilingual teaching materials.

Keywords: Teaching model · STEAM · Bilingual instruction in natural science curriculum · Content and language integrated learning

1 Introduction

Science, technology, engineering, art, and math (STEAM) literacy emphasizes students' STEAM reading and writing ability and the integration of students' knowledge to solve practical problems [1]. STEAM education originated from science, technology, engineering, and mathematics (STEM) education. STEM combines diverse subjects into integrated courses and emphasizes the interdisciplinary nature of students' learning process. The STEM education policy was initiated in the 1990s in the United States and subsequently implemented by three presidents of the United States. They promulgated relevant education policies and regulations and passed the STEM Act in the United States Congress to improve STEM literacy in the United States. In recent years, advocates of the STEM-to-STEAM movement have caused a worldwide shift toward STEAM education [2]. STEAM education is a teaching model that emphasizes an interdisciplinary curriculum comprising science, technology, engineering, art, and mathematics. STEAM curriculum design is guided by five components, namely cross-domain topic research, hands-on learning, life applications for stimulating students' curiosity, solving of real-life problems, and application of five senses in learning [3]. STEAM literacy emphasizes the development of literacy skills and cultivation of integrated knowledge among students. Through a STEAM education, students learn to adapt and continue developing their ability to solve practical problems [1]. Such an education also helps students to apply interdisciplinary concepts to solve real-world problems.

© Springer Nature Switzerland AG 2021
Y.-M. Huang et al. (Eds.): ICITL 2021, LNCS 13117, pp. 579–583, 2021.
https://doi.org/10.1007/978-3-030-91540-7_59

In response to globalization and international trends, Taiwan must improve the English proficiency and competitiveness of its people. To this end, Taiwan has developed a blueprint for becoming a bilingual country by 2030 [4]. Taiwan's Ministry of Education uses content and language integrated learning (CLIL) as its main teaching axis and actively promotes the teaching of English in small and medium learning areas [5]. CLIL is a teaching method that combines subject content with foreign language learning. In CLIL, subjects such as mathematics, natural science, and social science are taught in a foreign language to achieve the dual learning objectives of learning a language and domain knowledge by means of learning integration [6]. The cultivation of students' ability to use foreign languages to acquire new knowledge and communicate is a key aspect of CLIL. Currently, the CLIL pilot program in Taiwan is primarily implemented in elementary schools, particularly in the lower grades. Experimental courses mainly involve the fields of life curriculum, integrative activities, health and physical education, and the arts [5]. The goal is to allow students to familiarize themselves with a bilingual environment [7]. CLIL teaching is not equivalent to English teaching. For each subject, teachers can plan the ratio of Chinese language to English language instruction to suit their attributes and goals [5]. The development of a CLIL model suitable for the teaching environment in Taiwan is a topic that warrants discussion.

In the present study, an ICIL teaching model suitable for application in STEAM natural science courses in Taiwan was developed. The related curriculum uses the "plants in our daily life" theme to integrate natural science, English, integrative activities, mathematics, and art; it also encourages students to apply their imagination and curiosity to understand and describe phenomena in the natural environment. This curriculum design is a dual-objective learning model that incorporates subject content and language and uses the natural science component of STEAM education as its main curriculum design axis.

2 STEAM–CLIL Natural Science Curriculum

The STEAM–CLIL natural science curriculum proposed in the present study uses images of specific plants and plant landscapes (Table 1).

The author of the present study has applied the aforementioned teaching plan in a small community of natural science teachers who engage in practical teaching using

Table 1. STEAM–CLIL natural science curriculum

Teaching unit	Plants
Teaching objectives	Students can identify the parts and growth elements of plants
Teaching object	Third grade
Context analysis	This lesson plan does not emphasize full English instruction; Chinese is the main language of instruction for this teaching mode. Only essential natural vocabulary and key sentence patterns are taught in English
Natural sciences principal axis	Third-grade elementary school students have a complete conceptual understanding of the roots, stems, leaves, flowers, fruits, and seeds of the six major parts of the plant. Students have the basic ability to observe plants • Natural learning goals The student can correctly name plant parts

(continued)

Table 1. (*continued*)

Teaching unit	Plants
Target language	• Natural sciences academic vocabulary Root, stem, leaf, flower, fruit, seed, sunshine, air, water • Main key sentence pattern What plant parts do you see? • Social language "Good job," "repeat after me," "please raise your hand" English learning goals Labeling the parts of a plant in English Student can write out plant parts in English
Integrated learning	Students can use English to discuss plant parts in specific situations Student can write down the names of plant parts
Classroom management	The teacher uses English language phrases related to classroom activities Phrases used: "Repeat after me," "please raise your hand," "good job."
Lesson plan design	
Activity	Procedure and Practice
Warm-up	Question: "What is the effect of COVID-19?" Story: Freud and Rilke were walking in the mountains in 1913. Rilke liked the beauty of the mountains very much, but he couldn't feel happy because of this beauty. Freud told Rilke that "flowers that only bloom for one night will not appear less beautiful because of this." We must accept the feeling of loss to appreciate the beauty of flowers. Plants have the power to heal our soul Search: 1. Guide students to explore and identify plants on campus Show students a picture of the campus and state the following: T: Look at the picture T: This is a garden S: I see…(expected answers: Banyan tree, lavender, Rosemary) T: Do you see plants? S: Yes, I do/No, I don't 2. There are many plants around us in school T: What is the word plant in Chinese? T: What are plants? T: Plants are living things that grow from the earth T: Can you name the plants? T: Where are they? 

(*continued*)

Table 1. (*continued*)

Teaching unit	Plants
Natural principal axis	Observation: • Ask students to observe the plant T: What is this? S: It is a lavender plant T: Is it a plant? S: Yes, it is a plant T: What plant parts do you see? S: I see… 
Target language	The teacher asks a student to name plant parts Student can name plant parts This is the root This is the stem These are the leaves These are the flowers These are the fruits These are the seeds
Integrated learning	• The teacher shows the potted plants to students and points out the plant parts during a group competition • One lavender plant requires 0.16 square meters of planting area. How much planting area is needed to plant 15 lavender plants? The teacher asks each group of students to calculate and share their results and encourages them when they perform well • The moisture meter can measure soil moisture. Please write down the steps for using the Micro:bit program  1. Leave the Duplicate Detection box 2. Turn on the Pin analog signal reading 3. Open the "variables" field 4. Insert the soil moisture detector into the soil 5. Select "basic" to display numbers • The display and placement of plants influence our visual senses and emotional state when we learn to appreciate them "Please observe the following landscape image and talk about the change in your mood." Students then describe their mood changes after viewing the landscape image 
End activity	The teacher shows the plant and asks students to name plant parts

English. The author used simple and easily understood English sentences during the demonstration process. Teachers can flexibly adjust their lesson plans to suit their English ability and teaching goals.

3 Practical Implications

The present study uses a specific teaching plan to describe a STEAM–CLIL natural science curriculum. The proposal of this teaching model is expected to aid the development of a feasible plan for promoting the STEAM bilingual education policy in the natural science domain. It can be extended to other learning areas and used as a reference for research and development programs in other learning areas.

References

1. Zollman, A.: Learning for STEM literacy: STEM literacy for learning. Sch. Sci. Math. **112**(1), 12–19 (2012). https://doi.org/10.1111/j.1949-8594.2012.00101.x
2. STEM to STEAM Act of 2017, 42 USC 1862q § 3344 (2017). https://www.congress.gov/115/bills/hr3344/BILLS-115hr3344ih.pdf
3. Lu, C.C. Ma, S,Y.: Design STEAM course to train STEAM literacy of primary students: taking "animal mimicry beast" as an example. J. Res. Educ. Sci. **64**(3), 85–118 (2019). https://doi.org/10.6209/JORIES.201909_64(3).0004
4. Executive Yuan: Blueprint for developing Taiwan into a bilingual nation by 2030 (2018). https://www.ey.gov.tw/Page/448DE008087A1971/b7a931c4-c902-4992-a00c-7d1b87f46cea
5. Lu, Y.H., Yuan, Y.: A model of bilingual instruction in mathematics: a preliminary study. Taiwan J. Math. Educ. **7**(1), 1–26 (2020). https://doi.org/10.6278/tjme.202004_7(1).001
6. Coyle, D.: Supporting students in content and language integrated learning contexts: planning for effective classrooms. In: Masih, J. (ed.) Learning through a Foreign Language: Models, Methods and Outcomes. Centre for Information on Language Teaching and Research, London (1999)
7. Tsou, W., Kao, S., Chen, H.: Core principles of content and language integrated learning. In: Tsou, W., Kao, S. (eds.) Exploring CLIL: A Resource Book (2018)

Employing STEAM 6E Teaching Methods to Analyze the Academic Emotions of the Digital Video Practice Course

Yu-Chen Liang[1](✉), Koong Hao-Chiang Lin[1], and Cheng-Tsung Li[2]

[1] Department of Information and Learning Technology, National University of Tainan, Tainan 70005, Taiwan

[2] Department of Digital Media Design, Asia University, Taichung 413, Taiwan

Abstract. In order to solve the problems faced by students when employing traditional teaching. The study uses the STEAM 6E teaching methods for curriculum design, allowing students to create videos, and then analyzes the emotional changes of students at each stage. In this study, students are divided into 2 groups: the experimental groups and the control groups. The teaching strategy of the experimental group is to integrate the course content into the STEAM 6E teaching methods, while the teaching strategy of the control group is to use the general traditional teaching methods. The teaching experiment tool is video editing software. In the courses, students can create their own works through hands-on practice based on the Maker practical teaching philosophy and can continue to learn by sharing their works and creative ideas with other students afterwards. The emotional performance of each stage through AEQ is analyzed to explore the relevant research on the relationship between academic emotions when STEAM and Maker is combined with the STEAM 6E teaching methods. The results have shown that through STEAM 6E teaching methods, students, even with negative emotions in learning, can still feel hopeful and proud toward learning.

Keywords: STEAM 6E · Academic emotions questionnaire · Maker

1 Introduction

In the scenarios which employ traditional teaching, students will have negative emotions when encountering problems in learning, and then their learning motives and learning results are affected. Especially so for implementing courses, where students tend to give up easily and readily. For example, in traditional teaching, teachers will use preset themes, material and software to teach, and students will follow the steps designed by teachers. When students start to make videos on their own, they often encounter problems like can't come up with creative ideas, don't have the ability to find resources, and lacking the technology skill to complete the job. Therefore, this research tries to solve the problems encountered by students when learning by employing different teaching strategies. Recently the scientific education revolution is an ongoing issue in the world. It emphasizes the importance of search and implementation in the learning process,

© Springer Nature Switzerland AG 2021
Y.-M. Huang et al. (Eds.): ICITL 2021, LNCS 13117, pp. 584–592, 2021.
https://doi.org/10.1007/978-3-030-91540-7_60

making the students think like scientists to solve the relevant problems relating to future society and life science. US, HK, and Singapore all continue to promote technology-education-based STEAM courses revolution, to enhance the design and search abilities of the students and thus enhance the future competition edge of their country (Herschbach 2011; Long and Davis 2017; Maeda 2013) [5, 9, 11]. International Technology and Engineering Educators Association (ITEEA) has created a 6E teaching model about STEAM education to ensure that the T(technology) and E(engineering) parts of STEAM education are incorporated into courses learning, and thus can really be implemented in real life. Course teaching is one of the main activities of education, with teaching mode as the primary way to complete the course, cultivate and inspire students' academic emotions. Teaching mode is a paradigm or plan to build courses and assignments, to select teaching materials, and to assist teacher activities. Also, under certain guidance of educational thoughts, teaching and learning theories, teaching mode can, in some specific environments, be the stable relationship between teaching activities factors and the structural form of activity progression. Teaching mode can be classified from different angles. When looking from the angle of the main methods of implementing teaching mode, there is one with traditional ways and one with different strategies. Without exception emotion is involved in teaching part of the teachers and learning part of the students in educational scenarios. In 2002 Schutz and Lanehart pointed out that emotion is closely involved in every process of teaching and learning [18]. Therefore, it is important to understand emotions in educational scenarios. However, in traditional education concepts, emphasis is often put more on students' cognitive learning, and the impact of students' emotion in education scenarios is often neglected. In 2002, Pekrun, Goetz and Titz pointed out that there is little progression in studies on emotions impact on education scenarios, except for emotions concerning examination anxiety and attribution [14].

2 Literature Review

2.1 STEAM 6E Teaching Method

Now the STEM education has got a lot of attention from international education. STEM has broadened the learning environment and learning realm. It changes the way of teaching and learning, promotes the broad fusion of knowledge, and triggers innovation of knowledge. In 1960, SCIS proposed a basic teaching mode, a teaching process to scientific education, with 3 steps of exploration, invention, and discovery. In the field of technology education, Barry (2014) has proposed 6E teaching methods based on the 5E teaching circle, to strengthen the design and exploration ability in STEM education [1]. 6E includes Engage, Explore, Explain, Extend/Elaborate, Enrich, and Evaluate. Each section of 6E teaching methods represents a complete journey. Because students need to think constantly in the process, each section has embodied STEM educational ideas to some degree.

2.2 STEAM Courses Integration

STEAM consisted of the original STEM and the newly added video creation, which is also a form of art. With the educational spirit of makers, students can share ideas in different fields and implement the ideas into practices. Thus, this research incorporates both STEAM and the educational spirit and ideas of makers, to cultivate more cross-domain talents, to best meet the latest society and international trend, and to explore the plausibility of combining STEAM, maker education ideas, and video creating.

2.3 Academic Emotions

Academic emotions are the emotions, whether related to academic activity or results, generated by learners after they make controlled and value cognition evaluation about learning scenarios (Pekrun 2000; Pekrun, Goetz, Titz, and Perry 2002) [13, 14]. The idea of academic emotions was first proposed by Pekrun in 2002 [14]. It depicted the emotions experienced by students in the process of teaching and learning, and in academic activities. For example, academic emotions can be happiness when learning, or anxiety when taking examinations, etc. Thus, academic emotions include all the positive and negative emotions experienced in every link of the learning processes. Students have different academic emotions under different scenarios, and emotions also vary with time and scenarios (Efklides and Volet 2005) [3]. Using activation (activate, deactivate) and valence (positive, negative) as classifying factors, researchers divided academic emotions into 4 categories: positive activate, negative activate, positive deactivate, and negative deactivate (Pekrun et al. 2002) [14]. Positive activate academic emotions are positive academic emotions that are activate, such as happiness, hope, and price. Positive deactivate academic emotions are positive academic emotions that are deactivate, such as comfort, relax, and satisfaction. Negative activate academic emotions are negative academic emotions that are activate, such as anger, anxiety, and shame. Negative deactivate academic emotions are negative academic emotions that are deactivate, such as hopelessness and boredom.

2.4 Related Works

MacIntyre and Gardner (1991) found different tasks will cause different level of students' emotions of anxiety [10]. Jacob (1996) mentioned that learning scenarios is pertinent to emotions. Students who feel teachers' enthusiasm and positive feedback can have emotions of happiness [6]. The research of Frenzel, Perkrum and Goetz (2007) also shows pertinent relation between students' learning environment and their academic emotions [4]. Pekrun (2006) found that the self-regulated learning and creative solution also help with students' academic emotions of happiness [13]. Nummenmaa and Nummenmaa (2008) did research on academic emotions and e-learning and found that students' positive attitude toward the internet and collaborative learning is pertinent to their academic emotions of happiness [12]. Chia-Ling Sung and Yuan-Chen Liu (2019) show when students have greater motives, they will enjoy positive emotions more [2]. They're more likely to learn how to self-adjust, earn academic achievement, and acquire the ability to solve problems by themselves. Rolling (2016) pointed out that the main characteristics of combining STEAM courses with Project-Based Learning (PBL) are to design real-life problems and offer students the opportunity to come up with solutions through creativity selection and cooperation [17]. Quigley, Herro, Jamil (2017) thinks that real-life scenarios should combine with problem-solving and cooperative learning [16]. 6E

Learning by Design Model of STEM can cultivate students' abilities to create and apply through exploratory implementation activities. To sum up, we realize that students will have multiple emotions in the process of learning. And students' academic emotions are closely related to teachers' teaching methods in teaching scenarios, feedback to students, and learning tasks faced by students.

3 Methods

The processes of this research include initial research purpose and motive, related works collection, courses design, activities, data collection and analysis, statistical data, and final results.

3.1 STEAM 6E Courses Teaching Module

This course is for video creation, including theme selection, story creation, script creation, filming, editing, special effect post-production and public demonstration, etc. The scaffold of this course is STEAM 6E teaching methods, as shown in Table 1 (Lai et al. 2018; Lai and Chu 2016) [7, 8]. The teachers provide a clearly defined learning goal and standard at the beginning of six-week experiment period. There is a different learning

Table 1. STEAM 6E teaching methods.

STEAM 6E	Contents	Operation
Engage	Inciting students' interest. Heightening students' curiousity through prior knowledge or experience	Inciting interest through videos and past works
Explore	Offering students chances(data analysis, mutual discussion, brain storming)	Using ways of PBL to invoke self-learning and self-exploration
Explain	Providing students opportunities to rethink what they had learned before, in order to better understand the content of the theme and learned knowledge	Clarifying and understanding problems through courses of the principles and techniques for making movies
Engineer	Applying learned concepts into everyday lives through implementation, to gain better understanding of the cores of courses' theme	Using editing software (Vivavideo and PowerDirector) to make movies with plots
Enrich	Searching deeper into what the students had learned to solve deeper and more complex problems	Probing deeper into the subject of the learning process through problems discussion
Evaluate	Offering the opportunities for students and teachers to evaluate the effectiveness of learning and degree of understanding	Peer evaluation

theme for every week. Specific discussion tasks and expected results are set by teachers before learning activities begin, then students execute learning activities accordingly. In the six-week experiment period, there are six different tasks, each with a different learning theme.

3.2 Traditional Teaching Mode

For the traditional teaching team, teachers teach in courses through dictation according to schedule, and handle relative knowledge about teaching schedule. Teachers don't need to arrange or organize course activities. They only have to pass the knowledge on to students according to the teaching requirements. Students listen tentatively in the courses, do assignments and review what teachers had taught at home. Teachers will provide supplemental material and arrange time to reinforce students' practices.

3.3 Teaching Tools

VivaVideo is a multi-purpose editing App for beginners on the mobile. In courses teachers can let students get hands-on experience immediately through course content. PowerDirector 15 is the tool for after class practice. It is a professional video editing software with powerful editing functions and easy-to-use tools. It offers users new eye-catching special effects, fluent user experience, and ever-expanding texture libraries. Moreover, new users can learn how to use it rather quickly, and gain control over the video creating process with little effort.

3.4 Experiment Design and Research Tools

The subjects of the experiment are the 66 students in a southern university in Taiwan. The subjects are divided into 2 groups according to classes: 30 in the control group and 36 in the experimental group. In the teaching mode, the control group uses traditional teaching while the experimental group incorporates the STEAM 6E teaching methods into teaching. The research experiment lasts 6 weeks. AEQ learning emotion quantitative before-studying questionnaires are filled out before the experiment to inspect the little differences between 2 groups. After the 4th week courses, AEQ learning emotion quantitative during-studying questionnaires are filled out. After the 6th week courses, AEQ learning emotion quantitative after-studying questionnaires are filled out (see Fig. 1).

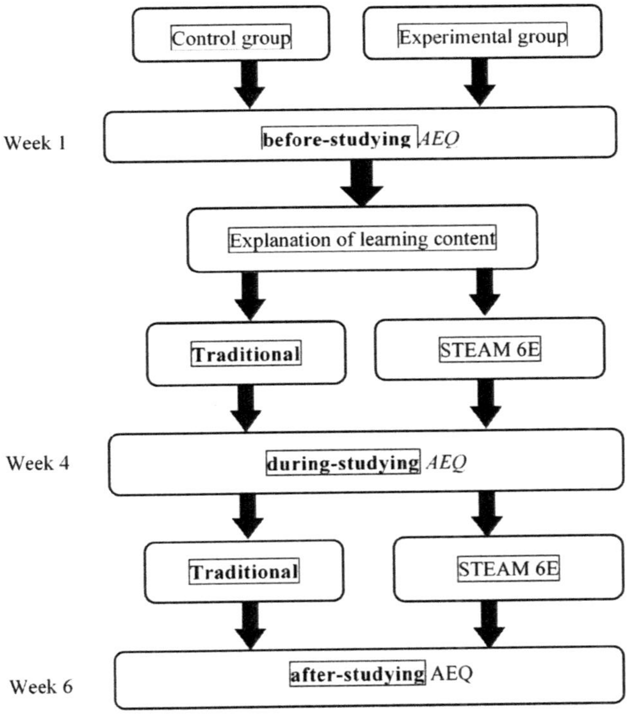

Fig. 1. Experiment process flowchart.

4 Results

4.1 Data Collection and Analysis

There are 66 effective samples in this research, mainly to explore the academic emotions between those who employ the STEAM 6E teaching method and those who don't. This research explores the differences in academic emotions between the 2 groups. Firstly, the before-studying, during-studying, after-studying questionnaire are analyzed. Then 8 types of academic emotions of 2 groups are analyzed. Because there are reverse questions in questionnaires, the reverse question should be reversed before doing the analysis.

4.2 AEQ Analysis

The purpose of this research is to understand the changes in academic emotions in the experiment group ($N = 36$) and control group ($N = 30$). According to the AEQ devised by Manual in 2005, quantitative questionnaires are divided into 3 parts, i.e., before-studying, during-studying, after-studying, totaling 75 questions. Included are 8 academic emotions: enjoyment, hope, pride, anger, anxiety, shame, hopelessness, and boredom. This questionnaire uses the 5-level Lickert scale.

The following is the analysis of before-studying, during-studying, after-studying academic emotions of the experimental group and the control group. This research compares the changes in academic emotions utilizing STEAM 6E teaching methods. Table 2 shows the result of academic emotions of independent sample t in different groups. Before-studying data of academic emotions shows nonsignificant difference between the experimental and the control groups. The data of the experimental group is $M = 3.31$, $SD = 3.0$. The data of the control group is $M = 3.44$, $SD = 0.34$. After analysis the result $p = 0.14 > 0.05$, showing nonsignificant. So, it can be implied that there is nonsignificant difference between the academic emotions of the 2 groups. During-studying data of AEQ shows a significant difference between the experimental group and the control group, with $t\ (65) = -12.47$, $p = 0.00*$. The data of the experimental group is $M = 3.20$, $SD = 0.2$. The data of the control group is $M = 2.64$, $SD = 0.23$. After-studying data of AEQ shows a significant difference between the experimental group and the control group, with $t(65) = -4.71$, $\mathrm{p} = 0.00*$. The data of the experimental group is $M = 3.60$, $SD = 0.48$. The data of the control group is $M = 2.75$, $SD = 0.51$. The p value is less than 0.05 for during-studying and after-studying, indicating a significant difference in the 2 groups. We can see in the process of learning; the learning goals are clear for both groups. However, the subjects' receptance of academic emotions are much more apparent in the experimental group, which uses STEAM 6E teaching methods.

Table 2. Independent t test of AEQ in different groups.

	M(*SD*)		*df*	*t*	*p*	*d*
	Control group ($N = 30$)	Experimental group ($N = 36$)				
Before studying	3.44(0.34)	3.31(0.30)	65	1.1	.14	0.41
During studying	2.64(0.23)	3.20(0.20)	65	−12.47	.00*	2.61
After studying	2.75(0.51)	3.60(0.48)	65	−4.71	.00*	1.72

$^{*}p < .01$

4.3 Analysis of 8 Academic Emotions

The results of AEQ from 2 groups are analyzed by 8 academic emotions, i.e., enjoyment, hope, pride, anger, anxiety, shame, hopelessness, and boredom. The changes of academic emotions between traditional and the STEAM 6E teaching method can be learned. Table 3 is the result of independent sample t test. The result of the analysis shows $p < 0.05$ for both groups. There are significant differences in 7 academic emotions (enjoyment, pride, anger, anxiety, shame, hopelessness, and boredom). But as for hope, the data in the experimental group is $M = 3.41$, $SD = 0.15$. The data in the control group is $M = 3.19$, $SD = 0.38$. It shows no distinct difference between the 2 groups. The analysis result $p = 0.12 > 0.05$, indicating there are nonsignificant difference differences between the 2 groups.

Table 3. Independent t test of 8 academic emotions in different groups.

	M(SD)		*df*	*t*	*p*	*d*
	Control group ($N = 30$)	Experimental group ($N = 36$)				
Enjoyment	3.19(0.45)	3.69(0.43)	65	−2.54	$.01^{**}$	1.14
Hope	3.19(0.38)	3.42(0.15)	65	−1.29	.12	0.79
Pride	2.71(0.15)	3.49(0.41)	65	−4.34	$.00^{**}$	2.44
Boredom	2.75(0.36)	3.10(0.21)	65	−2.75	$.01^{**}$	1.21
Anger	2.82(0.55)	3.30(0.12)	65	−2.58	$.01^{**}$	1.26
Shame	2.55(0.28)	3.22(0.31)	65	−5.34	$.00^{*}$	2.26
Hopelessness	2.73(0.44)	3.33(0.21)	65	−4.09	$.00^{*}$	1.79
Anxiety	2.74(0.51)	3.07(0.24)	65	−1.98	$.03^{**}$	0.85

$^{**}p < .01$, $^{*}p < .05$

5 Conclusions and Discussion

In this research a teaching activity is designed to combine maker and the STEAM teaching methods. Digital technology is incorporated with STEAM 6E teaching methods to enable students to fulfill maker spirit and ideas from learning and to experience changes of learning emotions at the same time.

The results show that by employing 6E teaching methods in STEAM teaching activities, students are provided with a more complete learning structure. In this structure, students' motives and interests are triggered in the Engage stage. PBL is utilized to invoke self-learning and self-exploring in the Explore stage. Teachers provide support and enthusiasm as guidance to students' thinking in the Explain stage. Students implement what they learned on real-life through practical operation in the Engineer stage. Students make deeper discussions to solve problems from all angles in the Enrich stage. A specific evaluation index is set to provide guidance for students in the Evaluate stage. Students can still feel hopeful and proud even when having negative emotions during learning. This corresponds with the conclusion mentioned by researchers that different tasks will generate different levels of emotions of anxiety [10], study environment is related to academic emotions [4, 6], and STEAM courses combined with PBL can offer opportunities for students to solve problems collaboratively [16, 17].

Through qualitative research, students' emotional reaction in every stage can be turned into text description in the future. With the analysis in this article, students' real emotional reaction is extracted and thus offers a chance for students to reflect. Also, this research can be used as base to further exploration of relations between anxiety and other learning emotions, providing feedback to teachers as design reference of STEAM 6E teaching methods courses.

References

1. Barry, N.B.: The ITEEA 6E learning ByDeSIGN TM model: maximizing informed design and inquiry in the integrative STEM classroom. Technol. Eng. Teach. **73**(6), 14–19 (2014)
2. Sung, C.-L., Liu, Y.-C.: A project on cultivating STEAM literacy: using 6E teaching strategy to teach elementary students to make "Simplest Electric Train." Second. Educ. **71**(1), 10–28 (2019)
3. Efklides, A., Volet, S.: Emotional experiences during learning: multiple, situated and dynamic. Learn. Instr. **15**(5), 377–380 (2005). https://doi.org/10.1016/j.learninstruc.2005.07.006
4. Frenzel, A.C., Pekrun, R., Goetz, T.: Perceived learning environment and students' emotional experiences: a multilevel analysis of mathematics classrooms. Learn. Instr. **17**(5), 478–493 (2007)
5. Herschbach, D.R.: The STEM initiative: constraints and challenges. J. STEM Teach. Educ. **48**(1), 96–122 (2011)
6. Jacob, B.: Achievement emotions in students' achievement in school students. Unpublished Master's Thesis, University of Regensburg, Germany (1996)
7. Lai, C.H., Chu, C.M.: Development and evaluation of STEM based instructional design: an example of quadcopter course. In: The First Annual International Symposium on Emerging Technologies for Education (SETE) Conjunction with ICWL 2016, 26–29 Oct 2016, National Cheng Kung University, Roma, Sapienza University of Rome, Rome, Italy. Springer International Publishing (2016). https://doi.org/10.1007/978-3-319-52836-6_20. eBook ISBN:978-3-319-52836-6
8. Lai, C.H., Chu, C.M., Chen, C.H.: An examination of online discussions quality of STEM based instruction. J. Internet Technol. **19**(6), 1943–1950 (2018)
9. Long, R.L., II., Davis, S.S.: Using STEAM to increase engagement and literacy across disciplines. STEAM J. **3**(1), 1–11 (2017). https://doi.org/10.5642/steam.20170301.07
10. MacIntyre, P.D., Gardner, R.C.: Investigating language class anxiety using the focused essay technique. Modern Lang. J. **75**(3), 296–304 (1991)
11. Maeda, J.: STEM+Art=STEAM. STEAM J. **1**(1), 34 (2013). https://doi.org/10.5642/steam.201301
12. Nummenmaa, M., Nummenmaa, L.: University students' emotions, interest and activities in a web-based learning environment. Br. J. Educ. Psychol. **78**(1), 163–178 (2008)
13. Pekrun, R.: A social-cognitive, control-value theory of achievement emotions. In: Heckhausen, J. (ed.) Motivational Psychology of Human Development, pp. 143–163. Elsevier, Oxford (2000)
14. Pekrun, R., Goetz, T., Titz, W., Perry, R.: Academic emotions in students' self regulated learning and achievement: a program of qualitative and quantitative research. Emot. Educ.: Spec. Issu. Educ. Psycholog. **37**(2), 91–105 (2002). https://doi.org/10.1207/S15326985EP3702_4
15. Pekrun, R.: The control-value theory of achievement emotions: assumptions, corollaries, and implications for educational research and practice. Educ. Psychol. Rev. **18**, 315–341 (2006)
16. Quigley, C.F., Herro, D., Jamil, F.M.: Developing a conceptual model of STEAM teaching practices. Sch. Sci. Math. **117**(1–2), 1–12 (2017)
17. Rolling, J.H., Jr.: Reinventing the STEAM engine for art + design education. Art Educ. **69**(4), 4–7 (2016)
18. Schutz, P.A., Lanehart, S.L.: Introduction: emotions in education. Educ. Psychol. **37**(2), 67–68 (2002)

Satisfaction of Engineering Design Thinking Course for High School Students

Charuni Samat[1](✉), Sathaporn Wongchiranuwat[2], Issara Kanjug[3], Pornsawan Vongtathum[1], Sumalee Chaijaroen[3], and Suchat Wattanachai[4]

[1] Division of Computer Education, Faculty of Education, Khon Kaen University, Khon Kaen, Thailand
[2] Doctor of Philosophy Student of Education Technology, Faculty of Education, Khon Kaen University, Khon Kaen, Thailand
[3] Division of Educational Technology, Faculty of Education, Khon Kaen University, Khon Kaen, Thailand
[4] Division of Surgery, Faculty of Veterinary Medicine, Khon Kaen University, Khon Kaen, Thailand

Abstract. The results of this study will be used to design and develop the engineering design thinking learning environment course and future teaching strategies for Engineering Design Thinking course. The participants (n = 40) of this study were high school students enrolled in a -week course on engineering design thinking course. Instrument of this study was a satisfaction survey form on teaching and learning management in the course. The results showed that high level satisfaction for all 3 dimensions: course management, the engineering design process task, and learning resources with the Engineering Design Thinking course. The problem of most students is that learners cannot access information of learning resources due to lack of equipment that can be used for some outside classroom learning. After which it closes by making recommendations for research aimed at enhancing design learning. The findings can be used for future improving learning design and based on the research results, this paper presents suggestions for developing learning environment that promotes engineering design and design thinking of learners, and guidelines for developing a learning model that responds to the future skills.

Keywords: Engineering design thinking · Satisfaction · STEM education

1 Introduction

The current educational model that focuses on promoting the STEM learning process focuses on the development of technology literacy for learners by focusing on the development of their ability to use, manage, assess and technology. One of the philosophies of technology education is teaching students to create a problem-solving process. This is considered an important skill for long-term life, because problem-solving skills that arise from learning figuring out a solution rational thinking until the decision making in order to lead the way to action In order to come up with an answer to that problem through

© Springer Nature Switzerland AG 2021
Y.-M. Huang et al. (Eds.): ICITL 2021, LNCS 13117, pp. 593–600, 2021.
https://doi.org/10.1007/978-3-030-91540-7_61

a problem solving process in technology studies such as research and development (Research & Development) or R & D, scientific methods and scientific inquiry (Scientific Methods & Scientific Inquiry), design process. Engineering (Engineering Design Process) or EDP, invention and innovation. (Interventions & Innovations), including artificial intelligence (Artificial Intelligent) or AI, etc.

The focus of STEM learning is the integration of engineering design concepts with students' learning of science, math, and technology, that is, as students engage in activities to develop their knowledge, understanding and practice science, math, and technology skills. Learners must have the opportunity to apply their knowledge to design methods or processes to solve problems related to daily life which is a product of engineering design processes.

The engineering design process is a problem-solving method that uses basic science, math, and engineering ideas to create optimal solution designs, plan and implement solutions, test, evaluate, and improve solutions, and provide a solution outcome. Our study looked at how satisfied students were with the Engineering Design Thinking Course, including the problems students experienced and the barriers that encountered. The results of this study will be used to design and development for learning environment course and develop future teaching strategies for Engineering Design Thinking course. This study may promote learners to be using problem-solving and creative thinking in their engineering design thinking, as well as design and develop a learning environment to enhance high school students' understanding of the engineering design process.

2 Literature Review

2.1 Engineering Design Thinking

Engineering design thinking is a STEM learning as Engineering Design Process and Design Thinking. Engineering design thinking is a fundamental skill in the field of engineering, and it should be promoted in school and tertiary education. Jonassen [1] describes problem solving as a design form that is an ill-structure problem solving. Alternative approaches and various solution approaches are typical in engineering designs [2, 3]. Engineering design is a model of learning management that encourages students to develop creative thinking and problem-solving skills. Learning management for learners according to the STEM approach is implemented according to the engineering design process, requiring learners to learn through the creative process. synthetic thinking and step-by-step action to solve problems or meet needs. Each step of the engineering design process encourages students to use creative and synthetic thinking to gather data and information that may be used, as well as articulating concepts to explain and communicate ideas to others who may simply understand concepts [4, 5].

2.2 Engineering Design Process

Engineers use the engineering design process to come up with a solution to a problem. Problem-solving techniques such as defining and delimiting an engineering problem, generating possible solutions, and optimizing the design solution are some of the steps. The design process is iterative, which means we repeat the processes as many times as necessary, improving so that we can go as learners recognize and explore different design possibilities to arrive at great solutions [5]. These steps aim to put a strong focus on collaboration and the value of the design that you generate. Therefore, you need these qualities to create new ideas, work with math and scientific concepts, run multiple iterations of tests, review data once testing has concluded and formulate solutions based on all information gathered from these steps [6–8].

The engineering design process is typically approached in these six steps [7, 8]:

Step 1 Problem Identification. Understanding the problem or situation. Analyze the problem situation's conditions and limitation. Define the problem's scope to develop a product or a strategy for solving problem.

Step 2 Related Information Search. Collection of scientific, mathematical, technological information and concepts related to problem solving and feasibility assessment, advantages, and limitations.

Step 3 Solution Design. Work with a team to brainstorm ideas and develop as many solutions as possible. Applying relevant information and concepts to product design or problem solving. Restrictions and conditions according to the specified situation.

Step 4 Planning and Development. Determining the sequence of steps of creating a product or method. Create a product or develop a method for solving a problem.

Step 5 Testing, Evaluation and Design Improvement. Testing and evaluating the usability of the product or method. The results may be used to improve and develop the most efficient solution to the problem.

Step 6 Presentation. Presentation of concepts and problem-solving steps of product creation or method development. Presenting products to others to understand and bring suggestions for further development.

2.3 Concept of Engineering Design Thinking Course

Teaching and learning for Engineering Design Thinking Course used a conceptual framework to design learning tasks. According to the engineering design process, there are 6 steps which are problem Identification, related Information search; collecting information related to the solution, solution design, plan and implement solutions, test, evaluate, and improve solutions or product designs and present a solution to the problem solution or product results. Sometimes the work may have to go back and forth to develop the work to be more efficient.

3 Purposes

To study the context of high school students' satisfaction with an engineering design thinking course.

4 Method and Result

4.1 Scope of Research

The developmental research design was employed [9]. This is to intensively study the process of developmental research design which comprises 3 research process as 1) design process 2) development process and 3) evaluation process. The Design Process was utilized in this study to present the results of the construct process Survey Research in the context of the learner; these results were then used to design and develop the engineering design thinking learning environment course.

4.2 Target Group of the Study

The participants were 40 high school students.

4.3 Research Design

The Descriptive research was employed in this study.

4.4 Research Instruments

The research instruments used to analyze this question were satisfied. There are 3 parts as follows: General information of the students. The satisfaction of studying in the teaching and learning of the Engineering Design Thinking course in the amount of 30, divided into 3 learning dimensions; course management, the engineering design process task, and learning resources. The questionnaire form: The Likert Scale choices is most satisfied, very satisfied, moderately satisfied, slightly satisfied, and not at all satisfied, The score is 5, 4, 3, 2, and 1, respectively. The last part, problems, obstacles and suggestions for teaching and learning are there are 9 open-ended questions.

4.5 Data Collection and Analysis

Analyze data with basic statistics. The mean and standard deviation were used. Information about problems, obstacles and recommendations for teaching and learning management were presented by collation.

4.6 Research Results

The results showed that satisfaction with the Engineering Design Thinking courses were as follows:

Part 1: General Information of the students. The general information of the students, which was found that most of the 40 students had a cumulative GPA. In good condition 3.00–3.49, 18 persons, accounting for 40.50%, the level is quite good, 10 persons, representing 27.00%, sufficient level, using 4 persons, representing 10.80%, very good level, number 2 people, representing 5.40% and not giving information to another 6 people, representing 16.20%.

Part 2: The satisfaction of studying in the teaching and learning of Engineering Design Thinking course. The findings indicate a high level of satisfaction with the Engineer Design Thinking course ($x = 4.31$, $SD = 0.23$). Additionally, satisfaction levels for all three dimensions (course management, engineering process task, and learning resources) were equally high ($x = 4.41$, $SD = 0.27$; $x = 4.45$, $SD = 0.31$; $x = 3.57$, $SD = 0.57$, respectively), as shown in Table 1.

Part 3: The problems in students' learning. The students' learning problems were mainly with the learners cannot access information of learning resources due to lack of equipment that can be used for some outside classroom learning, the learning time limitation, inadequate learning resources, unique product design is not creative and lack of examples that can be linked to solutions for design new product. The findings can be used for future improvements in design and development of the Engineering Design Thinking Course.

Table 1. Satisfaction with the engineering design thinking course.

Teaching and learning management	$\tilde{x}$	SD	satisfaction
a. Course management			
1. Helps students to achieve learning objectives	4.22	0.41	very satisfied
2. Help students to understand the content.	4.03	0.55	very satisfied
3. Encourage students to seeking knowledge on their own.	4.24	0.66	very satisfied
4. Enabling students to learn from the group members.	4.38	0.72	very satisfied
5. Increasing student learning efficiency.	4.35	0.58	very satisfied
6. Encourage students to learn together between members within the group.	4.62	0.54	most satisfied
7. Encourage students to learn together between groups.	4.49	0.60	very satisfied
8. Encourage students to have engineering design thinking.	4.51	0.60	most satisfied
9. Challenge students' abilities.	4.38	0.63	very satisfied
10. Encourage students to freely express their opinions.	4.51	0.55	most satisfied
11. Encourage students to participate in brainstorming of group members.	4.73	0.45	most satisfied
12. Encourage students to produce a new idea.	4.43	0.60	very satisfied
13.Encourage students to have skills in academic presentation.	4.38	0.49	very satisfied
14. Encourage students to be responsible for discovery of learning and reflection.	4.57	0.50	most satisfied,
The overall average of course management	**4.41**	**0.27**	**very satisfied**
b. The engineering design process task			
1. Students can ask critical questions.	4.68	0.47	most satisfied
2. Students participate in the operation of the group to achieve the objectives.	4.68	0.47	most satisfied
3. Encourage students to acquire skills in solving problems Conflict within the group.	4.62	0.49	very satisfied
4. Encourage students to acquire coordination research skills with others.	4.57	0.50	most satisfied
5. Encourage students to work with a team to brainstorm ideas and develop as many solutions as possible.	4.38	0.59	very satisfied
6. Encourage students to be responsible for assigned tasks.	4.68	0.47	most satisfied
7. Encourage students to select one solution and plan to move forward with it.	4.62	0.54	most satisfied
8. Encourage harmony between members within the group.	4.43	0.60	very satisfied
9. Encourage competition between groups.	3.42	1.13	Moderately satisfied
10. Encourage students to push yourself for creativity, imagination and excellence in design.	4.46	0.69	very satisfied

(continued)

Table 1. (*continued*)

Teaching and learning management	$\bar{x}$	SD	satisfaction
11. Encourage students to discuss and presentation how you could improve your solution.	4.35	0.58	very satisfied
12. There is a teacher as a coaching to promote friendship between teachers and students.	4.85	0.37	most satisfied
The overall average of the engineering design process task	**4.45**	**0.31**	**very satisfied**
c. Learning resources			
1. Textbooks and documents in the book are enough to search for information.	3.59	0.72	very satisfied
2. Internet system are enough to search for information.	3.50	0.69	very satisfied
3. There are enough lab or studying room to learn in small groups.	3.46	0.86	moderately satisfied
4. LMS system is suitable for online learning management.	3.73	0.76	Very satisfied
The overall average of learning resources	**4.31**	**0.23**	**very satisfied**

5 Conclusions

According to the above findings, the results of this study as shown above, as a guideline for improvement and development of teaching and learning management and further research. As a next step for future research would be to develop, the learning environment for engineering design thinking course. Conclusion for the application of the engineering design process as a strategy in teaching and learning to promote learning of youth to practice problem-solving skills step by step. Extension of existing knowledge to expand until new perspectives arise in solving a complete and correct problem and to develop products or methods that are competitive in business and to increase the intellectual abilities of Thai youths, which is a force in the development of the nation in the future.

Acknowledgement. This work was supported by the Academic and Research Affairs, Innovation and Cognitive Technology Research Center, Faculty of Education, and the Research and Technology Transfers Affairs Division, Khon Kaen University.

References

1. Jonassen, D.: Toward a design theory of problem solving. Educ. Tech. Res. Dev. **48**(4), 63–85 (2000)
2. Brophy, S., Klein, S., Portsmore, M., Rogers, C.: Advancing engineering education in P–12 classrooms. J. Eng. Educ. **97**(3), 369–387 (2008)
3. Foster, J., Kay, J., Roe, P.: Teaching complexity and systems thinking to engineers. In: The 4th UICEE Annual Conference on Engineering Education, Bangkok, Thailand (2001)
4. Dynn, C.L., Agogino, A.M., Eris, O., Frey, D.D., Leifer, L.J.: Engineering design thinking, teaching, and learning. IEEE Eng. Manag. Rev. **34**, 65 (2006)

5. Lin, K.-Y., Wu, Y.-T., Hsu, Y.-T., Williams, P.J.: Effects of infusing the engineering design process into STEM project-based learning to develop preservice technology teachers' engineering design thinking. Int. J. STEM Educ. **8**(1), 1–15 (2021). https://doi.org/10.1186/s40594-020-00258-9
6. Ulrich, K.T., Eppinger, S.D.: Product Design and Development, 4th edn. McGraw Hill, New York (2008)
7. STEM curriculum for K-12: Engineering Design Process (2020). https://www.teachengineering.org/design/designprocess. Accessed 22 May 2021
8. National Research Council: A Framework for K-12 Science Education: Practices, Crosscutting Concepts, and Core Ideas. The National Academies Press, Washington, DC (2012). https://doi.org/10.17226/13165
9. Richey, R.C., Klein, J.: Design and Developmental Research. Lawrence, New Jersey (2007)

Author Index

Abid, Mohsina 470
Amado, Cristina 49
Antoine, Melchior 389

Barroso, João 377

Carvalho, Diana 377
Chaijaroen, Sumalee 183, 189, 219, 422, 511, 593
Chang, Chi-Cheng 557
Chang, Jui-Hung 22
Chang, Pei-Yu 39
Chao, Mu-Fen 365
Chen, Chao-Chun 61
Chen, Hong-Ren 450
Chen, Huimin 252
Chen, Judy F. 303
Chen, Yingling 343
Cheng, Shu-Chen 498
Cheng, Wai-Khuen 131
Cheng, Yuh-Ming 102
Cheng, Yu-Ping 498
Chien, Pei-Ling 85
Chien, Yu-Cheng 39
Chou, Pao-Nan 170
Chung, Chih-Chao 102
Chung, Hsiang-Jen 3

Deng, Xiaoying 252

Faizi, Rdouan 548
Fayziev, Mirzaali 397
Francisco, Manuela 49
Frangou, Satu-Maarit 241

Gaevskaya, Elena 397
Gamlunglert, Romwarin 219

Hattingh, Marié 228
Hong, Zeng-Wei 131
Hooshyar, Danial 39
Howard, Grant R. 262
Hsu, Jane Lu 389
Hsu, Wen-Chiao 85
Huang, Sheng-Bo 161
Huang, Tien-Chi 85
Huang, Yong-Ming 61
Huang, Yu-Che 22
Huang, Yueh-Min 39, 498
Huang, Yu-Lun 196
Hwang, Wu-Yuin 67

Jakobsen, David 121
Jarungsirawat, Non 430
Jarungsiraway, Non 152
Jeng, Yu-Lin 161
Jitsopitanon, Jetbordin 183
Junruang, Chinnaphat 144

Kanjug, Issara 95, 144, 152, 206, 430, 593
Kiyani, Midhat Noor 470
Kroeze, Jan Hendrik 10, 262

Lai, Chin-Feng 22, 161
Lai, ChinLun 74
Lai, Mei-Jie 450
Lamsombat, Kodchakorn 95
Lee, Hsin-Yu 39
Li, Cheng-Tsung 584
Li, Chien-Kuo 365
Li, Zhe 252
Liang, Yu-Chen 584
Lin, Han 252
Lin, Hao-Chiang Koong 111
Lin, I-Chun 483
Lin, Jim-Min 131
Lin, Koong Hao-Chiang 584
Lin, Wei-Tsung 61
Lin, Yen-Ting 483
Lin, Yu-Hsuan 111
Liou, Jia-Wen 303
Liu, Hsin-Lan 111
Liu, Taoying 397
Lou, Shi-Jer 102
Luangsodsai, Arthorn 352

Martins, Paulo 377
Mashau, Nkhangweni Lawrence 262

Modimogale, Lloyd Letlhogonolo Koikoi 10
Moeikao, Nutthakarn 152, 430

Ness, Ida 461
Nunthaitaweekul, Pimwarun 219
Nurtantyana, Rio 67

Øhrstrøm, Peter 121
Opdal, Kathinka 461
Otajonov, Olimboy 397

Pillay, Komla 228, 521
Pinheiro, Margarida M. 567
Ploug, Thomas 121
Pongsuphan, Kriangsak 189
Prinsloo, Tania 521
Putra, Muhammad Trio Maulana 67

Quidwai, Noor Us Subah 470

Rintanalert, Thanawat 352
Rizwan, Azka 470
Rocha, Tânia 377
Rønningsbakk, Lisbet 293
Rudneva, Maria 548

Samat, Charuni 144, 152, 206, 333, 413, 430, 533, 542, 593
Sandborg-Petersen, Ulrik 121
Sandnes, Frode Eika 461
Santos, Vanda 567
Sari, Mega Kartika 323
Sathanarugsawait, Benjaporn 533, 542
Schmidt, LeAnne J. 274
Shadiev, Narzikul 397
Shadiev, Rustam 397
Shen, Wei-Wei 131
Shih, Ru-Chu 170
Shu, Yu 85
Singha, Pinyarat 413
Singkaew, Chan 422
Smuts, Corlia 439
Smuts, Hanlie 439
Song, Zong-Kun 131
Starčič, Andreja Istenič 161
Su, King-Dow 30
Su, Peiyao 252

Tang, Jih-Hsin 491
Thima, Samrit 511
Thorvaldsen, Steinar 121
Tseng, Ching-Yun 85

Väätäjä, Janne 241
van Staden, Cornè Johandia 10
Vongtathum, Pornsawan 183, 333, 413, 593

Wang, Tz-Chi 483
Wang, Wei-Tsong 323
Warden, Clyde A. 303
Wattanachai, Suchat 206, 333, 533, 593
Wei, Chih-Fen 491
Weilbach, Lizette 228
Weng, Ting-Sheng 365
Willliams, John 557
Wongchiranuwat, Sathaporn 206, 593
Wu, Mei-Hsin 491
Wu, Pei-Hsuan 22
Wu, Yu-Hsin 196

Yang, Fu-Rung 491, 579
Yang, Yeongwook 498
Yen, Wan-Hsuan 557
Yordanova, Zornitsa 283, 310
Yu, Sen-Chi 450

Zhong, Hua-Xu 22
Zhussupova, Roza 397